AF182756

Claiming a Promised Inheritance

Claiming a Promised Inheritance

A Comparative Study

ALEXANDRA BRAUN

OXFORD
UNIVERSITY PRESS

OXFORD
UNIVERSITY PRESS

Great Clarendon Street, Oxford, OX2 6DP,
United Kingdom

Oxford University Press is a department of the University of Oxford.
It furthers the University's objective of excellence in research, scholarship,
and education by publishing worldwide. Oxford is a registered trade mark of
Oxford University Press in the UK and in certain other countries

© Alexandra Braun 2022

The moral rights of the author have been asserted

First Edition published in 2022

Impression: 1

All rights reserved. No part of this publication may be reproduced, stored in
a retrieval system, or transmitted, in any form or by any means, without the
prior permission in writing of Oxford University Press, or as expressly permitted
by law, by licence or under terms agreed with the appropriate reprographics
rights organization. Enquiries concerning reproduction outside the scope of the
above should be sent to the Rights Department, Oxford University Press, at the
address above

You must not circulate this work in any other form
and you must impose this same condition on any acquirer

Public sector information reproduced under Open Government Licence v3.0
(http://www.nationalarchives.gov.uk/doc/open-government-licence/open-government-licence.htm)

Published in the United States of America by Oxford University Press
198 Madison Avenue, New York, NY 10016, United States of America

British Library Cataloguing in Publication Data

Data available

Library of Congress Control Number: 2022933050

ISBN 978–0–19–875725–2

DOI: 10.1093/oso/9780198757252.001.0001

Printed and bound by
CPI Group (UK) Ltd, Croydon, CR0 4YY

Links to third party websites are provided by Oxford in good faith and
for information only. Oxford disclaims any responsibility for the materials
contained in any third party website referenced in this work.

An meine Eltern

Acknowledgements

This book has been a long time in the making. It started off as something completely different: a research project on the use of contracts in the testamentary context and, in particular, a historical and comparative exploration of instances in which the law allows a testator to bind herself with respect to the distribution of her estate. Depending on the jurisdiction, a testator can do so in a number of different ways including, for instance, through a mutual will, an *Erbvertrag* (inheritance contract), or a contract to make a future will. Somehow my attention was captured especially by those instances in which a testator promises that she will make a will in which she will benefit a particular person, and the dynamics that such promises give rise to. I was particularly drawn to those cases (and stories) in which no formal contract could be established, but a promise had nonetheless been made and relied upon, and the promisee's expectation of an inheritance had been frustrated.

I soon discovered that while informal testamentary promises are not being paid much attention to in legal scholarship, they are nonetheless made and often litigated in ways that are not necessarily immediately obvious. I also realized that many families had stories to tell about instances in which promises to leave something by will had been made, but the promisees either believed that the law would not offer them any protection or decided not to litigate. I thus became fascinated by the complexity of the social, psychological, emotional, and legal context in which such promises are expressed, acted upon, and litigated in court. While at the start I focused my attention on a couple of jurisdictions, I began, in due course, to cast my net wider and explored case reports across a broader geographical area and in more than one legal tradition. It is the practice of comparison that led me to ask new questions and to look beyond some of the doctrinal structures in place, but also to pay greater attention to the interests and values at stake. And, so with time, the book grew into something that I could not myself have anticipated at first.

No book is written by one person alone. I owe enormous gratitude to many people and institutions. I started this book at the University of Oxford and completed it at the University of Edinburgh. My thanks go to my friends, colleagues, and students at St John's College, Lady Margaret Hall, the Institute of Comparative and European Law, and the Law School in Oxford, and my friends, colleagues, and students at the Law School at Edinburgh University who have welcomed me so warmly and supported me in so many different ways.

It would have been impossible to write this book without time to search, think, and write. I am therefore very grateful to the Alexander von Humboldt Foundation for funding a generous period of research leave that I spent in Germany (in 2013/

2014 and again in 2015) and during which much of the research was carried out, and much of the foundation laid, for the present book. I owe huge thanks to the Max Planck Institute for Comparative and International Private Law in Hamburg where I spent many happy months of that leave. The Institute provided not only a stimulating environment, but also gave me access to wonderful resources. I particularly thank Reinhard Zimmermann for his generous support and advice over many years and my fellow researchers at the Institute, many of whom have become close friends. I also thank Bucerius Law School in Hamburg where I was invited to spend the summer of 2015 working on this research project and, in particular, Anne Röthel, for her friendship, enthusiasm, encouragement, inspiration, and wise guidance.

Over the years, I had the opportunity to present some of the findings of this book in various research institutions. I would particularly like to thank: Anne Sophie-Hulin (now at the University of Ottawa), Robert Leckey, and Lionel Smith for inviting me to present my research at McGill University (in October 2015); Gregor Christandl (now at the University of Graz) for inviting me to spend time in Innsbruck (as a BritInn Fellow in June 2019) to work on and present my research; Gerardo Caffera (at the Universidad de la República, Uruguay) for initiating me to take part in the Jornadas Nacionales Uruguayas De Derecho Privado, 150 Años Del Código Civil Uruguayo (in November 2018), which allowed me to discuss my research with other civil lawyers; and Thomas Gallanis (at Iowa University) for inviting me to give the Hugh J and Frank Tamisiea Lecture in Trusts and Estates (in September 2019) and to present this research in a common law context. All these research stays and the conversations with colleagues and students in these institutions opened up new avenues for reflections, forced me to question some of my assumptions, and helped me sharpen the focus of my enquiry.

Over the many years that it took to complete this book, I also had many conversations with colleagues and friends, over coffee, a glass of wine, a meal, or during a walk, many of whom were prepared to share with me personal stories, directed my attention to cases I had missed, were happy to listen, and took time to read various drafts of chapters of this book. I have benefitted tremendously from conversations with these colleagues and friends, and the opportunity to test my thoughts in a safe environment. I was the lucky recipient of their advice and gentle redirection when I was going off track, and their generous encouragement when things did not go so well. So many have supported me and have been patient with me, and I am grateful for that. I cannot thank everyone, and I apologize in advance for omissions, but I would like to thank especially the following: Leyla Ahani, Amalia Amaya, Yeşim Atamer, Zenon Bankowski, François Barrière, Amin Benaissa, Sanja Bogojević, John Cairns, John Cartwright, Gregor Christandl, Giacomo Correnti, Paul Craig, Xon de Ros, Jenny Dix, Sionaidh Douglas-Scott, Neville Dowley, Jacques Du Plessis, Anatol Dutta, Isabel Fanlo Cortés, David Fox, Mark Freedland, Joshua Getzler, José Goicoechea, Christina Goldschmidt, Michele Graziadei, George

Gretton, Mauro Grondona, Zita Hadju, Catherine Jacqueson, Nils Jansen, Jan Kleinheisterkamp, Heinz-Jürgen Klöpper, Johannes Liebrecht, Maurizio Lupoi, Hector MacQueen, Jonathan Mance, Ben McFarlane, Ewan McKendrick, Jamie McKendrick, Michael Monoyios, Nicola Peart, Alexandra Popovici, Elspeth Reid, Kenneth Reid, Mathias Reimann, Jan Peter Schmidt, Ruth Sefton-Green, Lionel Smith, Stephen Smith, Angela Space, Bill Swadling, Shauna Thompson, Viviane Vagh, Prue Vines, Stefan Vogenauer, Neil Walker, Niall Whitty, and Alison Wood. I would also like to thank and remember Walter Paul Auer who is unfortunately no longer with us. I am further grateful to Ilke Meissner for invaluable assistance with the editorial side of things.

Finally, I would like to thank my family, and my parents, whom this book is dedicated to. I especially thank my boys, Maks and Tristan, for their endless patience, generosity, and support, and for their ability to be terribly silly, which has kept me sane.

Table of Contents

List of Abbreviations

A	Appellate Division Supreme Court (South Africa)
ABGB	*Allgemeines Bürgerliches Gesetzbuch* (Austrian Civil Code)
AC	Appeal Cases (UK)
ACT	Australian Capital Territory
AP	*Arbeitsrechtliche Praxis* (Germany)
ArbG	*Arbeitsgericht* (labour court, Germany)
Art(s)	article(s)
BAG	*Bundesarbeitsgericht* (Federal Labour Court, Germany)
BCCA	British Columbia Court of Appeal (Canada)
BCSC	British Columbia Supreme Court (Canada)
BeckRS	*Beck-Rechtsprechung* (Germany)
BGB	*Bürgerliches Gesetzbuch* (German Civil Code)
BGBl	*Bundesgesetzblatt* (Federal Law Gazette, Austria, Germany)
BGH	*Bundesgerichtshof* (Germany Federal Supreme Court)
BGHZ	*Entscheidungen des Bundesgerichtshofes in Zivilsachen* (Decisions of the Federal Supreme Court in Private Law Matters, Germany)
BT-Drucksache	*Bundestagsdrucksache* (Bundestag document, Germany)
Bull civ	*Bulletin des arrêts de la Cour de cassation, chambers civiles* (France)
Bull Inf C cass	*Bulletin d'information de la Cour de cassation* (France)
BW	*Burgerlijk Wetboek* (Dutch Civil Code, Belgian Civil Code)
CA	*Cour d'appel* (Court of Appeal, France); Court of Appeal (England and Wales); New Zealand Court of Appeal
Cass 1re civ	*Cour de cassation, Première chambre civile* (Court of Cassation, first civil chamber, France)
Cass 3e civ	*Cour de cassation, Troisième chambre civile* (Court of Cassation, third civil chamber, France)
Cass soc	*Cour de cassation, chambre sociale* (Court of Cassation, labour chamber, France)
Ch	Chancery Division (England and Wales)
cit	cited
comm	commentary
CPD	Cape Provincial Division (South Africa)
Defrénois	*Répertoire du notariat Defrénois* (France)
DP	*Dalloz périodique* (France)
DStR	*Deutsches Steuerrecht* (Germany)
E	High Court of South Africa, Easter Cape Division (South Africa)
ed(s)	editors
EDL	Eastern Districts Local Division (South Africa)
edn	edition
ErbSTB	*Der Erbschaftssteuer-Berater* (Germany)

ErläutRV	*Erläuternde Bemerkung zur Regierungsvorlage* (Austria)
EWCA Civ	Court of Appeal (Civil Division) (England and Wales)
EWCA	Court of Appeal (England and Wales)
EWHC	High Court (England and Wales)
Fam	Family Court of New Zealand
FamRZ	*Zeitschrift für das gesamte Familienrecht* (Germany)
ff	following
Gaz Pal	*Gazette du Palais* (France)
GP	*Gesetzgebungsperiode* (legislative period, Austria)
HC Wellington	High Court of New Zealand, Wellington (New Zealand)
HC	High Court of Justice (England & Wales, New Zealand)
HCA	High Court of Australia
HL	House of Lords (United Kingdom)
IEHC	High Court of Ireland (Ireland)
JCP G	*Juris-Classeur Périodique, Édition Générale* (France)
JCP N	*Juris-Classeur Périodique, Édition Notariale* (France)
jurispr.	*jurisprudence* (France)
KG OLGZ	*Kammergericht Entscheidungssammlung der Oberlandesgerichte in Zivilsachen* (Germany)
KG	*Kammergericht* (highest state court for the city of Berlin, Germany)
LAG	*Landesarbeitsgericht* (Regional Labour Court, Germany)
LG	*Landgericht* (District Court, Germany)
Man QB	Court of Queen's Bench for Manitoba
Man CA	Court of Appeal, Manitoba (Canada)
n	footnote
NICh	High Court of Justice Northern Ireland: Chancery Division
NJW	*Neue Juristische Wochenschrift* (Germany)
NJW-RR	*NJW-Rechtsprechungs-Report* (Germany)
no(s)	number(s)
NSW	New South Wales (Australia)
NSWCA	New South Wales Court of Appeal (Australia)
NSWSC	New South Wales Supreme Court (Australia)
NT	Northern Territory (Australia)
NZ	New Zealand
NZA	*Neue Zeitschrift für Arbeits- und Sozialrecht* (Germany)
NZCA	New Zealand Court of Appeal
NZHC	High Court of New Zealand
obs	observations
OCA	Court of Appeal for Ontario (Canada)
OGH	*Oberster Gerichtshof* (Austrian Supreme Court)
OLG	*Oberlandesgericht* (Regional Court of Appeal, Germany)
OLGR	*OLG-Report* (Germany)
OLGZ	*Entscheidungen der Oberlandesgerichte in Zivilsachen* (Decisions of the Regional Courts of Appeal in Private Law Matters, Germany)
ONCA	Court of Appeal for Ontario (Canada)

ONSC	Ontario Superior Court of Justice (Canada)
Ont CA	Ontario Court of Appeal (Canada)
OPD	Orange Free State Provincial Division (South Africa)
OR	*Schweizerisches Obligationenrecht* (Swiss law of obligations)
PC	Privy Council
Qld	Queensland (Australia)
QSC	Queensland Supreme Court
RAG	*Reichsarbeitsgericht* (Imperial Labour Court, Germany)
RAGE	Entscheidungen des Reichsarbeitsgerichts (Decisions of the Imperial Labour Court, Germany)
RD rur	*Revue de droit rural* (France)
RegE	*Regierungsentwurf* (government bill, Germany)
Rép Defrénois	*Répertoire Defrénois* (France)
RG	*Reichsgericht* (Imperial Supreme Court, Germany)
RJPF	*Revue juridique personnes et famille* (France)
RLDC	*Revue Lamy droit civil* (France)
RTD civ	*Revue trimestrielle de droit civil* (France)
SA	South Australia
Sask QB/SKQB	Saskatchewan Court of Queen's Bench (Canada)
SASR	South Australian State Reports
SCC	Supreme Court of Canada
Seuffert's Archiv	*J. A. Seuffert's Archiv für Entscheidungen der obersten Gerichte in den deutschen Staaten* (Germany)
SKCA	Saskatchewan Court of Appeal (Canada)
Tas	Tasmania (Australia)
TASSC	Supreme Court of Tasmania (Australia)
TGI	*Tribunal de grande instance* (Higher Court, France)
Trib civ	*Tribunal civil* (Civil Court, France)
UKHL	United Kingdom House of Lords
UKPC	United Kingdom Privy Council
UKSC	United Kingdom Supreme Court
Vic	Victoria (Australia)
VSC	Victoria Supreme Court (Australia)
VSCA	Victoria Court of Appeal (Australia)
WA	Western Australia
WarnRspr	*Warneyers Jahrbuch der Entscheidungen* (Germany)
WASC	Western Australia Supreme Court
WCC	Western Cape Court, (South Africa)
ZAWCHC	Western Cape High Court (South Africa)
ZEV	*Zeitschrift für Erbrecht und Vermögensnachfolge* (Germany)
ZGB	*Schweizerisches Zivilgesetzbuch* (Swiss Civil Code)

Introduction

I. Focus, objectives, and claims of the book

A. Object of the enquiry

This book examines those cases where a person is promised a future inheritance and, having acted on it, later discovers that the promise is unfulfilled. Such instances have long been part of social reality,[1] and continue to give rise to litigation.[2] Yet, as this book shows, the role and impact of promises of a future inheritance and how they are litigated are not always immediately visible.[3] In many ways, such promises give rise to testamentary arrangements that operate behind the scenes and that legal systems seem to be often suspicious of.

Promises of a future inheritance, often referred to also as testamentary promises, are typically made in the domestic or family setting. More specifically, they are made in the farming/agricultural and the household/care contexts, and usually in exchange for something in return. They tend to involve a mutual arrangement among individuals who are in a close relationship, and for this very reason the arrangement is frequently informal, meaning that it does not amount to a legally binding contract. Typical examples are cases where parents promise their daughter that if she looks after them in old age, they will provide for her in their will; or where a farmer reassures either a family member or a farm worker that if they continue to stay on the farm and to work for him for low or almost no wages, they will not regret it, as the farm will one day be theirs.

[1] See the references in the Roman texts mentioned in Chapter 2. Notably, Rudolf von Jhering mentions two testamentary promises cases in his *Collection of Legal Questions* (1904) 58, No 79. Testamentary promises are sometimes referred to also in novels. An example is Daniel Defoe's Moll Flanders (the mother promised that she would provide for Moll in her will). The British Magazine, *Punch* published cartoons titled 'One day son, all this will be yours'.

[2] Breitenbach AJ in the South African case *Naidoo NO and Another v Crowhurst NO and Others* (21732/2009) [2009] ZAWCHC 186; [2010] 2 All SA 379 (WCC) (1 December 2009) states 'It is not uncommon for people to promise to leave their property to others in their will and then not to do so'. Similarly, *Schaefer v Schuhmann* [1972] AC 572, 594 (Lord Simon of Glaisdale) (hereafter *Schaefer v Schuhmann*).

[3] This is, as we will see, partly because work carried out by family members is often invisible. See, among others, Philipps (2008) 85.

Claiming a Promised Inheritance. Alexandra Braun, Oxford University Press. © Alexandra Braun 2022.
DOI: 10.1093/oso/9780198757252.003.0001

In return for a promise of a future inheritance, promisees commonly perform a variety of services, or make financial payments or improvements to the promisor's property. In doing so, they frequently make both professional and personal sacrifices, which, irrespective of their tangible or intangible nature, can be of huge benefit to the promisor. For instance, in the earlier first example, acting on the prospect of the inheritance, the daughter may decide to move in with her mother and sell her own home, or to take the mother to live with her instead, which could potentially affect not only her professional but also her private life. She may also give up her job or revert to part-time employment. Similarly, in the second example, the prospect of inheriting the farm may induce the promisees not to insist on payments of wages and/or to omit looking for alternative employment. Confident in the fact that the farm will one day be theirs, they may also invest their own money, making improvements to the farmer's property or purchasing equipment. Were the promisors in these two examples to make the promised will and the will were to take effect, no problems would usually arise, except where nothing is left in the estate. However, were they to change their mind and fail to make the promised will, or, for whatever reason, the will would be invalid, the expectations of the promisees who have counted on the inheritance would be frustrated, unless they inherit under intestacy rules.[4] Hence, promises of an inheritance foster expectations which, if unfulfilled, can cause not just emotional hurt, but also significant economic detriment.

It is these cases, where a promise, understood broadly, was made and acted upon by the promisee, but the promise remains unfulfilled, that this book pays attention to. The book structures its analysis and argument around the stories of disappointed promisees and their unfulfilled expectations of an inheritance, and the question of whether and how legal systems protect their interests. It does so by drawing attention to, and comparing, the various, and often very diverse range of legal responses that a promisee can avail herself of across different legal traditions and what they require of her.

B. Aims of the enquiry

Given that testamentary promises concern a prospective inheritance, one might expect to locate the protection of promisees within succession law. Yet, succession laws are usually either entirely silent about them or prohibit them altogether. Many civil law jurisdictions expressly forbid legally binding promises in the form of pacts or contracts to make a will. In other words, for reasons that I will explore in Chapter 2, most civil law jurisdictions prevent a testator[5] from binding herself

[4] In this book, all of the promisors and promisees are 'she' unless a specific case is discussed in which case it will reflect the gender of the particular claimant or defendant.

[5] I am using the term 'testator' in a gender-neutral way.

as to the content of her future will. By contrast, common law jurisdictions generally allow for such contracts to be entered into, though usually without providing a specific set of provisions tailored to the testamentary context. Instead, they apply general contract law rules, but only few testamentary arrangements ever meet the contractual requirements, meaning that protection of promisees through contract law is often precluded.

Moreover, and this is crucial for the purposes of this enquiry, with the exception of New Zealand, most legal systems fail to specifically regulate informal testamentary promises, that is promises that do not amount to a legally binding contract. While in a civilian context this is not surprising given that many legal systems explicitly prohibit legally binding promises, it is interesting that common law jurisdictions have not followed the lead of New Zealand in regulating informal testamentary promises, leaving it instead to the courts to find solutions. Thus, in both civil and common law jurisdictions, when a promisee has acted on an informal testamentary promise, and her expectation of obtaining a future inheritance is disappointed, the question arises as to whether to protect her interests and, if so, how.

As the analysis in this book reveals, the decision as to whether or not to provide the promisee with relief is not straightforward, not least because it has implications for a variety of persons such as creditors of the promisor and third-party transferees, but also successors[6] who take under intestacy rules, a will, forced/compulsory heirship provisions, or those who benefit from a family provision order. The relief granted to the promisee could also potentially be perceived as challenging the promisor's testamentary freedom or undermining requirements of form for the transfer of property or testamentary dispositions. Consequently, any decision as to whether and how to provide redress involves a complex and delicate balancing act on the part of courts and legislatures.

Despite these difficulties, this book shows that many jurisdictions offer some form of protection to promisees who have acted on an informal promise of an inheritance, through the law of unjust or unjustified enrichment,[7] property, employment, or, to a lesser extent, family and succession law. Thus, most forms of redress analysed in this book were not designed to tackle instances of unfulfilled testamentary promises. In some cases that need not be a problem and may indeed free the promisee from having to prove a promise. This is, for instance, the case where the relevant doctrine is aimed at remunerating unremunerated services. At the same time, for that very reason, not all avenues of relief examined in this book account for the specificities of the setting in which promises of a future inheritance are expressed and acted upon.

[6] In this book, the 'successor' refers to those who inherit from the promisor, whether under the will, intestacy rules, or forced or compulsory heirship rules.

[7] This book uses the expression 'unjustified enrichment' when referring to French and German law and the expression 'unjust enrichment' with reference to common law jurisdictions.

The objective of this book is both to map and compare a number of forms of redress that are drawn from different areas of private law and from across both civil and common law traditions, and to evaluate them from the perspective of the promisee. The book assesses each form of redress on its own terms and against the background of other available forms, by examining: (i) the extent to which they are sensitive to the context in which testamentary promises are made, including: their informality and the fact that they may be implied from behaviour adopted over time; the long time lag that can lie between the promise and the promisor's death; the variety of motives (and emotions) that can underpin the behaviour of both the promisor and the promisee; and the importance of intangible benefits but also efforts and sacrifices that they can entail; (ii) the level of protection they offer to promisees (in terms of amount of the redress and the protection vis-à-vis third parties); and, (iii) their scope, that is whether or not they are capable of protecting a wide range of promisees.

This book therefore asks: When do courts grant relief and on what basis? What must a promisee prove and what difficulties does she face when bringing a claim? Which promisees are protected, and which are not, and how does the promisee's claim fare against third parties? What interests and values are at stake when deciding to protect the interests of (certain) promisees and what policy considerations underpin the individual avenues of redress?

The analysis in this book shows that not all forms of redress are available in all jurisdictions, but that in most jurisdictions, a promisee can seek redress in more than one way. Arguably, this is good news from her perspective, though we will see that some promisees have a greater choice than others.[8] Most private law doctrines examined are incapable of capturing all types of situations in which a testamentary promise remains unfulfilled. Even when promisees have a choice, as we will see, the nature of their relationship with the promisor, the type of performance provided in exchange for the promise, and their gender may affect the outcome, so that different promisees may receive a different treatment. In other words, some promisees face greater challenges than others—challenges that can potentially limit their chances of success or discourage them from bringing a claim. Moreover, while with certain forms of relief the promisee is granted a proprietary right, with others she is regarded as a creditor of the promisor's estate. And, sometimes, she is treated as a mere successor of the promisor who benefits after all of the promisor's debts have been paid.[9] This, then, has a significant impact on the degree of protection promisees are awarded vis-à-vis third parties. Thus, the legal framework mapped in this book is highly fragmented and sometimes lacks a principled approach or is incoherent and inconsistent.

[8] Chapter 2.

[9] For details, see Chapter 3 but also Chapter 7.

Besides comparing the various forms of redress a promisee may seek out, this book also reflects on the wider consequences of the state of the law. For instance, the analysis shows that because protection is sought by promisees through various doctrines of private law, wealth is distributed on the promisor's death through a number of different means other than succession law, such as enrichment law, the doctrine of proprietary estoppel, or employment law. In other words, wealth transfers on death do not merely occur through succession law.[10] This, then, has implications for both creditors and successors of the promisor and the administration of the estate. It further emerges that the application and adaptation of certain private law doctrines to the testamentary context can have implications for how these private law doctrines develop. We will see this, for example, when examining the way in which enrichment law has evolved in common law Canada, but also when analysing how the doctrine of proprietary estoppel has developed in England and Wales, or how § 612 *Bürgerliches Gesetzbuch* (hereinafter BGB) has been applied in Germany.[11]

Finally, this book also aims to raise broader questions concerning the following: the role of law in this context; the intersection between moral and legal obligations; the frontier between what is gratuitous and what is not, and hence the effectiveness of the distinction between bargains and gifts; questions of social justice; questions of gender and intergenerational equality; and the role of different conceptions of testamentary freedom. Ultimately, the book highlights the value of testamentary promises, and the importance of informal intergenerational exchanges of labour and wealth.

C. Significance of the enquiry

Since promisees can usually seek redress through a number of different doctrines, testamentary promises cases are hardly ever looked at collectively in legal scholarship. The literature examining gratuitous or gift promises does not usually consider promises made in the testamentary context, but instead deals primarily with promises of a lifetime gift.[12] Similarly, scholarship dealing with contract, property, enrichment, family, or succession law is also often silent on the point. In fact, promises of an inheritance are not usually defined as a distinct subject and in many ways represent a grey and neglected area. One could therefore gain the impression that they represent a marginal phenomenon in real life. As this enquiry seeks to show, however, this is not the case.

[10] This is also partly a consequence of the use of will-substitutes. See Braun & Röthel *Passing Wealth on Death* (2016).

[11] Chapters 6, 4, and 8.

[12] For details, see the analysis in Chapter 2.

For reasons that will become clearer later, while there is very little scholarship examining testamentary promises in the civil law context,[13] there is some literature dealing directly with such promises in common law jurisdictions.[14] In addition to Rosalyn Wells' fascinating doctoral dissertation,[15] Sarah Nield has published valuable articles in which she has examined some of the questions addressed in this book (especially in the care context) and compared some of the legal responses available in common law jurisdictions.[16] Brian Sloan has also examined some of the cases analysed here, in the context of an important book that focuses, however, on the protection of carers in common law jurisdictions, irrespective of whether or not there is a promise.[17] Yet, none of these works offers a comparative account of testamentary promises across both common and civil law traditions. There is therefore a considerable gap in the scholarly analysis of promises of an inheritance, both across various social contexts and legal traditions. This book seeks to address this gap in the literature by providing a collective examination of testamentary promises from a comparative perspective and through a particular lens.

D. The importance of adopting the promisee's perspective

This book examines promises of a future inheritance through the lens of the promisee. One of the reasons for doing so is that legal systems frequently privilege the perspective of the person who owns the property, that is to say that of the transferor, donor, or promisor. They do so, for instance, by requiring formalities for certain transfers of property both during lifetime and on death; by excluding the enforceability of promises of a gift or gratuitous promises unless there is consideration or form; by protecting testamentary freedom (including in some cases by preventing the deceased from legally binding herself with effect on death); and by putting in place presumptions against gifts (e.g. the presumption of a resulting trust) or presumptions that services rendered by family members are rendered gratuitously. That legal systems tend to privilege the promisor's perspective will become especially clear when examining the legal framework within which testamentary arrangements usually operate.

[13] Most civilian literature limits itself to an examination of the prohibition of succession pacts. Exceptions are De Giorgi *I patti sulle successioni future* (1976) and Miserre *Die 'culpa in testando'* (2002) 20.

[14] There is Bertel M Sparks' book entitled *Contracts to Make Wills: Legal Relations Arising Out of Contracts to Devise or Bequeath* (1956) (cited as Sparks *Contracts to Make Wills* (1956)), which provides a fascinating account of contracts to make wills in the US and in England, including their historical development, without, however, paying attention to informal promises. The book is a collection of a number of journal articles published in US legal journals. There is hardly any historical research in this field. For an important exception, see Hartog *Someday* (2012).

[15] Wells *New Approach* (2007). See also Wells 'Testamentary Promises' (2007).

[16] Nield (2000); Nield (2007). Also to be mentioned here is Davey (1988).

[17] Sloan *Informal Carers* (2012).

Adopting the promisee's perspective has other important benefits. First, moving our focus away from the discourse around the promisor's autonomy and her testamentary freedom, it will be possible to gain a better understanding of the complexities of the social and regulatory framework within which these types of testamentary arrangements are usually reached, acted upon, and litigated. This approach provides insights into the power-differential that distinguishes the relationship between promisor and promisee and the emotional and financial motivations that inform their behaviour and thus their arrangements. It further brings to the fore that what matters to a promisee is not just whether she can obtain what she was promised, and when her claim arises, but also how her claim ranks vis-à-vis creditors and successors of the promisor with an interest in the estate. By taking the promisee's perspective, we can also better appreciate the implications of informal property arrangements for families, including for the viability of their businesses and farms, and the difficult balancing act that courts have to undertake when faced with an unfulfilled testamentary promise. Finally, by looking at the forms of redress through the lens of the promisee, we gain insight into the values that underpin certain doctrines, and how they can change, and the interests that they protect. It also highlights how and when notions of family solidarity and societal expectations towards certain family members, including gendered assumption, play a role.[18]

E. Claims of the book

This book advances several claims. It argues that despite the relative lack of attention in the literature, both formal and informal testamentary promises fulfil an important and useful role for both promisors and promisees. They allow promisors to negotiate and secure a performance that can yield both tangible and intangible benefits, without losing control over their assets during their lifetime and without incurring any risks. At the same time, they allow promisees to potentially obtain benefits (e.g. in the form of a family home or a family business or farm) that can both exceed the value of their performance and have significant emotional value to them.

However, the book further claims that for a variety of reasons to do with the particular social and legal context in which these promises are expressed, promisees find themselves in a vulnerable position which promisors can easily take advantage of.[19] It argues that there is a significant power imbalance between the promisor and the promisee which is somewhat enhanced by the fact that, as already mentioned,

[18] See the discussion in Chapter 2.

[19] On the notion of 'vulnerability' in the family context and the importance of recognizing such vulnerability, see, especially, Wallbank & Herring *Vulnerabilities* (2014); Logar (2010); Fineman & Grear *Vulnerability* (2013); Gordon-Bouvier *Relational Vulnerability* (2020); Herring *Relational Self* (2020) chapter 2.

the law tends to privilege the perspective of the owner of the property. The enquiry further shows that while courts have, generally speaking, been open to providing redress to promisees whose expectations have been frustrated, the current legal framework sometimes overlooks or enhances the vulnerabilities of promisees of an inheritance. It does so, for instance, by placing undue importance on the motives of the promisee's performance, or by requiring her to show that her performance exceeds certain accepted societal expectations as to what is regarded as 'normal' in a given context.

This book thus argues that greater attention should be paid to the promisee's position and her vulnerabilities, and that ways should be found to protect her interests, even when there is no legally binding promise, that is a contract, in place. It contends that while the informality of testamentary promises creates a risk for both parties, it cannot be a valid objection against the protection of the interests of promisees lest we are prepared to accept the risk of an abuse of testamentary power on the part of the promisor. Equally, it argues that the need to protect the promisor's testamentary freedom should not be regarded as a bar to the promisee's protection. The book claims that, in certain circumstances, promisors (and their estates or successors)[20] should bear the consequences when informal testamentary promises remain unfulfilled, because promisors could otherwise exploit the vulnerability of promisees. This is the case where the promisor has expressed a promise (understood broadly), the promisee has acted on the promise to her detriment and the promisor accepts the promisees behaviour, thereby obtaining a benefit.[21] It is the combination of both the behaviour of the promisor and that of the promisee, looked at over time, that stops the promisor from changing her mind so that she is no longer free to dispose of her wealth as she pleases. Hence, the restriction of the promisor's freedom of disposition has its source in an obligation that she has voluntarily assumed by accepting the promisee's behaviour. What the courts do is enforce this obligation.

This is not to say that this book advocates a universal approach to testamentary promises cases. Indeed, it does not. Nonetheless, the book takes the view that the response to the challenges that especially informal testamentary arrangements pose should not be to forbid them, as some civil law jurisdictions have chosen to do. For a start, as mentioned earlier, testamentary promises fulfil an important function. Also, the analysis reveals that social practices do not conform to the legal framework and that legal rules, even where they are strict, do not manage to completely eradicate social practices.[22] This means that, irrespective of whether or not

[20] As for details of how the estate is administered in common and civil law jurisdictions, see Schmidt, *Itinera hereditatis* (2021).

[21] As Brereton J held in *Bovaird v Frost* [2009] NSWSC 337, [102]: 'The community expects testators ... to recognise the claims of those to whom they have made promises of support, particularly if those promises have been relied upon.'

[22] Resta (2014) 48.

prohibitions are in place, promises are being made informally and acted upon. For that very reason, the answer to the problems set out in this book cannot solely lie in admitting contracts to make a will. Indeed, this book argues that contract law does not provide the best answer. Even if both parties were prepared to enter into a legally binding contract, the promisee is unlikely to be able to dictate the conditions for the agreement, as her bargaining power is not equal to that of the promisor.[23] Also, because death is unpredictable, the parties would need to devise detailed conditions to deal with a number of unforeseeable circumstances. The reality of the cases analysed in this book shows, however, that much of what happens between the parties over a long period of time cannot be easily cast in contractual terms. Hence, insisting on formal arrangements misses the point. Instead, means of protection should be explored that are sensitive to the particular context in which testamentary promises are made and thus attuned to the specificities of these social practices, including the fact that they are often made informally.

This is not to suggest that promisors are necessarily mischievous. In fact, on the whole, instances in which courts have to deal with a devious promisor seem rare, though there may be cases that are simply not litigated. Therefore, the analysis does not invite the reader to ignore nor try to downplay the vulnerabilities of the promisor,[24] who is clearly exposed to certain risks, especially of undue pressure and influence from family members, as well as fraud. Rather, this book argues that the law is usually more acutely attuned to the risks that the promisor incurs and that the focus (and emphasis) of the law is therefore frequently one-sided. Thus, this book complements this traditional viewpoint by bringing into focus the (too often ignored) perspective of the promisee.

Instead of suggesting a legal solution that works for all contexts and across all jurisdictions, this book points out the various challenges informal testamentary promises entail. It explores what interests and values are at stake, and what context-sensitive factors courts should take into consideration when tackling this complex area of the law, so as to ensure that deserving promisees are not being left unprotected. These will be brought into sharper focus through a comparison of the various forms of redress available across areas of private law and jurisdictions.

23 See Thompson (2018) 623.

24 Others have, for instance, pointed out risks of undue influence. See Sloan *Informal Carers* (2012) chapter 7; Sloan in *Current Issues* (2016).

II. Methodological aspects

A. Centrality of cases

This book offers a contextual account of testamentary promises and of the ways in which courts tackle instances in which a disappointed promisee claims that she has acted on a promise of a future inheritance to her own detriment and that her expectation has not been fulfilled. The focus is on social practices that happen on the ground. Where possible, the analysis is centred on reported cases and the stories they reveal. These stories provide the reader with a number of insights into the dynamics of the relationships that can lead to such promises but also their breach, and how they are litigated.

Of course, litigation usually deals only with situations in which things go wrong, and thus where a testamentary promise is breached or where it is kept, but the will does not produce the desired effect. It is thus impossible to know, for example, how many instances there are in practice in which testamentary promises are kept and expectations satisfied, unless a claim is brought to invalidate a will made in compliance with such a testamentary promise, which is very rare.[25] However, this book does not dispute that promisors intend to keep their promises when they are made. Instead, it is interested in exploring those instances in which they remain unfulfilled, for whatever reason, and whether and how promisees can obtain redress and, in particular, obtain the promised inheritance.

It is equally impossible to know how many cases there are in which expectations remain unfulfilled, but the disappointed promisee has decided not to litigate her case.[26] Undoubtedly some promisees will feel uneasy about litigating against family members or close friends, especially given that it involves talking about intimate aspects of life, family quarrels, and financial matters.[27] It could also make them look greedy or ungrateful. Social pressure can be a strong disincentive to bringing a claim. Furthermore, in light of the fact that the legal position is, as we will see, complex and the promisee's chances of success often uncertain, some promisees may simply (and understandably so) be reluctant to go to court, especially if the financial costs of doing so are high. Thus, an unknown percentage of promisees may well accept their situation, sometimes as the price for family harmony.[28] However,

[25] This can sometimes happen in Italy, where legally binding testamentary promises are void and the invalidity also captures the corresponding will. See De Giorgi *I patti sulle successioni future* (1976) 160.

[26] Leslie (1999) 558 argues that, for instance, in the US, family members are unlikely to file a claim based on a testamentary promise. However, they may decide to contest the decedent's will, as this could be seen as acting on behalf of the testator.

[27] As McDonald J stated in the Irish case of *K v K* [2018] IEHC 615, [2]: 'Regrettably it will be necessary in this judgment to consider many aspects of the life of this family which, in the absence of a court hearing, would remain entirely private'.

[28] Hartog *Someday* (2012) 171. According to Hartog, at least in the past, in the US, daughters more than sons seem to have fallen into this category.

where the amount of wealth involved is substantial, and the harm or disappointment suffered is significant (e.g. because the promisee has performed services or work over the course of a long period of time or has positioned her whole existence on the assurances given to her), promisees may be prepared to risk upsetting intimate relationships and expose themselves vis-à-vis relatives, friends, and the public. This goes to show how important it is for promisees to know what protection is available to them and what risks they will have to take.

Finally, it is hard to determine how many of the cases have made it into the law reports,[29] and how many were settled. In other words, the picture that will be depicted in this book is inevitably incomplete. The reader should also be warned that law reports do not necessarily offer a balanced view, for the majority of cases deal with instances in which the promisor is no longer alive and is thus unable to tell her side of the story. The account of the facts is therefore potentially one-sided. Nevertheless, bearing in mind all those caveats, the cases provide important insights, not merely into social practices but also, crucially, into what goes wrong, what is at stake, and the attitude courts adopt towards promisees. For these reasons, cases are a central focus of this enquiry.

B. The value of taking a comparative approach

The core part of this book is built around the comparison of a range of different types of forms of redress that are available across different legal traditions and in different settings (ranging from the household/care to the agricultural/farming context) to a promisee who seeks to obtain the promised asset, and the considerations that play a role when courts grant or deny redress. Even though most forms of redress analysed were not designed to tackle cases of a breach of a testamentary promise, and, as we will see, proof of a promise is therefore not always required (and sometimes no mention of it is made in the proceedings),[30] they can potentially benefit a promisee whose promise is unfulfilled.

By comparing different types of legal responses through which promisees may potentially seek protection, a number of insights can be gained. It is first of all possible to see which of the various approaches examined in the book is more attuned to the testamentary context and the vulnerabilities of the promisee, irrespective of whether or not it was designed for that purpose. We can then understand the level of protection that promisees are given and what price they may have to pay if one approach is favoured, or chosen, over another. For instance, we will see that some promisees are better protected than others and that sometimes the law

[29] For instance, marriage promises were hardly ever reported. See Lettmaier *Broken Engagements* (2010) 10.

[30] Chapter 9, Section III.

differentiates between promisees even when they are equally deserving.[31] It will also be possible to see which factors have an impact on the likelihood of the success of their claim, and where possible obstacles may lie or even hide. For instance, it will emerge that due to societal expectations associated with certain types of work (i.e. domestic work) on the whole, women tend to be less well protected.

By structuring the analysis this way, we can also appreciate the many ways in which wealth is being transferred on death of a person. In other words, the analysis shows that the answer to the question of how testamentary promises are being tackled cannot be found solely by examining areas that belong formally to succession law. It is therefore important to study testamentary promises in a broader legal context and to acknowledge, for instance, the interconnectedness of succession law with other areas of private law.

The comparative outlook further allows us to establish points of legal and cultural convergences and differences across legal traditions, regarding the scope and level of protection across the board as well as of specific categories of promisees. The comparison shows, for instance, that the approaches offered map only partly onto different legal traditions. In other words, it is not the case that the common and civil law traditions offer completely opposite forms of redress. For instance, enrichment law is invoked across jurisdictions and legal traditions, though it does not lead to the same outcome in all jurisdictions, and it is not necessarily the approach that is most suitable from the perspective of the promisee. That said, the enquiry also shows that the likelihood of the promisee receiving the promised asset is higher in the common law tradition. This is partly linked to the fact that civil law jurisdictions examined in this book prohibit contracts or pacts to make a will so that a promisee who brings a claim does not usually see her promise fulfilled.[32] She will normally obtain monetary compensation based on the value of the performance, the promisor's enrichment, or receive something less. By contrast, in common law jurisdictions, an informal promise can lead to the transfer of the promised asset and in many cases it does. This is largely due to the role of equity and the discretionary powers that courts have in common law jurisdictions.[33] Nonetheless, even in the common law context, the approach that seems to prevail in most cases is to compensate the promisee for the work or services provided to the promisor, or to restore the promisor's enrichment, rather than to give effect to the promise by awarding a proprietary right.[34]

[31] See, for instance, the analysis in Chapters 3 and 6.

[32] Chapter 2.

[33] Chapters 4, 5, and 6.

[34] That is certainly true if we look at the New Zealand TPA 1949 (Chapter 7) and enrichment claims in common law Canada (Chapter 6), but less so if we consider English proprietary estoppel cases (Chapter 4). However, many of the proprietary estoppel cases concern work carried out on the farm rather than domestic or care services, so that there are other policy considerations at play.

The comparative analysis further brings to the fore that the responses available to a promisee are not necessarily the same within each legal tradition. It is, for instance, possible to see that in some common law jurisdictions the promisee is less well protected, be it in terms of available forms of redress, the type of award they can obtain, or their standing with regard to third parties. In England and Wales, the options are usually limited to proprietary estoppel or contract law, though contractual claims are now extremely rare. English courts have been restrictive in their interpretation of the family provision legislation, so that family provision orders will not usually provide much protection to promisees. On the other hand, in Australia, a promisee can seek redress in a number of different ways. She may be able to bring a contractual claim or may instead try to base her action on principles of enrichment law, proprietary estoppel, or make an application under the relevant family provision legislation. Also, on the whole, chances of obtaining the promised asset are probably higher in Australia, not least because, even in the case of a proprietary estoppel claim, courts are not limited by the proportionality principle, and because they tend to make wider use of the discretionary powers under the family provision legislation. In New Zealand, a promisee can resort to a variety of possible actions, including one based on the Law Reform (Testamentary Promises) Act 1949 (hereafter New Zealand TPA 1949).[35] While an award under the Act is unlikely to lead to a transfer of the promised asset, its scope is on the whole wide, capturing a variety of different situations. Thus, there is no uniformity in approach among common law jurisdictions.

Equally, among the civil law jurisdictions considered in this book, the forms of redress are not uniform and therefore the level of protection is not the same. For instance, in France, a promisee is less likely to obtain redress than, for example, in Germany or Austria, as there are fewer avenues available to her and these are often restricted to certain contexts or certain promisees. By way of an example, deferred wages (a *créance de salaire différé*) can only be claimed in the agricultural context and in any event only by the farmer's descendant or her spouse (and in very limited instances also the descendant's spouse) and only for work carried out for up to ten years.[36] Equally, in France, an enrichment claim can be brought only in very limited instances and the subsidiarity principle dictates that where other options are available, an enrichment claim is excluded.[37] Conversely, German law offers a greater array of options including a claim based on either employment law, alleging an informal employment relationship with the promisor,[38] or enrichment law,[39] but also, as a last resort, an adjustment based on § 2057a BGB, albeit only in the context of intestacy.[40] Austria, too, offers various avenues, including a new

[35] Chapter 7.
[36] Chapter 10.
[37] Chapter 9, Section III.
[38] Chapter 8.
[39] Chapter 9, Section II.
[40] Chapter 11.

statutory care legacy tailored to instances of care.[41] Again, the protection is not the same across all civil law jurisdictions examined.

Through the comparison it is further possible to gain insights into how legal change in this area has come about. The enquiry shows that developments in one jurisdiction have sometimes inspired developments or reforms in neighbouring jurisdictions. For instance, the German § 2057a BGB was inspired by Swiss law and was in turn an incentive for the introduction of the Austrian statutory care legacy in 2015. And it is possible that these developments have further influenced the drafters of the new Dutch Civil Code.[42] Imitation aside, in some cases developments in one particular area of the law are a response to gaps or perceived shortcomings in other areas of the law. For instance, we will see that one of the objectives behind the introduction of the *créance de salaire différé* in France in 1939 was to counter the tendency of French courts to facilitate the recourse to the *actio de in rem verso* in the farming context.[43] Equally, in Germany, the courts' extensive construction and application of § 612 BGB in the testamentary promises context was an expression of an attempt to counterbalance the application of the *condictio ob rem* by German courts to instances of unfulfilled testamentary promises.[44] On the other hand, the New Zealand TPA 1949 was a reaction to the harshness of contract law when applied to the testamentary context, and to some extent the same could be argued with respect to the doctrine of proprietary estoppel.[45]

Finally, comparing the various forms of redress also gives insights into why the law intervenes in certain cases or contexts, and how the rationale for this intervention can sometimes change over time. On the whole, the rationale underlying the various forms of redress can be grouped into the following: (i) preventing unconscionable behaviour/risk of exploitation; (ii) protecting reliance; (iii) remunerating unremunerated work; (iv) preventing the promisor's enrichment; and (v) treating the promisor's successors equally. These justifications aside, there also seem to be other broader policy reasons for intervening. For instance, in the farming context there is a need to keep farming viable, by ensuring that future generations stay on the farm, even if they cannot be immediately paid or the farm transferred to them. There is also a need to avoid fragmentation of farms (and agricultural business), which might explain why in many farm cases the promisee is likely to obtain the promised asset. On the other hand, in the care context, the concern is often to ensure that care is rendered in the family context so that the person in need of care is not put into a care institution and no professional carer needs to be employed. The analysis throughout this book pays attention to these various rationales.

41 Chapter 11.
42 Chapter 11.
43 Chapter 10.
44 Chapter 8.
45 Chapters 7 and 4.

In comparing the different ways in which a promisee can seek relief, this book examines jurisdictions in which there is, or has been, a meaningful amount of litigation and valuable approaches have developed, including primarily Australia, Austria, common law Canada, England and Wales, France, Germany, the Republic of Ireland, and New Zealand (with occasional references to Belgium, Italy, Jersey, the Netherlands, Scotland, and South Africa). Within each, it focuses on those avenues of redress around which there have been relevant legislative or jurisprudential developments.

Writing a book that compares a variety of different forms of redress belonging to various areas of private law and across more than one legal tradition inevitably poses certain terminological and linguistic challenges. This is even more so given that this book aims to speak to both common and civil lawyers, and legal scholars working across a range of different areas of law. Certain terms inevitably come with cultural baggage. Since this book is not (at least not purposefully) written from the viewpoint of any particular legal tradition or system, where possible it aims to employ terminology that cuts across legal traditions, except where individual forms of redress are being examined. This is, for instance, why this book does not normally speak of 'remedies', but uses rather the generic terms, 'forms of redress' or 'avenues of redress'.

III. Scope of the enquiry

A. The meaning of 'promise'

This book focuses on instances in which a person has made a promise of a future inheritance and the promise has been acted upon by the promisee but remains unfulfilled. For the purposes of this book, the term 'promise' is given a broad factual meaning so as to include not only legally binding promises in the form of a contract, or promises consisting in a speech act, but also informal representations, assurances, indications, and expressions of intentions that are, or can be, implied from the behaviour of the promisor. Thus, it matters not just what promisors say but also how they behave, and not just at a particular moment but also over time. The term is understood to encompass unilateral promises that are acted upon as well as bilateral (even if tacit) arrangements between the promisor and the promisee, who have reached some form of understanding, that is that the former will make a future testamentary disposition in favour of the latter in exchange for some performance.[46] This broad terminology allows the book to capture not only the

[46] Take, for example, the case where one person accepts services or performances from another person knowing, or at least suspecting, that the other's behaviour is motivated by an expectation to inherit something (in exchange) but refrains from saying anything to dispel the expectation. Although

array of different behaviours of the promisor over time, but also a wide range of forms of redress a promisee can seek.

Where the promise is express, it can be made either orally or in writing. Even when made in writing, this is not a will itself, for the promisor simply promises, albeit in writing, to make a future disposition. Irrespective of whether or not they are made in writing, testamentary promises may or may not turn into a contract.[47] Where a legally binding testamentary promise is referred to, this book speaks explicitly of a contractual promise to make a will.[48] In all other cases, it refers more generally to 'informal' testamentary promises (whether or not they are in writing).

B. What lies outside the scope of the book?

Bare expectations to inherit are not within the scope of this book. In the testamentary context, a person may well have developed, and relied upon, beliefs as to a future inheritance, even in the absence of an express or implied promise. This may be due to her relationship with the deceased, or other circumstances, such as the awareness that she is the only remaining relative,[49] or, for instance, the farmer's only son. In the farming context, especially, certain expectations can be nurtured, due to the social practice of land being passed on, and retained within the family (usually the male children) for several generations. In such cases, property can be regarded as merely in transition between successive family members. However, where no promise understood broadly was made, the cases fall outside the remit of this book, which focuses on instances where the promisee's performance is based on an expectation to inherit that is engendered by the promisor's behaviour. Equally, outside the scope of the enquiry are instances where a promise may have been made but the promisee has not provided any performance in exchange. In other words, the focus is on cases where there is a promise (understood broadly) and the promisee has provided a performance that was accepted by the promisor.

Given that this book only deals with promises to make future testamentary dispositions (which are to confer benefits on death of the promisor), donative promises in which the promisor promises to convey the promised asset during her

there is here no express promise on the side of the promisor, her behaviour is still relevant, as it fosters the expectations of the promisee.

[47] As for the requirements of such a fully blown contract to make a will, see Chapter 3. Writing is usually only required where the promise concerns land.

[48] In Germany and Austria, reference is sometimes made to the *Testiervertrag*. By contrast, in France and Italy, there is no specific term for a legally binding promise to make a will.

[49] Sometimes the expectation may be raised once the claimant acquires knowledge, even if only indirectly, of the fact that the deceased has made a will in her favour. This was the case in *Schaefer v Schuhmann* (n 2) but also *Guzzo v Catlin Estate* (1989) 38 BCLR (2d) 41 (BCCA). In OLG Köln 29 June 2017 – 16 U 106/16 the promisee was the sole heir and convinced he would ultimately inherit.

lifetime lie necessarily outside its scope. The same holds true of mechanisms that bring about an immediate lifetime transfer of rights to the promisee, such as gifts, or binding caregiving or maintenance agreements.[50] Equally excluded are inheritance contracts, such as the German *Erbvertrag*,[51] which represent testamentary dispositions that take effect on death but that are, in principle, immediately binding and thus irrevocable, so that a testator is no longer free to dispose of her assets as she pleases. The book further omits a discussion of mutual wills, which are wills made by two or more people, usually in favour of each other, who agree that they will not revoke the will without the other party's consent. Finally, the book does not include an analysis of the protection of spousal rights through patrimonial regimes or the protection of de facto partners through the finding of a constructive trust concerning the couple's home.

Where a will contradicts a promise, a promisee could contest the will, on the basis of lack of formalities, lack of capacity, duress, or undue influence (or unconscionable behaviour).[52] However, in many jurisdictions a will-contest is difficult. Furthermore, it would only be useful where the promisee benefits under intestacy rules, for only in that case would the estate go to her once the will is invalidated. In some instances, a promisee may further want to argue that the person who benefitted under the will or intestacy rules is unworthy or that forfeiture rules apply.[53] Again, such claims are often difficult to bring and would anyway only be advantageous where the estate will go to the promisee, should the person in question be found to be unworthy. For that reason, such claims are not analysed in detail.

Principles of extra-contractual liability do not normally come into play in this context, and it is usually uncommon to invoke rules concerning *negotiorum gestio*.[54] And, in any event, this book focuses on instances where a promise was made and leaves out cases in which a person acts for someone else (providing, for instance, gratuitous services) without being encouraged to do so in any form. The

[50] For the US, see Hall (2001–2002); Hall (2003); Kohn (2019). See further Hofri-Winogradow & Kaplan (1997) and Coore in *Ageing, Gender and Family Law* (2018) 34. For the civil law context see, for instance, the Italian 'contratto di mantenimento'. For details see Christandl in *Passing Wealth on Death* (2016) 144–145.

[51] § 1941 and §§ 2274ff BGB.

[52] For examples where the promisee has contested the validity of the will, see the Canadian case of *Lata v Rush*, 2012 ONSC 4543 and the Irish decision in *Naylor v Maher* [2012] IEHC 408. See also the English case of *James v James* [2018] EWHC 43 (Ch) where the claimant had also brought an estoppel claim but both were unsuccessful. Undue influence was pleaded in the Canadian case of *Huculak v Kallenberger et al* 2005 BCSC 239 but the claim (together with the *quantum meruit* claim) was rejected. However, in *Granger v Granger* 2016 ONCA 945 undue influence was found. Leslie (1999) 558 has argued that, in the US, will contests are the preferred vehicle for protecting disappointed expectations partly because it makes the promisee look less greedy.

[53] The will was contested, and a claim based on unworthiness was brought in the German case decided by the BAG 5 August 1963 – 65 AZR 79/63, NJW 1963, 2188.

[54] Miserre *Die 'culpa in testando'* (2002) 53; Ludyga (2009) 290.

law of partnerships too is also normally of little assistance to a promisee of a future inheritance,[55] and is therefore excluded from the analysis.

IV. The structure of the book

This book is divided into three parts. Part I outlines the background of the enquiry and introduces the reader to the promisee's perspective by examining both the social and legal context within which such promises tend to operate. It provides an overview of factual scenarios and problems emerging from cases and explores the motives behind the practice of testamentary promises and why they may remain unfulfilled. In doing so, this part offers insight into the complex web of power relationships that characterizes the setting in which such promises are expressed and highlights why it is important to protect the promisee. It further provides an overview of the various forms of redress that can be sought and the challenges that promisees face when bringing a claim. Finally, this part also illustrates why legal systems have struggled to regulate testamentary promises and what difficulties arise for courts faced with unfulfilled promises.

From this overview of the social context, as revealed by the reported cases from across several jurisdictions, and of the underlying legal framework, the book then moves on to an analysis of the available legal responses in Parts II and III. Here, the book examines and compares a wide range of different types of possible legal avenues across both the common and civil law traditions and evaluates them through the lens of the promisee. The order of analysis does not follow any particular jurisdiction. Rather, it groups the various forms of redress together, starting (in Part II) with those through which promisees can obtain the promised asset, and then moving on (in Part III) to those in which the promisee obtains monetary compensation based on either the value of her performance or the value of the promisor's enrichment. It ends with those forms of redress in which the law imposes an artificial limit to what the promisee can claim.

Structuring the book in this way is not without challenges. For instance, one difficulty with it is that with some forms of redress courts have a considerable amount of discretion, meaning that the relief granted may or may not lead to the promised asset being transferred to the promisee. For that reason, some cases may fit into more than one chapter (e.g. we will see this in proprietary estoppel cases, but also Canadian unjust enrichment law cases, or instances in which a family provision order is applied for). There is therefore a certain risk of artificiality of the

[55] See, however, the *stillschweigender familienrechtlicher Kooperationsvertrag* or *stillschweigender familienrechtlicher Vertrag* discussed in Miserre *Die 'culpa in testando'* (2002) 40–41. On the possibility of implying a partnership agreement where a son has worked on the farm of his father, see Kroeschell in *Göttinger Festschrift* (1961). US courts are generally reluctant to imply partnerships between husband and wife—see Philipps (2008) 81.

classification and one of overlap and repetition. At the same time, there are important benefits to grouping together the various forms of redress this way. It brings into view the circumstances under, and jurisdictions in which, a promisee is more likely to obtain fulfilment of the promise, which is ultimately what she will most want. It also helps to resist the formalist pull of some of the doctrinal categories and to get away from conceptual and terminological habits. In other words, it puts into sharper focus what the courts are actually doing, thereby allowing the reader to move beyond the formal label attached to the particular redress and its doctrinal structures, and to question the justifications for the intervention of the law in protecting the promisee's interest.

Both Part II and Part III pay attention to what a promisee needs to prove in order to be successful, how the award is quantified, and the possible challenges that a promisee may have to overcome. They also show why the law intervenes and whether the reasons for that have changed over time. They examine when the claim arises, how the promisee's position fares against that of third parties with an interest in the estate, and what forms part of that estate. This will reveal, once more, the complexity of both formal and especially informal testamentary arrangements.

PART I

INTRODUCING THE PROMISEE'S PERSPECTIVE

1
The social context

I. Introduction

Before examining, in Chapter 2, the legal framework within which testamentary promises usually operate, this chapter offers an insight into the social context in which they are made. It does so by drawing on information that can be gleaned from reported cases. The aim is to show the specificities of testamentary promises, but also the vulnerabilities of the promisee and why promisors should be held to their promises. For this reason, I will first examine the distinguishing features of testamentary promises before investigating the motivations that underpin the behaviour of both the promisor and the promisee, and finally, why testamentary promises may remain unfulfilled.

The picture that arises from the cases is complex because the facts are as varied as the relationships. Nonetheless, some common features emerge. First, promises of a future inheritance are principally made in a domestic or family setting, and most commonly in the farming/agricultural and the household/care context, and are for that very reason informal and often generic and vague. This, as we will see in the course of this enquiry, can pose difficulties for the promisee. Second, such promises are normally part of an intergenerational testamentary exchange. The paradigm testamentary promises case is that of a promise that is not wholly gratuitous.[1] As the analysis will show, the objective of such promises is frequently to persuade or induce the promisee to rely on the promise and, consequently, to act on it by providing (or continuing to provide) financial benefits, work, or services in the family business or on the family farm, as well as services in the household, including care services, emotional support, and companionship. This exchange does not exclude generosity or genuine intention on the part of the promisor. Indeed, the reward in the form of an inheritance can sometimes be quite generous, exceeding the value of the performance rendered by the promisee. This is the reason why testamentary arrangements can be attractive also for the promisee, even though she may have to wait a long time before she benefits.

Also, as the analysis will show, testamentary promises are usually intended seriously, meaning that the promisor intends to keep the promise at least at the time it is made. Nonetheless, promisors are normally in a position of considerable

[1] Atiyah *Promises* (1981) 143–146.

Claiming a Promised Inheritance. Alexandra Braun, Oxford University Press. © Alexandra Braun 2022.
DOI: 10.1093/oso/9780198757252.003.0002

power that makes it easier for them to be generous and, at the same time renders the promisee more vulnerable and susceptible to exploitation by the promisor. As this book will show, this power derives from the promisor's economic position, her information advantage, the fact that the transfer to the promisee usually only takes place on the promisor's death, that until then her will is freely revocable, and that her relationship with the promisee is usually one of trust and affection. Moreover, testamentary agreements tend to involve people with whom the promisor is in a close relationship, and who are more likely to rely on them even if they are made informally. Thus, testamentary promises permit promisors to secure benefits from people with whom they usually have a close relationship, while still maintaining control over their wealth for the duration of their lives.

Finally, the cases will also show that testamentary promises have been part of our social reality for many centuries, and that they continue to play a role even in an age where sophisticated estate planning is available. Even so, judging from the cases, it appears that promises of an inheritance cases do not usually involve the wealthiest strata of society,[2] but rather the middle and lower classes. Generally speaking, the wealthier people are the more likely they are to seek the advice of professionals for estate planning purposes. They are therefore probably less prone to making such promises, and probably also less likely to rely on them.

II. Core features of testamentary promises

A. Context and form of testamentary promises

Testamentary promises are primarily made in the domestic or family setting, rather than in a commercial setting. They often concern family members and occasionally also involve friends, housekeepers, or farm workers, who are sometimes regarded as part of the family. This explains why such promises are usually made informally,[3] even when it would be possible (and more prudent) to enter into a legally binding contract to make a will. In other words, generally speaking testamentary promises are made orally and involve an agreement that is reached over the course of many conversations, held over several months or even years. Occasionally they are repeated in conversations with third parties or are referred to in letters.[4] The informality of the agreement reached between promisor and promisee means that the

[2] In the past, formal testamentary promises appear to have involved the wealthier strata, as they were sometimes expressed in the context of marriage settlements and marriage promises; however, both of these are no longer that common.

[3] The German Bundesgerichtshof has acknowledged that testamentary promises are not generally put into writing. BGH 29 November 1965 – VII ZR 214/63, NJW 1966 540, 541.

[4] For example, *Synge v Synge* [1894] 1 QB 466 (hereafter *Synge v Synge*). In *Sullivan v Sullivan & Ors* [2006] NSWCA 312 a message inside a Christmas card was regarded as sufficient to establish a promise.

promise frequently lacks a level of precision regarding the exact subject matter[5] and the scope of the counter-performance. In other words, they are vague. As we will see later, this can create difficulties for the promisee.

Another central feature that emerges from the cases across various jurisdictions is that testamentary promises are often part, or take the form, of informal agreements or understandings whereby the promisee will obtain an inheritance *provided that*, or *because*, she offers something in return. In other words, the cases litigated usually involve a certain level of reciprocity. They show that promises of an inheritance are a useful means through which a promisor can decide how to pass, or distribute, her wealth on death,[6] while at the same time also securing benefits of all kinds. In some cases, the agreement can therefore look rather like a 'bargain'.[7]

Within the domestic environment, promises are most commonly expressed in the farming/agricultural and household/care contexts. In the case of farming, children are usually expected and required to help and work on the farm from a very young age and often for no reward. Typically, they leave school at an early age (most commonly when they are fourteen or fifteen years old) to work on the farm and some never leave, precisely because they are told that they will eventually inherit the farm. In such cases, their existence is often entirely based on the farm, which provides both a home and a means to sustain a living. Farming is after all a way of life. At the same time, help from the next generation is frequently the only way in which farms can survive, especially where they are small.[8] Thus, a promise as to the future transfer of the farm can ensure that it remains viable. While in the past farms may not always have been worth fighting for, this position has changed with the increase in real estate values.

[5] See section II.B.

[6] Lobley (2010) 840 argues that 'identification of a successor can act as a trigger for business development, and the existence of a successor can provide a powerful motivation for on-going investment in the business even into the old age of the retiring farmer'.

[7] For examples, see the Australian case *Vigolo v Bostin* (2005) 221 CLR 191 where a son worked in the family farm business run by his father. See also the English decision in *Seward v Seward* (Ch, 20 June 2014), where a couple had promised to leave their farm to their younger son if he complied with their request to transfer his half share in another property to his older brother, which he did. The Canadian Case of *Proulx v Daniels* 2001CarswellBC 657, (2001) BCSC 441; 104 ACWS (3d) 605 is another good illustration. Here the defendant and his wife made a proposal to the claimants, namely, that if the claimants came to live in Victoria, and cared for the Daniels in their home for the remainder of each of their lives, the Daniels would leave the claimants their home and its contents in their wills.

[8] Behrens J in an order of 15 November 1996 (first instance decision in *Re Pearce (Deceased) Re Pearce (deceased)* [1998] 2 FLR 705; [1999] 2 FCR 179; [1998] Fam Law 588 (hereafter *Re Pearce (Deceased)*) said that 'It was suggested that many farm children did similar amounts of work. It seems to me that this plaintiff did very much at the top end of the sort of work that farm children do, and he was the only child, and he was working very hard, in my view, but the fact that other farm children may also have done a substantial amount of work, does not in my view mean that there is no moral obligation on the parents to leave or to pass on part of the estate to the children. It seems to me that that is the basis on which small farms have been run, and that is the reason why children have worked for very little money on farms in the expectation, and in my view, subject to a moral obligation on their parents to pass on the farm to them.' On the difficulties when dealing with the transfer of farms, see the Victorian Law Reform Commission, *Succession Laws: Report* (2013) [6.163].

Testamentary promises are also frequently made in exchange for household/domestic and care services. In the nineteenth and early twentieth centuries, parents would often ask one of the daughters to stay at home to look after them in old age in exchange for a promise to leave her the family home.[9] Similarly, one could find cases in which testamentary promises were made to the housekeeper, sometimes in connection with a promise of marriage. Although such cases are no longer that common, longevity and increasing rates of dementia have rendered the need for private care even more pressing, showing the continuing utility of such promises in the care context. Again, the increase in the value of real property has made it worth litigating over the family home.

B. Content and object of testamentary promises

The content of testamentary promises usually consists of a promise to leave something by will. However, a promisor can also promise not to revoke an already existing will containing a bequest in favour of the promisee. Such cases[10] are frequently found in connection with mutual wills, that is to say wills in which both parties promise not to revoke their wills without the consent of the other.[11] However, these lie outside the scope of this book. It is equally possible for a promisor to undertake (to her intestate heir) not to make a will or not to sever a joint tenancy, so that the other tenant becomes absolutely and automatically entitled to the property through survivorship on death of the promisor. However, either of these instances rarely feature in the law reports.[12] A will aside, a promisor may also want to benefit someone through alternative means, such as an inheritance contract (*Erbvertrag*),[13] a life insurance policy, or a private pension scheme nomination.[14] Again cases involving such benefits are comparatively rare. However, given that wealth is increasingly invested in life insurance and pensions and retirement schemes, the object of testamentary promises may well change in the future as a result.

9 See Hartog *Someday* (2012) 81ff.

10 For example, see *Re Marsland* [1939] Ch 820 (hereafter *Re Marsland*) and *Palmer v Bank of New South Wales* [1974–1975] 133 CLR 150.

11 For an Australian example, see *Barns v Barns* [2003] HCA 9; 214 CLR 169; 196 ALR 65. In order for the doctrine of mutual wills to operate, it is necessary for there to be an express promise not to revoke the will. See *Re Goodchild (Deceased) and Another* [1997] 2 FLR 644.

12 For an example, see the Canadian case of *Henderson v Henderson* (1998) 52 BCLR (3d) 184 (BCSC).

13 See BGH 12 July 1989–VIII ZR 286/88, BGHZ 108, 256, 263 = NJW 1989, 2745.

14 Such alternative modes of benefitting someone on death are often referred to as 'will-substitutes'. See, especially, Braun & Röthel *Passing Wealth on Death* (2016) and Langbein (1983-1084). For a pension example, see the Canadian case of *Belvedere v Brittain Estate* 94 OR (3d) 655 (2009) OCA. For a life insurance example, see the German decision RG 20 March 1911, WarnRspr 1911, Nr 267.

Among all the various options just outlined, the most common and typical in practice is a generic undertaking by a testator to leave something on death, usually a will. In civil law legal systems, the promisor may promise to nominate someone as their heir, or to leave a legacy, without specifying exactly what the promisee is to receive. Equally, in common law systems, the promisor may undertake to benefit the promisee on her death, without necessarily specifying what she will leave or without even referring to a will. In fact, promises are often generic along the lines of: 'I will see to it',[15] or 'you don't have to worry about money, you'll be all right',[16] or 'I will look after you',[17] or '[…] some day when you have this farm you'll appreciate this',[18] or it is 'all going to be yours when I am gone',[19] or referring to the farm 'you're doing it for yourself, sure I can't take it with me'.[20] In such cases, the promisor seems to imply that she will make a testamentary disposition in favour of the promisee. However, where it is unclear exactly what was promised and how much the promisor intended the promisee to receive, the promisee may have difficulties establishing a claim.[21] Even where the promisor announces that 'this will all be yours one day',[22] specifically pointing at specific property, it can potentially be problematic to ascertain what 'this' actually refers to.[23] Indeed, the success of any court action and the degree of protection, including vis-à-vis third parties, can depend on how specific the promise is in identifying the benefit.[24] So the lack of specificity of some promises carries a risk that promisors could potentially exploit.

Quite often the promisor undertakes to leave her entire estate[25] or what is left, that is the residue, or a share of it. For instance, in some cases promisors may make statements along the following lines: 'if you stick with us you will have what is left',

15 *Jennings v Rice* [2002] EWCA 159 (hereafter *Jennings v Rice*).

16 *Re Basham* [1987] 1 All ER 405, [1986] 1 WLR (Ch) 1501 (hereafter *Re Basham*); *Jennings v Rice* (n 15); *Re William (deceased)* HC Wellington CP 866/92, 21 July 1994.

17 *Hamilton v Hamilton* [2003] NZFLR 883 (NZHC), [49].

18 *Sabey v Beardsley* [2013] BCSC 642, [23] and [25]. In the Irish case *Naylor v Maher* [2012] IEHC 408, the promisor repeatedly said 'you will be farming for yourself' when the claimant questioned the low wages he was receiving.

19 *Cook v Thomas* [2010] EWCA Civ 227, [35] and [72].

20 *K v K* [2018] IEHC 615, [7]. The uncle of the promisor had also said 'God, isn't it a grand farm, won't you have a fine farm in time to come, wont it be a lot more than we had when myself and your father started out with just the front?' In the Irish case of *McCarron v McCarron* (Supreme Court, unreported, 13 February 1997) (hereafter *McCarron v McCarron*) Murphy J held that the discussions between the farmer and the claimant were very limited and that they amounted to no more than an exchange in which the farmer said 'I suppose you are wondering about some compensation for your work' to which the claimant replied 'I suppose I will not be forgotten' in response to which the farmer said to the claimant 'you'll be a rich man after my day'. The Supreme Court held that there was a binding agreement.

21 See, for instance, *Layton v Martin* [1986] The Times 11 December 1985, [1986] Fam Law 212 where the deceased promised 'financial security'. The proprietary estoppel claim was unsuccessful.

22 *Jennings v Rice* (n 15) [9], [17].

23 In *Habberfield v Habberfield* [2019] EWCA Civ 890 (hereafter *Habberfield v Habberfield*) the promisor said that the daughter should receive a 'viable dairy farm at Woodrow', a farm in Somerset.

24 This could, for instance, not only be a problem if the promisee wants to base her claim on contract law but also where she intends to rely on the doctrine of proprietary estoppel.

25 *Antrobus v Antrobus* 2009 BCSC 134 (hereafter *Antrobus v Antrobus*).

or 'you know what Pa said ... that what was left would be yours if you stayed with us'.[26] Again such promises can be problematic from the point of view of a promisee for the degree of her protection may be reduced. For instance, Chapter 3 will illustrate that a promisee of a contractual promise to leave the residue estate will not be able to obtain specific performance of the promise.[27] She will also not be treated as a creditor, so that she benefits only after all debts have been paid, which is less than satisfactory from her perspective.

However, as will emerge in the course of this book, there are also many cases where the testamentary promise is specific as to the subject matter of the promise. This may, for instance, be a promise to leave a life interest in a property,[28] a particular asset, such as a business, or, more commonly, the home in which the promisor was living prior to her death, or her farm. Being at the receiving end of a specific promise can make things easier for the promisee, not just in terms of the burden of proof of the promise, or the available forms of redress and the relief granted, but also in terms of her protection vis-à-vis third parties.

What is promised can sometimes be of great economic value. This is evident when looking, for instance, at cases involving farms. In *Suggitt v Suggitt*, the son was held to be entitled to a farm and farmhouse valued at over £3 million.[29] Equally, in *Habberfield v Habberfield*,[30] the promisee was awarded £1.2 million, and in *Gee v Gee*, the value of the farm business and land at the heart of the contention was £8 million.[31] The considerable value of potential testamentary promises claims explains (at least in part) the promisor's reluctance to give up the entitlement or control during her lifetime, a point to which I shall return later,[32] but also why promisees may agree to the testamentary exchange. The value that they can obtain through an inheritance is often higher than what they could earn by way of labour. Yet, as the enquiry will show, the value of the promised inheritance for the promisee cannot just be measured on the basis of its economic value.[33]

C. Who makes testamentary promises and in favour of whom?

The cases also tell us that promises of an inheritance mostly involve family members (broadly understood) that pertain to different generations. They are made

[26] *Foster v Royal Trust Co* [1951] 1 DLR 147.

[27] For details, see especially Chapter 3.

[28] Examples are *Maddison v Alderson* (1883) 8 App Cas 467 (HL) (hereafter *Maddison v Alderson*) and *Synge v Synge* (n 4).

[29] *Suggitt v Suggitt* [2012] EWCA Civ 1140. In the English decision of *Bradbury v Taylor* [2012] EWCA Civ 1208; [2013] WTLR 29 (CA (Civ Div) (hereafter *Bradbury v Taylor*), newspaper reports indicate that the house awarded to the claimant was valued at £800,000. Mee (2013) 287.

[30] *Habberfield v Habberfield* (n 23).

[31] *Gee v Gee* [2018] EWHC 1393 (Ch).

[32] See section III.B.4.

[33] Conway in *Emotional Dynamics of Law and Legal Discourse* (2016) 35, 40, and 43.

primarily by parents, aunts and uncles, and occasionally siblings and cousins.[34] In other words, they tend to be made to children (including stepchildren and adopted children), nephews and nieces, and sometimes to siblings and cousins. They can also involve other family members, such as grandparents and grandchildren, spouses (including civil partners), cohabitants, and daughters- and sons-in-law.[35] Another, 'target' of such promises are friends, and occasionally also lodgers or neighbours, as well as farm workers, managers, or gardeners.[36]

In the past, testamentary promises were made in the context of marriage settlements, that is to a future spouse. In certain jurisdictions, it was, for instance, not uncommon for a father to make such a promise to a potential suitor in an attempt to 'persuade' him to marry his daughter or not to change his mind about a planned marriage. In other words, testamentary promises were a means to secure a marriage and were made in exchange of a marriage promise.[37] However, today, such marriage cases seem to have largely disappeared from the law reports. Generally, fewer claims appear to be brought by spouses and cohabitants across the various jurisdictions considered in this book. This is probably due partly to the fact that an increasing number of jurisdictions have put in place measures to recognize and compensate the work that spouses (including civil partners) and de facto partners perform in the context of the business or home of their deceased spouse or partner. In other words, the value of any improvements they make to the deceased's property, as well as the value of non-financial contributions, have been recognized to a greater extent.[38] Also, in the course of the past decades, at least spouses and civil partners have seen their succession rights increase, both in the case of intestacy and in case of testate succession,[39] so that they may have less of an incentive to bring a claim for breach of a promise made to them by their spouse or civil partner.

[34] *Thorner v Major* [2009] UKHL 18; [2009] 1 WLR 776 (hereafter *Thorner v Major*).

[35] In a case note to the decision of the BGH 22 March 2013 – V ZR 28/12, NJW 2013, 2025, Chris Thomale states that there is an increasing exchange between parents and daughters-in-law. Thomale (2013).

[36] For examples involving gardeners, see *Taylor v Dickens* [1998] 1 FLR 806 as well as *Jennings v Rice* (n 15). For a farm manager, see *Campbell v Griffin* [2001] EWCA Civ 990 (hereafter *Campbell v Griffin*). According to Wells *New Approach* (2007) 38–39, in Canada, in recent years more claims have been brought by persons unrelated to the deceased. Wells predicts this trend to continue given the social and geographical mobility, the increasingly unstable pattern of family relationships, and an increasing inability or unwillingness of relatives to provide care for members of their wider family.

[37] See, for instance, *Synge v Synge* (n 4); *Hammersley v De Biel* (1845) 12 Cl & Fin 45; *Coverdale v Eastwood* (1872) LR 15 Eq 121. In the last case, the proposal of marriage had already been accepted. See Lettmaier *Broken Engagements* (2010) 24 who argues that in seventeenth-century England, marriage was understood principally as a commercial speculation.

[38] The developments in England concerning family home constructive trusts seem to confirm this. For an overview, see McFarlane et al *Land Law* (2021).

[39] For an overview, see Reid, de Waal, & Zimmermann, 'Intestate Succession in Historical and Comparative Perspective' in *Comparative Succession Law 2* (2015) and Reid, de Waal, & Zimmermann, 'Mandatory Family Protection in Historical and Comparative Perspective' in *Comparative Succession Law 3* (2020).

Promises directed towards housekeepers[40] or servants also seem to belong to the past. They were sometimes treated as if they were part of the family, and not infrequently no formal employment contract existed between the parties.[41] Not only are housekeepers less common in those circles of society in which such promises are made, nowadays the housekeeper may also sometimes qualify as a de facto partner and as such enjoy greater protection, though not necessarily in the context of succession law where they are not usually treated in the same way as spouses and civil partners.[42] In fact, some of the older cases dealt with instances where (usually) a man was looking for someone (often a younger woman) to look after him and his household. Not infrequently, she was promised an inheritance, as well as marriage.[43]

One interesting question in this context is whether some people are more often the beneficiaries of such promises than others. The historian Henrik Hartog has suggested that, in the nineteenth and early twentieth century, women were frequently the 'target' of testamentary promises, and that such promises were a way of keeping one of the female descendants at home and to prevent them from getting married.[44] Also, housekeepers were usually female, but as mentioned, these days cases by housekeepers are rare. What is certainly noticeable is that in instances where a promise is made in exchange for care, household services, or companionship, the promisee is often, though not always,[45] a woman. By contrast, in cases in which the transfer of a farm is promised in exchange for work and improvements, the promisee is frequently a man, though there are some recent instances where the claim to the farm was brought by the farming daughter.[46]

D. What do promisees do in exchange?

As mentioned earlier, a central feature of testamentary promises is that they involve a certain level of reciprocity. Indeed, one claim put forward in this book is that promises of an inheritance usually come with strings attached. It is therefore

[40] Examples are *Maddison v Alderson* (n 28); *Schaefer v Schuhmann* [1972] AC 572 (hereafter *Schaefer v Schuhmann*) and *Hesjedal v Granville* 1993 CarswellSask 569, 117 Sask 111, 109 DLR (4th) 353.

[41] Hartog *Someday* (2012). For a case in which the servant became a lover, see *Greasley v Cook* [1980] 1 WLR 1306.

[42] See Reid, de Waal, & Zimmermann, 'Mandatory Family Protection in Historical and Comparative Perspective' in *Comparative Succession Law* 3 (2020).

[43] For an example, see the German case of KG 9 March 1970 – 12 W 817/70, KG OLGZ 1971, 22 = FamRZ 1970, 317.

[44] Hartog *Someday* (2012) 222. That power differentials based on gender operated systematically against women promisees was pointed out by Fellows (1992) 338.

[45] A notable example is the French decision of Cass 1re civ, 12 July 1994, JCP G 1995, II, 22425; JCP N 1995, II, 438, note Sériaux; Defrénois 1994, art 35950, 1511, note X Savatier.

[46] See *Habberfield v Habberfield* (n 23); *Davies & Anor v Davies* [2014] EWCA Civ 568; [2014] Fam Law 1252; *Mulholland v Kane* [2009] NICh 9 (8 September 2009) (hereafter *Mulholland v Kane*).

important to explore what people do, or are asked to do or to provide, in *exchange* for the promised inheritance.

The cases suggest that occasionally promisees pay money, which the promisor might use to purchase a flat or to renovate her business.[47] More common,[48] however, are cases in which the promisee incurs other types of expenses, for instance, in the form of investments on the promised property. Across the different jurisdictions examined, there are several judgments involving promisors who promised to transfer land or a house on their death, and because of that the promisee had started to make improvements to the property (through work or financial investments),[49] or to build on the land,[50] only to discover later that the promise was not kept.

Most widespread, however, is litigation involving promises of an inheritance made in exchange for services. There are many cases in which the promisee has performed domestic/household services, which range from companionship and emotional support, to running errands, shopping, cooking, cleaning, driving the promisor (e.g. to medical appointments), gardening, and carrying out maintenance jobs in the house, to actual nursing or care work. Equally common are cases in which the promisee has provided services or labour on a farm and, occasionally, in a family business,[51] be it an agricultural business, shop, pub, or restaurant.[52]

Where services in the household, care services, or work on the farm are involved, promisees often perform such services for a long period of time, in some instances even thirty or so years.[53] Also, in many farming or care cases, the performances and demands on the promisee tend to increase over time (e.g. at first the promisee performs some errands or minor labour and then with time is asked to do more and more).[54] Sometimes the promisee may agree to change or adapt her lifestyle. In certain instances, this can involve promisees (and their families) moving from one country to another,[55] or selling their own home,[56] or refraining from moving

[47] OLG Karlsruhe, 6 December 2001 – 9 U 47/01, ZEV 2002, 196 = DStR 2002, 1232. In this case, the claimant and her husband had given financial support to the parents of the claimant so that they could continue their photographic shop in exchange for the promise that they would receive the family home.

[48] For an unusual case, see *Whitehead v State Trustees Ltd* (2011) 4 ASTLR 528; [2011] VSC 424; BC201106685 where the promise was one to help the mother if she carried out the pregnancy and had the child (of another man).

[49] See, for instance, the Jersey case of *Pirouet v Pirouet* 1985–86 JLR 151 (hereafter *Pirouet v Pirouet*) or the German decision BGH 22 March 2013 (n 35). See also the Canadian cases of *Kreeft v Kreeft* 2001 Carswell BC 1458, 2001 BCSC 893, 39 ETR (2d) 233 and of *Cowderoy v Sorkos Estate*, 2012 ONSC 1921.

[50] BGH 29 November 1965 (n 3).

[51] *Re Abram* [1996] 2 FLR 379; [1997] 2 FCR 85; [1996] Fam Law 666.

[52] *Re Basham* (n 16); *Thorner v Major* (n 34).

[53] Examples are *In Re Callaghan, Decd In Re Callaghan, Decd* [1985] Fam; *Antrobus v Antrobus* (n 25); *Thorner v Major* (n 34); *Habberfield v Habberfield* (n 23).

[54] A good example is the Canadian case of *Schnogl v Balen Estate* 2005 BCCA 575; (2006) 21 ETR (3d) 32 (hereafter *Schnogl v Balen Estate*).

[55] For instance, in the New South Wales case of *Wakeling v Ripley* (1951) 51 SR (NSW) 183, the promisor persuaded his sister and her husband to leave England, to reside with him in Australia and to look after him. In *McDermott v McDermott* [2008] NICh 5 (10 March 2008) the promisor had convinced his son and daughter-in-law to leave the US for Northern Ireland.

[56] *Parker v Clark* [1960] 1 WLR 286 (hereafter *Parker v Clark*).

out of the promisor's home and purchasing their own place.[57] And in some cases, promisees take promisors to live with them, offering board and lodgings, in addition to providing other types of (often care) services.[58] There are also several cases in which the promisee gives up her job, or alternative job opportunities, to be able to perform the agreed services.[59]

In the farming context, the work required is often very challenging, not just physically but also in terms of time, leaving the promisee very little room for anything else. Equally, care work can be time consuming and demanding leaving no energy or free time for other pursuits. Thus, irrespective of the context, promisees may not just actively do (or pay) something for the promisor, they often also renounce prospects of a different job, of better earnings, of a social life, or even of a good marriage.[60] Sacrifices on the part of the promisee are therefore not necessarily only professional but also personal. They can be both tangible and intangible in nature. While it may be difficult to put a price tag on intangible sacrifices and efforts, they should be properly acknowledged and rewarded.

There are inevitably some cases in which the claimant has done little more than simply paying regular visits to the deceased or making regular phone calls. In such instance, the courts have (usually) rejected the claim.[61] However, most of the cases that we will come across in this book show an extraordinary level of devotion, commitment, effort, and trust on the part of the promisee. One important aspect to note here is that whatever form the promisee's performance takes, it is often of immense value to the promisor and her estate (and thus also to the promisor's successors). For instance, it can help to preserve or maintain the viability of a business or a farm. It can also enrich the estate, for example, where due to the promisee's care services it will not be necessary for the promisor to pay a professional carer or to cover the costs of a care home. In the farming context, the work provided by family members means that the farmer will not have to pay for labour when the farm may not generate sufficient revenue. Economic benefits aside, the promisor can also gain significant non-economic benefits, for the work or services can allow the promisor to be cared for by someone whom she trusts, and to stay (often until death) in a home that is the centre of her life. Equally, the benefits of being able to continue staying on a farm (run by the next generation), which is not just a place of work but also a social place and home, are just as valuable as economic ones.

[57] *Thompson v Thompson* [2018] EWHC 1138 (Ch).

[58] *Balkwill v Smith* (1957) 65 Man R 55, 21 WWR 474 (hereafter *Balkwill v Smith*).

[59] *Clarkson v McCrossen Estate* (1995) 122 DLR (4th) 239 (BC CA) (hereafter *Clarkson v McCrossen Estate*).

[60] See Hartog *Someday* (2012) 188. For an example, see *Mulholland v Kane* (n 46). The court found that the relationship with the deceased barred her from the prospect of marriage or lifelong partnership with other men.

[61] An example is the decision of the CA de Douai, Chambre 1, 15 October 2007 discussed in Chapter 9. See also the New Zealand case of *Stevens v Ryan* [2017] NZFLR 419 and the German decision of the ArbG Trier, 28 January 2015 – 1 Ca 522/14, Az 1 Ca 522/14 discussed in Chapter 8.

III. The rationale underlying informal testamentary arrangements

A. Introduction

As the discussion so far has shown, promisees are frequently asked, or expected, to 'earn' their future inheritance, through the provision of work, services, improvements to the property, or financial contributions. In other words, what they get, if they get something, they do not usually get for free, though all going well, their reward may be higher. Thus, as I have argued also elsewhere,[62] on the whole, promises of an inheritance are usually more likely to be self-interested than selfless. In sections III.B and III.C I explain in more detail why I hold this view. I will focus especially on the reasons underpinning both the undertaking of testamentary promises and the acting on such promises, so as to obtain a more comprehensive picture of the power imbalance that characterizes the relationship between promisor and promisee. We will see that the prospect of obtaining something in return is an important (if not the most important) motivation behind such promises. The analysis will in fact show that promises are usually made to induce the promisee to act in a way that benefits the promisor. In other words, promises can be purposefully used to obtain benefits without the promisor taking any personal risks. Unlike the promisee who has a lot to gain (where the promise is kept) but also a lot to lose (where the promise remains unfulfilled) in making the promise, the promisor has usually only to gain. This is the case even when the promisor intends to reward the promisee generously, thus even when the value of what is promised (and what the promisee may end up inheriting) may exceed the value of the promisee's performance. After all, the promisor will not usually bear any consequences. She is in a position of strength and can easily exploit the promisee's position, whose performance is normally motivated by a number of reasons, including the prospect of an inheritance but also love, affection, and trust. The promisee will therefore be more gullible and likely to find it difficult to refuse the proposal, or to ask for a formal commitment.

It should be said from the outset that the judicial narrative of the facts does not always offer a clear picture of the motives involved on either side. Also, the promisors are often no longer in a position to tell their side of the story. Nonetheless, what transpires very clearly from the cases is that the behaviour on either side is frequently informed by more than one motive,[63] and that motives can change over time. This multitude of motives can make it even more difficult to get to the heart of these promises, which straddle the boundary of what is gratuitous and what is not and thus what is expected to be remunerated and what is

[62] Braun in *L'abnégation en droit civil* (2017) 41.
[63] See more generally Farnsworth (1995) 360.

not. This will become relevant again later in Parts II and III of this book, where I will evaluate the various forms of redress that a promisee can resort to. We will see that some place weight, and in some cases arguably too much weight, on the motives that underpin the promisee's actions and, occasionally, also on those of the promisor.

B. Reasons for making testamentary promises

1. Altruistic v non-altruistic motives

Whether lifetime or testamentary, one obvious reason for making donative promises would seem to be purely altruistic motives, that is intentions to be kind and generous,[64] in our case to benefit someone with effect on death. But purely altruistic motives would appear to be rare in practice. Indeed, anthropologists, sociologists, and economists have long suggested that donative promises often entail an element of exchange,[65] in the form, for instance, of an enhanced reputation, more favourable treatment, respect, or esteem, but also economic benefits.[66] It is therefore important not to automatically assume that promises of an inheritance are motivated by pure altruism.

Although, in principle, these reflections apply not just to lifetime promises of a gift but also to testamentary promises, in this book I argue that the testamentary context involves somewhat different considerations, as a consequence of which they are even less altruistic. The cases we will come across in the course of this enquiry will show that, although promisors may sometimes express the promise for purely altruistic reasons, in most instances, promises are either aimed at rewarding a service or performance already received or (more frequently) at inducing a promisee to provide services or work, to invest in or make improvements to the promisor's property.[67] Frequently, testamentary promises are resorted to as a

[64] Leslie (1999); Posner (1997) 577, 581.

[65] Stoljar (1956) 249; Farnsworth (1995) 359; Baron (1988–1989) 190–198; Rose (1992); Leslie (1999) 557 who speaks of the illusory nature of the gift/exchange dichotomy; Zimmermann *Law of Obligations* (1996) 477–478; Zweigert & Kötz *Introduction to Comparative Law* (1998) 389. This view is confirmed by the studies by anthropologists such as Marcel Mauss, see Mauss *The Gift* (1967). However, in the sense that the gift still exists and that it cannot be reduced to reciprocity as well as that the social fabric is not founded solely on market exchange, see the sociologist Godbout *World of the Gift* (1998). Some economists too confirm that gifts are used as compensation. See, for instance, Bernheim et al (1985) 1045. See also the studies by Fehr & Schmidt in *Handbook of the Economics of Giving I* 2006); Fehr & Fischbacher (2003); Fehr & Gächter (2000) as well as Masson & Pestieau in *Is Inheritance Legitimate?* (1997).

[66] Weimar (1994) 790 mentions that towards the end of the twelfth century, Placentinus endorsed Papinian's contention (C 3 28 35 1) according to which 'fathers should gain the esteem of their children not by means of promises or contracts but on merit'.

[67] This was recognized, for instance, by Walker (2008) 239 who, speaking of care cases, refers to a quid pro quo. Speaking of farm cases, Voyce 'Testamentary Promises' (2014) 2 has argued that 'such promises should be seen as reciprocal understandings within the context of intergenerational exchange of labour and land'.

means of preventing someone from stopping their performance or of persuading them to continue to perform or behave as they have.[68] Suppose, for instance, that a child who has been helping on the farm wants to stop and to move away so as to start a professional career. One way to prevent this from happening might be to express a promise regarding her future entitlement or interest in the farm. In other words, announcing a future inheritance can induce the promisee to continue carrying out the work she has been doing and that she intended to cease doing.[69] A similar example could be given in the care context. Imagine a case in which a person (in practice often someone within the family) is helping in the household or running errands for an elderly person who is in increasing need of help. When the requests become too demanding the person may want to stop but a promise may induce her to continue assisting the promisor. Just like wills, promises of an inheritance are therefore a powerful estate planning 'tool',[70] and can be employed in a strategic manner.[71] It follows that in many testamentary promises cases the promisor and the promisee envisage some sort of economic exchange.

But promises of an inheritance are not only a means of obtaining economic benefits in the form of investments, work, or services. They can also be undertaken in order to exercise power and control over another person,[72] or to secure a variety of intangible benefits which are just as important. Sometimes the purpose of a promise is to persuade the promisee to remain living, or return to live, with their family of origin, or to prevent them from moving elsewhere. Historical studies show, for example, that in the US, from the mid-nineteenth to the mid-twentieth century, an explosive economy and shifting social opportunities drew the young away from home and that the elderly used promises of inheritance to keep their children at their side.[73] The historian Hendrik Hartog, who studied nineteenth- and twentieth-century case law of the state of New Jersey, found that parents, uncles, and aunts often responded to the desire of the young to move away by offering them the prospect of future ownership of property.[74] Similar motives are noticeable also in modern times, especially where the promisor is elderly and in need of either company or care, or both.[75] Thus, promises of an inheritance are

[68] Sparks (1954–1955) points out that informal agreements often concern a continuation of existing affairs.

[69] Shavell (1991) 402; Goetz & Scott (1980).

[70] See Braun in *L'abnégation en droit civil* (2017) 33. Locke *Second Treatise of Government* (2001) chapter VI, [72]; Bentham *Theory of Legislation* (1890) chapter 5.

[71] Braun in *L'abnégation en droit civil* (2017) 41.

[72] In *Gillett v Holt* [2001] Ch 210 (CA) 219 (hereafter *Gillett v Holt*), Walker LJ stated at page 228 that 'it is notorious that some elderly persons of means derive enjoyment from the possession of testamentary power'.

[73] Hartog *Someday* (2012) 55 explains that 'inheritance was the hook that mobilized the attention and the work of those family members', especially at a time in the history where old age became a goal.

[74] Hartog *Someday* (2012) 142.

[75] See, for instance, BGH 22 March 2013 (n 35) and the case note by Thomale (2013). See also *Jiggins v Brisley* [2003] EWHC 841 (Ch) and *Bradbury v Taylor* (n 29) where the promisor convinced the nephew and his reluctant wife to move to Cornwall.

sometimes made in order to influence the behaviour of the next generation, irrespective of the social security system in place. This can be motivated by a desire not to be alone, but also by an awareness that, with growing age, the promisor may well need assistance.

Again, the reasons I have outlined can explain both lifetime and testamentary promises. However, there are other considerations that are particularly prevalent in, or specific to, the context of promises of an inheritance, and that make them especially attractive to prospective promisors. One important feature of testamentary promises is that promisors do not have to give up anything during their lifetime and that the property will only pass to the promisee on the promisor's death. In other words, unlike with lifetime promises of a gift, a promisor of a testamentary promise is left with control over the property for the remainder of her life, which she can employ to secure a benefit, while at the same time being able to enjoy it. She does not bear the direct consequences of her promise, as she does not give anything away. Indeed, she can still freely dispose of her assets. Any consequences, if there are any, of the non-performance of the promise are usually borne by her successors, unless a lifetime claim is granted. As I will discuss in greater detail in Chapter 2, this would appear to be the principal reason why Roman lawyers regarded stipulations directed towards the appointment of a future heir to be against *bonos mores*.[76] This fact, coupled with the perceived remoteness of the death most of us have, may well lead a promisor to be even more generous.[77] In other words, the fact that no immediate action or sacrifice is required on the part of the promisor, may make it easier for her to give her assets away, though this is not to say that such promises are not intended seriously.[78]

Another important aspect to consider is that wills are by nature revocable, and that this is widely known. Hence, even if a promisor keeps the promise and makes the promised will, she can always revoke it and, in most legal systems, this freedom cannot be limited even if the testator wants to.[79] The free revocability of wills represents a special incentive for making a testamentary rather than a lifetime promise. In a sense, therefore from the perspective of the promisor, testamentary promises are more attractive and probably less altruistic than lifetime donative promises.

At the same time, it should also be acknowledged here that, at times, the promisor may have no choice but to make a promise. Referring in particular to the farming context in Australia, Malcolm Voyce has argued that '[a]ny intimation that the father was not prepared to give the farm to a working son would imply that, under the son's management, the farm would be run down'.[80] The son may also not

[76] Weimar (1994) 789, 796.
[77] See McFarlane in *Current Issues* (2016) 80.
[78] See Braun in *L'abnégation en droit civil* (2017) 30.
[79] Except, for instance, in Germany where a testator is bound by the mutual will and can bind herself through an *Erbvertrag*. See the discussion in Chapter 2.
[80] Voyce '"Domestic Promises"' (2014) 161.

be prepared to commit. In other words, the viability of a farm may be dependent on gratuitous help from family members and the only way to secure that may be to make a promise. Even so, the promise is not made for free, and the promisee's action will therefore benefit the promisor.

It may also be the case that some promises function as a reassurance that is expressed to maintain peace and to avoid conflict with members of the family. A promisor may, for instance, use promises as a defence mechanism to silence those who advance requests. Even so, there is no doubt that testamentary promises frequently represent an instrument through which promisors can, and often do, pursue self-interest. This becomes even clearer when exploring why such promises are announced to promisees.

2. Reasons for announcing future gifts

The fact that testamentary promises are not made solely out of sheer generosity, as they are often undertaken to achieve some trade-off, is, in my view, shown particularly by the fact that promisors announce the gift to the promisee during their lifetime.[81] Announcing a future gift in the form of an inheritance, can be, as mentioned before,[82] a useful means for a promisor to *induce* another person to provide something in exchange, except, of course, where the promise serves as an assurance that someone will be rewarded for performances rendered in the past. Announcing a future gift may also be an effective way of keeping promisees where they are and of persuading them to continue to work or provide for the promisor. For instance, in the English case of *Cowderoy v Cranfield* Morgan J stated that the testatrix believed that 'if she made a will in favour of Mr Cranfield and told him that she had done so, that would help her because he would be more likely to continue to visit her and care for her'.[83] This can also be seen in the English proprietary estoppel case of *Walton v Walton* where the son's complaints about his low wages were met with promises by his mother concerning the inheritance of the farm, which he relied upon by staying on the farm.[84]

Such (non-altruistic) economic motives may, however, be mixed with other considerations. For instance, announcing a future gift can also be a way of marking how valuable and important the promisee's assistance or relationship (friendship) is or was, or of expressing the promisor's gratitude openly and sometimes publicly. Hartog has argued that to announce a gift represents a way of communicating to a person that she is viewed as someone close and important to the promisor, much like a family member.[85] Thus, love and affection also play a role for the promisor.

[81] *Schaefer v Schuhmann* (n 40) is a good example in which the promisor informed the beneficiary when he made her read out the codicil that benefitted her. The case is discussed in Chapter 3.
[82] See section III.B.II.
[83] *Cowderoy v Cranfield* [2011] EWHC 1616, [147].
[84] *Walton v Walton* (CA, 14 April 1994) (hereafter *Walton v Walton*).
[85] See, Hartog *Someday* (2012) 105.

According to some law and economics scholars, announcing future gifts may also benefit the promisee in the sense that advance knowledge of a future transfer means that she can adapt her consumption decisions to the impending change in wealth.[86] However, besides the fact that the promisee would probably often favour immediate performance, a decision to act on the promise can sometimes turn out to be detrimental precisely because the promisor is not bound, not even when she makes a will. More convincing, it seems, is the argument that a promise increases the likelihood that the gift will be made in the future. Indeed, by verbalizing our intentions they become more real and only then may we feel bound to keep our word. As Mischkowski, Stone, and Stremitzer have shown '[t]he average sensitivity of subjects' willingness to perform to their counterparties' expectations is higher when they made a promise'.[87]

To summarize, there may be many reasons for announcing a gift. However, more often than not it is a way of inducing someone to behave in a particular way and, at the same time, of increasing the chances of reliance, thus to maximize the promisor's own benefit, and not least a way of simply feeling good. Even when a testamentary promise is expressed to reward or reassure someone who has already been providing services to the promisor, or to show how much the promisee's actions or her relationship with the promisor are valued, or because the promisor feels that she has no choice but to promise to give an inheritance so as to secure indispensable services or work, this should not detract from the fact that in such cases there is an exchange and that the act is not purely selfless. That holds true even in cases where the value of what is promised eventually exceeds the value of the counter-promise or performance, and even if the promisor is motivated also by other reasons, such as love, affection, and gratitude.

3. Motives for making informal rather than formal testamentary promises

The earlier analysis has shown that promisors are in a powerful position and can use the promise as a tool to obtain certain benefits in return.[88] Arguably all this could explain why they make informal rather than formal promises. However, I argue that these are not the primary explanations. Other factors are at play which have to do primarily with the social context in which such promises are made.

The principal reason for making informal promises seems to be that promisors do not usually want to enter into a legally binding contract.[89] Most simply prefer informal dealings to formal ones. Personal relationships themselves are premised on a number of mutual and simultaneous promises and actions, and the closer the relationship, the less likely it is that promises are articulated (or documented) in

86 Goetz & Scott (1980) 1267; Posner (1977) 412.
87 Mischkowski et al (2019) 690.
88 Fellows (1992) 332.
89 According to Hartog *Someday* (2012) 82, some testators would go to solicitors in order to draft wills that would appear to give effect to the promise, without however conveying the property.

a clear and formal manner.[90] Moreover, problems in succession communication within families are not uncommon, which explains also the vagueness of many testamentary agreements. According to some scholars, in the domestic context it is often best that some things are left unspoken.[91] It might also feel awkward to formalize an agreement between an aunt and her niece or a father and his son. Thus, in my view, the primary reason for expressing testamentary promises informally is often that they are expressed in the domestic/familial setting where agreements are not usually formalized.[92] It is also difficult to formalize an agreement that tends to stretch over many years and to set out detailed conditions to deal with unforeseen circumstances. And some promisors prefer to keep their options open and allow for contingencies that may cause them to change their mind. Moreover, in some legal cultures, people seem to shy away from formalizing testamentary intentions, also seen in low testacy rates.[93] This again may be due, *inter alia*, to mere superstition or simply uneasiness when confronted with the idea of one's own mortality.

The fact that promises are made informally does not, however, mean that promisors are not serious about the promises they make; they may feel that a moral obligation is just as binding as a legal one,[94] and/or that it would be superfluous or even 'insulting' to put the undertaking in writing, or to express it in contractual language. Having given their word, they may be convinced (at least at the particular moment at which it is expressed) that they will keep it. Even though a promisor may make a testamentary promise strategically to obtain some benefit in exchange, rather than merely to benefit the promisee, the cases suggest that most people actually intend to keep their promises, at least when they make them.[95] It is precisely because promises are made in the domestic context, that they are intended to be binding, albeit not necessarily legally binding. Thus, they are normally intended seriously, even though neither of the parties may have reflected upon the possibility of legal enforcement.[96]

90 Leslie (1999) 556. See also Brian (2002).

91 Leslie (1999) 572 has argued that the act of commodification strips the exchange of its value. See also Titmuss *The Gift of Relationship* (1971) 245.

92 Dixon (2019) 90: 'Families, just like couples, do not put things in writing'. Notice that in *Bovaird v Frost* [2009] NSWSC 337 (hereafter *Bovaird v Frost*) the promisor did not want anything in writing but was happy for friends of one of the promisees to be told of the agreement. See also *Hardwick v Johnson* [1978] 1 WLR 683, 688 where Lord Denning makes a similar point about other types of family arrangements, e.g. property arrangements between cohabitants.

93 For instance, in France, the testation rate does not appear to exceed 10%. See C Pérès, 'Intestate Succession in France' in *Comparative Succession Law 2* (2015) 34.

94 Kasirer (2001).

95 Braun in *L'abnégation en droit civil* (2017) 45. I will expand on this in section IV when I will turn to the reasons for why promises of an inheritance remain unfulfilled.

96 I will not here engage with the vast amount of literature surrounding the expectations governing promissory obligations in the context of close personal relationships. That promises can be intended seriously even if they do not amount to a contract is shown also by the doctrine of proprietary estoppel. See the analysis in Chapter 4.

Consequently, the informality is usually neither a sign of the selflessness nor of the maliciousness of the promisor, who wants to leave the promisee without protection, nor of a lack of seriousness. Rather, it is primarily determined by the context in which they are made. At the same time, the informality of the arrangement renders the promisee even more vulnerable because, on the one hand, it makes proof of the promise more difficult and, on the other hand, because it exposes the promisee to the risk that the promisor's demands will increase over time.

4. Motives for not making an immediate gift

If promisors are, as I argue, serious about their intention to benefit or reward the promisee on their death, a natural question is why do they not make immediate gifts? Why do they prefer making a promise to leave something on death, thereby deferring the gift to a later moment, or indeed, to the last possible moment? The answer to the question lies partly in what I said earlier. If a person makes a testamentary promise, she has little to lose for she does not usually have to give up anything herself.[97] This leads me to the next point.

Provided we are not in the realm of fraudulent promises, the most important reason for deferring the gift is that most people do not generally enjoy giving up control over what they have earned and accumulated during their lives. This is so especially when the promised property is all they have. Imagine, for instance, the situation in which an elderly promisor undertakes to transfer her home to the person who is providing care for her. It is perfectly understandable that she may want to continue living in her home until her death, and to retain full power and control over it until then. Otherwise, she could risk becoming dependent on others, in this case her carer.[98] Of course, there may be other ways of achieving this,[99] but they generally involve formalizing the agreement, and that is not usually what promisors want. And there is also the risk that the carer predeceases her.

But even where the promised property is not all the promisor has, she may still want to maintain control over it. Referring to the US, Hartog describes this reluctance to give up control and power of property too early as the 'King Lear problem'.[100] He argues that '[i]f property were transferred too quickly, too finally, too securely, then one placed oneself at the mercy of one's children. Nothing protected one. One could not trust to love or duty alone'.[101] In other words, a lifetime transfer would have exposed the person to the will and control of others. This fear seems to be shared by testators across legal systems, both past and present. It is, for instance, not uncommon in the farming context, and for several reasons; farmers

[97] Hyland *Gifts* (2009) 44ff.

[98] Sparks (1955) 2; see also Miller *The Machinery* (1996) 214.

[99] For instance, a usufruct would be an option but its creation requires formalities and the involvement of a member of the legal profession.

[100] Hartog *Someday* (2012) 33, 55; Weiner *Inalienable Possessions* (1992).

[101] Hartog *Someday* (2012) 55. Similarly, also Sparks (1955) 1.

can find it difficult to let go of the 'reins',[102] and in the words of some scholars 'to entrust his/her 'pension' to a younger family member'.[103] We can see this, for instance, in a number of cases dating back to the 1950s and 1960s where German farmers who had promised their farm to their sons preferred not to transfer their farms during their own lifetime, but instead elected to do so on their death, even though de facto the farms were being run together with the promisee.[104] Recent research shows that in England and Wales, more so than in other jurisdictions, older farmers are reluctant to delegate and transfer the farm earlier on. Gasson and Errington have defined this as the 'farmer's boy problem'.[105] I will return to this point in Chapter 4 where I analyse several farm cases. At the same time, it is important to mention here that unwillingness to transfer farm assets is not only common for fear about the farmer's financial future and loss of control.[106] It can also reflect a desire to continue work on a farm, which is often the promisor's life project, especially given that with the work comes a social status.[107]

Intrinsic to this argument is the fact that immediate gifts are not usually revocable and that promisors may prefer keeping their options open. While being happy for the promisees to perform their side of the bargain, they do not usually want to commit themselves too early. After all, relationships and circumstances can change, and promisors may prefer to allow for contingencies that might cause them to change their minds. Making a promise of a testamentary gift allows for this flexibility. The promisor can see how the relationship unfolds, for example, where a parent asks a child to move in together.[108] This argument carries particular weight where the promisor intends to transfer a farm or a business and wishes to test whether the collaboration/partnership with the promisee works, and whether the promisee is capable of carrying out the task or role to the satisfaction of the promisor.[109] That said, some promisors probably prefer maintaining full control for their life and possibly even beyond their grave,[110] and they may have specific views about what 'capable' means and how the business or farm should be run. For instance, in the New Zealand case of *Edwards v NZ Insurance Co Ltd*, Speight J mentioned that the deceased 'was perhaps reluctant to part with his powers as rapidly as his son may have wished and he was unable or unwilling to recognize

[102] Errington & Lobley (2002); Potter & Lobley (1992).

[103] See Uchiyama et al (2008) 43.

[104] For a discussion of such cases, see Kroeschell in *Göttinger Festschrift* (1961) 108 and Roemer (1957) 288. Gerckens (1955) 163 mentions the saying according to which: 'One does not get undressed until one goes to sleep'.

[105] Gasson & Errington *Farm Family Business* (1993) 42ff.

[106] See Leonard et al (2017); Conway et al (2016).

[107] Leonard et al (2017) 16 further mention that the lack of available retirement income may make some farmers reluctant to retire. Uchiyama et al (2008) 42 have found that in England, family farm businesses have traditionally been regarded as a pension fund for the older generation.

[108] This is argued by Battes (1969) 690.

[109] See Humbert (1956) 1858.

[110] On dead hand control see, among many, especially Friedman (2009).

the decline in his ability'.[111] The case dealt with the transfer of a business. While the father preferred doing things gradually, and to postpone the transfer for as long as possible, the son was apprehensive that his father would die still holding a substantial proportion of the shares in the business. The difficulty in cases like this lies partly in the fact that the younger generation has often different ideas about how the business should be developed. This highlights once more how tricky the position of a promisee can be in negotiating the transfer of the promised asset, in this case a family business.

Arguably, where the promisee has rendered services in favour of the promisor, the latter could choose to pay monthly wages rather than to reward the former by way of a transfer of property on death. However, the promisor may not always have the necessary financial means to do so.[112] Sometimes, all a testator has at her disposal are pension payments, which might be insufficient to cover, for instance, care or other services.[113] The same applies to cases where the income of a farm is not enough to pay wages to the worker.[114] Although farms can have significant capital value, sustaining a livelihood is often precarious and the financial situation delicate with little available cash. A solution might be to sell the property. But, converting a farm into cash would often mean destroying the very thing that is sought to be preserved, and might leave the promisor (and the promisee) without a home.[115] Thus, in some cases it is only natural that the promisor prefers to transfer the asset on her death.

It may further be the case that the promisor intends to leave a property which is worth far more than the value of wages. This is not always clearly spelt out by promisors and, of course, they are usually dead when the claim is brought. However, it is not difficult to imagine that wages might not always be perceived as representing the appropriate kind of reward, especially as the services are usually rendered by a child, niece or nephew, daughter- or son-in-law, friend, or partner. In these instances, a testamentary bequest might be viewed as more appropriate, especially as this allows for benefits to be transferred that exceed normal wages. A promisor is also likely to feel uneasy at the idea of stipulating, for instance, a formal employment contract with a close family member or a friend.[116] Again this would require

[111] *Edwards v NZ Insurance Co Ltd* [1971] NZLR 113, 114 per Speight J (hereafter *Edwards v NZ Insurance Co Ltd*).

[112] *Walton v Walton* (n 84); *Re Townley* [1982] 2 NZLR 87 (NZCA) 90.

[113] For an example, see the German cases LAG Hessen, 7 September 2010–12 Sa 1817/08, ZEV 2011, 434 and LAG Rheinland-Pfalz 27 July 2011–11 Ta 145/11, ErbSTB 2012, 10 = ZEV 2011, 549 where the pension was very low.

[114] *Re Pearce (Deceased)* (n 8) seems to have been such a case.

[115] Sparks (1955) 2.

[116] In *Guest v Guest* [2019] EWHC 869 (Ch), [63] (hereafter *Guest v Guest*), the promisor is reported to have said to the promisee (his son), who was paid the base rate set by the Agricultural Wages Board for the work on his father's farm, and who had complained that they were not enough to support his children, that he was 'somewhat saddened that you wish to be regarded as an ordinary employee rather than a valued member of the family'. See Hartog *Someday* (2012) 101 according to whom '[t]hey

formalizing the relationship but would possibly also involve payment of health insurance and pension benefits.

To summarize, there are a number of reasons why someone may prefer a testamentary promise over an immediate gift or regular salary payments, ranging from financial considerations or restriction to reasons of convenience, but also a realization that on death they can be more generous. At the same time, it is often a decision determined by fear of loss of independence, or a wish to maintain control. All in all, testamentary promises provide a convenient, easy, and cost-effective way for a promisor to be able to retain control over her estate until her death, while ensuring that benefits will accrue to her during her lifetime and that the promisee will benefit when she will be gone.

C. Reasons for relying on non-legally binding testamentary promises

Having analysed the reasons why people may want to make testamentary promises rather than lifetime donative promises or immediate gifts, and why they are usually informal, I will also briefly address what motivates the promisee's behaviour. In particular it is important to explore why promisees rely on promises that are made orally and in an indefinite and vague manner. Again, their motives will normally be mixed. While the prospect of a future inheritance obviously plays an important role,[117] the reason why promisees rely on a non-legally binding promise is usually because they know, trust, and/or love the promisor, or because it would be difficult for them to insist on a formal promise. Thus, love and affection do not exclude an expectation to inherit.[118] This is important because it highlights once more the vulnerabilities of the promisee and the potential room for abuse or exploitation. It is further important because, as the enquiry will show, with many forms of redress discussed in this book the promisee's motives matter and they can sometimes stand in the way of adequate protection. Thus, understanding what motivates promisees is critical.

It is likely that a good number of promisees will be unaware of their legal position and of the fact that in case of a breach of the promise, they may find themselves in a weak position.[119] Indeed, they may not know whether a legally binding

[promisors] did not want to see themselves as employers. They particularly did not want to "employ" their daughters and sons'.

[117] An example is OLG Karlsruhe, 6 December 2001(n 47).

[118] Zelizer (2000); Kohn (2019).

[119] But see Hayton (1987) 216 who argues that: 'Even if there is a distinct promise (of a non-contractual nature) to leave property by will, surely the promisee knows that he will only obtain the property if a valid will is made. If he acts to his detriment, this is in the belief he will only obtain the property *if* a will is made: too bad if it's not made'.

testamentary promise can be made. It is usually only when problems arise, for instance, when the relationship deteriorates, that promisees inform themselves about their legal position. As Melanie Leslie put it:

> family members rarely consider the legal rules when evaluating the motives of loved ones or determining whether to rely on them for support [...] Only when trust is lacking, and self-interest substantially dominates altruism, will family members worry about the legal enforceability of family obligations.[120]

In intimate relationships it is often difficult for parties to contemplate that things may go wrong and that they may fall out with one another. Afterwards, one is often wiser.[121]

Even where promisees are informed about the legal position and would prefer some form of written confirmation, they often have little or no choice.[122] If they ask for a formal assurance, they could well be unsuccessful. Some cases suggest indeed that where the promisee asks for an assurance, the promisor may either refuse to provide a formal confirmation or agree but never get around to providing it.[123] Asking for confirmation can also risk jeopardizing the relationship, which is not in the promisee's interest. As Devlin J said in *Parker v Clark*: 'it is easier to demand formal documents from a stranger than it is from a relative and friend'.[124] Courts thus seem to be conscious of the fact that promisees finds themselves in a vulnerable position.[125] For instance, in the English proprietary estoppel case of *Thorner v Major*, Lord Neuberger acknowledged extrajudicially that for the promisee (David), who had worked on his cousin's farm for about thirty years without being paid, to have sought to formalize the arrangement in contract 'would have

[120] Leslie (1999) 560.

[121] See Hartog *Someday* (2012) 144. The author mentions that when looking back, promisees often notice that they missed opportunities, gave up jobs and careers, did not undertake land sales, or put off marriages.

[122] Fellows (1992) 332.

[123] In the English case of *Gillett v Holt* (n 72), for instance, the claimant was seeking more formal assurances to which the testator replied that this was not necessary as it was all going to be his anyway. In *Bradbury v Taylor* (n 29) the wife of the promisee had wanted the security of a letter saying that the agreement was permanent, and that the promisor would not change his mind, but although he had agreed to provide such a letter, he never did.

[124] *Parker v Clark* (n 56).

[125] Nonetheless, occasionally some courts seem to have taken the view that the claimant ought to have done something to secure the entitlement. See a decision of the KG of 9 March 1970, KG OLGZ 1971, 22, 25 (n 43). See further Dobson J's words in the NZ decision in *Saunders v New Zealand Guardian Trust Company Limited HC Palmerston North* [2010] NZHC 1417 (HC), [47]: 'Even without any legal training, it is reasonable to expect that a promisee relying on a promise when providing services would suggest some qualification on the freedom of the promisor to resile.' See also the statement of the BGH 5 February 1957–V BLW 37/56, BGHZ 23, 249, 261 in relation to rural communities: 'Every farmer— with few exceptions— [knows] today that he can only determine his farm successor [...] by will, transfer contract (*Übergabevertrag*) or inheritance contract and that these transactions require form'.

risked harming the relationship with Peter (the promisor).'[126] Equally, in the New Zealand case of *Nealon v Public Trustee*, Jinlay J acknowledged that:

> [. . .] such agreements were generally made between close relatives, and the party rendering the service commonly found it difficult to have such essential requirements [that of a valid contract] satisfied by the other. To attempt to do so would savour of doubting the integrity and trustworthiness of that other. This might jeopardize the existing happy relationship between the parties, and so jeopardize the prospects of receiving a reward which was generally promised upon a generous scale.[127]

Where the promisee has already rendered certain services or made certain payments, she may be particularly reluctant to compromise her relationship with the promisor. It may also be that the promisee simply does not want to risk a confrontation with an authoritative family figure. It is in fact not uncommon for children or other younger family members to feel deferential towards a more senior family figure, or to be intimidated out of respect or fear.[128]

Rather than asking for the promise to be formalized, or for an immediate transfer to take place, the promisee could insist on getting compensation in the form of wages. However, as I pointed out earlier, the promisor may not have the necessary means and both parties may prefer not to be in a formal employment relationship.[129] Also, as *Walton v Walton*[130] shows, a request for the payment of wages may simply lead to further informal assurances about the future inheritance.

Furthermore, it has been suggested that some promisees do not want to look greedy and therefore refrain from expressing a request or demanding a more formal assurance. They possibly will also deem it inappropriate to talk about the details of an economic reward, and in particular an inheritance.[131] After all, many families never openly discuss financial matters,[132] including, for instance, the transfer of the family business or the family farm.[133]

[126] Lord Neuberger (2009) 542.

[127] *Nealon v Public Trustee* [1949] NZLR 148, 160.

[128] In the sense that relatives often feel a 'quasi-voluntary coercion' and that they do not feel in the position of rejecting the request out of pity and compassion, but also because of the intimate nature of the relationship, see Ludyga (2009) 290. In many legal systems there is a vivid discussion about the scope of private autonomy within intimate relationships. Herring in *Rights, Gender and Family Law* (2010); see also Röthel *Verträge in der Unternehmerfamilie* (2014); Sanders *Statischer Vertrag* (2008).

[129] See also Canaris (1967).

[130] *Walton v Walton* (n 84).

[131] See n 91.

[132] Some authors have shown that, for instance, in the farming context, the financial field is the last knowledge and decision-making domain to be delegated to the next generation. Thus, the next generation is frequently unaware of the financial situation. Anderson & Hepworth (1980).

[133] See *Guest v Guest* (n 116) [62] where the promisee had told the partnership's accountant that the farm succession had always been a difficult subject to broach with his father.

However, it is also conceivable that the promisee knows that the promise is not binding and that the will is revocable, and is thus aware of the risks, but that she does not worry, as she simply trusts the promisor.[134] After all, such promises are often made by people with whom the promisee has a particular relationship of trust and affection. The parties may therefore take the view that their word is sufficient. An interesting case here is the Irish case of *McCarron v McCarron* where the promisor (a farmer) had asked the promisee (his cousin) whether he wanted a formal agreement to remunerate him for his work by way of a provision in his will. The promisee replied, 'I will not put you out of your house or home' to which the promisor said, 'Right, ... we will leave it at that'. According to Murphy J:

> what is noticeable from the transcript ... was the natural courtesy ... which often results in an unwillingness to pursue discussions to a logical and perhaps harshly expressed commercial conclusion ... in some, particularly rural areas, a meeting of minds can be achieved without as detailed a discussion as might be necessary elsewhere.[135]

Trust aside, the promisee could be aware of her precarious legal position, but still be prepared to accept the risk of non-performance. After all, as noted earlier, an inheritance may be the only way of gaining wealth one would never be able to earn through hard work. In addition, the promised asset may also have important emotional value to the promisee, that is where the farm or home has been passed from one generation to the other.[136] She may therefore feel it is worth taking the risk.

However, there are also some promisees who would have acted the way they did in any event,[137] because their actions were driven first and foremost by altruistic motives, a sense of duty or deference, love and affection, or compassion towards the promisor, with the prospect of the inheritance being just an additional incentive or welcome side-effect. This, I will argue, should not stand in the way of compensation. In other words, we should not require a promisee to act, and to have to prove to have acted, only or primarily because of the prospect of inheriting something from the promisor—a point I shall return to in later stages of the book. In fact, in most cases, the promisee's motives will be mixed, and they often change over time. It is perfectly possible to think of a situation in which, at the beginning, a person renders certain services out of love, affection, or sense of duty, but with time, and as requests become more and more demanding, the behaviour of the

[134] In *Balkwill v Smith* (n 58) [9] Tritschler J stated that 'I accept plaintiff's statement that he [the promisee] never doubted Copeland would make provision for him in his will.'

[135] *McCarron v McCarron* (n 20) 9. An interesting example is, *Thorner v Major* (n 34).

[136] On the emotional attachment to property, see Conway in *Emotional Dynamics of Law and Legal Discourse* (2016) 42–44. See also Conway & Stannard in *Research Handbook on Law and Emotions* (2021) 229, 240–242.

[137] In some cases, the promisees are candid about that. For examples, see *Campbell v Griffin* (n 36); *Murphy v Burrows* [2004] EWHC 1900 (Ch); *Single v Macharski Estate* (1996) 3 WWR 23 (Man CA).

promisee becomes increasingly motivated by the prospect of a financial reward. It follows that, as is the case with the promisor, the promisee's behaviour is often determined by complex motives, including strategic financial considerations and altruistic concerns, as well as love and affection. This can, however, work against promisees where the law puts undue weight on subjective motives or requires that the prospective inheritance should be the only motive. The analysis will in fact show that where the prospect of an inheritance is just one of the many motivating factors (or not the principal one) it may sometimes be more difficult for a promisee to make out a successful case in court.

IV. Reasons why testamentary promises may remain unfulfilled

Thus far, I have looked at why testamentary promises are being made and why they are relied upon even if they are made informally. We have seen that both the behaviour of the promisor and that of the promisee can be motivated by a number of reasons. That said, there is clearly a power differential between promisor and promisee, meaning that the promisee has a lot to lose and the promisor a lot to gain.

In order to obtain a more comprehensive picture of the dynamics underlying testamentary promises, it is useful also to explore why promises remain unfulfilled. We will see that there are many reasons why a promisee may see her expectations frustrated. Some depend on the promisor, but others do not. Nevertheless, they show that promisors are usually serious about their promise, at least at the time when it is made.

A. The promisor changes her mind

The majority of cases involving testamentary promises appear to concern instances in which the alleged promise is either only partly kept or (most commonly) not kept at all. The reasons for this can be manifold, including that the promisor has changed her mind. This change of mind is expressed by either not making the promised testamentary disposition or, quite often, by making it but later revoking it. This shows that, at least at first, many promisors intend to keep their promises. If that is so, why do promisors change their mind and consequently their will? The reasons can be many[138] and, importantly, are not necessarily dependant on the promisors having some fraudulent design. As mentioned earlier, instances in which courts

[138] For an analysis of possible reasons that justify a change of mind, see Farnsworth in *Scintillae Iuris* (1994); Farnsworth *Changing your Mind* (1998).

are confronted with a rogue promisor seem to be rare,[139] though there may be cases which are not litigated. There are perfectly comprehensible reasons why a promisor no longer wishes to keep her promise. After all, the arrangements can depend on timing, and continued capacity and capability.[140] Likewise, there could be a change in the financial situation of the promisor, or that of another close family member. In some cases, the parties simply decide to enter into a new agreement.[141]

However, the change of mind is often also due to the parties falling out with one another.[142] Given that the time span between the moment of the promise and the promisor's death can stretch over many years, it is not altogether surprising that events happen that affect the relationship between promisor and promisee. There can be a number of reasons why the relationship between them may deteriorate, the responsibility for which can lie with either party. For example, the promisor may feel that the counter-promise is not being kept or performed at an appropriate level. It may be the case that her own expectations have changed and exceed what was initially agreed with the promisee. Since testamentary agreements between the promisor and promisee are usually generic, their expectations may have never been spelt out clearly, and this can pose difficulties. When the promisor's needs become too demanding for the promisee to handle, the promisee could complain, or decide to stop performing altogether, and this can then lead to a conflict.

The change of mind can also be due to changes in personality, as people tend to get more anxious and impatient with age.[143] However, quite often the clash is caused by changes in the promisor's or promisee's personal lives. In some cases, the promisor remarries, as was the case in *Clarkson v McCrossen Estate*,[144] and decides

[139] For examples, see two New Zealand cases. In *Jones v Public Trustee* [1962] NZLR 363 (NZCA) (hereafter *Jones v Public Trustee*) the New Zealand Court of Appeal found that the deceased had deceived his son and daughter in law, as his correspondence to other relatives revealed that he had changed his mind but nonetheless continued to repeat his promises to the promisees. In *Edwards v NZ Insurance Co Ltd* (n 111) 116 Speight J said 'I think he [the deceased] may have made the promise to Stanley [his son] as an inducement with no intention of carrying it out or, a more charitable view, that he wished in the meantime to tie Stanley up as tightly as possible and then possibly relent later if he found it convenient to do so and the spirit moved him—which it never did'. See also the Jersey case of *Pirouet v Pirouet* (n 49). In this case, relations between the claimant and his father became strained and the latter had raised the former's rent and gave him notice to quit two fields. The son asked his father if he planned further actions against him. The father assured his son that he had no further plans. Unbeknown to the son, however, the father had in fact changed his will, excluding the son from the disposable one third of the movable property and giving him only a usufruct in the farm.

[140] Hartog *Someday* (2012) 148.

[141] See *Higgins v Higgins* [2005] QSC 110 where a promise was made, and expectations had arisen, but then the expectations had ceased because the parties had entered into agreements for sale of the farmlands.

[142] This happened, for instance, in *Devereux v Devereux* 2 ETR 164. Changes in the emotional relationship occurred also in *Gillet v Holt* (n 72) 219, *Clarkson v McCrossen Estate* (n 59), *Antrobus v Antrobus* (n 25), and *Thorner v Major* (n 34).

[143] Wells *New Approach* (2007) 34. See *Jones v Public Trustee* (n 139) where North J speaks of 'an increasing sense of irritation which old people are often prone to feel towards those with whom they are in daily contact and to whom they owe the most'.

[144] *Clarkson v McCrossen Estate* (n 59). Here the promisor (the promisee's stepfather) married a woman twenty years his junior who he had met a few months earlier and whom he left the majority of his estate.

to change the will in favour of the new partner. More frequently, the change of mind is caused by the fact that the promisee has a new partner who the promisor does not like or approve of.[145] In some of the farm cases, the fallout is caused by a difference in views as to how the farm should be run and the farming business developed.[146]

B. Other reasons why testamentary promises may remain unfulfilled

Besides cases in which the promisor changes her mind and decides not to perform the promise or to revoke her will, there may be other reasons why the promise remains unfulfilled and the promisee's expectations are frustrated.[147] In some instances, the deceased was in the process of making the promised will but then suddenly died.[148] Also, some testators are simply forgetful,[149] or put off the writing of the will, possibly because they believe that they still have time to write it,[150] but then a sudden onset of mortal illness or dementia makes it impossible to fulfil their promise.[151] Some testators are superstitious and thus defer the writing of the will until the last possible moment.[152] This is not, of course, a justification that should release them from their liability, after all they made the promise and the promise has been acted upon.

The law reports also disclose cases in which a testamentary disposition was made but did not produce the desired effect.[153] This can be due to the fact that the promisor made a will that did not comply with the requisite formalities, be it as a result of a personal mistake, or the negligence of a legal advisor.[154] For instance, there may be an issue with the signature, the number of required witnesses may be incorrect, or witnesses may be completely absent.[155] While in some jurisdictions,

145 A good example is *Giumelli v Giumelli* [1999] 196 CLR 101 (HC). Problems arose when the promisee decided to marry a woman who his parents (the promisors) disapproved of, following which they refused to uphold their promises. See also *Jans v Jans* 2016 SKQB 275, where the relationships with the promisor started to sour with the arrival of the promisee's new partner.

146 For a good example, see *Brain v Harwood* [2014] NZHC 1092.

147 In *Bovaird v Frost* (n 92) there was a piece of paper, but it could not be found.

148 In *Re Basham* (n 16) the promisor had a stroke which led to his death within four days from making the promise. Even so he repeated the promise shortly before dying.

149 See *Balkwill v Smith* (n 58) [11].

150 *Schnogl v Balen Estate* (n 54). Here the testator made an unexecuted will.

151 In *Campbell v Griffin* (n 36) the promise was not kept due to mental illness of the promisor.

152 Hartog *Someday* (2012) 107; Atkinson *Handbook of the Law of Wills* (1937) 122.

153 In the German case BAG 30 September 1971 – 5 AZR 177/71, BAG AP No 27, the will was made but could not take effect because of the prior existence of interdependent mutual wills (*wechselbezügliche Testamente*).

154 In *Re Lowe* [1991] 1 NZLR 99 (NZHC), 103 the deceased had given instructions to the solicitors, but they were never put into effect.

155 In *Maddison v Alderson* (n 28) the promisor had made a will with the promised disposition and had signed it, but it failed for lack of attestation. In *Powell v Public Trustee* [2003] 1 NZLR 381 (NZCA) the amended copy of the will was not witnessed. In the Canadian case of *Hammond v Hammond* (1995)

courts take a lenient approach to problems concerning formalities (e.g. in Australia and in New Zealand where courts are provided with dispensing powers), in others (e.g. England and Wales) they are very strict so that the will could easily fail,[156] leaving the promisee in the position of having to bring a claim.

Occasionally the will may be void because the testator lacked the requisite capacity.[157] It can further happen that a will was made but cannot be found.[158] Finally, the promise may be kept, but the will in question is revoked by law. For instance, most legal systems provide that in the event of remarriage or divorce, dispositions in favour of the former spouse are automatically revoked.[159]

Thus, not all reasons why a promise of an inheritance remains unfulfilled are directly attributable to the promisor changing her mind. Irrespective of that, the cases suggest that most promisors are serious about the promise even though it was expressed informally and even if they later change their mind. Thus, to think of testamentary arrangements as arrangements that involve, on the one hand, a 'wicked' promisor and, on the other, a 'feeble' promisee would be misleading. The reality is usually much more complex. Even so, this does not change the fact that the promisor is always free to change her mind and to do so up until her death. And when she does, this is not only emotionally hurtful to the promisee[160] but also has financial implications for her. The promisor does not need to justify her decision to revoke her will; nor does she need to communicate it to the promisee. The free revocability of the will thus exposes the promisee to considerable risks and enhances the power that the promisor has over the promisee. The promisee can never be sure that the promisor will not change her mind and may well feel that she has to behave in a way that ensures that she does not fall out with the promisor.

7 BCLR (3d) 25 (BCSC), a will was made but the gift of the residue to the deceased's son had failed because his wife had witnessed the will.

[156] For a comparative overview of the position of courts in relation to wills, see Reid, de Waal, & Zimmermann, 'Testamentary Formalities in Historical and Comparative Perspective' in *Comparative Succession Law 1* (2011) 463ff. On the problems that a literal compliance with the Wills Act poses see, especially, Langbein (1975).

[157] *Byrne v Bishop* [2001] NZLR 780 (NZCA). Here the deceased lacked temporarily testamentary capacity when the will was executed.

[158] In *Re Archer* [1990] 3 NZLR 737 (NZHC), 742 apparently the will had gone missing when the house of the deceased had been burgled.

[159] Section 18 Wills Act 1837. Section 18B deals with the revocation by civil partnership. For an interesting English decision see *Re Marsland* (n 10). By contrast, in many US states, wills are revoked on divorce rather than on remarriage. In Germany, a testamentary disposition is invalid if the marriage was dissolved before the testator's death or if the conditions for a divorce from the marriage existed and the testator had applied for or consented to the divorce. See § 2077 BGB.

[160] On the emotional consequences of inheritance, see Conway in *Emotional Dynamics of Law and Legal Discourse* (2016).

V. Concluding summary

This chapter has explored the core features of testamentary promises and has highlighted that they are typically characterized by an element of exchange, usually between different generations. The promises are often deliberately made to secure financial contributions, work in the business or on the farm, all manner of domestic and care services, or emotional support and companionship. Therefore, promises of an inheritance challenge the distinction between bargains and gifts, and thus between non-gratuitous and gratuitous transactions. As Chapter 2 will show, legal systems attach importance to these distinctions on the basis of assumptions about the promisor's motives that are not, however, necessarily tenable. This is particularly visible when looking at the motives that underlie testamentary promises, which are rarely purely altruistic.

The analysis in this chapter has further shown that testamentary promises are often made informally and are generic and vague. Judging from the cases, instances where the parties will sit down at the kitchen table and establish in minute detail what the promisee is required to perform and what she will obtain in exchange are rare. If the promisee asks for a commitment, or insists on some form of security or guarantee, she risks jeopardizing the relationship without improving her own situation, especially where the promisor does not have the means, during her lifetime, to remunerate the promisee by way of payment of wages or transfers of wealth, or does not want to part with control over her assets.

I have argued that the informal and generic nature is not usually the result of an act of calculation on the part of the promisor, but rather a consequence of the fact that testamentary promises are expressed in domestic settings (and especially in the farming/agricultural or the household/care context), and usually involve close family members and friends. It is also difficult to frame the arrangement in contractual terms. However, we have also seen that, although promises of a future inheritance tend to be made informally, they are intended seriously, which is confirmed by the analysis of the reasons of why such promises can remain unfulfilled.

Yet, the informality enhances the risks that the promisee will be exploited. In fact, if the promise is broken, the informality can lead to difficulties in proving the promise. These difficulties are enhanced in legal systems that have rules in place that prevent the testimony of the promisee in relation to the existence of a promise to make a will.[161] Difficulties of proof aside, the informal nature of the testamentary arrangement also exposes the promisee to the risk of further requests from the promisor.[162] As Lord Walker pointed out extrajudicially in relation to assistance cases:

[161] See Chapter 2.

[162] Sparks (1954–1955) 69: 'Sometimes the prior relationship of the parties is relied upon to determine the services to be rendered.'

> Very few of the 'assistance' cases involve anything like a clear bargain at the outset of the relationship. That is not how human nature works. The claimant (the assister) and the defendant (the assisted) need to find out by experience how they get on. But over the years an understanding develops, sometimes fairly precise and sometimes imprecise, as to what is expected of the assister, and as to the quid pro quo which the assister can expect to receive sooner or later. What is expected often becomes more onerous over the years, as the assisted person becomes increasingly frail (as in Campbell and Jennings) or alcoholic (as in Ottey) or unable or unwilling to work in his business (as in Wayling or to some extent Gillett). The quid pro quo may be defined precisely (possibly even in writing, as in Ottey). It may change over the years as the defendant's business changes its location (as in Wayling and Gillett). On the other hand it may be highly ambiguous (as in Jennings).[163]

The quid pro quo aside, if the subject matter of the promise is not clearly defined, this may affect the nature of the award that a promisee is able to claim as well as her position vis-à-vis third parties.

However, the informality is not the only issue. The analysis has shown that the primary difficulty or problem from the perspective of the promisee is the significant power imbalance between the parties. The promisee has an information deficit and does not normally know whether the promisor owns the promised asset or is indebted when she undertakes the promise. Also, what she was promised may no longer be part of the estate when the promisor dies. Thus, when accepting to act on the promise, the promisee usually takes significant risks, amplified by the (potentially long) time lag between the moment of the promise and the promisor's death, and the substantial nature of the demands often placed on her.

The considerable time span that can pass between the moment of the promise and the death of the promisor merits emphasis. In some ways, this time factor represents an issue for both parties. On the one hand, the temporal disjunction between the promise and the promisor's death may mean that the promisor may be held to a promise that she made several years or decades prior to her death, though she does not usually suffer any consequences. On the other hand, the promisee usually has to wait a long time before obtaining any reward, often several decades and without any guarantee that the testator will ever provide for her. In other words, she does not receive any immediate reward but must continue to perform. What is more, the promisee can only act once it is clear that the promise has not been, or can no longer be, fulfilled, which is normally only the case on the death of the promisor, and all the while she is required to perform,[164] even if she entertains

[163] Walker (2008) 239.

[164] Sparks (1954–1955) 75 argues that '[i]n the usual contract to make a will the promisee has rendered full performance by the time the action is brought'.

doubts about the promisor's true intentions. The promisee may well have a suspicion that her expectations will be frustrated, for instance, because the parties have fallen out with one another. However, since technically speaking the promisor can perform the promise at any time up until her death, there is normally little a promisee can do, save where the promisor transfers the promised asset during her lifetime so as to render the promise nugatory, or tries to dispossess the promisee from the promised property (e.g. the home or the farm) or expressly intimates that she has changed her mind.[165] Even then, depending on the legal system, the promisee may not be able to obtain redress while the promisor is still alive, for as the enquiry will show, some forms of redress are available only on death.[166] A promisee could, of course, stop performing but there is a risk that that will diminish her chances of getting redress.[167]

This power differential characterizes many testamentary arrangements and is amplified by the fact that a promisee may feel bound by moral duties, love, and affection, or act out of deference and fear, which may make it more difficult for her to stop performing or to ask for payment. Sometimes all the promisee can do is to act and hope for the best.

A further feature of testamentary promises is that, in contrast to lifetime gifts,[168] wills are in principle always revocable.[169] This means that even when the promisor makes the promised will, the promisee's expectations might still be frustrated. Should the promisor explicitly promise not to revoke her will, which is legally permissible only in some jurisdictions, she could still break that promise and the validity of the new will would not be affected.[170] In fact, because of the principle of testamentary freedom, a court could not order the promisor to make the promised will but would be required to find other ways of protecting the interests of the promisee, usually by awarding damages for the loss suffered. There is no doubt therefore that the promisee can find herself in a vulnerable situation.

In Chapter 2 I will explore in greater detail the legal framework within which such promises operate. I will examine how succession laws approach such promises and the extent to which they protect the promisee. We will see that the picture

[165] However, there are a number of recent proprietary estoppel cases where the promisee has brought a lifetime claim because the parties have fallen out with one another. See Chapter 4.

[166] This is the case with the protection offered by the New Zealand Law Reform (Testamentary Promises) Act 1949 (Chapter 7), § 2057a BGB and §§ 677ff ABGB (both analysed in Chapter 11), and also the *créance de salaire différé* (Chapter 10) as well as the family provision legislation (Chapter 5).

[167] A good example is *Davies v Davies* [2015] EWHC 015 (Ch) on appeal see [2016] EWCA Civ 463, [33]. The daughter had left the farm on four occasions, often after an argument with her parents. At first instance HHJ Jarman found that the daughter had suffered a detriment. However, the Court of Appeal significantly reduced the amount awarded from £1.3 million to £500,000.

[168] In civilian jurisdictions they may be revocable where the donor finds herself in a situation of need or the donee is ungrateful. Hyland *Gifts* (2009) 513ff.

[169] An exception is mutual wills, but they fall outside the scope of this book.

[170] See Chapter 4.

is complex and that this can somewhat exacerbate the difficulties promisees face. What is more, most legal systems lack a specific framework capable of capturing informal testamentary promises, which compels promisees to seek redress by resorting to various doctrines of private law not all of which are open to all promisees or suited to the testamentary context.

2
The legal context

I. The general legal framework concerning gift promises

A. Introduction

So far, I have examined the core features of testamentary promises and their underlying motivations. I have illustrated why such promises are an attractive instrument for the promisee, but especially the promisor, and why the promisor is in a powerful position vis-à-vis the promisee, a position that can easily be exploited. The analysis has shown that testamentary promises can be a useful means to procure certain benefits in exchange for a promise of a future inheritance in which the promisor has little to lose but much to gain. It has also transpired that there is a significant power differential between the promisor and the promisee. This power differential, and the resulting vulnerabilities of the promisee, will emerge further in this chapter, where I will investigate in greater detail the legal framework within which such promises currently operate. We will see that legal systems have generally struggled with the regulation of promises of an inheritance and that the law tends to be suspicious of them and to privilege the promisor's position. Many civil law jurisdictions have tried to eliminate them altogether by prohibiting legally binding testamentary promises. In other words, they preclude a person from entering into a legally binding contract or pact in which she promises to make a future will or not to revoke it, though nothing usually prevents her from making an informal promise. In fact, the prohibitions have not stopped these social practices. Testamentary promises are still expressed, albeit informally, and others act on them. On the other hand, common law jurisdictions admit the validity of contracts to make a will. Yet, even in these jurisdictions such testamentary arrangements tend to be made informally. Consequently, courts in both legal traditions are confronted with informal testamentary promises and the difficulty of deciding whether and how to protect the promisee's interests. As we will see, such decisions are not easy, including because of the potential implications that they have for a number of people such as other promisees, creditors, successors or those with a moral claim against the estate, and third-party transferees.

Claiming a Promised Inheritance. Alexandra Braun, Oxford University Press. © Alexandra Braun 2022.
DOI: 10.1093/oso/9780198757252.003.0003

As this chapter will show, New Zealand aside, succession laws across jurisdictions do not explicitly regulate informal testamentary promises. Hence, when they remain unfulfilled, promisees must often seek redress outside succession law, by basing their claim on various doctrines belonging to different areas of private law that are not usually designed to tackle instances of unfulfilled testamentary promises. In principle, this is not necessarily negative, for the promisee is usually given a choice between different forms of redress and with some of them the promisee does not need to prove a promise, can bring an action during the promisor's lifetime, and/or is treated as a creditor. Nonetheless, resorting to doctrines rooted in various areas of private law also poses certain challenges not least because some doctrines are narrow in scope or are not tailored to the specificities of the setting in which such promises are normally expressed. For that reason, some promisees may have to overcome certain obstacles to obtain redress, which may well function as a deterrent or limit their chances of success. Also, not all forms of address are available to all promisees, so that some have a greater choice and sometimes therefore greater protection than others.

Technically speaking, testamentary promises fall within the broader category of gratuitous or gift promises. Before focusing on how legal traditions regulate both formal and informal promises of a future inheritance, it is therefore useful to briefly look more generally at how gratuitous promises are dealt with. This will allow us to appreciate the wider legal context within which testamentary promises are often analysed and discussed in the literature. It will emerge that the law tends to favour the perspective of transferors, donors, and promisors of gifts, and is generally speaking suspicious of gratuitous, including testamentary promises. However, the analysis will also show that the reasons for the circumspection are not entirely convincing. These have largely to do with certain assumptions about the motivations underpinning such promises (i.e. that they are intended to be gratuitous and are therefore an expression of irrational behaviour) which do not necessarily correspond to the reality. More importantly, these assumptions are even less compelling when it comes to promises of a future inheritance. As Chapter 1 has amply shown, testamentary promises are usually made in exchange for a performance and are therefore often 'non-gratuitous'. In fact, in the majority of cases they are at least partly self-interested. At the same time, it will also become clear that testamentary promises pose particular challenges from the perspectives of both the promisee and the courts. In other words, the analysis illustrates the complexities that distinguish testamentary arrangements and sheds light on the reasons why some legal systems have decided to try to do away with them by prohibiting legally binding contracts or pacts concerning the content of a future will. It also highlights the aspects that we should be mindful of when considering how to protect the interests of promisees.

B. The approach to lifetime promises to make gifts

Contrary to the position in relation to non-gratuitous promises, lawmakers have been reluctant to enforce gratuitous promises (sometimes referred to also as 'donative promises', or 'gift promises'[1]), usually treating them as actionable only when they take a particular form.[2] In fact, to some extent the law has been somewhat wary of and unfavourable, if not adverse, towards gratuitous acts,[3] including lifetime promises to make gifts. This seems to have been true of both common and civil law jurisdictions.[4] In continental Europe, for instance, in the past, a gift above a certain amount required *insinuatio* or registration before a court, so as to encourage deliberation.[5] Even today, promises to make gifts usually require some formalities, be that a deed, a notarial act,[6] or some other form of writing.[7] Similarly, in common law jurisdictions donative promises have been considered to be unenforceable because they lack consideration, unless they are made in the form of a deed.[8] That said, exceptions to the requirement of form have always existed. The *ius commune*, for instance, provided exceptions for donations to a charitable body and for those made to people on account of marriage. Some of these exceptions have been maintained in certain jurisdictions. In common law systems, exceptions have generally developed in favour of persons who have relied upon gratuitous promises.[9] Even in civilian legal systems, the lack of formalities could (and still often can) be cured by rendering the promised performance.[10]

There are several explanations of why legal systems deem it necessary to police gratuitous promises and to treat them differently from non-gratuitous ones.[11]

[1] Personally, I prefer the term 'gift promises' over 'gratuitous promises' because it tells us what was promised, not what the underlying motivation was. The term 'gift promise' is, however, sometimes also used to refer to the donation itself. Hyland *Gifts* (2009). For a list of possible gratuitous lifetime promises, including promises of gifts, see Gordley *Enforceability of Promises* (2001) 15ff.

[2] Zimmermann *Law of Obligations* (1996) 477; Zweigert & Kötz *Introduction to Comparative Law* (1998) 389ff.

[3] In the sense that gifts have been singled out for special treatment, see Dawson *Gifts and Promises* (1980); Kull (1992) 58; Resta (2014) 42 and 45.

[4] Zweigert & Kötz *Introduction to Comparative Law* (1998) 399; Gordley *Enforceability of Promises* (2001) 65, 337–339.

[5] Gordley *Foundations of Private Law* (2006) 352–353. For an analysis of the historical origins of the formalities prescribed for gifts and wills, see Baron (1988–1989) 160ff.

[6] See, for instance, §§ 518 and 2301 BGB for *Schenkungsversprechen* in Germany.

[7] Gordley *Enforceability of Promises* (2001) 338.

[8] Until recently, a deed required a seal. This is true of England and of many American jurisdictions. It is also possible for the donor to declare herself trustee in favour of the donee.

[9] For instance, through the doctrines of promissory and proprietary estoppel. See Stoljar (1956). Some authors have argued that, in the US, courts have been willing to enforce donative promises even in the absence of proof of an actual detrimental reliance. See Farber & Matheson (1985) 907–915 and Yorio & Thel (1991); Kull (1992) 41–46.

[10] Similarly, in some common law jurisdictions, the doctrine of part-performance can cure lack of formalities.

[11] There is an abundant literature on why unilateral promises, including gratuitous promises, are being looked at with suspicion. See, in particular, Gorla *Il contratto* (1954) 7ff; A D'Angelo *Le promesse unilaterali* (1996) 2ff; Eisenberg (1997).

A detailed analysis would exceed the scope of this book. Nonetheless, it is useful to briefly explore some of the arguments employed in this debate, and their relevance for the testamentary context and specifically for promises of an inheritance.

1. Irrational behaviour

The primary argument for enforcing gift promises only when they comply with certain formalities is usually that formalities serve not only evidentiary and channelling functions but also ensure that the promisor acts sensibly.[12] In other words, formality requirements are considered to provide, among other things, reliable evidence that the promisor really intended to be bound, and to prevent impulsiveness and lack of proper deliberation on her part.[13] Similar arguments apply to the requirement of consideration in common law jurisdictions, which is often described as evidence, or a sign, of seriousness.[14] However, as James Gordley observes, '[t]his explanation presupposes that there are more and less sensible ways of giving away property, and that deliberation helps a person to tell the one from the other',[15] which is debatable. Also, while it may be true that formality requirements can render persons more conscious of the fact that their actions have legal implications, which is one of the reasons why wills usually require stricter formalities,[16] the argument presupposes that gratuitous promises are necessarily made without deliberation. The concern would appear to be that the purported gift is obtained improperly on the basis that the promise is made without deliberation.[17] This conclusion is based on the assumption that, unlike non-gratuitous promises, gratuitous ones are 'frequently made in highly emotional states brought on by surges of gratitude, impulses of display, or other intense but transient feelings'.[18] Donors or promisors of gifts are therefore often regarded as persons prone to irrational behaviour.

However, this argument seems to overlook the fact that as anthropologists, sociologists as well as economists have shown, in many cases those making gifts, and gift promises, pursue some form of exchange and that people do not usually make such promises without receiving some form of benefit in return.[19] As Chapter 1

[12] Fuller (1941); According to Kull (1992) 58–59, in his book *Gifts and Promises* (1980), Dawson identified the reason for imposing formalities on the continent, rather than in a real hostility towards gift giving, in the principle of forced heirship.

[13] Zweigert & Kötz *Introduction to Comparative Law* (1998) 399. As to the various functions form can fulfil, see Gulliver & Tilson (1941) and, especially, Fuller (1941) critically discussed by Kull (1992) and Posner (1996) 1983ff.

[14] Fuller (1941); Zimmermann *Law of Obligations* (1996) 506.

[15] Gordley *Foundations of Private Law* (2006) 354–355.

[16] See *Comparative Succession Law 1* (2011). Other reasons are the need to prevent fraud and to facilitate evidence of the intent of the testator.

[17] See Eisenberg (1979) 5 who suggests that 'since the donative promisor tends to look mainly to the interest of the promisee, an informal donative promise is more likely to be uncalculated than deliberative'. Another concern seems to be problems of proof; see Rose (1992) 304.

[18] These are the words of Eisenberg (1979) 5. On this point see also Baron (1988–1989) 184ff and Wessman (1995–1996) 716.

[19] See especially Mauss *The Gift* (1967); Bourdieu *Logic of Practice* (1990) 98ff; Godbout *World of the Gift* (1998), and Masson & Pestieau in *Is Inheritance Legitimate?* (1997). For more details, see Braun in

has highlighted, this is especially true of promises of a future inheritance. A promisor resorts to making such promises to secure benefits of various kinds during her lifetime without at the same time losing control over her wealth, or normally suffering any consequences should the promise not be kept. Hence, testamentary promises frequently exhibit the features of an exchange, and are therefore usually (even) less altruistic than lifetime ones.[20] It follows that promises of an inheritance challenge not only the distinction between altruistic and non-altruistic motives, but also the separation between bargains and gifts. They represent a kind of *gratuité intéressée*.[21] Thus, advancing irrational behaviour as a justification for the imposition of formality requirements is even less convincing in the testamentary context. To insist on formalities for testamentary promises further misses the point that informality is a distinctive feature of such promises.[22] This book therefore argues that a lack of formality should not and cannot stand in the way of the protection of the promisee, lest we are happy to expose the promisee to the risk of exploitation and to accept that the estates of promisors are enriched at their expense.

Unsurprisingly, over the past decades, legal and law and economics scholars have also criticized the image of gifts (and gift promises) as purely altruistic transactions. Likewise, they have rejected the view that donors or promisors of gifts are 'weak'.[23] It is a well-known fact that there can be many reasons for making a gift, including the desire to avoid taxes or, in some legal systems, forced/compulsory heirship provisions.[24] Indeed, the line between gifts and bribes can be a fine one. Some scholars have thus suggested that a rigid distinction between gifts and exchanges is ultimately misguided.[25] For instance, while Carol Rose has acknowledged 'a leakage of gifts into exchanges',[26] Jane Baron has argued that the dichotomy between gifts and bargains is less a reflection of real differences than a construct.[27] Samuel Stoljar has also pointed to the fact that 'benevolent promises' (as he calls them) range from pure gift promises to promises that contemplate, encourage, and invite certain actions (sometimes reciprocal actions), capable of causing significant expectations as

L'abnégation en droit civil (2017) 31 where I discuss especially the position of economists with regards to the motives underpinning testamentary gift-giving. For a general discussion, see also Leslie (1999).

[20] See Chapter 1. See also, Braun in *L'abnégation en droit civil* (2017) 48.

[21] Here, I borrow the language of Guével in *Mélanges en l'honneur du professor G Goubeaux* (2009).

[22] See Chapter 1.

[23] Baron (1988–1989); Rose (1992) 295; Leslie (1999). Critical of the collapse of the categories of gift and exchange seems to be Eric Posner. He argues that although almost all gifts involve some form of reciprocation, the significance of reciprocation varies considerably from context to context. See Posner (1997). Of a trend to bury the gift speaks Kreitner *Calculating Promises* (2007).

[24] Zimmermann *Law of Obligations* (1996) 478 and Dawson *Gifts and Promises* (1980) 49ff, 192–193.

[25] See Rose (1992); Baron (1988–1989); Leslie (1999) 560, and Farnsworth (1995) who states that 'today, however, most significant gifts are made either to someone in one's family or circle of friends or to a charity. Those who make them are not motivated solely or even primarily by altruism'.

[26] Rose (1992) 309.

[27] Baron (1988–1989) 157. That said, Baron (195) also points out that to see gifts as exchanges is not necessarily to see them as 'bargains'.

well as significant loss.[28] Thus, we tend to lump together a broad range of different promises under the heading 'gift promises', but there are important distinctions to be made. As I have tried to show elsewhere,[29] the distinction between gifts and exchanges and the need for formalities for the former deserves greater scrutiny, especially in the testamentary context.[30]

2. Economic considerations

Another reason often cited for treating gift promises differently from non-gratuitous ones, and thus for imposing formality requirements on the former, is found in economic considerations, that is the alleged lack of social utility.[31] Richard Posner has argued that the law is reluctant to enforce gratuitous promises because the social cost of doing so (i.e. the administrative costs of enforcement and the likelihood of error) might exceed the gain of the promisee.[32] Indeed, gifts have been regarded by some scholars as being less 'useful', both socially and economically, than exchanges, or at least as comparatively unimportant.[33] Because of that, only those that are significant, that is to say those for which the benefits of compelling performance exceed the costs, deserve intervention by the legal system.[34] This differentiation is made through the imposition of formality requirements. However, unsurprisingly, this approach also has its critics.[35] Even though transactions in a bargain context may play a bigger role in the economy, it is questionable whether gratuitous transfers produce less economic utility.[36] It suffices to think for instance,

[28] Stoljar (1989–1990). This seems to be recognized by Article 1812 of the Quebec Civil Code which deals with lifetime gift promises and awards damages for the 'benefits which the beneficiary [of a promise of a lifetime gift] has granted and the expenses he has incurred in consideration of the promise'. Melanie Leslie has argued that 'most gratuitous promises implicate notions of reciprocity'. See Leslie (1999) 570.

[29] Braun in *L'abnégation en droit civil* (2017) 21.

[30] Baron (1988–1989) 197. Critical also Kull (1992) 49–50.

[31] In the 1940s, Fuller (1941) 799 wrote: 'it has been said that the enforcement of gratuitous promises is not an object of sufficient importance to our social and economic order to justify the expenditure of the time and energy necessary to accomplish it'. According to Hyland *Gifts* (2009) 322, 'the Common law has usually decided that the harm caused by the breach of a gratuitous promise is not fundamental enough to warrant its involvement … the principle requires some modification as it encounters practical realities'. Philipps (2008) 99, however, makes a good point when she argues that 'caregiving and domestic work is recognized as productive when done for pay, yet becomes economically invisible when unpaid'.

[32] Posner (1977) 414–415 according to whom 'gratuitous promises tend both to involve small stakes and to be made in family settings where there are economically superior alternatives to legal enforcement'. By contrast, Farnsworth (1995) 362 says that the 'role of such promises in contemporary society is anything but insignificant'.

[33] For a description of this view, see Eisenberg (1979) 3–6. That commercial promises are likely to be more socially valuable than gratuitous promises and that legal protection of the latter is, therefore, less justifiable is argued by Posner (1997).

[34] Kull (1992) 47.

[35] Critical of this approach are Baron (1988–1989) 188–189; Gordley *Foundations of Private Law* (2006) 355; Kull (1992) 49.

[36] Kull (1992) 56 further objects that consideration is a substitute for the primary validating formality of the seal and the seal validates all promises alike, whether gratuitous or not and thus irrespective of the costs and benefits.

of the benefits produced by philanthropic behaviour. Moreover, the growing economic relevance of the non-profit sector would suggest that arguments concerning the lack of economic importance should be at least viewed with caution. Finally, gift promises serve very useful purposes, which cannot be otherwise satisfied.[37] As this book will show, this is certainly true even more so of promises of an inheritance. They allow promisors and promisees to enter into a testamentary arrangement about the exchange of labour (frequently work rendered in the household or on the farm, or care services) or emotional support and wealth, that can serve the interest of both parties, albeit only if both are adequately protected.

3. Administrative costs

A final argument related to Posner's point outlined earlier is that the standardization produced by form reduces confusion and resulting administrative costs. If only those gifts which are formally executed are enforced, legal involvement is kept to a minimum.[38] However, this would leave many promisees unprotected. While 'enforcing' such testamentary promises has its costs, this enquiry illustrates that not enforcing them also has its costs, which are borne by those who, in reliance on the promise from someone whom they usually trust, provide a performance that is valuable to the promisor. In addition, imposing formalities makes little sense here because it clashes with the realities of social practice. Also, as the analysis in Chapter 3 will demonstrate, where the promise is formalized and a contract entered into, some jurisdictions assume that the promisor may have had an intention to circumvent family provision legislation,[39] or to be eligible for Medicaid.[40] In other words, formalizing the agreement may ultimately work against the promisee.

C. Summary

We have seen that as a consequence of the prevalent approach (i.e. the inherent suspicion) towards gifts and gift promises set out earlier, legal systems impose certain formalities for gifts and promises of a lifetime gift. But we also saw that the reasons for imposing formalities on gratuitous promises are not always compelling—even more so when it comes to testamentary promises. Such promises are usually part of an intergenerational testamentary exchange and less frequently an expression of purely altruistic motivations. In other words, they are not solely gratuitous but are a type of *gratuité intéressée*, so that the argument that they are a result of irrational behaviour is not really persuasive.

[37] It has, for instance, been argued that gifts are socially important because they are spontaneous, approximate and unspecifiable. Baron (1988–1989) 199.
[38] Baron (1988–1989) 189.
[39] See Chapter 3.
[40] Kohn (2019).

By requiring such formalities, the law prioritizes the perspective of the donors or promisors of the gift who, in principle, are not bound unless they comply with a certain form. However, the protection of the interests of donors and promisors is provided also in other ways. For instance, in common law jurisdictions, where there is lack of evidence of the intention of the transferor, the presumption of resulting trusts operates as a way of safeguarding the transferor in case of gratuitous transfers to another person or the purchase of property in the name of another person. The law thus favours a construction of the transfer that is least burdensome to the donor or promisor, though if the transfer is made to a child or spouse, the presumption is one of gift (often referred to as the presumption of advancement).[41] In particular, landowners have always enjoyed strong protection.[42] In the testamentary context such protection finds further expression in the principle of testamentary freedom, whereby a person is free to dispose of her wealth as she wishes and to change her mind until her death. Freedom of testation itself is protected through the enforcement of strict formality requirements but, as we will see, in some jurisdictions, also by preventing the testator from binding herself as to the contents of her will.[43] But what about the promisee? This book argues that the position of the promisee and her vulnerability is frequently overlooked and therefore examines this area through the lens of the promisee.

II. Formal testamentary promises

A. Common v civil law

As has emerged from the discussion so far, the legal position concerning lifetime promises to make a gift is that, so long as they comply with formality requirements, they are enforceable, and that the absence of form can be overcome by actual performance.[44] We further saw that the position is not altogether different in civil and common law jurisdictions. The same cannot be said with regards to testamentary promises, at least on a formal level.

In fact, the legal framework for testamentary promises is much more complex than that for lifetime gift promises, and the starting point is different in the two legal traditions. As this section will show, contrasted with lifetime promises to make gifts, testamentary promises are not necessarily actionable simply because

[41] For a comparison of the operation of the two types of presumptions in US law with the law in the Commonwealth, see Glister (2018). Scots law too has a presumption against donations of moveable property which can be rebutted. See MacQueen & Hogg (2012).

[42] McInnes (2016) shows, for instance, that rights in real property were always sacrosanct and for that reason, historically, those who improved someone else's land were not awarded relief.

[43] See section II.A.2.

[44] See nn 9 and 10.

they comply with formality requirements. On the contrary, succession laws of many civil law legal systems explicitly prohibit legally binding promises to make a future will. By contrast, common law jurisdictions recognize their validity. On a formal level, there is thus a significant difference in approach between common law jurisdictions on the one hand, and most civil law jurisdictions on the other, although underlying social practices tend to be similar in both traditions. This does not mean that promisees are left without protection. Simply their protection is in many cases found outside succession law, and more specifically in contract law, enrichment law, property law, employment law, or family law. Before looking at how informal promises are dealt with, I will explore some of the differences in approach between the common and civil law tradition with regards to formal testamentary promises and the reasons why many legal systems have chosen to reject their validity. This is critical in order to understand the approach courts take to informal testamentary promises and what aspects to be mindful of when trying to regulate them.

1. The common law context

Many common law jurisdictions recognize the validity of legally binding testamentary promises in the form of contracts to make a will or a bequest.[45] In other words, a promisor can enter into a contract with the promisee in which she promises to make a will, not to make a will or not to revoke it. This means that if the elements of a contract can be established, the promisor will be bound and the promise enforceable, so that in case of breach, the promisee can claim either damages or, in some cases, specific performance.[46] This does not mean that promisors cannot change their will. On the contrary, the will remains revocable. However, promisors can be liable for breach of contract if they change the will and breach their promise. Thus, by admitting contracts to make a will, common law jurisdictions acknowledge the possibility of, and allow for, a formal/binding testamentary exchange.

The earliest English cases involving such contracts (or covenants) to make a will date back to the seventeenth century,[47] and since then their validity has never been in doubt.[48] In the past, such contracts were sometimes made in the context of marriage settlements and marriage promises.[49] Not infrequently the father of the bride expressed such a promise to his daughter's future husband.[50] Contractual promises

[45] For a historical account of developments in England and the US, see Sparks *Contracts to Make Wills* (1956). However, it seems that, in the US, legislatures and courts have grown suspicious of family contracts for elder care and view them as non-binding. For a fascinating analysis, see Kohn (2019).

[46] Details of the protection will be provided in Chapter 3.

[47] The first reported English case is *Goilmere v Battison* (1682) 1 Vern 48; (1682) 23 ER 301, while the first reported US case on this subject dates back to 1785: *Izard v Middleton* 1 Desaus 116 (SC 1785).

[48] At the end of the eighteenth century, in *Walpole v Orford* (1797) 3 Ves Jun 402, 412; 30 ER 1076, 1081, counsel stated that '[n]o proposition is better settled than that a contract to leave by will is good'.

[49] Miller *The Machinery* (1996) 214. For examples, see *Synge v Synge* [1894] 1 QB 466 (CA) and *Fortescue v Hennah* (1812) 19 Ves 67; 34 ER 443.

[50] Learmonth et al *Theobald on Wills* (2021) 8–8006.

of an inheritance were also sometimes made in favour of housekeepers.[51] Both are less frequent today. Generally, judging from case law, contracts to make a future will appear to be less common in practice, at least in England and Wales,[52] though there is case law in other common law jurisdictions.

Contracts to make a will are regulated by general contract law rather than being the object of specific provisions tailored to the testamentary context. Thus, as we will see in greater detail in Chapter 3, for a legally binding contract to arise, contractual requirements such as offer and acceptance, intention to create legal relations, and consideration (or a deed), must be met. In addition, where the promise relates to land, the contract has to be made in writing. Again, law insists on formalities. Given the particular context in which testamentary promises are usually expressed,[53] meeting these requirements (including that of writing) often presents a significant challenge for promisees who may, as a result, not be able to avail themselves of contractual remedies. Formalizing the relationship is not what people (and especially promisors) normally desire in these circumstances. Also, the time differential between the promise and the promisor's death necessitates a certain flexibility so that it is difficult for the parties to cast the relationship in contractual terms. This leaves many promisees potentially without legal protection unless ways are found to protect their interests outside contract law. Thus, while not prohibiting contracts to make a will, common law jurisdictions impose strict requirements and high evidentiary standards, making it difficult to prove such contracts. For this reason, New Zealand has passed specific legislation dealing with informal promises, that is promises that do not amount to a contract to make a will.[54] Somewhat surprisingly, other common law jurisdictions have not followed in its footsteps. However, as this book will show, in the absence of specific regulations, a promisee can resort to other private law doctrines to obtain redress, and in some cases, this can even lead to an award of the promised asset.

2. The civil law context

In striking contrast to the picture that we find in common law jurisdictions, most civil law legal systems do not recognize the validity of contracts to make a will.[55] Indeed, irrespective of the form used, such contracts are usually explicitly forbidden, meaning that a testator cannot bind herself as to the content of her future will; nor is she able to make a legally binding promise not to revoke her will, or not to make one at all. Hence, while lifetime gift promises are admissible in civil

[51] See, for instance, *Fenton v Emblers* (1762) 3 Burr 1278; (1762) 97 ER 831 and *Schaefer v Schuhmann* [1972] AC. For examples from the US, see the study by the historian Hartog *Someday* (2012).

[52] For details, see Chapter 3.

[53] See Chapter 1.

[54] See Chapter 7.

[55] Exceptions are represented by Scotland, Greece and Turkey as well as some Nordic countries such as Denmark and Norway. For references, see Süss *Erbrecht in Europa* (2020). See also Dutta (2020).

law jurisdictions, provided that they comply with formality requirements, testamentary ones are usually not. The law is thus even harsher towards, and more suspicious of, testamentary promises.

The existence of prohibitions of contracts or pacts to make future wills may lead one to conclude that such promises are no longer expressed and that they have therefore ceased to pose challenges for the law. This is indeed the impression one gains from looking at succession law literature. However, this is not necessarily the case. Such prohibitions have not prevented promisors from expressing informal promises of a future inheritance and others from acting on, and seeking to enforce, them. Arguably, therefore, civil law jurisdictions have been unsuccessful in trying to legislate away this particular social practice. What they seem to have achieved is that there is reduced litigation but that may also have other reasons, that is forced/compulsory heirship provisions which in a way temper the risk that at least the closest family members who have provided services or work, or made financial contributions, go empty handed. In any case, reduced litigation does not mean that promises are not being made. Thus, regardless of whether or not legal systems admit the validity of legally binding promises to make future testamentary dispositions, in practice, informal testamentary promises are undertaken and relied upon, and the problem arises as to how to deal with cases when they remain unfulfilled. Consequently, in the absence of specific regulation, both in common and civil law legal traditions, promisees will usually resort to various doctrines of private law that vary in scope and that are not necessarily devised for the testamentary context.

Before exploring the options promisees have across jurisdictions when seeking redress, and any potential hurdles they may have to overcome, as well as the challenges that this situation poses for courts, I will briefly examine these prohibitions, their historical roots, their effect, and some of the reasons underpinning them. This will allow us to gain a better understanding of the interests the prohibitions aim to protect and thus the perceived threats that testamentary promises are seen to pose. We will see that the grounds for such prohibitions are not always convincing. Even so, one can also understand why some legal systems may have wanted to do away with them.

B. Prohibiting pacts/contracts to make a will

1. Historical roots of the prohibitions

The roots of the prohibitions of contracts (or pacts) concerning the content of a future will contained in many modern civilian codifications can be traced back to Roman law. Testamentary promises feature both in the Digest[56] and the Codex,

[56] The most ancient text is a fragment by Julian. D 45, I, 61. Jul. 2 ad Urseium Ferocem. See Schulz *Classical Roman Law* (1951) 206 and Vismara *Storia dei patti successori I* (1942) 77–78.

with sources relating to a number of different contexts. Promises to nominate someone as heir were, for instance, expressed in connection with an agreement constituting a *societas*, dotal pacts, and a compromise remitting debts.[57] All of the sources declare such promises void, irrespective of the context in which they were expressed. Even though some legal historians have argued that this is unsurprising, suggesting that Roman lawyers had a general aversion against pacts concerning a future succession,[58] the sources do not confirm that. As the legal historian Giulio Vismara has shown, Roman law never embraced a general prohibition of all types of succession pacts. It rather prohibited certain types of *pacta successoria* (succession pacts), among which featured pacts concerning the future content of a will and pacts not to revoke a will or not to make one.[59] This is important because the reasons behind the prohibitions are different, depending on the type of pact.

So what were the reasons justifying the prohibitions of promises to nominate someone as heir? The answer is somewhat contentious among Roman legal historians. It is generally agreed that such promises were seen as being *contra bonos mores*.[60] Two of the texts[61] explicitly state this. However, exactly why testamentary promises were considered against good morals, is a question that has divided legal historians. Vismara was of the opinion that the reason for holding these pacts against good morals was that they clashed with the testator's freedom of testation.[62] This would seem to find confirmation in some of the sources, which refer to the power to make a free disposition.[63] Vismara also mentions that in some instances, the prohibition was motivated by the desire not to allow for a violation of the legal order of succession, that is where the deceased intended to benefit more remote relatives.[64]

By contrast, for the legal historian Peter Weimar, obligatory transactions (stipulations) directed towards the appointment of an heir were contrary to good morals, because the consequences of a non-performance were borne by the heirs and not the deceased herself.[65] Only on death of the promisor did it become clear whether she had fulfilled her promise. This means that a promisor could freely undertake such obligations. If she fulfilled them, nothing could be said, and if she did not, her heir bore the consequences. Hence, according to Weimar, the reason for prohibiting such pacts did not lie in the fact that the Romans saw the pact as limiting

[57] For a detailed examination of the texts, see Vismara *Storia dei patti successori I* (1942) 77–86.
[58] See the authors cited by Vismara *Storia dei patti successori I* (1942) 77.
[59] Ibid. De Giorgi *I patti sulle successioni future* (1976) 19ff.
[60] D 45, I, 61 and C 8, 38, 4. See Kaser *Das Römische Privatrecht I* (1971) 677 and Kaser *Das Römische Privatrecht II* (1975) 475. Vismara *Storia dei patti successori I* (1942) 77–86. Weimar in *Miscellanea Domenico Maffei IV* (1995) 236. An English translation is published as Weimar (1994) hereinafter referred to.
[61] D 45, I, 61 and C 8, 38, 4.
[62] Vismara *Storia dei patti successori I* (1942) 84.
[63] D 17, 2, 52, 9 and C 2, 3, 15. Vismara *Storia dei patti successori I* (1942) 84.
[64] D 17, 2, 52, 9 discussed in Vismara *Storia dei patti successori I* (1942) 79.
[65] Weimar (1994) 790.

the promisor's testamentary freedom. In his view, the idea that agreements which restrict the testator's freedom of testation were *contra bonos mores*, and void, only developed in medieval jurisprudence. For Weimar it was scholastic jurisprudence, rather than Roman jurisprudence, that regarded binding dispositions in contemplation of death to be in conflict with the notion of testamentary freedom.[66]

The German legal scholar Robert Battes has further argued that the Romans wanted to avoid circumvention of strict formality requirements and to deter potential legacy hunters.[67] Although Battes does not support this claim with any evidence, Vismara has also pointed out that between the second and the fourth century CE there was an invasion of *captatores hereditatis*.[68] The prohibitions could therefore have been related also to a desire to address the risk of undue influence of the promisor, or of fraudulent allegations of testamentary promises. Thus, to conclude, it seems that there were different reasons why Roman lawyers regarded promises to nominate someone as heir as problematic. In section II.B.3 we will see that these reasons are only partly similar to those that informed the decisions of the drafters of many modern civilian codes to expressly prohibit such pacts.

2. Modern codifications

Prohibitions of pacts in which a testator promises to make a future testamentary disposition found their way into many modern civil law codifications. For instance, the Civil Codes of France, Germany, Italy, Spain, Belgium, the Netherlands, the Province of Quebec, and of several Latin American countries feature prohibitions that include (either explicitly or implicitly) legally binding promises of a future inheritance.[69] In many countries, the bar of such promises forms part of a general prohibition of the use of pacts and contracts in the succession context. This is, for instance, the case in Italy where Article 458 of the Italian Civil Code covers pacts by means of which a person promises to make a will, as well as pacts in which a person nominates an heir or attributes a legacy, and agreements to waive inheritance rights concerning a future inheritance. By contrast, in the French Civil Code the prohibition of such pacts is expressed in various codal provisions.[70]

However, not all civil law jurisdictions that prohibit contracts/pacts to make a future will also prohibit other types of pacts or contracts related to a future succession. This is the case of Germany. § 2302 of the German Civil Code expressly

66 Ibid, 796.

67 Battes (1978) 341.

68 Vismara *Storia dei patti successori I* (1942) 85. See also Raoul-Cormeil et al (2011) para 6.

69 It should, however, also be noted that many of these jurisdictions feature numerous exceptions to the prohibition which, in some cases, have thrown into question the relevance or desirability of the prohibitions. The position of mixed legal systems is not uniform. South African law prohibits *pacta successoria*. See *Borman en De Vos NNO v Potgietersrusse Tabakkorporasie Bpk* 1976 (3) SA 488 (A) and *McAlpine v McAlpine NO* 1997 (1) SA 736; *Van Aardt v Van Aardt* 2007 (1) SA 53 (E). Unlike South Africa, Scots law does not know of such a prohibition and both unilateral promises to make a will as well as contracts to make a will are valid. See Hutchison in *Exploring the Law of Succession* (2007).

70 See Articles 1130(2), 722, 1389 and 943 of the Code civil.

prevents a testator from undertaking a legally binding promise to make a future will, not to make one or not to revoke it. At the same time, the BGB allows a testator to enter into a legally binding inheritance contract in which she nominates an heir, and it allows for contracts through which a prospective heir waives her rights over a future succession.[71] This is in stark contrast to most civil law jurisdictions.[72] The difference in approach is intimately linked to the reasons that underlie the German prohibition of formal promises to make a future will, which leads me to the next point.

3. Rationale behind the prohibition

We have seen that there are conflicting accounts as to the reasons why promises to nominate someone as heir were considered invalid under Roman law. As for modern codal prohibitions, the rationale underpinning the various prohibitions is not uniform across jurisdictions and, to some extent, contested in most jurisdictions. Over the years, the prohibitions have been criticized by legal scholars and several jurisdictions have introduced exceptions to their prohibitions so that their purpose is somewhat undermined.[73] It is neither possible nor necessary here to enter into a detailed discussion of all the various justifications that are put forward across the many jurisdictions that enshrine such prohibitions. Nonetheless, for the purposes of this enquiry it is useful to point out some of the core arguments, for they allow us to gain a sense of the interests that the prohibitions aim to protect but also of the reasons why legal systems are generally sceptical towards testamentary promises.

In many jurisdictions the prohibition is seen primarily as an expression of the desire to protect the promisor's testamentary freedom and in particular the free revocability of her will. This is, for instance, true of France and Italy,[74] where such pacts are regarded as a means whereby the deceased limits rather than expresses her freedom to dispose freely of her assets until her death. The argument goes that, where a testator enters into a contract to make a will, she restricts her own freedom to change her mind up until her death, when in fact this freedom should be preserved. Also, because she will feel bound by the pact, her testamentary disposition would not be spontaneous.[75] For that reason, she should not be able to bind herself. Besides the fact that, arguably, entering into such a contract is an expression of that very freedom,[76] what this seems to show (once more) is that the law privileges the

[71] See §§ 2274ff BGB.
[72] Other exceptions are Austria and Switzerland which also recognize the validity of the *Erbvertrag*.
[73] This is, for instance, the case in France and Belgium, and to a limited extent also Italy. For a discussion see Braun 'Towards a Greater Autonomy' (2012). The Belgian succession law reform entered into force in September 2018 has eroded the prohibition even further.
[74] See De Giorgi *I patti sulle successioni future* (1976) 59ff; Zoppini *Le successioni* (2002) 173; Gazzoni (2001).
[75] Critical of the prohibition and this justification is Leleu in *Les relations contractuelles internationales* (1995).
[76] Dutta (2020).

perspective of the testator by ensuring that her freedom to change her mind is preserved until her death and that she is not bound as to the content of her future will.

However, this is not the full story. The prohibitions of contracts or pacts over a future succession also fulfil other purposes. They are also partly an expression of the desire to protect forced and compulsory heirship provisions from attempts by the testator to undermine them. As is well known, these provisions are aimed at providing certain members of the deceased's close family with an entitlement to a share in the deceased's estate even against her will, and thus to keep assets in the family. A testator could circumvent those entitlements by committing herself to leaving her estate to someone other than those entitled to a share. The view taken by many codifiers is that testators should not be able to contradict statutory provisions that determine the distribution of the estate in favour of certain family members. This is similar to one of the arguments we saw being raised in the context of Roman law. Thus, the prohibitions also protect the interests of forced/compulsory heirs. That there is a risk of such pacts being used to circumvent family protection is shown by the experience of common law jurisdictions. As we shall see in Chapter 3, some common law jurisdictions have felt the need to introduce provisions that prevent precisely the evasion of claims under the family provision legislation through contracts to make a will.[77] Of course, such prohibitions are not the only way to protect forced/compulsory heirship provisions from being undermined. There are anti-evasion mechanisms that can be used to prevent this from happening, without the need for a prohibition, as German law shows.[78]

Finally, the prohibitions are sometimes also described as an expression of the fear that pacts or contracts to make a will are being used to arrange the succession in conflict with the principle of equality of the treatment of descendants, which underpins some codal provisions on forced/compulsory heirship. In other words, such pacts could lead to a concentration of wealth in the hands of few, and some descendants could thus be treated better than others. This was one of the arguments that led to the exclusion of succession pacts from the French Code civil.[79] Whether this is a sound argument is debatable; after all nothing stops the deceased from leaving her disposal share to whomever she wants, so that equal treatment can never be fully achieved. Also, where one of the children has performed services on the parents' farm or looked after them in old age on the basis of a promise of an inheritance, the attribution of equal shares could lead to injustice. Precisely this argument has led to inroads into the general prohibition of such pacts in some jurisdictions, including in France.[80] Thus, prohibitions of contracts or pacts of a

77 See Chapter 3.

78 See Zimmermann, 'Compulsory Portion in Germany' in *Comparative Succession Law 3* (2020) 269, 286ff.

79 De Giorgi *I patti sulle successioni future* (1976) 37; Baudry-Lacantinerie & Barde *Traité théorique et pratique I* (1906) 308; Grimaldi *Droit Civil Successions* (2017) 286.

80 France introduced the possibility (Articles 920–930-5 of the Code civil) that the compulsory heir waives the right to bring an action of reduction against a disposition that infringes her share. One of

future succession can be seen as both protecting and at the same time hampering the promisor's testamentary freedom. They limit the possibilities that the deceased gives the property to whomever she wants in a way that is binding. Later in this book we will see that the argument of equality of treatment of descendants underpins some of the forms of redress made available in civil law jurisdictions that are aimed at compensating unremunerated work.[81]

Interestingly, in Germany, the objections to the provision in § 2302 BGB (which states that a contract by which a person agrees to make or not to make a *mortis causa* disposition, to revoke it or not to revoke it, is void) are different from those mentioned earlier.[82] Although the reason for prohibiting contracts to make a will in Germany has often been ascribed to the need to protect freedom of testation, there are alternative and perhaps more convincing explanations for the scope and function of § 2302 BGB. As a study by Robert Battes shows, the rationale for the invalidity of contracts to make a will in Germany does not really lie in the desire to protect testamentary freedom.[83] This is so even though the provision is entitled 'unlimited testamentary freedom' and traditionally many authors have referred to this freedom as the underlying reason. Rather, it is to be found in the fact that German law establishes a *numerus clausus* of testamentary forms that a testator can resort to in order to dispose of her assets.[84] She can either use a will or, if she intends to bind herself with immediate effect, she can resort to a testamentary contract (an *Erbvertrag*). For each of these German instruments, succession law mandates specific formalities. The purpose of § 2302 BGB is thus to protect the *numerus clausus* of testamentary instruments and to prevent, in particular, the circumvention of provisions regulating inheritance contracts through the use of contracts to make a will,[85] including the prescribed formality requirements,[86] and those provisions that establish when the testator can revoke the inheritance contract.[87] According to Battes, these should not be undermined by agreements that would be subject 'merely' to the general rules of contract law.[88] Battes' interpretation of § 2302 BGB is in line with the decision of the German legislature to admit inheritance contracts as well as mutual wills through which the testator can bind herself. It would also

the arguments used was that a parent may want to reward the child that is most deserving. See Braun 'Towards a Greater Autonomy' (2012) 466.

[81] For details, see Chapters 10 and 11.

[82] For a more detailed discussion, see Braun 'Formal and informal testamentary promises' (2012) 997–1001.

[83] Battes (1978) 337.

[84] Ibid, 346. § 2302 BGB is seen as a conclusive provision that defines the scope of the rules on the testamentary contract (*Erbvertrag*) and that gives it an exclusive position.

[85] Battes (1978) 346–347. See also Krebber (2004) 167.

[86] § 2276 BGB.

[87] As per §§ 2294 and 2295 BGB

[88] Battes (1978) 359. The argument of form is also used in Italy. See Caccavale in *Trattato del Contratto VI* (2006) 482 and Toti (1985).

explain why German courts are not concerned that a testator may feel bound by a formal or informal promise and therefore provide protection to promisees who have acted on a void contract to make a will.[89] This is different in Italy, where a promise of an inheritance may invalidate the future will—the justification being that testamentary dispositions should be spontaneous and therefore freely revocable until the last moment.[90] A will made in execution of even an informal promise would not be regarded as being spontaneous.

C. Summary

There are a host of reasons why many civil law legal systems have been suspicious of, and have thus positioned themselves against admitting, formal agreements (be it contracts or pacts) to make a future will. Even though these justifications are not always convincing and have come under significant scrutiny, a common justification is the desire to protect the testator's testamentary freedom and, in particular, the free revocability of her will. Here we see yet another way in which the law privileges the position of the person who owns the property and who gives it away (donor, promisor).[91] The analysis has, however, also revealed that such prohibitions are part of broader policy considerations underpinning succession laws in civil law jurisdictions, including the desire to treat descendants equally, to limit the number of testamentary forms, and to keep wealth in the family. The fact that form, the relationship with forced and compulsory heirship, and the principle of equality are all of concern highlights the complexity of the perceived challenges posed by testamentary promises. It also explains, perhaps, why certain jurisdictions wanted to do away with them—a point which will become even clearer in section III.D. But as the analysis in Chapter 3 will show, even in common law jurisdictions, contracts to make a will are sometimes seen with suspicion and precisely a means to circumvent potential family provision orders.

However, irrespective of whether or not one finds the justifications underpinning prohibitions of pacts or contracts to make a will compelling, they should not prevent the interests of promisees who have acted on a testamentary promise from being protected. In fact, in most jurisdictions promisees are not left without protection. Nonetheless, putting in place express prohibitions of legally binding promises of an inheritance inevitably has consequences for promisees. Not only do such prohibitions exclude the possibility of a formal agreement that could potentially

[89] For details, see Chapter 8 and Chapter 9, section II.

[90] Zoppini *Le successioni* (2002) 169. Toti (1985) 9 but also De Giorgi *I patti sulle successioni future* (1976).

[91] McBride *Humanity of Private Law I* (2019) at n 33 sees testamentary freedom as promoting the testator's flourishing. There are also other ways in which the perspective of the promisor is privileged, e.g. through a strict interpretation of formality requirements, and the interpretation of wills.

protect the promisee's interest more effectively, arguably they also exacerbate their vulnerability. For instance, as mentioned earlier,[92] in Italy, the prohibition can affect the validity of a will made in compliance with an (invalid) pact to make a will. In other words, if an Italian testator makes a will and those omitted from the will contest the validity of the will by arguing that it was made in compliance with (or execution of) a prior pact that is void, the will can be invalidated. Thus, even where the promisor wants to fulfil the promise that the law regards as void, she will be estopped from doing so.

More importantly, the prohibition implies that the promisee cannot, in principle, obtain the expectation interest because if courts gave effect to the informal promise, it could be argued that they would go directly against said prohibition.[93] As we will see, in Austria, Germany, and France, courts protect the interests of the promisee but only by providing some form of redress usually measured either on the basis of the value of the performance rendered by the promisee, or on the basis of the value of the enrichment obtained by the promisor, or less where they impose an artificial limit.[94] It follows that not only are these prohibitions incapable of preventing the social practice of expressing promises of a future inheritance, they can potentially also lead to inadequate protection of promisees. Whether that is justifiable is doubtful. Of course, one aspect to remember here is that in civil law jurisdictions, forced/compulsory heirship provisions ensure that at least those promisees who are close family members entitled to a share benefit from the deceased's estate. However, their share is not measured on the basis of the value of the promise or their performance but is instead fixed. Also, typically only descendants and the spouse or civil partner are entitled to a share.[95] Thus, in the civil law tradition, these prohibitions create difficulties that promisees in common law jurisdictions do not have to face. What is more, forced/compulsory heirship provisions can prevent promisors from rewarding those who are deserving, though arguably they can use the disposable share (i.e. that share of her estate that she can freely dispose of) for that purpose.

Merely abolishing such prohibitions and thus allowing parties to enter into a legally binding contract to make a will would not, however, fully address the problem that this book deals with. While having a prohibition in place arguably takes away from the parties the possibility of negotiating an exchange and agreeing on compensation, most families do not want to formalize such arrangements. As the experience of common law jurisdictions shows, testators usually make informal

[92] See n 87.

[93] Christandl, '§§ 677–678', in *Großkommentar zum ABGB* (2021) 219–220. Battes (1978) 366–368 has, however, argued that an entitlement to a right to compensation or restitution would not conflict with the prohibition enshrined in § 2302 BGB.

[94] For details, see the discussion in Chapters 8, 9, and 11.

[95] See Reid, de Waal, & Zimmermann, 'Mandatory Family Protection in Historical and Comparative Perspective' in *Comparative Succession Law 3* (2020).

promises even when they have the option of entering into formally binding contracts to make a will. While that could be explained (at least in part) with reference to the fact that the contractual requirements are burdensome, Chapter 1 has shown that the prevailing social practice is that of informality of such promises. The reason for the informality is both the context in which they are made but also the need for flexibility for the arrangement to work over time. Hence, requiring proof of the elements of a contract (including the need for writing in the case of land), as common law jurisdictions do, can place a heavy burden on promisees (who can do little where the promisor refuses to formalize the agreement) and fails to acknowledge the social reality. Again, the law prioritizes the perspective of the promisor, that is the property owner.[96] Also, as we will see in Chapter 3, framing the relationship in contractual terms is often difficult, also because of the potential time lag between the promise and the promisor's death, which would require parties to insert detailed conditions to deal with unforeseen circumstances. Other ways therefore have to be found to deal with informal testamentary promises.

III. Dealing with informal testamentary promises

A. Informal testamentary promises in civil and common law traditions

The analysis so far has shown that prohibitions of contracts or pacts to make a will have not prevented promisors from making informal testamentary promises and others from relying on them. In other words, the social behaviour has not conformed to the legal framework.[97] Also, in those jurisdictions in which such contracts are admitted, few promises are entered into formally and amount to a legally valid contract. However, most legal systems do not expressly regulate informal testamentary promises. The only real exception is New Zealand, which recognizes contracts to make a will while at the same time also expressly regulating informal testamentary promises. As we will see in Chapter 7, the relevant legislation in New Zealand acknowledges the informal character of many testamentary promises and ensures that those who provide work or services for the promisor in exchange for a promise receive reasonable compensation. This does not mean that in other jurisdictions that lack specific regulation, promisees are left without protection. Courts in both legal traditions have come to the aid of promisees who have acted on informal promises of an inheritance, and they have done so even in jurisdictions where legally binding promises of an inheritance are prohibited.

[96] This will become even clearer in Chapter 3.
[97] Resta (2014) 4.

The protection awarded to promisees is provided by drawing on and adapting various doctrines of private law that will be examined in Parts II and III. In the remaining sections of this chapter, I provide a brief overview of the various forms of redress that promisees may want to seek out, before exploring some of the main challenges that they face when bringing a claim. I then move on to showing that protecting promisees of informal testamentary promises is not without its problems. In fact, the testamentary context poses particular challenges, requiring courts to engage in a difficult balancing act. These should not, however, stand in the way of protecting the interests of promisees.

B. Range of possible forms of redress

1. A complex and fragmented picture

Because most legal systems lack specific legislation dealing with informal testamentary promises, when seeking a legal response, promisees resort to various general principles of private law. Consequently, the legal framework within which testamentary promises operate is necessarily complex and fragmented. What is more, the scope of these doctrines varies considerably and many of them are not specifically designed to deal with such cases.

In the majority of the cases the redress is sought on the basis of contract law, the law of unjust or unjustified enrichment, property law, and, to a lesser extent, employment law, family law, and succession law. For instance, where there is proof of a valid contract to make a will (in a legal system that recognizes such contracts) the claimant may obtain damages or specific performance. However, this is possible only in a few jurisdictions and even then the promise will not usually amount to a contract so that redress has to be sought outside contract law. In some jurisdictions it may be possible for a promisee to establish the existence of an implied employment contract with the promisor, so that she may be awarded an amount equivalent to lost wages. This option has been explored in civilian jurisdictions, such as Germany and Austria (and, at least in the past, also Italy), but interestingly not in the common law context. In France and Belgium there is also the possibility for a promisee who has worked on the family farm to claim that she is entitled to a deferred salary against the estate on the basis of the doctrine of the *créance de salaire différé*, though in these cases no actual contract is implied.

In many jurisdictions redress can be sought by arguing that the promisor was unjustly enriched at the expense of the promisee. This approach is adopted, in common law jurisdictions, such as Canada, Australia, and New Zealand, as well as in civil law jurisdictions, such as Germany, Austria, and France, though the scope of application varies across jurisdictions. In some of them it can only be invoked when no other claim is available.

In some legal systems, the interests of the promisee are offered protection also through property law. For instance, in the common law context, the doctrine of proprietary estoppel represents a popular form of redress. Although the equitable doctrine of proprietary estoppel, rooted in the detrimental reliance of the promisee on a promise, is formally only known to common law jurisdictions, some civil law scholars have suggested developing a similar protection of reliance interests based on equitable principles.[98] In the past, arguments similar to those underlying the doctrine of proprietary estoppel were invoked by German courts in cases where owners of a farm had informally promised to leave the farm to someone, usually the son, on death and courts have given effect to the informal promise.[99]

Lastly, redress can sometimes be sought through succession law. In jurisdictions with forced/compulsory heirship provisions in place, the risk of promisees going empty handed is somewhat tempered where they are entitled to a share in the estate. However, such provisions only protect promisees who are close family members. Also, forced/compulsory heirship is a usually a feature of civil law and mixed legal systems but not of common law jurisdictions. In common law jurisdictions a promisee could try to seek protection under the family provision legislation (which is functionally similar to forced/compulsory heirship provisions) by suggesting that the promisor has not made proper or adequate financial provisions for her. We will indeed see that a promise of a future inheritance, especially if it has been acted upon, can give rise to a moral duty on the part of the deceased to provide for the promisee.[100] However, the protection is usually limited. In Germany, promisees of testamentary promises may also try to obtain redress by demanding an adjustment of their intestate share on the basis of § 2057a BGB. Although the codal provision only applies on intestacy and benefits only descendants, it may be usefully invoked as a last resort. The Dutch Civil Code contains a similar provision (Article 4:36 BW) dealing with the distribution on intestacy, though unlike the German provision it entitles the applicant to compensation rather than a mere adjustment of the share. And in Austria, the promisee may be entitled to a statutory legacy but only where she has cared for the deceased and falls amongst those eligible to bring a claim (§ 677 ABGB). Thus, there are a range of possible avenues across jurisdictions that a promisee may want to pursue and that will be explored in this book.

[98] Miserre *Die 'culpa in testando'* (2002); Zankl *Gesetzliche Vorausvermächtnis des Ehegatten* (1996) 168ff.

[99] For an analysis, see Wöhrmann & Graß *Das Landwirschaftserbrecht* (2019); Lüdtke-Handjery & Jeinsen, *Höfeordnung* (2015); Roemer (1957); Wieacker (1956) and (1957); Kroeschell in *Göttinger Festschrift* (1961); Canaris *Vertrauenshaftung* (1971) 360–363.

[100] Chapter 5.

2. Choice of avenue

In practice, claimants will commonly invoke more than one doctrine so as to increase their chance of some form of redress.[101] However, not all forms of redress discussed in this book are available in all jurisdictions and to all promisees. Several of the solutions analysed here are available only in either common or civil law jurisdictions, though some feature in both. Some of the forms of redress are context specific (e.g. available only in the farming or care setting), while others are of a subsidiary nature, thus representing a means of last resort.[102] Also, not all represent independent causes of action,[103] and some of them are only available on death of the promisor, leaving the promisee without protection during the promisor's lifetime.[104] Finally, some forms of redress can only be relied upon where the promisee has acted on the promise by rendering, for instance, services, rather than providing financial support or incurring other expenditures, in the form of improvements to the promisor's property.[105] Thus, most private law doctrines are not capable of capturing all types of situations in which a testamentary promise remains unfulfilled.

Some promisees seem to have greater choice in terms of modes of redress. For instance, the comparison reveals that within the circle of close family members, descendants are potentially protected under all forms of redress examined in this book. In fact, some, such as the German § 2057a BGB, apply to descendants only. While the scope of the French *créance de salaire différé* has been extended to the spouse of the farmer, the protection provided to descendants is stronger. Equally, the Austrian statutory care legacy applies to a limited range of people and the same is true of the family provision legislation, which can only be invoked by those who are eligible under the provisions. Thus, depending on the nature of the relationship with the deceased, the range of avenues available may change. Even so, in most jurisdictions promisees have a choice, and where possible they will rely on more than one form of redress. The choice of the form of redress is important because it affects what the promisee has to prove to establish her claim. As section III.C will show, some may prove to be more challenging than others. In particular there are some recurring challenges that promisees face and that it is useful to outline here.

[101] A good example is the Irish case of *K v K* [2018] IEHC 615 (hereafter *K v K*) where the promisee brought a claim grounded in contract law, proprietary estoppel, and the family provision legislation.

[102] See the subsidiary nature of enrichment claims in France (Chapter 9), but also of § 2057a BGB (Chapter 11) which can only be invoked when no other claim is available.

[103] See § 2057a BGB discussed in Chapter 11.

[104] See the protection provided by § 2057a BGB, § 677 ABGB, the New Zealand TPA 1949, or the family provision legislation.

[105] An example is § 612 BGB (Chapter 8).

C. Recurring challenges for promisees

1. Introduction

A promisee who seeks to obtain protection in case of an unfulfilled testamentary promise faces a number of challenges in terms of proving her case. These challenges are determined partly by the informality and vagueness that frequently characterize such promises. But even where they are made formally, some jurisdictions exclude the testimony of the promisee or require corroboration.[106] The purpose of such provisions is to protect the estate from false claims,[107] but they can potentially also exclude valid claims.[108]

Irrespective of that, establishing a claim can be particularly difficult where promisees are asked to prove that: (i) what motivated their behaviour is the prospect of the inheritance or that they did not act out of love and affection; and/or (ii) what they have done exceeds not only potential duties they may have towards the promisor but also societal expectations towards them, so that what they have done goes above and beyond that which can normally be expected of them. In addition, some forms of redress also pose potential psychological barriers that may well function as a deterrent to bringing a claim or make life more difficult for a promisee who intends to bring a claim. These stumbling blocks will be briefly explored here but returned to in each chapter.

2. Role and relevance of the promisee's motivations

With some forms of redress, the motives underlying the promisee's behaviour are entirely irrelevant. This is true of the New Zealand Law Reform (Testamentary Promises) Act 1949 (hereafter the New Zealand TPA 1949) which was specifically tailored to the testamentary context.[109] Motives are further irrelevant for the purposes of establishing a claim to deferred wages on the basis of the French *créance de salaire différé*, an adjustment on the basis of the German § 2057a BGB, or compensation on the basis of the Austrian statutory care legacy regulated by §§ 677ff ABGB. This is because these latter forms of redress are not specifically aimed at dealing with instances in which the work or services were performed on account of a promise. Rather, the aim is to compensate unremunerated work and services rendered by certain family members for the benefit of the deceased, irrespective of any promise. Nonetheless, these forms of redress can come to the aid of promisees,

[106] See, for instance, the 'dead man's statutes' in the US which render any testimony showing that the decedent entered into an express oral contract inadmissible so that the promisee may have great difficulties proving her claim. Although in recent years the majority of states have repealed their respective dead man's statutes, some state courts still observe the repealed law. For an analysis, see Wallis (2005) and Tucker (2000).

[107] Gallanis & Gittler (2011–2012) 770ff.

[108] Beardsley (2001). For a critical analysis of the dead man's statutes, see Langbein (1975) 501ff.

[109] For details about the Act, see Chapter 7.

and, as we will see, not having to prove the existence of a promise can be beneficial for them since, due to the informality of such promises, that is often a difficult task.

However, with other forms of redress examined in this book, considerable weight is placed on the promisee's motives for acting the way she did. For instance, we will see that for the purposes of a proprietary estoppel claim, the promisee needs to have relied on the promise to her detriment, though the burden of disproving reliance is on the defendant, which makes things easier for the promisee.[110] In the case of an unjust enrichment claim brought under Canadian law, the promisee will need to prove the absence of a juristic reason, such as the absence of a donative intent. The same is true in France. With other forms of redress, she may have to show that there is a nexus between the expectation to inherit and the lack of compensation (e.g. in the case of a claim based on § 612 BGB), at which point the motives again play a role.

As the analysis in Chapter 1 has revealed,[111] informal testamentary arrangements usually involve people in a close relationship and the motives underpinning the promisee's behaviour are therefore generally mixed.[112] Asking promisees to prove their subjective motives thus has the potential of forcing them into proving something which is likely to be (at least partly) untrue and presenting themselves in a light that is not in line with their moral character. In addition, it has the potential to hurt others, especially where the promisor is still alive and the promisee is forced to argue that what she has done for the promisor was not for free. At best it can feel awkward and at worst it can present a deterrent for some (deserving) promisees.

Where the promisee is someone who is not a family member or close friend, it may sometimes be easier to assume that she has acted on the promise because it explains her performance. Surely a stranger would not have provided services or work for free were it not for a prospect of an inheritance. Indeed, in the Irish decision in *K v K*, McDonald J stated at para [103] that:

> An important underlying factor in that case [the decision of the Supreme Court in *McCarron v. McCarron* (Supreme Court, unreported, 13 February 1997)] was that it was impossible to explain how a person in the claimant's position would have been prepared to work long hours on the farm of a stranger without any form of remuneration whatsoever. It might be said that this factor is absent in the present case in that the plaintiff here was the eldest son of the deceased.[113]

[110] See Chapter 4, section II.B.

[111] On this point see also Zelizer (2000) who argues that many transactions involve a mixture of the economic and the intimate.

[112] This was the argument of the defendants in *Re Basham* [1986] 1 WLR 1498 (Ch), 1500.

[113] *K v K* (n 101).

It follows that family members are, on the whole, more likely to face an uphill battle when trying to establish a claim, yet they are also more likely to rely on the promise in the first place because of the trust and confidence they have in the deceased. This shows again the vulnerability of promisees who are in a relationship of trust with the promisor. By placing too much weight on motives, or taking a strict approach to the requirement of reliance or requiring a nexus between the promise and the promisee's performance, law risks rewarding those who act only or primarily on the basis of a promise. In particular insisting on the proof of reliance further overlooks the fact that in many of the scenarios examined the promise follows at a later stage; that is once the performance has commenced, to prevent the promisee from stopping her performance, or to entice her to continue or increase her services. In other words, the sequence is, as noted before, not always chronological,[114] and in many instances more than one promise is made over the course of several years so that some flexibility will be needed when evaluating reliance.

3. Societal expectations

Another recurring theme in this book is the challenges some promisees face due to expectations society nurtures towards them, including expectations about their motivations and about how they ought to behave. Such expectations are not always openly acknowledged or discussed, and they can change over time.[115] They will be reflected in the way courts interpret certain requirements a promisee must meet to be successful. Sometimes they also find expression in the form of legal presumptions whereby work carried out, for instance, by family members is automatically deemed to have been rendered gratuitously.[116] Overcoming such presumptions is possible but can be difficult. The burden lies with the promisee who will need to show that she has in fact not acted gratuitously.

In some cases, societal expectations are expressed in the form of legal duties. For instance, in Germany, direct relatives are under an obligation to support one another if they are in need.[117] And, due to § 1619 BGB, a child (even if adult) still belonging to the household of their parents and supported by them, has a duty to perform services for them in their household and business in a manner appropriate to the child's strength and position in life. When bringing an action, they therefore need to show that what they have done for the parent exceeds their duty.[118]

[114] This is something the New Zealand TPA 1949 usefully accounts for. See Chapter 7.

[115] Courts' perceptions of women's contributions to farms and households have changed and obtained greater recognition. In this sense see, for instance, Forbes-Chilibeck (2005) and Freedman (2010) 177. On the gender question, see also Fellows (1992); Korven (1993). See further Philipps (2008) 106–108 on the risk of romanticizing families as sites of altruism and solidarity, ignoring the potential for hierarchy and exploitation of unpaid market workers.

[116] For the US, see Kohn (2019) 220ff; Gallanis & Gittler (2011–2012) 770–771. For a historical analysis of the position adopted by Italian courts, see De Giorgi *I patti sulle successioni future* (1976) 165ff.

[117] See §1601 BGB.

[118] Here see Chapter 11 and the contrast between Germany and Austria.

In France too, children have a duty to pay alimony or maintenance towards their parents who are in need.[119] In order to demand an indemnity, their performance must therefore exceed the threshold of filial piety. As the analysis in Chapter 9 will show, what that means is not always clear.

Societal expectations will frequently depend on the relationship between the parties in question, the type of work or service carried out, and consequently, also the gender of the promisee. For instance, certain services are expected to be rendered gratuitously if the relationship between the parties is one of love and affection.[120] These expectations frequently differ depending on whether the particular service was rendered by a woman or a man, a spouse, a child or a more remote relative. Some cases, especially older ones, suggest that society and courts had certain expectations towards women and in particular wives, cohabitants, daughters, or daughters-in-law.[121] They were (and sometimes still are) expected to render certain services for free so that their claims were (and are) more easily denied.[122] This is partly because certain types of services or work are still often gender specific.[123] For example, women are more likely to provide care services or work in the home rather than to make investments in or improve the deceased's property. However, we know that the economic utility of work in the household, and of care, is generally insufficiently appreciated,[124] and that particularly female domestic labour is often underrated,[125] with some of it being dismissed as 'affective work'.[126] This is partly because law has often struggled to give value to intangible benefits, such as those that derive from domestic and care work.

Because law places greater value on certain types of work that is often carried out by men, for example, work on a farm or work that improves the value of the property itself, and thus often work that is externally more visible, or the financial benefits of which are more immediately tangible, women may sometimes find

[119] See Article 205 of the Code civil analysed in Chapter 9.

[120] Kohn (2019) 221.

[121] Hartog *Someday* (2012) 222. On the expectations courts have towards women, see Flynn & Lawson (1995) 117–118: 'All the behaviour which is placed in the realm of the domestic, no matter how arduous, will not amount to detriment because it can be expected of any woman in an intimate relationship with a man. Behaviour which takes the claimant outside the domestic realm is categorised as abnormal, and, in order to explain it, it must be placed in the context of a market-like transaction giving rise to a property interest.'

[122] See the reference in *Antrobus v Antrobus* 2009 BCSC 1341, [41].

[123] On the gendered definitions of space and the gendered distribution of unpaid socially reproductive labour, see Gordon-Bouvier (2019). That women perform on average 60% more unpaid domestic work than men is found by the Office for National Statistics, Women Shoulder the Responsibility of 'Unpaid Work' (10 November 2016) <https://www.ons.gov.uk/employmentandlabourmarket/peopleinwork/earningsandworkinghours/articles/womenshouldertheresponsibilityofunpaidwork/2016-11-10> accessed 5 November 2021.

[124] See especially Hoerder et al *Towards a Global History* (2015) 5ff; Sloan *Informal Carers* (2012) and Kohn (2019).

[125] See *Murdoch v Murdoch* [1975] 1 SCR 423. We see that with changes also in the area of constructive trusts in English law.

[126] The literature is rich. See especially Philipps (2008) 105; Wong (2007) 274–275 who has also shown that domestic work is often seen as 'labour of love'.

themselves in a worse position. As Ellen Gordon-Bouvier has put it, '[m]ale claimants can find it easier to convince the courts that their motivations for domestic work were financial rather than affectionate in nature'.[127] This may well explain why the French *Cour de Cassation* was prepared to grant an enrichment claim to the caring son in the seminal *arrêt Fouret* decision.[128]

What is more, because of the type of performances they have rendered, which are by their very nature less publicly visible, women are often less likely to be awarded a proprietary interest. For instance, we will see that they are less likely to benefit from the doctrine of part-performance (Chapter 3), for it requires a strong connection between the contract and the acts of part-performance undertaken—a connection that is often missing where the services are performed in the household or consist of care. For the same reason, in common law Canada they are also less likely to obtain a constructive trust in an enrichment claim, as a nexus between the work and the promised asset is required for there to be such a trust (Chapter 6). Thus, those who provide work on a farm, or improve the deceased's property, or make financial contributions are more likely to obtain their expectations fulfilled and, in the examples examined in this book, it is often men who provide such work. In the farming context there is frequently an expectation that family members, but especially boys, contribute because otherwise farming is not viable.[129] This might suggest that men might find it more difficult to bring a successful claim, though this is not borne out by the cases.[130] The reason for that may well be that there is an expectation that the eldest male child will take over the farm. In other words, expectations of primogeniture might still be looming in the background and advantage men.[131] In fact, overall women seem to be less likely to succeed in a farming business.[132] Thus, potentially, women could miss out in both contexts.

The nature of the relationship, gender, and type of performance aside, expectations may also depend on whether or not the promisee lives with the promisor and, if so, whether that is in the promisor's or the promisee's home. It seems that

[127] Gordon-Bouvier (2019) 14.

[128] See the analysis in Chapter 9.

[129] Korven (1993) 437 argues that especially in the context of farms, parents expect that one of their children will farm the land that may have been in the family for generations.

[130] See especially Chapter 4.

[131] Malcolm Voyce has argued that until the mid-1980s, in the case of conflicting claims under the family provision legislation, the sons who had worked on the farm of the parents would often be better off than other children, including those who had cared for the parents in reliance on a promise for a reasonable provision. However, from the 1980s onwards, courts seem to have changed their position so that no claimant automatically prevails, and adequate support is provided for all children even if that means selling the farm. Voyce 'Family Provision' (2014) and Voyce (1993). However, De Groot & Nickel *Family Provision in Australia* (2017) 86 have argued that this is not due to a change in community attitudes to the family farm but rather that these are atypical cases and that usually family provision orders are still modest.

[132] This is confirmed by Lobley (2010) 843 where the author refers to the very low numbers of daughters/daughters-in-law identified as successors by the farmer as being a problem of international concern. On the gender bias in relation to farms, see Goodnow & Lawrence (2010) 76.

where the promisee has moved in with the promisor, and the promisee has benefited from free accommodation, it can sometimes be more difficult to establish that what the promisee has done exceeds what could be expected of her, unless the promisee has, for instance, sold her own home. At the same time, by moving in it is sometimes also easier to establish the link that is required for certain proprietary interests to arise.[133]

Expectations can matter at different stages of proving a claim. With some approaches explored in this book, a promisee will be able to obtain redress only if she can prove that her performance exceeds what is regarded as *normal*,[134] or is out of the ordinary and goes beyond 'what was called for out of natural love and affection'. Whether that is the case usually depends on her relationship with the promisor, her gender, the type of work or service provided, and how substantial her performance was, both in terms of intensity and time. Here, the courts often require promisees to provide significant or extraordinary services with little clarity on what such a threshold may entail and without providing much by way of guidance.[135] In fact, the definition of 'normality' is often itself gendered.[136] This can be seen when it comes to care or domestic services, including companionship.[137]

Expectations may also affect whether or not the relationship can be fitted into a particular legal framework so as to provide the promisee with protection. In the 1960s Jan Kropholler argued, for instance, that when children work for their parents, the expectation is that this is a case of familial cooperation and that German courts do not usually assume there is a contract.[138] Thus, courts may be more reluctant to establish, for instance, an employment contract between a father and his daughter or son, or a spouse and her husband, or to find that parents have been enriched.[139] Equally, in Chapter 3 we will see that there is a legal presumption that agreements between relatives and friends are not intended to be legally binding. Again, the promisee will need to prove that there was, in fact, such an intention.[140]

However, over the years we can also observe changes to how society values unremunerated services in the family context, including care work and what it

[133] See the analysis in Chapters 4, 6, and 9.

[134] What is normal matters sometimes when looking at consideration in contract law, reliance in proprietary estoppel cases, the absence of a juristic basis in a Canadian enrichment claim, but also an adjustment of the intestate share based on § 2057a BGB.

[135] Here see the discussion of French enrichment law in Chapter 9.

[136] Wong (2007) 275.

[137] Gordon-Bouvier (2019) 11.

[138] Kropholler (1969) 249. Similarly, in the common law context, a presumption operates whereby, in the domestic context, parties do not have an intention to enter into a legal relationship so that no contract is found. See Chapter 3, section II.B.

[139] See Chapters 8 and 9. De Giorgi *I patti sulle successioni future* (1976) 165ff; Toti (1985); Ghezzi (1961) and (1976).

[140] For examples in the testamentary context where such an intention was found to be missing, see *Walton v Walton* (CA, 14 April 1994) and *Wayling v Jones* (1995) 69 P&CR 170 (CA). However, in both cases the estoppel claim was successful. See Chapter 4.

expects from certain family members. For instance, on the whole spouses or cohabitants who work in the business or home of their partner are being provided with greater protection.[141] This change may also be partly linked to changes in the way society conceives of the role of women (be they spouses, de facto partners, daughters, or daughters-in-law). In the past, so-called 'housekeeper cases' where a man promises a woman to make a testamentary disposition in her favour if she looks after him, could be found, for instance, in New Zealand, Australia, or Germany, but also England and Wales. Such instances are no longer that common today. In some cases, they have now turned into spousal claims by de facto spouses.[142] These changes in the protection of the promisee have also gone hand in hand with, or are a by-product of, changes in family law.[143]

Equally, for a long time, children were regarded as pension assets meaning that the expectations that parents, and more generally society, had towards them was that they would work and help in the household, family business, or farm. However, several of the legislative interventions that will be discussed in this book were aimed precisely at ensuring that certain unremunerated work carried out by descendants would be compensated. Despite these developments, in some cases we can still see certain gender biases at work, and a difference in treatment between improvements to property and care and domestic work, including emotional support and companionship.

4. Psychological barriers

A final aspect to be mindful of when examining the modes of redress examined in this book is that some of them may pose greater psychological barriers than others for promisees. Having to go to court is already a significant disincentive for certain promisees, both because of the costs involved and the need to share details about their personal life. In addition, having to prove their subjective motives for acting on the promise can, as noted earlier, sometimes cause significant embarrassment. For instance, with enrichment claims, a promisee will often have to prove the absence of a donative intent,[144] which may be psychologically difficult. While a proprietary estoppel claim requires reliance, it allows the promisee to emphasize her being a 'victim' or at least a virtuous person who has relied on the promise made by a person whom she trusted. Arguably, it might be easier psychologically for a

[141] This is, for instance, visible in the development of unjust enrichment law in common law Canada, the development of the family home constructive trust in England, the *société créée de fait* in France, as well as the *Innengesellschaft* in Germany. See the introduction of the *impresa di famiglia* in Italy in 1975. Paetel *Die erbrechtliche Ausgleichung von Pflegeleistungen* (2009) 93.

[142] For example, in Australia or New Zealand, where they can bring a claim under the family provision legislation. See Chapter 5. On de facto partners, see Nield (2007) 301.

[143] See, for instance, the Italian family law reform of 1975 which led to the recognition of work in the family business and that has changed litigation. But that is nothing new, for succession law is often changed through or as a reaction to changes in family law.

[144] Chapter 9.

promisee to say that she has been induced to act on the promise or been treated unfairly, than to prove that she had no intention to benefit the promisor. Requiring the promisee to provide proof of the fact that she has acted the way she has primarily because of the prospect of the inheritance (rather than out of love or generosity) or that her behaviour was not informed by a donative intent, even though it was performed for a relative or friend, can potentially also represent a deterrent to seeking redress.

From this perspective, some of the forms of redress that do not focus on the proof of the promisee's reliance (i.e. the New Zealand TPA 1949, the *créance de salaire différé*, or the Austrian care legacy based on §§ 677ff ABGB), and therefore do not focus on her motivations, may be preferable. Here, the person only needs to show that she has provided a certain performance that was unremunerated. However, the price is that she will usually only be able to obtain the value of the unpaid wages or, in the case of the Austrian care legacy, the value of the benefit of the performance for the deceased for up to three years.

Motives aside, proving some of the other requirements can also pose difficulties.[145] For instance, it may be psychologically more difficult for a claimant to argue that her parents have been enriched (as required in enrichment cases in Canada and France)[146] and she impoverished as a consequence, rather than that there was a common purpose which was frustrated (as with a German enrichment claim).[147]

The analysis in Chapter 5 will further demonstrate that to obtain a family provision order, in most jurisdictions, the promisee will need to show that she is in need of maintenance even though she is an adult, which may be rather uncomfortable to say the least. In fact, John Mee has argued that if a promisee tries to bring a family provision claim she will 'most likely have to rehearse the unglamorous part of being a "lame duck" '.[148] That may well function as a disincentive for bringing a claim. Thus, different forms of redress raise different psychological barriers. This is something that attention should be paid to when considering how to protect the promisee's interests.

D. Informal testamentary promises: difficulties for courts

So far, I have talked about the challenges promisees face when they bring a claim for breach of a testamentary promise and the need to be sensitive to their interests. However, as this book shows, dealing with and regulating testamentary promises

[145] Leslie (1999) 558 argues that, for instance, in the US, family members are unlikely to file a claim based on a testamentary promise as that may make them look greedy. However, they may decide to contest the decedent's will, as this could be seen as acting on behalf of the testator.

[146] See Chapter 6, and Chapter 9, section III.

[147] See Chapter 9, section II.

[148] Mee in *Landmark Cases* (2019) 192.

is not easy. When courts are asked to intervene, they are confronted with a number of difficulties inherent in the nature and form of testamentary promises and the context in which they are expressed. I will outline some of these difficulties below. The analysis shows that courts are often trying their best in very complex circumstances. In fact, on the whole they seem to be more generous towards promisees than many legal scholars seem to be. This is not to say that promisors should not be held to their promises or that promisees should not be protected; on the contrary. The point is rather that no simple and universal approach can be advocated.

1. Issues of evidence and proof

First, the cases discussed in this book will show that the informality of the testamentary agreement raises questions as to the type of evidence courts should admit, especially since the promisor is usually no longer alive at the time of litigation. As many promises are made orally, cases in which the promisee can produce something in writing are few.[149] In many cases the promise and its exact content have to be ascertained through oral evidence of either the promisee or third parties. Assessing such evidence poses its own problems and risks. As mentioned earlier,[150] some legal systems exclude the promisee's testimony in relation to the existence of promises to make a will. Where oral evidence of the promisee is excluded, external witnesses may be available, but issues can arise where the witnesses are not entirely reliable or credible,[151] have a different recollection of the facts, or have themselves an interest in the relevant estate.[152] Thus, courts will need to be cautious when assessing statements of witnesses (and not just that of promisees), not least because the promisor can often no longer provide her version of the facts, and because memories fade due to the long time lag that often lies between the promise and the trial. This was stressed by HHJ David Cooke in the English case of *Rawlings v Chapman*:

> The court must in my view be appropriately cautious in assessing witness evidence in relation to such representations. The most honest and genuine witnesses are bound to have difficulty in recollecting exactly what was said over such a long

[149] See the Australian case of *Sullivan v Sullivan & Ors* [2006] NSWCA 312 where a message inside a Christmas card was regarded as sufficient to establish a promise. In *Guest v Guest* [2020] EWCA Civ 387, [39] the assurance was evidenced by the fact that the promisor failed to correct the promisee during secretly recorded conversations.

[150] See section III.C.1.

[151] See *Granger v Granger* 2016 ONCA 945, [2] and *James v James* [2018] EWHC 43 (Ch). The issues of credibility and reliability was given much space to in *Jans v Jans* 2016 SKQB 275, [133]–[154].

[152] For instance, as far as New Zealand is concerned, at least in the beginning, courts expressed the need for caution when dealing with evidence in support of a testamentary promises claim, and required that, where possible, evidence be corroborated. See *Bennett v Kirk* [1946] NZLR 580, 583. However, their approach has relaxed over time. According to Patterson *Law of Family Protection* (2021) 242–243 '[c]ourts have tended to place great weight on the demeanour of the claimant as a witness and the circumstances which the evidence has disclosed'.

> period of time, and may come, perhaps unconsciously, to believe that it must have been in accordance with what they believe ought to have been said, or to correspond with subsequent discussions that they may have had with relatives or other interested parties. The need for caution is even more important in circumstances where the representor is dead or otherwise unable to give evidence and the witnesses who were present at the time have an interest in the outcome. Even if they do their best to recall accurately what was said, they may come to persuade themselves that the words used must have been such as would now support their case.[153]

Hence, the fact that the trial often takes place several years, or even decades, after the promise was first made can make it difficult for courts to ascertain the promisor's intentions and what the parties had agreed.[154] The situation is exacerbated by the fact that testamentary promises are not only expressed orally but are often also vague and generic. More specifically, the parties do not usually discuss the details of their arrangement, with the length and precise content of the performance by the promisee being left open,[155] and the exact amount of the benefit she is to inherit not necessarily established. In addition, the content of the promise may well change over time,[156] and the demands on the promisee increase. Thus, courts are frequently required to tease out the promise from several conversations that may have taken place over a long period of time.[157] In doing so, they also need to decide how much weight, if any, to place on the will or absence of a will or a potential sequence of wills. In other words, can or should a will be used to establish whether or not there was a promise? Does the fact that a will benefits a person make it more likely that a promise was made?[158] These are all questions that courts have to face.

2. Interests of third parties

A further challenge for courts derives from the fact that testamentary promises can be performed up until the promisor's death, so that claims are usually lodged

[153] *Rawlings v Chapman* [2015] EWHC 3160 (Ch), [34].

[154] Such problems arise also in legal systems which still admit oral wills such as Poland. See Zoll, 'Testamentary Formalities in Poland' in *Comparative Succession Law 1* (2011). The same holds true of legal systems (such as England and Wales) which recognize secret trusts.

[155] Sparks (1954–1955) 69 argues that '[s]ometimes the prior relationship of the parties is relied upon to determine the services to be rendered'. This seems to confirm my argument that the promise comes in to induce the promisee to continue performing.

[156] See *Giumelli v Giumelli* [1999] 196 CLR 101 (HC) where the parents had expressed three different promises.

[157] See what is said in Chapter 3 in relation to contracts to make wills. In *Gee v Gee* [2018] EWHC 1393 (Ch), [111] and [114] where Birss J found that 'looking at the evidence as a whole, I find that over a twenty-year period from the late 1980s until about 2009/10 his father JR made it clear to MJ that he would succeed his father as the farmer'.

[158] See *Guest v Guest* [2019] EWHC 869 (Ch), [245] where the judge found that the assurance was evidenced also by the terms of the 1981 will.

against her estate or her successors. Consequently, any decision about whether or not to grant the promisee an action inevitably affects a range of people, including other promisees, creditors[159] and successors of the deceased, whether they benefit under the will, intestacy, compulsory or forced heirship provisions, or from a family provision order.[160] Exactly how they are affected will depend on the type of redress that the promisee will obtain. For instance, if the promisee is treated as a creditor, those succeeding to the inheritance will be worse off. They will inherit less, and in some jurisdictions they will have to pay the debts of the deceased with their personal assets, unless they limit their liability.[161] The debt will also potentially affect the calculation of forced/compulsory heirship shares as well as any family provision order, which will be based on the net estate.[162] Yet, if the promisee is not treated as a creditor, she may never receive anything. In other words, what matters to the promisee is not simply how much she is awarded, that is whether her expectation interest is fulfilled, or whether she gets the value of her performance or of the promisor's enrichment, but also when her claim arises, and how her claim fares against that of others with an interest in the promisor's estate.

Creditors and beneficiaries aside, in some instances there are also the interests of third-party transferees of the promised asset to consider. Suppose a situation in which the promisor sells to a third party a title to a house she has previously promised to leave by will to the promisee. Under English law, the promisee may be able to bring a proprietary estoppel claim which can lead to a proprietary award (of the promised asset) but of course this can affect third-party transferees.[163] And where the promisee brings her claim already during the promisor's lifetime, for instance, because the parties have fallen out with one another, the courts also have to consider the position of the promisor and how she would be affected by the relief.[164]

Thus, courts face the difficulty of striking a balance between the interests of the promisee and the promisor and various third parties, including the promisor's successors. Sometimes it is the legislature that establishes how to strike this balance, but where courts are given discretion, it is usually up to them to decide which interests to prioritize. As this book shows, this can be difficult.[165] Matters become

159 Hartog *Someday* (2012) 170. According to the author, creditors of the deceased could claim that the claim for redress is only a family conspiracy aimed at avoiding the payment of a lawful debt.

160 For instance, in *Suggitt v Suggitt* [2012] EWCA Civ 1140 and in *Naylor v Maher* [2012] IEHC 408 not much would have been left for the sisters of the claimant to bring a family provision legislation claim against the estate.

161 See the discussion in Chapter 11.

162 The family provision legislations usually contain provisions preventing their circumvention through contracts to make wills, but there is nothing in these pieces of legislation dealing with court decisions that achieve a similar result. Thus, there are competing claims but whether that of the promisee or that of the dependant prevails often remains unclear. See Chapter 5.

163 McFarlane *Proprietary Estoppel* (2014) 487ff. For further details, see Chapter 4. Other interests involved, though not in a negative manner, are those of creditors of the promisee, who may have an interest in pledging the right, and those of heirs of the promisee, as the claim might be hereditable.

164 Here see some of the proprietary estoppel cases discussed in Chapter 4.

165 See, for instance, the discussion in Chapters 3 and 7.

especially complicated where more than one promise was made, and the promisees base their claim on different grounds and doctrines.[166] Finally, the court order may also have tax consequences or lead to social security payments for the parties.[167]

This does not mean that the promisee does not deserve protection, or that the promisor's successors should not bear the brunt of a breach of the promise, especially given that the estate is usually enriched by the promisee's performances, or actions. But it shows that decisions about whether or not and how to protect promisees have consequences for a number of people, and in many cases affect the distribution of wealth on death. This must be taken into account when evaluating how to protect promisees.

3. Other factors to be considered

Third-party interests aside, there are also other factors, including the promisor's interests, that courts must take into consideration when deciding whether to protect the promisee's interest and how. It has, for instance, been argued that where the promisee is awarded the promised asset, there is a potential clash with the principle of testamentary freedom. Whether or not there is such a clash will be examined in greater detail in relation to those forms of redress that allow for the protection of the promisee's expectation interest in the form of a proprietary transfer.[168] Suffice to say here that I argue that there is no such conflict because the courts are enforcing an obligation that the promisor has voluntarily assumed. In other words, by making a promise (understood broadly), and accepting that the promisee acts on it to her detriment, the promisor has limited her own freedom to change her mind.

In some instances, it has also been argued that the enforcement of informal promises clashes with formality requirements for testamentary dispositions or transfers of property more generally.[169] Arguably, the possibility of abuse or fraud against the promisor is heightened by the informality of the arrangements. In other words, there is a risk that allegations of such promises are falsely made, or that testators are unduly influenced by others and induced to make such promises by legacy hunters. We have seen that this was a concern raised by Roman scholars.[170] However, if we allow lack of form to stand in the way of the protection of promisees, then we leave them exposed to the risk of exploitation. Any promisor could always escape liability on the basis that the promise was not made formally. But,

[166] For an example, see *Bristow v Smith* [2013] NZHC 2866 discussed in Chapter 7.

[167] This is mentioned in some of the proprietary estoppel cases, including *Moore v Moore* [2016] EWHC 2202 (Ch); on appeal *Moore v Moore* [2018] EWCA Civ 2669. See also the discussions in Chapters 8 and 11.

[168] See especially the discussion in Chapter 4, section V.B.

[169] For details, see again especially the discussion in Chapter 4, section V.C.

[170] See what I said about Roman law at n 67.

as we saw, testamentary promises tend to be made informally because of the particular context in which they are made.

There are also wider policy considerations to be taken into account. For instance, if a legal system protects a promisee of a testamentary promise too readily, it could be argued that relationships will be commodified and that people may be encouraged to help others, not out of friendship or love, but because they know an award will likely be available.[171] But even if that were true, is the risk of commodification a sufficiently strong argument for leaving promisees without protection?[172] A contrary argument could also be made: if a legal system decides against protecting promisees, this may erode trust and induce people to act merely when they are legally bound. This, of course, assumes that most people are informed about the law and that the law determines their behaviour which, as we have seen, is questionable.[173] Thus, courts are faced with difficult decisions.

IV. Conclusion

This chapter has shown that on a formal level there is a difference in approach between civil and common law with regards to promises in the form of a pact or contract to make a will. While common law jurisdictions recognize the validity of such contracts and pacts, exceptions aside, civil law jurisdictions generally do not. However, regardless of these formal positions, in both legal traditions testamentary promises are usually made informally and, in the absence of specific regulations, promisees who have acted on them have to seek redress through the application of various doctrines drawn from different areas of private law. The framework in both legal traditions is therefore patchy. While this means that at least some promisees have a choice as to the legal basis of their claim, not all doctrines are attuned to the context in which such promises are generally made, and several are limited in scope. Some also pose challenges for the promisee in terms of burden of proof, especially where they require proof of the promisee's motives or that her actions exceed what is be expected of her. In other words, some forms of redress create greater obstacles than others for promisees who seek to claim a promised inheritance. And

[171] In the sense that commodifying donative promises corrupts the values connected to gift giving, see Eisenberg (1997) 847–848 and Leslie (1999) 560. See also the discussion in Hyland *Gifts* (2009) 322. See *Chan v Chan* 2014 BCSC 2422 per Mr Justice Myers at [64] on the monetization of family relationships. In *Strudwick Estate* 1996 CarswellBC 794; 21 RFL (4th) 185 (BCSC), Blair J found that 'the obligation here, it seems to me, arose from the familial bond between father and son which saw the pair working together on the farm to support themselves. As a matter of public policy, such limited economic activity as occurred in this case involving father and son ought to be encouraged without necessarily attracting a subsequent claim for unjust enrichment.' See further the discussion in *Jans v Jans* (n 151) analysed in greater detail in Chapter 6.

[172] Philipps (2008) 102; Silbaugh in *Feminism Confronts Homo Economicus* (2005) 348.

[173] See section III.A.

not all promisees are equally protected even when they seem equally deserving. This will become even clearer in Parts II and III of this book.

However, the analysis has also shown that when providing redress, courts need to consider a number of different interests and values and are required to undertake a delicate and difficult balancing act.[174] This might contribute to explain, perhaps, why some jurisdictions have decided to exclude the validity of legally binding promises of a future inheritance. That said, the success of such measures is doubtful in the sense that they have not been able to prevent people from making informal promises and others from relying on them, though they seem to have contributed to reducing the amount of litigation.

Parts II and III will analyse the primary avenues a promisee can pursue to obtain legal redress. The analysis will start by examining those doctrines through which the promise can be given effect to, and the promisee's expectations be fulfilled, by obtaining the transfer of the promised asset. I will then pass on to those doctrines through which the promisee can obtain compensation for the value of her performance or the value of the promisor's enrichment, or less. Each form of redress will be evaluated on its own terms and against the background of other available forms of redress. This will allow for a functional comparison across forms of redress and legal traditions.

[174] Sloan (2009) 155: 'Judges are charged with the unenviable task of balancing, on the one hand, issues including testamentary freedom, capacity, certainty and the potential for undue influence with, on the other hand, the arguable desirability of enforcing promises made to a long-suffering unpaid worker.'

PART II

OBTAINING WHAT WAS PROMISED

Introduction to Part II

In Part I of this book, I examined the social and legal background against which testamentary promises operate, pointing out the specificities and complexities of testamentary arrangements and the vulnerabilities of the promisee that are frequently overlooked. We saw that some legal systems have tried to address the problems that such arrangements raise by prohibiting legally binding testamentary promises. Such attempts have not been entirely successful, however, for promises of a future inheritance are still expressed, albeit informally. I further illustrated that the legal framework is highly fragmented because when such promises remain unfulfilled, and in the absence of specific regulation, redress is provided through various doctrines belonging to different areas of private law. While this is in some ways good news for promisees, it also poses certain challenges, not least because such doctrines are not usually tailored to the particular context in which testamentary promises are normally expressed and their scope is often limited. I have further pointed the reader to recurrent challenges that promisees face when bringing a claim, and that courts must confront, when dealing with unfulfilled testamentary promises.

In this part, Part II, I explore avenues which promisees can pursue to obtain the promised asset. As mentioned before, these avenues will be examined from the perspective of the promisee with a view to establishing how effective their protection is and who can benefit from it. The emphasis will lie on when the promisee can bring the claim, what she will need to prove to obtain redress, the potential challenges she may encounter in establishing a claim, how relief is established, and how her interest fares against that of third parties.

This part includes four chapters each examining a different form of redress all of which are drawn from common law jurisdictions. The reason for that is that in civil law jurisdictions, it is usually difficult to obtain the transfer of the promised asset.[1] The analysis starts with formal promises and then moves on to examine ways in which informal promises, that is promises that do not amount to a contract, can be given effect to. Chapter 3 deals with the protection offered by contract law. We will see that, where the validity of contracts to make a will is recognized,[2] which is

[1] An exception is the *Höferechtssprechung* referred to in Chapter 2.
[2] For details, see Chapter 2.

the case in many common law jurisdictions, a promisee may seek protection and, in particular, fulfilment of her expectation through the application of general principles of contract law. This will allow her to claim damages equivalent to the value of the promised asset and, in certain circumstances, specific performance of the promise. However, for such protection to be available, she must provide proof of a legally binding contract which, given the particular setting in which such promises are expressed, often represents a significant challenge. In fact, most promises are expressed informally, meaning that they are often generic and vague, subject to unspoken conditions, and not recorded in writing. Consequently, it will usually be impossible to establish a contractual relationship.[3] Unsurprisingly, case law dealing with contractual testamentary promises is sparse.

Where no contract can be established, promisees will want to pursue alternative and more flexible forms of redress that courts have developed, often through the application of equitable principles. Chapter 4 shows that in England and Wales, Australia, and the Republic of Ireland, the doctrine of proprietary estoppel has been increasingly invoked by promisees as a means of obtaining redress. The recent the decision of the High Court of New Zealand in *Carroll v Bates* (2018)[4] suggests that proprietary estoppel may also become a popular avenue in New Zealand. While the doctrine of proprietary estoppel is not without problems, on the whole, courts have been sensitive to the context in which such promises are being made and willing to protect the interests of a wide range of promisees. There are some Canadian proprietary estoppel cases. However, the analysis in Chapter 6 reveals that, under Canadian common law, the law of enrichment is usually the preferred vehicle. Here the doctrine of unjust enrichment has developed in a way that is sensitive to the testamentary context and because it is perceived of as an equitable doctrine, it involves considerable judicial discretion in setting the award. Nevertheless, obtaining an enrichment claim can be potentially difficult, not least because of the economic approach taken by courts as well as the relevance of both the promisee's motives and societal expectations. Even so, the advantage of both approaches (proprietary estoppel and enrichment) is that neither requires the promisee to establish a legally binding contract (be it in writing or not), but they can nonetheless lead to an award of the promisee's expectation interests. Thus, part of the reason for a decrease in contractual claims in common law jurisdictions, may well lie in the development of other legal doctrines more suited to dealing with testamentary promises.

These three approaches aside, in this part of the book (in Chapter 5) I also explore ways in which the family provision legislation can come to the aid of promisees by allowing her to obtain the promised asset. While the legislation was never

[3] For a recent Irish case in which a testamentary contract was found see *K v K* [2018] IEHC 615.

[4] *Carroll v Bates* [2018] NZHC 2463.

meant to tackle instances of broken testamentary promises, it may at times offer a means to obtain redress, though usually one of last resort. Indeed, a promise of an inheritance coupled with a performance on the part of the promisee can help establish a moral duty on the part of the promisor to make provision for the promisee in her will. However, the scope of the family provision legislation is such that it can only benefit those eligible under the legislation. Also, unlike with the other approaches examined in this part, the legislative claim only arises on the promisor's death and, at least in principle, only against the net estate. As a result, the protection that it provides is generally weaker than the protection under contract law, the doctrine of proprietary estoppel, or enrichment law. Even so, in certain instances it may come to the aid of promisees.

What will emerge is that unlike in civil law jurisdictions, in common law jurisdictions promisees of informal testamentary promises usually have more than one option to seek redress and a good chance to obtain what they were promised partly because of the considerable discretion exercised by courts in determining the relief. We will see that this is not uncontroversial and that objections have been raised, in particular, against the wide judicial discretion. In fact, some scholars have been concerned that the enforcement of informal promises leads to an inroad into promisors' testamentary freedom and that it clashes with the formality requirements that the law imposes on lifetime and testamentary dispositions.

3
Establishing the existence of a contract to make a will

I. Introduction

In most cases we will come across in this book it will be impossible for a promisee to establish a contractual relationship. Nonetheless, it is useful and important to commence the analysis of the various forms of redress by looking at contracts to make a will and the protection they offer. The analysis will show not only that the threshold that promisees must meet is high, including because testamentary promises concerning land must meet certain formalities to be valid, but also that contract law does not offer the best framework for this particular social practice.[1] While in principle it may be useful for parties to be able to negotiate their testamentary agreement, casting the relationship in contractual terms can be difficult not least because the length of the relationship is uncertain. Also, it does not avoid the risk of exploitation of the promisee which, in part, stems from the significant power differential that characterizes her relationship with the promisor.

Even when proof of a contract can be provided, the level of protection accorded by contract law very much depends on the exact content of the contractual promise and on the timing of the breach, meaning that the promisee may not necessarily obtain the promised asset or its value in the form of damages. The content of the promise further affects the nature of the promisee's entitlement, and thus her position vis-à-vis creditors of the deceased's estate and other third parties, such as potential claimants under the family provision legislation. In some instances the promisee will be regarded as a creditor but in others she will rank after creditors, reducing the chances of an effective protection. Thus, even where a contract can be established, promisees can still find themselves in a vulnerable position. In some jurisdictions, a contract can even operate against the promisee where there is a suspicion that the contract was entered into by the promisor merely to circumvent a possible family provision order,[2] or for the purposes of becoming eligible for Medicaid.[3]

1 That said, in Chapter 8 I will show that in Germany and Austria, it might be possible to imply services contracts from the parties' conduct.
2 See section IV.
3 Kohn (2019).

Claiming a Promised Inheritance. Alexandra Braun, Oxford University Press. © Alexandra Braun 2022.
DOI: 10.1093/oso/9780198757252.003.0004

To acquire a clearer picture of the benefits but also of the limitations of casting testamentary promises in contractual terms it is useful to consider the factual and legal requirements that a promisee must meet before considering the nature of the available forms of relief. The focus here will centre primarily on developments in English and Australian law, with occasional references to other common law jurisdictions.

II. The requirements of a legally binding contract to make a will

Contracts relating to the future content of a will can take the form of a contract to make a will, or not to make a will or not to revoke an existing will. This chapter focuses on contracts to make a will, for these are most common. While contracts not to revoke a will are also sometimes encountered, they are usually entered into primarily in the context of mutual wills, which fall outside the scope of this book.

Even though they relate to a future testamentary disposition, contracts to make a will are subject to general principles of contract law rather than a special set of rules specific to the testamentary context. Thus, for a testamentary promise to become a binding and enforceable contract, general contractual requirements such as offer and acceptance, intention to create legal relations, and consideration (or a deed) must be met. In addition, where the promise relates to land, usually the contract has to be in writing.

A. Offer and acceptance

The first requirement for a testamentary promise to be binding is the need for an agreement in law. Vague statements, such as a promise to reward services by a disposition in a will, along the lines of 'don't you worry, I shall see that you will be rewarded for your services' are usually not enforceable as contracts.[4] Something more precise and certain is required, though the promisor does not necessarily need to employ the term 'promise'. In light of the practices described in Chapter 1,[5] it will usually be difficult to find a clear offer.[6]

[4] See *Jennings v Rice* [2002] EWCA 159; [2003] 1 P & CR 100 where the first instance judge found that the terms of the offer were regarded as too vague and imprecise to amount to a contract. As we will see in Chapter 4, the estoppel claim was, however, upheld. See also *Sutherland v Towle* [1937] GLR 509 and *Higgie v Wilkinson* [1903] 23 NZLR 74 where the contractual claim failed because the promises were regarded to be too vague or uncertain. For an Australian example where no contract could be established because there was uncertainty in relation to timing and other aspects, see *Estephan v Estephan* [2012] NSWSC 52.

[5] Chapter 1.

[6] The promise can be accepted by way of acquiescence, for instance, by starting to perform the agreed service, but the performance has to relate to the testamentary promise. *Wakeham v Mackenzie* [1968] 1 WLR 1175 (Ch); [1968] 2 All ER 783 (hereafter *Wakeham v Mackenzie*).

Not only is it necessary that the intention of the parties is certain, the terms of the bargain between the parties must also be certain, including the duties of the promisee. But, as noted earlier, the understanding sometimes develops only over the years and is subject to changes, so that the parties rarely lay out the terms of their agreement with the precision required for a contract.[7] The subject matter of the promise must also be certain, that is it must be clearly ascertainable. It must indicate whether the testator intends to merely make a will, or whether she wants to leave a specific asset or a share or the whole of the residue on death. Simply declaring 'I shall benefit you in my will' or 'I shall provide you with financial security on my death' may not be regarded as certain enough for a successful contractual claim.[8] Quite often, however, testamentary promises are phrased precisely in such an indefinite and vague manner, and this may well work against the promisee's ability to establish a contract. In fact, because testamentary promises are often expressed in the family/domestic context, their content must frequently be teased out from several conversations, or various behaviours, which might have taken place over a long period of time.[9] As a result, identifying a sufficiently certain agreement between the parties is frequently a challenge.

B. Intention to create a legal relationship

Offer and acceptance aside, a promisee must also provide evidence of an intention to create a legal relationship. This can be difficult to establish given that there is a legal presumption that domestic agreements between relatives and spouses or civil partners are not intended to be legally binding.[10] Thus, courts are generally reluctant to find such an intention to create a legal relationship in this context, though they have been more open where such promises were made as part of a 'bargain',[11] or concerned property arrangements.[12]

[7] This was acknowledged by Barrington-Foote J in *Jans v Jans* 2016 SKQB 275, [224] and [226] (hereafter *Jans v Jans*): 'This provision was, in substance, a promise to take care of an aging parent. The particulars of what that means—which turn on matters such as timing, preferences and health—was necessarily left for "future accommodation", based on the needs and decisions of the parent.'

[8] In the Australian case *Horton v Jones* (1935) 53 CLR 475 (HC) (hereafter *Horton v Jones*), a promise to leave the deceased's 'fortune' was regarded as sufficiently certain. In *MacPhail v Torrance* (1909) 25 TLR 810, 811 an agreement to make an 'ample provision' was judged as being too vague.

[9] See Chapter 1. We see that below in the case of *Dable v Peisley* [2009] NSWSC 772 (7 August 2009) (hereafter *Dable v Peisley*).

[10] Beale *Chitty on Contracts* (2020) para 2-179-185. For examples in the testamentary context where such an intention was found to be missing, see *Walton v Walton* (CA, 14 April 1994) (hereafter *Walton v Walton*) and *Wayling v Jones* (1995) 69 P&CR 170 (CA). However, in both cases the estoppel claim was successful. For details, see Chapter 4.

[11] For examples, see *Parker v Clark* [1960] 1 All ER 93 (Assizes) 292 (hereafter *Parker v Clark*); *Re Edwards, deceased* [1958] Ch 168 (CA) (hereafter *Re Edwards, deceased*); *Wakeham v Mackenzie* (n 6). See also the Irish case *K v K* [2018] IEHC 615 (hereafter *K v K*) where the court found such an intention. Nonetheless, according to Sarah Nield, it is easier to establish an intention to create legal relations if, as for instance in *Wakeham* and *Parker*, the parties' relationship is not too close. See Nield (2007) 290.

[12] See *Bovaird v Frost* [2009] NSWSC 337, [52]. Sloan *Borkowski's Law of Succession* (2020) 55.

One reason frequently identified for the reluctance of the law to assume such an intention is that testamentary promises are often subject to unspoken and ill-defined qualifications in relation to what might happen in the future.[13] However, such qualifications are a consequence of the fact that there is usually a long time lag between the moment of the promise and the death of the promisor. The other point to make here is that in most cases the parties probably do not want to enter into a legally binding contract.[14] Thus, requiring such an intention can work against the promisee. It does not follow, however, that such promises are not intended seriously, nor that the promisee is undeserving of protection.

The question regarding the intention to create legal relations arose, for instance, in the Australian case of *Dable v Peisley* (2009).[15] Here the claimants had alleged a contract between themselves and the deceased, whereby the latter had agreed to make (and not to revoke) a will in their favour in exchange for which they had provided him with companionship, hospitality, personal services, and sometimes free food. While the parties were not related, there is evidence that the deceased had seen one of the promisees as a son. Despite the promise, the deceased changed his will, and his executors denied the claimants an interest in his estate. Ward J held that the contractual claim (as well as the proprietary estoppel claim) failed because the parties had *not* intended to enter into a legally binding contract. The judge reached the conclusion partly on the basis of the fact that the deceased had otherwise been pedantic in his documentation of personal loans he had made to the claimants so that a promise of this kind would have been out of character. In addition, he found that the promises were made from time to time, commencing in the late 1970s and continuing for about thirty years. According to Ward J:

> It might be thought that if the deceased had intended to commit himself legally to such a promise there would have been some mechanism by which, if there were to be a change in his circumstances or in the relationship with the Dables [the claimants] or the provision of services on the part of the Dables in the interim, then the question whether the promise were to stand (and, if not, how the services provided up to that time were to be recognised) would have been taken into account. Similarly, if, as seems to have happened in the last years of his life, the deceased found someone else to perform much of the services which had been provided by the Dables, then there would be issues as to whether it was open to him, from a contractual point of view, to do so if the arrangements between them were objectively intended to be characterised as a contract.

The judge found that a contract was unlikely to have been intended here because otherwise the deceased would have provided for the eventuality of a change of his

[13] *Walton v Walton* (n 10).
[14] See the analysis in Chapter 1.
[15] *Dable v Peisley* (n 9).

circumstances or the relationship with the promisees. Although in this case the existence of an agreement was arguably doubtful, one wonders whether it would have been possible for the promisor and promisees to predict the various contingencies and to provide for them in the contract—probably not. This is an important point to which I will return later.[16] The other objection raised by Ward J was that had there been such a contract, the parties would have been limited in their behaviour. Given the context in which testamentary promises are made, that may well be something both parties may not want. In other words, in the case of promises of an inheritance, not only is a contract not usually intended, due to the lack of flexibility, it may not necessarily be in the interest of either party to enter into such a contract.

C. Consideration

Unless the promise to make a will is made by deed, for it to be enforceable, consideration must be given. In principle, this is not a problem because testamentary promises are usually expressed in exchange for a performance on the part of the promisee. While in the past consideration was sometimes provided in the form of a marriage, in present times it is more likely to take the form of money, improvements to land, and especially work or services provided on the promisor's farm or in her business or home, including domestic or care services,[17] or a combination thereof.[18]

The problem that a promisee may face in establishing a contract is that it is sometimes difficult to draw a line between performances that constitute consideration and those that are provided out of love and desire to offer mutual support, and that can be expected given the particular relationship or circumstances. The issue arises because the parties are usually in a family or friendly relationship with one another, so that they may be prompted by a combination of motives, including the prospect of a future inheritance, but also feelings of love and affection.[19] Unlike strangers, family members and friends may therefore have a harder time proving that what they have done constitutes consideration.[20] An additional difficulty for the promisee can be that past services cannot be relied upon as consideration.[21] As we know, the promise does not always precede the performance but can be made at a later stage when there is a risk that the promisee will stop performing, or the

[16] See section VI.

[17] In *Irani v Irani* [2006] EWHC 1811 (Ch), consideration was found in Mrs Irani's promise not to proceed with her application for a lump sum payment order and a property adjustment order in respect of the property in question.

[18] *Buchko v Buchko* 1997 CanLII 10951 (SK QB) (hereafter *Buchko v Buchko*) and *Orange v Swierz Estate* (1986) 54 Sask R 195 (hereafter *Orange v Swierz Estate*) are interesting because the performance of the promisee included the provision of personal care of the aging landowner and not just farming.

[19] See the discussion in Chapter 1. See also Nield (2000) 87.

[20] On the problems of finding consideration, see Sparks (1954–1955).

[21] This problem is solved by the New Zealand TPA 1949 for it is irrelevant at what point the promise was made. See Chapter 7. The question arose in the Irish case *K v K* (n 11) [104] but McDonald J found

promisor's demands increase. All in all, therefore it is not easy for a promisee to meet the requirements that are necessary to establish a contract. These difficulties are enhanced by the formality requirements imposed in cases where the promise concerns land.

D. Formalities

If a person promises to leave a sum of money, shares or other financial instruments, or benefits deriving from a pension scheme or life insurance, no writing is required for the contract to be valid.[22] However, where the promise of an inheritance concerns land (including a house or a farm), which is often the case, it must be in writing,[23] meaning that the promisee has a further hurdle to overcome. This is a requirement across common law jurisdictions. For instance, in England and Wales, section 2(1) of the Law of Property (Miscellaneous Provisions) Act 1989 requires the contract to be in writing, to be signed by both parties and to contain all the terms of the bargain.[24] Thus, an exchange of letters will be insufficient,[25] but in most cases there will not even be a letter. Failure to comply with these requirements will render the contract void and not just unenforceable.

Prior to the 1989 Act,[26] in England and Wales, the equitable doctrine of part-performance, allowed the lack of writing to be overcome by a party's execution of the contract. In other words, where the promisee had performed her side of the agreement, the failure to comply with the formality requirement would not work against her. However, the doctrine operated only to enforce a contract that would have been valid, but for the formality requirements relating to land, which

that the promise was supported by 'fresh consideration moving from the plaintiff because the plaintiff remained involved in the farm and continued to work very long hours on the farm. In addition, he contributed his lorry to the sand and gravel business which was clearly a key part of the deceased's plans to generate income to pay off the bank.'

[22] Unless the promise concerns an equitable interest under a trust, in which case s 53(1)(c) of the Law of Property Act 1925 (hereafter LPA 1925) applies.

[23] The contract to make a will lacked writing, in *Young v Anderson* [1940] NZLR 239, *Nealon v Public Trustee* [1949] NZLR 148 (hereafter *Nealon v Public Trustee*), and *McCormack v Foley* [1983] NZLR 57.

[24] The rule set out in s 2 Law of Property (Miscellaneous Provisions) Act 1989 dates back to s 4 of the Statute of Frauds 1677, which was superseded by s 40 of the LPA 1925. Section 40 still applies to contracts made before 27 September 1989. The Statute of Frauds 1677 was introduced also in other common law jurisdictions.

[25] See *Commission for New Towns v Cooper (Great Britain) Ltd.* [1995] Ch 259 (CA). Under s 40 LPA 1925 a letter or a will were a sufficient memorandum because the provision stated that the agreement or a memorandum of the agreement needed only to be signed by the party to be charged. The same was true under the previous s 4 of the Statute of Frauds 1677. In fact, in *Synge v Synge* (1894) 1 QB 466 (hereafter *Synge v Synge*), discussed later, the letter was sufficient evidence of the contract.

[26] It would seem that the Law of Property (Miscellaneous Provisions) Act 1989 has abolished it, even though the statute itself has not expressly said so. For details, see Beale *Chitty on Contracts* (2020) para 5-039. That said, the doctrine of part-performance applies to contracts entered into before 27 September 1989.

as we saw is already difficult to prove. Also, it came to the aid of the promisee only where there was a strong connection between the contract and the acts of part-performance undertaken. In other words, the performance of the promisee had to be done unequivocally with reference to a sufficiently certain contractual agreement. In the context of testamentary promises, the test of 'unequivocal referability' could be more easily fulfilled where the promisee had, for instance, worked on the promised farm or carried out improvements to the promised property, rather than cared for the deceased or worked in her household. In the latter cases, courts would frequently decide against applying the doctrine and refuse to enforce the contract. Thus, the doctrine normally assisted promisees, often men, who provided work or made improvements to property that were regarded as financially valuable (and were visible), and not those who provided care or other domestic services, often women.[27] Thus, some promisees were better off than others. I will illustrate this point by discussing three testamentary promises cases. All three involve women who provided household services. Only in one case did the court find that there was a sufficient link to establishing a part-performance on the part of the promisee so that the lack of writing did not stand in the way of a contractual claim.

The first case is *Maddison v Alderson* (1883), which is also the case in which the test for part-performance was first established.[28] It illustrates well what many of the testamentary promises cases used to look like at the time. Mrs Elizabeth Maddison had lived for several years as the housekeeper in the service of Mr Alderson, who had promised her a life interest in a house he was to inherit, in return for which she accepted not being paid any wages and gave up the prospect of getting married. Although the promisor had made the will and signed it, it was void due to lack of attestation. The promisee brought a contractual claim founded on the oral agreement with the deceased. However, her claim failed partly because, according to the court, there was no contract for mutual consideration. The House of Lords concluded that even if there had been, and although the woman had wholly performed her part by serving till the promisor's death without wages, her service was not unequivocally and in its own nature referable to any contract and was not such a part-performance as to take the case out of the operation of section 4 of the Statute of Frauds. The court thus took the view that the services rendered by the claimant, even without receiving wages were not 'such an act as to be in itself evidence of a new contract, much less of a contract concerning her master's land'.[29] In other words, the required 'connection' was missing,[30] and the lack of writing was regarded as fatal, even though Mrs Maddison had worked for twelve years without wages in the belief engendered by Mr Alderson that she would benefit on his death.

[27] See the discussion in Chapter 2, section III.C.3.
[28] *Maddison v Alderson* (1883) 8 App Cas 467 (HL).
[29] Ibid, 480–481 (Lord Selborne LC).
[30] Ibid, 478.

The case thus shows that domestic labour, frequently carried out by women, has often been underrated.[31]

However, eighty-five years later, in *Wakeham v Mackenzie* (1968), Stamp J was prepared to find a sufficient act of part-performance[32] in a case in which a widower (Mr Ball) had orally agreed with a widow, Mrs Margaret Elizabeth Wakeham, that if she gave up her council flat, moved into his house and looked after him and his home for no wages, he would leave his house and contents to her in his will. Once Mr Ball died, Mrs Wakeham found out that he had made no disposition in her favour and therefore brought a claim against the executor claiming specific performance of the agreement. The court found that giving up her home and moving into the home of the promisor, looking after him and his home, and putting money towards food were acts which referred to the alleged oral agreement made by the promisor.[33] Although the promisee had rendered services similar to those performed by Mrs Maddison, in this case, the doctrine of part-performance was applied. The difference in treatment seems to have been caused partly by the fact that by the time *Wakeham v Mackenzie* was decided, the requirements of an unequivocal 'connection' for the purposes of the doctrine of part-performance had become more relaxed.[34] However, it is also the case that in the course of the past century the attitude of courts towards the value of domestic and care services seems to have changed, at least in some settings.[35] Another factor seems to have been that in *Wakeham v Mackenzie* the claimant had given up the council flat in order to move in with the deceased.

This reading of the case seems to be confirmed by the decision in *Re Gonin* (1979). In this case, a daughter had been asked by her parents to take compassionate release from the Air Ministry, where she had worked, to look after them. Walton J concluded that the daughter's acts were *not* sufficiently related to her parents' house so as to justify her contractual claim.[36] He distinguished *Wakeham v Mackenzie* on the grounds that in *Re Gonin*, the daughter who had been living in Air Force accommodation, had not given up any house of her own, but simply

[31] Chapter 2, section III.C.3.

[32] *Wakeham v Mackenzie* (n 6).

[33] Ibid, 1181: 'The expression "must be referred to some contract" used by Upjohn L.J. in *Kingswood Estate Co. Ltd. v. Anderson* [1963] 2 Q.B. 169 (CA) 189, cannot exclude any act which could possibly be referable to love or affection, for whenever a man goes into possession of land he may be there by the grace and favour of another.'

[34] This was confirmed by the House of Lords in *Steadman v Steadman* [1976] AC 536 (HL), 542–543 (hereafter *Steadman v Steadman*) which dealt with a compromise agreement between husband and wife. The court found that a payment of money could in special circumstances amount to a sufficient act of part-performance to call the equitable doctrine into play.

[35] Kohn (2019) argues that, at least in the US, there has been a growing recognition of the value of care work when it comes to parental childcare. We also see a growing recognition of the value of household contributions in the context of a divorce or the break-up of cohabitants (in common law jurisdictions e.g. through the development of the common intention constructive trust). As for the civil law, see the legislation analysed in Part III of this book.

[36] *Re Gonin* [1979] Ch 16.

returned to her parents' home in order to look after them. It was further argued that, since the daughter had moved in with her parents rather than strangers, the likelihood of there being a contract, especially one concerning land, was low.[37] The fact that she was a family member mattered and seems to have worked against her. Walton J found that 'in a family situation of this nature one would not expect to find any strict contractual bond between parents and daughter, the whole resting much more on the good faith of each side without there being any intention on either side to enter into strict legal relationships.'[38] In other words, the question of part-performance aside, Walton J had doubts about whether there had been any intention to enter into a contract in the first place.

What these cases show is that while the doctrine of part-performance came to the aid of promisees who, for instance, improved the promisor's property, it did not really help those who cared for the deceased or provided services in her household, except in *Wakeham v Mackenzie* where the promisee had given up her entitlement to a council flat, and had thus suffered a financial prejudice. This shows again that domestic labour has often been treated as lacking in economic value. It is further noticeable that in all three cases the promisee was a woman, although only one (*Re Gonin*) was a family member and precisely that may have worked against her.

As mentioned earlier, the doctrine has been abolished in England and Wales so that oral promises relating to land can no longer be enforced even if there is part-performance, further enhancing the vulnerability of certain promisees. The doctrine of part-performance is, however, still in place in other common law jurisdictions, including in common law Canada, though there seems to be disagreement among courts as to the correct test for part-performance. In some provinces it is said to operate only if there is proof of a contract, and the performance unequivocally concerned the promised property and not just the contract itself.[39] Even so, there are several Canadian cases in which oral contracts to make a will have been enforced by invoking the doctrine of part-performance.[40] These are, however, primarily cases where promisees, usually men, have made improvements to the promisor's property or farm, rather than providing domestic or care services. In the latter cases, promisees would seem to base their claim on enrichment

[37] Ibid, 31.

[38] Ibid, 34.

[39] This would seem to emerge from *Thompson v Guaranty Trust Co* [1974] SCR 1023 (SCC) (hereafter *Thompson v Guaranty Trust Co*) and *Brownscombe v Public Trustee of Alberta*, 1969 CanLII 86 (SCC), [1969] SCR 658 (hereafter *Brownscombe v Public Trustee of Alberta*). It has been suggested therefore that Canadian courts are even stricter in their interpretation of the doctrine. For an analysis of the differences, see Granger (1969). However, some authors have also pointed at case law showing that certain Canadian courts have adopted a more liberal approach following the direction of the House of Lords decision in *Steadman v Steadman* (n 34). See Nozick (1978) 167–168 and Friedman (1980).

[40] For examples, see *Brownscombe v Public Trustee of Alberta* (n 39); *Thompson v Guaranty Trust Co* (n 39); *O'Neil v Lunn Estate*, 98 ACWS (3d) 332 [2000] OJ No 2698 [26] (Ont SCJ); *Sheldrake v Sheldrake* 2008 CarswellOnt 196; [2008] OJ No 150 (Ont SCJ); *Jans v Jans* (n 7); *Buchko v Buchko* (n 18); *Orange v Swierz Estate* (n 18).

law, but as we will see, only occasionally will they be able to obtain the promised asset because for a constructive trust to arise there is need for an established link between the contribution (performance) that founds the promisee's action and the promised asset.[41]

Whether writing is required for promises to leave the residue estate or a share thereof, which may well contain land, is currently uncertain, as there is conflicting authority.[42] In some cases, the courts have been prepared to characterize the promise as being unrelated to land, even though land was part of the promisor's estate at the time of the promise. However, in other cases, they have not, so that the protection of the promisee's interest remains unclear. Overall, establishing a contract to make a will is not a simple matter for a number of reasons, including the need to comply with formality requirements where the promise relates to land. Whereas in some jurisdictions the doctrine of part-performance can come to the aid of promisees, this is not the case for all promisees. Accordingly, formality requirements can stand in the way of a protection of a promisee's interest through contract law.

III. Breach of a contract to make a will

A. Introduction

Even if a promisee manages to prove the existence of a contract, protection in case of breach of contract may not always lead to the promisee's expectation interest being fulfilled. As the analysis will show, it very much depends on the content of the testamentary promise and on when the promise was broken, that is during the lifetime of the promisor or on death.

Before considering the type of relief available to a promisee in such cases, it is important to briefly clarify what constitutes a breach of promise. While the answer may seem to be obvious, this is not necessarily the case. Generally, where the promise is one to make a will, which I am focusing on here, the breach can arise by not making the promised will, or by making a will that benefits someone else. The promise may also be broken because the will is made but revoked or because it turns out to be void, for instance, due to a failure to comply with the formality

[41] See the analysis in Chapter 6.

[42] In *Birmingham v Renfrew* (1937) 57 CLR 666 (HC) 677, which concerned a contract to make mutual wills, the High Court of Australia held that the contract did not have to be in writing because the promise related to unascertained property i.e. to property of whatever character at the time of death. In the sense that a contract relating to the whole estate does not have to be in writing, see also the Australian case *Palmer v Bank of New South Wales* [1973] 2 NSWLR 244. In the Canadian case *Racette v Bearden* (1977) 1 ETR 211 (Sask Q B) the promisor promised to leave his farm to his partner and in general to provide security for her in his will, and the Saskatchewan Queen's Bench concluded that the promise did not concern land. By contrast, in *Horton v Jones* (n 8) the High Court of Australia held that the promise to leave the entire fortune was void due to the lack of writing, given that 'fortune' also included a specified interest in land.

requirements, as was the case in *Maddison v Alderson* discussed earlier.[43] This may be attributable to a personal mistake of the promisor or negligence of her estate planner.

Whether the promisor is liable for breach of the promise depends on whether it is a promise to merely make a will, to leave the residue estate or a share of it, or rather to leave specific property to the promisee. Technically speaking, a promise to merely make a will or to leave the residue or a share of it is not, in principle, regarded as being breached where a will was made but subsequently revoked.[44] By contrast a promise to pass specific property to the claimant is usually regarded as only performed when the will takes effect, as the promise is treated as an obligation to ensure that the promisee will take the said property on the promisor's death.[45] In this case, revocation of the will, even when automatic, for example, due to remarriage (or divorce in some jurisdictions) of the promisor, represents a breach, and the promisor is liable for breach of contract. It is argued that, where the revocation is automatic, the promisor can still make a new will and, if she fails to do so, she is in breach.[46] This distinction between cases in which the promise is merely one to make a will, or to leave the residue estate or a share in it, rather than one to pass a specific asset seems, however, to be somewhat arbitrary and to unfairly differentiate between promisees merely on the basis of the wording of the promise, meaning that those who are promised a specific asset are likely to be better off. This is especially problematic given how vague and generic testamentary promises usually are.

Finally, a promisor may also be liable for breach of the promise where she disposes of the promised property during her lifetime, thereby placing herself in a position of no longer being able to perform the promise. If the promisor dies intestate but the promisee is a beneficiary under intestacy rules, there is no breach, for her share under intestacy counts as a satisfaction of the whole or *pro tanto* of the liability under the promise, depending on the amount received.[47] Thus, in this case, the contract is treated as being performed by allowing the property to come to the promisee under the intestacy of the promisor,[48] and the promisor is not liable.

In sections III.B and C below I will discuss the forms of relief that a promisee may obtain in case of a breach of contract. I will start with a discussion of instances in which the breach of the promise is discovered on the death of the promisor, because those are the cases most common in practice. I will then explore those cases in which the breach occurs during the promisor's lifetime. We will see that the protection is less strong where the breach occurs, and the claim is brought, during the promisor's lifetime, for

43 See n 28.
44 Nield (2007) 289.
45 Miller *The Machinery* (1996) 212.
46 Margrave-Jones *Mellows Succession* (1993) 25, para 3.29. See *Robinson v Ommaney* (1883) 23 Ch D 285 (CA).
47 Martyn et al *Theobald on Wills* (2021) para 8-106.
48 Ibid.

in such a case the promisee is seen to obtain an accelerated benefit. Protection is also weaker where the promise is a promise to simply make a will or to leave the residue or a share in it, rather than one to leave a specific asset. Again, the law differentiates between promisees even when they might be equally deserving.

B. Forms of relief after the death of the promisor

Technically speaking, a contract to make a will does not prevent the promisor from making a new will that revokes the promised will, or that contradicts the promise. Indeed, a will made in breach of a contract to make a will is perfectly valid and is admitted to probate.[49] However, where there is a contract, courts will give effect to the agreement, so that the promisee may seek relief in the form of damages or specific performance, either from the estate (through the personal representative), or from the beneficiaries under the will, residuary legatees or those who take on intestacy. The type of relief available on the death of the promisor, and thus the degree of protection afforded to the promisee, depends, as already mentioned, on the specific content of the promise. I will start with instances in which the promise was one to leave a specific asset and where the protection is strongest.

1. Promise to leave a specific asset

If the promisor has promised to leave a specific asset, a life interest, or a fixed amount, the amount of damages awarded is represented by the value of the promised property.[50] Where the circumstances are appropriate, specific performance might be available to the promisee.[51] Where that is the case, the court will order the personal representative, or the beneficiary under the will or legatee or intestate successor, to convey the property according to the contract, or otherwise to give effect to the contract.[52] This was, for instance, the case in *Wakeham v Mackenzie* mentioned earlier, where part-performance led to a claim against the deceased's executor and an award of specific performance in favour of Mrs Wakeham. What is more, where the promise relates to a specific asset, the promisee will be treated like

[49] *Re Heys* [1914] P 192 (P); *Aimers v Taylor* (1897) 15 NZLR 530. In the latter case the promise was one not to revoke an existing will.

[50] See *Hammersley v De Biel* (1845) 12 Cl & Fin 45 and *Synge v Synge* (n 25).

[51] As to the scope of the remedy, see Beale *Chitty on Contracts* (2020) paras 27-011ff. Specific performance is not granted where the contract is made by deed, as it will be enforced by damages only. In this sense Margrave-Jones *Mellows Succession* (1993) 18, para 3.10. Specific performance was not granted in *Jans v Jans* (n 7) [247] but that was because, in this case, the promisee would not have been in a position to have a cooperative relationship with his brother (the defendant in the case), who had also worked on the farm. Here, see the analogy with the proprietary estoppel cases discussed in Chapter 4 that require a clean break.

[52] Examples are *Goilmere v Battison* (1682) 1 Vern 48; (1682) 23 ER 301; *Coverdale v Eastwood* (1872–1873) LR 15 Eq 121 (Ch) (hereafter *Coverdale v Eastwood*); *Wakeham v Mackenzie* (n 6) and *Re Edwards, deceased* (n 11).

a creditor so that her interests will prevail over the interests of those who benefit under the will, though we will see that this does not necessarily apply when the promise is kept, the promised will is made, but someone else has made an application for a family provision order against the estate.

2. Promise to leave the residuary estate or a share in it

Where, on the other hand, the promisor simply promised to make a will, or to leave the promisee the entire residuary estate, or a share in it, specific performance will *not* be available. Although the promisee is entitled to claim damages, these will be calculated on the basis that the estate may be taken to satisfy debts.[53] It follows, that in the case of a generic promise, the amount of damages awarded is likely to be lower than the value of what was promised. More importantly, the promisee will be treated like a beneficiary of the estate, rather than a creditor. The reason for that is that the contract to leave the residue, or a share in it, is regarded as referring to the deceased's net estate,[54] which is only ascertained *after* satisfaction of the interests of any creditors.[55] This may well mean that the promisee does not receive any property on the death of the deceased, because the assets may be required for the payment of the deceased's other liabilities.

It further means that the promisee benefits after successors under the will. However, William A Lee has argued that a promisee 'should not be postponed to legatees or devisees under the will, as a residuary beneficiary ordinarily is, for if he were so postponed the promisor would be able, by making substantial legacies and devisees, to render his promise nugatory'.[56] The argument seems convincing. There is, of course, the risk that if the contractual promisee were to get the whole of the residuary estate, nothing would be left for testamentary legatees. However, this seems justified by the fact that the promisee's claim arises already during lifetime (and is thus to be seen as a debt incurred by the promisor), and that she has usually done something in exchange for the promise, resulting in an enrichment of the estate. Irrespective of that, the promisee of a contract to leave the residue will only take what is left after a family provision order has been made.[57]

As mentioned before, in practice, promises are often vague, and they may change over time, so that it may not always be clear whether the promisor intended to make a specific disposition, or to leave merely what is left, that is the residue. In other words, the promisee may find it difficult to prove that a specific asset was promised so that specific performance may not be available to her. However, it

[53] In this sense Margrave-Jones *Mellows Succession* (1993) 23, para 3.25.

[54] *Schaefer v Schuhmann* [1972] AC 572 (hereafter *Schaefer v Schuhmann*), Lord Cross of Chelsea.

[55] See *Jervis v Wolferstan* (1874) LR 18 Eq 18 (Ch) 26 (hereafter *Jervis v Wolferstan*) where Sir George Jessel took the view that 'everybody taking a residue must know that he takes it subject to the testator's liabilities and takes the risk of its afterwards turning out that there are undiscovered liabilities'.

[56] Lee (1971) 360.

[57] As far as the position vis-à-vis claimants under the New Zealand TPA 1949 is concerned, Chapter 7 shows that courts are given the power to balance them.

appears that when in doubt, courts have tended to give effect to the arrangement as an obligation to ensure that the property passes to the claimant on death rather than as a mere obligation to make a will or to leave what is left.[58] In this regard, courts seem to have been favourable towards promisees.[59]

To summarize, when there is evidence of an enforceable contract and the promise concerns a specific asset, the promisee enjoys considerable protection in the case of breach of contract, being able to obtain either damages (based on the value of the expectation interest) or, in some cases, even specific performance of the agreement. She will then be treated as a creditor of the estate, which puts her in a better position than beneficiaries under a will or intestacy, or any applicants under the family provision legislations. By contrast, where the promise is to leave the promisee the residue or a share in it, the protection is less robust, for only damages can be obtained and their value is likely not to be equivalent to the value of the promised inheritance. Also, the promisee will not be regarded as a creditor of the estate but rather as a beneficiary of the estate who takes after all creditors have been satisfied, legacies have been paid, and any family provision orders have been made.

C. Forms of relief during the lifetime of the promisor

Sometimes the promisee's interests are frustrated already during the promisor's lifetime, for instance, because the promisor sells the property object of the contractual promise, gifts it to someone else, or transfers it on trust. Where the promisee is aware of such actions and seeks to stop the promisor from breaching her promise or to obtain another remedy, the level of protection depends again on the content of the promise but also on whether the third party is a *bona fide* purchaser for value without notice.

1. Promise to leave a specific asset

Where the promise is one to leave specific property, rather than to leave the residue or a share in it, the current position seems to be that if the promisor puts herself in a position of no longer being able to perform the contract, by disposing of the promised asset, an action may be brought against her during her lifetime.[60] In other words, the promisor's actions are seen as inconsistent with the agreement. This is because, as mentioned, a contract to make a specific provision in a will is treated not merely as an obligation to make a will containing such a provision, but as an obligation to ensure that the promisee will take the promised property on the

[58] In this sense, Margrave-Jones *Mellows Succession* (1993) 16, para 3.4, but also Nield (2000) 90.

[59] For instance, in *Synge v Synge* (n 25) the court was prepared to read the letter which said 'I leave house and land to you for lifetime' as referring to a house and land in Devonshire.

[60] *Synge v Synge* (n 25); *Schaefer v Schuhmann* (n 54).

promisor's death.[61] For this reason, the promisor may not donate the property, or settle it on trust for herself for life with the remainder to go to someone other than the promisee. The contract is regarded as broken at the time of the disposal of the asset, at which point the promisee can bring a claim for breach of contract.[62]

This was confirmed by the English Court of Appeal decision in the 1894 case of *Synge v Synge*, in which a future husband had made an ante-nuptial promise, in consideration of marriage, to leave by will a house and land to his future wife (Lady Synge) for her lifetime. However, sometime later he conveyed his whole estate and interest in the property to his daughters. At that point his wife brought a claim seeking a declaration that she was entitled to damages for breach of contract. The agreement was contained in a letter by the husband to his future spouse written prior to their marriage. At that time, a letter was sufficient to provide the required formalities for a contract,[63] something which is no longer the case. The question arose as to whether the letter amounted to a contract. The court found that it did and granted Lady Synge's contractual claim against the transferees of the estate, calculating the damages on the basis of the value of the life estate which she would have been entitled to, had she survived her husband. Although in *Synge v Synge* the claim led to the award of damages, the court also held *obiter* that:

> Courts of Equity . . . can decree that the heir or devisee in such a case [that is where the promise relates to a defined piece of real property] to convey the land to the widow for life, and under the Trustee Act can make a vesting order, or direct that someone shall convey for him if he refuses.[64]

Thus, the Court of Appeal did not exclude the possibility that courts could compel the devisee of the promised asset to convey the property to the promisee under the contract, with the exception of *bona fide* purchasers for value without notice. This position was confirmed decades later by the Privy Council in *Schaefer v Schuhmann* (1972):

> If the contract is to devise or bequeath specific property the position of the promisee during the testator's lifetime is stronger than if the contract is simply to leave a legacy. If the testator sells the property during his lifetime the promisee can treat the sale as a repudiation of the contract and recover damages at law which will be assessed subject to a reduction for the acceleration of the benefit and also if the benefit of the contract is personal to the promisee subject to a deduction for the contingency of his failing to survive the promisor. But if he can intervene before a

[61] Miller *The Machinery* (1996) 212.
[62] *Jones v Martin* (1798) 5 Ves 266n; 3 ER 560 (hereafter *Jones v Martin*).
[63] Statute of Frauds 1677, s 4.
[64] *Synge v Synge* (n 25) 471.

> purchaser for value without notice obtains an interest in the property he can obtain a declaration of his right to have it left to him by will and an injunction to restrain the testator from disposing of it in breach of contract: *Synge v Synge* [1894] 1 QB 466. No doubt if the property is land he could also register the contract or a caution against the title.[65]

It seems that so long as the promise is one to leave specific property, courts can intervene to prevent substantial *inter vivos* dispositions aimed at defeating a promise of an inheritance.[66] As the majority in *Schaefer v Schuhmann* pointed out, in such cases it might even be possible for the promisee to obtain an injunction to restrain the testator from disposing of her property in breach of contract.[67]

Where the lifetime claim is one for damages rather than specific performance, the amount of the damages would appear to be calculated by taking into account debts as well as potential interventions by the court under the family provision legislation.[68] The damages awarded are thus subject to a reduction for the acceleration of the benefit and, if the benefit of the contract is personal to the promisee, subject to a reduction for the contingency of her failing to survive the testator.[69] Other contingencies too may be taken into account when calculating damages, such as the fact that the promised asset might be destroyed before the will takes effect.[70]

All of this shows that where damages are sought during the promisor's lifetime, the protection is potentially weaker compared to the cases where relief is sought on the death of the promisor. From the perspective of the promisee, arguably it is therefore preferable that the promisor breaks the promise by not making the promised will, rather than by making a lifetime transfer of the promised property, except that in the former case the promisee has to wait until the promisor's death before bringing a claim without a guarantee that there will be something left in the estate worth fighting over.

2. Promise to leave the residue or a share in it

What is the position when the promise is one to leave the residue or a share in it and the promisee brings a claim during the promisor's lifetime? Case law seems to be conflicting. On the one hand, there are some older cases that suggest that the promisor is free to dispose of her property during her lifetime as she wishes,[71] on the basis that there is no implied term that the residue will be of any given

[65] *Schaefer v Schuhmann* (n 54) 585–586.
[66] This was held also in *Jones v Martin* (n 62); Nield (2000) 91.
[67] *Schaefer v Schuhmann* (n 54) 586.
[68] Margrave-Jones *Mellows Succession* (1993) para 3.25.
[69] *Schaefer v Schuhmann* (n 54) 586.
[70] This was the case in *Parker v Clark* (n 11).
[71] See *Jarman on Wills* (1910) 28. This is confirmed by *Needham v Smith* (1828) 4 Russ 318; 38 ER 825 and *Coverdale v Eastwood* (n 52). This includes subsequently acquired property, see *Needham v Kirkman* (1820) 3 B & Ald 531; 106 ER 755.

size.[72] Although the promisor cannot make testamentary dispositions that defeat the promise, she appears to be able to make lifetime dispositions that achieve the same result.[73] Following this approach, the promisee is worse off simply because the promise is one to leave the residue of the estate or a share in it, rather than a specific asset.

However, in a dissenting judgment delivered in the Privy Council decision in *Schaefer v Schuhmann*, Lord Simon had stated that:

> even where a share of the residue is promised, the testator will not be permitted fraudulently (in the sense used in equity) to render his promise nugatory by making substantial gifts inter vivos or by way of specific legacy (*Gregor v. Kemp* (1722) 3 Swan. 404).[74]

Thus, if Lord Simon's position were to be followed, even where the promise is one to leave the residuary estate rather than a specific property, the promisor would not be able to make a substantial gift intended to make the promise nugatory, but could only dispose of her property *inter vivos* in the normal course of events. This position seems to find support in some older decisions where the courts have defeated attempts to evade a promise by way of lifetime gifts.[75] From the perspective of the promisee, this approach would no doubt be preferable.

IV. Promisees of contracts to make a will vis-à-vis applicants of a family provision order

I have already mentioned that, depending on the nature of the promise, the contractual promisee is treated either as a creditor or as a beneficiary of the estate and that this categorization affects the strength of her protection vis-à-vis others with an interest in the estate. But what happens if the contractual promise is kept and the promised will is made? The question becomes relevant where, on the death of the promisor, an application is brought for a family provision order against an estate with insufficient funds. Is the property that is the subject matter of the testamentary disposition in favour of the promisee available as part of the estate which

[72] *Jervis v Wolferstan* (n 55). Miller *The Machinery* (1996) 212.

[73] While this is not the place to go into further detail, it is interesting to note that this has given rise to a dispute as to which dispositions are to be qualified as testamentary and which are not, especially where they do not take the form of a will, as is the case with will-substitutes. The issues arose in *Fortescue v Hennah* (1812) 19 Ves 67, 71; 34 ER 443, 71 (hereafter *Fortescue v Hennah*) and *Logan v Wienholt* (1833) 1 Cl & Fin 611; 6 ER 1046 but also in *Palmer v Bank of New South Wales* (1975) 133 CLR 150.

[74] *Schaefer v Schuhmann* (n 54) 599.

[75] See, for instance, *Fortescue v Hennah* (n 73) as well as *Lewis v Madocks* (1803) 8 Ves 150; 32 ER 310 where an agreement to settle personal property was not allowed to be evaded by investing in the purchase of land.

may be redistributed under the family provision legislation? As Gleeson LJ put it in the Australian High Court decision in *Barns v Barns* (2003):

> [the issue] has divided judicial opinion from the earliest days of such legislation. It has never been the subject of authoritative decision by this Court, but it has been the subject of inconsistent decisions of other courts, including inconsistent decisions of the Privy Council.[76]

It is interesting in this regard to note that, at least in Australia and New Zealand, contracts to make a will have been frequently described as a means for the deceased to increase the debts and liabilities that are payable out of the estate on her death and thus to avoid claims of family members with a moral claim against the estate.[77] The assumption seems to be that such contracts are necessarily entered into in bad faith rather than being an expression of the willingness of some testators to bind themselves as to the content of their future will. This appears to suggest that a contractual promise is less genuine than an informal promise, which is ironic given that the law usually insists on form to show seriousness of intention of the promisor,[78] and for that reason requires formalities for contracts to make a will concerning land, though there are also other considerations underpinning such requirements. Consequently, if the promisee is *lucky* enough, in the sense that the promisor is willing to commit and to put something in writing, and the promise is kept, she risks that her interest competes with the interests of those who have a moral claim against the estate.

Going back to Gleeson LJ's aforementioned point, while some courts have taken the view that the assets object of a contract to make a will that was executed do not form part of the estate for the purposes of a family provision order, others have taken the exact opposite view, holding that they have a power to interfere with the testamentary disposition and thus to redistribute such assets.[79] The leading case in support of the first position is the Privy Council decision in *Dillon v Public Trustee of New Zealand* (1941), which dealt with an appeal from New Zealand.[80] Without entering into too much detail, in this case the deceased had agreed to bequeath his farm lands on trust to his children and executed a will giving effect to the agreement. Subsequently he remarried, and, on his death, his widow brought a claim under the Family Protection Act 1908 (NZ),[81] arguing that what she had received

[76] *Barns v Barns* [2003] HCA 9; 214 CLR 169; 196 ALR 65, [18] (hereafter *Barns v Barns*). See, the cases cited by Lee (1972), where the bench was divided on the particular question.

[77] Foster (1998–1999) 112 n 203 cites cases that suggest that, in the US, courts have looked at the contracts with misgivings and suspicion.

[78] See the discussion in Chapter 2.

[79] For an examination of the cases, see Lee (1971) and Sheppard (1985).

[80] *Dillon v Public Trustee of New Zealand* [1941] AC 294 (PC) 304–305 (hereafter *Dillon v Public Trustee of New Zealand*).

[81] The Act has been superseded by the Family Provision Act 1955.

under her husband's will was not adequate provision for her 'proper maintenance and support'. She thus requested the court to exercise its discretion to order further provision for her out of the deceased's estate. The Supreme Court of New Zealand gave judgment in favour of the widow but, on appeal, the Court of Appeal of New Zealand held that the court had no discretion to order further provision in her favour. When the case came before the Privy Council, the Committee concluded in favour of the widow that the benefits given under the will pursuant to the agreement were subject to redistribution by the courts under the family provision legislation.[82] Consequently, in this case the contractual promisees were not treated as creditors whose debt had to be paid prior to making any order under the family provision legislation, and thus lost out.

The decision of the Privy Council in *Dillon v Public Trustee of New Zealand* is problematic because promisees whose promise was fulfilled would seem to be worse off than promisees whose promise was broken. Precisely this argument was raised by the Chief Justice in *Dillon v Public Trustee of New Zealand*,[83] but rejected by the Committee of the Privy Council on the basis that where the promise is breached, the promisee would not necessarily be awarded the value of the property but a reduced amount based on a calculation of a redistribution due to the application of the Family Protection Act 1908.[84] Thus, the Privy Council did not share the view that the promisee is worse off where the promise is kept. It took the view that irrespective of whether or not the promise is fulfilled, the Act 'affects the unqualified operation of a contract to make a will'.[85]

However, the decision in *Dillon v Public Trustee of New Zealand* was met with criticism,[86] and thirty years on in *Schaefer v Schuhmann*[87] the Privy Council, this time dealing with an appeal from New South Wales, departed from its earlier decision. In this case, the deceased had retired from business, was in poor health, and was living by himself. He therefore engaged a housekeeper whom he told that if she looked after him until his death, he would leave to her by will his house, which he did. Indeed, he had asked her to read the codicil to him and then executed the document at the bank that day. So, in this case, the promisee was informed of the testamentary disposition in her favour, evidently to ensure that she would be aware of it and rely on it.[88] From that day until the testator's death the housekeeper

[82] *Dillon v Public Trustee of New Zealand* (n 80) 303.

[83] *Dillon v Dillon Public Trustee* [1939] NZLR 550, 559, per Myers CJ: 'The effect of the decision appealed against is that where A enters into a contract with B, for valuable consideration, that he will by his last will and testament devise certain lands to B, and A subsequently marries and actually performs his contract, B is to be in a worse position than if A had committed a breach of his contract. It would be an extraordinary thing if our law permitted such a result.'

[84] *Dillon v Public Trustee of New Zealand* (n 80) 304–305.

[85] Ibid, 305. The point was addressed and rejected in *Schaefer v Schuhmann* (n 54) 587.

[86] Oughton *Tyler's Family Provision* (1997) 314 n 18 with references.

[87] *Schaefer v Schuhmann* (n 54).

[88] On this particular point see the analysis in Chapter 1, section III.B.2.

received no wages. The testator also made provision in his will for his three sons and four daughters. After the will was proved, the four daughters claimed that adequate provision had not been made for their proper maintenance, and they applied to the court for that to be done out of the estate under section 3(1) of the Testator's Family Maintenance and Guardianship of Infants Act 1916–1954. At first instance, Street J considered the financial circumstances of the applicants and, feeling bound by *Dillon*, held that three of them had made out cases for relief under the Act. He therefore ordered that their legacies be increased and that the burden be met partly by, and be a charge on, the property given to the housekeeper, and partly by interests received by the three sons equally. The housekeeper contended that the court had no jurisdiction to place any of the burden of such orders on the property given to her but that the whole burden should come out of the residuary estate left to the three sons.

On Appeal, the Privy Council, by a majority (of four out of five), held in favour of the housekeeper. The Judicial Committee took the view that *Dillon v Public Trustee of New Zealand* was out of line with earlier English and Australian authority,[89] and, given that the case was decided thirty years earlier, and had received both judicial and academic criticism, it chose not to follow it. Lord Simon of Glaisdale, dissenting, agreed with the position that the Privy Council had taken in *Dillon v Public Trustee of New Zealand.* Perhaps in somewhat melodramatic fashion, he pointed out that the effect of overruling *Dillon v Public Trustee of New Zealand* was that the New South Wales statute was to be construed:

> to countenance the following situation: a widower is left with two infant children; he proposes marriage to another woman, promising to bequeath her the whole of his estate if she will accept him; she does accept him on these terms; he dies shortly afterwards; the court is powerless to order any provision out of his estate for his infant children. The legislatures of the various jurisdictions concerned may wish to consider this situation.[90]

One problem with this position is that Lord Simon of Glaisdale does not differentiate between situations in which the contract is concluded to make a family provision claim nugatory and those in which there is no such intention on the part of the promisor. In fact, judging from case law, the example he gives seems to rarely materialize in practice. Also, his Lordship seems to overlook the fact that a contractual promisee deserves protection for she will have provided consideration. Of course, Lord Simon does not suggest that the contractual promisee goes empty-handed,

[89] See, for instance, the decision of the Full Court of the Supreme Court of New South Wales in *Coffill v Commissioner of Stamp Duties* (1920) 20 SR (NSW) 278.

[90] *Schaefer v Schuhmann* (n 54) 594.

but the disposition in her favour will have to be reduced and that needs to be justified. Where the family provision order is sought by a promisee of a testamentary promise made by the deceased,[91] and the promisee has provided a performance in return for the promise, arguably it is right that they share the risk. But if that is not the case, it is unclear whether the applicant's financial needs alone are sufficient to justify the interference, especially given that, England and Wales aside, in other common law jurisdictions courts interpret 'financial need' in a flexible manner, and that in New Zealand, the requirement has been altogether abandoned.[92] Also, even if the applicant were in need, it could be argued that this could be due to their own doing, and not merely due to misfortune.[93]

Irrespective of the merits of the dissenting judgement in *Dillon v Public Trustee of New Zealand*, it is clear that the two Privy Council decisions take opposite views as to whether the power under the family provision legislation extends to property that is subject to a contract to make a will that was executed. Partly, the different approaches reflect, as Rosalind Croucher says 'different ways of viewing family provision legislation'.[94] This has also emerged from case law that has followed since. In fact, the Privy Council decision in *Schaefer v Schuhmann* has not brought an end to the debate. As far as Australia is concerned, in *Barns v Barns*,[95] by a majority (of four out of five) the High Court of Australia decided to reject the Privy Council decision in *Schaefer v Schuhmann* and to follow the earlier decision in *Dillon v Public Trustee of New Zealand* instead.[96] It concluded that legislative amendments were not needed to intrude upon a contract to make a will through the vehicle of family provision legislation, but that the court could do so as a matter of construction of the legislation.[97] By contrast, Callinan J who dissented, held that it was a matter for Parliament to decide whether to upset the agreement the deceased had entered into. Consequently, in Australia, the promisee under a contract to make a will that was executed may see the testamentary disposition made in her favour reduced so as to allow for the order to be made.[98]

Since *Barns v Barns* does not apply in New Zealand, *Schaefer v Schuhmann* is still the law. This means that, in New Zealand, courts do not have the power to interfere with the will that executes a contract to make a will on the basis of the Family Protection Act 1955. Indeed, the decision of the Privy Council in *Schaefer v Schuhmann* was followed by the Supreme Court of New Zealand in *Re Webster*

91 See Chapter 5.
92 Chapter 5.
93 Here, see the discussion in Chapter 7, section IV.B.
94 Croucher (2005).
95 *Barns v Barns* (n 76).
96 Croucher (2005).
97 Ibid, 272.
98 Dal Pont & Mackie *Succession* (2017) 677.

(1976),[99] and by the Court of Appeal in *Breuer v Wright* (1982).[100] Importantly, in *Breuer v Wright* (1982), the New Zealand Court of Appeal took the view that:

> these are not matters for resolution by the Courts but, should it seem necessary, for attention by Parliament. The one comment that should perhaps be made is that the principle enunciated in the Schaefer case is not concerned to protect some piece of contractual window dressing, carefully designed for no other purpose than to defeat just claims under the legislation, but as that judgment makes plain with bona fide enforceable contracts made for valuable consideration.[101]

Thus, unlike Lord Simon in *Schaefer v Schuhmann*, here the court acknowledges that not all contracts to make a will are by definition intended to defeat the family provision legislation and, importantly, that the contractual promisee will have provided consideration in exchange for the promise. It was also of the opinion that the issue should be addressed by Parliament, which is what happened in England and Wales. In fact, two years after the Privy Council decision in *Schaefer v Schumann*, the English Law Commission considered the issues.[102] It took the view that a distinction had to be drawn between contracts to leave property by will where the intention of the promisor is to defeat a claim for family provision, and those where there is no such intention. It suggested that courts should be given a power to interfere with contracts but only where there was an intention of the promisor to defeat a claim for financial provision, taking into account any valuable consideration which has been given for the contract.

In reaching this conclusion, the English Law Commission was inspired by legislation that had already been in place in Canada.[103] Its recommendations were implemented into section 11 of the Inheritance (Provision for Family and Dependants) Act 1975 which establishes that the court has the power to make an anti-evasion order, and that property that is the subject of a contract to leave a bequest may be brought into the net estate, provided that the contract was for less than full value and made with the intention to defeat a family provision claim.[104] Only then will the promisee be affected. Much will thus depend on whether full consideration has been given,[105] and what that means. Where no valuable consideration was given or promised in exchange for the contractual promise of the deceased, a

[99] *Re Webster* [1976] 2 NZLR 304.
[100] *Breuer v Wright* [1982] 2 NZLR 77.
[101] Ibid, 86.
[102] The Law Commission *Second Report on Family Property: Family Provision on Death* (Law Com No 61) 1974, paras 222–242.
[103] In particular, the Canadian Draft Uniform Relief Act, s 16, which was based on similar provincial legislation. See *Oosterhoff on Wills* (2016) 892–897.
[104] Such contracts include mutual will contracts but exclude contracts to die intestate.
[105] See Oughton *Tyler's Family Provision* (1997) 315ff.

presumption operates whereby there is an intention to defeat the Act.[106] But these cases will be rare, for as we saw in Chapter 1, there is usually an exchange involved. In fact, Article 11 has been rarely invoked.

Even so, it is important to note again that not all contracts to make a will are treated in the same way and that there is no assumption that they are all entered into to circumvent any duties the deceased may have had under the family provision legislation. Contractual promisees should not be automatically worse off.[107]

V. Evaluating contractual claims from the perspective of the promisee

From the perspective of a promisee, a successful contractual claim can no doubt have certain benefits. The main advantage is that damages are awarded as of right and, where the promise is one to leave a specific asset, they are calculated on the basis of the expectation interests, that is to say the prospective inheritance. Also, where the promise is specific, the promisee may even obtain the equitable remedy of specific performance, which is often what the promisee will want. It is desirable especially where the promisor is insolvent.[108] Importantly, she will be treated as a creditor. Furthermore, if the promisor puts herself in a position of no longer being able to perform the promise, a claim for breach of contract may be brought already during the lifetime of the promisor. The fact that, at least in principle, expectation interests are fulfilled makes the relief predictable with the added advantage of making it easier for the parties to settle the claim which, as will be seen, can pose a potential problem with other forms of redress (i.e. proprietary estoppel but also unjust enrichment claims in Canada).[109]

However, we also saw that where the promise is simply one to leave the residue or a share in it, the promisee's protection is much less robust, both on death and especially during lifetime. Damages will be available but will be calculated on the basis that the estate may be taken to satisfy debts. Thus, not all promisees of a contractual promise may be able to obtain the promised asset or its value. Also, where the promise is a generic one, the promisee is seen as a beneficiary of the estate rather than as a creditor. And, if the contract is kept and the promised will made, the contractual promisee may see her testamentary disposition reduced by a family provision order. This is certainly the case in Australia, though not in New Zealand,

[106] Section 12(2). According to Oughton *Tyler's Family Provision* (1997) 318, 'the inclusion of the rebuttable presumption was erroneous and was the result of trying to combine two different and essentially incompatible approaches' one of which was the Canadian one.

[107] As to possible conflicts between contractual promisees and claimants under the New Zealand TPA 1949, see Chapter 7, section IV.

[108] Lee (1971) 360.

[109] Chapters 4 and 6.

and in England and Wales it depends on whether or not the contract was for less than full value and made with the intention to defeat a family provision claim. As noted earlier, this is somewhat ironic because it would seem that the promisee is likely to be better off when the promise is broken, for then she will be treated as a creditor so long as the promise was one to leave a specific asset. Thus, not only are some breaches more 'beneficial' than others from the perspective of the promisee (i.e. a breach on death rather than during the promisor's lifetime), it may also be 'better' for her if the contractual promise is breached rather than kept, which seems absurd. Also, the protection is dependent on how specific the promise is, which is often down to luck.

It follows that establishing a contract does not necessarily mean that the promisee benefits from greater protection, which may well make contracts to make a will less attractive and encourage claimants to pursue other avenues of redress even if a contract can be proven. In fact, it is probably no coincidence that recently there has been an increase in cases in which claimants have invoked the doctrine of proprietary estoppel.[110] It may also mean that where a testator intended to use a contract to make a will to avoid a family provision order against her estate, she will now be looking for other avenues including, for instance, setting up a trust.[111]

All this assumes, of course, that the parties, and especially the promisor, are willing to enter into a legally binding contract in the first place, which is not necessarily the case. In fact, we saw that in most cases the parties prefer not to formalize the arrangement, so that it is usually difficult to prove the existence of a contract.[112] As noted, the agreement and thus the intention has to be sufficiently specific, not only in relation to the subject matter of the promise, but also regarding the obligations assumed by the parties.[113] In addition, testamentary contracts concerning land require writing. Whilst this requirement shields the promisor against the risk of fraudulent allegations, it works to the considerable disadvantage of the promisee, who is already in a weaker position, for she is not in control of the promised property. Although in some jurisdictions, part-performance offers a way around such formality requirements, so that even oral contracts can be enforced, its availability very much depends on the type of performance rendered by the promisee. As we have seen, domestic and care services are often insufficiently related to the promised asset. This means that there is again a differentiation between promises—those performing domestic and care services, often women, are less likely to establish the existence of a contract.

[110] Chapter 4.

[111] Peart (2008) 379.

[112] 'Such contracts are not easily proved in fact and when proved are likely to run into legal difficulties' says Devlin J in *Parker v Clark* (n 11) 291.

[113] For a case in which no such agreement and no such intention was found, see *Taylor v Dickens* [1998] 1 FLR 806 (Ch).

V. Conclusion

In this chapter we have seen that in many common law jurisdictions, promisors can make a contractual promise to make a will. However, the analysis has also revealed that it is often difficult for promisees to establish such a legally binding contract. Only a limited number of promisees will therefore receive protection under contract law. This was pointed out by Finlay J in the New Zealand decision in *Nealon v Public Trustee* (1949) when describing the situation in New Zealand:

> The need thus emphasized for a valid and enforceable contract as the basis for a successful claim gave rise to much injustice. Honourable understandings were defeated by the necessity for that completeness and exactitude or the necessity of form, which the law required as essentials to the validity and enforceability of contracts. Compliance with these essentials to validity and enforceability was, in the ordinary course of things, difficult to secure, for such agreements are generally made between close relatives and the party rendering the services commonly found it difficult to have such essential requirements satisfied by the other. To attempt to do so would savour of doubting the integrity and trustworthiness of the other. This might jeopardise the existing happy relationship between the parties, and so jeopardise the prospects of receiving a reward which was generally promised upon a generous scale.[114]

It almost appears as if the law safeguards the interests of those promisees who manage to get, or insist on, not only a clear agreement as to the obligations of both parties as well as the subject matter of the promise, but also such an agreement being reduced to writing. In other words, it rewards promisees who are lucky, courageous, or strategic, or all three. After all, promisees who insist on satisfying those requirements risk, as Finlay J pointed out, jeopardizing their relationship with the promisor.[115] Yet, in some common law jurisdictions, contracts to make a will have been viewed with suspicion, that is as a means for the deceased to increase debts and liabilities that are payable out of the estate on her death, and thus a way to prevent a potential family provision order.

Aware of the fact that few promisees will be able to establish such a contract, New Zealand has introduced specific legislation in the form of the Law Reform (Testamentary Promises) Act 1949 (hereafter the New Zealand TPA 1949) regulating informal promises of an inheritance. The legislation was a reaction precisely to the hard cases caused by the application of contract law rules to the testamentary promises context discussed by Finlay J earlier.[116] Whether, and to what extent, the

[114] *Nealon v Public Trustee* (n 23) 160.
[115] See also the discussion in Chapter 1.
[116] For details, see n 114.

Act represents a satisfactory answer to informal testamentary promises cases will be discussed in Chapter 7. However, even outside New Zealand, it has been argued that the context in which testamentary promises are usually expressed, 'is one in which strict notions of contract formation and formulation are inappropriate'.[117] Indeed, in *Re Welch*, the Judicial Committee of the Privy Council conceded that 'the shortcomings in the evolution of the common law can still result in hard cases in England'.[118] Some legal scholars have therefore advocated in favour of legislation along the lines of the New Zealand TPA 1949,[119] which does not require the promisee to prove the existence of a contract. However, outside New Zealand, no other jurisdiction appears to specifically regulate informal testamentary promises. In the absence of specific legislation, common law courts have responded to the harshness of some of the contract cases by developing more flexible forms of redress, through the application, for instance, of the doctrine of proprietary estoppel and, in some jurisdictions, unjust enrichment, which will be examined in the following chapters.

But even if the parties are willing to formalize their agreement, casting the promise in contractual terms is neither ideal nor easy also for other reasons. Although contracts to make a will can be useful because the parties can agree their respective obligations and the consideration, in all types of contexts (e.g. farming or care), the problem is that it is difficult for the parties to foresee all eventualities and to plan for contingencies. This is especially so because the performance is not necessarily immediately sequential to the promise, but also because there is often a long time lag between the moment (or moments) of the promise and that of the promisor's death, and much can happen during that time. For that reason, the testamentary agreements are frequently subject to unspoken qualifications. In addition, the power differential between the promisor and the promisee is such that it is unlikely that the promisee can dictate the conditions.

117 Nield (2000) 91. See also Stoljar (1989–1990) 35.

118 *Re Welch* [1990] 3 NZLR 1 (PC) [40].

119 Nield (2000) 103; Nield (2007) 305; Davey (1988) 110; Sloan *Informal Carers* (2012) 240; Wells *New Approach* (2007). By contrast, Ben McFarlane takes the view that that legislation is not necessary in England and that the doctrine of proprietary estoppel is well equipped to deal with testamentary promise cases. See McFarlane in *Current Issues* (2016) 77.

4
Establishing detrimental reliance on the promise

I. Introduction

In the absence of a contractually binding agreement over a future inheritance, or where proof of such an agreement might be difficult, one way for a promisee of a testamentary promise to obtain the promised asset may be to invoke the equitable doctrine of proprietary estoppel. The promisee can argue that the promisor has made a promise which she has relied upon to her detriment, and that the promisor should therefore be estopped from reneging on the promise, even though it was expressed informally, because it would be unconscionable for the promisor to go back on her promise. Such a course of action is available in many common law jurisdictions and captures many of the cases that form the subject matter of this book. The rationale for intervening is to prevent unconscionable behaviour on the part of the promisor and to protect the promisee's reliance on her promise.

The equitable doctrine of proprietary estoppel has its origins in English law where it has developed especially over the course of the past forty or so years,[1] but has also gained ground in other common law jurisdictions such as Australia, New Zealand, common law Canada,[2] and the Republic of Ireland. Although the doctrine has a wide scope of application, including the commercial context, 'many of the English cases crucial to its development ... involved an alleged testamentary promise'.[3] This would appear to have affected how the doctrine itself has developed.

The first English case in which the doctrine of proprietary estoppel was invoked in a testamentary promises context was *Re Basham*, which dates back to 1986.[4] The case is interesting because a contractual claim would have been difficult here (and was indeed not brought), not least because the promise made by the promisor was oral. In this instance, the promisee had worked for her stepfather, helping him to

[1] For an overview of the developments, see McFarlane *Law of Proprietary Estoppel* (2020).

[2] Interestingly, the cases seem to stem primarily from the province of Ontario. See *Belvedere v Brittain Estate* 2009 ONCA 1; 306 DLR (4th) 754 (Ont CA) in which the Ontario Court of Appeal rejected the claim because the promisee had not relied upon the promise nor suffered any loss. The proprietary estoppel claim was rejected also in *Schwark Estate v Cutting*, 2010 ONCA 61; 316 DLR (4th) 105. For successful cases, see *Cowderoy v Sorkos Estate*, 2012 ONSC 1921, *Zapfe v Zapfe*, 2015 ONSC 6508 and *Love v Schumacher*, 2014 ONSC 4080.

[3] McFarlane in *Current Issues* (2016) 77.

[4] *Re Basham* [1987] 1 All ER 405 (Ch); [1986] 1 WLR 1498 (hereafter *Re Basham*).

Claiming a Promised Inheritance. Alexandra Braun, Oxford University Press. © Alexandra Braun 2022.
DOI: 10.1093/oso/9780198757252.003.0005

run his business for over thirty years without receiving any payment. She did so on the oral assurance that she would inherit his property (which included a house) when he died. The promisee's husband did not get on well with the promisor. Nonetheless, he too provided food for the promisor, kept his garden in order and helped him with work around the house. The promisee had also bought carpets for the house and laid them herself, and she had regularly prepared meals for her stepfather. The stepfather died intestate, most likely not because he did not intend to keep his promise, but because he suffered from a severe stroke which led to his death within four days. During those four days he had confirmed, and indicated again by signs, that he wanted to make a will leaving money to the promisee's son and that the promisee was to have his house. However, the will was never made. On the death of the promisor, the promisee filed a claim against two of the promisor's nieces, who took the estate on intestacy, claiming that she was absolutely and beneficially entitled to the house, the furniture, and other property. Edward Nugee QC, sitting as a High Court judge, found that the claimant had successfully established that there had been a promise and that she had acted to her detriment in reliance on the belief, encouraged by the deceased promisor, that she would ultimately benefit from his property. The judge further found that, and this is important for the purposes of this enquiry, that the reliance did not have to be a belief relating to an existing right but that it could also concern a future right over an inheritance. Consequently, the stepdaughter was granted title to the promisor's residuary estate, including his house, although there had only been an oral promise. Thus, the lack of formality was not a bar to her claim.

Several other cases have followed since in which promisees of an informal promise of an inheritance have invoked the doctrine of proprietary estoppel. Although, the doctrine finds application in a variety of contexts, it is noticeable that in England and Wales, litigation mostly involves promisees who have carried out work on the promisor's farm in exchange for a promise of the farm,[5] and

[5] *Gillett v Holt* [2001] Ch 210 (CA) (hereafter *Gillett v Holt*); *Walton v Walton* (CA, 14 April 1994) (hereafter *Walton v Walton*); *Thorner v Major* [2009] UKHL 18; [2009] 1 WLR 776 (hereafter *Thorner v Major* 2009); *Suggitt v Suggitt* [2012] EWCA Civ 1140 (CA) (hereafter *Suggitt v Suggitt* 2012); *Davies v Davies* [2015] EWHC 1384 (Ch) (hereafter *Davies v Davies* 2015) and *Davies v Davies* [2016] EWCA Civ 5463 (hereafter *Davies v Davies* 2016); *Moore v Moore* [2018] EWCA Civ 2669 (hereafter *Moore v Moore* 2018); *Habberfield v Habberfield* [2019] EWCA Civ 890 (hereafter *Habberfield v Habberfield* 2019); *Thompson v Thompson* [2018] EWHC 1138 (Ch) (hereafter *Thompson v Thompson*); *Gee v Gee* [2018] EWHC 1393 (Ch) (hereafter *Gee v Gee*); *Guest v Guest* [2020] EWCA Civ 387 (hereafter *Guest v Guest* 2020). See also the unsuccessful claims in *Cook v Thomas* [2010] EWCA Civ 227 (hereafter *Cook v Thomas*); in *James v James* [2018] EWHC 43 (Ch) (hereafter *James v James*) and in *Shaw v Shaw* [2018] EWHC 3196 (Ch) (hereafter *Shaw v Shaw*). There are also several Irish cases dealing with farms, such as *Finnegan v Hand* [2016] IEHC 255; [2016] 3 JIC 1002 (hereafter *Finnegan v Hand*); *Coyle v Finnegan* [2013] IEHC 463; [2013] 10 JIC 2502 (hereafter *Coyle v Finnegan*); *Naylor v Maher* [2012] IEHC 408; [2012] 9 JIC 1401 (hereafter *Naylor v Maher*); and *K v K* [2018] IEHC 615 (hereafter *K v K*). For Australian examples, see *Waddell v Waddell* [2011] NSWSC 1174, (2012) 292 ALR 788 (hereafter *Waddell v Waddell*); *Lieschke v Lieschke* [2003] NSWSC 743 (hereafter *Lieschke v Lieschke*); and *Re Mahoney* [2015] VSC 600.

therefore involve, more often than not, men rather than women.[6] An explanation for this rise in farming cases may be that, as research shows, more than in other jurisdictions, in England and Wales, older farmers are reluctant to delegate and transfer their farm earlier on. In other words, they prefer to maintain control and postpone the transfer (and their retirement) to a later point in time, sometimes their death. While the next generation will usually prefer an earlier transfer, from the perspective of the farmer, the testamentary promise is a useful way of planning the succession of the farm without having to give up control. As mentioned in Chapter 1, Gasson and Errington have defined this as the 'Farmer's boy problem'.[7] Another reason for an increase in cases involving farms is perhaps also that the value of land holdings and real property has dramatically increased over the past forty years, so that claims are worth bringing.[8]

Farming aside, some cases deal with various forms of improvements to property belonging to the promisor,[9] work carried out in the context of her business,[10] or domestic/household and care services.[11] Just like a contractual claim, the scope of the doctrine of proprietary estoppel is broad enough to encompass a myriad of factual situations. While at the start of the 1970s, establishing the existence of a contract was probably still essential for a promisee to be able to obtain some form of redress in England and Wales,[12] this is no longer the case.[13] Claims based on the doctrine of proprietary estoppel have partly replaced those in which the claim is founded on contract law. The analysis will show that although the doctrine is sometimes invoked together with a contractual claim,[14] more often than not it is relied on in instances in which a contractual claim would have been difficult or simply impossible.

[6] Exceptions are *Davies v Davies* 2016 (n 5) and *Habberfield v Habberfield* 2019 (n 5).

[7] Gasson & Errington *Farm Family Business* (1993); Errington & Lobley (2002); Potter & Lobley (1992).

[8] In *Thompson v Thompson* (n 5) the value of the farm had increased from £255,000 in 1989 to £1.2–1.4 in 2018.

[9] See *Bradbury v Taylor* [2012] EWCA Civ 1208 (hereafter *Bradbury v Taylor*); *Vukic v Grbin* [2006] NSWSC 41; *Estephan v Estephan* [2012] NSWSC 52 (hereafter *Estephan v Estephan*); and *Evans v Evans* [2011] NSWCA 92 (hereafter *Evans v Evans*).

[10] *Re Basham* (n 4) and *Lothian v Dixon* (Ch, 28 November 2014) (hereafter *Lothian v Dixon*). For an unsuccessful case relating to a family business, see *McDonald v Rose* [2018] EWHC 445 (Ch).

[11] *Jennings v Rice* [2002] EWCA 159 (hereafter *Jennings v Rice*); *Estephan v Estephan* (n 9). Lord Walker extra-judicially discusses some of these cases that he defines as 'assistance' cases. Walker (2008) 234.

[12] Lloyd LJ in *Thorner v Major* [2008] EWCA Civ 732, [32] (hereafter *Thorner v Major* 2008).

[13] Nowadays instances in which a contract is alleged tend to concern primarily cases regarding promises to make mutual wills. Examples are *Fry v Densham-Smith* [2010] EWCA Civ 1410 and *Charles v Fraser* [2010] EWHC 2154.

[14] In *Giumelli v Giumelli* [1999] 196 CLR 101 (HC) (hereafter *Giumelli v Giumelli*), the contractual claim failed, but the estoppel claim was granted. In *Ashton v Pratt* (No 2) [2012] NSWSC 3 both the contract and the estoppel claim failed. In *Smith v Taylor* [2006] NSWSC 162 the judge granted the estoppel claim and was of the opinion that he did not need to ascertain whether there was a contract or a constructive trust.

The surge of proprietary estoppel claims is not entirely surprising, given that in England and Wales, in the absence of writing (required if land is involved), a contractual claim is precluded because the doctrine of part-performance is no longer available to promisees.[15] Also, a proprietary estoppel claim dispenses with the need to prove the existence of a contract, including an intention to create a legal relationship and the requirement of writing, where applicable. Although the relief does not necessarily lead to an award of what was promised, there are several English, Irish, and Australian cases in which promisees have successfully invoked the doctrine of proprietary estoppel and obtained what had been promised to them by the deceased. What is more, even though the promisee has to meet certain requirements, as we will see, on the whole, courts have been fairly liberal in interpreting them. This has not gone unnoticed in legal scholarship and, as we shall see in greater detail later,[16] developments have attracted criticism from those who fear that the doctrine has been taken too far, the court's discretion in these cases is too wide, and the relief awarded (at times) too generous, so that the doctrine could potentially undermine fundamental principles of property and succession law.

The aim of this chapter is to examine the scope of the doctrine of proprietary estoppel, what requirements promisees must meet, how awards are being quantified, and to evaluate the extent to which the doctrine is capable of protecting the promisee's interests in an effective manner. The analysis will focus primarily on developments in English law, where there has been a host of cases, with some references to Australian and Irish cases. We will see that, while some aspects of the operation of the doctrine are still uncertain, on the whole, the doctrine is sensitive to the context in which informal testamentary promises are being expressed and able to protect the interests of a wide range of promisees. The analysis will also show that while some scholars are critical of the development of the doctrine of proprietary estoppel, many of the objections raised are unfounded or can be overcome.

II. The requirements

As Robert Walker LJ has put it in *Gillett v Holt* (2001), the 'doctrine of proprietary estoppel cannot be treated as subdivided into three or four watertight compartments'.[17] Much is still contentious, and academic attempts to map the law in this area are fairly recent.[18] However, there is agreement that three requirements must be satisfied: an assurance, reliance, and detriment. While these must be chronologically ordered, they are usually closely related and sometimes overlapping.

[15] See Chapter 3, section II.D.
[16] See below section V.
[17] *Gillett v Holt* (n 5) 225.
[18] For a comprehensive study, see McFarlane *Proprietary Estoppel* (2020).

Unconscionability seems to permeate all three elements but is not regarded as an additional requirement.[19] While 'the court must look at the matter in the round',[20] it is important here to consider each requirement in turn. We shall see that courts have tended to interpret the three requirements in a broad manner, taking into account the context in which the testamentary arrangements are taking place.

A. A promise

For a promisee to succeed, the promisor needs to have made an express or implied promise of an inheritance.[21] Although courts have used different expressions, sometimes referring to promises, and sometimes to representations, assurances, or encouragements, they have been clear that a promisee's reliance on her own belief is not enough, and neither is a mere intention of the promisor to leave something by will. For that intention to produce any effect, a will must be executed in the form required by law.[22] In other words, courts draw a distinction between a statement of current intentions concerning a future conduct and a *promise* of that conduct.[23] While the line may often be a fine one, only the latter will suffice for the purposes of a proprietary estoppel claim.

Even though proof of an express or implied promise is required, unlike with a contractual claim, there is no need to prove an intention to bring into existence a legally binding contract.[24] This is important because, as we have seen, the parties often lack such an intention. Writing is also not required, which makes this doctrine more suitable to the testamentary context and attractive to promisees. Even if a promisor, prompted by the promisee, refuses to enter into a formal contract, or to commit a promise to writing, this will not, by itself, preclude a claim.[25] For instance, in the English case of *Gillett v Holt* (2001), the promisor had declined to comply with the request to provide something in writing to confirm his promise, but this did not stand in the way of a proprietary estoppel award. Equally, the promisee's awareness that the will itself can be revoked does not bar a claim. Finally, as the decision in *Guest v Guest* (2019) shows,[26] even the fact that a promisor later writes a

[19] This is argued by McFarlane in *Jurisprudence of Lord Hoffmann* (2015) 353. This view is not, however, shared by Dixon in *Modern Studies II* (2003).

[20] *Gillett v Holt* (n 5) 225.

[21] This chapter will only deal with cases of estoppel by promise and omit cases of estoppel by acquiescence or representation. See McFarlane *Proprietary Estoppel* (2020) ch 2. McGee *Snell's Equity* (2020) para 12-036-12-036a.

[22] See Lloyd LJ in *Thorner v Major* 2008 (n 12) [68]. The formality requirements for wills are set out in s 9 of the Wills Act 1837.

[23] See, *James v James* (n 5) [24].

[24] This was clarified by Hoffmann LJ in *Walton v Walton* (n 5) where his Lordship rejected the first instance judge's finding that there is a need for the words to have intended to create a legal obligation. See also the Australian case *Evans v Evans* (n 9).

[25] McGee *Snell's Equity* (2020) para 12-042.

[26] *Guest v Guest* [2019] EWHC 869 (Ch) (hereafter *Guest v Guest* 2019) [12].

letter accompanying his new will (in this case made after the parties had fallen out with one another), in which she says, 'I have never promised any of my children any sort of inheritance', does not prevent the finding of a promise.

1. ... that is clear and unequivocal ...

Although the promise can be oral and implied from conduct, it must be sufficiently clear and unequivocal. Sufficient clarity depends on the context;[27] even vague or indirect promises that would not establish a contractual claim can sometimes suffice. The doctrine of proprietary estoppel therefore is able to capture many of the testamentary promises cases in which the existence of a contract cannot be established. For instance, in the seminal decision of *Thorner v Major* (2009), the House of Lords was faced with a claim from a man (David Thorner) who, for nearly thirty years, had done substantial work on the farm of his father's cousin (Peter Thorner), without being paid.[28] Peter Thorner had made various oblique remarks (including handing over to David Thorner in 1990 an insurance policy bonus notice with the words 'that's for my death duties') which led David Thorner to expect that he would inherit the farm. Although Peter Thorner had made a will in favour of David Thorner, he had later destroyed the will and eventually died intestate so that the property went to his next of kin. At that point, David Thorner claimed that Peter Thorner's estate was bound by conscience to give him the farm by way of proprietary estoppel. At first instance, John Randall QC found that a claim of proprietary estoppel had been established and thus ruled in favour of David Thorner. The Court of Appeal, however, allowed the defendants' appeal on the grounds that the deceased's implicit statements did *not* amount to a clear and unequivocal representation upon which he had intended the claimant to rely. David Thorner appealed, and the House of Lords reversed the Court of Appeal decision in his favour. The court found that whether a representation had sufficient clarity to establish a propriety estoppel claim, was dependent on *the context* in which it had been made. The court held that the specific context of that case was unusual because it concerned two taciturn and undemonstrative men who communicated obliquely but understood each other well.[29] While a contractual claim would have no doubt failed in this instance, an estoppel claim did not, so that David Thorner was awarded the farm and associated assets of a net value that the Court of Appeal estimated at £2.1 million. Thus, in *Thorner v Major*, the House of Lord adopted a wide interpretation of the notion of 'promise', stressing the importance of the context in which the representations or assurances were made, including the personality of

[27] *Thorner v Major* (n 5) [56] where Lord Walker of Gestingthorpe states: 'the relevant assurance must be clear enough. What amounts to sufficient clarity, in a case of this sort, is hugely dependent on context'. See also [84]–[86] (Lord Neuberger of Abbotsbury).

[28] Ibid.

[29] *Thorner v Major* (n 5) [26]. Communication problems between the promisor and promisee also existed in *Guest v Guest* 2019 (n 26) [230].

the parties and their interaction and communication.[30] This suggests that while, in general, the domestic context works against the promisee when she tries to establish a contract to make a will, this is not necessarily the case with a proprietary estoppel claim because the court is able to take into account the circumstances in which the promise was made, including the particular relationship and character of the parties. However, as I will discuss, this does not mean that societal expectations do not play a role.

A similarly liberal approach to the notion of promise was taken by the Court of Appeal in *Suggitt v Suggitt* (2012), a controversial case decided a couple of years later.[31] The claimant was the son of a farmer who, upon his death, left his entire estate to one of his daughters with the express wish that if at any time his son showed himself capable of working or managing the farmland, it should be transferred to him. The son contended that during his life his father had repeatedly promised the farm to him on his death, and that he was therefore entitled to part of the estate that was comprised of farmland, buildings, and a business bank account. As a child, he had helped his father on the farm and partially completed a course to learn farming skills. He argued that he had also assisted his father in doing jobs on the farm, save for a period when they had become estranged because he had not received any wages. He filed a claim against the executors of his father's estate (one of his sisters and his father's accountant) based on proprietary estoppel. Even though Roger Kaye QC, sitting as a High Court judge, regarded the father's assurances as 'opaque to say the least',[32] he awarded the promisee the farmland and a property to live in, for an aggregate value of some £3.3 million, though not the money in the business accounts nor the other assets beyond incidental farm machinery.

The decision was taken on the basis that 'it was more likely than not that the deceased had repeatedly promised his son that he would inherit his farm'. Although the evidence of such testamentary promises was arguably even less clear-cut than in *Thorner v Major*, Roger Kaye QC was prepared to find a promise. On appeal, Arden LJ, with whom Sullivan LJ and Sir Nicholas Wall concurred, found that the court could not interfere with the finding in the first instance (i.e. that there had been an unconditional promise as well as reliance and detriment) unless the judgment was perverse or clearly wrong, which it did not find to be the case. The appeal was rejected.

The two cases show that where a contractual claim would almost certainly fail, with the aid of equity, a promisee may still be able to obtain the promised inheritance, which can be of significant economic value, by basing her action on the doctrine of proprietary estoppel. Finally, they demonstrate that context plays an

30 This is noticeable also in *Gee v Gee* (n 5) [116]: 'JR was a man of his word, not given to idle discussions about such things and not given to changing his mind at all. When JR talked about matters of this kind, which was not often, he meant what he said and expected people to understand that.'

31 *Suggitt v Suggitt* 2012 (n 5).

32 Ibid, [45].

important role and that depending on the context, courts are willing to find that a promise has been made even if it has to be implied from indirect statements and conduct. This is confirmed also by the first instance decision in *Thompson v Thompson* (2018) where the promisee was unable to identify precise words used on precise occasions, but was nonetheless able to establish a promise.[33]

The facts that (i) courts are willing to imply promises from vague statements[34] and (ii) what amounts to a promise depends on the context can undoubtedly benefit the promisee. At the same time it inevitably creates a certain level of uncertainty especially given that the same words have given rise to a claim in some cases but not in others.[35] For instance, in *Cook v Thomas* (2010), the Court of Appeal found that the deceased's words, that the property is 'all going to be yours when I am gone', did *not* amount to a testamentary promise.[36] Yet the words were virtually identical to those expressed in *Gillett v Holt*, where the applicant had been successful. Although the Court of Appeal in *Cook v Thomas* noted the similarity in wording, it distinguished *Gillett v Holt* on the basis that the circumstances were different,[37] including the facts that in *Gillett v Holt*: (i) the claimant's relationship with the promisor was not a familial one; and (ii) the services were rendered over many years, that is over thirty rather than six years. Similar words were also used in *Wayling v Jones* (1995)[38] and in *Jennings v Rice* (2002),[39] and in both cases the claim was granted. Here the context in which the words were spoken is again important.[40] Sometimes the context clearly speaks against a promise. This was, for instance, the case in the English decision of *James v James* (2018),[41] where the testator was generally reluctant to make any commitments.[42] In fact, various letters that the accountant had written to the claimant referred to the fact that his father (who was

[33] *Thompson v Thompson* (n 5) [149]: 'Although this is not a case where it is possible to pinpoint a specific occasion on which this promise or assurance was given, I am satisfied that it is a very long standing promise or assurance, repeated within the family and to Gilbert, (and others) on many many occasions from when he was fairly young and starting to work full time on the Farm. I am satisfied that these promises or assurances were made by both Parents consistently over time.'

[34] In other common law jurisdictions courts are also willing to interpret the requirements of a promise broadly, so as to take into account the context. This is shown, for instance, in the Australian case of *Sullivan v Sullivan & Ors* [2006] NSWCA 312 where the deceased had written inside a Christmas card to his sister that he would provide her with a home 'to live in as long as you like', which was to be her 'home for life', with the requirement to pay minimal rent after the first year. At first instance the claim was rejected but on appeal, the Court of Appeal of New South Wales found that the representation in the Christmas card had been sufficiently certain, though the court did not provide the promisee with her expectation interest. Another example is *Lieschke v Lieschke* (n 5).

[35] For instance, while the Court of Appeal in *Thorner v Major* 2008 (n 12) did not find a promise, the House of Lords did (n 5). In *Walton v Walton* (n 5), the first instance judge did not find a promise while on appeal the Court of Appeal did.

[36] *Cook v Thomas* (n 5).

[37] Ibid, [76].

[38] *Wayling v Jones* [1995] 2 FLR 1029 (hereafter *Wayling v Jones*).

[39] *Jennings v Rice* (n 11).

[40] *James v James* (n 5) [33].

[41] The decision was reviewed critically by Carroll (2018).

[42] *James v James* (n 5).

still alive) had not been prepared to talk about his future intentions.[43] In the words of the judge, '[t]hat was not his character. As Sam [the claimant] himself recognised and admitted, he [the deceased] wanted to preserve his freedom of action as long as he possibly could'.[44]

However, precisely because context plays a role, and words are examined in the light of that context, including the nature of the relationship between the parties, societal expectations come into play. In this respect, McFarlane has argued that an alleged promise will be easier to find where the claimant has, for instance, embarked on a course of conduct which, in the absence of any promise would be difficult to explain, for example, to work on a farm for no pay for a long period of time.[45] The aforementioned cases illustrate that the fact that a promisee is not a close family member (as was the case in *Gillett v Holt* but also in *Jennings v Rice*) can play a role, as it is assumed that someone unrelated to the promisor would not have performed certain services for free especially when they are rendered over a long period of time. Other promisees, particularly family members, could thus have greater difficulties proving the promise, unless what they do exceeds what is regarded as *normal*.[46] That said, the most recent farming cases involving children do not suggest that that is the case, though in many of them the promisee's performance was substantial not just in terms of daily efforts but also length of time.

2. … that is reasonably understood as seriously intended

Although it is not necessary for the promisee to believe that the promise was legally binding, it has to be reasonable for her to conclude that the promise was seriously intended. This confirms, as I have argued in Chapter 1,[47] that promisors can seriously intend a promise without intending to be legally bound, and thus without framing the promise in contractual terms. But when can a promisee reasonably believe a promise to be seriously intended? The answer depends again on the context. The factual context must make it reasonable to believe that the person expressed a commitment to making a testamentary gift. McFarlane argues that 'the mere fact of a promise having been made in a family context does not render such a belief unreasonable'. I would go a step further and argue that it is precisely *because* the promise is made in the family context that the belief that there is a commitment should be regarded as reasonable. After all, we are more likely to leave property to those who are close to us. For that reason, we are more likely to trust a gift-promise made by a family member or someone close to us. Were the promise to leave a future inheritance to come from a perfect stranger, it would surely be less reasonable to regard it as seriously intended.

43 Ibid, [25]–[26].
44 Ibid, [37].
45 McFarlane in *Current Issues* (2016) 89.
46 See the discussion in Chapter 2, section III.C.3.
47 See Chapter 1.

That said, the promise does not have to be irrevocable. The promisor does not have to say that she regards the testamentary promise as irrevocable. Rather, the promise becomes irrevocable once detriment on the part of the promisee is established.[48] This is important in that the promisee neither needs to show that the promise was intended to be irrevocable, which is not easy to do, nor that the promisor assumed the obligation, and thus became bound, during her lifetime. I shall return to this point later when refuting the argument that a proprietary estoppel award infringes the promisor's testamentary freedom.[49]

3. The subject matter of the promise

So far, we have seen that courts have been willing to find a promise for the purpose of an estoppel claim even when the words used are vague and generic, or when it needs to be implied from the circumstances. But how specific must the subject matter of the promise be? The answer is still somewhat contentious, at least in England and Wales. It is clear that changes to the character or the extent of the property will not defeat a claim. It is uncertain, however, whether the promise has to identify a particular asset. If that were the case, many testamentary promises cases could not be addressed through the doctrine of proprietary estoppel.

In *Re Basham*, being the first English proprietary estoppel case dealing with a promise of an inheritance,[50] the court found that the promise need *not* concern a specifically identified asset.[51] In fact, in that case, the promise was to leave the promisee the 'deceased's property', which included a house but also other assets. However, this position was called into question by Lord Walker in the House of Lords decision in *Thorner v Major*, also referred to earlier, where his Lordship stated that:

> it is a necessary element of proprietary estoppel that the assurances given to the claimant (expressly or impliedly, or, in standing-by cases, tacitly) should relate to identified property owned (or, perhaps, about to be owned)[52] by the defendant … It is the relation to identified land of the defendant that has enabled proprietary estoppel to develop as a sword, and not merely as a shield.[53]

48 See *Gillett v Holt* (n 5) 227–229 where *Taylor v Dickens* [1998] 1 FLR 806 (Ch) (hereafter *Taylor v Dickens*) was disapproved. See also *Uglo v Uglo* [2004] EWCA Civ 987, [9].

49 See section V.B.

50 *Re Basham* (n 4).

51 In *Mulholland v Kane* [2009] NICh 9 the promise did not concern a specific part of the property, but this did not stand in the way of a proprietary estoppel claim. See McFarlane *Proprietary Estoppel* (2020) 101.

52 In the recent decision of the Canadian Supreme Court in *Cowper-Smith v Morgan* [2017] 2 SCR 754, the promise regarded an ownership interest in a house. The Court of Appeal for British Columbia held that because this was a promise over a future interest the claim should fail, but the Supreme Court of Canada found differently. The majority held that a proprietary estoppel claim can arise even where a promisor had no ownership interest in the property at the time the promise was made.

53 *Thorner v Major* (n 5) [63]. In *Southwell v Blackburn* [2014] EWCA Civ 1347, [7] Tomlinson LJ found that 'the promise must be of a right in relation to identified land'.

This interpretation would suggest that if a promisor promised to leave all or part of her residuary estate, the promisee may not be able to avail herself of the protection provided by the doctrine of proprietary estoppel. However, according to McFarlane, 'Lord Walker's concerns notwithstanding, there is no reason for adopting a general rule that a proprietary estoppel claim can never arise from a promise to leave B all or a specified part of A's residuary estate.'[54] In fact, McFarlane and Sales maintain that the line of authority invoked by Lord Walker in *Thorner v Major* provides no real support for this limitation,[55] and I tend to agree with them.

Arguably, recent cases show that the contrary is indeed true. The entire estate was, for instance, promised in *Lothian v Dixon* (2014),[56] and the proprietary estoppel claim was nonetheless granted. In *Suggitt v Suggitt*, mentioned earlier, the promise was vague in the sense that it referred to 'farmland', but again this was not regarded as problematic. In *Davies v Davies* (2016) the content of the promise to the daughter changed throughout the years, at times including the entire farm and, at others, involving a share in the company.[57] This did not prevent the court from granting her claim, though, as we will see later,[58] it affected the relief she was granted. Equally, in *Guest v Guest*, the expectations shifted and diminished over time, as the promisee first assumed that he would take over the entire farm and later realized that he would inherit it jointly with this brother.[59] This did not, however, prevent his claim. Indeed, Judge Russen QC stressed that, 'the equitable doctrine obviously admits of more flexibility, in terms of certainty of interest, than the law of contract' and that 'uncertainty over the specific interest to be acquired, in the identified property, should not be fatal to a proprietary estoppel claim'.[60] In *Habberfield v Habberfield* (2018), where the promisor said that the daughter should receive a 'viable dairy farm at Woodrow', which was a large farm, this was not regarded as an obstacle to the daughter's claim. Birss J stated that:

> I have asked myself whether the fact that the representations were not understood to promise 100% of the farm to Lucy or promise something specific about the circumstances surrounding a conveyance, mean that they were not sufficiently certain to be relied on. I find that they are sufficiently certain. They were focussed

[54] McFarlane in *Current Issues* (2016) 87.

[55] See McFarlane & Sales (2015) 621ff.

[56] *Lothian v Dixon* (n 10).

[57] *Davies v Davies* 2016 (n 5). Interestingly, in *Habberfield v Habberfield* [2018] EWHC 317 (Ch) (hereafter *Habberfield v Habberfield* 2018) [225] Birss J distinguished the facts from those in *Davies v Davies* with 'a series of different expectations and mutually incompatible expectations over the years (cf Lewison LJ para 48). In this case a single promise was made albeit in different guises and reinforced over a single long period.'

[58] Section III.B.

[59] *Guest v Guest* 2019 (n 26) [142]–[143]. In *Gee v Gee* (n 5) [119] the fact that the representations did not enter into the details of shareholdings or land holdings did not render them uncertain.

[60] *Guest v Guest* 2019 (n 26) [237]–[240]. The sentence 'one day this will all be yours' was judged to be specific enough to identify the farm.

> on something concrete, the dairy farm. The fact that one could not draw a bright line at some point in the 1980s or 1990s and say that land on one side had been promised to Lucy whereas land on the other side had not been, does not undermine their seriousness nor does the fact that the precise way in which the transfer would be undertaken was undecided.[61]

Thus, for the judge, the promise was sufficiently certain with regards to the subject matter.[62] If a proprietary estoppel claim can be brought even though the promisee was promised unspecified property, or the entire estate or part of it, then she seems to be better off where the promise does not amount to a contract. For, as we saw in Chapter 3,[63] if there is a contract to leave the residuary estate, the promisee can only ever obtain damages and not specific performance, and she is treated as a beneficiary under a will rather than as a creditor, meaning that her position vis-à-vis third parties is weak. By contrast, with a proprietary estoppel claim she may be able to obtain a proprietary remedy capable of binding third parties, placing her in a very strong position vis-à-vis third parties, including creditors and third-party transferees.

B. Reliance

The second requirement for a successful proprietary estoppel claim is reliance on the promise. Reliance establishes the connection between the promise and the detriment that the promisee would suffer if the promisor were free to go back on her promise.[64] While the claimant needs to prove the promise and the detriment, the burden of proof regarding the lack of reliance is on the promisor or her successors.[65] Once it has been established that a promise has been made, the defendant is required to show that the promisee did *not* rely on it in any respect.[66] This helps the promisee, who would otherwise have to prove her motives, which can be factually difficult and, as noted earlier, also embarrassing, for the motives are likely to be mixed.[67]

The exact test to be applied by the courts in determining whether a particular action or inaction of the promisee amounts to reliance is somewhat uncertain.

61 *Habberfield v Habberfield* 2018 (n 57) [105].
62 Ibid, [206].
63 Chapter 3.
64 McFarlane *Proprietary Estoppel* (2020) 145ff.
65 In *Walton v Walton* (n 5) Hoffmann LJ stated that 'as Balcombe LJ said in that case: "Once it has been established that promises were made, and that there has been conduct by the plaintiff of such a nature that inducement may be inferred, then the burden shifts to the defendants to establish that he did not rely on the promises . . ."'.
66 Malek *Phipson on Evidence* (2013) para 5-40. See *Wayling v Jones* (n 38) 173.
67 See the discussion in Chapter 2.

The question was addressed by the Court of Appeal in the unreported English case of *Walton v Walton* (1994). The court upheld the claim of a son who had worked for low pay, long hours, and almost twenty-nine years on a family farm that belonged to his mother.[68] He had spent money on maintenance and improvements to the farm, 'on the assumption that the land would one day be his'. The son had frequently complained about his low wages and his mother had consistently met those complaints by assuring him that his reward lay in the future: her stock phrase was that 'You can't have more money and a farm one day'. As is so often the case in litigation involving promises of an inheritance, over the years the relationship between the mother and son deteriorated. The judge described the mother as a difficult person whose behaviour drove not just her son, but also her friends, away. When the mother died, the son discovered that she had attempted to sell the farm during her lifetime and that she had made a will that did not include him. At that point he brought a proprietary estoppel claim. Unlike the first instance judge, who found against the son, the Court of Appeal established that there had been a promise and that the son had acted in reliance on the promise by incurring expenses and making sacrifices he would not otherwise have made. Similarly to what Hoffmann LJ had already done in the earlier decision of *Wayling v Jones*, he examined the element of reliance as follows:

> when a promise has been made, one does not test reliance by asking what the plaintiff would have done if it had never been made. One asks what he would have done if, the promise having been made, he had been told that it would not be kept.[69]

In the case in question, Hoffmann LJ concluded, and Glidewell LJ agreed, that all three requirements, including reliance, were satisfied, and that the claimant should obtain the farm subject to the existing mortgage.[70] This suggests that, as is the case with the requirement of a promise, when considering reliance, courts take the context into account. However, as Lloyd LJ noted in *Thorner v Major*, one of the difficulties for the promisee may be that 'the relationship between the parties is often such that it could plausibly be argued that the recipient of the statement would have done just the same whether or not the statement had been made'.[71] The promisee may thus find herself in the difficult and awkward position of having to defend herself by arguing that she acted not out of love, but rather because of the promise and the prospect of the inheritance.[72] At the same time, one could indeed argue that

68 *Walton v Walton* (n 5).
69 Ibid.
70 McFarlane in *Jurisprudence of Lord Hoffmann* (2015) 336, criticizes the family friendly departures from the standard causation tests.
71 *Thorner v Major* 2008 (n 12) [63].
72 See the analogy with the difficulties promisees encounter in the context of an enrichment claim discussed in Chapters 6 and 9.

by putting the question as suggested by Hoffmann LJ—what the promisee 'would have done had she been told that the promise would not be kept'—the answer will most likely be that 'they would have left the farm' or that they would have 'stopped the performance of care services'. This somewhat tempers or pre-empts the risk of an argument that the promisee would have worked on the farm or the business anyway out of love and affection. In other words, posing the question in these terms arguably assists the promisee.

Also, and importantly, the courts have taken the view that the promise need not be the *sole* reason for why the promisee performed a certain service,[73] it being perfectly acceptable that she may have had more than one motive to act as she did.[74] In *Campbell v Griffin & Ors* (2001), the Court of Appeal found that mixed motives did not stand in the way of a finding of reliance. The claimant had admitted under cross-examination that 'he would not in any event have ignored his elderly landlord ... if he had been lying on the floor, and had not eaten for two days'.[75] Robert Walker LJ concluded that 'it would do no credit to the law if an honest witness who admitted that he had mixed motives were to fail in a claim which might have succeeded if supported by less candid evidence'.[76] Similarly, in *Murphy v Burrows* (2004) it was found that the claimant would have done some of the work (i.e. looking after the promisor's pigs, driving him to the pub on Fridays, taking meals, and having his washing done) anyway out of a sense of 'family obligation'. Again, this did not stand in the way of the judge finding an estoppel.[77] Also interesting is *Wayling v Jones*,[78] for the court upheld the claim to the promised inheritance despite the fact that the claimant had stated that he would have stayed with the promisor even if no testamentary promise had been made.[79] However, it has been argued that it may have mattered in this case that the claim involved two homosexual men who at the time could not have benefitted from a family provision order.[80] And the decision has been criticized for being based on the judge's gendered assumptions about what

[73] McFarlane *Proprietary Estoppel* (2020) 163–164. According to McFarlane, in *Grundy v Ottey* [2003] EWCA Civ 1176 (hereafter *Grundy v Ottey*) it was not clear whether the promise had caused the promisee to change her behaviour, and yet the claim was granted. McFarlane in *Current Issues* (2016) 96.

[74] This was, for instance, the case in *Thorner v Major* (n 5) discussed in section II.A.1 and *Walton v Walton* (n 5) discussed in section II.B.

[75] *Campbell v Griffin Ors* [2001] EWCA Civ 990 (hereafter *Campbell v Griffin Ors*).

[76] Ibid, [29]. See also *Gill v Woodall & Ors* [2009] EWHC 3778 (Ch), [516].

[77] *Murphy v Burrows* [2004] EWHC 1900 (Ch).

[78] *Wayling v Jones* (n 38). The case is further interesting because the courts went a step further speaking of a presumption of reliance. The presumption is referred to also in *Greasley v Cooke* [1980] 1 WLR 1306 (CA). This approach assists the promisee, though it also broadens the scope of the doctrine. *Wayling v Jones* was indeed criticized for indulging the promisee and for distorting the principles of proprietary estoppel. See McFarlane *Proprietary Estoppel* (2020) 195. That said, it appears to have gained little acceptance amongst the judiciary. McGee *Snell's Equity* (2020) para 12-043.

[79] *Wayling v Jones* (n 38).

[80] See McFarlane in *Current Issues* (2016) 95. As we will see in Chapter 5, family provision legislation provides for the maintenance of certain members of the family or dependants of the deceased, who have not been adequately provided for either in the deceased's will or on intestacy. The legislation may provide a route for some promisees to obtain some form of redress.

could be expected from a male claimant in the context of a caring relationship with a property owner.[81] Even so, the fact that the promise must not represent the sole motive is crucial from the perspective of the promisee, as otherwise many promisees would fail to bring a successful claim. It also shows that the courts are aware of, and take into account once more, the context in which these promises are made.

To summarize, while there is need to show reliance, the burden of proof to show its lack is on the defendant. This helps the promisee, though she may still have to prove that she acted because of the promise and not solely out of love and affection. Also, the promise does not have to be the sole motive for the promisee's behaviour. However, just as we have seen with contractual claims, when establishing a proprietary estoppel claim, societal expectations concerning certain types of work, certain relationships, and gender can sometimes work against a promisee.

C. Detriment

Promise and reliance aside, the third requirement to be met is detriment. Reliance and detriment often overlap and are therefore not easily distinguishable. However, despite being closely connected, they must be satisfied individually.[82] While '[r]eliance is what a person does on the faith of some matter ... detriment is usually the result'.[83] There must also be a causal link between the two, and there must be a sufficient link between the promises relied upon and the conduct which constitutes the detriment.[84] This does not mean that the conduct giving rise to the detriment must be directly related to the promisor's land,[85] which was necessary for the operation of the doctrine of part-performance as discussed in Chapter 3.[86] Again, this is significant, as it would otherwise disadvantage those promisees who, in reliance on the promise, provide domestic or care services, rather than improving the deceased's property.

Case law concerning testamentary promises reveals that the detriment can consist, for example, in not being paid for one's personal services, in the expenditure of money or the making of improvements to the promisor's property (i.e. on a farm), in being prevented from buying, or living in, their own house,[87] in choosing not to take up another career path,[88] or in moving in with the promisor.[89] Thus,

[81] See Flynn & Lawson (1995) 121, who have argued that it is less likely that a female non-owning claimant who was in Wayling's situation would have been successful.

[82] *Suggitt v Suggitt* 2012 (n 5).

[83] Ibid, [35].

[84] In *Jones v Watkins* (26 November 1987, unreported), Slade LJ said that 'the more vague the promise alleged, the more clear should be the evidence of detriment incurred in reliance on the promise'.

[85] McGee *Snell's Equity* (2020) para 12-044.

[86] Chapter 3, section II.D. In Chapter 6 we will see that a similar link is necessary for the court to establish a constructive trust in common law Canada.

[87] See *Thompson v Thompson* (n 5) [157].

[88] *Davies v Davies* 2015 (n 5) where the son did not become a police officer.

[89] *Bradbury v Taylor* (n 9).

detrimental reliance is not merely a financial matter.[90] It is also recognized that the promisee may have made personal sacrifices and given up the possibility of a different and better life.[91] Again, this suits the context in which testamentary promises are made. For instance, in *Davies v Davies* the Court of Appeal found that had the daughter left her parents' farm '[s]he would have been able to work shorter hours in a working environment of her choosing. Furthermore, she would have been free of the difficult working relationship she had with her parents.'[92] In *Henry v Henry* (2010), the Privy Council held that the detriment did not merely consist of the fact that by remaining on the plot of land the promisee had benefitted the promisor with food and care, but also that he had 'effectively deprived himself of the opportunity of a better life elsewhere'.[93] Thus, courts consider not only professional but also personal sacrifices, including those that come with relocating to a different place.

This emerges also from the decision in *Bradbury and Taylor* (2012).[94] After the death of his wife, the promisor had lived alone in his large house in Cornwall. With time he became increasingly concerned about living alone and therefore sought to persuade his nephew and the nephew's wife to leave Sheffield and to move to Cornwall together with their two children, and to live with him, on the basis of an oral promise that he would leave the house to them. A few years later relations soured, and the promisee eventually discovered that the uncle had changed his will and no longer intended to leave the property to them as promised. The uncle sought a declaration that the nephew and his wife had no beneficial interest in the property and were no more than licensees or tenants. He died a few months later, and, when the matter came to trial, Judge Griggs found in favour of the couple, holding them to be entitled to receive the house subject to the payment of inheritance tax. The judge found that the promisees had moved to the property in Cornwall on the basis of the uncle's promises that he would leave the house to them subject to certain conditions, including that they had to continue living there for seven years after his death. The judge determined that despite the fact that the promisee had obtained a number of benefits, the move to Cornwall, in addition to contributions made to the promisor's care, and improvements to the property, amounted to detrimental

[90] In *Jennings v Rice* (n 11) the promisee gave up his spare time. Thus, there is no need to give up an employment. See also the Canadian case of *Sabey v Beardsley* 2013 BCSC 642, [63] (Meyers J) where the claimant had given up what he wanted to do in life (to become a professional dressage rider) and had oriented his work in a way to stay as close as possible to the farm.

[91] The detriment can also consist of giving up a potential claim against the deceased. For instance, in the Australian case *Harrison v Harrison* [2013] VSCA 170 (hereafter *Harrison v Harrison*), the daughters of the deceased had been induced to give up a claim for relief under Part IV of the Administration and Probate Act 1958 (Vic). The difficulty was therefore to establish whether such a claim would have been successful had it been brought.

[92] *Davies v Davies* 2016 (n 5) [65].

[93] *Henry v Henry* [2010] UKPC 3; [2010] 1 All ER 988, [61]–[62] (hereafter *Henry v Henry*).

[94] *Bradbury v Taylor* (n 9).

reliance, such that the promisee was entitled to the whole of the property. The decision was upheld on appeal.[95]

The level of detriment incurred is ascertained through a holistic analysis. This also means that disadvantages suffered by the promisee are weighed against any countervailing advantages,[96] such as, for instance, free accommodation that the promisor provides for the promisee. Thus, while moving in with the promisor can represent detriment, it must be weighed against benefits that derive from free accommodation.

The detriment has to be that which would be caused to the promisee if the promisor were free to act entirely as she wishes and must be judged at the point where the person who has given the assurance seeks to go back on it.[97] Because the promisee's potential detriment is not necessarily assessed immediately after her reliance, the promisee's reliance does not have to be immediately detrimental.[98] At the same time, countervailing benefits acquired after that initial reliance must also be taken into account when evaluating the detriment.[99]

Again, overall courts seem to take a liberal approach to the finding of such detriment. For instance, on the basis of the facts in *Suggitt v Suggitt*, discussed earlier,[100] it is arguably questionable whether the son had suffered any real detriment. Even though the first instance judge found that he did not work as hard, or as long, as, for instance, the claimant in *Thorner v Major*, he concluded that the son had 'positioned his whole life on the basis of the assurances given to him'.[101] While John Mee is right in pointing out that '[t]he work John [the son] did on the farm was limited by the fact that his father, having no faith in him to run the farm, had leased most of it to third parties',[102] the son did not do a good job and was on the whole a disappointment. He had had effectively run away to York and spent his inheritance from a great aunt before returning to the farm when the money had run out. In a way, the son had little choice but to return, which makes it at least questionable whether there was detrimental reliance. Yet, the promisee was awarded the farm, which is one of the reasons why this decision has been criticized in legal scholarship.[103] This suggests that the approach of the courts to the quantum of the relief is not always

95 Ibid, [26]. Although Lloyd LJ's judgment does not refer to the relevant figures, newspaper reports indicate that the house was valued at £800,000.

96 *Henry v Henry* (n 93) [51].

97 *Gillett v Holt* (n 5) 232.

98 McFarlane *Proprietary Estoppel* (2020) 235.

99 McFarlane in *Jurisprudence of Lord Hoffmann* (2015) 345. This was confirmed by the Court of Appeal in *Jennings v Rice* (n 11).

100 Section II.A.1.

101 *Suggitt v Suggitt* [2011] EWHC 903 (Ch), [59]. For a critical analysis of the case, see Mee in *Landmark Cases* (2019) 202.

102 Mee (2013) 283.

103 Another decision often criticized is *Bradbury v Taylor* (n 9). Mee (2013) 281 argued that the court allowed a claimant to succeed 'in circumstances where it is questionable whether the defendant's representation could appropriately form the basis of a proprietary estoppel claim'. While McFarlane recognizes that Bradbury is a borderline case, he nonetheless thinks that the Court of Appeal decision is justifiable, because it would be difficult to explain why the promisee and his family moved, if not for the existence of a promise. See McFarlane in *Current Issues* (2016) 89.

consistent in the sense that even in cases where the detriment is perhaps less substantial, a promisee may be able to obtain the expectation interest, which leads me to the next point, the relief.

III. Determining the relief

Unlike in case of a breach of a contractual promise, in a proprietary estoppel claim the choice of relief is flexible, for the courts have a broad discretion. However, this discretion must be exercised by taking a principled approach. The doctrine of proprietary estoppel does not operate to impose a duty on the promisor to put the promisee in the position that she would have been in had the promisor performed her promise.[104] Rather, unlike in the case of a breach of contract, the promisor is liable to ensure that the promisee suffers no detriment as a result of her reasonable reliance on the promise.[105] The court must therefore look at the circumstances in each case to decide in what way the equity can be satisfied. For that reason, a proprietary estoppel claim can lead to a variety of reliefs that range from an award of a proprietary right in the estate (e.g. where the promisee obtains the disputed property) to a monetary award. The important question is what is the court's starting point and what are the criteria that it should apply in exercising its discretion?

In this section I will try to answer both of these questions. The analysis will show that, especially in England and Wales, the answer is not straightforward because courts are not in agreement as to the starting point, which creates a level of uncertainty. We will, however, also see that irrespective of that, in most of the testamentary promises cases judged so far, the promisee seems to have been awarded a proprietary interest, often equivalent to the expectation interest. This then explains why this form of redress is attractive for, and frequently sought after by, promisees, for as we will see later, the protection that the promisee enjoys in the case of a proprietary award can be strong.

A. Proportionality of the relief

In Australia,[106] and it appears also in New Zealand,[107] the fulfilment of the promisee's expectation interest seems to be the *prima facie* relief. However, it is

[104] McFarlane in *Jurisprudence of Lord Hoffmann* (2015).

[105] Ibid.

[106] This is the case since the High Court decision in *Giumelli v Giumelli* (n 14). See also *Delaforce v Simpson-Cook* [2010] NSWCA 84, [59] (hereafter *Delaforce v Simpson-Cook*). More recently, see also *McNab v Graham* [2017] VSCA 352, [75]–[77]; *Mould v Canale* [2017] VSC 793, [45]; *Browne v Browne (No 2)* [2017] WASC 375, [94], [104]; *Ryan v Ryan* [2016] TASSC 4, [48]–[50]. Dal Pont, *Equity and Trusts* (2015) 363–375.

[107] In *Carroll v Bates* [2018] NZHC 2463, [74], [78] Dunningham J stated that: 'I take account, too, that this is not a case where there is a context of commercial interest where certainty of property rights

unclear what the exact position is in England and Wales.[108] In *Jennings v Rice*, Walker LJ held that, where the understanding between the parties is judged to be reasonably clear and 'assurance and reliance had a consensual character not far short of a contract ... the court is likely to vindicate the claimant's expectations'.[109] However, where that is not the case, either because the expectation is uncertain or regarded to be disproportionate to the detriment, the position seems to be that equity is to be satisfied in another way. This was the conclusion reached by the Court of Appeal in *Jennings v Rice*.[110]

In this case, the promisee had provided household and personal services for nearly thirty years to an elderly person who was childless (Mrs Royle). Besides doing gardening, the promisee (Mr Rice) ran errands, took the lady shopping, and, at a later stage, also helped her wash, dress, did her shopping, and slept overnight at her house. Although in the beginning the promisee received payment, at some point the elderly lady stopped the payments, telling him not to worry about it as 'he would be alright' and that 'this [the house in which she was living] will all be yours one day'. However, years later Mrs Royle died intestate, at which point the promisee brought alternative claims against the estate on the following bases: (i) a claim under the Inheritance (Provision for Family and Dependants) Act 1975 (hereafter the 1975 Act) seeking a family provision order;[111] (ii) in contract; and (iii) under the doctrine of proprietary estoppel. At first instance, Judge Weeks QC rejected the claim under the 1975 Act and, unsurprisingly, also the breach of contract claim, for the terms of the offer were regarded as too vague and imprecise to amount to a contract. However, he found in favour of the promisee under the doctrine of proprietary estoppel. He concluded that there had been a promise and that the promisee had acted to his detriment in giving up his spare time to look after the elderly lady. Judge Weeks QC awarded the promisee £200,000, which represented the estimated cost of full-time nursing care.[112] The promisee appealed maintaining that he should be awarded the whole estate valued at £1,285,000. However, the Court of Appeal dismissed the appeal holding that there must be proportionality between the award and detriment.[113] More precisely, Walker LJ stated that:

should prevail. Rather, relief is sought in a family context where I consider there is more flexibility to ensure that the wishes of those family members now deceased are carried out without unnecessary legal hurdles being placed in their way.'

108 McGee *Snell's Equity* (2020) paras 12-047ff. In Ireland the position is not entirely clear. Judging from the recent decision in *K v K* (n 5) the courts seem to aim at fulfilling the expectation interests.

109 *Jennings v Rice* (n 11) [45]. It was confirmed also in later cases, including *Thompson v Thompson* (n 5) [161].

110 *Jennings v Rice* (n 11). The net value of the estate was £1.285 million. The house and furniture were valued at £435,000.

111 For details as to how the 1975 Act may come to the aid of promisees, see Chapter 5.

112 As to the position prior to *Jennings v Rice* (n 11), see Mee in *Modern Studies V* (2009) 389.

113 *Jennings v Rice* (n 11) [36]. Aldous LJ identified it as the 'most essential requirement'. As to the origins of the concept of proportionality in this context, see McFarlane *Proprietary Estoppel* (2020) 437.

> if the claimant's expectations are uncertain, or extravagant, or out of all proportion to the detriment which the claimant has suffered, the court can and should recognise that the claimant's equity should be satisfied in another (and generally more limited) way.[114]

This reference to proportionality by Walker LJ seems to have been the source of much confusion and continuing debate amongst academics and judges. In fact, exactly what 'proportionality' means is somewhat unclear,[115] there being doubts as to whether proportionality has a positive rather than a negative role to play.[116] In other words, it is uncertain what the starting point for the court's assessment should be: the reliance or the expectation interest. According to one approach, proportionality plays a positive role in that the remedy has to be proportionate to the detriment. The essential aim of the discretion is therefore to ensure that the claimant's reliance interest is protected, so the expectation interest is not the starting point. This is the conclusion the Privy Council reached in *Henry v Henry*. The committee relied on Robert Walker LJ's [as he then was] statement in *Campbell v Griffin & Ors* that 'the court had to look at all the circumstances in order to achieve the minimum equity to do justice to the claimant'.[117]

By contrast, in *Suggitt v Suggitt*, discussed earlier, Arden LJ held that the proportionality principle 'does not mean that there has to be a relationship of proportionality between the level of detriment and the relief awarded'.[118] Instead, her Ladyship suggested that the correct question is whether the claimant's expectation, if granted, is 'out of all proportion to the detriment'.[119] In other words, the starting point is the promisee's expectation interest,[120] and a departure is only permitted where such a remedy would be disproportionate. Thus, in Arden LJ's view, the concept of proportionality plays only a negative role.[121] For that reason, in *Suggitt v Suggitt* the promisee was not just awarded the unpaid element of his work on the farm, but the farm as well as a number of houses adjacent to it, called Wellfield. This particular interpretation of the proportionality principle is controversial in

[114] *Jennings v Rice* (n 11).

[115] On proportionality, see Gardner (1999); Gardner (2006) and the response by Mee in *Modern Studies V* (2009) 404–407.

[116] Mee in *Modern Studies V* (2009) 399–400. For an analysis also McFarlane *Proprietary Estoppel* (2020) 47ff. Also controversial is whether it must be proportionate both to the expectation and the detriment or just the detriment.

[117] *Henry v Henry* (n 93) [52]. In *Campbell v Griffin Ors* (n 75), Walker LJ weighed the disadvantages which the claimant had suffered by reason of his reliance, against the advantage of the rent-free accommodation, which did not extinguish the equity but led to the award of a fixed sum of £35,000.

[118] *Suggitt v Suggitt* 2012 (n 5) [44]. Mee (2013) 285 is of the view that the reasoning of Arden LJ is flawed.

[119] *Suggitt v Suggitt* 2012 (n 5) [44]. See also *Gill v Woodall* (n 76) [547].

[120] This was criticized by Mee in *Modern Studies V* (2009).

[121] This view had been adopted also in Australia. See *Delaforce v Simpson-Cook* (n 106) where the court emphasized that in *Thorner v Major* (n 5), the House of Lords had not talked about proportionality. The approach was followed in *Harrison v Harrison* (n 91).

legal scholarship.[122] Nonetheless, it has been followed in a number of later cases. For instance, in *Davies v Davies*,[123] Judge Jarman QC, sitting as a judge of the Chancery Division, asked himself whether the promisee's interest in the farm was out of all proportion to the detriment suffered and, having concluded that it was not, awarded him the farm (though not the bungalow on the land). In another recent farm case, *Gee v Gee* (2018), Birss J declared that 'the appropriate approach is to base the remedy on the expectation, not the financial value of the measurable parts of the detriment'.[124]

B. The sliding scale

The question of the quantum of the award was specifically addressed again in *Davies v Davies*.[125] In the first part of the proceedings, Judge Jarman QC established that the promisee,[126] one of the daughters of the promisors, who had worked on their farm for long hours at low wages over the course of many years (though with long interruptions) in reliance on their assurances that the farm would one day be hers, had a valid claim for equitable relief based on proprietary estoppel.[127] While the daughter had pitched her claim at her expectation that she would succeed to the farming business, and thus claimed £4.4 million, her parents contended that a cash award of £350,000 would suffice. During the second part of the proceedings, dealing with how the equity should be satisfied, Judge Jarman QC took the expectation interest as the starting point but then concluded that the proportionate remedy would be a lump sum in the amount of £1.3 million. The judge regarded this as a fair reflection of the promisee's expectation (which changed over time) and the detriment without, however, explaining exactly how he had reached this conclusion. The decision was appealed and the appeal was granted.[128] Lewison LJ, with whom both Underhill and Patten LLJ agreed, argued that in *Jennings v Rice* Walker LJ had established that in cases where the claimant's assurances and reliance had a consensual character not far short of a contract (and in this case a number of different promises had been made over a certain period of time), the court could still take the claimant's expectations as a starting point.[129] However, referring to the passage from Walker LJ's opinion cited

[122] Mee in *Modern Studies V* (2009) 399–400. See further McFarlane in *Jurisprudence of Lord Hoffmann* (2015 and McFarlane in *Current Issues* (2016) 92 who is of the view that proportionality should play a positive role.
[123] *Davies v Davies* 2015 (n 5).
[124] *Gee v Gee* (n 5) [144].
[125] *Davies v Davies* 2015 (n 5).
[126] Ibid.
[127] The Court of Appeal upheld this finding on the preliminary issues. See *Davies v Davies* [2014] EWCA 568.
[128] *Davies v Davies* 2016 (n 5).
[129] Ibid, [40]. Rather critical of that approach is McFarlane *Proprietary Estoppel* (2020) 406ff.

earlier,[130] Lewison LJ then added that:

> What is not entirely clear from this passage is what the court is to do with the expectation even if it is only a starting point. Mr Blohm suggested that there might be a sliding scale by which the clearer the expectation, the greater the detriment and the longer the passage of time during which the expectation was reasonably held, the greater would be the weight that should be given to the expectation. I agree that this is a useful working hypothesis.[131]

Thus, Lewison LJ thought that the sliding scale suggested by counsel for the promisee would be a useful way to approach the quantification of the relief. The greater the detriment and the longer the passage of time during which expectation was held, the greater the weight was to be given to the expectation interest. This approach would usually favour the promisee, but not in this case because the Court of Appeal found that Judge Jarman QC had applied far too broad a brush and that he had failed to analyse the facts with sufficient rigour. After a careful (though arguably overly meticulous) analysis of the various representations made, as well as the benefits the claimant had obtained (in the form of free accommodation and expenses), Lewison LJ decided to significantly reduce the judge's award from £1.3 million to £500,000. The reduction seems to have been partly motivated by the fact that the promisee had left the farm on two separate occasions. According to the judge, this suggests that she had given up the expectation and that the assurances no longer mattered ('served to wipe clean any previous assurances').[132] However, such a conclusion sets a problematic precedent, as it does not differentiate between cases in which the relationship turned sour due to the behaviour of the promisor (which appears to have happened in *Davies v Davies*, where the parents disliked the promisee's choice of partners) and those in which the breakdown is attributable to the promisee. It would be absurd if the promisee had to stay, for instance, where the promisor behaves unreasonably or it is clear that the promise had been broken because the property had been transferred to someone else.

Irrespective of that, what judges will make of this sliding scale in future cases is unclear. In *James v James*, Judge Paul Matthews (sitting as Judge of the High Court) said that he would agree with Arden LJ's (more generous) interpretation of the proportionality test that takes the expectation interest as the starting point,[133] expressing doubts as to 'how far a "sliding scale" approach would be useful'.[134] In *Guest v Guest*, Judge Russen QC found that 'the sliding scale should not be deployed as a scalpel unless, perhaps, the initial assurance was so uncertain as to not

[130] *Jennings v Rice* (n 11) 119.
[131] *Davies v Davies* 2016 (n 5) [41].
[132] Ibid, [33]. For a criticism, see Tattersall (2016) 240.
[133] *James v James* (n 5) [51].
[134] Ibid, [52].

really justify much of a place on it'.[135] By contrast, in *Habberfield v Habberfield*, Birss J appears to agree with Lewison LJ's view that it is useful for a court to operate on the basis that the longer the expectation was reasonably held, the greater would be the weight given to the expectation. That said, he suggested:

> a refinement to paragraph 41 derived from the article by McFarlane and Sales which is referred to in Lewison LJ's judgment. … They … propose a 'hybrid' model as follows: 'The relief afforded to B under the promise-detriment principle is protection in respect of B's detrimental reliance, unless and until any performance he or she rendered under a reciprocal arrangement with A of which A's promise forms part amounts to substantial performance by B of the return A wished to secure by making the promise.'[136]

In other words, in this case (unlike in *Gee v Gee* cited earlier),[137] Birss J seems to prefer the approach whereby the starting point is the detrimental reliance rather than the expectation interest, unless the promisee has provided substantial performance of the agreement with the promisor. But, of course, what 'substantial' means is not always clear and will depend on the context, so that it is doubtful that this approach is more helpful. Applying this reasoning to the facts in question, Birss J concluded that, in this case, where a daughter had worked on a farm for thirty years for low pay on the basis of her father's assurances that she would receive a 'viable dairy farm at Woodrow', merely compensating the claimant for reliance losses would not be equitable and that, absent strong contrary reasons, she should receive compensation based on the promise made to her. A cash payment of the value of the farmland and farm buildings, around £1.2 million, was thus ordered and the appeal against the decision rejected.[138]

Thus, it seems that the proposal by Lewison LJ of a sliding scale has not brought greater clarity to the debate and it is therefore still unpredictable whether in England and Wales, a court will take the promisee's expectation rather than her reliance interest as the starting point. Irrespective of this, as we will see, quite often promisees seem to be able obtain their expectation interest.

135 *Guest v Guest* 2019 (n 26) [156]. By contrast, on appeal (*Guest v Guest* 2020 (n 5)), Floyd LJ at [52] agreed with Lewison LJ that a sliding scale was a useful working hypothesis 'although I would not regard this list of scaling factors as more than important examples of the considerations which come into play'.

136 *Habberfield v Habberfield* 2018 (n 5) [228]. The article the judge was referring to is McFarlane & Sales (2015).

137 See n 129.

138 *Habberfield v Habberfield* 2019 (n 5).

C. Relevant factors when quantifying the relief

Irrespective of what the exact starting point for the quantification of the relief is, in *Jennings v Rice* Walker LJ stated that when quantifying the award, a court will take into account a variety of factors, including, for instance:

> the court's recognition that it cannot compel people who have fallen out to live peaceably together, so that there may be a need for a clean break; alterations in the benefactor's assets and circumstances, especially where the benefactor's assurances have been given, and the claimant's detriment has been suffered, over a long period of years; the likely effect of taxation; and (to a limited degree) the other claims (legal or moral) on the benefactor or his or her estate. No doubt there are many other factors which it may be right for the court to take into account in particular factual situations.[139]

I cannot here explore all the criteria that are relevant to the exercise of the court's discretion. However, it is interesting to refer to those that have played a role in testamentary promises cases. Among those explicitly mentioned by Walker LJ is the need for a clean break, which is sometimes required where the promisor is still alive, or the trial involves siblings who are required to work together on the farm but have fallen out with one another. The desire to obtain a clean break affected the way in which relief was quantified in *Guest v Guest*, where family relations had broken down, and there was no prospect of the parties continuing to work on the farm and living together in close proximity.[140] The promisee was awarded a lump sum payment, even though this would likely result in the need to sell the farm, which the promisors were still living on but which they had promised to leave to the promisee. Reference to a clean break was also made in *Gee v Gee*, another farm case. Nonetheless, the judge decided against a lump sum payment that would have achieved such a clean break, because of the risk that the value of landholding would rise dramatically, meaning that the promisee would lose out. In other words, by awarding the promisee a proprietary interest, she could benefit from such an increase. This seems an important consideration to take into account when considering what the adequate redress should be. At the same time, where relationships have soured, it is likely that they could not agree as to what to do with the property, including whether to sell it or not, so that a cash payment may be more appropriate.

Another factor mentioned by Walker LJ is possible claims (legal or moral) that other people may have against the promisor's estate.[141] In some cases, courts have indeed considered the impact that the relief would have on the promisor but also

139 *Jennings v Rice* (n 11) 52.
140 *Guest v Guest* 2020 (n 5) [88]. See also *Habberfield v Habberfield* 2018 (n 5).
141 *Jennings v Rice* (n 11) [52]. See McFarlane in *Current Issues* (2016) 94.

on other members of the family. For instance, in *Guest v Guest*, Judge Russen QC suggested that Walker LJ's caveat in *Jennings v Rice* about proportionality 'covers not just the idea of disproportionate benefit to the claimant but also a disproportionate burden to the property-owner and others who may have interests in the property'.[142] And, in the Court of Appeal's decision in *Moore v Moore* (2018),[143] the impact that the son's entitlement by way of proprietary estoppel to his father's share in the assets and business of a farm was going to have on his parents (the promisors) during the remainder of their lives was a central consideration.[144] In the Australian decision in *Giumelli v Giumelli* (1999), the court opted for payment of a sum representing the value of the promised lot, because this would have less of an impact on third parties.[145] Interesting in this respect is also *Gee v Gee*, where Birss J took into account the effect his judgment was going to have on the promisee's sister, even though she was not a party to the litigation.[146] The suggestion that courts should take into account claims by others when ascertaining the extent of the right acquired by the promisee has attracted criticism in legal scholarship.[147] After all, the purpose of the doctrine of proprietary estoppel is to prevent detrimental reliance rather than to achieve equality and fairness amongst those with an interest in the estate. Certainly, from the perspective of the promisee, taking into account the interests of claims by others is not desirable as it reduces the likelihood that the promisee will obtain the promised asset. This complexity arises, for instance, where the interest of the promisee clashes with that of an applicant under the family provision legislation, who is in financial need. However, as Chapter 5 will show, financial need is not a necessary requirement in all common law jurisdictions and in some jurisdictions courts take a flexible approach to the requirement, so that it is unclear why the relief should be adjusted and a promisee be worse off.[148] By contrast, where the promisee brings a claim already during the promisor's lifetime, it is arguably right that an adjustment is made. Notably, in several of the recent English proprietary estoppel cases promisees have brought the claim not on death

[142] *Jennings v Rice* (n 11) [148].

[143] *Moore v Moore* 2018 (n 5).

[144] According to Dixon in *Modern Studies II* (2003) 182, in *Campbell v Griffin* (n 75) 'a monetary award was granted in order to be even-handed between the claimant and the persons benefiting under the deceased's will as the court did not want a property claim clogging the title and keeping the other beneficiaries out of their money'.

[145] *Giumelli v Giumelli* (n 14).

[146] *Gee v Gee* (n 5) [162]. The question also arose in *Habberfield v Habberfield* 2019 (n 5) [84] because the first instance decision meant that the elderly promisor (eighty-two years old) had to leave the house which has been her home for over forty years for the farm was likely to have to be sold in order to fulfil the equity and guarantee a clean break. But Lewison LJ felt that [84] the order that the judge made was within his discretion.

[147] Gardner (2006) 501. Mee in *Landmark Cases* (2019) 208 argues that 'there is no obvious scope within the doctrine of proprietary estoppel to weigh up the competing merits of the claims of those who would otherwise be entitled'. McFarlane in *Current Issues* (2016) 94 is doubtful.

[148] Chapter 5. See also the discussion in Chapters 3 and 7.

but during the promisor's lifetime,[149] primarily because the parties had fallen out with one another.[150] In such cases, the courts have stressed that the promisee's expectation is a future one and that she has not performed until the promisor's death, which is usually what she has agreed to do. In other words, the promisee is claiming an accelerated interest. By benefiting earlier, she is shielded from the risk that there is nothing left on the death of the promisor, something which should be taken into account.

Another important factor that courts consider when quantifying the award is, as the analysis has already revealed, whether the promisee has obtained any mutual benefits such as free accommodation or free board. This could be potentially problematic for promisees who have lived with the promisor,[151] which is not uncommon both in farm but also care cases—an issue promisees would not encounter if the promise amounted to a legally binding contract. That said, in *Gee v Gee*, the free accommodation was not regarded to be a benefit to be taken into account when quantifying the relief but was seen instead as 'given to him [the promisee] as a result of his status as a family member, not as compensation for time and effort spent farming'.[152]

Another related question is whether any potential claim the promisee might have, for instance, under the family provision legislation should reduce the amount awarded. The answer is unclear. Arden LJ recognized in *Suggitt* that such a claim by the promisee was pending but concluded that no particular value could be attached to it. According to McFarlane:

> given the nature of the 1975 Act as a statutory last resort, a proprietary estoppel claim, should be determined first, and without reference to possible claims under that Act. As a result, a court should reject C's argument that the extent of the right acquired by B can be reduced by the possibility of a 1975 Act claim.[153]

[149] See *Gillett v Holt* (n 5), *Seward v Seward* (Ch, 20 June 2014) (hereafter *Seward v Seward*), and *Davies v Davies* 2016 (n 5). In *Clarke v Meadus* [2010] EWHC 3117 (Ch), [74], Warren J confirmed: 'That is not to say that effect cannot be given to an estoppel before the time when the promise falls due. In a case where a claimant has a clear right to expect that a property will be left to him by another, an attempt to circumvent a promise to that effect by changing the will or by selling the property may give rise to enforceable rights even before the death of the promisor. It all depends on the facts of the case.' Also see *Habberfield v Habberfield* 2018 (n 5) where the principal bone of contention at first instance was whether the cash payment to the promisee should be deferred until the promisor's death. The judge rejected the argument on the basis that the desperately difficult situation in which the promisor found herself was of her own making. However, note the Canadian case *Granger v Granger* 2016 ONCA 945 in which the Court of Appeal of Ontario upheld the first instance decision in which the judge excluded the estoppel claim on the basis that it was premature, as the promisor had not yet died.

[150] *Moore v Moore* 2018 (n 5), *Gee v Gee* (n 5), and *Guest v Guest* 2019 (n 26).

[151] See *Campbell & Griffin & Ors* (n 75) and *Bradbury v Taylor* (n 9).

[152] *Gee v Gee* (n 5) [125].

[153] McFarlane in *Current Issues* (2016) 93.

That must be right. As we shall see in Chapter 5,[154] claims under the 1975 Act are usually brought when all other avenues are failing. Also, a family provision order would not protect the promisee in the same way because the claim only exists against the net estate so that the promisee would be paid after any creditors.

Thus, while courts have considerable discretion, the exercise of the discretion is guided by a number of factors. That said, it is undeniable that the current uncertainty as to the starting point for determining the relief is highly unsatisfactory. Even so, the next part shows that in most cases, courts have been generous when granting relief, which is probably, at least in part, why some legal scholars have been critical of the liberal interpretation of its requirements.

D. The reality of testamentary promises cases

Even though the starting point for determining the relief has sometimes been the promisee's reliance rather than expectation interest, the reality is that in the majority of the English testamentary promises cases in which a proprietary estoppel claim has been upheld so far, a proprietary interest has been awarded that reflects the promisee's expectation interest either in full or, at least, in large parts.[155] Thus, in many cases, the award has been of considerable economic value. There are only a few instances in which the award was limited to the reliance interest.[156] Even when courts have decided against an order for the transfer of the promised asset, for instance, in order to obtain a clean break, the monetary award has often exceeded the reliance interest.[157] In Ireland, too, there are examples where the farm has been awarded.[158] Equally, in Australia, where the proportionality test does not

[154] Chapter 5.

[155] This was the case in *Re Basham* (n 4), *Gillett v Holt* (n 5), *Walton v Walton* (n 5), *Thorner v Major* (n 5), *Suggitt v Suggitt* 2012 (n 5), *Bradbury v Taylor* (n 9), and *Moore v Moore* 2018 (n 5) but also *Thompson v Thompson* (n 5). The expectation was also fulfilled in *K v K* (n 5) but here the court granted the contractual claim. Nonetheless, it confirmed that, even if based on estoppel, the promisee should be entitled to the ninety acres he was promised. In *Gee v Gee* (n 5), the judge based the relief not on the detriment, but on the expectation interest. However, because the promisee had been paid wages, and due to other factors, the promisee was awarded 52% of the company shares and 46% of the land. See also *Gill v Woodall* (n 76) where the High Court said that had it not set aside the will for undue influence, it would have awarded the farm and farming business and the money in the family account. In *Jiggins v Brisley* [2003] EWHC 841 (Ch) the minimum equity was the flat.

[156] *Jennings v Rice* (n 11). In *Powell v Benney* [2007] EWCA Civ 1283 only the expenses were paid back. See also *Habberfield v Habberfield* 2018 (n 57) and *Davies v Davies* 2016 (n 5).

[157] See, for example *Guest v Guest* 2019 (n 26), where the court decided in favour of a monetary award equivalent to a substantial part of the farm to allow for a clean break. A monetary award was also awarded in *Habberfield v Habberfield* 2018 (n 57) for tax reasons, but also because a transfer would have had the inevitable consequence that the promisor would have had to leave her home, for the parties had fallen out with one another. While a sale of the farmhouse was still likely, the judge thought that a cash award allowed for the possibility of not having to sell it [258].

[158] *Naylor v Maher* (n 5). In *Finnegan v Hand* (n 5), White Michael J placed a lot of emphasis on *Thorner v Major* (n 5) though thinking (wrongly) that in *Thorner v Major* the House of Lords found a remedial constructive trust. The judge therefore awarded a constructive trust over half of the farm, half the value of the stock and machinery and miscellaneous items sold, rather than the entire estate, as this

apply, there have been numerous cases where promisees have been able to obtain the promised asset,[159] sometimes by way of a constructive trust.[160] As shown by the Australian case of *Estephan v Estephan*, this is not only true of farm cases[161] but also where the promisee has provided care services.[162]

Why have courts tended to award a proprietary right that reflects the expectation interests in full or at least in part? There are several possible explanations. Aside from the fact that, as Walker LJ mentioned in *Jennings v Rice*, the expectation interest may sometimes be easier to determine than the detriment,[163] in some cases it is arguably the only means to fully redress or at least come close to fully redressing detriment, for example, where the promisee has provided work or services over a long period of time or has made substantial professional and personal sacrifices. In many of the farm cases discussed, the promisee will have spent most of her life on the farm and have based her entire life plans on the expectation to inherit the farm. As Birss J pointed out in *Habberfield v Habberfield*, 'although part of it [the detriment] was quantifiable, compensation for having been committed to the farm for three decades and not building a different life elsewhere was not'.[164] In other words, in some of these cases it is difficult to fairly quantify the detriment,[165] especially when consisting also of personal sacrifices. Moreover, frequently promisees are in their late forties or even in their fifties and early sixties, and it would be difficult for them to start all over again and to find alternative employment. As Hoffman LJ said in *Walton v Walton*:

> He [the claimant] cannot have his life over again. If he does not get the farm, he will have to start again at the age of nearly 50, whereas if Mrs Walton had never promised him the farm, he might by now have established himself in some other way. So it would be unjust, or in the language of equity 'unconscionable' for the plaintiff now to be turned off the land.[166]

This point goes back to the nature of the detriment suffered. In the many farm cases analysed in this chapter, the detriment is often considerable, not least because

would be an injustice to the deceased's next of kin. By contrast, in *Coyle v Finnegan* (n 5) the judge did not grant the expectation interest because the deceased had retained a discretion to vary the will. He held, however, that the claimant, who had worked on the deceased's farm, should have a charge or lien on the lands for a sum equivalent to a reasonable remuneration for his services on the basis of the doctrine of proprietary estoppel.

[159] Burns (2001) 132.
[160] *Saliba v Tarmo* [2009] NSWSC 581 (23 June 2009). See Dal Pont *Equity and Trusts* (2015) 342–343.
[161] For a farm case, see *Waddell v Waddell* (n 5).
[162] *Estephan v Estephan* (n 9).
[163] Walker LJ in *Jennings v Rice* (n 11) [51].
[164] *Habberfield v Habberfield* 2018 (n 57) [225].
[165] On appeal, Lewison LJ too felt that 'the three decades of her life that Lucy spent on the farm are not susceptible of quantification'—see [60].
[166] *Walton v Walton* (n 5).

those who know that they will one day own the farm are likely to invest greater effort. The detriment is therefore not ordinarily to be satisfied merely by a monetary payment. That said, there is no doubt that, unlike with domestic or care work, the financial value of the type of work carried out on a farm (which is usually visible) is generally more directly recognized.[167] There is also the additional argument that some farms have been in the family for generations and awarding a share may lead to a fragmentation of the farm,[168] which is generally undesirable, though as we saw, in *Habberfield v Habberfield*, that did not stop the judge from making a monetary award.[169]

This is not to say that where the promisee performs household or care services she should not obtain the expectation interests. On the contrary, in the care context, one could argue that courts should award the expectation interest because care can involve a huge emotional and personal investment on the part of the promisee that cannot be satisfied by merely awarding the costs of hiring a nurse. Also, the benefits that a promisor may obtain from being able to stay and die at home, and being nursed by close family members, can be immensely valuable. However, it is perhaps worth noting that one of the few English cases in which the reliance interest was awarded (i.e. *Jennings v Rice*) was a care case. Finally, another reason for awarding the expectation interest might be that some of the testamentary promises cases we have come across in this chapter 'have a consensual character falling not far short of an enforceable contract'.[170] As Walker LJ said in *Jennings v Rice*, in such cases, the court is likely to vindicate the promisee's expectations.[171]

However, what matters from the perspective of a promisee is not just whether or not she can obtain the promised asset, but also what her position is vis-à-vis third parties—an aspect which I shall address in section IV.

IV. Nature of the right of the promisee

If a promisee is awarded a monetary payment, she will be treated as a creditor who competes with other unsecured creditors and will benefit prior to any successors who benefit under a will or on intestacy. If, however, the proprietary estoppel claim results in the award of a property right, the promisee is in an even stronger position,

[167] See the discussion in Chapter 2.

[168] Though notice that in *Thorner v Major* (n 5), the successful promisee subsequently sold the farm to the supermarket chain Sainsbury's, which later obtained planning permission for a large supermarket.

[169] See section III.B.

[170] *Jennings v Rice* (n 11) [45], [50].

[171] See section III.A. *Seward v Seward* (n 149) represents a clear 'quasi-bargain' case. Birss J characterized *Habberfield v Habberfield* 2018 (n 57) as a 'quasi-bargain' case. In *Davies v Davies* 2016 (n 5) [43] and in *Gill v Woodall* (n 76) [542] reference is made to the bargain or 'quasi-bargain cases'. Even when the details are not clearly articulated by the parties, it is arguable that an exchange or 'bargain' of some sorts still exists. Braun in *L'abnégation en droit civil* (2017) 41.

for she takes prior to unsecured creditors. Also, her rights can take priority over the interests of third-party transferee,[172] though a distinction must be drawn between a donee and a purchaser and in particular a *bona fide* purchaser for value without notice whose interest will always prevail.

A further distinction must be drawn based on whether the third party acquires a right to the promised asset *after* or *prior* to the court order in favour of the promisee. *After* a court order has been made in favour of the promisee, and a third party acquires the asset from the promisor, the transferee will be bound by the promisee's right. *Prior* to the court order, the promisee is said to have an equity by estoppel. But what exactly does that mean? The law in the area is not entirely clear. However, the prevailing position in legal scholarship seems to be that where the promisee is awarded a proprietary right, in England and Wales, a further distinction must be made between registered and unregistered land.[173]

Where the land is unregistered and the property is given away through a lifetime gift, the equity attaching to the property binds the successor, even if she has no notice of the equity. By contrast, where registered land is concerned, the position depends on the interpretation of section 116(a) of the Land Registration Act 2002. The provision states that in relation to registered land, an equity by estoppel, 'has effect from the time the equity arises as an interest capable of binding successors in title (subject to the rules about the effect of dispositions on priority)'. Thus, even before the court orders in favour of the promisee, the 'estoppel equity' can bind third parties.[174]

In *Henry v Henry*, mentioned earlier, a case where the promisor had sold the interest in an agricultural land (which had been the object of a testamentary promise) to a third party who was registered as the legal owner, the Privy Council agreed with the conclusion of the Court of Appeal of the Eastern Caribbean Supreme Court that 'any equity acquired by [the promisee] in respect of the plot is an overriding interest' within the meaning of section 28 of the Land Registration Act (St. Lucia), and therefore binding.[175] However, the court also clarified that '[t]he Board does not rule out the possibility that cases may arise in which the particular circumstances surrounding a third party purchase may, notwithstanding the claimant's overriding interest, require the court to reassess the extent of the claimant's equity in the property'.[176] Thus, the decision of the Privy Council suggests that, in some cases, the promisee may not prevail after all. Unsurprisingly, the decision has been criticized on the basis that it requires the court 'to reinvent

[172] For a comprehensive analysis, see McFarlane *Proprietary Estoppel* (2020) 476–494.

[173] See *James v James* (n 5) where part of the deceased's property was unregistered land and part was registered.

[174] McGee *Snell's Equity* (2020) para 12-053. On the interpretation of s 116(a) of the Land Registration Act 2002, see Bright & McFarlane (2005).

[175] *Henry v Henry* (n 93) [54].

[176] Ibid, [56].

the wheel by using broader notions of unconscionability to determine when C [the transferee] might be bound'.[177]

V. Concerns about the impact of developments in this area

A. Introduction

The developments in the area of proprietary estoppel have come under academic scrutiny both because courts have on the whole been flexible in interpreting its requirements but also because of the way they have exercised their discretion in granting relief.[178] This is seen as problematic because of the degree of protection that the promisee enjoys. It has, for instance, been argued that if such claims are too readily granted, vague statements made by the deceased could become the basis for a claim,[179] and promises may be alleged or found even where none were ever made.[180] Also promises may become difficult to deny when a person has provided substantial services to, or work for, the deceased. John Mee, for instance, has argued that in light of the fact that these cases often span a long period of time in which it was envisaged that the claimant will inherit 'it will nearly always be possible for a claimant to cobble together some remarks, or alleged remarks, made over the years by the deceased defendant which a sympathetic court' will be receptive to.[181] What is more, as Judge Jarman QC pointed out in the High Court decision in *Davies v Davies*:

> It is easy to assert such oral promises when the person making the promises has passed away, when the only other witness is elderly and not available to give oral evidence, when there is little contemporaneous documentation and none that directly refers to such promises. It is right in those circumstances that the assertions should be treated with care and even suspicion.[182]

[177] McGee *Snell's Equity* (2020) para 12-053.

[178] Kerridge *Parry and Kerridge* (2016) 120 who finds that in *Suggitt v Suggitt* 2012 (n 5) and *Bradbury v Taylor* (n 9) the 'property awarded appears to be disproportionate to any detriment suffered by the claimant'. See also Mee in *Landmark Cases* (2019) 199 and Mee (2009) 381–382; Mee (2013) 283–287. See also Davey (1988) 110, who criticized the fact that it may be used to give binding effect to a non-contractual promise. See further Hayton (1987) and Dixon (1999). Most of the criticisms have been addressed and persuasively rejected by McFarlane in *Current Issues* (2016).

[179] Kerridge *Parry and Kerridge* (2016) 117.

[180] On this see Hayton (1987) 216.

[181] Mee in *Landmark Cases* (2019) 201.

[182] *Davies v Davies* 2015 (n 5) [9]. In *Gillett v Holt* [1998] 3 All ER 917 (Ch) 929, Carnwath J warned that 'particular care is needed where considering proprietary estoppel in the context of an alleged promise to make a will'.

There is thus a concern that promises are too readily found at the expense of the promisor who is often prevented from telling her story. However, if the requirements that a promisee must meet are clearly defined, then the risk can be contained. Supporters of the doctrine have indeed called for a principled approach and clearly defined strands and categories so as to avoid overextension of the doctrine of proprietary estoppel.[183] This is in the interest of promisors, their successors, and creditors, as well as third-party transferees, but potentially also the promisees, for if some courts are too lenient, others may well return to a stricter approach along the lines of the one adopted in the past.[184]

Mee has further argued that it is comparatively rare for courts to show real sympathy for the testator and other characters therefore get marginalized.[185] He suggests that it may be 'more fulfilling to dispense discretionary justice to the parties before the court than to feel obliged to apply, in a more mechanical way, the strict rules of property law and succession law'.[186] Courts may therefore more easily neglect the interests of those who benefit under the will, intestacy rules or applicants under the family provision legislation. McFarlane raises a similar point where he argues that courts may be too generous when interpreting the requirements or the effect of the doctrine of proprietary estoppel in the testamentary context because a court may well take the view that someone who takes under a will or intestacy has less of a reason to complain.[187] While there may be some truth to this, arguably those who take under a will or intestacy have little reason to complain. After all they usually only ever benefit when all debts are paid, and the promisee is a debtor. All the court does here is to enforce an obligation that the promisor has voluntarily assumed towards the person, who in reliance on a promise, has suffered a detriment. By contrast, those taking under the will or intestacy usually get something for free. Moreover, the estate is normally enriched by the promisee's performance and the beneficiaries under the will or intestacy thus benefit from the promisee's behaviour. It must also be remembered that the purpose of the doctrine of proprietary estoppel is not to obtain a fair and equal distribution of the estate. Besides, we have seen that in some cases the courts actually do consider the interests of the promisor and third parties when establishing the relief, including when they consider solutions that would lead to a clean break.[188] Thus, the doctrine does not undermine succession law, though it may affect a claim that some family members may bring based on the family provision legislation.

[183] McFarlane in *Current Issues* (2016). Clear criteria are favoured also by Lloyd LJ in *Thorner v Major* 2008 (n 12) [69], who speaks of the need for 'a certain degree of rigour of analysis'.

[184] See *Taylor v Dickens* (n 48).

[185] Mee in *Landmark Cases* (2019) 208.

[186] Mee (2013) 297.

[187] McFarlane in *Current Issues* (2016) 78.

[188] See section III.C.

This view is also taken by McFarlane,[189] who has argued that '[t]he possibility of such a liability does not only reduce the risk of A's abuse of that power [i.e. the power to make promises and to drop hints], it may also, somewhat paradoxically, assist A [the promisor]'.[190] In McFarlane's view, which I agree with, the doctrine reinforces the promisee's motivation for acting in particular ways requested by the promisor, for she knows she will be protected.

Another not uncommon argument is one articulated by Mee who fears that:

> The existence of an open-ended discretionary estoppel jurisdiction may lead to family quarrels becoming exponentially more bitter through a descent into litigation. A family member who feels ill-used upon a relative's death may be inclined to swallow his disappointment and get on with his life until he learns of the possibility that, if the court sees things this way, he may obtain a remedy against the other people in the family.[191]

It is true that some cases have received a certain level of publicity in local newspapers,[192] and that the stories told tend to emphasize the generosity of the relief. However, this does not necessarily mean that family quarrels will become more bitter. The costs that a claim involves are usually considerable and, combined with the fact that one would need to render so many private details public, will often act as a deterrent. Also, the same argument could be raised against other forms of redress discussed in this book. That said, it is true that litigation based on the doctrine of proprietary estoppel has increased in England and Wales, and that we can now also see cases being brought in other common law jurisdictions. But this does not mean that the promisees in these cases are or were not deserving. In fact, it is likely that prior to this jurisprudential development, many cases were simply not litigated even if deserving, because contractual claims were almost always impossible. In any event, the fear of increased litigation cannot be a strong argument against providing protection given the vulnerabilities of promisees. Rather, it emphasizes once more the need to have clear requirements for an estoppel claim to arise.

Some authors have further argued that because the outcome is generally unpredictable,[193] it is not only difficult for the parties to settle a claim,[194] there can

[189] McFarlane in *Current Issues* (2016) 78.

[190] Ibid, 85.

[191] Mee (2009) 383 and Dixon (2019) 91. The floodgate argument is sometimes mentioned by courts. See n 195.

[192] In *Habberfield v Habberfield* 2018 (n 57) [81] the claimant explained in cross-examination that 'she was unaware that a claim of this kind could be brought until, after those events, she heard about a newspaper article concerning the *Davies v Davies* case'. See also *Shaw v Shaw* (n 5) in relation to which the claimant is reported as the 'cow-hating son'; see *The Times*, 29 November 2018. On this particular point, see also Mee in *Landmark Cases* (2019) 209.

[193] The problem of the unpredictability of the remedy in proprietary estoppel cases was raised by Honey & Evans (2007).

[194] Mee in *Landmark Cases* (2019) 209; Mee (2009) 383; McFarlane in *Current Issues* (2016) 88 and Kerridge *Parry and Kerridge* (2016) 120; Sloan *Informal Carers* (2012) 48.

also be little incentive to settle,[195] for the prospects of success are difficult to determine. While it is true that courts have sometimes expressed regret where parties have failed to settle their dispute and spent significant sums on court fees and legal advice,[196] as with other forms of redress where courts have discretion, the flexibility has its benefits. It allows courts to take into consideration the context but also, for instance, a change of circumstances since the promise was made, or other considerations.[197]

Finally, it has often been argued that the doctrine proprietary estoppel could provide a means of circumventing testamentary freedom and, where a proprietary award is made, also a means to elude the formality requirements for both testamentary dispositions and lifetime transfers of property.[198] This is one of the reasons why in *Thorner v Major*, the Court of Appeal overturned the first instance judgment and denied the claim. Lloyd LJ stated that the fluidity and flexibility of proprietary estoppel:

> [created] dangers unless the established requirements of proprietary estoppel are applied with a certain degree of rigour of analysis. Otherwise not only the strict requirements of the Wills Act as to how to give effect to testamentary intentions, but also the basic proposition of freedom of testamentary disposition, might be subverted, so that A could be found much too readily to be subject to an obligation to dispose of particular property in a particular way, giving B a claim which would take effect not merely to give B the expected legacy or devise, but also to give B a stronger right to it than if he or she had merely been made a beneficiary under a duly executed will but with no relevant promise or representation.[199]

The issue has been raised primarily because the protection that the doctrine affords promisees with regards to third parties is strong. In the pages that follow, I will explore both the claim that testamentary freedom is infringed and the claim that the requirements of the Wills Act 1837 are being circumvented, because they are core to this inquiry. In fact, as the analysis in Chapter 2 has shown, among the reasons for prohibiting contracts to make a will in many civil law jurisdictions, is the desire to protect testamentary freedom and to ensure that the *numerus clausus* of testamentary dispositions and their formality requirements as established by succession law are not evaded.[200] In the following pages I will argue that neither argument

[195] The floodgate argument was invoked by Lloyds LJ in *Thorner v Major* 2008 (n 12) [69] and [75]. The argument was, however, dismissed by Lord Walker in the House of Lords decision (n 5) [60]. His Lordship took the view that cases like this would be fairly rare. We know that this is not the case.

[196] In *Suggitt v Suggitt* 2012 (n 5) [66]. Another case is *Moore v Moore* 2018 (n 5) [1] where Henderson LJ pointed to the fact that the legal costs of the dispute were estimated at £2.5 million.

[197] For example, the fact that the promise was procured by a misrepresentation or misconduct by the promisee. See McGee *Snell's Equity* (2020) para 12-045.

[198] McFarlane in *Current Issues* (2016).

[199] *Thorner v Major* 2008 (n 12) [69].

[200] See the discussion in Chapter 2.

is ultimately convincing; nor can it stand in the way of protecting a promisee's interests.

B. Circumventing testamentary freedom?

Sometimes promissors and their successors object to the claim by arguing that the promisor's testamentary freedom will be infringed should a claim be granted.[201] But is testamentary freedom really infringed here? I would argue that it is not. It is certainly the case that in some proprietary estoppel cases courts have made an order that has conflicted with the promisor's last will. But that is unsurprising, for it is precisely by making a will that omits the promisee that promises are often broken. It does not, however, follow that the promisor's testamentary freedom is encroached upon by the court. It is not a construct of the courts, but rather that of the promisor herself who has expressed the promise, thereby voluntarily assuming an obligation which she is not free to ignore because the promisee has relied on the promise to her detriment. In other words, the court does not restrict testamentary freedom but merely gives effect to an existing obligation.[202]

One could, of course, argue that where a court gives effect to an informal promise (as opposed to a contract) by awarding the promisee the promised asset, a promise which was perhaps never intended to be legally binding is *de facto* turned into an enforceable contract with the consequence that the promisor is no longer in a position to change her mind. More importantly, while a contract may be terminated, with an informal promise the promisee may have difficulties revoking her promise. While the promisor could simply tell the promisee that she has changed her mind, this is perhaps more difficult in cases where, as in *Gee v Gee*, no specific moment could be identified in which the promise was made,[203] but the court inferred the promise from a series of circumstances. Yet, once the promisee had relied on the promise and the promisor had accepted the performances, the promisor was bound. Even though the facts of *Gee v Gee* are arguably peculiar, it is not uncommon for courts to reconstruct the promise on the basis of a number of assurances made over a long period of time. Arguably, this makes revocation more difficult. Nonetheless, it seems to me that the vulnerability of the promisee must trump the promisor's freedom to change her mind because she has accepted the promisee's performance.[204] Again, this speaks in favour of having clear requirements for an estoppel claim to arise.

201 *Guest v Guest* 2019 (n 26) [15].
202 McFarlane in *Current Issues* (2016) 82.
203 *Gee v Gee* (n 5).
204 In *Thorner v Major* (n 5) [55] Lord Walker stated that 'the landowner's standing by in silence serves as an element of assurance'.

It has further been argued that the impression that estoppel 'is being used against him [the promisor] to curtail his future freedom of disposition'[205] is even more acute in cases such as *Gillett v Holt* where the claim is brought during the lifetime of the promisor, usually because the parties have fallen out with one another. Martin Dixon has indeed interpreted *Gillett v Holt* as a case where 'proprietary estoppel operated, in effect, to prevent the future testator from changing his will so as to deny the claimant an inheritance that he had been long promised'.[206] But the point is that the testator has herself forfeited that possibility because she has accepted the performance and has benefitted from it.[207]

C. Circumventing formality requirements for testamentary dispositions

Another concern that has been raised in relation to the enforcement of informal testamentary promises is that by transferring the promised asset to the promisee, courts allow the parties to forgo formality requirements foreseen both for testamentary dispositions but also for lifetime transfers of land.[208] It is not possible nor useful here to enter into the debates about the functions of formality requirements. Suffice to say, and as already pointed out in Chapter 2,[209] formalities primarily protect the person who owns the property, and is about to give it away, from the dangers of informality, such as fraud and undue influence, though there are also other considerations at play like the need for legal certainty of the transfer and the need for evidence of the parties' intentions.[210]

Of course, if one were to argue that such formality requirements imposed by property or succession law stand in the way of the protection of the interests of the promisee, then we would be fighting a lost battle because this is an area in which informality represents the norm. As we have seen, insisting on formalities can turn into a problem for the promisee, which is why the New Zealand Law Reform (Testamentary Promises) Act 1949 (hereafter the New Zealand TPA 1949) does not require a written contractual promise. Nonetheless, it is important to clarify

[205] Ibid.

[206] Dixon (2008).

[207] What Dixon seems to criticize most is that the courts do not provide a satisfactory explanation of the underlying rationale for employing estoppel to curtail testamentary freedom, for, in his view, they do not clarify exactly what role unconscionability plays and what it means. His concerns appear to be directed more at the risk of abuse and of finding a promise where none was made.

[208] In fact, legally binding contracts to make a will must comply with formality requirements where the contract concerns an interest in land. That said, the doctrine of part-performance has sometimes offered protection even in the absence of such writing. See Chapter 3, section II.D.

[209] See Chapter 2. Fuller (1941). On the function of testamentary formalities see, Reid, de Waal, & Zimmermann, 'Testamentary Formalities in Historical and Comparative Perspective' in *Comparative Succession Law 1* (2011) 432.

[210] See Chapter 2.

why an award based on proprietary estoppel does not in my view infringe formality requirements, whether those required for testamentary dispositions or lifetime transfers.

Dixon, who has been generally critical of the developments in the area of proprietary estoppel, has asked: 'Why can promises, conduct or assurances that do not comply with the law's requirements of form be upheld, even in supremacy to dispositions which do meet those requirements?'[211] One answer is that the promisee is in a vulnerable position that warrants protection.[212] Another is that if courts could not ignore what is said in the promisors' last will, and hold them accountable for their earlier informal promises, promisors could simply make a will to defeat any promise they have ever made. In other words, promisors could rely on the lack of formalities of their promise to defeat the promisee's claim despite having benefitted from the promisee's performance[213]—more importantly, as mentioned earlier, the promisors' liability arises already during her lifetime. Thus, the will disposes of property that is no longer theirs to dispose of.[214] Also, one should not forget that in some jurisdictions such as Australia and New Zealand, though not in England and Wales, the formality requirements for wills are not strictly enforced because courts have dispensing powers.[215] They can therefore admit to probate documents that do not comply with the formality requirements.

With regards to the formalities imposed by the English Wills Act 1837 or equivalent legislation in other common law jurisdictions, it has been argued that if the promisee's expectations are fulfilled, it is as if the deceased had made a will.[216] But clearly the promisee's claim is not based on a testamentary disposition made by the promisor. It is based on the promisor's *inter vivos* promise. McFarlane has addressed the point by arguing that 'the effect of the former [a court order] can be seen as equivalent to the writing, or rewriting, of a will, so as to dispose of particular property to B. An equivalence of outcomes, in any particular case, does not of course mean that any two doctrines necessarily overlap conceptually.'[217] This must be right. Although the effect is the same, it does not mean that there is an infringement.

211 Dixon (2008) 68.

212 Sloan *Informal Carers* (2012) 79 has also made the point that, '[i]n the testamentary context, it is surely the case that the claimant trusted the deceased to comply with the formality requirements.'

213 Nield (2000) 88.

214 McFarlane in *Current Issues* (2016) 82: 'Proprietary estoppel operated to impose a liability on A, arising during A's life, and did not depend on any actual or assumed testamentary transfer.'

215 Peart, 'Testamentary Formalities in Australia and New Zealand' in *Comparative Succession Law 1* (2011) 349.

216 Hayton (1987) makes this point in relation to *Re Basham* (n 4). He seems to suggest that unlike in cases of a mutual will, where there is a promise to make a will, here there is no fraud as the promisee must have known that in the absence of a will, he would not have received anything.

217 Ibid, 90.

Thus, most of these arguments do not seem to speak against a protection but rather in favour of clearly defined requirements and clear guidelines as to how courts are to exercise their discretion when quantifying the relief.

VI. Evaluation from the perspective of the promisee

From the examination in this chapter it is clear that, from the perspective of the promisee, the doctrine of proprietary estoppel presents a number of benefits, especially, but not only, when looked at against the background of the contractual approach examined in Chapter 3. First, there is no need to prove a legally binding contract which, as we have seen, can be arduous and has often led to hard cases. Moreover, there is no need for the agreement to be in writing, even where the testamentary promise involves land. This fits the testamentary context, given that such promises are often made orally. What is more, on the whole, courts, whether in England and Wales, Australia, New Zealand, or the Republic of Ireland, have been prepared to interpret the requirements of a promise, reliance and detriment, in the specific context.[218] They have been willing to infer a promise from a number of statements or events, sometimes taking place over a longer period of time. Although the authority is not conclusive, it would seem that the doctrine of proprietary estoppel applies also when the promise does not relate to specific property but is a promise to leave the residuary estate. This is important. We have also seen that the detriment does not have to be financial in nature, that the conduct does not have to relate to the promised asset, and that the promise does not have to be the only reason for the conduct of the promisee, which is crucial because the promisee's motives are often mixed.[219] While the promisee must have relied on the promise to her detriment, the burden of proof of the reliance is on the promisor and the way the question is usually posed by courts is to the advantage of the promisee, though she may still have to defend herself by arguing that she has acted because of the promise. Thus, unsurprisingly, at least so far, instances in which the claim has been denied are comparatively rare.[220]

From the perspective of the promisee, the development of the doctrine of proprietary estoppel is to thus be welcomed, especially because the relationship (and hence the performance) often evolves over a long period of time so that it is difficult to frame the relationship in contractual terms. Also, it is frequently difficult

[218] As noted in *Thorner v Major* (n 5) [80], 'the meaning to be ascribed to words passing between parties will depend, often very much, on their factual context'.

[219] This is welcomed by Thompson (2003) 163.

[220] The claim was unsuccessful in *Uglow v Uglow* [2004] EWCA Civ 987; *MacDonald v Frost* [2009] EWHC 2276 (Ch); *Taylor v Dickens* (n 48); *Wrights v Waters & Anor* [2014] EWHC 3614 (Ch), and *McGuinness v Preece and Ors* [2016] EWHC 1518 (Ch). More recently, see also *James v James* (n 5) and *Shaw v Shaw* (n 5).

for her to insist that the parties enter into a formal contract or that the agreement be reduced to writing. For instance, in *Gillett v Holt*, the promisee had asked for something in writing to confirm that the farm would be his, but his request was met with the reply that 'that was not necessary as it was all going to be yours [his] anyway'. Sometimes the promisee may prefer immediate payment but again she may find it difficult to ask for such payment.[221] For example, in *Davies v Davies*, the daughter, Eirian, had asked for money for her services and her mother had simply responded that she should not 'kill the goose that lays the golden egg'. In *Walton v Walton*, complaints as to low wages simply triggered further promises or restatements of the promise from the promisee's mother. Similarly, in *Jennings v Rice*, the first instance judge noted that, when Mrs Royle was challenged by Mr Jennings about her failure to pay him, her reply was always '[h]e did not need to worry about that, he would be alright and she would "see to it"'.[222] Thus, not only might the insistence on formalities or compensation jeopardize the relationship, it may also not lead anywhere and simply trigger further promises. This is not to say that promisors necessarily act in bad faith, even though in *Jennings v Rice*[223] the trial judge had expressed doubts to that effect. Equally, one could argue that the fact that in *Davies v Davies*[224] the promisee was shown a draft will with her name on it and was led to believe that a partnership agreement had been signed, was a sign of mischievous intent on the part of the promisors, regardless of the fact that the Court of Appeal did not pay much attention to this detail. Instead, it insisted that this was only a draft will and that the promisee was aware of the fact that executed wills were different but nonetheless stayed on the farm. This is concerning because it suggests that the court had not taken into account that the promisee had trusted the promisors, her parents. Even so, promises can remain unfulfilled for a number of reasons, including because a will lacks attestation or because the promisor suddenly dies before she could make the will.[225]

Another benefit of the doctrine of proprietary estoppel is that, just like the contractual approach, it can be invoked irrespective of the type of performance the promisee has rendered in exchange for the promise of an inheritance (i.e. whether household or care services, services in a business, improvements to land, work on a farm, etc). Its scope is broad enough to capture a wide range of promises. It is thus more flexible and comprehensive than other approaches that will be analysed later in this book, even though, at least in England and Wales, it is often invoked in farm cases. Moreover, just like a contractual claim, but unlike some of the other type of claims analysed in this book,[226] an estoppel claim can be brought both on death

[221] See the comments in Chapter 1.
[222] *Jennings v Rice* (n 11) [9].
[223] Ibid, [46]: 'Mrs Royle was prone to saying different things at different times and, perhaps deliberately, couched her promises to Mr Jennings in non-specific terms.'
[224] *Davies v Davies* 2016 EWCA (n 5) [47].
[225] *Re Basham* (n 4) is such a case. See the discussion in Chapter 1, section IV.B.
[226] See, for instance, the New Zealand TPA 1949, but also § 2057a BGB and § 612 BGB.

and during the lifetime of the promisor, for instance, when the promisor is transferring the property to third parties by way of gift or sale in breach of the promise, or the parties fall out with one another. In such a case, the courts may, however, make allowance for the fact that the promisee obtains an accelerated effect.

Finally, the discretion courts have in establishing the award, while inevitably cause of some uncertainty, works for the testamentary context where rigid criteria do not always do justice to the complexity of some of the cases.[227] We saw that there can be good reasons for awarding the promised asset and that courts tend to award the expectation interest where the expectation and the detriment are clear, or the case has consensual-like (or quasi-bargain/contractual-like) features. The outcome is often the same, if not better, as it would have been had the promisee brought a successful contractual claim, or had there been a will giving effect to the promise, which is partly why the doctrine of proprietary estoppel has come under fire from some commentators.[228] That said, unlike with a breach of contract, mutual benefits (e.g. in the form of free accommodation) may be taken into consideration when establishing the award. Even so, on the whole the doctrine has less of an economic focus than, for instance, an enrichment claim.[229]

However, where the promisee is awarded a proprietary right, such a right binds third parties so that the claimant is ranked above creditors. In fact, even before the court orders in favour of the promisee, the 'estoppel equity' can bind third parties.[230] Thus, depending on whether the award is personal or proprietary in nature, the promisee will either rank as a creditor or better, which is of great advantage to her.

That said, the doctrine of proprietary estoppel is not without problems from the perspective of the promisee. While courts take into account the context, this is precisely where accepted societal expectations can play a role and work against certain promisees. Also, it is uncertain whether or not the promise must relate to 'specific, identified property'. However, the biggest uncertainty, at least in England and Wales, relates to the quantification of the relief, where it would be important to have clearer guiding principles for courts. Finally, it is debatable whether courts should take into account the interest of the promisor but also that of third parties when determining the relief.

227 The flexibility was welcomed by Thompson (2001) 86.
228 See section V.
229 See Chapters 6 and 9.
230 McGee *Snell's Equity* (2020) para 12-053 and s 116(a) of the Land Registration Act 2002. See section IV.

VII. Conclusion

This chapter has illustrated that through the doctrine of proprietary estoppel, common law courts have found a way to aid testamentary promisees who are unable to prove the existence of a contract. Even where a contract can potentially be proven, promisees may have an incentive to bring an estoppel claim. This is especially so in England and Wales, where the difficulties of bringing an enrichment claim, and the stricture with which courts have interpreted the requirements that must be met for a family provision order, leave the promisee with few other options.[231] In other common law jurisdictions, such as Australia or New Zealand, but also common law Canada, promisees have other avenues at their disposal.[232] Yet a proprietary estoppel claim is nonetheless attractive, given that the promisee can bring a claim already during the lifetime of the promisor, but especially given that that courts can award a proprietary remedy, in which case the promisee is in a strong position with regards to third parties.

All in all, it would seem that when applying the doctrine of proprietary estoppel courts are attuned to the specificities of the testamentary context and that the doctrine is able to capture cases where a contractual claim would not have been available.[233]While, in principle, the domestic context works against the promisee when she tries to establish a contract to make a will, both with regards to the requirement of consideration and that of an intention to create a legal relationship, this is not necessarily the case with a proprietary estoppel claim because the court is able to take into account the circumstances in which the promise was made, including the particular relationship and character of the parties, the variety of motives but also intangible benefits.

[231] Mee in *Landmark Cases* (2019) 191–192 also reminds us that it is rather difficult to challenge a will on the basis of undue influence or lack of capacity.

[232] Promisees can seek a family provision order discussed in Chapter 5, or bring an enrichment claim (see Chapter 6) and, in New Zealand, their position is protected through the TPA 1949 (see Chapter 7).

[233] McFarlane in *Current Issues* (2016) 85 argues that 'the doctrine thus has the principled flexibility necessary to deal with the concerns raised by a testamentary promise intended to benefit B only many years after having been made by A.'

5

Establishing the moral duty of a promisor to provide for the promisee

I. Setting the scene

Another way in which the promisee of an unfulfilled testamentary promise may try to seek redress, though only in common law jurisdictions, is by bringing a claim under what is commonly referred to as the family provision legislation.[1] I have already mentioned this legislation in Chapter 3, where I discussed when and how a family provision order may affect the interests of a contractual promisee.[2] In this chapter, I explore the extent to which the legislation may come to the aid of promisees.

The family provision legislation was first introduced in New Zealand in 1900,[3] and from there has found its way into the Australian jurisdictions,[4] England and Wales,[5] the Republic of Ireland,[6] and the common law provinces of Canada.[7] The New Zealand legislation was specifically designed for widows and dependent children who had been omitted from the wills of their husbands and fathers in neglect of their moral duty towards their family.[8] It provided courts with the power to order a provision out of the estate of the deceased who had not made adequate

[1] For a detailed account of how and why common law jurisdictions introduced this type of family protection, rather than one based on fixed shares, see Reid, 'Mandatory Family Protection in the Common Law Tradition' in *Comparative Succession Law 3* (2020) 704ff.

[2] See Chapter 3, section IV.

[3] Testator's Family Maintenance Act 1900 (NZ). The story of that legislation is skilfully explained by Reid, 'Mandatory Family Protection in the Common Law Tradition' in *Comparative Succession Law 3* (2020) 718ff. See also the fascinating analysis provided by Atherton (1990). The 1900 Act has been amended many times and the core provisions are now to be found in the Family Protection Act 1955 (NZ).

[4] Widows and Young Children's Maintenance Act 1906 (Vic); Testator's Family Maintenance Act 1912 (Tas); Testator's Family Maintenance Act 1914 (Qld); Testator's Family Maintenance and Guardianship of Infants Act 1916 (NSW); Testator's Family Maintenance Act 1918 (SA); Guardianship of Infants Act 1920 (WA); Testator's Family Maintenance Ordinance 1929 (NT); Administration and Probate Ordinance 1929 (ACT).

[5] Inheritance (Family Provision) Act 1938. Current legislation is contained in the Inheritance (Provision for Family and Dependants) Act 1975 (hereafter the 1975 Act).

[6] Succession Act 1965 (Ireland) (hereafter the 1965 Act), s 117. For a commentary, see Spierin *Succession Act* (2017).

[7] For details, see Popovici & Smith, 'Family Provision in Canada' in *Comparative Succession Law 3* (2020) 507ff.

[8] For details, see Peart & Vines, 'Family Provision in New Zealand and Australia' in *Comparative Succession Law 3* (2020) 450ff; Croucher (2005).

Claiming a Promised Inheritance. Alexandra Braun, Oxford University Press. © Alexandra Braun 2022.
DOI: 10.1093/oso/9780198757252.003.0006

provision for their proper maintenance and support. Hence, the legislation has its roots in the financial need of close family members (and especially of widows and children) although, at least in its origins, it was also a reflection of the desire to prevent dependence on the State.

Over time, the scope of the New Zealand legislation (and to some extent also that of the equivalent legislation in other common law jurisdictions) has expanded through an extension to intestacy.[9] Hence, in many jurisdictions an application can be brought both where the deceased has made a will that does not adequately provide for the applicant, and where a will is missing or invalid. Also, with time, the category of those entitled to bring a claim has been expanded,[10] and certain applicants have become almost automatically entitled to a claim.[11] This is certainly true of New Zealand, where an increasing number of successful claims based on the family provision legislation are being brought by adult children who are not in need.[12] These and other developments have cast doubts on the rationale underpinning the legislation.

Be that as it may, the purpose behind the family provision legislation has never been to tackle instances where expectations of an inheritance are frustrated due to the breach of a testamentary promise,[13] nor to compensate work performed by family members.[14] Rather, its primary objective has been to provide for the maintenance of certain family members or dependants of the deceased who have not been adequately provided for. Thus, just like civilian forced or compulsory heirship, family provision orders operate even against the deceased's will. Nonetheless, in some cases promisees have successfully sought protection through the family provision legislation.

Due to the wide discretionary powers that courts are given under this type of legislation, the award can vary from monetary payments to a proprietary interest in

[9] In all Canadian jurisdictions, except British Columbia and Nova Scotia, it is possible to claim family provision on intestacy. See Popovici & Smith, 'Family Provision in Canada' in *Comparative Succession Law 3* (2020). By contrast, the Irish Succession Act 1965 is limited to claims under a will. However, a report of the Irish Law Reform Commission launched on 30 May 2017 by Ms Justice Baker has proposed to change this. Irish Law Reform Commission, *Report on section 117 of the Succession Act 1965: Aspects of Provision for Children* <https://www.lawreform.ie/news/report-on-section-117-of-the-succession-act-1965-aspects-of-provision-for-children.758.html> accessed 5 November 2021.

[10] See Reid, 'Mandatory Family Protection in the Common Law Tradition' in *Comparative Succession Law 3* (2020) 735 who shows how, at least initially, the surviving spouse was marked out for favourable treatment.

[11] McGregor-Lowndes & Hannah (2009) argue that disinheritance is almost impossible in Australia and that adult children are now entitled to an award almost as of right. See also Croucher (2007).

[12] Peart & Vines, 'Family Provision in New Zealand and Australia' in *Comparative Succession Law 3* (2020) 468. However, stepchildren are eligible under s 3 only if they were being maintained by or dependent on the deceased at death. That requirement is strictly construed in *Re Hilton* [1997] NZLR 734.

[13] *State Trustees Ltd v Whitehead* [2012] VSCA 274, [155] (hereafter *State Trustees Ltd v Whitehead*), per Neave JA: 'The purpose of the Act is not to give effect to promises made by testators, but rather to make orders which adequately provide for the maintenance and support of those for whom a testator has a moral responsibility to provide.'

[14] In *Re Coventry (deceased)* [1980] Ch 461 (Ch), 474–475 Oliver J held that '[i]t is not the purpose of the Act to provide legacies or awards for meritorious conduct'.

the deceased's estate. In the majority of cases, it will consist in a monetary payment. Yet, as the analysis will show, at least in Australia and in the Republic of Ireland, promisees have sometimes been able to obtain the promised inheritance, with courts ordering the transfer of the promised farm or family home. For this reason, I discuss the family provision legislation in this part of the book, even though this form of redress is often used by promisees as a last resort.

While the legislation does not only apply to promisees, in this chapter I focus only on cases that were brought by testamentary promisees. We will see that the promises examined were sometimes made in exchange for domestic and care services,[15] improvements to the promisor's home,[16] or work in her business.[17] However, most of the family provision cases involving promisees deal with promises made in exchange for work on the deceased's farm.[18] This, then, may explain why almost all the claims were claims brought by adult sons and why, in some cases, they got the farm. Irrespective of that, in this chapter I analyse which promisees can bring a claim and what requirements they must meet in order to be successful. We will see that a promise of a future inheritance can be important in a court's finding that the applicant has not been adequately provided for. It can trigger a moral duty on the part of the deceased to provide for the promisee, especially where the promise has been acted upon, which are the cases at the heart of this enquiry. For this reason, some Australian judges have drawn a parallel between the family provision legislation and the doctrine of proprietary estoppel, analysed in Chapter 4. However, while there may well be some commonality in the theoretical underpinnings to be found in the notion of unconscionability, the analysis will show that the scope, the requirements, and the degree of protection provided are very different.

It will not be possible, nor necessary, here to cover all jurisdictions that feature cases in which the family provision legislation has been resorted to by promisees. Also, in most jurisdictions the promisee is likely to pursue alternative claims. For instance, because New Zealand has enacted a statute dealing specifically with cases of breach of informal testamentary promises, it is less likely that a promisee will have, or want, to rely on the family provision legislation in order to obtain redress, though she may well pursue both avenues.[19] Equally, although in common law

[15] Such cases are, however, less common. For examples, see *Espinosa v Bourke* [1999] 1 FLR 747 (CA) (hereafter *Espinosa v Bourke*) and *In Re Callaghan, Decd* [1985] Fam 1 (hereafter *In Re Callaghan, Decd*).

[16] *Vukic v Luca Grbin, Estate of Zvonko Grbin* [2006] NSWSC 41 (hereafter *Vukic v Luca Grbin*).

[17] *Re Abram (deceased)* [1996] 2 FLR 379; [1997] 2 FCR 85; [1996] Fam Law 666 (hereafter *Re Abram (deceased)*); *Coates v National Trustees Executors and Agency Co Ltd* (1956) 95 CLR 494 (hereafter *Coates v National Trustees Executors and Agency Co Ltd*).

[18] See, for instance, *Re Pearce (deceased)* [1998] 2 FLR 705; [1999] 2 FCR 179; [1998] Fam Law 588 (hereafter *Re Pearce (deceased)*); *In the Goods of Breen (deceased), Breen and Kennedy v Breen and Others* (High Court, 5 May 1995), [1995] Lexis Citation 5760 (hereafter *In the Goods of Breen (deceased)*); *RG v PSG* [1980] ILRM 225 (hereafter *RG v PSG*); *Frey v Frey* [2009] QSC 43 (hereafter *Frey v Frey*).

[19] See Chapter 7. In *Hamilton v Hamilton* [2003] NZFLR 883 (HC), the grandson had sought redress through the Law Reform (Testamentary Promises) Act 1949 and, alternatively the Family Protection Act 1955 (NZ).

Canada it is not excluded that a family provision claim is pursued as an alternative to other actions, a promisee of an informal testamentary promise will normally bring a contractual claim, an enrichment claim or a proprietary estoppel claim.[20] For this reason, in this chapter, particular focus will be placed on case law drawn from England and Wales,[21] the Republic of Ireland and, especially, Australia, where a good number of promisees have been able to obtain redress through the family provision legislation leading, in some cases, to an award of what they were promised.

The purpose of this chapter is neither to provide a detailed discussion of the legislation in the various common law jurisdictions, nor to evaluate the success of the legislation aimed at protecting the interests of family members. What is of relevance to this enquiry is understanding the extent to which the legislation can come to the aid of a promisee and whether or not it is attuned to the specificities of the context in which testamentary promises are made. The analysis will show that the family provision legislation can be helpful for promisees because the legislation neither requires proof of a promise (whether express or implied) nor of detrimental reliance. Hence, the promisee's motives and the timing of the promise are entirely irrelevant. Also, in some cases the promisee may be able to obtain the promised asset. At the same time, we will also see that there are reasons why the legislation is often only invoked when other avenues fail, for example, because the protection is limited not just in terms of its scope (so that only a limited number of promisees could ever rely on it) but also in terms of degree, including vis-à-vis third parties. The analysis will further show that, for instance, English courts have been strict in their construction of the requirements that must be met for a family provision order, which they regard as interfering with testamentary freedom.[22] This is in stark contrast to their approach to the interpretation of the requirements for a proprietary estoppel claim.[23] Thus, in England and Wales, promisees will often opt for a proprietary estoppel claim instead, unless the promise is too vague or the detrimental reliance too tenuous for such a claim. By contrast Australian,

[20] In common law Canada, a contractual claim is possible also when the contract lacks writing for the doctrine of part-performance still operates. See Chapter 3, section II.D. In practice, promisees will often pursue more than one claim, as in *Guzzo v Catlin Estate* (1989) 38 BCLR (2d) 41 (BCCA) where the claimant had brought two claims, one based on the lack of adequate provision for the proper maintenance and one based on the enrichment of the deceased.

[21] In *Jennings v Rice* [2002] EWCA 159, a claim based on the family provision legislation was brought together with one in contract and one based on proprietary estoppel. In *Suggitt v Suggitt* [2012] EWCA Civ 1140 the court referred to a pending claim under the 1975 Act. In *Habberfield v Habberfield* [2018] EWHC 317 (Ch) the claim was based on the doctrine of proprietary estoppel and, alternatively, on the 1975 Act. Because the proprietary estoppel claim was granted, it was not necessary for the court to decide the claimant's position under the 1975 Act.

[22] Although, in England and Wales, there are only a handful of cases where a promisee of an inheritance has successfully brought a claim under the 1975 Act, sometimes the legislation has been invoked together with, or in alternative to, a proprietary estoppel claim.

[23] See Chapter 4.

and Irish, courts seem to be more flexible, both when interpreting the conditions for an order, but also when establishing the quantum.

II. Scope and prerequisites

A. Eligible parties

In order to seek a family provision order, the promisee must be among the category of those eligible to such a claim. The category varies across jurisdictions. Generally, such claims are available to children and the surviving spouse or civil partner of the deceased. As noted earlier, while initially the legislation was only aimed at protecting the surviving spouse and children, the scope has been extended over the years. In fact, in some jurisdictions, it also includes a former spouse who has not remarried, cohabitants, and parents, as well as other dependants of the deceased.[24] While the list of potential applicants under the family provision legislation has grown over time, the scope of the legislation is not as broad as that of the doctrine of proprietary estoppel, which I examined in Chapter 4, or that of enrichment law in common law Canada, which will be discussed in Chapter 6.

B. Lack of adequate or reasonable provision for the applicant

For a promisee to be successful, it is not sufficient to fall among the category of those eligible to bring a claim. Something more is required in the form of the lack of adequate or reasonable provision.[25] In most jurisdictions the applicant must be in financial need. An exception is New Zealand. Although, as mentioned earlier, in the beginning the aim of the family provision legislation was to protect the interests of widows and children in financial need, this is no longer the case. In 1962, financial need was formally abandoned as a prerequisite,[26] and since then there has been a tendency to protect applicants, including adult children as of right.[27] This

[24] This is, for instance, true of England and Wales: s 1(1) of the 1975 Act. In Canada, the situation varies from province to province. For details, see Popovici & Smith, 'Family Provision in Canada' in *Comparative Succession Law 3* (2020). In the Republic of Ireland, the protection offered by s 117 of the 1965 Act is restricted to children, but this is because the surviving spouse is already entitled to half of the estate where there are no children and a third where there are children. Details are provided by Reid, 'Mandatory Family Protection in the Common Law Tradition' in *Comparative Succession Law 3* (2020).

[25] Reid, de Waal & Zimmermann, 'Mandatory Family Protection in Historical and Comparative Perspective' in *Comparative Succession Law 3* (2020) 737ff, 747.

[26] *Re Harrison* [1962] NZLR 6 (CA).

[27] Peart & Vines, 'Family Provision in New Zealand and Australia' in *Comparative Succession Law 3* (2020) 468; Peart & Borkowski (2000) 336. By contrast, in Canada, in many cases, adult children may only claim if they are unable to earn a livelihood. See Popovici & Smith, 'Family Provision in Canada' in *Comparative Succession Law 3* (2020).

development seems to be the result of the fact that the New Zealand legislation speaks not merely of 'maintenance' but mentions also 'support'. Courts have read 'support' to take a wider meaning than 'maintenance' and to mean 'sustaining, providing comfort'.[28] Thus, adult promisees, who are often those who seem to rely on the legislation, have an easier task in New Zealand compared to other jurisdictions.

Although the language employed by the relevant family provision legislation across Australian jurisdictions varies, with some speaking of 'maintenance and support'[29] and others establishing that an order can be made where 'adequate provision for the proper maintenance, education or advancement in life' is lacking,[30] financial need is still a prerequisite. Yet, over time Australian courts seem to have constructed 'financial need' in a flexible manner[31] so that adult children are now more likely to succeed than in the past.

Financial need is also a necessary requirement in the Republic of Ireland but again courts have been relatively flexible in interpreting the requirement.[32] This is because the duty of the deceased is not one to make 'adequate provision' but to make 'proper provision', which is not limited to making a reasonable provision for children who are dependants. Thus, the position of an adult child under section 117 of the Succession Act 1965 seems to be better than the position under the equivalent 1975 Act in England and Wales. Despite the fact that the scope of the family provision legislation has also been widened in England and Wales, the decision of the UK Supreme Court in *Ilott v Mitson* (2017),[33] concerning the claim of an adult daughter, has shown that the power that English courts have to intervene and interfere with a will is still very much dependent on the applicant's financial needs.

However, as a recent comparative study has pointed out, '[b]eginning with New Zealand in 1909, a number of countries (Australia, Canada, Ireland) now make use of a "moral duty" test to help determine the "adequacy" or "reasonableness"

[28] See *Williams v Aucutt* [2000] NZFLR 532 (CA), [52] per Richardson P:

> 'Support' is an additional and wider term than 'maintenance'. In using the composite expression, and requiring 'proper' maintenance and support, the legislation recognises that a broader approach is required and the authorities referred to establish that moral and ethical considerations are to be taken into account in determining the scope of the duty. 'Support' is used in its wider dictionary sense of 'sustaining, providing comfort'. A child's path through life is supported not simply by financial provision to meet economic needs and contingencies but also by recognition of belonging to the family and of having been an important part of the overall life of the deceased. Just what provision will constitute proper support in this latter respect is a matter of judgment in all the circumstances of the particular case.

[29] For example, Succession Act 1981 (Qld), s 41.

[30] Succession Act 2006 (NSW), s 59.

[31] *Jones (a pseudonym) v Smith (a pseudonym)* [2016] VSCA 178, [33] and [66] acknowledging that 'need' is a relative concept.

[32] It should be noted here that the Irish Law Reform Commission, *Report on section 117 of the Succession Act 1965* (n 9) has recommended that the law should be reformed, specifically as it applies to adult children. Among many other things, the proposal suggests that the court should presume that the deceased made proper provision for adult children.

[33] *Ilott v Mitson* [2017] UKSC 17; [2017] 2 WLR 979.

of the will vis-à-vis the applicant'.[34] In other words, the establishment of a moral duty would appear to be particularly relevant where the claim is brought by an adult child.[35] For instance, in *Re IAC* (1990), the Irish Supreme Court concluded that a mature applicant 'will have a heavy onus to discharge',[36] and that she has to establish a positive failure of moral duty on behalf of her parent.[37] In England and Wales, proof of impoverished circumstances will not be enough to succeed.[38] Adult children may have to show special circumstances or a moral obligation,[39] but proving the existence of a moral obligation on the part of the deceased is not an easy endeavour. Indeed, in England and Wales, adult children will often find it difficult to bring a successful claim, even if they manage to prove the existence of a moral obligation on the part of the deceased.[40] For that reason, the legislation is frequently invoked only as a fallback.

It is precisely when applying the moral duty test that a promise of an inheritance can play an important role. In other words, a promise, even if vague, can help establish such a duty on the part of the deceased promisor and show that she has not made adequate or reasonable financial provision in the promisee's favour, especially where the promise was acted upon and the promisee has, for instance, made contributions or provided services.

To conclude, New Zealand aside, in other common law jurisdictions the promisee has to show that she is in need of maintenance in order to demonstrate that the promisor has not made adequate, reasonable, or proper financial provision in her favour. However, in Australia and the Republic of Ireland, the court's approach to the requirement of financial need seems to be more relaxed than in England and Wales. To ascertain whether the provision is inadequate or unreasonable, courts generally look at whether the deceased had a moral duty towards the applicant, especially where adult children are involved. And for the purposes of establishing such a moral duty it matters whether the deceased has made a testamentary promise in favour of the applicant or whether the latter has provided a performance for the former.

[34] Reid, de Waal & Zimmermann, 'Mandatory Family Protection in Historical and Comparative Perspective' in *Comparative Succession Law 3* (2020) 747.

[35] Miller (1995) 30; Sloan *Informal Carers* (2012) 197–198.

[36] *In Re Estate of IAC decd* [1990] 2 IR 143.

[37] Spierin *Succession Act* (2017) 323.

[38] Sloan *Borkowski's Law of Succession* (2020) 337.

[39] Kerridge, 'Family Provision in England and Wales', in *Comparative Succession Law 3* (2020) 396.

[40] Ibid, 332. For a comparison between English law and the law in New Zealand, see Peart & Borkowski (2000). See also Sloan in *Future of Family Property in Europe* (2011) 251.

C. Relevance of the promise of an inheritance and of the promisee's contribution

As mentioned earlier, the purpose of the family provision legislation has never been to tackle testamentary promises cases, nor to reward unremunerated work carried out in the family context. In fact, a promisee does not need to prove a promise of an inheritance, nor that she has provided work or services for the promisor or made contributions to her estate. Yet we also saw that promises that the deceased has made to an applicant, and contributions made by the latter, can play a significant role when establishing that the deceased had a moral duty towards her. This helps to determine whether the provision that the deceased has made for the applicant (or that she receives through intestacy) was 'adequate' or 'proper', and whether she has a claim.

For the purpose of establishing a moral duty, promises do not have to be express nor specific, nor do the contributions have to be of a financial nature. It is therefore perhaps unsurprising that promisees of unfulfilled informal testamentary promises have sometimes relied on the legislation in order to obtain redress.

There are several English,[41] Irish,[42] and particularly Australian cases[43] in which courts have found that, where a person was *induced* by the deceased to believe that they would inherit the property through a promise, the latter was under a moral duty to provide for them especially where they acted on the promise. This was explicitly stated, for instance, in the Australian case of *Alexander v Jansson* (2010), where Brereton J (with whom both Basten JA and Handley AJA agreed) held that:

[41] See *Espinosa v Bourke* (n 15) where the promisee's father had promised that her mother's portfolio of shares would be left to her on his death.

[42] For example, in *In the Estate of ABC, XC v RT* [2003] 2 IR 250, 263, Breen J confirmed that: 'Special circumstances giving rise to a moral duty may arise if a child is induced to believe that by, for example, working on a farm, he will ultimately become the owner of it, thereby causing him to shape his upbringing, training and life accordingly.' Another Irish case in which the promise mattered is *RG v PSG* (n 18). The decision will be discussed later (see the text at n 82), because in this case the farm was awarded. For a recent case, see *K v K* [2018] IEHC 615, [133] (hereafter *K v K*). According to McDonald J: 'The plaintiff was led to believe that he would receive an interest in the farm. That was very clearly a consideration to which the deceased, as just and prudent parent, ought to have borne in mind when it came to making her will.'

[43] See Brereton J in *Vukic v Luca Grbin* (n 16) [38]: 'Promises made and expectations raised by testators have always been regarded as relevant to the ascertainment of what is proper provision for a claimant ... This is particularly so where a claimant has relied to his or her detriment on any such promise or expectation.' Brereton J took the same position in *Bovaird v Frost* [2009] NSWSC 337, [111]. See further *Forsyth v Sinclair* [2010] VSCA 147, [98] per Neave JA, with whom Redlich JA and Habersberger AJA concurred: 'Whilst Part IV of the Act does not give the Court power to make an order simply to give effect to the intention or promise of a deceased person to provide for someone else, such a statement of intention is not an irrelevant consideration.' For other examples where the promise mattered, see *Frey v Frey* (n 18) [190] and *Whitehead v State Trustees Ltd* (2011) 4 ASTLR 528; [2011] VSC 424, [338] (hereafter *Whitehead v State Trustees Ltd*); *Coates v National Trustees Executors and Agency Co Ltd* (n 17) 523.

> Promises made and expectations raised by testators have always been regarded as relevant to the ascertainment of what is proper provision for a claimant ... though this may be more so where a claimant has relied to his or her detriment on any such promise or expectation.[44]

The decision is particularly interesting because in this case the successful family provision claim was brought not by a child, but by the ninety-four-year-old mother of the deceased. Among the factors the New South Wales (NSW) Court of Appeal considered in her favour were various statements attributed to her son to the effect that she would be able to live in the property (which they had held as tenants in common) until she died. It is important to mention that the NSW Family Provision Act 1982, which the claim in *Alexander v Jansson* was based on, explicitly mentioned among the factors courts should take into account when evaluating whether there is a claim, any contribution an applicant has made whether of a financial nature or not to the 'acquisition, conservation or improvement of the deceased property'.[45] The NSW Succession Act 2006, which superseded the 1982 Act, further increased the list of factors and added that a court should also take into account (both when deciding whether the person in whose favour the order is sought to be made is an eligible person, and whether to make a family provision order, but also the nature of any such order), 'evidence of testamentary intentions of the deceased person including statements made by the deceased person'.[46] Thus, the NSW legislation explicitly acknowledges that not only contributions made by the applicant but also a promise of a future inheritance made to her are determinative in establishing a moral duty on the part of the deceased to provide for the applicant.

An interesting English case in which the court found that the promise of an inheritance, and the work the promisee had performed by acting on the promise were relevant for the purposes of establishing the promisee's claim, is *Re Pearce (Deceased)* (1998).[47] From the age of six to sixteen the promisee had worked on his parents' sheep farm without pay and was repeatedly told by his father (the deceased) that he would leave the farm to him on his death. The promisee left home at sixteen to get a job, having been told by the deceased that he could not pay him to work on the farm. Nonetheless, the promisee continued to help on the farm when he could without pay until he joined the army aged twenty-two. On the death of the father, eight years later, he brought an application under the 1975 Act on the grounds that his father had not made reasonable provision for him in the will. The father had made a will but had left all his property to the defendant, his former cohabitant. The first instance court held that the deceased had a moral obligation

[44] *Alexander v Jansson* [2010] NSWCA 176, [18].

[45] Family Provision Act 1982 No 60 (NSW), s 9(3)(a)(i) superseded by the Succession Act 2006 No 80 (NSW), s 60(2)h.

[46] Succession Act 2006 (NSW), s 60(2)j.

[47] *Re Pearce (deceased)* (n 18).

towards the son, that the obligation continued until the deceased's death, and that it did not end when the son left home aged sixteen because in doing so the son had acted reasonably. The moral obligation was created by the substantial unpaid work that the son had rendered in acting on the promises made to him by his father. For this reason, and in light of the financial needs of the son, the court awarded him £85,000 free from inheritance tax (the value of the estate being judged at £285,000). The Court of Appeal dismissed the appeal. It noted that although 'there is no invariable prerequisite that a moral obligation or some other special circumstance must be shown' in this case, a 'particular moral obligation' did arise from the 'very substantial amount of work carried out by the applicant coupled with the promises that were made to him by the deceased'.[48]

Similarly, in the Irish case of *In the Goods of Breen (Deceased), Breen and Kennedy v Breen and Others* (1995),[49] one of the sons of the deceased (who had fourteen children) sought relief under section 117 of the Succession Act 1965 on the grounds that his mother failed in her moral duty to make proper provision for him, 'having promised to do so'.[50] On leaving school, the son had worked full-time for his parents on the family farm for eight years between the age of fourteen and twenty-two. He was not paid by them except for his keep at home, and he received about £3 per week in Social Welfare payments ('farmers dole'). While other family members helped out on a part-time basis, the son was the only one to work full-time. He was encouraged to do so by his mother's promise that 'she would give me the farm later on'. The son stopped working on the farm when his father returned to working full-time on the farm and no longer needed his services. Indeed, he told the son that he should 'go off and get a job for himself'.[51] At the time of his application, the son was unemployed and thus in financial need. Barr J found that the son had made a 'significant sacrifice'[52] by working without reward for eight years on the family farm, and that he had done so on the promise by his mother that she would look after him. The judge noted that, in so working, the applicant was deprived of the chance for further education which some of his brothers took up. Unlike some of his brothers, he was not given a site for a house by his parents; nor was he given any reward for his employment on the farm. Barr J therefore concluded that the deceased had failed in her moral obligation to the son who was entitled to £4,000 to supplement the 'farmers dole' he had received.

Even though promises of an inheritance are not technically speaking a requirement, these cases show that coupled with work or services performed by the promisee, such promises matter when establishing that the deceased had a moral duty to provide for the applicant. This does not, however, mean that the promise and the

48 Ibid, 711.
49 *In the Goods of Breen (deceased)* (n 18).
50 Ibid.
51 Ibid.
52 Ibid.

promisee's performance are necessarily sufficient to establish a claim, they are just two among many factors that help to establish whether the deceased had a moral duty and thus whether the provision for the promisee was adequate or reasonable. Also, New Zealand aside, the promisee still needs to show that she needed maintenance or support,[53] though in Ireland and in Australia the requirement of financial need is interpreted in a more flexible manner, at least compared to England and Wales. Now that we have seen what a promisee must prove to avail herself of the family provision legislation, let us look at the types of awards and orders courts can make.

III. Establishing the award

A. Providing adequate and proper maintenance and support

Just as with proprietary estoppel, and the New Zealand Law Reform (Testamentary Promises) Act 1949, which I will examine in Part III, under the family provision legislation, courts have a wide discretion when making an order. How far courts go in exercising their discretion varies across jurisdictions. Relative legislation usually refers either to the adequate provision for the 'proper maintenance and support',[54] the 'maintenance, education or advancement in life of the eligible person',[55] or the 'proper provision for the child in accordance with his means'.[56] What counts as 'adequate' and what as 'proper' seems to depend on the circumstances of the case. However, it appears that courts have generally used 'proper' to allow for a more liberal provision.

We saw that with regards to the Republic of Ireland the duty of the deceased is one to make 'proper provision', which is not limited to making a reasonable provision.[57] And we saw that in New Zealand, and to some extent also in Australia, there

[53] See the Australian case *Higgins v Higgins* [2005] QSC 110, where the application was not based on financial need but rather on the lack of recognition of work that the applicant argued he had carried out in reliance on a promise by his parents. The claim was rejected. That the promise is insufficient to substantiate a family provision claim was confirmed also in *Flocas v Carlson* [2013] VSC 221, [295] (dealing with a mutual will), where McMillan J concluded that:

> I am not satisfied that the existence of agreement or representation to leave Robert's interest to the plaintiff by will can establish a moral responsibility on the part of Marjorie to provide for the plaintiff. The existence of a promise of this nature, if proved, may indicate what provision might be adequate in the circumstances. Such a promise might, in certain circumstances, suggest the kind of relationship that might justify an order for further provision. It cannot of itself, however, support the existence of a responsibility to make further provision. That responsibility must rest on the nature of the relationship between the deceased and the claimant and the claimant's need, not upon the existence of a promise not honoured or an assurance departed from.

[54] Family Protection Act 1955 (NZ), s 4(1).

[55] Succession Act 2006 (NSW), s 59(2).

[56] See the Irish Succession Act 1965.

[57] See section II.B.

has been a move away from pure financial need.[58] Indeed, in *Bosch v Perpetual Trustee Company, Limited* (1938), in an appeal to the Privy Council from an order of the Supreme Court of NSW, Lord Romer stated that:

> The use of the word 'proper' in this connection is of considerable importance. It connotes something different from the word 'adequate'. A small sum may be sufficient for the 'adequate' maintenance of a child, for instance, but having regard to the child's station in life and the fortune of his father, it may be wholly insufficient for his 'proper' maintenance.[59]

This is not, however, the case in England and Wales, where all applicants (except the spouse and civil partner) can only ever claim 'reasonable financial provision', meaning 'financial provision as it would be reasonable in all the circumstance of the case for the applicant to receive his maintenance'.[60] This was recently confirmed by the Supreme Court decision in *Ilott v Mitson* (2017) according to which '[t]his limitation to maintenance provision represents a deliberate legislative choice and is important'.[61] In the eyes of the majority of the court, it 'demonstrates the significance attached by English law to testamentary freedom'.[62] In other words, for the Supreme Court maintenance is still key and is the only reason that justifies the inroad into testamentary freedom. What maintenance means is, of course, uncertain, for the term is rather vague. However, Lord Hughes (with whom Lord Neuberger, Lady Hale, Lord Kerr, Lord Clarke, Lord Wilson, and Lord Sumption agreed), held that although the concept of maintenance is broad, and while it is not limited to subsistence, 'it cannot extend to any or everything which it would be desirable for the claimant to have. It must import provision to meet the everyday expenses of living'.[63] Hence, in most English cases, the promisee will obtain only a monetary payment limited to the promisee's needs.

Irrespective of that, in exercising the discretion, courts are again guided by a number of factors (many of which are relevant already when establishing the claim) that are either determined by the court or by statute. In some cases the list is endless and, as others have already pointed out, the longer the list of factors, the more complex and costly the whole trial will be.[64] These factors usually include the

[58] As for New Zealand, see *William v Aucutt* [2000] 2 NZLR 479.

[59] *Bosch v Perpetual Trustee Company Limited* [1938] AC 463 (PC), 476.

[60] This is established by the 1975 Act, s 1(2)(b). By contrast, in the case of current spouses or civil partners, ss 1(2)(a) and (aa) state that reasonable financial provision is what would be reasonable for the applicant to receive, whether or not required for maintenance. Section 3(2) adds that courts have discretion to have regard to the provision that the spouse or civil partner might have been expected to obtain in the event of divorce or dissolution. Thus, the legislation is more generous towards spouses and civil partners who should not find themselves worse off on death than they would have been on divorce. See Kerridge, 'Family Provision in England and Wales', in *Comparative Succession Law 3* (2020) 395.

[61] *Ilot v Mitson* (n 33) [13].

[62] Ibid, [13].

[63] Ibid, [14].

[64] Ibid, 748.

financial needs of the applicant, any obligations or responsibilities which the deceased had towards her and others, the size and nature of the estate, the conduct of the applicant, and, in several jurisdictions, any promises the deceased has made to the applicant or any contributions that the latter has made to the deceased's estate.[65]

Thus, while neither the promise nor the contribution that the promisee has made in acting on the promise represent the basis for an award, they are among the factors to be taken into account at the stage of the quantification. An interesting case in this context is *State Trustees Ltd v Whitehead* (2012),[66] decided by the Court of Appeal in Victoria. Here the promise was an unusual one. The promisor promised to provide for the promisee and her son (born from another relationship) if she carried out the pregnancy and kept the child. The first instance judge found that a claim had been established and ordered that the applicant should receive provision in the sum of $450,000, and that a sum of $400,000 be paid into Court to be held by the Senior Master for the benefit of her son until he attained the age of eighteen years.[67] The decision was appealed and the Victorian Court of Appeal was asked to consider whether the first instance judge had erred in saying that the award under the relevant family provision legislation should reflect the promise that the deceased had made to help the promisee and her son. The appeal was dismissed. The court found that the judge had not erred in his findings because he had not determined the amount solely by reference to the promise, having given detailed consideration to the financial resources, earning capacity and financial needs of the beneficiaries.[68] Thus, what is adequate depends, among other things, on the size of the estate, the promise, and the promisee's action, as well as her financial needs. In order to establish these needs, the court will take into account mutual benefits in the form of lifetime or testamentary gifts she has received.[69] Just as with proprietary estoppel claims, mutual benefits are taken into account when deciding the extent of the family provision order.

B. Type of possible orders

The orders that courts can make to provide for the applicant are flexible. In the case of England and Wales, the orders themselves can take the form of periodical payments, the transfer of lump sums, the transfer or settlement of property,

65 See, for instance, Succession Act 2006 (NSW), s 60.
66 *State Trustees Ltd v Whitehead* (n 13).
67 *Whitehead v State Trustees Ltd* (2011) (n 43) [338].
68 *State Trustees Ltd v Whitehead* (n 13) [156].
69 The 1975 Act, s 3(1) requires the court to consider the 'financial resources and financial needs' of any applicant or beneficiary, which will include the destination of any pension benefit. See, for instance, *P v G (Family Provision: Relevance of Divorce Provision)* [2004] EWHC 2944 (Fam), [2006] 1 FLR 431 where the court formulated an award which took account of the fact that the applicant had already received benefits from the deceased's pension.

and the variation of ante- or post-nuptial settlements in favour of the applicant.[70] Australian legislation provides similarly. For instance, in NSW the order may, amongst other things, consist of the application of specified existing or future property, thus leading to the award of a proprietary right,[71] which is a point I explore later. In the Republic of Ireland, the court may order that such provision shall be made for the child out of the estate as the court thinks just.[72] Lastly, in New Zealand, courts may order a lump sum, a periodical or another type of payment, and also a transfer of property.[73] Thus, courts have a range of powers including the power to fulfil the promise, which is of course in the interest of the promisee.

C. Cases in which the promise was given effect to

While courts have the power to transfer property, normally an order under the family provision legislation will consist of a monetary payment. This is particularly the case in England and Wales where, on the whole, courts have been comparatively less generous in terms of awards. Again, this is in stark contrast to the court's approach in the context of proprietary estoppel claims, which may have to do with the fact that the courts see the family provision legislation as directly interfering with testamentary freedom.[74]

By contrast, there are some Australian and Irish cases in which promisees have obtained what was promised in the form of a proprietary right, in either the farm or the family home.[75] I would like to single out three examples in which the promisee has been able to obtain the expectation interest. An interesting Australian farm case that involved a promise of an inheritance and that led to the award of the farm was decided by the Supreme Court of Queensland. In *Frey v Frey* (2009) three sons had worked the father's lands for decades and without adequate compensation but on the basis of a promise that they would all one day inherit from their father. The youngest son, Edward, had an expectation that his father would leave him one of several grazing properties (*Ashton Grove*), based on promises the latter had made to him.[76] Indeed, in two previous wills the father had left *Ashton Grove*

70 The 1975 Act s 2(1).

71 Succession Act 2006 (NSW), s 65. Under s 62 of the same Act, the court can also make an order restraining the final or partial distribution of an estate pending its determination of an application for a family provision order.

72 The 1965 Act, s 117(1).

73 Family Protection Act 1955 (NZ), s 5(2). New Zealand courts rely on the general provision in Family Protection Act 1955 (NZ), s 4(1), which refers to 'any provision the court thinks fit'. They can thus transfer a percentage share of the estate or a life interest in a property or the property itself.

74 See, however, the discussion in Chapter 4 on the point that some judges see proprietary estoppel relief as an infringement on testamentary freedom.

75 For an Australian case, see *Hughes v National Trustees, Executor and Agency Company of Australasia Ltd* 143 CLR 134 (1979) 134, 148 (Gibbs J). For a New Zealand case, see *B v Adams* (2005) 25 FRNZ 778 (FC), where the widow obtained half the farm.

76 *Frey v Frey* (n 18).

to Edward, but in the last will he left him a mere $25,000. When the father died, Edward brought a claim under the family provision legislation. Although the claim was brought late, Lyons J, felt that the delay had been adequately explained and thus heard the case. The judge found that 'promises made by testators are regarded as relevant'[77] and that Edward had a strong moral claim against the father's estate. What is more, Lyons J awarded Edward *Ashton Grove* together with 110 megalitres of water. In other words, his expectation interest was fulfilled. Why no proprietary estoppel claim was brought in this case is unclear, especially given that counsel of the promisee had pointed out the similarity between the unconscionability underpinning both proprietary estoppel and the moral duty under the family provision legislation.[78] However, in this case it would not have made much of a difference.

Another Australian example is the decision of the Supreme Court of NSW in *Vukic v Luca Grbin, Estate of Zvonko Grbin* (2006),[79] which involved a dispute over a family home. On several occasions, and over the course of many years, Ina Vukic had been told by her parents, who lived between Australia and Croatia, that if she continued to live in the family home, maintain it, and pay all the expenses, her father, who had returned to Croatia, would in his will leave her a three-quarter interest in the house in Australia. Ina remained in the house, maintained it, and paid all the outgoings, because she believed that her father would leave her three-quarters of the house. When she resigned from the Department of Community Services where she had worked, she received a lump sum superannuation pension payment of about $58,000, which she expended on the maintenance, conservation, and improvement of the house. Later on she undertook further improvements, linking the back flat to the main house. Her father had made a will but had left his house (worth about $770,000) to be divided into six equal parts of which Ina (the promisee) was going to receive only one. She brought a claim arguing that she was entitled to an equitable estate by way of estoppel in the house, arising from her detrimental reliance on representations made to her by the deceased to the effect that she would upon his death inherit a three-quarter interest in it. Alternatively, she claimed provision out of the estate pursuant to the Family Provision Act 1982 (NSW). The court concluded that both claims were founded. What is notable in this case is that, for the purposes of establishing whether there was a claim under the 1982 Act, the court highlighted the relevance of both the promise and Ina's reliance on it. Brereton J appealed to the concept of conscionability which, as we have seen, underpins all three requirements of proprietary estoppel. Indeed, the judge spoke of a philosophical analogy between the family provision legislation and proprietary estoppel:

[77] Ibid, [190].
[78] Ibid, [191].
[79] *Vukic v Luca Grbin* (n 16).

> The requirements of conscionable behaviour which inform the doctrine of equitable estoppel are philosophically closely analogous to the concept of 'moral duty' which has traditionally informed the exercise of jurisdiction under the Family Provision Act and its predecessors and, some of the observations in *Singer v Berghouse (No 2)* notwithstanding, continues to do so [*Vigolo v Bostin*; *Palmer v Dolman* [2005] NSWCA 361, [74]].[80]

The judge concluded that, in this case, conscionable behaviour required the deceased father to satisfy the expectation of his daughter, an expectation that was engendered by his promise. The case is further interesting because the promisee had submitted that rather than granting relief upon the basis of the doctrine of proprietary estoppel, it was 'preferable to proceed under the Family Provision Act, chiefly because of the more convenient statutory remedies provided by that statute'.[81] The reason for that is that section 10 of the Family Provision Act 1982 (NSW) authorizes court orders making 'consequential provisions for other eligible persons and beneficiaries in such a manner and to such extent as the Court thinks necessary to adjust all the interests concerned and to do justice in the circumstances'. In fact, what the judge effectively did in this case is to substitute the interests that the deceased had left in his will to the mother and one of the siblings of the promisee in the house, with monetary legacies charged against the house, which he awarded to the promisee. In other words, the judge vested the property in the applicant subject to charges in favour of the defendants. In doing so he varied the will, which he could not have done on the basis of the doctrine of proprietary estoppel. The thinking behind the judge's decision was that otherwise the daughter's continued occupation of the house would have been at the mercy of the defendants who could have appointed a trustee for sale. The adjustment was thus beneficial to the promisee without, however, leaving defendants without protection.

The last case I want to mention here is the Irish farm case of *RG v PSG* (1980),[82] in which the promised asset was again awarded. The promisee was the deceased's eldest son and the defendants his two brothers. The promisee left school at age fourteen to work on the family farm. When he married, his wife moved into the family home and although at the time they wanted to move to a nearby farm (at Harristown) owned by his mother, they were persuaded not to move because 'the home farm would be his eventually'.[83] Carroll J found that the applicant was always

80 Ibid, [38]. The same judge made the same statement in *Alexander v Jansson* (n 44) [18]. A similar position was taken also by Zelling J in *Re Anderson (deceased)* (1975) 11 SASR 276. In *Frey v Frey* (n 18) [191] A Lyons J noted that there was some force in counsel's submission that 'the requirements of unconscionable behaviour which inform the doctrine of equitable estoppel are closely analogous to the concept of "moral duty" and that unconscionable behaviour is highly relevant to what is proper provision for a plaintiff'.

81 *Vukic v Luca Grbin* (n 16) [35].

82 *RG v PSG* (n 18).

83 Ibid.

encouraged by his parents to believe that the farm would be his one day and that '[t]his was repeated to him by his father less than a week before he died'.[84] The judge further found that the son had worked on the farm every day of the year for over thirty years. Although the household expenses came out of the cheques when stock was sold, and if he or his wife needed money for special purposes, they could ask for it, and use the family car, the promisee was not paid for his work but was given only a little pocket money. In light of these circumstances, Carroll J concluded that the deceased had failed in his 'moral duty to the promisee to make proper provision for him and provide him with a means of livelihood from farming reasonably comparable with what he enjoyed before the death of the testator',[85] and that this would not be satisfied by a third share in the estate as per the intestacy rules. 'Farming is the only occupation know to the Plaintiff since the age of 14' the judge found. The judge also took account of the defendants' circumstances and held that they were still 'entitled to expect some share in their father's estate both for their own benefit and to help with their children's education'. The judge then divided up the deceased's assets, awarding the promisee the vast majority, which consisted of the house and all its contents, all personal effects of the deceased, all farm machinery, the car, and all stock on the farm, and all but approximately forty acres of the land.

Hence, in this case, the promisee was effectively given what he had been promised, that is the farm. The promise aside, in this case it was more practical to award what was promised and it was arguably the only way to do justice, given how substantial the promisee's services had been. Certainly, it was the only way to guarantee the promisee's maintenance. Had the farm been split up, the promisee would not have been able to carry on with the farming and, given that he was forty-seven years old when he brought the claim, changing jobs would not have been easy. As Carroll J noted, the reduction of the farm by forty acres would still 'enable him [the applicant] to carry on farming, not to the full extent as before but hopefully he will have a reasonable living on the reduced acreage'.[86] Thus, just as we saw with regards to proprietary estoppel,[87] there may be a variety of reasons, both practical and policy based, that can lead a court to awarding the expectation interest in the form of a proprietary interest in the deceased's property, especially where the property in question is a farm.[88]

To summarize, the analysis has shown that promises of an inheritance matter not just when establishing whether there is a moral duty on the part of the testator, and thus whether there is a claim, but can also sometimes play a role when

[84] Ibid.
[85] Ibid.
[86] Ibid.
[87] Chapter 4.
[88] In *Salmon v Osmond* [2015] NSWCA 42, dealing with a family provision order, the deceased was under the impression that the larger legacy to the daughters might place the viability of the farm in jeopardy which is something the court took into consideration.

quantifying the award and thus determining the order. It is therefore sometimes possible that the promisee's expectations are fulfilled, including because awarding the promised asset is more practical or because it is the only way to ensure adequate and proper maintenance, for example, where a farm is involved, and the applicant has based her entire life on the farm. Also, a fragmentation of the farm may make farming unviable and therefore speak in favour of a transfer of the entire farm or of a substantial part of it. In addition, the fact that some judges have sought a link between the family provision legislation and equitable estoppel may also have played a role when they quantified the award. In other words, it may have led them to base greater weight on the promise. For instance, one cannot but have that suspicion in the two Australian decisions, *Frey v Frey* and especially *Vukic*, both of which were discussed earlier. In this context, it is interesting to mention that in the Irish case of *K v K* (2018),[89] McDonald J said that there is no distinction between the extent of the remedy to be granted under section 117 of the 1965 Act on the one hand and the extent of the remedy to be granted in respect of the testamentary contract and related proprietary estoppel claim on the other. In this particular case it was not necessary to make an order under section 117 because the judge had found in favour of a contract. Nonetheless, the statement is important. It confirms that in the Republic of Ireland, family provision orders can involve a transfer of the promised inheritance. It may also suggest that Australian judges are perhaps not alone in seeing a commonality between family provision and proprietary estoppel, which brings me to the next point.

IV. Family provision v proprietary estoppel

The analysis has shown that some Australian courts have suggested that the requirement of an unconscionable behaviour, which informs the doctrine of equitable estoppel, is philosophically closely analogous to the concept of 'moral duty', which informs the exercise of jurisdiction under the Family Provision Act 1955. However, while unconscionability may be a common feature underpinning both claims, at least to some extent, it is unclear whether the analogy is really helpful.[90] Certainly in both cases courts have considerable discretion in determining the relief, and the fact that the deceased has made a promise which was acted upon, can

[89] *K v K* (n 42).

[90] See Dal Pont & Mackie *Succession* (2017) 669 who are also critical. They argue that:

> Yet the utility of the analogy is unclear. Not only is the threshold for 'unconscionable conduct' that triggers estoppel comparatively high, reference to moral duty in the context of family provision is not ordinarily directed to moral disapprobation of the deceased. And if there is unconscionable conduct of the kind that raises an estoppel, there seems little need to interfere, via legislation with freedom of testation. What the cases suggest, rather, is that promises or assurances that are by themselves insufficient to raise an estoppel may, when coupled with other relevant matters, go to what is proper provision.

play a role in establishing a moral duty on the part of the deceased to provide for the applicant, but it is not determinative. However, the threshold for unconscionable conduct in the case of a proprietary estoppel claim is higher than that required for establishing the breach of a moral duty for the purposes of a family provision order. Also different is the way in which the award is established. It is thus useful here to point out these differences with a view to establishing how beneficial family provision claims can be from the perspective of a promisee of a future inheritance and how well they cater for the specificities of the context in which such promises are made.

One advantage of a family provision claim is that while the promise and the promisee's performance in exchange matter for the purpose of establishing whether the provision made was inadequate or unreasonable, unlike in an estoppel claim, the motives underpinning the applicant's behaviour are entirely irrelevant. In other words, in the case of a family provision claim, there is no need to show that the promisee has relied upon the promise. For that reason, the promisee's performance can precede the promise or the promisee's motives can be of an entirely different nature. The fact that the promisee's motives are irrelevant is of considerable advantage for, as noted earlier,[91] establishing one's motives can not only be challenging but also emotionally and psychologically difficult. At the same time, as John Mee has argued, if a promisee tries to bring a family provision claim she will 'most likely have to rehearse the unglamorous part of "lame duck"'.[92] That may well function as a disincentive for bringing a claim. Also, while in the case of proprietary estoppel claims courts have been prepared to imply promises from the behaviour of the parties, and to take into account the particular context, including the personality of the parties, the promise must still be reasonably clear and unequivocal and it must be reasonably understood as seriously intended.[93] By contrast, for the purpose of establishing the promisor's moral duty, the promise can be very vague. Thus, it seems that the threshold that the promisor's behaviour needs to meet in order for it to be unconscionable, and for her to be estopped from changing her mind, is higher with the doctrine of proprietary estoppel. In some circumstances, a family provision claim may therefore be preferable. However, an application under the family provision legislation can only be brought by those eligible under the legislation,[94] that is certain family members and dependants, and only on death of the promisor. By contrast, an estoppel claim can be brought by anyone who, in reliance on a promise of a future inheritance, has suffered detriment, and already during

[91] See the discussion in Chapters 2 and 4. But see also Chapter 6.

[92] Mee in *Landmark Cases* (2019) 192.

[93] For details, see Chapter 4, section II.A.2.

[94] It is worth remembering that as the scope of the legislation has expanded, some promisees can now seek protection under it and no longer need to find redress by invoking, for instance, the doctrine of proprietary estoppel. See Chapter 4. According to some legal scholars this explains why in certain cases courts have been flexible and liberal in their interpretation or finding of the requirements for an estoppel claim.

the promisor's lifetime. What is more, in an estoppel claim, the personal financial circumstances of the applicant are entirely irrelevant. In other words, the promisee does not need to show that she is in financial need and that the testamentary provision made was therefore inadequate, though as we have seen, this is no longer a requirement in New Zealand, and in Australia and the Republic of Ireland, the requirement is interpreted somewhat broadly.

In addition, the short time period within which the claim under the family provision legislation has to be presented can pose a potential obstacle. For instance, in most Australian jurisdictions the time limit is six months from death, in New Zealand twelve months,[95] and in England and Wales, as well as in the Republic of Ireland, six months from the date on which representation with respect to the estate of the deceased is first taken out.[96] Thus, in practice, it may sometimes be too late for such a claim. The reason for such short time limits lies in the interests of an efficient estate administration but can clearly work against promisees, who may have to resort to other means of redress. That said, in some jurisdictions, extensions of time have been granted unless the estate is finally distributed, and this has happened in some of the testamentary promises cases, including in *Frey v Frey*.[97]

More importantly, an application under the family provision legislation is one against the deceased's net estate, so that the claim cannot be brought during the lifetime of the promisor. Difficulties can therefore arise where the promisor has made a lifetime transfer. In such cases, a promisee will need to resort to other forms of redress. As a further consequence of the fact that the claims are against the net estate, the promisee ranks after creditors and an award will only be made after all debts have been satisfied and provided that something is left in the estate. This also means that in the case of competing claims, for example, where an enrichment claim or an estoppel claim are brought by another promisee, the interests of the applicant under the family provision legislation will usually succumb.[98] This is important and may well be a reason why a promisee may prefer to pursue other forms of redress, and, in particular, a proprietary estoppel claim. That, said, as Chapter 3 has shown, where the interest of the applicant under the family provision legislation conflicts with that of a contractual promisee who benefits under the will, depending on the jurisdiction, the former may well prevail.[99]

Also, because the family provision claim is one against the net estate, the order may not be able to capture lifetime or *mortis causa* dispositions that the deceased has made. However, anti-avoidance mechanisms have been put in place so that in

[95] Family Protection Act 1955 (NZ), s 9(1).

[96] The 1975 Act, s 4 and Succession Act 1965 (Ireland), s 117(6).

[97] See also *Price v Smith* [2004] 1 NZLR 354 (CA). For an Australian example, see *Coates v National Trustees Executors and Agency Co Ltd* (n 17).

[98] See *Smith v Taylor* [2006] NSWSC 162 where the son had brought a claim under the family provision legislation and the daughter a crossclaim based on proprietary estoppel. The arrangement with the daughter was enforced and the applicant eventually received further provision.

[99] For details, see Chapter 3, section IV.

some jurisdictions, the powers of courts under the family provision legislation can, for instance, extend to property disposed of in execution of a contract to make a will or through a *donatio mortis causa*.[100] For instance, NSW has made changes to its laws whereby an applicant can ask the court to determine that property that was passed without full valuable consideration during the three years prior to the testator's death increases the estate available for the purpose of a family provision claim.[101] In England and Wales, discretionary orders can include a gift *mortis causa* as well as property the deceased owned jointly. Conversely, pension death benefits or life insurances policies held on trust are usually excluded.

In terms of award, despite the discretion courts have with both forms of redress, in the case of the family provision legislation, maintenance and support still represent the primary objective, though we saw that in some jurisdictions courts have been prepared to give the term 'proper' a wider meaning.[102] The promise of an inheritance and the promisee's performance usually represent simply two out of many other factors to be taken into account when quantifying the award, and the value of the promise will not usually represent the starting point or basis for the order. In fact, in most cases the promisee will probably obtain a monetary payment and in some jurisdictions, this will be limited to the amount that is needed for the purpose of their maintenance. Also, among the factors that a court must consider are moral duties that the deceased may have towards others. While such duties are among the factors that Walker LJ had mentioned in *Jennings v Rice* dealing with a proprietary estoppel claim, the extent to which they should matter in such a claim is controversial.[103]

Thus, a proprietary estoppel claim may often be the first port of call especially given that, as we saw in Chapter 4, courts seem to frequently award a proprietary interest. Yet, as demonstrated by *Vukic v Luca Grbin*, the promisee may have an interest in an award under the statutory provision, where a variation of the promisor's will is desirable. Even so, all in all, there is no doubt that a proprietary estoppel claim will usually offer a higher degree of protection, and that it captures a broader range of promisees.

V. Conclusion

In this chapter we have seen several instances in which promisees of unfulfilled testamentary promises have sought protection through the family provision legislation. What might explain this development? In most of the cases in which

[100] Family Protection Act 1955 (NZ), s 2(5); Succession Act 1981 (Qld), s 41(12).
[101] Succession Act 2006 (NSW), ss 75–93 and 80.
[102] Both in Australia and in Ireland.
[103] See the discussion in Chapter 4, section III.C.

promisees have resorted to the family provision legislation, a contractual claim would have failed from the outset, not least because of the lack of writing or a lack of certainty as to the terms of the contract.[104] In some of them a proprietary estoppel claim would probably also have been met with difficulties, either because the promise would not have been sufficiently clear and unequivocal,[105] or because it would have been difficult to prove that the detriment came about as a result of the reliance on the promise. Yet, because over time the scope of the family provision legislation has been extended, and courts have put emphasis on finding a moral duty, by paying attention to any promise made by the deceased or contributions and services provided by the applicant in return for such promise, arguably family provision claims have become increasingly attractive from the perspective of a promisee, in particular in some jurisdictions. This is so especially given that the threshold for unconscionable behaviour required for a proprietary estoppel claim seems to be higher but also because, even under the family provision legislation, courts have the power to make proprietary awards. Also, due to anti-avoidance rules, in some jurisdictions the power of courts has been extended so as to capture property which is the subject matter of will-substitutes, including contracts to make a will. Another aspect that promisees might appreciate is that, at least in England and Wales, the discretion under the 1975 Act is apparently rarely exercised in open court, and more usually by masters and district judges in chambers, where decisions are not reported (and cannot be unless leave is given), so that the cases are not usually public.[106] Similarly, in the Republic of Ireland applications based on section 117 of the 1965 Act are to be heard *in camera*.[107] This could help promisees who are reluctant to make family life public and who may otherwise be dissuaded from pursing a claim. Finally, some of the cases examined in this chapter have shown it is possible to demand 'compensation' for work or services carried out as a minor,[108] which is not possible with other claims examined in this book.[109]

Is this development to be welcomed? As mentioned before, the family provision legislation is regarded as a restriction of the deceased's testamentary freedom in the sense that it can work even against the deceased's will. For that reason, in *Illot*

[104] For instance, lack of certainty of the terms but also of an intention to create a legal relationship was found in *Lewis v Lewis* [2001] NSWSC 321 (1 May 2001), [68]–[69]. The estoppel claim also failed, but the court found in favour of the claimant on the alternative claim under the Family Provision Act 1982.

[105] In *Re Leach (deceased)* [1984] FLR 590, 606 the first instance judge found that the applicant 'rightly in my view, does not seek to use this incident as something upon which to found some sort of equitable estoppel'. In *Re Abram (deceased)* (n 17) (391) there was no clear promise. The court held that a statement by the testator in the latter years of her life that the applicant should not worry as 'everything will be alright', while accepted by the applicant as an assurance that the house would be his, was 'too slender a peg upon which to hang any positive assurance'. What is more, in this case the assurance came after the applicant had left the business and his mother had changed her original will. Under the 1975 Act, the son was able to receive 50% of the nest estate which was settled on him for life on protective trusts.

[106] This is stated by Judge Roger Cooke in *Re Abram (deceased)* (n 17) 388–389.

[107] Section 119 of the 1965 Act.

[108] See *In Re Callaghan, Decd* (n 15) and *Re Pearce* (n 18).

[109] See, for instance, the *créance de salaire différé* discussed in Chapter 10.

v Mitson, the UK Supreme Court was reluctant to allow claims by adult children unless they are in financial need. Thus, such an interference is generally justified by the fact that the applicant needs maintenance. However, we saw that over time, in some jurisdictions, the scope of the legislation has been extended beyond financial needs, and in the case of New Zealand, the requirement was abolished. Does this entail that the developments described in this chapter (i.e. the fact that the family provision legislation can be resorted to by promisees) unduly compromise the deceased's testamentary freedom?[110] I would argue that it is not, for reasons that I have mentioned earlier. While the legislation was not designed for this purpose, what courts are doing here is to give effect to obligations voluntarily assumed by the deceased. The fact that the order leads to the transfer of proprietary interest, therefore achieving the same result, does not change this. In other words, by making a promise the deceased herself has limited her own freedom. The fact that the promisee's interest is protected through the family provision legislation rather than the doctrine of proprietary estoppel or enrichment law does not change this. Also, if the basis for the claim is a moral duty, why should the deceased's moral duty to provide for the applicant only arise if the latter is in need and not also (or perhaps especially) if she has acted on a testamentary promise.

Whether the family provision legislation is the 'best' way to deal with these types of cases is another question, especially in jurisdictions where, as in New Zealand, there is specific legislation in place aimed at dealing with informal testamentary promises. Certainly, from the perspective of the promisee, other forms of redress provide greater protection. Given recent developments in the area of proprietary estoppel, it is unlikely that there will be many future cases in which the family provision legislation will be invoked by a promisee, except perhaps where there is a lack of a clear promise or assurance, or where detrimental reliance is difficult to prove. Where that is the case, another option may be enrichment law, which will be the focus of Chapter 6.

[110] McGregor-Lowndes & Hannah (2009); Croucher (2007) 200 has argued that '[f]amily provision is, in my view, right out of hand. It is on a slippery slope where adults are concerned'.

6
Establishing the promisor's enrichment in Canadian law

I. Scope and background

One interesting aspect that emerges from the analysis of this book is that in many civil and common law jurisdictions promisees can seek redress through enrichment law. One common law jurisdiction where enrichment law has been very prominent in providing protection to promisees of testamentary promises is common law Canada, which represents the focus of this chapter.

In common law Canada, contracts to make a will can be validly concluded and, unlike in England and Wales, a promisee's claim is aided by the fact that the doctrine of part-performance still operates.[1] This means that a contract to make a will concerning land may be enforceable even if it is not in writing, so long as there is proof of a contract, and the promisee's performance unequivocally concerned the promised property and not just the contract itself. Where a contract can be established, the promisee might be better off pursuing a contractual claim, as she is more likely to obtain the promised property.[2] However, as we saw in Chapter 3,[3] the level of protection that a promisee enjoys under contract law depends on the subject matter of the promise and on when the promise is breached. Thus, establishing a contract does not automatically lead to the award of the promised asset or to damages that reflect its value. Where no such contract can be proven, a promisee is not left without protection. It is often possible to bring a proprietary estoppel claim, and Chapter 4 has shown that there is Canadian case law concerning promises of a future inheritance in which the doctrine has been invoked. Even so, in common law Canada, the default way for a promisee to claim redress is to bring a claim based on the unjust enrichment of the promisor.[4] This is especially the case outside the farming context where it can be difficult to establish a sufficient link to the promised property in the form of contributions or improvements, so that lack of

[1] See Chapter 3, section II.D.

[2] The doctrine of part-performance applied, for instance, in *Jans v Jans* 2016 SKQB 275 (hereafter *Jans v Jans*), in *Buchko v Buchko* 1997 CanLII 10951 (SK QB) (hereafter *Buchko v Buchko*), and in *Orange v Swierz Estate* (1986) 54 Sask R 195 (hereafter *Orange v Swierz Estate*).

[3] See Chapter 3, section III.

[4] Oosterhoff et al *Oosterhoff on Wills* (2016) 122.

Claiming a Promised Inheritance. Alexandra Braun, Oxford University Press. © Alexandra Braun 2022.
DOI: 10.1093/oso/9780198757252.003.0007

any writing of the testamentary arrangement poses a problem for promisees and can deny them protection under contract law.

The recourse to enrichment law in cases in which a person's expectation of a future inheritance is frustrated is possible also in other common law jurisdictions, such as Australia.[5] However, the instances of such claims seem to be comparably fewer than in Canada, with most claims being based on contract law, the doctrine of proprietary estoppel, or the family provision legislation, all examined in Part II. And, since New Zealand has specific legislation in place, there are generally fewer claims in which promisees resort to the law of unjust enrichment to obtain redress.[6] In England and Wales, there seems to have been only one published case so far in which a promisee has invoked enrichment law alongside the doctrine of proprietary estoppel, but both claims were rejected.[7] Thus, while enrichment claims are a possibility, outside common law Canada promisees tend to seek other form of redress.

The fact that in common law Canada promisees frequently seek an enrichment claim is likely to be primarily due to both the fact that enrichment can come about through domestic and care work, and the flexibility of the relief in this jurisdiction. Although a successful claim normally leads to a monetary award, given the discretion courts enjoy in common law Canada, the monetary award is usually higher than the value of the promisor's enrichment. Moreover, in some cases it may be possible for the promisee to obtain the promised asset by way of a remedial constructive trust. I therefore examine Canadian enrichment cases in this final chapter of Part II and not in Part III, which deals with instances in which a promisee merely obtains the value of the performance or the restitution of the promisor's enrichment, or less.

The reason why the Canadian doctrine of unjust enrichment is so flexible and attuned to the testamentary setting is that it covers a broad range of contexts,[8] and many of the cases that were crucial to its development have concerned instances of a break-up of,[9] in particular, cohabitations. Consequently, under Canadian law some of the requirements are more flexible compared to other common

[5] For examples of Australian unjust enrichment cases in the testamentary promises context, see *Stinchcombe v Thomas* [1957] VR 509 (Victoria SC) and *Reynolds v McGregor* [1973] 1 QL 314.

[6] For examples of New Zealand cases, see *Van der Berge v Giles* [1979] 2 NZLR 111 (NZ SC) and *Stratulatos v Stratulatos* [1988] 2 NZLR 424 (NZ HC).

[7] *Cook v Thomas* [2010] EWCA Civ 227. Some authors have contemplated applying enrichment law in order to tackle cases in which testamentary promises have been frustrated, and more specifically cases in which promisees have provided care. See Wells 'Testamentary Promises' (2007) 75 but also Nield (2007); Sloan 'Unjust Enrichment Claims' (2011); Sloan 'Due Rewards' (2011) and Sloan *Informal Carers* (2012) 121ff, 134–135. Brian Sloan has, however, made the point that in England and Wales, the law of unjust enrichment may not be sufficiently developed yet to support a claim by a carer.

[8] For a list of instances that are covered by the doctrine, see McLachlin in *Restitution Past, Present and Future* (1998) 277.

[9] Chalmers (2017) 5ff. The historical development of the cause of action is analysed by Litman (1988) 407.

law jurisdictions, and, although courts use the language of restitution, the relief awarded is, as mentioned, not merely based on the value of the enrichment. Indeed, the doctrine is perceived as an equitable doctrine that involves considerable judicial discretion in setting the award.

What is interesting from the perspective of this book is that the first case in which the Supreme Court of Canada recognized unjust enrichment as a distinct legal doctrine was precisely a case involving the breach of a testamentary promise.[10] In *Deglman v Guaranty Trust Co of Canada and Constantineau*, which dates back to 1954, an aunt had made an oral promise to her nephew that she would make adequate provision for him in her will, and leave him her house, on condition that he would render certain services as she might from time to time request. Accordingly, the nephew took his aunt in her own or his car on trips to Montreal and elsewhere, and on pleasure drives. He did odd jobs in the houses she owned and ran errands and minor services for her personal needs. When the aunt died intestate, the nephew argued that he had fully performed his part of the agreement so that he should obtain the value of the promise, even though the promise had been made orally. Both the trial judge and the Court of Appeal of Ontario allowed specific performance of the oral contract on the basis of the doctrine of part-performance. However, the decision was overruled by the Supreme Court of Canada which found that the nephew's acts were insufficient to support a claim based on part-performance, for none of them were unequivocally referable to the promised property. Thus, the effect of the Statute of Frauds 1677 that required the testamentary contracts to be in writing could not be avoided in this case. Instead, the court awarded a *quantum meruit* claim for the value of the services he had provided.[11]

Deglman is the first in a long line of cases in which Canadian courts have been prepared to give redress to promisees of informal testamentary promises on the basis of enrichment principles, awarding either a monetary award or a restitutionary proprietary award in the form of a constructive trust. The cases concern a number of different scenarios, ranging from promises made in exchange for improvements to the deceased's property,[12] work on the promisor's farm,[13] and more frequently, domestic services or care provided for the promisor.[14] Hence, unlike

[10] *Deglman v Guaranty Trust Co of Canada and Constantineau* [1954] SCR 725 (hereafter *Deglman v Guaranty Trust Co of Canada*).

[11] The value of services awarded was $3,000. In the report of the decision of the Ontario Court of Appeal [1953] OWN 665, the value of the promise is given as $15,656.67.

[12] In *Schnogl v Balen Estate* 2005 BCCA 575; (2006) 21 ETR (3d) 32 (hereafter *Schnogl v Balen Estate*) the promisee carried out maintenance work in the house and the yard and provided personal services. In *Kreeft v Kreeft* 2001 BCSC 893; 39 ETR (2d) 233 (hereafter *Kreeft v Kreeft*) the four promisees had helped with the building of their father's auto body shop.

[13] In *Ogle v Ogle* 2005 SKCA 14; (2005) 248 DLR (4th) 626 the claimant had worked on the promisor's farm. The extension of constructive trusts to protect, in particular, the rights of farm children whose expectation to inherit the farm was frustrated, is advocated by Korven (1993).

[14] In some cases, the promisee had moved in with the promisor: *Schnogl v Balen Estate* (n 12). In others, the promisor had moved in with the promisee: *Guzzo v Catlin Estate* (1989) 38 BCLR (2d) 41; 33

Chapters 4 and 5, this chapter deals chiefly with promises made in exchange for services carried out in the home or assistance or care for the promisor, which will often, though not only, be performed by female promisees. In exchange for performances from the promisee, promisors usually promise to make a testamentary disposition in their favour, to leave a piece of property (e.g. their home), but sometimes also money and, occasionally, the benefits of a retirement scheme,[15] or the proceeds of an insurance policy.[16] Thus, just like contract law and the doctrine of proprietary estoppel, but unlike the family provision legislation analysed in Chapter 5, Canadian enrichment principles are broad enough to cover a wide range of testamentary promises cases, which is not necessarily the case with other remedial approaches analysed later in this book.[17]

The purpose of this chapter is to explore what a promisee needs to prove in order to establish a successful enrichment claim and how courts quantify the relief, with a view to establishing the extent to which this doctrine is able to deal with the specificities that distinguish such promises and thus to protect the interests of promisees in an adequate manner. The analysis will show that, while in common law Canada enrichment law is able to capture instances where the enrichment has come about through performances rendered by a promisee who is acting on a promise of a future inheritance, it is not always straightforward to establish such a claim. Although a promisee does not need to prove a contract, promise, detrimental reliance, or financial needs, she needs to prove an enrichment, a corresponding deprivation, and the absence of a juristic reason for the enrichment. In doing so she faces potential challenges, though the existence of a testamentary promise can be crucial in this regard. What is more, a proprietary award is not necessarily available to everyone, even if their performance has been substantial. We will also see that compared to proprietary estoppel claims, here there is a greater focus on tangible benefits and thus on the financial aspects of both the enrichment and the deprivation[18] (e.g. in the form of lack of opportunities). In addition, the promisor has certain defences available that can prevent an enrichment claim from being successful. Thus, while in common law Canada an enrichment claim can be useful from the point of view of a promisee, it also has its limitations, so that

ETR 163 (BCSC) (hereafter *Guzzo v Catlin Estate*). For a detailed and excellent analysis of the range of claims, see Wells *New Approach* (2007) and Wells 'Testamentary Promises' (2007).

[15] See *Belvedere v Brittain Estate*, 2009 ONCA 1; 306 DLR (4th) 754 (Ont CA) (hereafter *Belvedere v Brittain Estate*) where the claim was, however, dismissed. In *Henderson v Henderson* (1998) 52 BCLR (3d) 184 (BC SC) (hereafter *Henderson v Henderson*), the promisor had promised not to sever the joint tenancy of property purchased together with the promisee.

[16] See *Richardson Estate v Mew* 2009 ONCA 403; 310 DLR (4th) 2, though the action was dismissed along similar lines of *Belvedere v Brittain Estate* (n 15).

[17] See Chapters 8, 10, and 11.

[18] *Peter v Beblow* [1993] 1 SCR 980, 989–990 (hereafter *Peter v Beblow*): 'This Court has consistently taken a straightforward economic approach to the first two elements of the test for unjust enrichment.'

promisees may want to explore the possibility of a contractual or proprietary estoppel claim. A family provision claim will usually be brought only as a last resort.

II. Requirements a promisee must meet

For an unjust enrichment claim to be successful under Canadian common law, three requirements must be met:[19] (i) an enrichment on the part of the promisor; (ii) a corresponding deprivation on the part of the promisee; and (iii) the absence of any juristic reason for the enrichment. Each requirement will be looked at in turn, but we will see that, from the perspective of the promisee, the requirement of the absence of a juristic reason for the enrichment (including the defences available to the promisor in that context) is potentially the most difficult to meet. Not only does the promisee have to show what motivated her behaviour, societal expectations as to what can be regarded as normal or usual behaviour also play a role.

A. An enrichment

Canadian courts have established that a claimant must prove a tangible enrichment which can be both positive or negative in nature. An example of a negative enrichment is where the benefit conferred on the defendant spares her an expense she would otherwise have had to undertake.[20] The enrichment can come about through contributions or improvements to the deceased's property, but also work on a farm or in a business, and importantly also through domestic/household and care services.[21]

That domestic/household and care services are covered by the doctrine was explicitly stated by the Supreme Court of Canada in the seminal decision of *Peter v Beblow* (1993),[22] and confirmed by numerous cases dealing specifically with domestic services performed in exchange for a promise of a future inheritance.[23] Of particular interest in this regard is the decision of the Court of Appeal of British Columbia in *Clarkson v McCrossen Estate* (1995),[24] which was followed

[19] As Mr Justice Myers stated in *Chan v Chan* 2014 BCSC 2422, [64] (hereafter *Chan v Chan*): 'Nor are unjust enrichment cases wills variation claims without a will: it is not enough to conclude that a child may have been unfairly dealt with in the context of a parent's death. The elements of unjust enrichment must be made out.'

[20] See *Peel (Regional Municipality) v Canada* [1992] 3 SCR 762 (SCC) and *Kerr v Baranow* 2011 SCC 10; [2011] 1 SCR 269, [38] (hereafter *Kerr v Baranow*).

[21] By contrast, in Germany the question was raised as to whether the *condictio ob rem* is even applicable to services. See Chapter 9, section II.

[22] *Peter v Beblow* (n 18). See also *Kerr v Baranow* (n 20) [42].

[23] But already in *Deglman v Guaranty Trust Co of Canada* (n 10) the services rendered were of domestic nature and the same was true in *Balkwill v Smith* (1957) 65 Man R 55, 21 WWR 474 (Man QB) (hereafter *Balkwill v Smith*). See further *Guzzo v Catlin Estate* (n 14).

[24] *Clarkson v McCrossen Estate* (1995) 122 DLR (4th) 239 (BC CA) (hereafter *Clarkson v McCrossen*).

in a number of later cases.[25] Here a stepdaughter had cared for her mother and her stepfather over many years, providing a variety of services (including cooking meals, housework and nursing, numerous trips to the hospital, telephone calls, and visits) without remuneration. The mother and stepfather had consistently told the promisee that the family home would be hers, which is why she had not bought her own place when the opportunity arose. She felt that her employment as a hairdresser gave her the flexibility that was required to be able to look after them and did not therefore seek out other employment opportunities, but instead reduced her working hours. When her mother died, the promisee continued to look after her stepfather for about ten years. However, they fell out with one another when her stepfather informed her that he would get married to a woman twenty years his junior, whom he had met only a few months earlier, and that they had chosen to marry on a day and place (California) which made her attendance at the wedding impossible. The marriage took place and, a few months later, the stepfather died. Before that, and nine days prior to his death, he signed a will. The will, which was typed by the deceased's newly wedded spouse, left a small legacy of $1,000 to his stepdaughter, and the household furnishings and a motor vehicle to his new spouse, with a direction that the residue of his estate (which included the family home) be divided equally between the new spouse and his son by a former marriage. The value of the estate was approximately $280,000 of which $200,000 represented the value of the family home. The promisee brought a claim founded on the promisor's unjust enrichment. Her claim was granted, and the decision of the trial judge (who awarded her $125,000) was upheld by the British Columbia Court of Appeal on the basis that, while the stepdaughter did not expect to be paid for her services during the stepfather's lifetime, she had lived all her life in the expectation, which was engendered by the promise, that on her stepfather's death she would inherit the whole of his estate.

Similarly, in *Antrobus v Antrobus* (2009),[26] the eldest daughter of a couple had carried out household chores for a period of over thirty years, had cared for her younger siblings, alongside working for her parents' business, without pay, in return for which she was promised that she would be the sole heir and receive their entire estate. When the promisee realized that her parents had conveyed the promised property to themselves and their other three children in joint tenancy, and that they had executed a trust agreement with respect to their other assets to similar effect, she brought an enrichment claim. The claim was granted.

[25] *Single v Macharski Estate* (1996) 3 WWR 23 (Man CA); *Proulx v Daniels* 2001 CarswellBC 657, (2001) BCSC 441; 104 ACWS (3d) 605 (hereafter *Proulx v Daniels*); *Schnogl v Balen Estate* (n 12); *Moyes v Ollerich* 2005 BCCA 518; (2005) 21 ETR (3d) 40 (hereafter *Moyes v Ollerich*). In *Lata v Rush* 2012 ONSC 4543 (hereafter *Lata v Rush*), the claimant provided personal care but also work in the household. The Ontario Superior Court of Justice recognized that housekeeping, cooking, and personal care can enrich the promisor.

[26] *Antrobus v Antrobus* 2009 BCSC 1341 (hereafter *Antrobus v Antrobus* 2009); and *Antrobus v Antrobus* 2010 BCCA 356 (hereafter *Antrobus v Antrobus* 2010).

Thus, the promisor's enrichment can come about in many ways, not just through financial contributions, or improvements to property, which means that the scope of the doctrine is quite broad. That said, the enrichment has to be tangible, with courts taking an economic approach. For that reason, while household and care services can enrich the promisor, as far as mere companionship and other supportive services are concerned (e.g. emotional support through telephone calls and visits), case law is conflicting.[27]

B. A corresponding deprivation

The second requirement for a successful claim is a deprivation corresponding to the promisor's enrichment.[28] In the majority of the cases analysed in this chapter, the deprivation will come about through work or services performed for the promisor. Just like the enrichment, the deprivation has been interpreted widely by the courts so as to include loss of opportunities, such as the loss of the opportunity to find a better employment, or to purchase a home,[29] but also to get married and, importantly, personal sacrifices (e.g. in the form of the loss of free time), though the latter are unlikely to be sufficient on their own. A good example of such personal sacrifices is *Chan v Chan* (2014),[30] where the Supreme Court of British Columbia found that the son's deprivation consisted in the fact that the care he had provided to the deceased mother had cost him time but also that it had had a negative impact on his personal relationship with both a former girlfriend and his wife. Similarly, in *Clarkson v McCrossen Estate*, discussed earlier, the court took into consideration not only the fact that the daughter had forgone the opportunity to purchase her own home, but also that she had given up 'the opportunity to go and reside with or near her gentleman friend in a distant city in the United States'.[31]

That said, too great an emphasis by some courts on the loss of job opportunities or a better salary could be potentially detrimental to promisees who are not in employment or do not have such opportunities,[32] or who provide services in their

[27] See Wells 'Testamentary Promises' (2007) 44–45. Notice, however, that while in *Clarkson v McCrossen* (n 24) the promisee had phoned the parents almost daily for long stretches of time, and had paid them frequent visits, her services went beyond that which is why she obtained redress. Thus, in this respect, the New Zealand legislation seems to be more generous because it extends to cases of emotional support. See Chapter 7.

[28] In *Kerr v Baranov* (n 20) [39].

[29] See *Schnogl v Balen Estate* (n 12) [21] (Prowse JA).

[30] *Chan v Chan* (n 19).

[31] *Clarkson v McCrossen* (n 24) 249 (Hinds J).

[32] See *Hammond v Hammond* (1995) 7 BCLR (3d) 25 (BCSC). However, in this case no promise could be established, and the services were only rendered for four months prior to the mother entering a care home. Compare with § 2057a BGB discussed in Chapter 11 which, prior to the 2009 reform, required the claimant to have given up the possibility of professional income. See also French unjustified enrichment law in Chapter 9, section III.

spare time. As Rosalyn Wells put it, this could have 'the effect of devaluing the very real benefit for the defendant of domestic and caring services'.[33] There are, however, also cases where the fact that the promisee was not in employment did not constitute a bar to the enrichment claim.[34] Again, the case law is somewhat conflicting.

C. The absence of a juristic reason for the enrichment

The third requirement is the absence of a 'juristic reason' for the enrichment of the promisor. This requirement seems to be less straightforward than the other two and can create potential difficulties for promisees of testamentary promises because it does not necessarily take into account the fact that, since the promises are made in the domestic context, the promisee's behaviour is often motivated by a number of reasons.

Since the Supreme Court of Canada decision in *Garland v Consumers' Gas Co* (2004),[35] which reformulated the requirements for juristic reasons, a two-step process is in place. First, the promisee must prove that there was no juristic reason for the promisor's enrichment justifying retention of the benefit on her part. Second, the promisor is then given a chance to deny recovery by invoking the reasonable expectations of the parties, as well as moral and public policy considerations that speak against an award.[36] I will explore both stages.

1. The first stage

As to the first step in the process, there are established categories of juristic reasons for an enrichment the absence of which the promisee needs to prove, such as: (i) an intention to make a gift; (ii) the existence of a contract with the promisor; (iii) a disposition of law (such as where a benefit is awarded by intestate succession rules); or (iv) other valid common law, equitable, or statutory obligations on the part of the promisee. In practice, it is probable that for family members, who are frequently most likely to enter into an informal testamentary arrangement, the first and the fourth reasons create the greatest difficulty. By contrast, a housekeeper, or other promisees outside the family circle, may have difficulties proving the absence of a contract.[37] In the pages that follow, I will focus primarily on the absence of an intention to make a gift, the presence of a contract, and the absence of valid common law, equitable, or statutory obligations which concern more directly the cases this

[33] Wells 'Testamentary Promises' (2007) 47.

[34] Ibid. In *Lata v Rush* (n 25) the claimant had a full-time job but regularly cleaned the house and performed a number of chores, besides carrying out maintenance work.

[35] *Garland v Consumers' Gas Co*, 2004 SCC 25; 237 DLR (4th) 385.

[36] *Kerr v Baranow* (n 20) [43] (Cromwell J).

[37] *Hesjedal v Granville* 1993 CarswellSask 569, 117 Sask R 111, 109 DLR (4th) 353 (Sask QB). Here the plaintiff had worked for forty-six years as the housekeeper for the deceased for which she received wages. The court found that she had been employed.

book focuses on. We will see that whether or not the promisee is successful often hinges on the nature of the relationship between the parties, how substantial the performance is, and the clarity of the promise.

a) Proving the absence of an intention to make a gift

In proving the absence of a juristic reason, promisees must prove that when acting as they did, they did not intend to make a gift. This is not always easy. As we saw, motives are often mixed, and the fact that the promisee cares for and loves the promisor does not exclude that she also expects to inherit. Also, having to prove the absence of a donative intent can be awkward. It has the potential of forcing the promisee into proving something which is likely to be (at least partly) untrue and presenting themselves in a light that is not in line with their moral character. In addition, it has the potential to hurt others, especially where the promisor is still alive. At best, it can feel awkward, and at worst, it can present a deterrent for some (deserving) promisees.

If the promisee is in a long-term marital or quasi-marital relationship with the promisor, there seems to be a presumption that the services provided are to be paid for. In other words, a presumption of unjust enrichment operates.[38] In many Canadian provinces, the position of spouses is further enhanced through legislation for the division of family property that allows a claim for property division on the death of a spouse.[39] This means that persons in such relationships may find themselves in a better position than, for instance, children or other family members who will have to bring an enrichment claim and prove the absence of donative intent.

Whether the promisee had such a donative intent was, for instance, debated in *Chan v Chan* (2014), where, as mentioned earlier, a son had provided care and household services for his mother while also contributing to the household expenses. Mr Justice Myers found that the services were not intended as a gift to his mother. In doing so the judge observed that '[i]n the context of families the determination of what amounts to unjust enrichment is difficult because family life—particularly between a parent and child—often involves mutual contribution and aid: some mutual sacrifice is a normal part of family life'.[40] Although the judge noted that 'courts must be wary of allowing the "monetisation" of family claims', he also found that 'there may come a point where the conferring of benefits exceeds the expectations of the parties regarding normal family life'.[41] Thus, if the promisee renders a performance that goes beyond what is 'normal', there is an absence of a donative intent. What exactly should be regarded as part of a *normal* family

[38] Wells 'Testamentary Promises' (2007) 51.

[39] See Popovici & Smith, 'Family Provision in Canada' in *Comparative Succession Law 3* (2020) 511–512.

[40] *Chan v Chan* (n 19).

[41] Ibid, [64]–[65].

life and what exceeds it is of course a matter of contention and culturally relative, very much depending on societal expectations that in turn depend on the context, the relationship between the parties, and often also the gender.[42] In this case, Mr Justice Myers found that the threshold had been exceeded, because the son had taken on both the role of husband for his mother and that of father for his nephew for about twelve years. The judge further found that the son had been promised a share in the property and that he had provided a level of care which increased over time, and this, according to the judge, was at least in part motivated by the promise that the claimant should have a share of the house.[43] So it seems to matter not just how substantial the services provided were, both in terms of duration and intensity, but also whether there is a promise, though the promise and thus the expectation to inherit does not have to be the only or primary motive.[44]

In an earlier case, *Schnogl v Balen Estate* (2005), the gift argument was defeated by the fact that it was clear that the services rendered by the promisee, a tenant of the promisor, were provided on the basis of an expectation to inherit the deceased's house—an expectation which had been created by the deceased's representations.[45] Again, the promise mattered. In this case, the promisee (Mr Schnogl) had lived in the basement flat below the deceased's house (the Balen's) for over twenty-five years, during which he developed a filial-like relationship with them. He paid nominal rent and half of the utility bills. He often ate with them and paid for the food they shared. Mr Schnogl did the gardening, cut the grass, painted the trim on the house, repaired the fence, and did other maintenance work. He also spent money on the house. A couple of times, Mr Schnogl considered moving out and buying his own home, but Mr Balen dissuaded him, telling him that someday the house would be his. Two or three months before he died, Mr Balens went to see a lawyer about making a new will. While the lawyer drew up the will for him, leaving Mr Schnogl $10,000, and the right to live in the house for ten years, Mr Balens never signed it so that his old will took effect which did not include Mr Schnogl. Both the first instance judge and the Court of Appeal found that Mr Balens had promised to leave Mr Schnogl the property by way of inheritance and that this was why he had provided those services and given up opportunities to purchase his own home. Mr Schnogl did not therefore have a donative intent.

42 Also see the discussion in Chapters 7 and 8.

43 *Chan v Chan* (n 19) [66].

44 Yet, in *Strudwick v Strudwick Estate* 1996 CarswellBC 794; 21 RFL (4th) 185 (BCSC), [14] (hereafter *Strudwick v Strudwick Estate*), Blair J said that '[t]here is no evidence, as in *Clarkson* (supra), that Anthony Strudwick's involvement in the farm was performed by him solely in expectation that he would receive the farm'. However, in *Strudwick* the problem was also that the services rendered were not considered substantial enough, as they were rendered first on a part-time basis after school and then on a full-time basis for three years after which the claimant had left the farm.

45 *Schnogl v Balen Estate* (n 12) [160]–[161]. The donative argument was also rejected in *Jans v Jans* (n 2) [290].

Apart from the nature and extent of the services provided by the promisee, both *Chan* and *Schnogl* show that evidence of a clear promise on the part of the promisor plays an important role in refuting the argument that the promisee's performance was provided gratuitously. Thus, while a claimant does not need to have to prove the existence of a promise, if there is a promise it will be easier to establish the absence of a juristic reason. But, of course, promises of a future inheritance are frequently vague, so that some promisees may have a more difficult time gaining protection through enrichment law.

b) Proving the absence of a contract with the promisor

Besides raising the point that the services were intended as a gift, in the aforementioned *Schnogl* case, the representatives of the estate also argued that the promisee had rendered the services under a contract whereby his rent had been reduced on account of his services, and that this had provided a juristic reason for the promisor's enrichment. The contract argument was, however, rejected by the courts on the grounds that Mr Schnogl had developed a filial-like relationship with the promisors, the Balens.[46]

Thus, a contract was unlikely here because of the nature of the relationship between the parties. This confirms that establishing a contract in the domestic context may create difficulties, though in this case it worked in favour of the promisee. Here, the nature and quality of the relationship assisted the promisee in proving that there was no contract and thus no juristic basis for the promisor's enrichment. However, as noted earlier, the contract argument could potentially stand in the way of a housekeeper from obtaining redress.[47]

c) Proving the absence of common law, equitable, or statutory obligations owed by the promisee

Other juristic reasons for the promisor's enrichment can be common law, equitable, or statutory obligations that the promisee owes the promisor. A few years ago, Wells showed that in some Canadian testamentary cases the rent-free use of the defendant's property sometimes created informal family obligations on the part of the promisee that precluded a claim in respect of improvements to the property.[48] However, since the Supreme Court of Canada decision in *Kerr v Baranow* (2011), it would seem that mutual benefits such as rent-free living should be considered only at the second stage of the two-step process required in order to prove absence of a juristic reason.[49] That this applies also to testamentary promises cases has been

46 *Schnogl v Balen Estate* (n 12) [157]–[159].

47 See n 37.

48 Wells 'Testamentary Promises' (2007) 51–52 citing *Murfitt v Jones* 2004 BCSC 988, where the juristic reason was the equitable obligation that the claimant owed due to the fact that he had lived rent-free on the farm for nineteen years. However, in this case the court found that the alleged testamentary promise had not been made.

49 *Kerr v Baranow* (n 20).

confirmed by the Court of Appeal for Ontario in *Granger v Granger* (2016).[50] In this case, the court held that mutual conferral of benefits should not be taken into account until the burden has shifted to the defendant in the second stage (the defence/remedy stage). In very limited circumstances only should mutual conferral of benefits be taken into consideration to indicate the parties' reasonable expectations in proving the absence of a juristic reason for enrichment.

Sometimes a family obligation seems to have been inferred from the family bond between the parties,[51] especially that between a parent and a child. This was the case in *Strudwick v Strudwick Estate* (1996),[52] where the son had worked first part-time after school, then for three years full-time on his father's farm. The son then left the farm, visiting the farm only once or twice a year for about forty years. Blair J found that:

> the obligation here, it seems to me, arose from the familial bond between father and son which saw the pair working together on the farm to support themselves. As a matter of public policy, such limited economic activity as occurred in this case involving father and son ought to be encouraged without necessarily attracting a subsequent claim for unjust enrichment.

This suggests that there is an expectation that children help with work on a farm or in the household, and that their performance therefore needs to exceed a certain threshold to show the absence of a juristic reason for the enrichment. This has already emerged when discussing the need to prove the absence of a donative intent. But this case also confirms that with enrichment claims courts tend to focus on economic activity.

The existence of societal expectations, in this case towards children, was alluded to also in *Antrobus v Antrobus*, where counsel for the promisors had argued that in the 1960s and 1970s, family members, and in particular eldest daughters, were expected to help in the family.[53] For that reason they argued that the daughter's claim should be denied. However, the Supreme Court of British Columbia rejected the argument and concluded that:

> It is part of family life that family members assist one another—perhaps pitching in to help out younger siblings or aging parents, or helping with meal preparation and household chores. Children, teenagers and young adults living with their parents are often expected to do their share in keeping the household running. Working together for the common good of the family, spending time to help

50 *Granger v Granger* 2016 ONCA 945, [50].
51 Wells 'Testamentary Promises' (2007) 52.
52 *Strudwick v Strudwick Estate* (n 44) [15].
53 *Antrobus v Antrobus* 2009 (n 26) [26].

> other family members, without any expectation of monetary compensation, is generally part of the meaning of 'family'. It is not the norm, and the law does not contemplate, that family members will do a forensic accounting during their lifetimes and make sure that no one was disadvantaged in the overall exchange of services. However, the facts that I have found place this case clearly outside of the usual exchange that is part of family life. Linda was called upon by her parents to take on a greatly disproportionate amount of the work in the home during her teenage years.[54]

While the Supreme Court of British Columbia rejected the promisor's argument, it referred to what lies 'outside the usual exchange that is part of family life'. Establishing when the performance is 'unusual' or beyond what is 'normal' is, as mentioned earlier, precisely where the difficulty lies. In this regard, *Antrobus v Antrobus* suggests that the duration and intensity of the work or assistance provided by the promisee will often be crucial in supporting her claim. Thus, it seems that certain promisees, and, in particular, close family members, may have greater difficulties proving that there was no obligation (arising from the benefits received or the family bond) to provide assistance and thus no juristic reason for the promisor's enrichment. However, at this point, the difficulties for the promisee are not yet over, for there is a second stage to the test.

2. The second stage

Once the promisee has given proof that there is no juristic reason for the promisor's enrichment, the promisor has an opportunity to argue that the promisee should not receive the relief sought on the basis that her expectations were not reasonable or legitimate, or that they conflicted with public policy. Here, the promisor has defences that are not, for instance, available to her in the context of a proprietary estoppel claim, which is something to consider when choosing how to seek redress. Let us look at both of these in turn.

a) The promisee's expectations (to inherit) are not reasonable or legitimate

In *Garland* (2004), the Supreme Court of Canada stated that 'at the second stage of its analysis of juristic reasons it [the court] must take into account the reasonable expectations of both parties'.[55] Applied to the testamentary context, this means that the promisor or her successors may want to argue that what the promisee did is no more than what could be expected of her given her particular relationship with the promisor, and that the promisee's expectations to inherit are therefore unreasonable or illegitimate. Thus, societal expectations that arise on the basis of the nature of the relationship between the promisor and the promisee again play a role.

[54] Ibid, [185]–[186].
[55] Wells 'Testamentary Promises' (2007) 57.

For a claim to be successful, the services performed by the promisee and, consequently, the benefits received by the promisor, will have to be 'substantial' in nature. As I said earlier, it is often difficult to know what 'substantial' means.

As the analysis has shown, promises of a future inheritance can help the promisee in establishing that her performance was not intended as a gift. Equally, such promises can create reasonable expectations on the part of the promisee that services will be remunerated,[56] and thus defeat the promisor's defence that the promisee's expectations are either unreasonable or illegitimate. In *Antrobus v Antrobus* the claimant's parents had made promises to their daughter that she would receive their entire estate. Hence, Madam Justice Lynn Smith found that 'neither the reasonable expectations of the parties nor public policy provide a juristic reason for the enrichment of Joan and William Antrobus [the promisors] in this case'.[57]

In *Clarkson v McCrossen Estate*, examined at the beginning of this chapter, the court elaborated on what is meant by reasonable and legitimate expectations. Although the trial judge had found that the services rendered by the stepdaughter over many years were given out of love and affection, and not because she expected to be paid, he also concluded that there was an expectation to inherit because promises had been made to her that the family home would be hers. Thus, while the promisee did not expect to be paid during the promisor's lifetime, she had only stayed because she expected to inherit and, in light of the promise, her expectation was legitimate.

b) Conflict with public policy

Another defence the promisor can try to resort to in order to object to a promisee's claim is that the promisee's expectations were in conflict with public policy.[58] However, this argument has been rejected where a promise was made and the promisee had acted on the promise for many years. For instance, in *Antrobus v Antrobus*, counsel had argued that to allow the daughter's claim in that case 'would be to open a Pandora's box of claims by children for compensation for chores they performed while living with their parents'.[59] They suggested that the reasonable expectations of the parties aside, public policy provided the juristic reason for the enrichment in this case. But Lynn Smith J rejected the argument. In her view, the case was unusual because of the onerous workload imposed on the promisee while she was a child, the long-term extensive services that she continued to provide for many years, and the explicit promise of an inheritance.[60]

[56] We have seen that in *Clarkson v McCrossen* (n 24) but also in *Schnogl v Balen Estate* (n 12). See text at n 45.

[57] *Antrobus v Antrobus* 2009 (n 26) [219].

[58] For a useful articulation of public policy see, Freedman (2010) 191ff.

[59] *Antrobus v Antrobus* 2009 (n 26) [217].

[60] Ibid, [218].

In *Jans v Jans* (2016), involving a family dispute as to who should inherit the family farm, counsel for the defendant (Jay Jans) submitted that finding in favour of the promisee (his brother, Bryce Jans) would have 'a catastrophic effect on family farms, as family members expect to and commonly share the burden of farm work ... this essential element of family life will be undermined if the courts find that it results in an enforceable right to the farm or compensation'.[61] However, the court rejected the argument on the basis that the promisee had spent almost his entire life, and a good deal of his money, building the ranch, and that he did so on the basis of his father's promise that he and his brother would ultimately each get half of it. It concluded that '[f]inding unjust enrichment in these circumstances will not break new legal or social policy ground or undermine the usual family arrangements. The fact that parents and child recognize and act on their mutual family obligation on family farms does not mean it is not open to the court to find unjust enrichment, where appropriate'.[62]

As we saw earlier, both the floodgate argument and the argument that relationships would be monetized have sometimes been invoked also against proprietary estoppel claims, but what role such considerations should play is highly questionable.[63] It certainly cannot be an argument against protecting promisees from the risk of exploitation. Rather, it speaks in favour of clearly defined requirements that the promisee must meet.

D. Summary

The analysis thus far has shown that a promisee needs to prove an enrichment and a corresponding deprivation, with the courts taking an economic approach to both elements. In addition, she needs to prove the absence of a juristic reason. Where a promisee provides work or services (including domestic and care services) in exchange for a promise it is usually possible to establish an enrichment and a corresponding deprivation. However, depending on the nature of the relationship between the parties, it may be difficult for a promisee to prove the absence of a juristic basis for the enrichment. Some promisees may struggle to prove that they had no donative intent, that the enrichment was a consequence of certain informal family obligations owed towards the promisor who could have therefore expected certain performances from them, or to defeat the objection that their expectations were unreasonable or illegitimate. At the same time, the presence of a promise can help overcome some of these hurdles especially where the performance was substantial and carried out for several years.

[61] *Jans v Jans* (n 2) [291].
[62] Ibid, [292].
[63] See Chapter 4, section V.A.

The analysis has shown that in the context of the evaluation of the lack of a juristic reason, courts frequently refer to what is 'normal', 'usual' or 'unusual' given the particular relationship and context. But when are performances to be considered 'unusual', or 'out of the norm'? When can one say that work or services were substantial and thus exceeded the expectations of the parties regarding normal family or farm life? Here, societal expectations based on the type of the relationship, the gender, and type of work carried out by the promisee play a significant role and can operate against certain promisees. For instance, in the household, parents are likely to expect more from their daughters than their sons, while in the farming context, expectations may be higher towards sons. On the other hand, those outside the family may encounter the problem that it is more difficult for them to deny the existence of a contract. As we saw earlier, in *Schnogl* it helped that the relationship between the tenant and the promisors had become a filial-like one. By contrast, we saw that when it comes to services rendered in marital and quasi-marital relationships, there is a presumption of unjust enrichment and there is no need to prove the absence of a donative intent. It thus seems that it may well be more difficult for certain promisees to prove their claim.

III. When does the claim arise?

An important question is, when does the promisee's claim arise? The answer is that the claim crystalizes when it is clear that the promise has been breached, which is usually the moment of the death of the promisor.[64] However, an entitlement to restitution may accrue at any point during the lifetime of the promisor, where the promisor has acted in a way that renders the promise nugatory.[65] For instance, we saw that in *Antrobus v Antrobus*, the daughter had brought the claim when she discovered that her parents had conveyed the real property, which they had promised to leave to her in their will, to themselves and their other three children in joint tenancy and had executed a trust agreement with respect to their other assets to similar effect. When the claim reached the Court of Appeal for British Columbia the promisors objected to the daughter's claim for restitution because in their view the action had not yet accrued.[66] They argued that so long as they were alive, the

[64] *Clarkson v McCrossen* (n 24) [61].

[65] In *Kreeft v Kreeft* (n 12), the promisor's sons brought a claim when the father transferred the property into the joint names of him and his new wife in breach of the promise. Similarly, in *Proulx v Daniels* (n 25), the daughter brought a claim against the stepfather, one of the promisors. They had fallen out with one another and he had asked her to move out of his home, because he did not want to continue with the agreement that the stepdaughter and her husband would care for him. Also, in *Henderson v Henderson* (n 15), the promisee brought the claim when the promisor breached the promise not to sever joint ownership of the property.

[66] Here, see the analogy with *Habberfield v Habberfield* [2018] EWHC 317 (Ch) which is an estoppel case discussed in Chapter 4.

promisee had no entitlement to restitution, and that until then, they had a juristic reason to retain enrichment.[67] However, the Court of Appeal rejected their argument on the basis that any juristic reason for the retention of the enrichment ended when they established the trust arrangement as a means of defeating the daughter's entitlement to restitution.[68] Thus, just as with proprietary estoppel and with contractual claims, but unlike with family provision orders[69] and other forms or redress analysed later in the book,[70] here the promisee is protected already during the promisor's lifetime, which is of great advantage.

IV. The available awards

Canadian courts have understood the doctrine of unjust enrichment as an equitable doctrine that provides them with considerable judicial discretion. Thus, differently to what we will see to be the position in Germany and France, the promisee does not necessarily obtain merely the restitution of the value of the enrichment of the promisor. In many cases, courts go beyond mere restitution,[71] awarding either a monetary award that is higher than the value of the enrichment, or sometimes a proprietary award by way of a constructive trust.[72]

When doing so, courts take into consideration reciprocal benefits, for instance, in the form of free accommodation but also lifetime gifts and legacies. In this section I will explore the available awards. I will start with proprietary awards, for that is usually in the interest of the promisee, also because the protection with regards to third parties is greater.

A. Proprietary awards

Promisees usually prefer to obtain a proprietary relief for that will provide them with a stronger protection vis-à-vis third parties. However, a proprietary award will only be granted where a monetary award is considered to be inadequate.[73] A constructive trust is further precluded where there is no established link between the contribution (performance) that founds the promisee's action and the promised asset. In *Kerr v Baranow*, the Canadian Supreme Court held that:

[67] *Antrobus v Antrobus* 2010 (n 26) [29].
[68] Ibid, [32].
[69] See Chapter 5.
[70] See Chapters 7, 10, and 11.
[71] On the proprietary relief, see McInnes *Canadian Law of Unjust Enrichment and Restitution* (2014) ch 32. Waters et al *Waters' Law of Trusts in Canada* (2021) ch 11.
[72] See Chapter 9.
[73] *Peter v Beblow* (n 18) [24] (McLachlin J). *Kerr v Baranow* (n 20) [47].

> the plaintiff must demonstrate a 'sufficiently substantial and direct' link, a 'causal connection' or a 'nexus' between the plaintiff's contributions and the property which is the subject matter of the trust ... A minor or indirect contribution will not suffice (*Peter*, at p. 997). As Dickson C.J. put it in in *Sochran*, the primary focus is on whether the contributions have a 'clear proprietary relationship'[74]

Such a link can be more easily found where the promisee has, for instance, improved the promised property,[75] or has worked on the promised farm, though as mentioned earlier, such cases are frequently argued on a contractual basis especially since in common law Canada the doctrine of part-performance can overcome the lack of writing. By contrast, a link is often less likely to be established where the promisee has provided domestic or care services, which is what happened in the majority of the cases discussed in this chapter. Simply because of the nature of the services or work performed, some promisees will be able to obtain a proprietary interest while others will not. This is problematic. Just like with the doctrine of part-performance,[76] here the law provides greater protection to those who have, for instance, made improvements to or worked directly on the promised property, and whose work is therefore more visible.[77] As it happens, this type of contribution is often made by men rather than women who are more likely to provide domestic and care services. Consequently, they are less likely to obtain a proprietary award.

That said, in *Peter v Beblow*, a case dealing with the break-up of a cohabitant couple (and not a testamentary promise), McLachlin J pointed out that in family cases a monetary award may be insufficient because the claimant's efforts have established a special link to the property.[78] McLachlin J approved the finding of a sufficiently direct connection between the housekeeping, childcare, and home maintenance services and the house in which the couple had lived to support a finding of a constructive trust in that case. Thus, one of the effects of the decision of the Canadian Supreme Court in *Peter v Beblow* has been to weaken the strength of the link that must be found between the services rendered and the property claimed. The court treated 'the assets as a pool', the property being interpreted 'as all of the family assets'.[79] Given that the statement concerned services rendered in the context of a cohabitation,[80] it is unclear whether and to what extent it applies to instances where services or work are performed on the basis of a testamentary

[74] *Kerr v Baranow* (n 20) [51].
[75] An example is *Kreeft v Kreeft* (n 12).
[76] Chapter 3.
[77] See the discussion in Chapter 2.
[78] *Peter v Beblow* (n 18) 988 (McLachlin J). However, according to Freedman (2010) 173, the proprietary relief is not to be preferred given the inherent risk of prejudicing the legitimate rights of third parties in the property.
[79] On this point, see Smith (2015) 49.
[80] *Peter v Beblow* (n 18) 997.

promise. However, there is no reason why it could not apply also to the work or services that, for instance, a child, or any other claimant, provides in the promisor's home, though care services may still pose difficulties for they are not usually related to the property.

In *Schnogl*, discussed earlier, the trial judge established a sufficient link with the property, but in that case not only had the promisee (the tenant of the promisors) performed services of a personal nature, he had also provided maintenance work around the house and yard, in some cases at his own expense.[81] The trial judge therefore found a constructive trust. This was confirmed by the British Columbia Court of Appeal, even though it reduced the extent of the interest in the promised house from a 90% to a 66 2/3% undivided interest in the house, on the basis that the constructive trust was out of proportion with the enrichment of the promisor and her estate, and the corresponding deprivation suffered by the promisee. However, the court agreed with the trial judge that there was a sufficiently strong link between Mr Schnogl's overall contributions and the property to establish a constructive trust, also because the promisee had lived in the promisor's property to provide for them. This would suggest that providers of personal and care services might potentially be able to establish such a link, at least where the promisee has lived with the promisor in the promised home.

But what if the promisee takes the promisor to live with her? In an earlier decision of the British Columbia Court of Appeal in *Guzzo v Catlin Estate* (1989),[82] the court judged the link to the assets of the estate insufficient, for in this case the promisee had provided maintenance and care support for her mother in the promisee's own home. A constructive trust was denied, despite the fact that the daughter had assisted her mother for twenty-seven years. The court held that the trial judge's finding, that the assets of her mother's estate were subject to a constructive trust in the amount of $50,000, was inappropriate and that a monetary judgment in the amount of $50,000 ought to have been awarded instead (the estate had a net value of approximately $100,000). This could suggest that, where the promisee hosts the promisor, rather than the other way around, the promisee is less likely to be awarded a proprietary interest Yet, in *Antrobus v Antrobus*, the link between the services performed by the claimant and the real property owned by the defendants was deemed insufficient even though the promisee had lived in her parents' (the promisors') home where she carried out services over a period of thirty years consisting principally in household services but also assistance in the parents' business. The Supreme Court of British Columbia did not provide a detailed explanation of its decision to deny a constructive trust beyond saying that there was no apparent reason why a monetary award would have been inadequate,

[81] *Schnogl v Balen Estate* (n 12). Similarly, in *Buchko v Buchko* (n 2) and *Orange v Swierz Estate* (n 2) the promisee provided personal care to the aging landowner.

[82] *Guzzo v Catlin Estate* (n 14).

and that this was not a case where the promisee had improved a piece of real property with unique features. This decision shows again that domestic/care work is generally undervalued but also that the courts' approach is not always consistent.

By contrast, in *Proulx v Daniels* (2001),[83] the same court found a constructive trust in favour of the promisees who had moved in with the promisors and provided substantial care to them on the strength of a promise that they would receive the home after the defendant's death. After four years the surviving promisor changed his mind and frustrated the arrangement after which point the promisees brought a claim. The reason why the judge found a constructive trust seems to lie partly in the fact that the promisees had sold their own property and had moved in with the promisors, where they stayed for four years, during which time they were available twenty-four hours and maintained the house and the property. Another factor that mattered for the purpose of establishing a constructive trust was that in this case the promisor had a fixed income limiting his ability to pay a monetary award. Dorgan J felt that '[i]n this case it is unfair to require Mr. Daniels [the promisor] to attempt to satisfy a monetary judgment when it is possible to defer the plaintiffs' receipt of a remedy until after Mr. Daniel's death'.[84] Also, the judge was concerned with the way the promisor dealt with his assets, which may have made a monetary award potentially unenforceable. For all these reasons, the judge concluded that a monetary award was inadequate, and that the promisor held the house on trust for the promisees, subject to his right to occupy the house until his death or until he vacated the property, whichever occurs first. Thus, in this case, the court felt that a constructive trust would be in the interest of both parties.

The fact that a constructive trust arises does not mean that the promisee automatically obtains the full expectation interest. The claimant may only obtain a share in the property as in *Schnogl*, referred to earlier,[85] or the trust may arise with regards to a certain amount. Nonetheless, a constructive trust is highly desirable. While a monetary award creates a debt against the estate, meaning that the promisee is ranked as an ordinary unsecured debtor who ranks better than successors under the will or on intestacy, as well as applicants made under the family provision legislation, where there is a constructive trust, the promisee has a proprietary right that binds third parties. She might be given priority over some of the creditors for her interest may predate their claim.[86] But when the constructive trust arises is subject to debate. Does it arise when it is clear that the promisor has not kept his promise, that is to say at the moment at which a duty to make restitution occurs,[87]

[83] *Proulx v Daniels* (n 25).
[84] Ibid, [29].
[85] *Schnogl v Balen Estate* (n 12).
[86] Korven (1993) 455. For a detailed discussion of the situation of creditors, see also Paciocco (1989) and Waters (1990–1991); Waters et al *Waters' Law of Trusts* (2021) ch 11, 591–592.
[87] In *Clarkson v McCrossen* (n 24) [76], Hinds J stated that '[i]f a constructive trust arises when the duty to make restitution occurred, and not on the date that it is decreed by a court then in my view the alternative remedy of a monetary award must arise on the same date'. See also Paciocco (1989) 316.

or at the moment when the court decrees the trust? Canadian courts seem to prefer the former approach, which has, however, attracted academic criticism,[88] precisely because of its potential implications for creditors. If the court were to backdate the trust,[89] it could deplete the estate, leaving nothing not just for successors under a will or intestacy but also unsecured creditors. However, according to Wells, Canadian courts are unlikely to impose a constructive trust to satisfy a claim of unjust enrichment when creditors are involved.[90]

Thus, predicting when a promisee can obtain the promised asset through a constructive trust seems difficult. While such services can give rise to an enrichment claim, it seems that they are unlikely to establish the link that is required for a constructive trust to arise. In most cases dealing with domestic or care services promisees will therefore be awarded a monetary award except perhaps if they have moved in with the promisor. However, as we will see, the monetary award is not necessarily based on the value of the enrichment.

B. Monetary awards

Where a monetary award is considered sufficient to remedy the unjust enrichment, or the required link for a constructive trust is missing, which will be the case in many instances where the testamentary promise is made in exchange for domestic or care services, there are two possibilities. The court can calculate the relief on a *quantum meruit* 'value received' (or 'fee-for-service') basis and look at the commercial value of the services that were rendered. Alternatively, it can calculate the award with greater flexibility on a 'value survived' basis, meaning that it can go beyond the commercial value of the services, and take into account, for instance, the value of the promise. Following the Supreme Court of Canada decision in *Kerr*, it is not automatically the case that a monetary award needs to be calculated on the basis of the 'value received'.[91] On the contrary, the court expressed a preference for monetary awards to be calculated on a 'value survived' basis, which is in the promisee's interest. *Kerr* concerned, as noted earlier, a claim brought by a cohabitant on the breakdown of the relationship and was not a testamentary promises case. The question is therefore what consequences will ensue for such cases.

It would appear that already following on from *Clarkson v McCrossen Estate*,[92] which predates *Kerr*, the value survived method has been used in many

[88] Paciocco (1989).
[89] *Rawluk v Rawluk* [1990] 1 SCR 70 (SCC), 101–107 (McLachlin J).
[90] Wells 'Testamentary Promises' (2007) 65.
[91] In *Kerr v Baranow* (n 20) [58]ff the Supreme Court found that 'restricting the money remedy to a "fee-for-service" is inappropriate for four reasons: First, it fails to reflect the reality of the lives of many domestic partners. Second, it is inconsistent with the inherent flexibility of unjust enrichment. Third, it ignores the historical basis of *quantum meruit* claims. Finally, it is not mandated by the Court's judgment in *Peter*.'
[92] Wells 'Testamentary Promises' (2007) 61.

testamentary promises cases. This was true in *Moyes v Ollerich Estate* (2005),[93] where the promisee was awarded $125,000 in addition to a bequest received under the will. In *Antrobus v Antrobus*, the trial judge, Lynn Smith J, had arrived at the figure of $190,000, which corresponded to a third of the estate,[94] which she reached by applying essentially both methods of calculation. However, the Court of Appeal for British Columbia criticized Lynn Smith J for confusing the two methods and not choosing one over the other.[95] It therefore reduced the award to $100,000, which is arguably not much given that the promisee had worked for the family for over thirty years and considering that the promises that had been made to her.

The Court of Appeal for British Columbia also stated that there appear to be differences in the approach between that Court and the Ontario Court of Appeal to the quantification of unjust enrichment claims. In fact, while the Court of Appeal for British Columbia seems to accept both methods, requiring lower courts to identify which approach they applied,[96] the Ontario Court of Appeal would appear to confine the calculation of a monetary award to the value received approach. In other words, the Ontario courts seem to be stricter when quantifying the award.[97]

Clearly, a focus on the 'value survived' is beneficial for testamentary promisees.[98] The flexibility that courts have allows them to take into consideration lost opportunities or other types of detriment, as well as the promisee's expectations. At the same time, it also means that courts will take into account mutual benefits, and that they can balance the interests of both the promisee and the promisor or her successors which may not be in the promisee's interest. And, as we have seen to be the case with proprietary estoppel claims, flexibility inevitably creates a certain level of uncertainty.

V. Evaluation from the perspective of the promisee

From the perspective of a promisee, an enrichment claim in common law Canada has several advantages. First, it does not require the promisee to prove the existence of either a contract or a promise, whether or not in writing, though as we saw, the existence of a promise matters for the purposes of demonstrating the absence of a juristic reason for the enrichment. A promise can be indicative of the lack of a donative intent, but also of the fact that the promisee's expectation to inherit was legitimate and reasonable. Unlike in the case in a proprietary estoppel claim, there

93 *Moyes v Ollerich* (n 25).

94 See, in particular, *Antrobus v Antroubus* 2009 (n 26).

95 Ibid, [35].

96 *Wilson v Fotsch* 2010 BCCA 226; [2010] BCJ No 850 (QL), [53].

97 See, for instance, *Lata v Rush* (n 25) [66].

98 In *Henderson v Henderson* (n 15), the British Columbia Supreme Court held that measuring the constructive trust on the basis of the value received approach is inappropriate.

is no need to demonstrate reliance so that the performance can be rendered prior to the promise. There is also no need to prove that the promisee was in financial need, as would usually be required for an adult promisee to obtain a family provision order (called dependant's relief legislation in Canada).

An enrichment claim can be brought both during the lifetime and on the promisor's death. This is an advantage over a family provision order which is only available on death of the promisor. Also, and crucially, Canadian courts see the doctrine of unjust enrichment as an equitable doctrine, which provides them with a discretion not only to order restitution but also to compensate for the loss or occasionally, even, to fulfil the promisee's expectation interest, sometimes in the form of a proprietary interest. Where that is the case, the promisee is in a strong position vis-à-vis third parties. That said, we have seen that a proprietary relief through a constructive trust is not frequently awarded, even when, as in *Antrobus v Antrobus*, services were performed for many years and in the promisor's household. For a constructive trust to arise, there is a requirement of a specific link between the promisee's performance and the promised property, and this can fail if the promisee has provided domestic or care services. Also, monetary awards are often regarded as adequate. Nonetheless, the relief is usually higher than the value of the enrichment, as Canadian courts frequently grant an award based on the 'value survived' approach, in which case they can take into account the promisee's expectations. Thus, the rationale is not merely the restitution of the enrichment.

Just as with proprietary estoppel, the broad discretion of the court makes the outcome less predictable, though precisely this discretion can work in favour of promisees. Where the enrichment claim is satisfied by a monetary award, the judgment creates a debt against the estate which ranks equally with the claims of ordinary unsecured debtors. Such a judgment debt takes priority over successors whether under the will or intestacy, as well as any applicants for a family provision order, who can only bring a claim against the net estate.[99] Finally, while when establishing the relief courts take into account mutual benefits in the form of gifts or legacies and free accommodation (and for the purposes of establishing a constructive trust apparently also claims and interests of creditors), they do not have to take into account moral claims that others may have against the promisor's estate, which is an advantage over a family provision order.[100]

Nonetheless, this type of claim also poses certain challenges for a prospective promisee. First, the promisee will have to prove an enrichment and corresponding deprivation. While it is the case that courts interpret enrichment and deprivation widely, both of which can come about through domestic or care services, courts tend to take an economic approach. In addition, the promisee needs to prove the

[99] Popovici & Smith, 'Family Provision in Canada' in *Comparative Succession Law 3* (2020) 521.

[100] For instance, a claim brought under the New Zealand TPA 1949. See Chapter 7. See also family provision orders examined in Chapter 5.

absence of a juristic reason for the promisor's enrichment, which, as we saw, involves various stages and is quite complex. Depending on how substantial the performance was, and on how clear the promise, this can prove more or less difficult. Because the promisee's motives are often mixed, she may fail to show that her actions were not intended as a gift, and that she has not acted out of a family obligation towards the promisor. She may also struggle to defeat the argument that her expectations of an inheritance were illegitimate or unreasonable. Thus, the nature and duration of the promisee's performance and the existence of a promise matter a great deal. Equally, the nature of the relationship between the parties (and also their gender) can play a role in terms of expectations that society holds. Arguably one can expect certain behaviour from certain people, especially family members.[101] In other words, particular performances are regarded as 'normal' among people with a close familial bond, for example, parents and children, who may therefore have greater difficulties establishing a claim. In fact, we saw that a spouse is often in a privileged position. Thus, while in common law Canada an enrichment claim is no doubt a very useful form of redress for testamentary promisees, it has certain limitations which may well push them towards other forms of redress.

[101] *Strudwick v Strudwick Estate* (n 44) [15].

Concluding summary of Part II

In Part II, I have explored four possible ways in which a promisee may be able to obtain the promised inheritance. All four examples are drawn from the common law tradition. This is not a coincidence. As I discussed in Chapter 2, many civil law jurisdictions explicitly prohibit contracts to make a will, not to make one or not to revoke the will. Thus, a promisor is prevented from binding herself as to the future of her will. While promisors may make informal promises and promisees may obtain some form of redress, they are not usually awarded the promised asset. By contrast, in common law jurisdictions, promisees have a good chance to obtain what they were promised, partly because courts frequently have considerable discretion when determining the relief. To obtain the promised asset, promisees normally have more than one option to obtain redress, and several of them are broad in their scope so that they can potentially capture a wide range of promisees.

Where the parties have entered into a contract to make a will, it is usually possible to have the promisee's expectations fulfilled through specific performance or damages. However, we also saw that it is not easy to establish a contract and that the level of protection contract law provided depends on the content of the promise and on when the breach has occurred. Where a contract is difficult to prove, including because there is lack of writing, which is often the case, the doctrine of proprietary estoppel can be an effective means to obtain the promised inheritance, especially in jurisdictions and cases where the doctrine of part-performance does not come to the aid of promisees. This does not mean that the doctrine of proprietary estoppel is without problems, especially in England and Wales, where the proportionality test has given rise to conflicting case law concerning the way in which relief is to be determined. Also, we saw that societal expectations concerning certain types of work, certain relationships, and gender can sometimes work against a promisee. Nonetheless, on the whole courts have been sensitive to the context in which such promises are being made (including the fact that motives are often mixed), and willing to protect the interests of a wide range of promisees by taking a liberal approach to the interpretation of its requirements and taking into account intangible benefits. Thus, the doctrine of proprietary estoppel accommodates the social practice of informal family arrangements and provides a response to the harshness of contract law and of formality requirements. What is more, in most of the cases that we analysed in Chapter 4, the promisees had their expectation interests satisfied. It is therefore unsurprising that this approach has been increasingly sought out by promisees especially considering that, where the promisee is awarded a proprietary interest, she is in a very strong position vis-à-vis creditors and other third parties. This is true not just in England and Wales, but also in the Republic of Ireland, Australia, and to some extent New Zealand and Canada. However, it is noticeable that the cases in which promisees were able to obtain the promised asset were frequently farm cases where there are wider policy considerations at play and the promisee's work is more visible.

Similarly, in common law Canada, the doctrine of unjust enrichment has developed in a way that is sensitive to the domestic context, including the testamentary one, though proving an enrichment and corresponding deprivation and, especially, the absence of a juristic reason for the enrichment, can sometimes be difficult. While Canadian courts value intangible benefits, on the whole, the approach is economic. An advantage is that Canadian courts have considerable discretion in making an enrichment award. As we saw, the award is not limited to the restitution of the enrichment but is often higher and can potentially even consist of a proprietary award. Both the doctrine of proprietary estoppel and the doctrine of unjust enrichment are indeed based on equitable principles, which provide courts with considerable discretion. While this can create uncertainty, on the whole, it has led to enhanced protection for promisees.

Even so, when compared to the doctrine of proprietary estoppel, proving an enrichment claim in Canada would seem to be more complex and there is a greater focus on the financial aspects of both the enrichment and the deprivation. What is more, while detrimental reliance is crucial to a proprietary estoppel claim, and the promisee's reliance matters, it is for the other party to prove absence of reliance. In other words, once it has been established that promises have been made, the promisor is required to show that the promisee did *not* rely on it in any respect.[1] However, in the case of an enrichment claim, a promisee usually needs to show the absence of a donative intent, which may be difficult, not least from a psychological point of view, especially where the promisor was a family member. Depending on the relationship it may also be difficult to prove that the expectation was legitimate. The focus here is often on what is 'normal', but, as we saw, what that means is not always clear.

These three options aside, in this Part I also examined ways in which the family provision legislation can come to the aid of promisees. We saw that the deceased's promise and the promisee's performance can help establish a moral duty on the part of the former to provide for the promisee. However, compared to the other forms of redress examined, the legislation has the disadvantage that its scope is limited and that an application can only be made on the death of the promisor and only against the net estate. Thus, while a family provision order may sometimes

[1] See Chapter 4, section II.B.

lead to an award of the promised inheritance, in most cases it will be an avenue of last resort.

From the perspective of the protection vis-à-vis third parties, a proprietary estoppel claim that leads to a proprietary award and an enrichment claim resulting in a constructive trust provide the greatest protection. But even if they lead to a monetary payment, the promisee ranks as a creditor. That is not necessarily the case where the promisee establishes a contract to make a will, for if the contract is one to leave the residue estate or a share in it, the promisee will benefit only after all the debts have been paid. The position of a claimant under the family provision legislation is also less strong, for the claim is brought against the net estate after the deceased's debts have been paid. That said, where the funds are insufficient, in some common law jurisdictions, courts have the power to re-allocate assets transferred by way of will-substitutes, including contracts to make a will.

The analysis has shown that the fact that it is possible to obtain the promised asset by way of a proprietary award has invited criticism from certain scholars, especially where courts enjoy considerable discretion. In particular, we have seen that some scholars have expressed concerns that the promisor's testamentary freedom, or formality requirements for the disposition of land, are being circumvented. However, the analysis has also shown that these objections can be overcome.

In Part III, I will explore other means through which the promisee may be able to seek redress, but without being able to obtain the promised asset. I will examine instances where the legal response takes the form of a monetary payment based on the value of the promisee's performance, the enrichment of the promisor, or something less, for example, because the law imposes an artificial limit.

PART III

OBTAINING LESS THAN WHAT WAS PROMISED

Introduction to Part III

Part II dealt with forms of redress through which promisees may be able to obtain the promised inheritance, thus being put in the same position as if the promise (or their expectation) had been fulfilled. It showed that courts tend to award what was promised by way of a proprietary interest only in certain instances, and rare exceptions aside, only in common law jurisdictions. While promisees are often unable to rely on the protection offered by contract law, we saw that the doctrine of proprietary estoppel and, in the case of common law Canada, the doctrine of enrichment law can provide significant protection to promisees of informal testamentary promises, including vis-à-vis third parties. We further saw that in some cases, promisees may be able to obtain the promised asset by relying on the family provision legislation. In fact, what all three forms of redress have in common is that they provide courts with considerable discretion in determining the award, which can range from a monetary payment to the award of a proprietary interest.

Part III deals with forms of redress through which the promisee cannot obtain the promised asset, but may rather be granted a monetary award based on the value of the promisee's performance, the value of the promisor's enrichment, or something less, for instance, because the law imposes an artificial limit on the amount that can be claimed.[1] Chapter 6 has shown that although a claim founded on the principles of Canadian enrichment law may sometimes lead to the imposition of a constructive trust, more frequently courts opt for a monetary award, either on the basis of the value received, that is the value of the services or performance rendered, or more often, the value survived that takes into account lost opportunities or other types of detriment suffered by the promisee, as well as her expectation interest. In principle, some of these instances would fall within the scope of this chapter. However, because the requirements have already been examined,[2] these Canadian cases will not be discussed again here. Equally, claims based on the doctrine of proprietary estoppel, examined in Chapter 4, may provide the claimant with less than her expectation interest where that is regarded sufficient to grant

[1] This is the case for the *créance de salaire différé* examined in Chapter 10, where the descendant can only claim up to ten years' worth of wages, and the Austrian statutory care legacy analysed in Chapter 11, in which case the carer can claim the value of her services for up to three years.
[2] See Chapter 6.

appropriate relief.[3] Again, these cases would fall within this part of the book, but the requirements will not be repeated here.

Instead, this part examines a variety of other avenues that promisees can explore to obtain compensation. We will see that, even though the promisee may not be able to obtain the promised asset, there are often several means through which she may obtain at least some form of redress. Most are the product of legislative developments, and three of those examined in this part stem from the area of succession law. Unlike in Part II, the focus here lies especially on forms of redress available in civil law jurisdictions. An exception is Chapter 7, which deals with claims brought on the basis of the New Zealand Law Reform (Testamentary Promises) Act 1949 (hereafter the New Zealand TPA 1949). This is the only legislation directly dealing with the protection of the interests of promisees of informal testamentary promises. On the basis of this legislation, in theory, promisees may obtain redress up to the value of the promised inheritance. However, the reality is that they are normally awarded less, for the New Zealand TPA 1949 provides that the promisee may be awarded 'such amount as may be reasonable, having regard to all the circumstances of the case'.[4] For this reason, the legislation is examined here and not in Part II.

Another approach explored in this part, and one which promisees can pursue in some civil law jurisdictions, is to argue that the relationship between the promisor and the promisee is one of employment, so that the provisions dealing with service contracts apply. Where such an employment contract can be implied, a promisee may be able to demand the payment of outstanding wages (including holidays) for her work. Such claims feature, for instance, in Germany, where courts have shown a sensitivity to the vulnerabilities of promisees by adapting codal provisions regulating service contracts to instances where a promisee has provided services by acting on a promise of a future inheritance.[5] However, as we will see, the problem with this particular approach is that it only protects promisees who have performed services and does not capture those who act on the promise by making, for instance, a financial payment or improving the promisor's property. Also, those who are in an intimate or familial relationship with the deceased may potentially find it more difficult to have a contract implied. Interestingly such an approach is not evident in common law jurisdictions but is more readily found in the civil law context. Austria is one such example, where occasionally promisees successfully argue that a service contract is to be implied.[6] And, prior to the 1975 family law

[3] As was, for instance, the case in *Jennings v Rice* [2002] EWCA 159. For analysis see Chapter 4.
[4] TPA 1949, s 3(1).
[5] § 612 BGB.
[6] The provision that is relied upon is § 1152 ABGB.

reform,[7] which among other things introduced a regulation of work family members provide in the context of a family business (*impresa familiare*),[8] Italian law reports featured case law in which an employment relationship was found to exist between the promisor and the promisee.[9] Even so, the focus here will rest primarily on German law.

Also included in this part of the book is the analysis of cases in which the monetary award is based on the value of the promisor's enrichment. In particular, I examine the availability of such claims in civil law jurisdictions, where they can represent an important (and sometimes the only) means of obtaining redress, even though it is only ever possible to obtain restitution of the promisor's enrichment. The focus will rest on German as well as French law, where there have been interesting developments. While it will emerge that enrichment law is often not the most suitable form of redress, seeing that the requirements are not always easy to meet and the promisor has potential defences, it can sometimes be a useful means of redress.

To conclude, this part considers three further forms of redress, drawn from three different civil law jurisdictions. The first to be examined is the French *créance de salaire différé*. We will see that it is a popular form of redress. However, its scope is limited to the farming context, and it is available only to descendants of the farmer and, to a limited extent, the descendant's spouse and the spouse of the deceased farmer. Other family members, or those outside the family, are thus left without compensation. What is more, the wages are limited to ten years' worth of work. In addition, in Chapter 11 I explore adjustments based on the German § 2057a BGB, and entitlements arising from the care legacy provisions (§§ 677ff ABGB) recently introduced into Austrian law.

Unlike the New Zealand TPA 1949, neither of these three legislative solutions was developed to tackle specifically informal testamentary promises, and thus no mention is made of promises. A promisee may nonetheless rely on them to obtain some form of compensation for unremunerated work or services rendered for the deceased on the basis of a promise of a future inheritance. While their scope of application is relatively narrow, and the protection offered rather limited, these legislative interventions are interesting because they represent attempts to acknowledge the importance of work and services provided by certain family members for the deceased, and thus contributions to the estate, including in two cases in the form of domestic and care services. To some extent, then, this suggests that there has been a move towards greater recognition of the economic value of domestic labour, including care.

[7] Law no 151 of 19 May 1975.
[8] See Article 230-*bis* Codice civile.
[9] For an analysis, see De Giorgi *I patti sulle successioni future* (1976).

7

Establishing a claim under the New Zealand Law Reform (Testamentary Promises) Act 1949

I. Introduction: background and rationale

In New Zealand, it is possible for a contract to make a will to be validly concluded,[1] and where no such contract can be established, promisees can invoke the doctrine of proprietary estoppel.[2] Both avenues were discussed in Part II. The analysis has shown that both may lead to the award of the expectation interest in the form of a proprietary interest. In addition, a promisee could also bring an enrichment claim.[3] However, in New Zealand, the majority of the testamentary promises cases are, at least so far, litigated through the Law Reform (Testamentary Promises) Act 1949 (hereinafter TPA 1949).[4] This is a piece of legislation unique to New Zealand that is aimed precisely at protecting the interests of those who have provided work or personal services in return for an informal promise of a testamentary disposition in their favour.[5]

The jurisdiction conferred by the TPA 1949 had its genesis in section 3(1) of the Law Reform Act 1944 (hereafter the 1944 Act).[6] The 1944 Act was a legislative response to a number of cases[7] in which contractual claims brought by promisees

[1] *Fleming v Beevers* [1994] 1 NZLR 385; *Bristow v French* HC Christchurch 17 August 2012.

[2] See *Carroll v Bates* [2018] NZHC 2463 (HC) (hereafter *Carroll v Bates*).

[3] For examples of New Zealand cases, see *Van der Berge v Giles* [1979] 2 NZLR 111 (NZ SC) and *Stratulatos v Stratulatos* [1988] 2 NZLR 424 (NZ HC).

[4] New Zealand Law Commission, *Succession Law: Testamentary Claims*, NZLC Preliminary Paper 24 (Wellington 1996) (hereafter New Zealand Law Commission *Succession Law* (1996), [292].

[5] For a detailed discussion of the TPA 1949, see Patterson *Law of Family Protection* (2021) ch 13.

[6] For an analysis of the 1944 Act, see Campbell (1947). The TPA 1949 did not alter any of its core principles, though it clarified that the promise need not be for a specified amount, that it may relate to both real and personal property, and, that it need not be in writing. The Law Reform (Testamentary Promises) Act 1961 conferred wider discretionary powers on the court when deciding the award which, as we will see, has had an impact on the underpinning rationale. For a discussion of why changes were introduced in 1949 and in 1961, see Sheppard (1985) 175–176.

[7] For an example in which the contractual claim failed because the promise was regarded to be too vague or uncertain, see *Higgie v Wilkinson* [1903] 23 NZLR 74. In *Te Ira Roa v Materi Omipi* [1919] NZLR 681; [1919] GLR 492, the claim was rejected because the court concluded that the deceased's cousin had worked on her farm on the understanding that he would receive a legacy rather than being paid. In *Young v Anderson* [1940] NZLR 239, the claim was barred due to a lack of writing.

Claiming a Promised Inheritance. Alexandra Braun, Oxford University Press. © Alexandra Braun 2022.
DOI: 10.1093/oso/9780198757252.003.0008

of testamentary promises had been unsuccessful,[8] either because they were too vague, so that no offer, acceptance, or intention to create a legal relationship could be found, or because they lacked writing. One good example of such a case is *Sutherland v Towle* (1937). Here a woman, Mrs Sutherland, had provided the deceased, Mr Hastings, and his wife, with unpaid domestic and nursing services over a period of about five years, and incurred personal costs to provide such services. She did so on the deceased's express but oral promise to compensate her in his will.[9] The first promise was made when the promisee had just finished work for the deceased in the form of papering a room and whitewashing a ceiling. In response to her complaint about the lack of payment, Mr Hastings replied, 'I could not afford to pay a man. You have no need to grumble, you are getting well paid for this. I have made provision for you in my will, and when the time comes to settle up you will be well paid'. Three more promises followed along the same lines. Yet, in the end, Mrs Sutherland was not provided for in the deceased's will. The Supreme Court of New Zealand rejected Mrs Sutherland's contractual claim even though it found that there had been a clear promise, and despite the fact that it recognized the injustice its decision would lead to in this case. Ostler J concluded that:

> The law is clear that a person who does work for a testator on the understanding that he is to be paid by a legacy under that testator's will has no claims against his executors if he fails to provide the promised legacy. I do not think that the law is equitable, and in this case I feel that it will work an injustice. But it is clearly the law and my duty as a Judge is to follow the law.[10]

Thus, even if rather unwillingly, Ostler J resolved that the law did not permit the promisee's claim. That the judge could have reached such a conclusion is somewhat puzzling, for it is not entirely correct to say that there was no claim in any event, at least where a contract could be proven.[11] In any case, demonstrating the elements of such a contract is often difficult in practice, because the promisee needs to prove a clear offer and acceptance, consideration, an intention to create a legal relation, and, where the subject matter is land, also writing.[12] These difficulties were acknowledged by the Court of Appeal of New Zealand in *Nealon v Public Trustee* (1949) decided a few years later.[13] Commenting on the importance of the 1944 Act, Jinlay J pointed out that:

[8] For a discussion of the genesis of the 1944 Act, see Coote in *Essays in Law* (1965); Nield (2007) 298; Patterson *Law of Family Protection* (2021) 213–214; Pearson *Testamentary Promises Act* (2011).

[9] *Sutherland v Towle* [1937] GLR 509.

[10] Ibid, 511.

[11] Coote in *Essays in Law* (1965) 4–10 has argued that the decision was based on a misleading passage in Halsbury. He has further pointed out that New Zealand judges have later ascribed the failure to award redress in some of the cases to other reasons, including the lack of form of the agreement and the fact that the performance was gratuitous or the promise too vague. On this point, see also Peart (1991) 77.

[12] Chapter 3.

[13] *Nealon v Public Trustee* [1949] NZLR 148 (hereafter *Nealon v Public Trustee*).

> The need thus emphasized for a valid and enforceable contract as the basis for a successful claim gave rise to much injustice. Honourable understandings were defeated by the necessity for that completeness and exactitude or the necessity of form, which the law required as essential to the validity and enforceability of contracts. Compliance with these essentials to validity and enforceability was, in the ordinary course of things, difficult to secure, for such agreements are generally made between close relatives and the party rendering the services commonly found it difficult to have such essential requirements satisfied by the other. To attempt to do so would savour of doubting the integrity and trustworthiness of the other. This might jeopardise the existing happy relationship between the parties, and so jeopardise the prospects of receiving a reward which was generally promised upon a generous scale.[14]

The Court of Appeal stressed both the challenges promisees had been facing in bringing a claim for breach of contract and the problems of fitting testamentary promises within a contractual framework. The decision is important also for another reason: it recognizes that testamentary promises are made in the domestic context, often among close relatives, where insisting on certain formalities can put the promisee in an awkward position or potentially compromise the relationship.

The New Zealand Parliament also acknowledged the problems with the state of law, which the 1944 Act was intended to remedy. In the Law Reform Bill, the Minister of Justice, Mr Mason, stated that: 'A person might work for a long time and render services ... over many years in the faith of that expectation, and yet be defeated in respect of it, and have no remedy of any sort'.[15] This was not just due to the fact that promisees would often be unable to provide written evidence, but also due to the fact that promises would often be vague. Hence, in *Bennett v Kirk* (1946), Fair J reported that:

> until 1944 ... there was no power for the court to make any such provision, unless there had been a specific contract binding in law on the deceased, and in terms so definite and certain that the court was able to give effect to them. There had been many deserving cases where that legal contract had not been made because the promises were made in vague language. They were often definite enough as to the promise, but vague or uncertain as to the kind or extent of the benefits promised.[16]

Thus, the 1944 Act, and the TPA 1949 which reformed the former, were aimed at remedying some of the harshness of contract law by enabling promisees to bring a

[14] Ibid, 160.
[15] Parliamentary Debate (23 November 1944) 267 NZPD HR 299–300, at 299.
[16] *Bennett v Kirk* [1946] NZLR 580, 582 (hereafter *Bennett v Kirk*).

claim where it would have been difficult for them to prove the existence of a legally binding contract to make a will. A further aim of the legislation was to try to avoid any abuse of (testamentary) power by the promisor,[17] and thus to temper the risk that testators would 'obtain services under some form of deceit'.[18] Indeed, in the Court of Appeal decision in *McCormack v Foley* (1983), Cooke P described the rationale of the legislation as follows:

> The mischief which it was designed to remedy was largely the tendency of testators to persuade people to render services to them by promises later found to be too vague to establish at common law contracts enforceable against the estate. It also overcame evidential difficulties under the Statute of Frauds. It did not displace the common law as to testamentary contracts but created a new discretionary jurisdiction similar in that the object was to enforce the deceased's 'promises'—an expression itself liberalised during the history of the statutory jurisdiction.[19]

Just like the legislature, courts in New Zealand were thus aware of the risk of exploitation and the need to avoid that promisors would induce others to provide services for them without providing them with adequate remuneration.

Given that one of the purposes of the TPA 1949 was to protect promisees in cases where a contractual claim would have failed, the requirements for a successful claim had to be different and adapted to the testamentary context. In the following pages I will examine these requirements before turning to the question of how courts quantify an award under the TPA 1949, with a view to establishing the extent to which it is capable of protecting the interests of promisees in an adequate manner. We will see that on the whole, the TPA 1949 is tailored to the context in which testamentary promises are being made and thus minimizes many of the difficulties that promisees have otherwise to overcome when seeking redress. For instance, the promise can be vague and does not need to be in writing, and the notion of work and services has a wide meaning so as to capture also intangible benefits that a promisor may receive. Also, and importantly, the promisees motives are entirely irrelevant. At the same time, unlike with other forms of redress, the analysis will also reveal that promisees hardly ever obtain the promised property, that their claim only arises on death of the promisor, and that they are not usually treated as creditors, so that their protection vis-à-vis third parties is somewhat limited. While initially the purpose of this legislative intervention was to enforce informal promises, and to remedy the harshness of contract law, with time the rationale underpinning the TPA 1949 has changed so that the primary objective now is to compensate

[17] See Pearson *Testamentary Promises Act* (2011) 15 who sees the act as having a deterrent function.

[18] *Parata v McGowan* [1994] NZFLR 937, 943 (Williamson J) (hereafter *Parata v McGowan*).

[19] *McCormack v Foley* [1983] NZLR 57 (CA), 61 (hereafter *McCormack v Foley*). Most recently, these observations were endorsed in *Tawhai v Govorko* [2015] NZHC 2874, [59] (hereafter *Tawhai v Govorko*).

the promisee for unremunerated services rendered in return for a promise, and to do so principally on the basis of the objective benefit that has arisen to the promisor. This brings the TPA 1949 much closer to a claim for the restitution of the enrichment, with the consequence that the protection under the Act has weakened over time, so that some promisees may wish to seek redress through other means.

II. Requirements

In order to succeed under the TPA 1949, which as we said superseded the 1944 Act, an applicant must prove that: (i) she has provided services to, or performed work for, the deceased; (ii) there was a testamentary promise by the deceased; (iii) there was a causal connection between the promise and the services provided; and (iv) the promise was not, or not entirely, fulfilled, in the sense that the deceased failed to make the promised provision or to otherwise remunerate the promisee.[20] In the following sections, I examine each of these requirements. It will become clear that, generally, the threshold is not high. This does not mean, however, that the legislation does not pose potential difficulties, for instance, where the promisor's motives play a role.

A. Work or services

The first requirement to be met is that the promisee has provided 'work' or 'services' for the deceased. Neither of these terms are defined in the TPA 1949, but courts seem to have taken a broad view of what constitutes the necessary 'work' or 'service', with the effect that the TPA 1949 captures a wide range of situations. Indeed, in *Tawhai v Govorko* (2015), the High Court of New Zealand held that the words are to be given 'a large and liberal construction to achieve the remedial objectives of the Act'.[21] They include work and services that provide both tangible and intangible benefits but also single acts such as a surrender of rights.[22] It is worth mentioning here that the claimant does not have to be the person who provided the services or to whom the promise was made to.[23]

[20] TPA 1949, s 3(1).

[21] *Tawhai v Govorko* (n 19) [48]. See also *Ireland v Grant* [2014] NZHC 1523, [28] (hereafter *Ireland v Grant*).

[22] In *Tucker v Guardian Trust and Executors Co of New Zealand Ltd* [1961] NZLR 773 (SC), 776, in return for a promise to leave him the house, the promisee had disclaimed a legacy (hereafter *Tucker v Guardian Trust*).

[23] TPA 1949, s 3(1). See *McMillan v New Zealand Insurance Co Ltd* [1956] NZLR 353 (SC). In *Atkinson v Samuels* (unreported, High Court Auckland CIV 2006-404-7878, 30 May 2008) (hereafter *Atkinson v Samuels*), the High Court was prepared to treat the services by the three siblings as a group. In *Bishop v Public Trustee* [2001] NZFLR 413 (HC), [56] Nicholson J stated that the value of the services of each applicant should not be considered in isolation but in the context of the services provided by the family as a whole.

Doubts have sometimes been raised as to what constitutes 'services'.[24] Although on several occasions courts have explicitly confirmed that 'services' include companionship, affection, and emotional support,[25] it is not always clear where the line should be drawn. This was the case in *Re Welch* (1990),[26] the first and only Privy Council decision interpreting the TPA 1949. Here the stepson had assisted (in his spare time) with the deceased's transport business for a period of about five or so years and had assumed and performed the role of a son of the deceased. The deceased had been generous in return, giving the stepson a parcel of land on which to build a house, and arranging jobs for him. The deceased had also made a promise that a share in the business, and his house and furniture, would go to the stepson. However, he died intestate, and the stepson therefore brought an action. At first instance, Williams J found that acting as a son to the deceased qualified as a service for the purposes of the TPA 1949 and awarded him a large sum for his services. However, on appeal, which focused on the quantum, the Court of Appeal held, among other things, that the evidence provided pointed to nothing more than a 'normal' family relationship between stepfather and stepson, and that the award had therefore to be reduced, especially in light of the reciprocal advantages obtained by the stepson. The Privy Council agreed with this approach, describing the services provided by the stepson as 'natural incidents and consequences of life within a close family group' that should not be brought within the concept of 'services', or else the scope of the TPA 1949 would be strained.[27] The Privy Council therefore rejected the appeal.

While *Re Welch* is an important and highly influential decision,[28] it has not prevented other courts from rewarding a promisee for family or domestic services, including companionship, affection, and emotional support, under the TPA 1949. New Zealand courts have regularly held that such services can form the basis of a claim,[29] but only if they go beyond 'what is normally to be expected of a relative, a member of the same household, a neighbour or a friend'.[30] In other words, services need to exceed a certain threshold. Exactly what one can normally expect of a relative or a friend, and when the threshold is exceeded, is, however, not always easy to

[24] *Samuels v Atkinson* [2010] NZFLR 980 (CA), [46] (hereafter *Samuels v Atkinson*); see in particular *Tucker v Guardian Trust* (n 22). Patterson *Law of Family Protection* (2021) 224–226.

[25] *Tawhai v Govorko* (n 19) [48]. *Byrne v Bishop* (2001) 20 FRNZ 609, [2001] NZLR 780, [6] (hereafter *Byrne v Bishop*) and *Thwaites v Keruse* (1993) 11 FRNZ 19, 23 (hereafter *Thwaites v Keruse*).

[26] *Re Welch* [1990] 3 NZLR 1 (PC) (hereafter *Re Welch*).

[27] Both the Court of Appeal and the Privy Council distinguished the facts from those in *Hawkins v Public Trustee* [1960] NZLR 305 (SC) where the deceased wanted his family name and business to be carried on by a worthy successor. The grandson had changed his name, had become the full-time manager of the promisor's farms, in exchange for a promise that he would leave him at first the whole and then a quarter of the estate. This was held by Shorland J to constitute 'services' under the TPA 1949.

[28] For an analysis of the influence on subsequent decisions, see Peart in *Landmark Cases* (2019).

[29] *Saunders v New Zealand Guardian Trust Company Limited HC Palmerston North* [2010] NZHC 1417, [17] (hereafter *Saunders v New Zealand*).

[30] *Byrne v Bishop* (n 25) [6]. *Murray-Kendall v Wilson* [2014] NZHC 885 (2 May 2014), [43]; *Atkinson v Samuels* (n 23) [61].

establish. The crux of drawing the line,[31] as we have seen, is not a problem unique to this particular remedial approach.[32]

It helps when the services rendered by the promisee have enabled the promisor to stay out of institutionalized care.[33] Otherwise, the specific relationship between the parties, and potentially the gender of the promisee, also matter. Courts in New Zealand have taken the view that there is a need to ascertain not only what can be expected in 'normal families' but also what is 'normal' within the particular family in question.[34] Thus, just as is the case with the doctrine of proprietary estoppel,[35] under the TPA 1949, the context is significant. While that might make the existence of a claim less predictable, it is important that courts have scope to evaluate the requirements in the proper context. The need to consider the context, was, for instance, stressed by the Court of Appeal decision in *Thwaites v Keruse* (1993), where the following example was provided:

> Companionship, affection, cohabitation may properly be regarded as 'services' in some circumstances where, for example, the promisor is elderly or lonely or in poor health. But that cannot be so in the case of young people simply sharing together the pleasure of each other's company in a common household.[36]

The context mattered in *Re Fagan (dec'd)* (1999).[37] In this case, an adopted son had alleged that he had provided care and companionship, maintenance of the home, and financial advice to his biological father for about four years on the basis of a promise that he would be rewarded in the form of a testamentary disposition. The son argued that, while these services would be regarded as natural incidents of a relationship between a biological son and his father, they should be seen in quite a different light, given that he had been adopted by his stepfather. The court agreed, and the claim was upheld.

In *Samuels v Atkinson* (2010), the three claimants had provided primarily companionship, affection, and emotional support to their parents' friends (the Atkinsons) on the promise that they would be rewarded. Indeed, they acted as a 'surrogate' family for the promisor. In addition, one of the claimants, the daughter, had also physically cared for the deceased in that she had cooked for him, cleaned his home, taken him for medical check-ups, and assisted with personal accounts

31 This is pointed out by the Court of Appeal in *Samuels v Atkinson* (n 24) [50].

32 Here, see the parallel with Canadian enrichment law discussed in Chapter 6. See further the discussion of § 2057a BGB in Chapter 11 and of French enrichment law in Chapter 9, section III.

33 In *Kite v May* [2001] NZFLR 514 (HC) (hereafter *Kite v May*), the housekeeper became the de facto partner and cared for the deceased, enabling him to stay out of institutionalized care. See also *PH v GH* [2013] NZHC 443. It was also a factor in *Tawhai v Govorko* (n 19) [58].

34 *Saunders v New Zealand* (n 29) [9]; *Tawhai v Govorko* (n 19) [49].

35 See Chapter 4.

36 *Thwaites v Keruse* (n 25).

37 *Re Fagan (dec'd)*; *Walker v Fagan* [1999] NZFLR 222 (HC), 236.

and cash handling for about four years. The Court of Appeal agreed with the first instance judge who had found that, given the promisor's childlessness, the intangible benefit of having 'surrogate' children was 'something extra'.[38] Thus, when establishing whether the threshold is exceeded, the specific context matters and intangible benefits are taken into account.

An example where the services provided were regarded as insufficient is *Re Stevens (deceased)* (2017).[39] In this case, Woolford J found that odd jobs, the payment of small sums of cash (e.g. up to $100 at Christmas time, the purchase of a television and DVD player for the deceased), frequent telephone calls and visits made by the stepson and his wife over a period of about two years, that provided the deceased with emotional support, as well as occasional trips to the shops and doctors, were no more than the natural incidents of a family relationship.[40] Emotional support provided from a distance will also normally be insufficient. For instance, in *Saunders v The New Zealand Guardian Trust Company Limited* (2010), the High Court held that:

> whilst emotional support can add to services related to the physical well-being and care of a promisor in failing health and in respect of her property, it is more difficult to characterize emotional support [in this particular case in the form of phone calls, regular contact by mail, including cards, flowers and gifts on birthdays and at Christmas] from a distance, simply on its own, as a qualifying service. In the absence of a defined need by the promisor for such support, and some acknowledgment that it went some way to fulfilling such a need, I consider that such a service will not qualify.[41]

Thus, a line is drawn where the courts do not consider the performance substantial enough. It follows that what is to be regarded as 'normal' often depends on the duration and the type of services performed by the promisee.[42] Where the

[38] *Samuels v Atkinson* (n 24) [80]. In the *Estate of Coyne (Deceased)* [2005] NZFLR 678 (Fam), [44] the court considered that the claimant's services could include his efforts in maintaining and fostering cordial relationships with this stepmother and stepsiblings.

[39] *Re Stevens (deceased)*; *Stevens v Ryan* [2017] NZFLR 419, [18]–[22]. Similar services were provided by the claimant in the case of *Blumenthal v Stewart* [2016] NZFLR 647, where the claim was also denied. At [107] Ellis J commented that in relation to the plaintiff's claim, these situations can fall 'within the rock of the FPA [Family Provision Act] and the hard place of the TPA [Law Reform (Testamentary Promises) Act]'. In this case the claimant did not qualify as a 'stepchild' for the purposes of the FPA.

[40] The type of services rendered here seem similar to those provided in the decision of the LAG Rheinland-Pfalz, 6 August 2015 – 5 Sa 123/15, BeckRS 2015, 72666 based on § 612 BGB where the claim was also rejected. The decision is discussed in Chapter 8. See also the French decisions Cass 1re civ, 6 July 1999, JCP G 1999, I, 189, no 3, obs R Le Guidec and Cour d'appel Nîmes, Chambre civile 1, section B, 21 June 2012, RG no 11-02235, where the enrichment claim was rejected. For details, see Chapter 9, section III.

[41] *Saunders v New Zealand* (n 29) [50]. See also *Samuels v Atkinson* (n 24) [77]–[80].

[42] In *Parata v McGowan* (n 18), the nephew had helped the deceased and his late wife with friendship, support, and regular visits, particularly in times of trouble or ill health, and had done so for many years. The services were held to go beyond what would normally be expected of a nephew.

performance is not substantial, the best option for a promisee is probably to try to apply for a family provision order, but to do so they must, of course, fall among the category of those who are eligible.[43]

B. A promise

It is not sufficient for a promisee to have provided services. The second requirement for a claim under the TPA 1949 to be successful is an express or implied promise[44] to make a testamentary provision in favour of the promisee, and not to reward her, for instance, in some other way.[45] In other words, a promise of an inheritance rather than a promise to make a lifetime gift or to pay wages is required for the TPA 1949 to apply.

The term 'promise' has a wide meaning and is defined in section 2 of the TPA 1949 as 'any statement or representation of fact or intention'. The arrangement need not amount to a legally binding contract,[46] which is important. This was not always the case. In the immediate aftermath of the enactment of the 1944 Act, some courts adopted a 'contractual' approach to the interpretation of section 3 of the 1944 Act.[47] However, in *Nealon v Public Trustee*,[48] dealing with the interpretation of section 3 of the preceding 1944 Act, O'Leary CJ considered that, because of the remedial objects of the legislation, the case was one calling for a large and liberal construction and interpretation of these terms. Consequently, in his view, the word 'promise' was not to be used in a technical, contractual sense, but to be understood as an assurance, undertaking, declaration, or intimation to make some testamentary provision. Thus, the legislation was clearly intended to cover a wide range of testamentary promises cases. Gresson J, who agreed with O'Leary CJ, also rejected the contractual analogy declaring the TPA 1949 to apply to promises which lack the features that would make them enforceable in law.[49] On this basis, the court further concluded that section 4 of the Statute of Frauds 1677, which required writing of contracts to make a will concerning land,[50] had no application in such a claim meaning that even where the promise concerns land, no written proof of the promise is required under the Act.[51] Not only is there no need for a contract, the promise does not have to be in writing either.

43 For details, see Chapter 5.
44 As for a case in which the promise was implied, see *Jones v Public Trustee* [1962] NZLR 363, 372–373, and 376 (hereafter *Jones v Public Trustee*).
45 See, for example *Tawhai v Govorko* (n 19) [60]; *Ireland v Grant* (n 21) [27]; *Saunders v New Zealand* (n 29) [10].
46 *Ireland v Grant* (n 21) [26]; *Saunders v New Zealand* (n 29) [10].
47 These are the words of Coote in *Essays in Law* (1965) 10. See also Peart (1991) 78.
48 *Nealon v Public Trustee* (n 13).
49 Ibid, 164–165.
50 See the discussion in Chapter 3.
51 While this was unclear under the 1944 Act, the TPA 1949 clarified the point in s 3(1)–(2). In *Nealon v Public Trustee* (n 13) the claim had failed at first instance on the grounds that the promise

This more liberal interpretation is without doubt preferable from the perspective of the promisee and vital if the TPA 1949 is to remedy the harshness of contract law and to take account of the fact that, as discussed in Chapter 1,[52] in the domestic context, parties tend not to consider the legal consequences of their dealings, nor to discuss legal enforcement, and that testamentary promises are often vague. It would also seem to be more consistent with the underlying rationale of the Act, as pointed out by the court in *Nealon v Public Trustee*.[53] The debate that had emerged around the correct interpretation of the term 'promise' was eventually settled when the 1944 Act was reformed in 1949, which introduced a broad definition of 'promise'.[54] Hence, in *Byrne v Bishop* (2001) the Court of Appeal stated that:

> The term 'promise' under the Act covers declarations which might not fall within a dictionary definition of that word and certainly goes beyond any contractual context (*Jones v Public Trustee* [1962] NZLR 363). It includes a statement or representation of present fact ('I have done X for you in my will') or intention ('I will do X for you in my will') made either before, during or after the services or work occur (s3(2)).[55]

Consequently, since then, courts have protected promisees even in the presence of very imprecise and vague statements that would not amount to a contract.[56] For instance, in *Re William (deceased)* (1994), statements such as 'you'll be all right' associated with visits and personal assistance were regarded as sufficient.[57] In *Saunders v The New Zealand Guardian Trust Company Limited* (2010) the claimants had different recollections of the promise, including that they would 'always be looked after financially' or that the deceased 'would leave her estate to us girls'.[58] Dobson J was satisfied that the claimants' recollections were sufficient to constitute a promise by the testator that she would leave 'either "her estate" or a substantial portion of it to them in her Will'.[59] Nonetheless, in the end, the claims were rejected,

related to land and was not in writing. The New Zealand Court of Appeal held, however, that writing was not required.

52 Chapter 1.

53 In *Tawhai v Govorko* (n 19) [60], the High Court of New Zealand stated that: 'In keeping with the remedial intention of the Act, the courts have been prepared to interpret even very imprecise statements made by a deceased person as promissory in order to grant relief where a reasonably plain case has been made out.'

54 For an analysis of how the courts moved away from this contractual approach, see Coote in *Essays in Law* (1965) 10–13.

55 *Byrne v Bishop* (n 25) [8].

56 Patterson *Law of Family Protection* (2021) 236–238. In *Allender v Gordon* [1959] NZLR 1026 (CA), 1030 the court found that, in the circumstances in which they were said, the words of the deceased that her son would be 'properly rewarded' or 'suitably rewarded' were sufficient to amount to a promise.

57 *Re William (deceased)* HC Wellington CP 866/92, 21 July 1994.

58 *Saunders v New Zealand* (n 29) [42]–[44].

59 Ibid, [45].

though on the basis that the services remained within the bounds of normal familial services. In *Re Collier-Cambus (Deceased)* (1994) a promise was found in the deceased's statement to his stepson that he did not need to make a will 'as you are my family'.[60] In *Atkinson v Samuels* (2008),[61] one of the promises at issue was said to be a promise to one member of the family to 'do something else' for her,[62] and interpreted as 'a promise to make some provision' in the will for her.[63] Finally, in *Hamilton v Hamilton* (2003), evidence of one of the claimants was to the effect that 'during the ... years that Michael and I cared for him on many occasions he would say I was not to worry and he would look after Michael and I and the children'.[64] The court found that, given the context, these words were sufficient to substantiate a claim:

> In the context of an aged man, without available assets or other capacity to 'look after' Ms Cressey the inference drawn by her is inevitable—that within the meaning of s2 of the Testamentary Promises Act he was making a 'statement or representation of ... intention' and thus promising testamentary provision. And I am satisfied that the nexus is inevitable from the circumstances.[65]

Again, we can see that the context matters, but also that promises can be vague, even where the vagueness extends to the subject matter of the promise. The 1949 reform of the legislation clarified that it is not necessary for the promisor to indicate the exact amount she intends to leave to the promisee.[66] Section 3(1) explicitly provides that the claimant must prove a promise to make a testamentary provision 'whether or not the provision was to be of a specified amount or was to relate to specified real or personal property'. In some cases, the promise relates to a specific asset, be it a farm, half the profits of the sale of a property or the property (if not sold), or shares in a company that owned a farm, and so on. That said, the aforementioned examples show that, more often than not, promises are vague in terms of the precise subject matter of the testamentary disposition.[67]

To summarize, as the High Court of New Zealand stated in *Ireland v Grant*, '[t]he promisor need not to do a lot to make a promise',[68] which is perhaps unsurprising given that the TPA 1949 was meant to remedy the harshness of contract law

60 *Re Collier-Cambus (Deceased)* [1994] NZFLR 520 (HC) (hereafter *Re Collier-Cambus*).
61 *Atkinson v Samuels* (n 23) [5].
62 Ibid, [45].
63 Ibid, [82].
64 *Hamilton v Hamilton* [2003] NZFLR 883 (HC), [49] (hereafter *Hamilton v Hamilton*).
65 Ibid, [50].
66 This is confirmed by Speight J in *Edwards v NZ Insurance Co Ltd* [1971] NZLR 113, 116 (hereafter *Edwards v NZ Insurance Co Ltd*): 'How much was not stated but, of course, an amount need not be specifically defined for the promise to be enforceable.'
67 See nn 57–65.
68 *Ireland v Grant* (n 21) [27]. The court further noted that in *Gibson v Gibson HC Dunedin* CP9/90, 15 April 1992, per Tipping J mere nodding of the head was enough.

and its requirement of offer and acceptance, an intention to create a legal relationship, but also proof of writing in the case of land.

C. A nexus between the services and the promise

The third requirement for the application of the TPA 1949 is a nexus between the promise and the work or service performed by the promisee. The nexus can either be express or, more commonly, be inferred from the circumstances.[69] In establishing the nexus, it is important to note that, under the New Zealand legislation, the promisee's motives for providing the service or work are entirely irrelevant.[70] This represents a significant difference to, and advantage over, the doctrine of proprietary estoppel,[71] but also Canadian enrichment law,[72] given that the motives matter when it comes to providing the absence of a juristic reason for the enrichment. In other words, the link is not dependent on whether or not the promisee acted out of love or because of the prospect of a future inheritance. There is no need to prove reliance. Though not explicitly mentioned in the TPA 1949, this is established by case law. For instance, in *Re Lamb* (1993),[73] Williamson J expressed difficulty with the concept that work, or services lovingly given should be worth less than those contractually given. Equally, in *Byrne v Bishop* (2001), the Court of Appeal stated that '[i]t would be repugnant if the fact that the services or work were performed out of a generous spirit and not for mercenary reasons or in the hope of reward should count against claimants by way of depriving them of a claim or devaluing it'.[74] In *Hamilton v Hamilton*, the fact that the deceased's former partner had acted not for reward was no bar to the award.[75] On the contrary, the court referred to the 'virtue of [the services] being provided out of love and duty rather than for reward'.[76] The fact that the promisee's motives do not play a role is no doubt beneficial to the promisee, for, as pointed out in Chapter 1, in most cases, the promisee's motives will be mixed, and the promise may represent but one of the reasons for her behaviour. This illustrates again that the New Zealand legislature has taken account of the context in which testamentary promises are often made.

Given that the promisee's motives are irrelevant, and there is no need to prove reliance, the promise does not have to precede the performance of the services.[77]

[69] *Byrne v Bishop* (n 25). In *PZ v JC* [2006] NZFLR 97 (Fam), such a nexus was lacking.

[70] *Tawhai v Govorko* (n 19) [71]; *Byrne v Bishop* (n 25) [10]. See also *Edwards v NZ Insurance Co Ltd* (n 66) 116 where Speight J noted that the claimant 'with a candour which did him no harm in my eyes, agreed that the probably would have gone into the transaction in any event and he himself had some misgivings as to whether or not his father would honour his word'.

[71] See Chapter 4.

[72] See Chapter 6.

[73] *Re Lamb* [1993] NZ Recent Law 208.

[74] *Byrne v Bishop* (n 25) [10].

[75] *Hamilton v Hamilton* (n 64) [48].

[76] Ibid, [51].

[77] TPA 1949, 3(2)(a).

In other words, the services or work must take place during the deceased's lifetime (section (3)(1)) but can occur before or after the making of the promise. The timing is irrelevant. This is important, given that in many of the testamentary promise cases there is no clear arrangement about when work or services are to start. As I pointed out in Chapter 1,[78] it is not uncommon for a person to start looking after the promisor, or to start working on her farm or in her business, and for the promise of a reward to be made at a later stage, often to ensure that the promisee's performance continues. In fact, as the New Zealand Law Commission has acknowledged, '[t]his rule is particularly important in cases where services begin at a lower level, but gradually increase as the will-maker becomes older. The parties' initial intentions may not be a reliable indication of whether the benefit should be paid for'.[79]

However, whilst the motives of the promisee are irrelevant, those of the promisor matter, which is different from all other forms of redress examined in this book and potentially problematic from the promisee's perspective. In *Atkinson v Samuels*, the High Court of New Zealand stated that '[t]he nexus between promises and a service must be objectively determined and the focus must be on the promisor (the deceased) rather than the promisee'.[80] In other words, the promise must indicate an intention to *reward* the promisee for her services. As the High Court of New Zealand commented in *Tawhai*, this does not mean that the promisor must say 'if you care for me, I will leave you my entire estate', but there must be a nexus.[81] Although establishing the promisor's motives can be just as difficult as establishing those of the promisee, and there is potentially a risk that non-existent intentions are attributed, judging from case law, it seems that it is not in itself fatal that the promisor's motives are mixed. They are normally found to be lacking only if the promise was made *solely* out of love and affection, though case law is not entirely conclusive.

In *Saunders v The New Zealand Guardian Trust Company Limited*, the nexus was lacking because, according to the court, the promise of an inheritance was given out of love and affection and without any need for services or work in return.[82] This was based on the finding that the promisor's 'statements were freely volunteered at times when she was in good health, enjoying life and in particular enjoying the close and positive family relationship she had with "the girls"'.[83] This reasoning could suggest that a nexus can only be established if the promisor is in difficulty or under pressure, but a promisor can intend to reward the promisee even though the

[78] See Chapter 1.

[79] New Zealand Law Commission *Succession Law* (1996), [308].

[80] *Atkinson v Samuels* (n 23) [76].

[81] *Tawhai v Govorko* (n 19) [73]; *Ireland v Grant* (n 21) [30].

[82] *Saunders v New Zealand* (n 29) [46]. Dobson J found that 'there is no suggestion that Clarice's promise was made to procure any work or services from "the girls" but that they were freely volunteered at times when she was in good health'.

[83] Ibid.

promisor is in good health and enjoys the promisee's company. One does not exclude the other and is acknowledged in many other cases.[84]

In *Re Welch*, examined earlier, where the stepson provided assistance in the deceased's business (and assuming and performing the role of a son), the Privy Council, just like the Court of Appeal,[85] could not find the required nexus. This finding was partly corroborated by the fact that there was a discrepancy between the value of the deceased's assets and the value of the services, if any, provided by the stepson. For the committee, the discrepancy 'underlines that the predominant motive of the deceased in making the representations was affection for his stepson and the latter's family, and the natural tendency to give effect to ordinary family expectations'.[86] However, to suggest that too generous a promise excludes an intention to reward the promisee is potentially problematic, because a promisor may well want to reward the promisee but also leave her more than the value of the performance received. Again, one does not exclude the other. In fact, a testamentary promise can represent a useful tool through which a promisor can try to leave at least what the service may have been worth, but possibly more. And why should a promisor not be able to do so? Also, depending on how long the promisor lives, the promise may or may not be out of proportion, so that it is difficult to judge the promisor's intention when the promise is breached. However, the two decisions have to be read in the specific context, and it is unclear to what extent they represent the general position, as case law in this area is inconclusive. What they confirm, however, is that the rationale behind the NZ TPA 1949 is no longer the enforcement of the promise.

D. Lack of remuneration

The fourth and final requirement for an award to be granted is that the services or work provided by the promisee must not have been rewarded either by way of a testamentary provision or otherwise,[87] for example, a lifetime gift. However, as Pearson states, '[t]he mere fact that the testator has paid wages or made gifts to the claimant during his lifetime will not necessarily rule out a claim. These are only remuneration if they were made in recognition of the services for which remuneration was promised'.[88] This requirement may be potentially difficult to establish where the promise is vague, or where the services are intangible and a precise

[84] An example is *Samuels v Atkinson* (n 24).

[85] The NZ CA states that 'in all probability [the stepfather's motives] must have been due simply to the natural love and affection he felt for him'. *Re Welch* [1989] 2 NZLR 1, 8.

[86] *Re Welch* (n 26) 7–8. Here, see also the words by Dobson J in *Saunders v New Zealand* (n 29) [52]: 'Another consideration in assessing services is the relativity between the conduct characterised as "services" provided in return for the promise, and the value of the promise as claimed'.

[87] S 3(1) TPA 1949. See *Tawhai v Govorko* (n 19) [89].

[88] Pearson *Testamentary Promises Act* (201) 20.

monetary assessment cannot be made.[89] In order to establish whether the services were unremunerated, and thus for there to be a claim 'there has to be a "netting off" of the respective benefits and burdens ... Although it is awkward, and in a sense distasteful in respect of close personal relationships, to have to "net off" the balance of benefits and burdens in a case like this, the court has to do the best it can if the principles of the Act are to be properly observed'.[90] If the benefits received by the promisor exceed those received by the promisee, the unremunerated balance requires an award, which leads me to the next point, that is the quantification of the relief.

III. Quantifying the award

A. Enforcement of the promise or reward for the service?

Initially, the TPA 1949 required promises for specific sums and property to be honoured in full,[91] which might explain why courts required proof of a contractual promise. Indeed, early decisions contained references to the fact that the rationale behind the legislation was to *enforce* the promise.[92] This approach was clearly in the interest of the promisee, but it had the potential of affecting family members and dependants and other third parties with an interest in the estate, for example, claimants under the family provision legislation. This was seen as problematic so that, in 1961, the TPA 1949 was changed to provide courts with greater powers to take those interests into account. At that point the protection of the promisee was weakened.

The new section 3(1) of the TPA 1949 provides that, to the extent that the deceased failed to make the testamentary provision or to otherwise remunerate the claimant, the claim shall be:

> enforceable against the personal representatives of the deceased in the same manner and to the same extent as if the promise of the deceased were a promise for payment by the deceased in his lifetime of such amount as may be reasonable, having regard to all the circumstances of the case.

This means that in all cases courts should now award *such amount as may be reasonable*, having regard to all the circumstances of the case. Hence the promisee no longer necessarily receives what she was promised, even if the promise was specific. Where the deceased has made a promise to leave the promisee either real or

[89] See *Powell v Public Trustee* [2003] 1 NZLR 381, [31]–[33] (hereafter *Powell v Public Trustee*).
[90] See *Samuels v Atkinson* (n 24) [77] and [78] but previously also *Powell v Public Trustee* (n 89) [31].
[91] The 1944 Act, s 3(1).
[92] See text at n 47.

personal property, in theory, courts have a discretion to award all or part of that property to the claimant.[93] However, they are unlikely to do so where, for instance, those with a moral claim against the estate may be affected.

At least since 1961, cases in which the promisee has obtained what she was promised have been rare.[94] Courts are more likely to make an award in the form of a lump sum, a periodical or other payment for less than the value of the promise,[95] which is more akin to what courts do under the family provision legislation, though the rationale of the legislation is different. This is so despite the following dictum of Cooke J in the Court of Appeal decision in *Re Townley* (1982):

> the power to make a full or partial vesting order has been in the legislation since 1949. There is nothing in the wording to suggest that Parliament meant it to be used only exceptionally or sparingly. In inflationary times I think that when a promise relates to real property the Court should normally consider carefully whether the fairest order may not be to vest the specific property at least in part in the claimant.[96]

From the perspective of the promisee the fact that she will hardly ever obtain her expectation interest is no doubt unsatisfactory, especially when her performance was substantial or rendered for many years. It is certainly not in line with the initial rationale behind the TPA 1949, which was intended to temper the harshness of contract law by *enforcing* informal testamentary promises. This is not achieved if the deceased only ever sees her reliance interest fulfilled. However, the rationale has changed over time so that the aim is no longer to enforce the promise but rather to compensate the promisee for the value of the benefit received by the promisor.

One could argue that this allows for the equal treatment of all promisees, irrespective of whether or not the promise is to leave the deceased's estate, or a share in it, or to leave a specific asset, which, as we saw, can lead to very different outcomes under contract law.[97] Also, because courts no longer award the expectation interest, they can perhaps be less strict when interpreting the meaning of 'promise' or 'services' or when establishing a nexus, which indeed they seem to be. But does this mean that promisees will be awarded the value of their performance even when it exceeds the value of the promise? I will turn to this question in the next section.

93 TPA 1949, s 3(3).

94 Patterson *Law of Family Protection* (2021) 214 and Peart (1991) 81. Exceptions are *Bennett v Kirk* (n 16) and *Jones v Public Trustee* (n 44). See further *Re Beazer (Deceased)* [2001] NZFLR 557 (NZHC) and *Re Hanlon* [2000] NZFLR 227 (NZHC). In *Public Trustee v Bick* [1972] 1 NZLR 301 (CA), the High Court awarded the promisee the house of the deceased, but the Court of Appeal awarded a monetary sum which it held was a reasonable amount for the services rendered. In *Ireland v Grant* (n 21) 112 the Court concluded that the promisees should receive 50% of the farm despite the promise being that they would get the farm.

95 TPA 1949, s 3(4).

96 *Re Townley* [1982] 2 NZLR 87 (CA), 89 (hereafter *Re Townley*).

97 Chapter 3.

B. What represents the upper limit?

I mentioned earlier that the courts must award such amount as may be reasonable having regard to all the circumstances. This means that they have a broad discretion as to the quantum of the award.[98] How do New Zealand courts go about establishing what is a reasonable award? It seems that the upper limit is always what was promised,[99] even if the value of the performed service or work is higher. For instance, in *Re Collier-Cambus (Dec'd)* (1994), the High Court considered whether a sum greater than the amount promised can be awarded. Tipping J held that: 'It would be a curious anomaly if, following a complete failure to make any testamentary provision or provide other remuneration, the claimant could obtain more than the promise'.[100] It has further been argued in legal scholarship that if a higher award could be made, this would be contrary to the legislature's intention as expressed in the subtitle to the Act: 'An Act to make better provision for the *enforcement of promises* to make testamentary provision in return for services rendered'.[101]

However, given that the rationale is no longer the enforcement of the promise, it is unclear why the value of what was promised should represent the upper limit.[102] This seems particularly problematic where the promisee has provided substantially more than the parties had originally envisaged.[103]

C. Criteria courts must take into consideration

While courts have a significant degree of discretion in determining the award, in establishing what is a 'reasonable' award, they must have regard to a particular set

[98] *Re Welch* (n 26) 6.

[99] These restrictions were outlined in *Re Collier-Cambus* (n 60) 146, where Tipping J stated that:

> In a case, however, where there is a promise of a specific amount or of specific real or personal property, there are two limitations on the amount which can be awarded. First the amount cannot be more in value than what was promised and second it must be reasonable. The Court will not automatically award the amount specified or the specified real or personal property. It will only do so if that is fair recompense for the services. If the amount promised is greater than what is reasonable only such lesser amount as is reasonable may be awarded.

For an example of a case where the court has awarded more than the value of the promise, see *Re Murtagh, Mahe v NZ Guardian Trust Company* [1989] BCL 1557, where Doogue J awarded the claimant (the deceased's sister) almost ten times the value of the property promised.

[100] *Re Collier-Cambus* (n 60) 524.

[101] Peart (1991) 81.

[102] This is one of the reasons why in 1996, the New Zealand Law Commission recommended removing the need for a promise and focusing on the service provision, that is restitution for unremunerated services. See New Zealand Law Commission *Succession Law* (1996) 81, [296]. In fact, it is not the upper limit in the case of other forms of redress that are disconnected from the promise e.g. § 612 BGB discussed in Chapter 8. By contrast, it could not be higher with a proprietary estoppel claim.

[103] Wells 'Testamentary Promises' (2007) 308.

of statutory criteria set out in section 3(1) of the TPA 1949.[104] The provision requires courts to take into account:

> all the circumstances of the case, including in particular the circumstances in which the promise was made and the services were rendered or the work was performed, the value of the services or work, the value of the testamentary provision promised, the amount of the estate, and the nature and amounts of the claims of other persons in respect of the estate, whether as creditors, beneficiaries, wife, husband, civil union partner, children, next-of-kin, or otherwise.[105]

Although this list provides some guidance, it does not offer an indication as to what the starting point should be, what weight to award to each of the criteria listed, or in what order they should be considered. As a result, there seem to be discrepancies between the awards courts make under the TPA 1949.[106] This has been criticized for the reason that such inconsistencies lead to uncertainty about the quantum, which make attempts to settle the cases more difficult.[107] This is an argument we have come across before in relation to proprietary estoppel claims where courts also have considerable discretion.[108] It is submitted that the argument is not particularly strong. Where courts are granted discretion, some level of uncertainty is inevitable. This has the advantage, however, of allowing courts to take into account the particular context.

Looking at case law, the determination of a reasonable amount will often depend on a number of factors, including how substantial the services or work were, the value of the estate, and potential interests of third parties in the estate.[109] The starting point frequently seems to be the value of the services,[110] though it would

[104] The list seems in many ways similar to the one Walker LJ set out in the context of a proprietary estoppel award. See Chapter 4, section III.C.

[105] In *Powell v Public Trustee* (n 89) [10] the Court of Appeal considered each of these elements in turn and reached the conclusion that the award provided at first level had to be curtailed by three quarters. For a discussion of the case, see Richardson (2003). See also *Re Welch* (n 26).

[106] Pearson *Testamentary Promises Act* (2011) n 111 has argued that '[w]hen enacting the Act, Parliament was reluctant to establish any definite rule or measure in order to maximise fairness between the parties of each case'. See the Parliament Debates (23 November 1944) 267 NZPD HR at 300; (6 October 1949) 288 NZPD HR at 2597.

[107] *Humphrey v New Zealand Guardian Trust* [2004] NZFLR 179, [65], per William Young J.

[108] Chapter 4.

[109] Pearson *Testamentary Promises Act* (2011) 27. In *Ireland v Grant* (n 21) the court took into account the nature of the promise, the significant work performed, the services rendered, the expenses incurred in reliance on that promise, the nexus between the promise and those matters, the significant *inter vivos* dispositions made to the promisees by the promisor by way of gift, and the finding that the promisee probably contributed around 50% to the cottage cost (on the farm) (see [122] and preceding paragraphs). The Court concluded that the promisees should receive 50% of the farm (at [112]). In *Tawhai v Govorko* (n 19) the court took into account: (i) the promised distribution under the last will known to the promisee (which was not the final will); (ii) what was given to the promisee under the final will; and (iii) what benefits the promisee received during the lifetime (the court noted the other recipients were dear friends of the testator and elderly).

[110] Peart (1991) 81.

appear that the monetary calculations of such services are often rather vague. In fact, courts do not usually clearly articulate how they value the services or work provided. In the Privy Council decision of *Re Welch*, Sir Robin Cooke disclaimed absolute precision in making an award suggesting that 'it will often be impossible or inappropriate to weigh in any nice scales services or work on the one hand and testamentary reward on the other'.[111] Hence, 'the value of the services supplied is commonly an issue'.[112]

In evaluating the services, courts have often looked at what was promised, for this guides them as to the deceased's own estimation of the value to him of the services.[113] Patterson has argued that 'where the deceased's subjective appraisal of the value of the services is greater than what objectively those services might be worth, as much weight as possible should be given to the deceased's assessment as its reasonable in all the circumstances'.[114] I agree with him because the promise is usually a determining factor for the promisee's behaviour. Other matters included in the quantification of the relief are reciprocal/mutual benefits, such as testamentary gifts provided by the deceased or wages, but also free accommodation and lodgings. As I said earlier, only unremunerated benefits require an award. In this context, it is interesting to note that benefits in the form of companionship that the promisee receives also count as reciprocal benefits.[115]

Finally, also relevant to the determination of the award are other legitimate claims on the estate, such as those of creditors or beneficiaries under a will, as well as claims under the family provision legislation. Section 3(1) explicitly refers to the nature and amounts of the claims of other persons in respect of the estate, whether as creditors, beneficiaries, spouses, civil union partners, children, next-of-kin, or otherwise. In other words, the award will depend on how many other people may have a claim against the estate. Some of the criteria introduced with the 1961 reform therefore operate as a safeguard for the deceased's creditors and others with an interest in the estate. This is not usually in the interests of the promisee. It is similar to the state of affairs under the family provision legislation and is a clear disadvantage if compared to other forms of redress.[116]

111 *Re Welch* (n 26) 7. In *Byrne v Bishop* (n 25) [51] the NZ CA agreed with the first instance judge that the mental and physical value of what the promisor received was priceless and that '[i]n their very nature services of this kind, particularly companionship and love, are really beyond a monetary calculation'.

112 Dal Pont & Mackie *Succession* (2013) 27.

113 Patterson *Law of Family Protection* (2021) 244.

114 Ibid, 214.

115 See *Powell v Public Trustee* (n 89) [31], where the court stated that '[i]f tangible services have been partially "remunerated" by reciprocal benefits, the same approach must logically be taken. As intangible services like companionship qualify as services, reciprocal benefits of a like kind must equally qualify as partial remuneration'. See also *Re Archer* [1990] 3 NZLR 737 (NZHC), 747.

116 Whether it is one of the factors in proprietary estoppel claims is disputed. See Chapter 4, section III.C.

Does this mean that the promisee's claim prevails over that of others with an interest in the estate and, if so, when? I will address these questions in section IV. The answer is important if there are insufficient funds to provide for everyone. We will see that there is currently considerable ambiguity in this regard.

IV. The nature of the right of the promisee under the TPA 1949

A. The position vis-à-vis creditors

1. Introduction

A claim under the TPA 1949 can only be brought on the death of the promisor, which is different to many other remedial approaches that I have addressed so far (e.g. the contractual approach, proprietary estoppel, and enrichment law). This is one of the most significant limitations of the TPA 1949. For instance, where the promisor sells the property to a third party during her lifetime, the promisee is potentially left without protection. This also suggests that the promisee is not to be regarded as a creditor. Indeed, the general position is that the promisee is *not* treated as a creditor of the estate. Rather, the award is *deemed to be a bequest by the deceased* to the promisee. This is expressly provided in section 4(2)(b) of the TPA 1949 (through amendments introduced in 1961), which establishes that a successful claimant under the TPA 1949 ranks *after* the deceased's creditors.

Nonetheless, it would seem that a court order based on the TPA 1949 may affect an executor's ability to meet creditor's claims in full. Section 3(1) of the TPA 1949 provides that a claim is 'enforceable against the personal representatives of the deceased in the same manner and to the same extent *as if* the promise of the deceased were a promise for payment by the deceased in his lifetime'. This wording suggests that the interest of the promisee is akin to a lifetime debt and that the claim therefore concerns the deceased's gross rather than net estate. This can also be inferred from section 3(5) of the TPA, as reformed in 1961, which states that:

> The incidence of any payment or payments so ordered shall, unless the court otherwise determines, fall rateably upon the whole estate of the deceased, or, in cases where the authority of the court does not extend or cannot directly or indirectly be made to extend to the whole estate, then to so much thereof as is situated in New Zealand.

This interpretation indicates that the promisee competes with creditors even though, as we have seen, section 4(2)(b) explicitly provides that the claimant is deemed to have received a bequest by the deceased. Support for this analysis can be gleaned from the New Zealand Court of Appeal decision in *McCormack v Foley*

(1983),[117] where Cooke J held that a claim under the TPA is a claim against the gross estate, and not the net estate. Although the judge acknowledged that section 3(5), reproduced earlier, cannot safely be treated as having major significance in this regard, in the judge's view, this conclusion can be inferred especially from section 3(6), which provides that:

> The court shall have power, after hearing such of the parties as may be affected as it thinks necessary, to exonerate any part of the estate of the deceased from the incidence of any such payment or payments, to determine priorities as between any benefit awarded by the court to the claimant under this Act and the beneficial interests of any other person or persons in the estate of the deceased person, and to make such provision as it thinks fit as to the incidence of the whole or any part of the debts, testamentary expenses, and duty in respect of the estate of the deceased

Section 3(6) thus seems to indicate that under the TPA 1949, New Zealand courts have considerable discretion both in making decisions as to the incidence of the whole or any part of the debts, and in determining priorities as between the person claiming under the TPA 1949 and the interests of any other person or persons with a beneficial interest in the estate of the deceased person, including creditors. But, as we will see, not every creditor is treated in the same manner. New Zealand courts seem to distinguish between trade creditors and other creditors such as promisees under a contract to leave a specific asset who, as we have seen in Chapter 3,[118] are creditors.

2. The position vis-à-vis trade creditors

When considering specifically the relationship with trade creditors, certain *obiter* remarks made by Cooke J in *McCormack v Foley* indicate that, although the claims of trade creditors would most likely take priority over those of a promisee who invokes the TPA 1949, they do not have automatic priority:

> So, under subs (1), in determining the quantum of an award the Court is to have regard inter alia to other claims in respect of the estate; and these include, I think, claims under contractual rights. It would seem to follow that a simple unsecured contractual claim, such as a tradesman's debt, would fall to be considered. The tradesman is a creditor. But normally in exercising the discretion to fix a reasonable amount under the Act the Court would allow for the payment in full of trade and other inter vivos debts. Whether the rights of such creditors could ever

[117] *McCormack v Foley* (n 19) 65 (Cooke J).
[118] Chapter 3.

> properly be affected by an award under the Act is a question which can be left open unless and until it arises.[119]

Thus, a claimant under the TPA 1949 could potentially rank prior to any unsecured trade creditors. However, Richardson J was more cautious as to the scope of the discretion of the courts under the TPA 1949, noting that:

> there is no express power to determine priorities as between the holders of the testamentary promises benefit and ordinary creditors of the deceased. And the power to provide for the incidence of debts is a facilitative provision. Notwithstanding the apparent breadth of the discretion under subs (5) I have reservations as to the power of the court to direct in the case of a solvent estate that debts should be recoverable only from a designated part of the estate if that part is insufficient to discharge the debts and in that way to affect the value of those debts.[120]

It thus appears that the judges of the Court of Appeal were not in full agreement as to the exact scope of the powers awarded by sections 3(5) or 3(6) of the TPA 1949 vis-à-vis trade creditors, but since Cooke J used the term 'normally', it seems that the interests of trade creditors will prevail. This, of course, is not desirable from the perspective of a promisee and means that the protection under the TPA 1949 is less strong than that provided through a proprietary estoppel claim or an enrichment claim.

But what about other creditors? The question has often arisen in situations where courts were asked to balance the interests of competing promisees, one of which is a contractual promisee. In fact, it is possible that a promisor makes more than one promise and that therefore more than one promisee advances a claim against the estate (sometimes against the same asset), though not necessarily on the same grounds. Where that is the case, whose interest will prevail? We will see that this question arises both when the contractual promise has been broken, but also when it was kept and the promisor has made the promised will in favour of the contractual promisee, which are the cases I shall discuss first. Either way it seems that courts have the power to balance the interests for the benefit of the claimant under the TPA.

3. The position vis-à-vis a contractual promisee: the promise is kept

A clash between the interests of a claimant under the TPA 1949 and those of a promisee under a contract to make a will (or not to revoke the will), whose promise was fulfilled, has arisen in the aforementioned case of *McCormack v Foley*. Here

[119] *McCormack v Foley* (n 19) 65 (Cooke J). See also McMullin J at 76.
[120] Ibid, 71 (Richardson J).

the deceased had contracted not to alter an existing will (rather than to make a particular testamentary disposition in favour of the promisee) whereby he had devised certain farm assets to his brother. The promise was kept, and the will was not revoked. So far so good. However, after the testator's death, his sister had brought a successful claim under the TPA 1949, on the basis that over many years she had kept the deceased's household and provided special care that his diabetic condition required, in exchange for which he had promised that he would make a testamentary provision for her. As it turned out, the sister's award could only be satisfied by encroaching on the farming assets, which had been the subject of the contract not to make a will. Thus, the question arose as to whether the interest of the contractual promisee, the deceased's brother, was stronger than that of the sister who was basing her claim on the TPA 1949 and who, in principle, is to be seen as a legatee. At first instance, the payment under the TPA 1949 was charged against the share of the deceased's brother who was the beneficiary under the will that was made in execution of the contract not to revoke the will. The brother appealed the decision, and the Court of Appeal dismissed the appeal. It found that, because of the powers conferred by sections 3(5) and (6) of the TPA 1949, the first instance judge was right in doing so. Richardson J justified this interference with the deceased's will on the basis that:

> [i]n the case of a contract not to revoke or alter a will it cannot possibly be said that the original will was made in the performance of a binding contract and there can be no doubt that the person for whom testamentary provision was made will have a beneficial interest in the property which is devised or bequeathed to him. Whether he [the deceased's brother] takes that beneficial interest under the will alone or by the combined effect of the will and the contract, he must be regarded as a beneficiary in the estate within s 3(1).[121]

Although technically speaking in this case the will cannot be said to have been made in performance of a binding contract, it seems that the distinction made by Richardson J can lead to unjust results. It suggests that, had the will been made in execution of a promise to make a will, rather than one not to revoke the will, things would have been different and the brother better off. However, as we will see, later decisions put this inference into question.

Richardson J's conclusion further suggests that, had the will been revoked and the contractual promise broken, the brother (the contractual promisee) would have been in a stronger position than his sister who was the beneficiary of an informal promise, for the former would have been treated as a creditor.[122] This means that in some circumstances, a contractual promisee will want to hope that the

[121] Ibid, 69.
[122] See Chapter 3.

promisor will not give effect to the contractual promise so that she can bring a claim for breach of contract. That is absurd. However, subsequent case law which will be analysed in the next section has established that even when the contractual promise is broken, the interest of the contractual promisee does not necessarily prevail over the interests of a promisee of an informal promise. This is not the place to go into a more detailed analysis. However, it is interesting to note that, even though Richardson J saw the difficulties that his interpretation was giving rise to, he found that it was justified:

> There are two answers which may be made. The first is that the award of damages would need to reflect the risk that had the will not been altered the testamentary promises payment might have been charged against that property. The second admittedly partial answer is that the legislature has foreseen the usual case where the testator has complied with his contractual obligations and in that situation it has determined that the claims of that beneficiary have to be balanced against those of the testamentary promises claimant. It is perhaps unfortunate that when it made those substantial changes to s3(6) and s 4(2)(b) in 1961 Parliament did not expressly direct its attention to the exceptional case of a deceased who has left his personal representatives to face a claim for breach of contract.[123]

Admittedly, Richardson J spoke specifically about contracts not to revoke an already existing will. But what about contracts to make a will that are performed? Twenty years later, in *Hamilton v Hamilton* (2003),[124] the High Court of New Zealand dealt with a case in which a testamentary promises award under the TPA 1949 risked eroding a testamentary gift of a farm, which was made in execution of a prior contractual promise to make a will, in favour of one of the deceased's grandsons in recognition of his work and services. To be specific, this multipartite case involved a number of conflicting claims: (i) those of two elderly daughters who had brought a maintenance claim under the Family Protection Act 1955 (hereafter FPA 1955); (ii) that of the former wife of one of the grandsons who had cared for the deceased in the last seven years of his life, and who had brought a claim based on the TPA 1949; and (iii) that of the grandson who was the beneficiary under the will and who had been contractually promised the farm and worked on it all his life. Thus, unlike in *McCormack v Foley*, one of the interested parties was a beneficiary under a will made in execution of a prior contract to make a bequest, rather than a promise not to revoke the will.

Baragwanath J held that none of the claims had any automatic preference over the other,[125] and that the fulfilled contractual promise did not necessarily take

[123] *McCormack v Foley* (n 19) 72.
[124] *Hamilton v Hamilton* (n 64).
[125] Ibid, [60].

priority over the unfulfilled informal testamentary promise,[126] nor any claims under the FPA 1955. Thus, *Hamilton v Hamilton* shows that, although the will was made in execution of a contract to make a will (rather than a contract not to revoke the will), the court has the power to interfere with the will for the benefit of the claimant under the TPA 1949. Baragwanath J went a step further than Richardson J in *McCormack v Foley*. At the same time, he also protected the interests of the beneficiary of the farm under the will, both on the grounds that he had been promised the farm and had done much over the course of thirteen years to earn what was left to him in the will, and that it was the express will of the testator that he would receive the farm.

4. The position vis-à-vis a contractual promisee: the promise is broken

What about cases where the contractual promise is broken? Remember that in *McCormack v Foley*, Richardson J suggested that such a scenario would be evaluated differently. The problem arose in *Bristow v Smith* (2013),[127] decided about thirty years after *McCormack v Foley*, which again involved more than one promisee. In this case the High Court of New Zealand had to deal with a claim under the TPA 1949 brought by one of the sons (Timothy) on the basis that his mother had promised that she would transfer the remaining 1000 'B' shares she held in a company to him in exchange for which he and his wife had farmed the company's property. The particular question the court was asked to decide was whether the claim under the TPA 1949 could be satisfied from funds that belonged to a creditor of the estate. Notably, the creditor in question was the claimant's brother (Barnabas), who was a creditor of the estate by virtue of a judgment debt for a successful claim he had brought against the mother's estate for breach of contract to make a bequest. Indeed, in the past, the deceased mother had covenanted to leave to her son Barnabas her 1000 'B' shares in the company in return for a settlement of Barnabas' testamentary promises claim against his father's estate, but she had not fulfilled her promise. In other words, the subject of the broken covenant was a settlement relating to another testamentary promise made by the deceased father.

The question posed to the High Court was whether Barnabas was a 'genuine creditor', to be treated the same way as a trade creditor of the estate referred to by the Court of Appeal in *McCormack v Foley*. The court's assumption seemed to have been that if Barnabas was a genuine creditor—in the same vein as a third party or trade creditor of the estate—then he would take priority, because his debt would be required to be settled as far as the assets of the estate might extend, prior to any distribution under the will or settlement under the TPA Act 1949.[128] Gendall J

[126] The carer had not been promised the farm, but the deceased had told her that he would 'look after them' (meaning her and her family).

[127] *Bristow v Smith* [2013] NZHC 28667.

[128] Ibid, [27].

proceeded on the basis that 'there does not seem to be any express power in the *Law Reform (Testamentary Promises) Act* to direct that any award made under that Act shall be borne by creditors'.[129] Nonetheless, he concluded that because of sections 3(5) and (6) of the Act, the court had the power 'to determine that the incidence of a payment ordered in favour of a claimant under a testamentary promises legislation would not necessarily fall rateably upon the whole of the deceased's estate',[130] and that it had 'in the appropriate circumstances the ability to confer priority to a testamentary promises over some creditors'. 'This is especially so where the creditor, like Barnabas here, is a non-trade creditor'.[131] Gendall J therefore concluded that he had jurisdiction to direct that 'any provision made for Timothy under the testamentary promises legislation here could be satisfied from funds that would otherwise be paid by the executors of the estate to Barnabas as a creditor'.[132]

Thus, the court in *Bristow v Smith* distinguished between different types of creditors and took the view that, although the contractual promisee of a specific asset is a creditor, she is not to be treated in the same way as a trade creditor and that the court can balance the competing interests, even though this is not a case where the promise was kept, and the promised will executed. Thus, in this case the court again went a step further. The decision shows that a contractual promisee cannot rely on the fact that she is a creditor. If her claim clashes with that of a claimant under the TPA 1949 it does not automatically prevail irrespective of whether or not the promise was kept. Rather, the contractual promisee shares the risk that there are insufficient funds. In some ways, this development is to be welcomed as, arguably, both promisees have provided a performance which has enriched the estate, so that it is justifiable to balance their interests and not to treat a contractual promisee better than a promisee who has acted on an informal promise. However, it suggests that courts in New Zealand are suspicious of contracts to make wills, which is ironic given that form is often required as a sign of seriousness on the part of the promisor.[133] At the same time it also means that, at least in this context, the law does not privilege formal promises over informal ones.

B. The position vis-à-vis applicants under the FPA 1955

As far as potential conflicts with a claim under the FPA 1955 is concerned,[134] in *Hamilton v Hamilton* referred to earlier,[135] Bragwanath J held that no claim has

129 Ibid, [39].
130 Ibid, [41].
131 Ibid, [42].
132 Ibid, [45].
133 See the discussion in Chapters 2 and 3.
134 In *Edwards v NZ Insurance Co Ltd* (n 66) 118 Speight J seems to suggest that a claim under the FPA 1955 would have to be taken into account when establishing an award under a competing claim under the TPA 1949.
135 *Hamilton v Hamilton* (n 64).

an automatic preference over the other. In other words, courts have discretionary powers to balance the competing claims and to provide a result that does justice to all the parties. Yet, as Chapter 3 has shown,[136] in case of a conflict between a claim under the New Zealand FPA 1955 and a contractual claim brought by a promisee against the estate, unlike Australian courts, New Zealand courts do not have the power to interfere with the will that executes the contract to make a will. There is thus a lack of consistency, as in this case contractual promisees are treated better than informal ones.

Not everyone, however, agrees with this position. Bill Patterson has argued that a claim under the FPA 1955 should be given preference over a claim under the TPA 1949, especially where the estate is small. In his own words 'more attention may be desirable to the fact that family protection legislation imposes a restriction on testamentary freedom and that the former should therefore be accorded more consideration given the obligations imposed by the FPA 1955'.[137] In making this argument, Patterson appeals to the rationale underpinning the family provision legislation. However, given that in New Zealand financial need is no longer a requirement for a family provision order,[138] why should an applicant under the FPA 1955 take priority over a claimant under the TPA 1949 who has performed work or services for the benefit of the promisor? After all, even if the applicant were in need, it could be argued that a person may be in need due to their own doing, and not merely due to misfortune. A balancing of interests is perhaps justifiable where the applicant under the FPA 1955 has also acted upon a testamentary promise. In such a case, a conflict arises between the interests of two promisees and arguably one should not be better off than the other.

C. Summary

Notwithstanding the fact that section 4(2) of the TPA 1949 establishes that the promisee's award is *deemed to be a bequest by the deceased*, and that she is not therefore a creditor, her position is not always clear. As between a promisee who brings a claim under the TPA 1949 and a trade creditor, the interests of the latter usually prevail. From the promisee's perspective, this is unsatisfactory, and a clear restriction compared to some of the other forms of redress analysed in this book (e.g. an enrichment claim or a proprietary estoppel claim). In fact, once creditors have been paid, there may not be much left to be distributed. This is similar to the problem that applicants under the family provision legislation face, for their application is also made against the net estate.

[136] Chapter 3, section IV. See the decision in *Breuer v Wright* [1982] 2 NZLR 77.
[137] Patterson *Law of Family Protection* (2021) 221.
[138] Chapter 5, section II.B.

However, as between a promisee who acts on the basis of the TPA 1949 and a promisee who is party to a contract to make a bequest, whether it has been executed (as was the case in *Hamilton v Hamilton*) or breached (as was the case in *Bristow* v *Smith*), case law determines that New Zealand courts have a power to balance the interests of promisees so that claimants under the TPA 1949 could take priority, even though they are not technically speaking creditors. This suggests that in the absence of clear legislative guidelines, over time, New Zealand courts have enhanced the protection of the promisees under the TPA 1949 at least with regards to contractual promisees, who share the risk that there is not enough in the estate.

While discretionary powers necessarily entail a level of uncertainty, there seems to be a need to provide courts with greater guidance, not only with regard to the position of the claimant under the TPA 1949 vis-à-vis applicants under the family provision legislation, but also when it comes to other promisees who bring a claim based on unjust enrichment principles or proprietary estoppel.[139] At the moment, a review of succession law in New Zealand is under way, and it is hoped that the TPA 1949 will be retained, but that this particular aspect will be clarified.

V. Conclusion

The New Zealand TPA 1949 was clearly tailored to the testamentary context which, as we said, does not usually fit the contractual approach. Promises neither have to be specific nor do they have to be in writing. Redress can be given even for services performed prior to the making of the promise, for the motives behind the promisee's performance are irrelevant.[140] In other words, there is no need to prove reliance on the promise and the fact that the promisee may have, for instance, acted also (or even only) out of love and affection does not undermine her claim. The legislation makes allowance for the fact that motives can be mixed and also recognizes that the sequences between a promise and the promisee's performance may not be chronological.

From the perspective of a promisee, a claim under the TPA 1949 also has other advantages. The interpretation by the courts of both the notion of 'promise', and that of 'work' and 'service', has been, generally, expansive. Cases captured by the TPA 1949 have included instances of work carried out in a business of the deceased,[141] maintenance and improvement of farms,[142] but most commonly care or domestic services, including day-to-day assistance (in the form of preparing meals, visits, cleaning, shopping, assistance with medical appointments), and in some

139 That the state of the law in this regard is highly unsatisfactory has been pointed out by Peart (2008) 377.

140 Nield (2007) 299ff.

141 *Re Lowe* [1991] 1 NZLR 99 (NZHC).

142 *Re Townley* (n 96).

instances also companionship and emotional support, though a certain threshold must be exceeded.[143] Thus, on the whole, the TPA 1949 covers a wide range of situations and values both tangible and intangible benefits, taking less of an economic approach than, for instance, enrichment claims usually require.[144] At the same time, a line has to be drawn somewhere, and the Privy Council decision in *Re Welch* has tried to do that by reference to what is 'normal' in the particular context. However, as we saw, establishing what is 'normal', can pose difficulties because different expectations come into play.

Even so, all in all, it is perhaps unsurprising that the TPA 1949 has received praise by some New Zealand judges,[145] and has been advocated as a possible solution by scholars in other common law jurisdictions.[146] Nonetheless, the legislation also has its weaknesses,[147] especially since over the years it has been reformed in a way that is less protective of the promisee's interests. First, while the promisee's motives do not matter, they can have an impact on whether or not a nexus can be established. More importantly, the claim only arises on the promisor's death. Thus, the promisee lacks protection under the TPA 1949 where the promisor disposes of the asset by way of a lifetime transfer.[148] While in that case she may explore other avenues (e.g. a proprietary estoppel claim or an enrichment claim), this may not always be possible. Third, as it stands, the promisee is unlikely to obtain what was promised. This is not only because the reward has to be reasonable in the circumstances, but also because the legislation explicitly requires that entitlements of other interested parties, such as creditors and other claimants towards whom the deceased may have had a moral duty, must be taken into consideration. Thus, a court is unlikely to award the expectation interest even where the promise was specific. This may be justified by the fact that the purpose of the TPA 1949 has changed since 1961 and is no longer to enforce the promise, but to compensate the promisee for the value of the benefit accrued to the promisor. Yet, where, for instance, a promisee grossly undervalues the services provided, for example, because the promisee has provided services for longer than initially expected, courts can award no more than the amount specifically promised.[149] This is difficult to

[143] See *Atkinson v Samuels* (n 23) [55].

[144] See Chapters 6 and 9.

[145] Hammond J described it in *Kite v May* (n 33) 518 as a 'beneficient' provision.

[146] Sloan *Informal Carers* (2012) 240ff; Davey (1988) 110; Nield (2000) 103; Nield (2007) 305. Wells 'Testamentary Promises' (2007). By contrast, McFarlane in *Current Issues* (2016) 77 takes the view that legislation is not necessary in England and Wales because the doctrine of proprietary estoppel is well equipped to deal with testamentary promise cases.

[147] This is one of the reasons why the New Zealand Law Commission has considered reform of the statute. See New Zealand Law Commission *Succession Law* (1996), [298].

[148] In a letter to the New Zealand Law Commission, Brian Coote had suggested reforming the TPA 1949 so as to enable promisees to bring a claim during the testator's lifetime. See New Zealand Law Commission, Property Law and Equity Reform Committee, Working Paper on Proposals for Reform of the Law Reform (Testamentary Promises) Act 1949 (1974).

[149] Peart (1991) 81. Here, see *Samuels v Atkinson* (n 24) [74] (per Hamond J). The CA criticized awarding what was promised because this leads to effectively a specific performance of the testator's promise.

justify, given that the rationale behind the TPA 1949 has changed. Another significant limit in terms of the strength of protection is that a claimant under the TPA 1949 is not in principle treated as creditor, meaning that her claim is one against the net estate, though in some cases her claim may potentially prevail over (or at least does not automatically succumb to) that of certain creditors and others with a moral claim against the estate. Finally, one aspect that I have not yet mentioned is that any action based on the TPA 1949 must be commenced within twelve months after the personal representative of the deceased took out representation.[150] The time period for bringing an action is thus relatively short, though not as short as the one usually prescribed by the family provision legislation.[151]

Nothing stops a promisee from bringing a separate contractual claim,[152] or from bringing both claims in one action, though she will only be provided with one remedy. A contractual claim may be advantageous, because of the measure of the award, which does not, for instance, include the consideration of other claimant's interests. That said, few of the cases discussed in this chapter are likely to fit the contractual approach, which is one of the reasons why the TPA 1949 was introduced in the first place. Also, the protection under contract law depends on how specific the promise is. The recent decision in *Carroll v Bates* (2018) shows that a proprietary estoppel claim may be a valuable option for a promisee, especially because the courts can grant a proprietary right and order the transfer of the promised asset.[153] Such a proprietary right provides strong protection against third parties. In addition, the claim can be brought during the promisor's lifetime. While that may mean that the court takes into account the fact that the promisee will obtain an accelerated benefit, the promisee will not have to wait until the promisor's death, which is important, for instance, in cases where the parties have fallen out with one another or the promisor intends to dispose of her asset.[154]

Unlike what was initially feared,[155] it would seem that the TPA 1949 has not become an ill-used remedy.[156] Yet, the legislation has been criticized by some legal scholars who argue that it imposes a significant limit on the promisor's testamentary freedom,[157] especially in light of the fact that very vague statements can constitute a promise. This view seems to be shared by some judges.[158] However, is there really an infringement of testamentary freedom? For the reasons I have mentioned earlier,[159] when making a promise and accepting that the promisee acts on

[150] TPA 1949, s 6.
[151] See Chapter 5, section IV.
[152] See TPA 1949, s 3(8).
[153] *Carroll v Bates* (n 2).
[154] See Chapter 4.
[155] For references to some criticisms both from within and outside Parliament, see Burns (1965).
[156] Nield (2000) 89.
[157] Peart (2007); Peart (2008) 361. See further Davis (1950).
[158] In *McCormack v Foley* (n 19) [68] (Richardson J).
[159] See Chapter 4 and Chapter 5.

it, the promisor voluntarily assumes an obligation which the court gives effect to on the basis of the TPA 1949. In fact, the TPA 1949 requires there to be a promise, work and services, and a nexus between the two.

The confusion may partly stem from the fact that the promise is one to make a testamentary provision, the promisee's claim arises only on the death of the promisor (just like the family provision claim), and that the order is classified as a bequest. The argument of the encroachment on testamentary freedom can further be understood if one considers that in the New Zealand literature, the TPA 1949 has often been examined against the background of the FPA 1955, which operates even against the deceased's will.[160] In addition, just as with the FPA 1955, under the TPA 1949, courts have discretionary powers and the concern seems to have been that such powers are used to impose the court's view of what a particular testator should have done.[161] While it is the case that New Zealand courts have interpreted the requirements of the TPA 1949 in a liberal fashion, they hardly ever enforce the promise (which is, for instance, different to what we have observed to be the case in proprietary estoppel cases), so that it is less clear why the discretion has been so strongly criticized, especially given that it allows courts to balance a number of competing interests. In fact, while the initial purpose of the TPA 1949 was to enforce informal promises that would not amount to a contract, it now compensates promisees for their services, thereby placing emphasis on the objective benefits obtained by the promisor, so that it increasingly resembles an enrichment claim.[162] This gradual erosion of the protection of a promisee is not, however, in her best interest.

[160] See Chapter 5. See Coote in *Essays in Law* (1965) 13.

[161] Peart (1991) 78 seems to be concerned that the TPA 1949 is used to cure the imperfections of the FPA 1955 Act.

[162] In this sense, see Peart in *Landmark Cases* (2019) 229.

8
Establishing an employment relationship

I. Background

The discussion in Chapter 2 has shown that German law explicitly denies the validity of contracts or pacts in which a testator promises to make a will, not to make one or not to revoke it.[1] However, the prohibition enshrined in § 2302 BGB does not avoid problems of informal promises of an inheritance being made and acted upon by promisees. As mentioned earlier, like many civil law jurisdictions, German law has compulsory heirship provisions in place, meaning that certain close family members will be entitled to a share of the deceased's estate.[2] Arguably, this somewhat mitigates the risk that certain family members go empty handed, but it does not necessarily mean that they obtain what they were promised or the value of their performance. Promisees may therefore want to explore other avenues.

There are two main ways in which a promisee of an unfulfilled testamentary promise would usually seek protection under German law: the promisee can either argue that the promisor has been enriched at her expense (an option which will be explored in Chapter 9) or, and this is more common, she can argue that her relationship with the promisor is to be characterized as an employment relationship. In other words, the promisee can ask the court to imply a service contract between her and the promisor and claim payment of unpaid wages. This latter approach is the focus of this chapter. We will see that, since the 1960s, German courts have tended to compensate promisees who have provided services on the basis of an informal promise of an inheritance, through the application of the provisions regulating service contracts, that is §§ 611(1) BGB and 612 BGB.[3] They have done so in cases where a person has for years provided services on the assumption, accepted by the deceased, that she would benefit under the will of the latter,[4] but

[1] See Chapter 2, section II.A.2.

[2] Zimmermann, 'Compulsory Portion in Germany' in *Comparative Succession Law 3* (2020) 269.

[3] For a useful discussion of the developments, see Kössinger, '§ 1' in *Handbuch der Testamentsgestaltung* (2015) Rn 134–135; Müller-Glöge, '§ 612 BGB Vergütung' in *Münchener Kommentar zum BGB* (2020) Rn 13ff; Miserre *Die 'culpa in testando'* (2002) 35ff. A similar trend seems to have taken place in Austria. For details, see Bydlinski in *Festschrift zum 60. Geburtstag von Walter Wilburg* (1965). Similarly, an employment contract can be implied in Swiss law under article 320(2) OR. For Italy, see Ghezzi (1976); Ghezzi (1961).

[4] BAG 5 August 1963 – 5 AZR 79/63, AP No 20, zu § 612 BGB = BB 1963, 1297 (with a note by Hueck) = NJW 1963, 2188; BAG 18 January 1964 – 5 AZR 261/63, AP No 22, zu § 612 BGB (with a note by Mayer-Maly); BAG 24 June 1965 – 5 AZR 443/64, AP No 23, zu § 612 BGB (with a note by Bydlinski) = FamRZ 1965, 609; BAG 14 July 1966 – 5 AZR 2/66, AP No 24, zu § 612 BGB (with a note by

Claiming a Promised Inheritance. Alexandra Braun, Oxford University Press. © Alexandra Braun 2022.
DOI: 10.1093/oso/9780198757252.003.0009

the expectation has remained fulfilled. The redress in these cases is a monetary award based on the average salary that is normally paid for the particular services in question. Thus, the promisee will not usually obtain what she was promised. At the same time, implying a service contract at least ensures that she receives compensation for her efforts. In addition, depending on the length of service, the wages could potentially exceed what she was promised.

Whether or not an employment relationship can be found depends on a number of factors, including the nature of the promisee's performance. Most importantly, a promisee must show that she has provided services. Thus, where the promisee has acted on the promise by, for instance, paying a sum of money to the promisor, providing other financial contributions, or by building on the promisor's land, rather than performing services, it will not be possible to imply such a service contract. For this reason, it is clear that, irrespective of the merits of this particular form of redress, it can only capture certain types of breach of testamentary promises.

Where the performance does not consist of services, a promisee may seek out other forms of redress by arguing, for instance, that the promisor was enriched at her expense (something I will explore in Chapter 9) or, as a last resort and in very limited circumstances only, by invoking § 2057a BGB (a provision which will be analysed in Chapter 11). However, this chapter will show that from the point of view of a promisee an action grounded in the law regulating service contracts is frequently preferable.[5] This is partly because, on the whole, German courts have interpreted the requirements for the claim in a liberal manner, but also because the promisor lacks defences that would, for instance, be available to her in an enrichment claim. Also, mutual benefits in the form of free accommodation in the promisor's home do not affect the quantification of the wages. Thus, in many ways this is an approach that benefits promisees.

This chapter analyses how German courts have gone about implying service contracts. It examines what the promisee needs to prove and how the award is quantified with a view to exploring the extent to which this approach is capable of protecting promisees and cater for the specificities of the setting in which such promises are made. We will see that German courts have adapted a provision that was never meant to deal with instances of unfulfilled testamentary promises and have done so in a way that is for the most part sensitive to the particular context, except for the fact that subjective motives and societal expectations can occasionally hinder a promisee from obtaining compensation. The reason why German courts have adapted § 612 BGB is that they regard it as inequitable to leave someone

Diederichsen); BAG 28 September 1977 – 5 AZR 303/76, AP No 29, zu § 612 BGB = NJW 1978, 444. See also BGH 23 February 1965 – VI ZR 281/63, NJW 1965, 1124 = FamRZ 1965, 317, 319.

[5] Prior to the 1960s, German courts preferred compensating the promisee of a testamentary promise by applying principles of unjustified enrichment and, in particular, the *condictio ob rem*, as codified in § 812 I 2, 2 BGB. See Chapter 9, section II.

without protection when they have acted on an expectation to be compensated in the form of an inheritance and that expectation was engendered by a promise. In fact, it has been argued that the courts are protecting foremost the promisee's trust engendered by the promisor and thus her reliance on the promise.[6]

II. The application of employment law to testamentary promises cases

The starting point for a promisee to obtain redress under German employment law are two codal provisions: § 611(1) and § 612 BGB.

§ 611(1) BGB states that:

> By means of a service contract, a person who promises services is obliged to perform the services promised, and the other party is obliged to grant the agreed remuneration.

And § 612 BGB, dealing specifically with the remuneration of service contracts, establishes that:

> Remuneration is deemed to have been tacitly agreed if, in the particular circumstances it is to be expected that the services were rendered only for remuneration.
>
> If the amount of remuneration is not specified, then if a tariff exists, the tariff remuneration is deemed to be agreed; if no tariff exists, the usual remuneration is deemed to be agreed.

The original purpose of § 612 BGB was to protect those who, on the basis of a service contract, have provided unpaid services, which are of a kind that would normally warrant remuneration, but without having reached an agreement as to the payment. Thus, § 612 BGB was never meant to address cases where an agreement about the payment exists (e.g. in the form of a future inheritance), but is, for instance, void due to the effect of § 2302 BGB, which prohibits contracts in which the deceased promises to compensate the promisee through a future testamentary disposition. Neither was the provision intended to deal with cases where the testamentary promise was entered into informally. Nonetheless, from the 1960s onwards, the German Federal Labour Court (*Bundesarbeitsgericht*; hereafter BAG)[7]

[6] Miserre *Die 'culpa in testando'* (2002) 40.

[7] See the decisions cited in n 4. According to Lieb *Ehegattenmitarbeit* (1970) 72, the BAG has based this U-turn on earlier cautious attempts to solve cases on the basis of § 612(1) BGB. See further Canaris (1967) n 3. One such early example is RAG 1 March 1939, ARS 35, 173 concerning services rendered by a housekeeper on the basis of a testamentary promise.

applied § 612 BGB precisely to instances where a testamentary agreement was reached between the promisee and the promisor but was void or unenforceable.

As will be seen later, the extension of the scope of § 612 BGB beyond what the drafters of the German Civil Code had originally envisaged is one of the reasons why some German legal scholars have described this jurisprudential development as doctrinally unsound.[8] Nonetheless, the *Bundesgerichtshof* (hereafter BGH) soon followed the BAG in its interpretation, and extension, of § 612 BGB to testamentary promises cases.[9] Both federal courts have since continued to imply service contracts where a person has provided services on the basis of an expectation, accepted by the promisor, to be remunerated by way of a testamentary disposition in their favour, and the service was not adequately compensated.[10]

German courts have justified this extensive interpretation of § 612 BGB on the grounds that the type, scope, and duration of the services provided by promisees is not only often similar to those performed by full-time employees, but also carried out under the direction of another person (the promisor) and therefore within the scope of the provisions on service contracts.[11] In addition, courts have argued that in testamentary promises cases, the party performing the services has a clear expectation to be compensated and has no intention to provide them for free.[12] Thus, both federal courts have recognized the need to protect promisees who have acted on testamentary promises, albeit (only) through a monetary award.

III. Requirements for a protection under the law of service contracts

For § 612 BGB to apply, promisees must prove the following: (i) that they have performed services on the basis of an expectation to be remunerated in the form of a future transfer or allocation of property rights (in our case by way of a testamentary disposition); (ii) that this expectation was known to (or identifiable by) the other party (the promisor); (iii) that the services were not or not adequately compensated during the promisor's lifetime; and (vi) that there is a direct link between

[8] See section III.B.

[9] BGH 10 March 1964 – VI ZR 230/62 (unpublished). In BGH 23 February 1965 (n 4) the court stated that the position previously held by the RAG (RAGE 22, 24, [29]), that principles of unjustified enrichment should apply, is henceforth abandoned.

[10] In some of these cases, the promised testamentary disposition was either never made or was invalid, or revoked, or the promise was held to be void because of § 2302 BGB. In the case BAG 30 September 1971 – 5 AZR 177/71, BAG AP No 27, zu § 612 BGB the will could not be made because of the prior existence of interdependent mutual wills (*wechselbezügliche Testamente*) that were binding on the testator.

[11] BAG 15 March 1960 – 5 AZR 409/58, AP No 13 zu § 612 BGB = FamRZ 1960, 361 (with a note by Hueck).

[12] Ibid. See also Lieb *Ehegattenmitarbeit* (1970) 72.

the inadequate or missing payment of such services and the expectation.[13] Each of these requirements will be explored in turn. We will see that among these requirements, the first is perhaps the most complex one, for there are a number of factors that play a role. In addition, the last requirement, that of a direct link, can also pose challenges because subjective motives of the promisee may matter at this stage.

A. Provision of services on the expectation of a future compensation

1. Type of services and role of the promisee's motives

As noted earlier, for a service contract to be implied, it is important that the promisee has provided services and not, for instance, made payments to the promisor, or paid for the construction or improvement of a property that belongs to the promisor. That said, not every type of service automatically leads to a claim based on § 612 BGB. It must be a type of service that in the particular circumstances could only be expected in return for remuneration. Whether this was the case will depend on the circumstances of each case, but will be judged on a purely objective basis, without considering the subjective beliefs or motivations of the parties.[14] In other words, courts take into consideration the common usage/customs, the type, scope, and duration of the service, the profession and economic situation of the promisee, as well as the relationship between the parties.[15]

German courts have been prepared to grant an award based on § 612 BGB in cases in which, in exchange for a promise of a future inheritance, a person has worked on a farm[16] or has provided domestic services for the promisor. For instance, in a case dating back to 1971, the deceased's sister-in-law was running his household for about eight years in exchange for only food and lodgings, because he had promised to include her as an heir in his will.[17] The will was made, but it

[13] These requirements were set out in BAG 14 July 1966 (n 4). See further, LAG Hessen 22 December 2009 – 12 Sa 1363/02, BeckRS 2010, 71883, part B. Notice that the BAG did not differentiate between cases in which the compensation in the form of an inheritance or legacy was formally agreed, but ineffective due to § 2302 BGB, and those in which the inheritance was never formally promised (meaning there was no contract).

[14] See for instance, RAG 19 April 1939 – ARS 36, 162ff; BAG 17 August 2011 – 5 AZR 406/10, NZA 2011, 1335, Rn 20; LAG Rheinland-Pfalz 6 August 2015 – 5 Sa 123/15.

[15] RAG 19 April 1939 (n 14) mentions the type of activity, the scope and the duration. See further BAG 5 August 1963 (n 4); BAG 24 June 1965 (n 4); BAG 14 July 1966 (n 4). Müller-Glöge, '§ 612 BGB Vergütung' in *Münchener Kommentar zum BGB* (2020) Rn 6.

[16] See BAG 18 January 1964 (n 4). In BAG 24 June 1965 (n 4) the nephew had worked on the farm of his uncle expecting that he would inherit the promised farm, but the uncle had changed his mind. In BAG 28 September 1977 (n 4) the claimants had worked on an agricultural estate that was managed by the deceased. The claim was rejected because it was statute barred.

[17] BAG 30 September 1971 (n 10). See also LAG Berlin-Brandenburg 18 December 2008 – 14 SA 1098/08, BeckRS 2011, 67075 where the claim was, however, rejected. In this case the lodger had an employment relationship with the promisor (an elderly lady) on the basis of which he carried out all sorts of services, including gardening, work in the house, cooking lunches, etc. They agreed that he would pay reduced rent and that she would leave him her flat, but later he was made redundant and she reneged

turned out to be ineffective because the promisor had previously made a mutual will, which was binding on him. The promisee brought a claim based on § 612 BGB and was awarded redress. As will be seen later, if the same services are rendered by the deceased's partner the outcome may be different.[18] A more recent decision of the Regional Labour Court (*Landesarbeitsgericht*; hereafter LAG) of Hesse (2010) also concerned services provided in the household, in this case by a housekeeper who had been paid very little but who had continued to perform services because she had been promised the deceased's home. Again, the promisee was able to bring a successful claim.[19]

Whether care services can be compensated on the basis of § 612 BGB is subject to some debate,[20] especially where, as I will show, there is a close relationship between the promisor and the promisee. Thus, some promisees may be worse off than others. Doubts as to the remunerability of care services were raised following a first instance decision of the District Court (*Landgericht*; hereafter LG) of Heidelberg of 2009,[21] in which the court rejected the claim of a promisee who had cared for his brother. The action was based both on § 612 BGB and enrichment law (§ 812 BGB) but rejected on both accounts on the basis that the care was provided primarily for reasons of family solidarity, that is the inheritance was not regarded to be the decisive motive. The first instance decision is problematic not least because both the BAG and the BGH have repeatedly held that the assessment should be made objectively, and that the parties' subjective motives should not play a role when establishing whether an employment contract can be implied.[22] This is, however, not the only case where a German court has made explicit reference to, and based its decision on, the subjective motives of the promisee.

An interesting case in this regard is the decision of the Employment Tribunal (*Arbeitsgericht*; hereafter ArbG) of Trier.[23] Over a period of about three years, the claimant had kept the deceased (her husband's aunt) company over coffee and had occasional fifteen-minute telephone phone conversations with her. She had also taken her to the doctor, the bank, and the supermarket, but for these trips the deceased aunt had reimbursed the costs.[24] After the aunt destroyed the will in which

on the promise. The claim was rejected both because the lodger had already received what was owed to him, and because § 612 BGB does not operate if there is already an employment relationship in place.

[18] See section III.A.2.

[19] See also LAG Hessen 7 September 2010 – 12 Sa 1817/08, ZEV 2011, 434. The promisor had made the promised will but had later revoked it. Services rendered by a person working in the household were remunerated also in RG of 15 May 1916, WarnRspr 1917, Nr 14, 21. In this case the promisee had given up the possibility of an advantageous marriage, which would have guaranteed her maintenance.

[20] Doubts have been expressed by Trappe & Renners (2012) and by Roth in *Recht der Älteren* (2013) 473.

[21] LG Heidelberg 3 February 2009 – 1 O 148/07, Az 1 O 148/07.

[22] The decision was, in fact, criticized by Dienstbühl (2009).

[23] ArbG Trier 28 January 2015 – 1 Ca 522/14, Az 1 Ca 522/14.

[24] The claimant had alleged that, in total, she had spent 351 hours with her husband's aunt over a period of about three years.

she had nominated the claimant and her husband as heirs, they brought an action against her. The action was rejected on the basis that the type of services provided were not of a nature for which one can expect remuneration and invoke § 612(1) BGB. The case is interesting because, at first instance, the ArbG of Trier stated, among other things, that although there seems to have been a conversation between the parties about assistance and a possible testamentary disposition, it could not be assumed that the assistance provided by the claimants was given solely in the expectation to inherit and not also on the basis of other social reasons. Thus, once more, the subjective motives of the claimant were taken into consideration, and they were decisive in rejecting the claim. On appeal, the claimant argued that what she had done for the husband's aunt was *not* done out of kindness and that it went against reason to assume that someone who is not in a close relationship with another person would carry out similar performances for several hours a week. This is interesting because it represents one of the few cases I have come across in which a promisee was not reluctant to put forward this argument. Be that as it may, on appeal the LAG Rhineland-Palatinate (*Rheinland Pfalz*) rejected these arguments on the basis that even though the claimant may not have performed the services on the basis of kindness, or a relationship of kinship, it does not follow that the claim must be upheld.[25] Importantly, the LAG Rheinland Pfalz reiterated that, unlike what was suggested by the first instance court, the motives of the claimant are irrelevant, and that an objective standard is to be applied. It concluded that, on the basis of general moral considerations, the services provided by the promisee were not of a kind that are normally remunerated.[26] This is another example of where courts have referred to what society regards as 'normal'. Again, the type and intensity of the services as well as the relationship between the parties mattered.

Thus, as is the case with other types of redress discussed in this book (e.g. see the Canadian unjust enrichment cases discussed in Chapter 6 but also the New Zealand Law Reform (Testamentary Promises) Act 1949 (hereafter New Zealand TPA 1949) examined earlier), the question of whether or not services or work provided are of a nature that can be expected to be remunerated is an interesting one and often arises in the domestic context and especially where the benefits of the services are intangible (e.g. in the case of companionship or emotional support), and the relationship between the parties is close. Where the services are not substantial, it is likely that a court will decide against an award. However, as already mentioned, courts also consider other factors such as the profession and economic situation of the promisee, as well as the relationship between the parties.

[25] LAG Rheinland-Pfalz 6 August 2015 (n 14). The court further rejected the possibility that an award can be granted on the basis of *negotiorum gestio* or unjustified enrichment.

[26] The words employed by the court are that such services are 'not usually remunerated or compensated from a general moral and ethical point of view'.

2. Role of the relationship between the parties

Although little is said about this in German legal scholarship, it seems that German courts have sometimes been reluctant to grant redress, not merely because of the promisee's subjective motives (even though they should not play a role), or the nature of her services, but also because of the nature of the relationship between the promisee and the promisor, especially, it seems, where care and domestic/household services had been provided. Thus, we see again that domestic/household and care services are often undervalued, though there have been notable changes.

In this context, an interesting decision is one dating back to the 1970s. In this case, a woman had for eight years cared for, and looked after, the household of a man twenty years her senior. When he died, she argued that she had gratuitously cared for the deceased only because he had promised that he would marry her and that, should they get married, she would become his sole heir. The *Kammergericht* (the highest state court for the city of Berlin) concluded that it would be unusual to find an employment relationship between two people in a relationship as close as the one between the claimant and the deceased, for they were meant to get married.[27] The Court held that where household and care services are provided, and there is a close relationship between the parties, an employment relationship can only be found in exceptional circumstances. Unfortunately, the court did not specify what might count as 'exceptional circumstances'. It simply stated that an employment contract could be found in other domestic situations, and that:

> In case law … an employment relationship is generally only established if the person concerned has cooperated almost full time in the business of the other. In the case of work in the household, however, where there is a close personal relationship between the parties, it is only possible to speak of an employment relationship in very special circumstances. These are not present in the current case.[28]

Thus, the *Kammergericht* placed emphasis not only on the type of relationship but also on the fact that that the claimant had looked after the promisor in her spare time, and that she worked in the household rather than, for instance, the deceased's business. Had she performed her services in the business, the outcome would likely have been different. This goes back to the point made earlier that law tends to place less value on less-visible domestic work.[29] However, one must also bear in mind that the decision dates back to 1970.

[27] KG 9 March 1970 – 12 W 817/70 KG, OLGZ 1971, 22 = FamRZ 1970, 317.

[28] KG 9 March 1970, OLGZ 1971, 22, 24 (n 27). Here see also all the cases regarding work carried out by the son on the father's farm mentioned by Günther *Das Rechtsverhältnis* (1966) 5ff who suggests that between the 1920s and 1940s, German courts would hardly ever find an employment relationship but explain the services and work rendered on the basis of the familial bond.

[29] See Chapter 2.

In a more recent decision of 2001, the Higher Regional Court (*Oberlandesgericht*; hereafter OLG) of Cologne concluded that the care services provided by a cohabitant could not be remunerated on the basis of § 612 BGB because they were of such a nature that they could not have been provided with an expectation to obtain remuneration. The claimant had cooked for the deceased, had ensured that he would follow a strict diet, had done the washing for him, and had kept him company. Although her claim was granted at first instance, on appeal the OLG Cologne concluded that such services are usually provided for free by a spouse or, in this case, a cohabitant, especially where, as was the case here, the deceased had covered all the expenses for their support and maintenance.[30] Thus, the nature of the relationship matters, especially where care is involved.

Yet, there are also cases where German courts have held that care services can merit compensation, both where there had been a marital-like relationship,[31] and a friendship between the promisor and the promisee.[32] In fact, the BAG has been clear that the fact that there is a relationship of love or friendship between the parties does not, in principle, preclude the finding of a service contract.[33] Nonetheless, sometimes the line between what is a family like collaboration (*familienhafte Mitarbeit*) and what is an employment relationship can be a difficult one to determine, especially for partners and children, but also other relatives such as siblings.

3. Duties owed by certain family members

When considering whether particular services were rendered on the basis of an expectation to be remunerated, it is further important to note that German law imposes certain duties on certain family members. Hence, irrespective of the nature of the service and the relationship between the parties, one must consider whether the relationship between the promisor and the promisee is one that triggers such duties. Where that is the case, the services for which the award is sought must exceed the legal duty the claimant is under, otherwise a claim based on an implied employment relationship is precluded.

For instance, under German law, relatives in the direct line are under an obligation to support one another if they are in need.[34] In addition, according to § 1619

[30] This is in stark contrast with the position in common law Canada where the presumption is that certain services provided by spouses or partners in a marital-like relationship give rise to an enrichment. See the analysis in Chapter 6.

[31] BAG 24 September 1960 – 5 AZR 3/60, AP No 15, zu § 612 BGB; BAG 25 January 1963 – 5 AZR 178/62, AP No 21 zu § 612 BGB. In both cases there was a marital-like relationship between the parties.

[32] See RG 4 November 1914, Seuffert's Archiv 70, 272 (No 149). The RG remitted the case to the appeal court. It rejected the judgments in the previous two instances, which had found that the services had been rendered out of friendship, confirming that care services provided by a woman for the deceased could be compensated. The claim was based both on § 612 and § 812 BGB.

[33] See cases cited at n 31.

[34] See § 1601 BGB. Prior to 1976, in Germany, wives had a duty to work in the business of the husband. The duty, which was later imposed also on the husband, was, however, abolished for both. For an examination of the relevant provisions, see Burckhardt *Ausgleich für Mitarbeit eines Ehegatten* (1971).

BGB, a child (even if an adult) still belonging to the household of its parents and supported by them, has a duty to perform services for them in their household and business in a manner appropriate to the child's strength and position in life.[35] This duty to contribute, which children owe only to blood relatives, and not, for instance, to step-parents,[36] can potentially stand in the way of a compensation based on § 612 BGB. Although the fact that the promisee is under such a duty does not exclude the possibility that an employment relationship could arise,[37] it is necessary that the performance exceeds such duties.[38] At the same time, the absence of a duty of assistance or contribution does not automatically lead to an award either.[39]

To conclude, as the analysis has so far revealed, there are a number of factors that courts will take into account when establishing whether the services were provided in the expectation of a future remuneration or transfer, including the nature of the relationship between the parties and the nature of the services provided. While subjective motives do not normally play a role, and the test is an objective one, we saw that some courts have taken them into consideration. However, the type of services rendered in the cases in question may explain this approach, at least in part. In fact, household/domestic and care services are not necessarily treated in the same manner as work carried out in a business or on a farm.

B. The need for a tacit agreement

It is not sufficient that the promisee has performed services which, given the particular circumstances, could only be expected in return for future remuneration. The promisor must also have known about it. Although there is no need to provide proof of an express promise, and it is not necessary that the deceased has *induced* the other party to perform certain services, the parties must have 'agreed', even if only tacitly, upon the compensation in the form of an inheritance.[40] A mere subjective belief on the part of the person providing the services that she will be rewarded will not suffice.[41] It follows that unilateral expectations, and the mere performance of unrequired services, will not give rise to a claim under § 612 BGB. What matters is that the promisor recognized or should have recognized, given all

[35] On the duty to collaborate and its relevance in the context of promises of a compensation, see Fenn (1968) 292; See further Enderlein (2000). For a comparison of French and German law on contributions made specifically by spouses, see Rödl *Ehegattenmitarbeit* (1988).

[36] RAG 15 September 1937, ARS 31, 3 and RAG 26 September 1939, ARS 22, 24.

[37] BAG 30 August 1973 – 5 AZR 122/73, AP No 28, zu § 612 BGB = NJW 1974, 78, 78 did not question whether a service contract could exist between a father and his daughter.

[38] Preis, '§ 612 BGB' in *Erfurter Kommentar zum Arbeitsrecht* (2020) Rn 30. LAG Köln 20 April 1990 – 4 Sa 120/90.

[39] OLG Nürnberg 24 November 1959 – 2 U 136/59, FamRZ 1960, 119.

[40] LAG Rheinland-Pfalz 6 August 2015 (n 14): 'A secure prospect or even a commitment ... is not required'.

[41] BAG 19 February 1970 – 5 AZR 241/69, AP No 26 zu § 612 BGB = NJW 1970, 1701.

the circumstances, or have been aware of the fact that the person performing the services had a unilateral expectation to be remunerated, and that the promisor accepted this and the services.[42] In this sense, the burden of proof on the promisee is not particularly onerous.

It is unclear whether the tacit agreement has to concern only the type of compensation (in our case, in the form of a testamentary disposition) or whether the parties must have reached an agreement as to the employment relationship as such, including the type of services to be provided and their duration, but also other details such as holidays or fiscal treatment. Judging from case law, it appears that German courts have been prepared to imply the existence of a general agreement. Only in few cases have they been able to find an express agreement about the details of the employment relationship.[43] In the majority of cases, promises, assurances or statements about the future inheritance were made, without any reference to holidays, protection in case of illness, let alone the fiscal position of the promisee. This confirms that testamentary arrangements are often vague with many aspects left undefined. But it also shows that German courts have been sensitive to the context in which such arrangements are made, including the informality of such promises, and have been willing to find ways to protect promisees even in the absence of specific arrangements.

This has attracted criticism from some authors on the grounds that, in principle, § 612(1) BGB only involves a fiction as to the agreement about the compensation, and not also one about the existence of the employment relationship itself.[44] Others have criticized the application of § 612 BGB because it goes against the original purpose of the provision which was not meant to provide redress in cases in which there is an agreement (e.g. that the service would be rewarded by way of a testamentary provision), but the agreement is void because of the operation of § 2302 BGB, or unenforceable because it was entered into informally.[45] Although a number of authors have welcomed the application of § 612 BGB in these instances,[46] several have criticized courts for neglecting other available avenues, that is to say redress based on principles of enrichment law and, in particular, the *condictio ob rem*, which I will discuss in Chapter 9.[47] However, the analysis in

[42] BAG 14 July 1966 (n 4). The court declared that 'such an express promise is not necessary, rather a mutual expectation or even the unilateral expectation of the employee can suffice if the employer recognises or must nevertheless recognise it'. See also Miserre *Die 'culpa in testando'* (2002) 38.

[43] See BAG 24 June 1965 (n 4) and LAG Berlin-Brandenburg 18 December 2008 – 14 SA 1098/08), in which there was such an agreement.

[44] Canaris (1967) 165. See the discussion in Miserre *Die 'culpa in testando'* (2002) 37 and Preis, '§ 612 BGB' in *Erfurter Kommentar zum Arbeitsrecht* (2020) Rn 22–23. Critical also Fenn (1968) 296.

[45] Beuthien (1969) 166. Critical also Canaris (1967) 165 and Lieb *Ehegattenmitarbeit* (1970) 74. By contrast, see the opinion of Preis, '§ 612 BGB' in *Erfurter Kommentar zum Arbeitsrecht* (2020) Rn 22–23.

[46] Favourable Nikisch *Arbeitsrecht I* (1961) 327; Preis, '§ 612 BGB' in *Erfurter Kommentar zum Arbeitsrecht* (2020) Rn 21–22 and Müller-Glöge, '§ 612 BGB Vergütung' in *Münchener Kommentar zum BGB* (2020) Rn 14.

[47] Among these are Canaris (1967); Lieb *Ehegattenmitarbeit* (1970) 73–85; Bydlinski in *Festschrift zum 60. Geburtstag von Walter Wilburg* (1965); Beuthien (1969) 165ff; Fenn (1968) 296, 297; Fenn

Chapter 9 will show that, from the perspective of a promisee, an enrichment claim is often less desirable.

C. Lack of an adequate compensation

Another requirement for § 612 BGB to come into play is that the services must have been provided by the promisee without having been adequately compensated by the promisor during her lifetime, which is also a condition for a number of other forms of redress.[48] The cases deal either with situations in which the person was not remunerated at all, or was remunerated, but not in an adequate manner, for example, where the promisee was only provided with food and lodgings, or some pocket money. In order to ascertain whether the compensation was adequate it is not sufficient to compare what the promisee received with what is usually paid for that particular service. Instead, courts will consider the circumstances of the specific case, including the economic situation of the promisee.[49]

Entirely irrelevant for the purposes of the application of § 612 BGB is the question as to why the promisee was not compensated as promised. This can be due to the fact that the testamentary disposition lacked the required form, or the fact that the will was in conflict with a prior and binding mutual will.[50] However, where a promisee is promised the transfer of a farm but rejects it, she cannot later ask for a monetary compensation for her services on the basis of § 612 BGB, unless there are objective reasons for rejecting the transfer, for example, because the transferred asset did not correspond to what she was promised.[51]

D. The need for a nexus

A final requirement is the need for a direct relationship between the lack of compensation or payment and the expectation. A direct link is present when it can be determined that were it not for the promise, the person providing the services would have stopped performing or would have asked for payment.[52] In other

Mitarbeit (1970) 215. More recently, Wendehorst, '§ 812' in *Beck'scher Online-Kommentar BGB* (2017) Rn 90.

[48] See the discussion of § 2057a BGB and §§ 677ff ABGB in Chapter 11.

[49] BAG 14 May 1969 – 5 AZR 457/68, AP No 25 zu § 612 BGB (with note by Schnorr von Carolsfeld). On this point, see Müller-Glöge, '§ 612 BGB Vergütung' in *Münchener Kommentar zum BGB* (2020) Rn 16 and Preis, '§ 612 BGB' in *Erfurter Kommentar zum Arbeitsrecht* (2020) Rn 25.

[50] See, BAG 30 September 1971 (n 10).

[51] BAG 20 September 1978 – 5 AZR 365/77, BAG AP No 32, zu § 612 (which is, however, not a testamentary promises case). Preis, '§ 612 BGB' in *Erfurter Kommentar zum Arbeitsrecht* (2020) Rn 27.

[52] Preis, '§ 612 BGB' in *Erfurter Kommentar zum Arbeitsrecht* (2020) Rn 26. Vogelsang, '§ 67' in *Schaub Arbeitsrechts-Handbuch* (2019) Rn 19. LAG Köln 20 April 1990, LAGE BGB § 612 Nr 4, Rn 24ff (n 38).

words, if the person would have continued to provide services even in the absence of an agreement on payment, the required causal link can potentially be difficult to establish. Although the expectation to inherit (on the basis of the tacit agreement) does not have to be the sole reason for the service,[53] it appears that it must be a significant one. This, of course, can pose not just a practical but also a potential psychological hurdle for a promisee—one that she does not have to overcome in the case of the New Zealand TPA 1949 discussed in Chapter 7.

Thus, while the promisee's subjective motives do not (in theory) matter when establishing whether the promisee has performed services on the basis of an expectation to be remunerated in the form of a future testamentary disposition, they could potentially present an obstacle at this stage. Yet, there is surprisingly little judicial discussion on this point.

IV. When does the claim arise?

In Chapter 7 I mentioned that one important limitation of the New Zealand TPA 1949 is the fact that it only provides protection on the promisor's death. As far as a claim based on § 612 BGB is concerned, it normally arises immediately after the service is provided,[54] which is also when the limitation period of three years starts to run. However, since the agreement between the parties concerns a prospective inheritance, it is usually only on the death of the promisor that the promisee will know whether the promisor has actually kept the promise and made the promised testamentary disposition in her favour. How can this be reconciled with the fact that the period of limitation of three years runs from the moment at which the claim arises?[55] German courts have solved the dilemma by resorting to a fiction—they assume that the parties have agreed that compensation for the services would be deferred until the promisor's death (or the moment of the opening of the will). It is at this point that the limitation period starts to run and the amount of the wages is established on the basis of § 612(2) BGB.[56] This suggests that in this regard German courts have recognized the peculiarities of the context in which testamentary arrangements are made and that they are conscious of the need to protect the promisee.

Where the promise is revoked during the promisor's lifetime,[57] and the implied service contract terminated, the time limit runs from the moment of revocation, so

[53] LAG Köln 20 April 1990 (n 38) and BAG 14 July 1966 (n 4).

[54] This is established by § 614 BGB. See also Wendehorst, '§ 812' in *Beck'scher Online-Kommentar BGB* (2017) Rn 90 and Miserre *Die 'culpa in testando'* (2002) 38.

[55] § 195 BGB.

[56] BGH 23 February 1965, NJW 1965, 1224, 1225 (n 4). As for the problems that may arise in determining the compensation, see BAG 28 September 1977 (n 4).

[57] Preis, '§ 612 BGB' in *Erfurter Kommentar zum Arbeitsrecht* (2020) Rn 31 citing BAG 28 September 1977 (n 4).

long as it was clearly and unequivocally communicated to the promisee. This was determined in a case in which the claimants had spent their spare time working for free on the agricultural property of the promisor, who had promised that after his death, they would be adequately compensated. After seven years, the promisor decided to let his property to another person and the claimants stopped working on it.[58] At that point they demanded payment of wages for their services, which the promisor, however, refused. On the promisor's death they discovered that he had not provided for them in his will and therefore brought a claim against his sole heir for compensation based on § 612 BGB. In the first instance, the claim was rejected, but the decision was reversed on appeal. The promisees appealed the decision of the LAG, and the BGH upheld the appeal on the grounds that the period of limitation had run from the moment at which they had demanded payment from the promisee, which the promisor had refused. The BGH concluded that, in order to be successful, both parties would have had to intend for the payment to be deferred until the death of the promisor.[59] In other words, both parties must have continued to assume that the promise would be fulfilled. However, given the promisor's behaviour in this case no such shared will could be found.

And what happens if during her lifetime the promisor disposes of the asset that she had promised to leave to the promisee in her will? In a decision of 30 August 1973, the BAG established that, in principle, the promisor is free to dispose of her property if there are 'proper' reasons for doing so,[60] though the court did not elaborate on the meaning of 'proper reason'. In this particular case, the daughter brought a claim based on § 612 BGB for compensation arguing that she had worked in her parents' household for fourteen years and had helped in her father's business for ten to twelve hours per day. She had done so without being remunerated because her father had told her that she would inherit from him and that, in particular, he would purchase a construction site for her. Instead, he had transferred the parents' entire estate to her brother and were now living on a small pension that prevented them from remunerating her. The daughter therefore argued that her brother had to fulfil the parents' obligation towards her. Her claim was rejected. The BAG held that a promisee cannot bring a claim during the promisor's lifetime, and demand immediate payment, for she too is bound by the implied agreement whereby the payment is deemed to be deferred up until the moment of the promisor's death. While it is true that both parties are bound, and that the agreement was to benefit the daughter on their death, here the promised asset was transferred to the son,

58 BAG 28 September 1977 (n 4). For another case in which the claim was statute barred, see BAG 5 August 1963 (n 4).

59 So also BAG 19 February 1970 (n 41).

60 BAG 30 August 1973 (n 37). For the court, the risk that a promisor will not be able to fulfil the promise lies with the promisee. From the outset the person performing the services must take into account the fact that the person receiving the services can exercise her right to dispose of her assets or to consume them and this right is not limited by the agreement between the parties.

thereby making it impossible to fulfil the promise. Asking the promisee to wait until the promisor's death in these circumstances seems problematic, as it exposes her to the risk of exploitation. Thus, the fact that German courts are prepared to imply an agreement that compensation is deferred until death of the promisor, so as to extend the protection provided by § 612 BGB, may well mean that the promisee is left without protection during the promisor's lifetime. However, the BAG also noted that things may be different where, unlike in this particular case, the promisor disposes of the property in an arbitrary manner, and her action is likely to frustrate a later claim for the payment of wages. Thus, the decision leaves open the possibility that a promisee can bring a claim against the promisor (or transferee) where the court finds that the transfer was not justified by a 'proper reason'.

V. Quantifying the award

The amount of the redress the promisee can obtain in cases in which an employment relationship can be implied is established on the basis of § 612(2) BGB.[61] The provision states that:

> If the amount of remuneration is not specified, then if a tariff exists, the tariff remuneration is deemed to be agreed; if no tariff exists, the usual remuneration is deemed to be agreed.

But what is understood by 'usual remuneration'? In a case in which a woman had worked as a housekeeper, first for the couple and then for the surviving spouse,[62] the LAG Hessen (2010) concluded that, because work in the household depends strongly upon local usages and customs, courts must not look merely at the established wages but should also consider the level of payment typical for the particular economic area,[63] as well as the level of income of the households in the particular region. In this case, the promisee had at first worked for payment, but then without remuneration on the basis of a promise that she would one day receive the house. The promisor had only a small pension and would not have been able to pay wages. She had made a notarial will leaving the house to the promisee but later changed her mind.

Importantly, unlike under the New Zealand TPA 1949 discussed in Chapter 7, the value of the promised estate does not represent the upper limit in the case of a claim based on § 612(2) BGB. Thus, if the value of the due wages is higher than that of the promised amount or asset, the promisee will be in a better position if the

61 BGH 23 February 1965, NJW 1965, 1224, 1225 (n 4).
62 LAG Hessen 7 September 2010 (n 19).
63 Ibid, 437.

promise is breached. What is more, the wages may exceed what was left when the promisor died. This seems to emerge from a controversial decision of the BAG of 30 September 1971,[64] where the court found that what counts as 'usual wages' does not depend solely on the value of the estate. In fact, the court awarded more than the value of the estate, which is one reason why the decision was met with criticism among legal scholars.[65] Consequently, the promisor's heirs could potentially be liable for the debt, unless they have limited their liability. In fact, while a promisee basing her claim on the New Zealand TPA 1949 does not count as a creditor of the promisor's estate, a promisee basing her claim on § 612 BGB does, which has significant implications for the promisee and third parties with an interest in the estate. In fact, the source of her credit is not the succession but rather the service contract,[66] and the award counts as a *Nachlassverbindlichkeit* (estate liability) as per § 1967 BGB.

It should further be noted here that because the relationship implied is one of employment, the promisee is also entitled to paid leave. However, the LAG Hessen in the same case mentioned earlier, has established that, unless a specific agreement can be proven, § 612(2) BGB does not automatically entitle the promisee to a reimbursement of the expenses she may have incurred by reason of the services provided, including, for example, travel costs.[67] At the same time, benefits she may have received during the performance of the service, such as lodgings and food, are not detracted from the amount of the wages. Hence, it does not matter that the person has lived rent-free with the promisor. From the viewpoint of a promisee, this is of course highly beneficial and differentiates this particular form of redress from many others examined in this book, such as claims based on the New Zealand TPA 1949,[68] enrichment claims,[69] or, as we will see later, § 2057a BGB. However, normal rules on income tax apply and,[70] depending on the case, both parties may have to make social security payments, which in some cases can be considerable.

But what about other benefits that the promisee may have obtained? What if the promisee is a compulsory heir and thus entitled to a share in the estate by right? It seems that the compulsory share is not taken into account when quantifying the award. This seems right, for by invoking § 612 BGB, the promisee is seeking compensation for services rendered while acting on a promise of an inheritance. By

64 BAG 30 September 1971 (n 10).

65 BAG 30 September 1971 (n 10), BAG AP No 27, zu § 612 BGB. Beuthien seems to argue that if one bases the claim on the agreement, then one cannot obtain more than what was promised.

66 BAG 30 September 1971 (n 10). The BAG has explicitly established that a claim based on § 612 BGB is a *dienstvertraglicher Anspruch* and not an *erbrechtlicher Anspruch*.

67 Ibid.

68 Chapter 7.

69 Chapters 6 and 9.

70 Coester '§1619 BGB' in *Staudinger, Kommentar zum BGB* (2007) is rather critical (Rn 54) stating that the approach based on § 612 BGB leads to horrendous payments (*Nachzahlungspflichten*). See also Fenn *Mitarbeit* (1970) 228; Fenn (1968) 294.

contrast, the compulsory share is due irrespective of merits or need and is also payable to those compulsory heirs who have not provided any services. Thus, the two grounds of entitlement are and should be treated as entirely separate. We will see in Chapter 9, that this is not so where the promisee brings an enrichment claim,[71] or demands an adjustment based on § 2057a BGB (examined in Chapter 11), which is another reason why a claim based on § 612 BGB may be more attractive to a promisee.

What about lifetime gifts or other types of benefits such as life insurance proceeds? In a decision dating back to 1964,[72] the BAG dealt with a case where a person had provided unpaid work on the basis of an expectancy that he would inherit the deceased's house. However, instead of the house, he received the proceeds of a life insurance. The court held that it depends on the circumstances, whether and to what extent the proceeds and other benefits need to be accounted for.

VI. Conclusion

This chapter has explored how employment law can come to the aid of promisees who have performed services on the basis of a promise of a future inheritance. This, as we have seen is, for instance, possible in Germany (as well as in Austria) where courts have interpreted § 612 BGB in a way that makes it applicable to the testamentary promises context. One of the advantages of basing a claim on § 612 BGB is that the threshold to establish a successful claim is on the whole not particularly high because courts have adopted a liberal interpretation of most of the requirements. There is no need to prove the existence of a contract or an express promise and the agreement does not have to be in writing. So long as the promisee has provided services in the expectation of a future inheritance and this was known and accepted by the other party (the promisor), German courts are willing to imply a service contract as well as an agreement that the payment of the wages is deferred, though that is not without its problems because it may prevent a promisee from bringing a lifetime claim. Also, the analysis has shown that those who are in an intimate or familial relationship with the deceased may potentially find it more difficult to prove that the services they provided are of a type which, given the particular circumstances, could only be expected to have been provided in return for remuneration. This may mean that their services have to be more substantive and that they must exceed any obligations they may have towards the promisor.

[71] Chapter 9.
[72] BAG 18 January 1964 (n 4).

As far as the amount of the redress is concerned, the promisee cannot obtain what was promised. The promisee can only be awarded what she would have earned had she been employed by the promisor, including leave pay. However, under German law, a promisee can rarely obtain what was promised, unless a farm is involved, and the court finds that there is an informal contract for the transfer of the farm (*Höfevertrag*).[73] This is, as I mentioned before, a consequence of the prohibition of contracts in which the promisor binds herself as to the content of her will. Should a court enforce such an agreement, this would go directly against the prohibition.[74]

Unlike, for instance, the case with a claim brought on the basis of the New Zealand TPA 1949, where an employment contract is implied, the promised inheritance is not the upper limit. Thus, the promisee could potentially obtain wages that exceed the value of what she was promised. Also, what the deceased leaves behind does not represent the upper limit either. In fact, here the promisee is treated as a creditor.[75] Her interest must therefore be treated as prevailing over those of the promisor's successors, whether testate or intestate, which is beneficial from the promisee's perspective.

One limitation of this form of redress is that if the claimant incurred expenses, a separate agreement for the compensation would need to be established. However, any mutual benefits (e.g. in the form of accommodation or food) do not prevent a claim, nor are they considered when quantifying the award, which as Chapter 9 will show, is different with an enrichment claim. Thus, from the promisee's perspective, which is what this book is primarily concerned with, this approach is potentially more advantageous than an enrichment claim, for under German law she can only obtain restitution of the value of the enrichment, and the promisor may have certain defences that are not available if a service contract is implied. The problem is rather that § 612 BGB does not offer an all-encompassing solution, given that it applies only to services and potentially not all services. It does not cover instances where the promisee has made financial contributions or improved the promisor's property. Thus, some testamentary promises will not easily fit within its scope and other avenues may have to be pursued.[76] Also, it is unclear whether a lifetime claim is available given that an agreement to defer the payment until death is implied. Another potential difficulty would seem to be that the implication of a service contract could lead to substantial payments of taxes and social contributions.

Even so, in extending the application of § 612 BGB, German courts have generally shown a willingness to protect the promisee's interest and an awareness that

[73] See Chapter 2.
[74] See the discussion in Chapter 2.
[75] BAG 30 September 1971 (n 10).
[76] Including the *condictio ob rem* discussed in Chapter 9, section II and a claim based on § 2057a BGB discussed in Chapter 11.

there is a risk of exploitation of promisees of informal testamentary arrangements. It seems that, at least in some cases, they have granted redress on the basis of § 612(1) BGB so as to spare the promisee from having to bring a claim based on the principles of unjustified enrichment.[77] However, it appears that the true concern is to protect the promisee's reliance on the promise that she will inherit in the future.

[77] This is suggested by Richardi & Fischinger, '§ 612 BGB' in *Staudinger, Kommentar zum BGB* (2011).

9

Establishing the value of the promisor's enrichment in German and French law

I. Recovering the promisor's enrichment

The discussion in Chapter 6 has already revealed that in common law Canada, promisees who cannot establish the existence of a contract often seek redress by claiming that the services provided, payments or improvements made, or other actions they have performed in exchange for a testamentary promise have enriched the promisor. At least in part, this is the result of an acknowledgement by Canadian courts that an enrichment can come about through the performance of domestic/household and care services. In addition, Canadian courts have considerable discretion in determining the relief, which does not necessarily lead merely to the restitution of the enrichment. On the contrary, the promisee will usually obtain more than the value of the enrichment and, in some cases, even the promised asset, by way of a constructive trust, which makes this an attractive form of redress for promisees. For this reason, the Canadian cases were examined in Part II. This chapter analyses instances where the promisee obtains no more than the value of the enrichment, but without relating any Canadian decisions where that was the case. Instead, it focuses on the availability of such claims in civil law jurisdictions where they can represent an important (and sometimes the only) means of obtaining redress.[1] More specifically this chapter explores how and when the law of unjustified enrichment can come to the aid of a promisee of a testamentary promise in Germany and France, with occasional references to Austrian law.

[1] In some mixed legal systems too, an enrichment claim may be available in cases where a person makes a transfer in the expectation of being made an heir. See, for instance, the South African cases *Martin v The Estate of Petzer* 1912 CPD 849 dealing with an improvement case on a farm, and *Salzer v Salzer* 1919 EDL 221 and *De Villiers v Estate Odendaal* 1921 OPD 7 concerning assistance with a farm. However, it appears that in South Africa, such an action is only possible in cases of a transfer where restitution of property, rather than a benefit in the form of a domestic or care service, is claimed. See Du Plessis *Unjustified Enrichment* (2012) 188–189, who argues in favour of an extension of the scope of the *condictio causa data causa non secuta* so as to capture also services cases. On testamentary promises in Scots law, see Hutchison in *Exploring the Law of Succession* (2007) 226. In the Scottish case of *Gray v Johnston* 1928 SC 659, 1928 SLT 499, involving a testamentary promise, a recompense based on enrichment law was excluded. But changes were brought about through *Harris v Douglas* (14 February 2013) unreported, *OH Harris v Sales' Executors* 2003 GWD 7–186; noted [2004] RLR 243 and *Shilliday v Smith* 1998 SC 725; 1998 SLT 976 suggests that an enrichment claim may no longer be excluded. See MacQueen (2019).

Claiming a Promised Inheritance. Alexandra Braun, Oxford University Press. © Alexandra Braun 2022.
DOI: 10.1093/oso/9780198757252.003.0010

As the analysis of Chapter 8 has already shown, in Germany, testamentary promises cases are usually addressed through the application of § 612 BGB by implying a service contract. Only occasionally are they based on enrichment law and, more specifically, § 812 BGB. Enrichment law is, however, resorted to where a claim based on § 612 BGB proves difficult or is precluded, for example, because the promisee's performance does not consist of services but rather of a transfer of assets or an investment in, or improvement to, the promisor's property. In such cases, an enrichment claim may be the only option if the promise remains unfulfilled, though Chapter 11 will analyse situations in which § 2057a BGB can be of assistance. In Austria, a promisee can also resort to the *condictio causa data causa non secuta* (also called *condictio ob rem*), by analogy with § 1435 ABGB.[2] And, as we will see, in recent years, French courts have granted claims based on the *actio de in rem verso* in the testamentary context, though in very limited circumstances. Nonetheless, from the perspective of a promisee, this is an important development and therefore deserves attention in this book.

Due to the differences in the scope and requirements of the respective doctrines in Germany and Austria on the one hand, and France on the other, they will be analysed separately. We will see that, although enrichment law can sometimes offer protection, its application is generally limited, especially in France. This is not merely due to the principle of subsidiarity, whereby the claim can only be brought if the promisee has no other way to satisfy it, but also because French courts have been reluctant to extend the scope of the current protection beyond specific circumstances.

More generally, it will emerge that, because of the relevance of mutual benefits (e.g. in the form of free accommodation) in the context of both establishing the claim and quantifying the recoverable amount, and the availability of defences on the part of the promisor, it may be desirable for a promisee to seek out other forms of redress. With an enrichment claim, the promisee may have greater difficulties establishing the claim and potentially obtain less than she would with other forms of redress. This is partly due to the fact that with an enrichment claim there is usually a greater focus on financial aspects, with courts taking an economic approach when assessing the enrichment and the impoverishment, which makes it generally less suitable to the testamentary context. Also, the motives of the promisee and societal expectations can play a role when establishing whether there was a legal basis for the enrichment. This seems to be especially true of French law, where the potential practical and psychological hurdles involved when proving the promisor's enrichment may arguably be even higher than, for instance, in German law.

[2] In Austria, a further option is a claim based on §§ 677ff ABGB but only if the promisee has provided unremunerated care for the promisor during the last three years prior to the promisor's death. See Chapter 11.

II. Recovering the promisor's enrichment in German law

A. Introduction

Chapter 8 has shown that,[3] from the 1960s onwards, in Germany, the majority of cases dealing with the breach of a promise of an inheritance have been dealt with on the basis of § 612 BGB, classifying the relationship between the promisor and the promisee as one of employment. Prior to that, redress was normally provided through § 812 BGB, though admittedly, the reported cases dealing with such promises were very few.[4]

When examining § 612 BGB we saw that its application to the testamentary promises context has been criticized by several authors, some of whom argue that a response based on enrichment law would be better tailored to such cases,[5] not least because of the fictions that the application of § 612 BGB requires. Nonetheless, for reasons that will emerge more clearly later, in Germany § 612 BGB seems to remain the preferred approach. However, where § 612 BGB is not applicable,[6] for instance, because the promisee's performance consists of a transfer of assets, or an investment in, or improvement to, the promisor's property,[7] rather than of services, a promisee who wishes to seek redress may have no choice but to argue that her performance has enriched the promisor. Exactly which of the two *condictiones* enshrined in § 812 BGB (the *condictio sine causa* (§ 812 I, 1, 1 BGB) or the *condictio causa data causa non secuta*, commonly referred to also as the *condictio ob rem* (§ 812 I 2, 2 BGB), can be invoked depends on whether or not the promise amounts to a contract.

Where the parties had an intention to enter into a legally binding contract to make a will, which is void due to the prohibition of legally binding promises contained in § 2302 BGB,[8] the promisee who has performed her side of the agreement,

[3] Chapter 8.

[4] Examples are RG 20 March 1911, WarnRspr 1911, 303 No 267; RG 11 May 1942, WarnRspr 1942, 228ff, 231; RAG 10 May 1939, ARS 36, 287; RG 26 September 1939, RAG ARS 22, 24. For an overview of developments in Germany, see Canaris (1967); Bydlinski in *Festschrift zum 60. Geburtstag von Walter Wilburg* (1965) discussing both German and Austrian law; Lieb *Ehegattenmitarbeit* (1970) 71ff.

[5] See Beuthien (1969). See Fenn (1968) 297; Fenn *Mitarbeit* (1970) 215, who is in favour of the application of § 812 I 2, 2 BGB even though he argues that the provision is better suited for single patrimonial exchanges than for services relationships. See further Söllner (1963) 39; Esser *Schuldrecht II* (1969) 356 though he includes only cases where there is a '*Leistung*' (performance); same for Medicus *Bürgerliches Recht* (2011) 353. Weber (1989) 30 argues that the application of § 812 I 2, 2 BGB to situations where the promise cannot be enforced on the grounds of public policy reasons (for instance, because of § 2302 BGB) should be limited to cases were a clear and actual agreed purpose can be found. More recently, see Wendehorst, '§ 812' in *Beck'scher Online-Kommentar BGB* (2017) Rn 90. For a summary of the arguments against the application of § 612 BGB, see Chapter 8, section III.B.

[6] One claim seems to exclude the other. In this sense, see BAG 5 March 1963 – 5 AZR 79/63, BAG AP Nr 20, zu § 612 = NJW 1963, 2188, 2189.

[7] For an example, see BGH 29 November 1965 – VII ZR 214/63, BGHZ 44, 321 = NJW 1966, 540.

[8] Discussed in detail in Chapter 2.

may be able to invoke § 812 I 1, 1 BGB, which codifies the *condictio sine causa*.[9] It establishes that:

> A person who obtains something as a result of the performance of another person or otherwise at his expense without legal grounds is under a duty to make restitution to him.

In practice, cases where § 812 I 1,1 BGB comes into play in the testamentary context are very rare. More common are instances in which there was no legally binding contract to make a will, either because the parties knew about the prohibition of such contracts[10] or because one, or either, of them lacked the intention to enter into a legally binding contract. After all, in domestic cases parties often shy away from formalizing the relationship or agreement. Where there is no intention to create a legally binding contract, but an informal promise to leave an inheritance was made, the promisee who has provided the agreed performance may be able to obtain redress on the basis of the *condictio ob rem*, also referred to as *causa data causa non secuta*, which is codified in § 812 I 2, 2 BGB.[11] It provides that:

> This duty [to make restitution] exists also if the legal grounds later cease to exist or if the result intended by the performance in accordance with the contents of the legal transaction does not occur.

This particular provision deals with the restitution of performances which were provided on the basis of an agreed purpose (e.g. the testamentary gift), but where the purpose fails to occur (*Nichteintritt des bezweckten Erfolges* or *Zweckverfehlung*), in our case because the deceased has not upheld the promise to benefit the promisee in her will.

Since testamentary promises cases are more likely to be captured by the *condictio ob rem*,[12] rather than the *condictio sine causa*, the focus of the remainder of this part of the analysis of German law will lie on § 812 I 2, 2 BGB. However, before analysing its specific requirements, it is useful to briefly note that the scope and purpose of the *condictio ob rem* have long been controversial in German legal scholarship.[13] While in the eyes of some legal scholars it represents a historic relic,[14]

9 Lieb *Ehegattenmitarbeit* (1970) 111 n 8; Muscheler *Erbrecht I* (2010) 336.

10 Miserre *Die 'culpa in testando'* (2002) 56 takes the view that even a layman knows that such contracts, especially when stipulated informally, are not admissible.

11 Söllner (1963) 39.

12 In BGH 12 July 1989 – IVa ZR 174/88, BGHZ 108, 256 the court held that besides a claim based on § 812 I 2, 2 BGB, there would also be a claim based on § 812 I 1,1 BGB, without further explanation, however.

13 Lieb *Ehegattenmitarbeit* (1970) 110–111. Lorenz, '§ 812' in *Staudinger, Kommentar zum BGB* (1996) Rn 10.

14 Caemmerer in *Festschrift für Ernst Rabel I* (1954) 346. See Thomale *Leistung als Freiheit* (2012) 179ff, who examines the historical roots of the claim.

which has little reason to exist,[15] others have argued that it causes more problems than it solves.[16] Thus, German courts are addressing some cases of broken testamentary promises by relying on a codal provision whose nature and purpose, and thus justification, is generally speaking contentious in German legal scholarship. Nonetheless, several scholars have argued that enrichment law is better suited to address testamentary promises cases than § 612 BGB.[17]

B. Application in the context of testamentary promises

In the testamentary context,[18] the *condictio ob rem* has been successfully invoked where the promisee has improved the deceased's property,[19] has paid money to the promisor,[20] or has provided services in her business,[21] or home/household.[22] Interestingly, very few of the decisions concern care cases.[23] This is probably due to the fact that cases where an informal promise is made in exchange for care services are likely to fit more easily under the scope of § 612 BGB (examined in Chapter 8) or § 2057a BGB (explored in Chapter 11). Promisees in all of these cases are usually close family members (e.g. descendants, a nephew or niece, cohabitants, or a stepdaughter), friends, or, especially in the past, the deceased's housekeeper.

In what follows, I will examine what requirements a promisee must meet to be able to rely on the *condictio ob rem* and how relief is quantified. The purpose of this enquiry is to establish whether and to what extent the *condictio ob rem* is capable of protecting the interests of promisees. We will see that German law (and Austrian law) places the focus on the identification and frustration of an agreed purpose, thereby taking account of the mutuality of the testamentary arrangements discussed in this book. For that reason, it has perhaps less of a financial angle than, for

[15] Weber (1989) 30 suggests that it has a reason to exist but only in very limited cases. See also Kupisch (1985) 169. Further critical is Jansen (2016) 145.

[16] Danneman *Unjustified Enrichment* (2009) 48.

[17] See text at n 5.

[18] Other cases in which the *condictio ob rem* has been invoked involve work carried out in the business belonging to the spouse or the promisor of a marriage promise.

[19] BGH 29 November 1965 (n 7). See also OLG Koblenz, 8 November 1988 – 3 U 176/87, NJW 1990, 126.

[20] See OLG Karlsruhe, 6 December 2001 – 9 U 47, ZEV 2002, 196 = FamRZ 2002, 918 and BGH 22 March 2013–V ZR 28/12, NJW 2013, 2025.

[21] RAG 10 May 1939, ARS 36, 287, where a nephew had helped in the business of his uncle who had promised him that he would benefit him in his will. In RG 11 May 1942, WarnRspr 1942, 228ff, 231 the son had worked in the father's bakery who had promised him that he would take over the bakery and the land.

[22] RG 20 March 1911, WarnRspr 1911, 303.

[23] An example is RG 4 November 1914, Seuffert's Archiv 70, 272 (No 149). The claimant had cared for the deceased for about seven years and on his death brought a claim based on both § 612ff and § 812 BGB. Although she lost in the first two instances, the RG upheld her appeal and remitted the decision back to the appeal court. On this point, see Lieb *Ehegattenmitarbeit* (1970) 71ff.

instance, the French approach, which will be considered in section III. That said, many of the successful German cases have involved a financial contribution.

C. Requirements of the *condictio ob rem*

For a claim based on the German *condictio ob rem* to be successful, it is necessary for the promisee to provide evidence of: (i) a performance; (ii) an actual, even if tacit, agreement about the purpose of the said performance; and (iii) the frustration of the agreed purpose.[24] The same requirements are imposed by Austrian law.[25] Each requirement will be analysed in turn. We will see that the second requirement has given rise to some debate in legal scholarship as well as to conflicting case law.

1. A performance

In order to be successful, the promisee needs to prove that she has rendered a performance, though what counts as a *performance* under German law is contentious in legal scholarship. Some German legal scholars have, for example, expressed doubts as to whether the *condictio ob rem* should apply to instances in which services are provided. In fact, unlike in Canada, the provision is often seen as being a better fit for cases in which a transfer of money has taken place.[26] Nonetheless, there are cases in which § 812 I 2, 2 BGB has been applied by the courts in the context of services rendered in the household or home.[27] For instance, in a case decided by the *Reichsgericht* (German Imperial Court) back in 1911, the promisee (a housekeeper) had worked in the household of the promisor for about eighteen years and had helped with the agricultural business in exchange for accommodation and food, but without being paid any wages or receiving any other form of compensation. On the promisor's death, the housekeeper argued that the deceased had been unjustly enriched because she had provided the services on the expectation that he would compensate her, by nominating her as his heir, leaving her a legacy, or in some other form. She further argued that the promisor was fully aware of the fact that the future compensation in the form of an inheritance was the purpose of her service. The court upheld her claim.

Where the *Bundesgerichtshof* (hereafter BGH) has applied the *condictio ob rem* to cases where a promisee has incurred expenditure on the improvements to a piece of property belonging to the promisor in the belief that she would acquire

24 Lorenz, '§ 812' in *Staudinger, Kommentar zum BGB* (1996) 148.

25 Lurger, '§ 1435 ABGB' in *ABGB-ON* (2016) paras 6 and 10. If the promisee is a carer then a claim based on § 1435 ABGB may be useful where the requirements of the care legacy discussed in Chapter 11 cannot be met or the carer wants to claim compensation for care that exceeds three years. § 1435 ABGB can also be invoked outside care cases, e.g. in the case of work carried on a farm. Here, see Christandl, '§§ 677–678' in *Großkommentar zum ABGB* (2021) 199, 217–218, Rn 54.

26 Canaris (1967) 167.

27 See RG 20 March 1911 (n 22).

ownership of the property (either through a lifetime or testamentary gift),[28] this has been criticized.[29] It has been questioned whether in such cases one can speak of a 'performance', and in particular of a performance meant to enrich the promisor.[30] The argument has been made that where a person improves the quality of a building, or incurs expenses in relation to a piece of land, on the basis of a promise that she will receive it either during lifetime or on death of the promisor, the promisee intends to improve her own future property, and not that of the promisor.[31] Similar arguments have been raised against the application of the *condictio ob rem* to cases where a person has provided services in a business, which she expects to inherit. However, one could object that, at least at the time the services are performed, the payment is made, or the improvement carried out, there is an enrichment of the property belonging to someone else.[32] Also, a promisee can never be certain that the asset will become hers, not even when the promised will is made, for it can always be revoked. Thus, the argument against the application of the *condictio ob rem* in these cases is not particularly convincing, and indeed, courts have applied the *condictio* in these instances.

2. A shared purpose

a) No contract or writing required

The second requirement that needs to be satisfied by the promisee is that the performance was undertaken with a specific purpose in mind. In other words, the parties must have agreed that the performance would be compensated in the form of a benefit under a will or an inheritance contract.[33] As with § 612 BGB,[34] the fact that the promisee has a duty to collaborate in the business or the household of the promisor, or to support her, does not exclude the possibility of an enrichment claim so long as there is proof that there was an agreed purpose between the parties, that the purpose was frustrated, and that the performance exceeded such a duty.[35] Equally, in Austria, where children and parents also have a duty to assist

[28] See BGH 29 November 1965 (n 7); BGH 12 July 1989, BGHZ 108, 256, 263 (n 12) involving a case of an improvement of a house on property belonging to the mother-in-law who had nominated her daughter-in-law (and wife of the claimant) as sole heir by means of a binding inheritance contract (*Erbvertrag*) but later sold the house to her daughter.

[29] Lorenz, '§ 812' in *Staudinger, Kommentar zum BGB* (1996) 148 Rn 112.

[30] The argument seems to have received support from Söllner (1963) 30 and Esser *Schuldrecht II* (1969) 356. On this distinction and the differences in opinion between the judiciary and the academics without, however, deciding one way or the other, see BGH 16 October 1969 – VII ZR 145/69, NJW 1970, 136.

[31] Lorenz, '§ 812' in *Staudinger, Kommentar zum BGB* (1996) 148 Rn 112.

[32] Lieb *Ehegattenmitarbeit* (1970) 115.

[33] An inheritance contract (*Erbvertrag*) is not a contract to make a will. Rather it takes the same content of a will but, unlike a will, is binding on the testator (see § 1941 BGB). We have seen in Chapter 2, section II.B.3 that while contracts to make a will are not admitted under German law, inheritance contracts are, even though they restrict the testator's freedom of testation.

[34] See Chapter 8.

[35] Kropholler (1969) 241ff, 250; Damrau (1969) 581. For a discussion of the interaction between § 1619 BGB and the *condictio ob rem*, see Enderlein (2000).

one another,[36] work and services, including care services, can give rise to an enrichment claim, even if they are under such a duty, provided the services are substantial.[37] As is the case with other forms of redress examined in this book,[38] the difficulty will often be establish what 'substantial' means and thus what the norm is and when it is exceeded. Austrian courts seem to be in agreement that comprehensive care of a relative who is in permanent rather than temporary need of care exceeds the duty of assistance.[39]

While there is need for an agreed purpose, there is no need to prove an express promise of an inheritance, nor the existence of a contract to make a will. In fact, in Germany, such a contract would be void on the basis of the prohibition enshrined in § 2302 BGB.[40] What is more, § 812 I 2, 2 BGB would not apply if a contract could be established.[41] This was confirmed by a decision of the BGH dating back to 1965, where a nephew had built an extension on the land of his aunt who had promised that he would inherit the land.[42] The aunt had duly made a will nominating the nephew as her heir. However, after their relationship had deteriorated, she revoked the will and made a new will that no longer benefited him. Seven days later she died. The nephew's enrichment claim was granted at first instance but rejected on appeal by the Higher Regional Court (*Oberlandesgericht*, hereafter OLG) on the basis that there was no legally binding juridical act between the parties, and that the deceased had intended to reserve her freedom of testation until the last moment. However, the BGH overturned the OLG decision and reinstalled the decision of first instance. It found that, although an agreement is required for § 812 I 2, 2 BGB to apply, there is no need for a contractual agreement, as otherwise the *condictio ob rem* would not come into play. Importantly, the court further acknowledged that, in testamentary promises cases,[43] agreements are not generally put into writing. Thus, here the BGH demonstrates an awareness that testamentary promises are usually made in an informal manner, and agrees that the protection should not depend on the presence of such writing.

What the exact content of the agreement between promisor and promisee has to be is unclear and its nature is to some extent controversial among academic

[36] § 137 ABGB. See further the duties imposed on spouses by § 90 ABGB.

[37] OGH 24 May 2016 – 8 Ob 37/16y; OGH 24 January 2019 – 6 Ob 175/18f; OGH 20 February 2020 6 Ob 6/20f. Deixler-Hübner in *Erbrecht und Vermögensnachfolge* (2018) 378.

[38] For instance, with Canadian unjust enrichment law (Chapter 6), the New Zealand TPA 1949 (Chapter 7), and § 612 BGB (Chapter 8).

[39] Christandl, '§§ 677–678' in *Großkommentar zum ABGB* (2021) 217–218, Rn 54.

[40] For a discussion, see Chapter 2, section II.B.2. Unlike the German BGB, the Austrian ABGB does not explicitly rule out the validity of a contract to make a will. Nonetheless contracts to make a will are regarded as invalid.

[41] If there is a legal basis for the claim because the performance was rendered on the basis of a contract to make a will that is void, a claim based on the *condictio ob rem* is excluded. Instead § 812 I 1,1 BGB comes into play. See BAG 5 March 1963, NJW 1963, 2188, 2189 (n 6) and BGH 23 February 1965 – VI ZR 281/63, FamRZ 1965, 317, 319.

[42] BGH 29 November 1965 (n 7).

[43] Ibid, 541.

writers,[44] but this is not the place to enter into the details of that debate. Case law suggests that the agreement can be vague and that the agreed purpose does not have to be specific in the sense that the subject matter of the promise does not have to be specified,[45] which is beneficial from the perspective of the promisee and shows that courts are attuned to the specific context in which testamentary promises are made.

b) *Purpose or motive?*

In some instances in which German courts were prepared to find an agreed purpose, legal scholars have drawn a distinction between a purpose and a motive, thus questioning the appropriateness of awarding redress. This is true of so-called improvement cases referred to earlier.[46] For instance, in the aforementioned BGH decision of 29 November 1965 the claim was upheld because the court found that there had been an agreement as to the pursued purpose.[47] However, some legal writers have criticized the decision, arguing that the prospective inheritance represented not the purpose pursued by the construction of the house, but rather the motive.[48] In other words, they took the view that the case displayed a lack of a synallagmatic connection, and that the promisee should not have been able to recover under the *condictio ob rem*.[49]

This reasoning seems to have been based on the fact that, in this case, the building was constructed *after* the aunt had made the will which she later revoked. Thus, the gist of the commentary appears to be that there is a difference between a person providing a service *in order to* inherit or *because* she knows that she will inherit. It can be objected, however, that the promisee has acted on the promise. What is more, the promisee's performance may well have the purpose of ensuring that the promisor (testator) does not change her mind and revoke the will. Also, this argument seems to overlook the fact that a will is always revocable, which is why a promisee will never be certain to inherit, something that the BGH pointed out.[50]

44 See Thomale *Leistung als Freiheit* (2012) 183. For some scholars, the discussion concerning the legal nature of the agreement is relevant because of the potential conflict with § 2302 BGB discussed in Chapter 2, section II.B.2. See Miserre *Die 'culpa in testando'* (2002) 60, who argues that § 2302 BGB was only intended to prevent a legally binding obligation to make a will and not also a non-binding promise to make a will as such.

45 See RG 20 March 1911, WarnRspr 1911, 303 where the nature of the compensation was vague e.g. in the form of an inheritance, legacy, or other compensation.

46 See section II.C.1.

47 BGH 29 November 1965 (n 7).

48 Larenz & Canaris *Schuldrecht II* (1994) 154; Canaris (1967) 168. Similarly, Medicus *Bürgerliches Recht* (2011) 353, and Söllner (1963) 31ff.

49 Larenz & Canaris *Schuldrecht II* (1994) 154.

50 See n 42.

c) The agreement can be implied

The pursued purpose must be shared, and thus be an *agreed* purpose. While a unilateral purpose, which is not communicated to the other person, will not suffice,[51] the agreement can be tacit and implied from the circumstances of the case. German courts have taken the view that a tacit agreement is to be implied where the promisor is aware of the expectation to inherit nurtured by the promisee (who is providing the performance) and, through her conduct, the promisor intimates that she approves or assents to the agreed purpose.[52] If the promisee intends to accept the performance, but not the premise on which the performance was rendered and which she is aware of, she must say so. If she remains silent, then the principle of good faith demands that her conduct is to be understood as an acceptance.[53] Put differently, the fact that the promisor has accepted a service (or a payment) in the knowledge that the other person had an expectation to inherit, and has not expressed any objections, can indicate approval or a sharing of the purpose.[54]

That a tacit agreement can be implied is, of course, important from the perspective of the promisee because promises are not always expressly made. It thus seems that in applying the *condictio ob rem* German courts have been sensitive to the testamentary context, and, in particular, the fact that testamentary promises will rarely be in writing or be expressed in the form of a contract. They also take account of the mutuality of such testamentary arrangements. This seems to be confirmed by a decision of the OLG Karlsruhe of December 2001.[55] Here, the claimant and her husband had given financial support to her parents while the parents were running a camera store, later when the business was being wound up, and afterwards. In order to do so, they had to borrow money from a bank. On the death of the mother, who had died after the father and left the house to the claimant's sister, the claimant argued that she and her husband would never have provided the financial support were it not for the promise that they were going to receive the house, which comprised two flats. They argued that without their financial help the family home would have been subject to compulsory auctioning and that the respondent (the sister), who had inherited the house, was therefore unjustly enriched. The sister

[51] Wendehorst, '§ 812' in *Beck'scher Online-Kommentar BGB* (2017) Rn 92 argues that the fulfilment of the purpose (in our case the inheritance) represents a condition subsequent so that the agreement establishes that the other party can keep the performance until the moment in which it is clear that the agreed purpose does not occur or is not attained. The BGH in its decision of 22 March 2013 (n 20) [22] argued that the basis for the claim is the fact that the condition subsequent materializes.

[52] This sounds very similar to the tacit agreement required for the purposes of the application of § 612 BGB, discussed in Chapter 8.

[53] This is clearly stated in BGH 29 November 1965 (n 7). See further BGH 12 July 1989 (n 12) 2747. But compare with the decision of BGH 19 January 1973 – V ZR 24/71, NJW 1973, 612, 613 = FamRZ, 181, 182, which is, however, not a testamentary promises case. It states that there was no duty to expressly disagree with the partner. However, here the respondent had expressed a different purpose from the one envisaged by the claimant.

[54] BGH 22 March 2013 (n 20) [26]. For Austrian law, see Schauer in *Handbuch Familienrecht* (2015) 715. Christandl, '§§ 677–678' in *Großkommentar zum ABGB* (2021) 217–218, Rn 54.

[55] OLG Karlsruhe, 6 December 2001 (n 20).

objected on the basis that the claimant was adequately compensated by the fact that she and her husband had been living rent-free in one of the flats in the house. At first instance, the claim was granted, but only in part. On appeal, the OLG Karlsruhe decided that the claimant should be awarded a higher sum.

Upholding the claim, the court took into account the fact that the claimant and her husband had no property of their own and that they did not earn a substantial income. Under these circumstances, and since there had been no explicit agreement, and in particular no written one, the court concluded that all participants must have understood, as a matter of course, that the financial support was provided in order to preserve the family wealth and also to protect the interests of the promisee to later receive the value of half of the house. The court found that it would be unrealistic to think that the payments were accepted without any agreed purpose in mind, especially since one of the witnesses had heard the father say that the claimant's husband would get the property. It further found that the interest on the bank loan taken out by the promisees and other payments they had made exceeded the value of an appropriate rent for the flat in which they had lived. An agreement was therefore implied. What is interesting here is that the court did not exclude that an agreement was reached simply because the parties were close family members. On the contrary, the court seemed to assume that given their financial condition, the promisees would not have made the payments, and that the promisors would not have accepted such payments without an agreement. As we will see in the next section, this is not necessarily the approach other German courts have taken, though in those cases the promisees have often provided domestic services rather than financial payments, as was the case here.

d) Link between the performance and the agreed purpose

Before moving on to the third requirement, it is important to mention the nexus between the performance and the agreed purpose. In some of the older cases involving an enrichment claim by a testamentary promisee, it seems that at least some courts found it difficult to establish an agreed purpose where the relationship was a close one,[56] and they therefore rejected claims by insisting on the presence of a strong link between the performance and the agreed purpose. They have sometimes done so by placing emphasis on the subjective motives of the promisee. In other words, some courts have found that the agreed purpose (in our case, the future inheritance) must be the reason for the promisee's performance. This was the case in two decisions of the *Kammergericht* (the highest state court for the city of Berlin), which were mentioned already in Chapter 8. While they date back to the early 1970s, and need to be read in context, it is worth recalling them here because they highlight some of the difficulties that some promisees have faced and that are

[56] Again we see a similarity with the cases that are based on § 612 BGB and which were discussed in Chapter 8.

not unique to German law, especially where the services provided are care and domestic/household services and the relationship between the parties is close.

In the first case decided in 1970,[57] the promisee, the partner of the deceased, had looked after the twenty-year-older deceased for about eight years. She had taken care of his household and cared for him during his illness without, however, living with him. The couple had intended to marry but, for a variety of reasons, they never did. When the promisor died, the promisee brought a claim against the promisor's heirs arguing that her services were provided on the basis of a promise that he would marry her and that, should they get married, she would become his sole heir. The claimant's action was founded on both § 612 BGB and § 812 BGB but was unsuccessful on both accounts. As mentioned in Chapter 8, the application of § 612 BGB was excluded because, according to the court, where domestic services are provided and there is a friendly relationship between the parties, an employment relationship can only be found in exceptional circumstances.[58] The enrichment claim was also rejected on several grounds. First, the court held that there was no evidence of an agreement concerning the pursued purpose, only of unilateral expectations. Also, in the eyes of the court, the promisee had not provided the services solely on the basis of the promises, something that the court found the deceased was aware of. The court pointed out that the deceased had not promised to marry the promisee *because* of the care services and that, even if he had mentioned that she should be his sole heir, there was no reason to believe that there was a link between that promise and the care. The court placed importance on the motivations of both parties. Finally, the court also found that what the claimant had done was *normal* for people whose intention is to marry and that, in order to be successful, the claimant should have done something that went beyond what is common and appropriate. What exactly would have been required on her part was not, however, specified. Arguably, she had done all she could and certainly all that was asked of her. This goes to show again that societal expectations can play an important role, especially where the services provided are of a domestic nature, and the relationship is one of affection, similar to the position for claims based on § 612 BGB.[59]

In the second decision of the *Kammergericht* of 16 September 1971,[60] a woman had brought a claim against the heir of the deceased, for whom she had cared for about ten years. The promisee and the deceased were both retired and although they were not a couple, the claimant had lived (rent-free) with the deceased, taking care of him and his household. On the promisor's death, the promisee brought an enrichment claim arguing that shortly after she had started to look after the

[57] KG 9 March 1970 – 12 W 817/70, KG OLGZ 1971, 22 = FamRZ 1970, 317.
[58] Chapter 8, section III.A.2.
[59] See Chapter 8.
[60] KG 16 September 1971 – 12 W 1675/71, OLGZ 1972, 424.

promisor and his household the latter had promised her that, in exchange for her performances, she would have a lifelong right to live in the house and that she would inherit some of his savings. A year prior to his death he had made another promise to the effect that he would leave her 75% of his estate. The claimant alleged that she had some writing confirming the promise but was unfortunately unable to produce the relevant evidence. Both at first instance and on appeal, the courts rejected the claim. The *Kammergericht* found that the link between the service provided by the claimant and the promise to leave her 75% of the estate was not strong enough to establish a claim. Although the deceased and the claimant were not living in an intimate relationship, from what the claimant said, there were no reasons to believe that the services were rendered for reasons other than the personal relationship existing between the parties who lived together. According to the court, the agreed purpose of the performance (in this case the expectation to inherit) must represent a core element of the agreement. Although there may have been a link in this case, it was judged to be too tenuous to justify an award. The court further held that the link is strong enough when the services are provided *solely* on the basis of the deferred benefit.[61] But as mentioned earlier, in reality that will hardly ever be the case because the promisee's actions are usually motivated by more than one motive, especially if there is a personal relationship. Interestingly, the court also pointed out that the promisee had performed some services *before* the promise was made, suggesting that the timing of the promise mattered. This is a problem with testamentary promises cases because events are not always chronological. In other words, the promise does not necessarily precede the start of the performance. The court concluded that not only had the promisee neither shown nor argued that she had looked after the promisor *because* of the promise, there was also no agreed purpose. As with the previous case, the court failed to find a nexus as well as an agreement.

Interestingly, in the 1971 decision the *Kammergericht* found that in this case one could have expected that the claimant would have done something to ensure that she would benefit on the promisor's death, for instance by insisting on a binding inheritance contract.[62] However, this is in stark contrast to what the BGH stated in the 1965 decision involving an aunt and her nephew, which was discussed earlier,[63] where the court acknowledged the reality of testamentary promises and thus their informal nature.[64] As we know, it is very difficult for promisees to insist on a legally binding promise. Not only could their persistence jeopardize their relationship

[61] Ibid, 425.

[62] Similarly, the KG 9 March 1970, OLGZ 1971, 22, 25 (n 57) makes reference to the fact that the claimant has done nothing to secure her interest in the estate.

[63] BGH 29 November 1965 (n 7). See Section II.C.2.a).

[64] This seems to be somewhat confirmed also by the decision of the OLG Karlsruhe, 6 December 2001 (n 20).

with the promisor, the promisor may also regard it as unnecessary to put the promise in writing or simply refuse to do so.

Both cases suggest that societal expectations play a role and that a successful claim depends on the nature of the relationship between the promisee and the promisor. In one case they were a couple, and in the other they were not, but were living together. The two decisions further confirm that the importance and benefits of domestic services are often undervalued, and, as we know, often such services are, as was the case here, provided by women. However, both decisions must be read in the context and date back to the 1970s. In fact, later testamentary promises cases do not appear to require the promisee to prove that the agreed purpose represented the sole or core reason for the performance. Hence it remains somewhat unclear to what extent it is problematic that the performance is motivated not solely by the (agreed) purpose, but also by a sense of duty or feelings of friendship.

3. Frustration of the agreed purpose

The *condictio ob rem* can only be invoked when the agreed purpose has been frustrated. In the scenarios discussed in this book this will normally be the case when the promisor dies, and the promisee discovers that the promise was not kept. That said, the promise may sometimes be breached during the lifetime of the promisor, for instance, where she disposes of the promised asset. In this regard it is useful to mention a decision of the BGH of March 2013.[65] The case is interesting not merely because it deals with the question of when the claim arises but also because the claimant was not the promisee himself (who had died) but his surviving spouse.

A family had lived rent-free in the deceased's mother's home (the promisor). After the death of the son (the promisee), his mother brought a successful claim for eviction against her daughter-in-law (the claimant in the case) requiring her to leave the house. She further made a will leaving all she had to one of her daughters. When the mother-in-law (the promisor) died, the daughter-in-law brought a claim against the heir (her sister-in-law) arguing that her husband had invested €250,000 in his mother's house on the basis of a promise that he and his wife could live rent-free in the house for their lifetime, and that her husband would be nominated as his mother's sole heir. The question for the court was whether the deceased had a claim against his deceased mother, and, if so, whether this claim had passed to his surviving spouse. While the claim of the surviving spouse was denied in the first two instances, the BGH upheld her appeal.[66]

This BGH decision is important for a number of reasons. First, the BGH confirmed that the claim based on § 812 I 2, 2 BGB (the *condictio ob rem*) arises only when it is clear that the agreed purpose can no longer be attained. In this case that

[65] BGH 22 March 2013 (n 20).

[66] Though granting the appeal, the BGH remitted the case back to the appeal court for the purpose of ascertaining whether there was an agreement as to the purpose and the amount of the redress.

was when the promisee predeceased his mother because at that point it was clear that he could no longer inherit from her. It follows that the agreed purpose can be frustrated not only because the promisor omits to make the promised testamentary disposition, or disposes of the promised asset during her lifetime,[67] but importantly also because the promisee predeceases the promisor. However, while the claim arises at that point, the court found it becomes definitive only on the promisor's death because the agreement between the parties was that the promisee would only inherit the property on death of his mother. The BGH thus distinguished two stages:[68] first, the stage when the right to a claim arose, in this case the moment of the promisee's death, and second, the stage when the claim crystallized or became actionable, that is when the promisor died without having fulfilled her promise.

Regarding the question as to whether or not the claim had passed to the daughter-in-law, that is the promisee's surviving spouse, the BGH held that even though the claim was only actionable on the promisor's death, the right of the promisee to request restitution was hereditary.[69] In the eyes of the court, the fact that, had the mother made the promised will in favour of her son, his entitlement under her will would not have passed to his heirs was irrelevant to the decision. The case is not one dealing with rights against the estate of the mother-in-law grounded in succession law, but rather one regarding claims for restitution of what had been performed. In other words, the promisee is to be treated as a creditor and not as a beneficiary under a will. Consequently, the promisee's surviving spouse finds herself in a better position than the promisor's heirs and legatees who will benefit only once the promisor's debts have been paid.[70]

While the decision has obviously benefited the promisee's surviving spouse, it has solicited a number of critical reactions among legal scholars, not least because the court distinguished between the two stages mentioned earlier.[71] It is difficult to know whether this approach will be followed. What is clear is that the fact that the promisee predeceases the promisor does not mean that the promisor is free to dispose of her property. If she does dispose of it, an enrichment claim can be brought against her estate by the promisee's successors.

[67] Confirmed recently by OLG Köln 29 June 2017 – 16 U 106/16.

[68] BGH 22 March 2013 (n 20) [21]–[22].

[69] BGH 22 March 2013 (n 20) [23]. The BGH drew an analogy with duties that arise out of so-called 'incomplete legal relationships' as per the decision of the OLG Düsseldorf 19 April 1996 – 7 U 96/95, FamRZ 1996, 1440, 1441.

[70] As to how debts are paid, see Schmidt, *Itinera hereditatis* (2021). It further means that the claim has to be brought within thirty, rather than three, years. In fact, if it is a claim grounded in succession law, § 195 BGB would apply and it establishes a limitation period of three years (though there are exceptions: see §187 Abs 1 Nr 1 BGB).

[71] See the case note by Kroppenberg (2014), who agrees with the result but not with the reasoning of the court, which she judges as doctrinally untenable.

D. Type of redress and quantification

Under German law, a claimant relying on the *condictio ob rem* will obtain a monetary award measured on the basis of the market value of the performance (*Wertsatz*). The market value of the performance mentioned in § 818(2) BGB is the objective value, which is usually lower than what a worker would have received as adequate remuneration under § 612 BGB.[72] In fact, in the case of the implication of an employment relationship, the promisee can obtain payment of the wages commonly paid for the particular type of work, which depend on the local custom and level of payment typical for the particular economic area.[73] In addition, she can claim payment for leave.

In the BGH decision of March 2013 mentioned earlier, where the son had invested money improving his mother's property but had predeceased her, the BGH held that, while the award should compensate the promisee not only for the material used, the wages paid, and his own work, the compensation was to be measured on the basis of the increase in value of the debtor's (the promisor's) property which has come about as a result of the promisee's measures.[74] Although in this case the BGH did not mention that the fact that promisee and his family had lived rent-free should be taken into account, which has been criticized in legal scholarship,[75] courts usually take into consideration benefits in the form of other testamentary dispositions in favour of the promisee, lifetime donations, or rent-free living.[76] This, as we have seen, is not the case where the claim is granted on the basis of § 612 BGB.[77]

Equally, other benefits in the form of a compulsory share that the promisee may be entitled to, seem to be taken into account. Thus, unlike in France,[78] in a claim based on the *condictio ob rem* in Germany the redress is reduced if the claimant is entitled to a compulsory share in the estate of the deceased promisor,[79] which as we saw is not the case where the claim is based on § 612 BGB. However, this is problematic for the promisee's compulsory share is entirely dislodged from the

[72] Hence, for Canaris, to compensate work or services through the law of unjustified enrichment is unsatisfactory. Canaris (1967) 167.

[73] See Chapter 8, section V.

[74] BGH 22 March 2013 (n 20) [27].

[75] Thomale (2013) criticized the fact that the person could live in the home and that part of the agreement which was fulfilled had not been taken into account by the court. Critical also Grziwotz (2013) 474.

[76] See BGH 5 October 1967 – VII ZR 143/65, NJW 1968, 245 = FamRZ 1986, 23, though this is not a testamentary promises case. See also BGH 29 November 1965 (n 7) 542 where the courts says that the claimant is entitled to the difference between the benefits obtained and the disadvantages suffered. See also Fenn (1968) 298.

[77] See Chapter 8, section V.

[78] See section III.F.

[79] Schwab, '§ 812 BGB' in *Münchener Kommentar zum BGB* (2020) Rn 482. The same would not seem to be the case where the claim is based on § 812 I, 1, 1 BGB. See OLG Karlsruhe 6 December 2001, FamRZ 2002, 918, 919 (n 20).

merits of her enrichment claim. The compulsory share is due irrespective of merits or need, and is therefore also payable to those compulsory heirs who have not provided any services or work, or made contributions to the deceased's property.

E. Defences

Another disadvantage of an enrichment claim vis-à-vis a claim based on § 612 BGB is that the promisor (or his successors) may have certain defences. § 818(3) BGB provides that the liability to undertake restitution or to reimburse the value is excluded to the extent that the recipient is no longer enriched. This is, however, not the only defence that a promisor can raise. § 815 BGB further states that a claim is excluded where the pursued purpose was objectively impossible, and the promisee (who was rendering the performance) was aware of that and has prevented the realization of the success by acting against good faith.[80] However, such cases will be rare in the testamentary context. Thus, there may be more than one reason why a promisor may be able to avoid liability.

As we have seen from the aforementioned BGH decision of March 2013, according to the BGH, the fact that the promisee predeceased the promisor cannot represent a defence, as this situation is not captured by § 815 BGB.[81] Thus, the promisee's successors could still bring a claim in this case.

F. Summary

From the perspective of a promisee, to seek redress for breach of a testamentary promise through the principles of German unjustified enrichment law can be attractive, but also has its limitations, though, of course, in some cases the promisee has no other option. The requirements for a successful claim are overall not particularly burdensome.[82] Even though legal scholars are in disagreement as to whether services rendered by acting on a testamentary promise can be compensated by way of an application of the *condictio ob rem*, it would seem that courts have adopted a relatively wide meaning of performance. Also, in terms of the agreed purpose, courts do not require writing, nor a contractual agreement. What is needed is that the promisor recognizes that the other person is acting with an expectation to inherit, and that she accepts her performance. Acceptance of the performance in the awareness of the pursued purpose is thus sufficient. The agreed purpose does not have to be specific, meaning that the subject matter of the promise does not have

[80] Esser *Schuldrecht II* (1969) 356.
[81] BGH 22 March 2013 (n 20).
[82] See Miserre *Die 'culpa in testando'* (2002) 59.

to be specifically defined. However, in some cases problems have arisen where the prospect of the inheritance was not the primary purpose, which can be the case where the relationship is a close one. The fact that the promisee has to prove the frustration of a shared purpose rather than that the promisor was enriched at her expense, and that there is no juristic reason for the enrichment, as is the case in both Canada and France, arguably poses fewer practical and psychological stumbling blocks.[83] That said, we have also seen that the nature of the relationship and type of performance provided by the promisee have sometimes had an influence on the outcome of her claim.

The claim can be brought as soon as it is clear that the agreed purpose is not attainable, thus also during the promisor's lifetime, which is not the case with many other forms of redress analysed in this book (e.g. the New Zealand TPA 1949, but also the Austrian care legacy and § 2057a BGB analysed in Chapter 11), and the limitation period only starts running from the moment at which the promise is frustrated. Unlike with § 612 BGB, there is no need to resort to fictions (of an agreement to defer payment of the salary).[84] Also, if the promisee predeceases the promisor, the claim is not prevented but passes to her heirs. As is the case with § 612 BGB, the claimant is a creditor and is thus in a stronger position than those entitled to an inheritance under intestacy or a will,[85] or as we will see, an intestate heir demanding an adjustment of her share under § 2057a BGB. The same is true under Austrian law, for a claim based on § 1435 ABGB is considered to be like any normal debt owed by the estate vis-à-vis third parties and therefore takes priority over legacies.[86] Claims where the promisee is treated as a creditor are preferable, especially where the estate is left without assets, for in Germany and in Austria, the heirs may well have to pay for it unless they limit their liability.[87]

However, in terms of the relief, the promisee only ever obtains the value of the enrichment, which is likely to be lower than what the promisee would have received as adequate remuneration on the basis of § 612 BGB.[88] Interestingly, the fact that an enrichment claim may lead to a lower award, was at the centre of a scholarly debate that unfolded in the 1960s, with some scholars arguing that even

[83] See Chapters 6 and 9.

[84] See Chapter 8, section IV.

[85] The exact nature of debt is debated in Germany. See Küpper, '§ 1967 BGB–Erbenhaftung, Nachlassverbindlichkeiten' in *Münchener Kommentar zum BGB* (2020) Rn 14. In a controversial decision, the OLG Karlsruhe, 6 December 2001 – 9 U 47 (n 20) concluded that the unjustified enrichment claim brought by a promisee on death of the promisor was *not* an *Erblasserschuld*. Rather the debt was treated as a *Nachlasserbenschuld*, that is a debt that the successor has incurred and for that reason is *not* to be taken into account when, and detracted before, calculating the shares of compulsory heirs. See § 2311 BGB.

[86] Fischer-Czermak in *Das neue Erbrecht* (2015) 41ff; Jöchl (2016).

[87] See here the explanation in Chapter 11.

[88] Hence for Canaris (1967) 167, to compensate work or services through the law of unjustified enrichment is unsatisfactory.

in an enrichment claim courts should award the value of the wages.[89] However, the debate has not led to a change, and German courts do not have the discretion that, for instance, Canadian courts have in this context.[90]

A further disadvantage from the promisee's perspective is that mutual benefits in the form of free accommodation, or a compulsory share are deducted in an enrichment claim. Also, the promisor may use § 818(3) BGB or § 815 BGB to escape liability while a claim based on § 612 BGB does not allow for any defences. All in all, from the perspective of a promisee, in Germany, an enrichment claim is not preferable to a claim based on § 612 BGB, even though it can pass to a successor. That said, sometimes the promisee may have no alternative, in which case a claim based on § 812 BGB might provide her with the value of the promisor's enrichment.

III. Recovering the promisor's enrichment in French law

A. Background and context

As the analysis in Chapter 2 has shown, just like many other civil law jurisdictions, French law regards as invalid pacts or contracts over a person's future succession, including those in which a person promises to make a will, not to make one, or not to revoke an existing will.[91] This does not mean that promises of an inheritance are not made in practice, nor that promisees of informal promises are necessarily left without any form of redress. However, unlike in Germany, in France courts do not openly acknowledge that such promises are being made either in violation of the prohibition or informally. In fact, in France, when seeking redress, promisees are unlikely to make reference to any promises made to them. One possible explanation for that is that they want to avoid falling within the scope of the prohibition. Mentioning the promise entails the risk that the testamentary agreement (and potentially the will made in execution of such agreement) is regarded as void, even if made informally. In fact, in France one of the primary rationales underpinning the prohibition is that the promisor's testamentary freedom, including the freedom to change her mind, should not be limited.[92] While German law knows of a similar prohibition, the rationale behind it is not that the deceased should not feel bound

[89] Beuthien (1969) 165, 173 has argued, for instance, that courts should and could base the scope of the unjustified enrichment claim of the employee on the basis of the amount of the wages, for the employer is enriched not by the result of the work but by the wages she did not have to pay. Fenn (1968) 297–298 expressed himself in favour of greater flexibility, and suggested calculating the amount of the redress not merely on the basis of the value of the promisor's enrichment, but on the basis of what a person might normally obtain in the form of wages for a particular service (he refers to other situations in which the courts have been willing to do so).

[90] Chapter 6.

[91] Chapter 2, section II.A.2.

[92] Grimaldi *Droit Civil Successions* (2017) 286. Another rationale is the principle of equality of the heirs.

but rather that, if she wants to bind herself, she should choose the form that the law makes available to her, that is the inheritance contract.[93] For this reason, in Germany, there is no concern that promisors feel bound, and courts do not see informal promises as problematic, and indeed explicitly address the possibility of such promises. We saw that when examining the protection that German courts provide through the implication of a service contract between the promisor and the promisee, or enrichment law.[94]

Of, course, as with other civilian jurisdictions, the fact that the promisee is often a close family member means that, at least in some cases, compulsory heirship can mitigate the consequences of an unfulfilled promise by providing the promisee with a share in the estate. That said, in the case of France, compulsory heirship operates primarily in favour of descendants, with the spouse obtaining a share only in their absence.[95] Even where the promisee is a compulsory heir, she may want to seek redress when the promise remains unfulfilled, for the share depends on the number of descendants.

Since 1939, in France, certain promisees are in a position of demanding payment of a 'deferred salary' (*créance de salaire différé*) against the promisor's estate.[96] This deferred salary can be claimed in addition to the promisee's compulsory share. However, as Chapter 10 will show, this is only possible where the promisee is a descendant, the spouse of the descendant, or the spouse of the deceased farmer, and has worked on the farm without being remunerated or taking a share in the profits. In fact, the *Cour de cassation* has generally been reluctant to extend the legislative protection to, for instance, domestic work whether provided in the agricultural context or elsewhere.[97] Thus, outside these specific contexts, promisees may want (or have) to base their claim on enrichment law, for there is little else they can do.

In this section of the chapter, I consider the way in which French enrichment law can come to the aid of a testamentary promisee, even though the relevant case law does not refer to promises, and there is no need to provide proof of a promise. We will see that in the course of the past decades there have been some interesting developments in France whereby enrichment claims have been granted in both the agricultural and care context. However, these developments are restricted to very specific circumstances, leaving promisees in a number of situations without protection. In the pages that follow, I will examine these developments in greater detail, with a particular focus on case law concerning the protection of the interests of children who have assisted their parents. The analysis will show that, while for a long time French courts were reluctant to protect their interests, since 1994 children who care for their parents in old age may be able to demand restitution of the

[93] Chapter 2, section II.B.3.
[94] Chapter 8.
[95] See Pérès, 'Compulsory Portion in France' in *Comparative Succession Law 3* (2020) 78, 96.
[96] See Chapter 10.
[97] Terré et al *Droit civil* (2014) 1010, n 5.

value of their parents' enrichment. However, we will also see that such a claim is available only in limited circumstances and only where no other claim is available to them. Also, while in the beginning French courts appear to have been benevolent towards children bringing such a claim, more recently, courts seem to have been stricter in their interpretation of the requirements for a claim. The analysis will further show that French courts seem to place a lot of emphasis on financial aspects when requiring proof of an enrichment and an impoverishment. In addition, the promisee needs to prove that her assistance exceeds the demands of filial piety, which is not without problems. As a consequence, the French approach arguably poses even greater practical and psychological hurdles than, for instance, the German approach analysed earlier, which focuses on the proof of an agreed purpose and its frustration. Unsurprisingly, French notaries have argued in favour of a legislative intervention in the field and thus increased protection of children who assist their parents. In fact, arguably, the current jurisprudential development, while a welcome development, does not sufficiently protect those who have looked after their parents, especially if they have acted on a promise.

B. The *actio de in rem verso*

For a long time, the French Code civil lacked a general action for the recovery of an unjustified enrichment,[98] only regulating the two traditional quasi-contracts: the *negotiorum gestio* and the *condictio indebiti*.[99] Nonetheless, in 1892, the French *Cour de cassation* recognized a new general action, separate and independent from the *negotiorum gestio*.[100] For a long time, this action, which is often referred to as the *actio de in rem verso*, was regulated by case law. However, in the course of the reform of the French law of obligations that was implemented in 2016, this case law was codified in Articles 1303–1303-4 of the Code civil, under the heading 'L'enrichissement injustifié' (unjustified enrichment), rather than the previous heading 'enrichissement sans cause' (enrichment without legal ground or basis).[101] Thus, the action, which was originally the result of a jurisprudential development, is now codified. The principal requirements of this general *actio de in rem verso* are as follows: an enrichment on the part of the defendant and a corresponding (correlative) impoverishment of the claimant, together with the absence of a legal justification (or legal basis).[102]

[98] Terré et al *Droit civil. Les obligations* (2019) 1362ff.
[99] Articles 1371–1381 of the Code civil prior to the recent reform of 2016.
[100] Req 15 June 1892, DP 1892, 1596, S 1893, 1, 281, Grands arrets, t 2, no 239.
[101] L'ordonnance no 2016-131 of 10 February 2016 which was ratified by Law no 2018-287 of 20 April 2018. For a contextual analysis of the new provisions, see Descheemaeker (2017).
[102] Descheemaeker (2017) 87.

Already prior to the 2016 reform, due to a jurisprudential development that started in 1994, the *actio de in rem verso* was applied to the testamentary context and in particular to cases where children have cared for their parents in old age. Before exploring the requirements as developed by French courts, and examining whether and to what extent this action may come to the aid and is able to protect the interests of promisees, it is useful to understand the context and how the developments in this area have come about.

C. Applying enrichment law in the agricultural context

As mentioned earlier, in France, in the agricultural context, relief is often sought through the *créance de salaire différé* discussed in Chapter 10. Where the conditions for the application of the *créance* are not met, the French *Cour de cassation* has sometimes been willing to grant an enrichment claim, both in the agricultural context and beyond. For instance, in a controversial decision of March 1995,[103] the *Cour de cassation* granted an *actio de in rem verso* in favour of the daughter-in-law of a farmer. Despite the fact that she had helped her parents-in-law on their farm, she was unable to avail herself of the *créance de salaire différé* in her favour. The reason for that was that the relevant legislation requires that both the descendant and his or her spouse must have worked on the farm at the same time.[104] Thus, where, as in this case, the descendant has not worked on the farm, the surviving spouse will not be able to claim the deferred salary, even though she has herself worked on the farm and thus meets all the other requirements. Unable to rely on the 1939 legislation, the daughter-in-law sought redress arguing that the deceased farmer had been unjustly enriched by her work, and her claim was upheld.[105]

In another case of 2003, the *Cour de cassation* overturned the decision of the Court of Appeal of Grenoble which had rejected an *actio de in rem verso* brought by a son who had collaborated for twenty years in the threshing business (*activité de battage*) of his father, a business which his father had run alongside his farming activity. The claimant had been unsuccessful at first because the Court of Appeal of Grenoble held that his enrichment claim could not be brought in order to make up for the fact that the action aimed at establishing a *créance de salaire différé*

[103] Cass 1re civ, 14 March 1995, JCP G 1995, II, 22516, note F Roussel; JCP N 1995, II, 1433, note Moreau; RTD civ 1996, 160, note J Mestre; RTD civ 1996, 215, note J Patarin; D 1996, jurispr. 137, note Barabé-Bouchard; Defrénois 1996, 468, note J-L Fillette.

[104] For greater details, see Chapter 10.

[105] The decision of the *Cour de cassation* generated mixed reactions among legal scholars. For instance, some authors felt that the judgment was putting into question the subsidiary nature of the unjustified enrichment claim. Fillette (1996). See also Roussel (1996) [12], who contests the finding of the court that the conditions for a *créance de salaire différé* were not given in this case. By contrast, others regarded the decision as an expression precisely of the principle of subsidiarity because the daughter-in-law lacked the possibility of bringing a claim in her own right. See the case note by J Mestre (1996) RTD civ 160, 161. Favourable, though cautious, seems Patarin (1996).

was statute barred because the five-year limitation period had already passed.[106] However, the *Cour de cassation* took a different view and granted restitution of the enrichment.

The agricultural context aside, in some cases the *Cour de cassation* has applied enrichment law also in the artisanal context. For instance, in 1993 the court granted the enrichment claim of the descendant of a rural artisan, whose claim fell entirely outside the scope of the 1939 legislation, which does not in fact capture artisans, or work carried out in the context of any other type of small enterprise.[107] Although the *Cour de cassation* was not prepared to apply the 1939 legislation, it was willing to grant the descendant an enrichment claim to compensate him for his work in the family business.

Thus, sometimes, the *Cour de cassation* has been prepared to uphold an enrichment claim in situations that are analogous to those who would usually be captured by the 1939 or related legislation,[108] and occasionally even outside the specific agricultural context.[109] But such instances have been rare.

D. Applying enrichment law in the domestic context

1. Introduction

In the domestic context too, over the years, enrichment claims have sometimes come to the aid of family members. Since the 1960s, in France, the *actio de in rem verso* has, for instance, protected spouses (often the wife) living in a patrimonial regime of separation of assets and who have assisted the other spouse in the exercise of their profession (often the husband) without receiving any compensation.[110] The claim can be brought both against the spouse, in case of divorce, or the heirs, in case of death,[111] and either way the enrichment can be brought about through domestic work. A similar protection has been granted to cohabitants who have assisted their partner in the exercise of their profession, have made investments in their partner's property, or have sacrificed their career in order to look after the

[106] Cass 1re civ, 17 September 2003, no 01-16349. Concerning the relationship between an action aimed at claiming the *créance de salaire différé* and an unjustified enrichment claim, see Castella (2010).

[107] Cass 1re civ, 20 December 1993, JCP 1994, II, 22307, case note F Roussel; JCP N 1995, II 536; D 1995, somm 46, note M Grimaldi.

[108] For instance, in case of work carried out on the farm belonging to the sister and brother-in-law. See Cass 1re civ, 13 May 1975, Bull civ I, no 158.

[109] For instance, in the case in which a son had collaborated in the commercial business of the father. See Dijon, 16 March 1874, DP 1876, 2, 203.

[110] Cass 1re civ, 15 March 1960, Bull civ I, no 154, 123 and Cass 1re civ, 9 January and 30 May 1979, D 1981, 241, note A Breton.

[111] See Savatier (1994), text at n 17.

family.[112] I mention this here because we will see later that this development has had an influence on the jurisprudential developments examined in section III.

In fact, since 1994,[113] the *Cour de cassation* has been granting enrichment claims brought by children who have provided assistance to their parents in the domestic context. More precisely, it has upheld claims by children (and not those of other family members) who have assisted their parents in old age to a degree that, in the eyes of the court, went above and beyond the normal degree of filial compassion. This chapter will show that the 1994 decision (the *arrêt Fouret*) has initiated a jurisprudential development that has now consolidated. While none of the French cases mentions a promise, and indeed proof of a promise is not required, this development is interesting and important for this enquiry, for it can offer a way for certain promisees to obtain redress, even though only up to the value of the promisor's enrichment. In the remainder of this chapter, I therefore analyse the jurisprudential developments that started in 1994. But before doing so, it is useful to briefly outline the situation children found themselves in before then.

2. The protection of assistance in the domestic context prior to 1994

Prior to 1994, children who had provided domestic assistance to their parents were largely left without protection, except for the fact that since the 1970s, French courts have been allowing children who provide for their parents, when they are in a situation of need, to lodge a claim for reimbursement against their siblings. Article 205 of the French Code civil establishes that children have a duty to pay alimony to their parents (or other ascendants) when they are in financial need, that is because their resources are insufficient to cover housing, food, or care. But what happens when the alimony is paid by some but not all descendants? Case law has established that, where there is more than one child, the child who has provided for the parents, and thus fulfilled her duty under Article 205 of the Code civil, can bring a claim against the other siblings who are co-debtors of the duty to provide alimony. The child can do so either during the life or on death of the parents.[114] The amount that the performing child can recover from her siblings is established by taking into account the financial possibilities of the other children (the co-debtors).[115] For this reason, what she can recover may be lower than the expenses she has incurred or the value of the expended efforts, let alone the value

[112] Cass 1re civ, 19 May 1969, Bull civ I, no 187. See Malaurie *La Famille* (2011) 220–222; Terré & Fenouillet *Droit civil. La famille* (2018) 345–346. Where cohabitants can prove the existence of a *société de faite*, an enrichment claim is excluded. Here see similarities with the German *Innengesellschaft*.

[113] Cass 1re civ, 12 July 1994, Bull civ 1994, I, no 250; JCP G 1995, II, 22425; JCP N 1995, II, 22425 note A Sériaux; Defrénois 1994, art 35950, 1511, note X Savatier; RTD civ 1995, 373, no 13, note J Mestre.

[114] Cass 1re civ, 29 May 1974, Bull civ I, no 125, D 1975, 482; Cass 1re civ, 15 March 1972, Bull civ I, no 88. For details, see Montoux (2005). Cass 1re civ, 20 May 1974, D, 1975, 482, case note Magnin. For a discussion, see Mauger-Vielpeau (2010).

[115] Cass 1re civ, 29 May 1974, D 1974, somm 111.

of any promises made. And, in any event, the child who has supported the parents can only claim the sum exceeding her own duty, and only where the parents were in financial need. Thus, Article 205 of the Code civil will only be of assistance to a limited number of children.

The exact source of the child's entitlement against the siblings is not entirely clear and has been debated both by courts and in legal scholarship. While the courts have founded the redress either on the principles of *negotiorum gestio* (*gestion d'affaires*)[116] or on the parents' enrichment,[117] the majority of French legal scholars appear to identify the rationale of the claim in the principles of subrogation enshrined in Article 1251(3) of the Code civil.[118] In other words, they see the performing child as subrogating into the parents' right to maintenance. Whatever the underpinning rationale may be, the action founded on Article 205 of the Code civil is not an action against the parents' estate and the debt is not one of the estate but rather a personal debt of those children who had a duty to pay alimony to their parents but who did not fulfil it.

Outside these instances, for a long time, French courts refused to assist children who had provided care for, or assistance in the household of, their parents, including through the law of unjustified enrichment. The arguments usually invoked against an enrichment claim were primarily twofold: (i) what the child had done or provided for was but an expression of her moral obligations[119] towards her parents, and cannot therefore give rise to a right to compensation;[120] or (ii) the assistance provided was motivated by a donative intent, which prevents the application of the law of unjustified enrichment.[121] The argument was thus that the assistance provided was not without a legal basis, because either the performance was due (on the basis of a moral obligation) or motivated by an *intention libérale*. As discussed in earlier parts of this book,[122] similar arguments are often made in other jurisdictions and can pose obstacles to a claim by family members who are usually the ones

[116] CA Colmar, 15 March 1938, S. 1938, 231; *contra*: Req, 6 November 1899, DP 1899, 1, 559 – T civ Mamers, 3 November 1955, D 1956, jur, 32.

[117] Trib civ Bar-le-Duc, 5 June 1943, D C 1944, 18, with critical note G Ripert; Pierron (1949); *contra*: CA Versailles, 29 September 1989, 2e esp, préc.

[118] See e.g. Lescaillon (1990).

[119] These are enshrined in Article 371 of the Code civil.

[120] For an example, see Tribunal de grande instance d'Avesnes-sur-Helpe in a decision of 23 January 1962, JCP G 1963, II, 13279 (case note R Savatier); D 1963, 253 (case note J Prévault). For a discussion of the developments in this area, see Chamoulaud-Trapiers *Les fruits et revenus* (1999) 761ff, as well as Rivier in *Les Enjeux De la transmission entre générations* (2005) 141ff, 148–149ff. More recently, see the decision of the CA d'Aix-en-Provence, 9 June 1992, JCP N 1995, II, 1658 on appeal this decision was, however, overturned by the *Cour de cassation* in the *arrêt Fouret* discussed later.

[121] Cass 1re civ, 16 February 1960, Bull civ I, no 105. In this case the sister had cared for the deceased during a long and last illness. It resulted by her own admission that she had acted gratuitously. The court therefore rejected the claim. In some older cases the claim was rejected on the grounds that there was a '*pacte familial coutumier*' between the parties that would represent a sufficient ground for the unpaid labour. See the Trib civ de Pau, 22 March 1940, Gaz Pal 1940, 1, Jurisprudence, 475.

[122] See, for instance, the discussion of Canadian enrichment law in Chapter 6, but also the discussion of proprietary estoppel claims in Chapter 4.

to whom testamentary promises are made. But precisely because they are family members, their motives will often be mixed. Also, because they are family members, society nurtures certain expectations towards them and the law imposes legal and moral duties on them.

The position of the French courts against an enrichment claim in these cases was criticized by several legal scholars who have judged the approach as being too restrictive and argued that, at least in certain instances, some form of redress should be granted.[123] For instance, already in 1943, Georges Ripert[124] suggested a legislative intervention along the lines of the 1939 legislation regulating the *créance de salaire différé*.[125] And, criticizing a decision of the *Tribunal de grande instance* D'Avesnes-sur-Helpe of 1963,[126] in which the court rejected the enrichment claim on the basis that the daughter who had cared for her father for three years prior to his death had simply fulfilled her moral duty towards him, René Savatier argued that courts 'must prevent one of the children from becoming a serious victim of their own sacrifices'.[127] We will see that this is what the *Cour de cassation* decided to do, albeit another thirty years later, using precisely the language of 'filial piety'.

3. The *arrêt Fouret* and its impact

Whether or not the criticism referred to earlier was instrumental in bringing about the jurisprudential change is unclear. What matters is that, in a seminal decision of 1994, the French *Cour de cassation* held that the son who had assisted his parents during the last years of their lives, and in a manner that exceeded the requirements of filial compassion, was entitled to a claim against the estate on the basis that the deceased had been enriched.[128] The son had looked after his parents continuously, sparing them the need to be placed in a retirement home, and sacrificing his own professional future so as to be able to look after them. During the process of the liquidation and distribution of his parents' estate, the son had requested compensation which met with opposition from his sister. Because the parents were not technically speaking in need, the duty to pay alimony referred to earlier did not arise and a claim based on Article 205 of the Code Civil against his sister was therefore precluded. Instead, the son decided to base his claim on his parents' enrichment.

The *Cour d'Appel* of Aix-en-Provence[129] rejected the son's claim arguing that, even if the services provided by the son had exceeded the normal measure of filial

[123] For an examination of the criticism, see Chamoulaud-Trapiers *Les fruits et revenus* (1999) 762–763.

[124] Ripert (1949) 147.

[125] Trib civ Bar-le-Duc, 5 June 1943 (n 117).

[126] TGI Avesnes-sur-Helpe, 23 January 1962 (n 120) 254. Critical J Prévault, D 1963, 254ff.

[127] R Savatier, Defrénois 1963, art 28419, no 5, 553.

[128] Cass 1re civ, 12 July 1994, JCP G 1995, II, 22425; obs A Sériaux; Defrénois 1994, art 35950, 1511, note 5 Savatier.

[129] CA d'Aix-en-Provence, 9 June 1992 (n 120).

piety, he had merely acted in fulfilment of his moral and personal duties towards his parents. In other words, the moral obligations enshrined in Article 371 of the Code civil, which establishes that a child owes honour and respect to her parents, represented the reasons for the son's actions so that a claim for restitution was excluded. However, the *Cour de cassation*, held differently in its judgment commonly referred to as the *arrêt Fouret*. It concluded that:

> the moral duty of a child towards his parents does not in itself exclude compensation for the aid and assistance provided to them, to the extent to which they exceeded the demands of filial piety, the services provided freely have given rise both to an impoverishment of the child and a corresponding enrichment of the parents.[130]

Thus, the highest court in France acknowledged that the requirements of filial piety, expressed in Article 371 of the Code civil, have a limit that can be surpassed at which point the parents can be said to have been enriched. In reaching this conclusion, the *Cour de cassation* expressly referred to the line of cases in which the same court had agreed to compensate spouses whose dedication was judged to exceed their obligation to provide assistance to their partner and to contribute to the expenses of the marriage.[131] As noted earlier, since the 1960s, the law of unjustified enrichment has come to the aid of spouses[132] living in a patrimonial regime of separation of assets, as well as cohabitants, who have worked in the business of their partner. The notion of 'contribution' employed in these cases is usually broad and includes domestic contributions which can therefore give rise to an impoverishment and a correlative enrichment.[133] By extending this reasoning to children who assist their parents in old age, the *Cour de cassation* recognized the need for compensation of children's services.

The *arrêt Fouret* was followed in several subsequent cases. For instance, in a decision of January 1999, the *Cour de cassation* upheld the claim of another son who had housed the bedridden deceased, thereby saving significant costs that could have burdened the estate.[134] A few months later,[135] the *Cour de cassation* upheld the claim of a daughter who had supported her mother, who was suffering from a long-term illness, during the ten years preceding her death. Her efforts prevented

[130] In the words of the court 'le devoir moral d'un enfant envers ses parents n'exclut pas une indemnité pour l'aide et l'assistance apportées, dans la mesure, où ayant excédé les exigences de la piété filiale, les prestations librement fournies avaient réalisé à la fois un appauvrissement pour l'enfant et un enrichissement corrélatif des parents'.

[131] The duty to assist one's spouse is enshrined in Article 212 of the Code civil.

[132] See section III.D.1.

[133] Cass 1re civ, 4 March 1980, Bull civ I, no 75; Rép Defrénois 1980, art 32448, 1299, obs Champeois; Cass 1re civ, 20 May 1981, Bull civ I, no 175; Rép Defrénois 1981, art 32750, 1324, obs Champenois.

[134] Cass 1re civ, 5 January 1999, no 96–20151, JCP G 1999, I, 189, no 3, obs R Le Guidec; JCP N 1999, 722, note J-F Pillebout; RTD civ 2000, 605, no 2, obs J Patarin.

[135] Cass 1re civ, 6 July 1999, JCP G 1999, I, 189, no 3, obs R Le Guidec.

the deceased from having to employ someone or to be placed in a retirement home, and the daughter was therefore awarded 313,000 francs (about €50,000), which was not an insignificant sum at the time.[136]

The recourse to the *actio de in rem verso* in these instances is now considered a consolidated doctrine, to the point that references are being made, both in legal scholarship and in case law, to a *créance d'assistance* (a debt of assistance), a term that would appear to derive from the *créance de salaire différé* mentioned earlier and discussed in greater detail in Chapter 10. However, this is not to say that children are always successful. In fact, the threshold that they have to meet is quite high. In the following pages we will see what a claimant has to prove. Because this is an area of French law that is still developing, it currently lacks conceptual and theoretical systematization. Due to the dearth of scholarly work in the area,[137] much has therefore to be gleaned directly from case law which, given the style of French judgments, poses certain challenges. Even so, we will see that, as the discussion of the *arrêt Fouret* and the two 1999 decisions has already shown, there is a clear focus on the economic imbalance between the two parties, which can disadvantage certain promisees.

E. Requirements for a claim of a child to succeed

The *arrêt Fouret* has established that, in order to be successful, a claimant must prove: (i) an enrichment on the part of the parents; (ii) a corresponding impoverishment; and (iii) that she provided assistance that exceeds the demands of filial piety. As will be seen, these requirements cannot be neatly compartmentalized. The analysis will further show that of the three requirements, the third one is perhaps the most difficult to meet, as it is not always clear exactly what the promisee needs to do to exceed the threshold of her moral duty towards her parents.

1. Enrichment of the deceased parent

To succeed, a child will first of all need to prove that the assistance provided has led to an enrichment of the deceased parent. Here we see a difference to the German approach where the focus lies on proving that a performance has been rendered on the basis of a shared purpose which remains frustrated, though as we saw, that is not necessarily always easy either.[138]

Care but also other domestic or household services are regarded as being capable of enriching the parents, which is important given how frequently testamentary promises are being made in exchange for such services. However, the

[136] The claim was further upheld in Cass 1re civ, 28 March 2006, no 03-14455.
[137] Descheemaeker (2017) makes this point more generally about this area of French law.
[138] See section II.

cases also suggest that provision of support in the form of the running of mere errands, emotional support or visits, even if regular, will not suffice to establish a claim.[139] It is noticeable in this regard that in successful cases, French courts have frequently referred to the fact that, due to the assistance provided by the child, the parent has avoided spending money on a nursing home or a professional carer to assist them at home.[140] In principle, it is not excluded that courts take into account personal intangible benefits that are derived from being able to be cared for in a familial context, and to die in one's own home. Yet, judging from the cases, so far at least, the focus seems to lie on financial benefits. Of course, from the perspective of the promisee this is problematic in several respects. Arguably, a focus on financial enrichment could make it difficult for a promisee to establish a claim where the deceased had substantial financial means of her own, enough to pay for a retirement home or professional care in her own home.[141] Also, non-financial benefits can be just as important and valuable to the promisee, even if it may be difficult to put a price tag on them.

What is interesting to note here is that in several cases where the claim was granted, the claimants had taken the parent to live with them in their own home. While this is not a necessary nor a sufficient requirement for a claim to succeed, we will see that moving in with the parents may well preclude a claim, including on the basis that there is no impoverishment or that there is a juristic reason for the enrichment.[142]

2. Impoverishment of the performing child

An enrichment aside, the child will also need to prove a correlative impoverishment on her part. The jurisprudential development seems to suggest that the impoverishment can derive both from expenses incurred by the child in providing support (i.e. supply of food, transportation, etc) or losses suffered in the form of the promisee's loss of job opportunities, the denial of a promotion or, more generally, the lack of time to invest in her career. For instance, in the seminal *arrêt Fouret*, the impoverishment consisted in financial losses caused by the sacrifice of a professional future on the part of the son. In other successful cases, the claimants had given up their job so as to look after their parents, though this is not a necessary requirement. This was clarified by the *Cour de cassation* in a decision of May 2014 in which the court granted an appeal against a decision of the Court of Appeal of Rennes which had rejected the enrichment claim on the basis that the daughter

[139] CA de Douai, Chambre 1, 15 October 2007 says mere visits to the retirement home are insufficient.

[140] Cass 1re civ, 6 July 1999 (n 135).

[141] This was, for instance, the case in Cass 1re civ, 27 Mars 2007, no 05-15855 where the claimant was unsuccessful in showing an enrichment. Interestingly this is another case where the child had lived with the parents and thus benefited from free accommodation.

[142] See section E.2.

had not given up her profession in order to assist her parents.[143] According to the *Cour de cassation*, by doing so, the Court of Appeal of Rennes had imposed a condition that is not essential.

Whether other types of sacrifice of a more personal nature on the part of the promisee, such as giving up personal time, amount to an impoverishment is unclear. Case law seems to suggest that they do not. Yet, we know that care often involves significant personal investments on the part of the carer, and that there are forms of redress where that is being taken into consideration.[144] Again, the focus appears to be on financial aspects.

Even if impoverishment can be proven in the form of expenses incurred, loss of professional opportunities, or else, it may not be regarded as significant enough to support a claim if the child has, for instance, received benefits, such as, compensation in the form of financial contributions, lifetime gifts, testamentary dispositions, or other types of mutual benefits, such as rent-free accommodation,[145] rental income from a property,[146] or the possibility of free storage of materials at the parents' home.[147] In a decision of 23 January 2001,[148] the *Cour de cassation* found that a child who had obtained advantages in the form of a legacy and rent-free living was not impoverished. Thus, unless the assistance was of significant nature, where the claimant had lived with the parents rather than taking them to live with her, the claim is often less likely to be successful.[149] This was confirmed also by a decision of 1 April 2015. Here a son had assisted his parents with whom he had lived all his life. While living with his parents he had been provided with food and lodgings,[150] without having to contribute to the living expenses. In the eyes of the court, it is because the son benefited from a pension that he decided not to work, which meant that he was in a position to look after his parents. He did not therefore make a professional sacrifice, nor did he incur any expenses. Hence, the court found that there was no impoverishment, and the claim was denied. Interestingly, the court referred again to professional sacrifices despite the decision of 2014 mentioned earlier making it clear that this is not a condition for a successful claim.[151]

[143] Cass 1re civ, 14 May 2014, no 12-25735. Here notice that prior to the 2010 reform, a claim based on the German § 2057a BGB required the descendant who cared for the parent to be able to show a professional sacrifice. See Chapter 11.

[144] For example, see the New Zealand TPA 1949 discussed in Chapter 7, but also proprietary estoppel claims discussed in Chapter 4.

[145] A Romani (2018) para 78. An example is Cass 1re civ, 27 Mars 2007, no 05-15855.

[146] Cass 1re civ, 4 December 2013, no 12-20260. Here the son could cash in rental income for several years.

[147] Cass 1re civ, 22 October 2014, no 13-24581. In this case, the son had also benefited from financial contributions to work for his exclusive use and benefit.

[148] Cass 1re civ, 23 January 2001, no 98-22937, Bull civ I, no 9, 6; JCP N 2002, no 11, 1194, note R Le Guidec. See also the comment of Libchaber (2001).

[149] Cass 1re civ, 20 Mai 2009, no 08-17344 where the claimants could live rent-free. The *Cour de cassation* overturned the appeal decision and reprimanded the court of appeal for not taking that into account. See also Cass 1re civ, 27 March 2007, no 05-15855.

[150] Cass 1re civ, 1 April 2015 no 14-15774.

[151] Cass 1re civ, 22 October 2014 (n 147).

Thus, mutual benefits can make it difficult to prove that there is impoverishment, because the performance may well be seen as 'counterpart' for the benefits received.

3. Assistance exceeding the demands of filial piety

The third requirement set out in the *arrêt Fouret* to be met by the child is that she must have assisted the parent, and her assistance must have exceeded the demands of filial piety. What exactly counts as assistance is not clearly defined, though it is certain that the assistance provided must exceed the moral obligation towards her parents as enshrined in Article 371 of the Code civil. However, just as with other forms of redress discussed in this book,[152] the difficulty lies in establishing at what point the demands of filial piety are *exceeded*. While some French authors have spoken of the need of an extraordinary devotion or sacrifice,[153] others have referred to a total dedication of the child.[154] However, this seems very demanding and would leave most children without a claim.

Unfortunately, case law provides little guidance in this respect, though, on the whole, courts seem to be less strict than some legal scholars.[155] Even so, different courts can take a different view as to what can be expected of a child and whether her performance has exceeded her moral duty towards her parents. Judging from case law, simply living with one's parents is insufficient to warrant an enrichment claim. If anything, living with the parents in their own home may work against the claimant, for as we saw, it may be difficult to prove impoverishment, and it could be argued that her behaviour does not exceed the demands of filial piety.[156] In other words, the threshold appears to be higher where the child lives with the parents and benefits from rent-free accommodation. In the decision of the *Cour de cassation* of 23 January 2001, mentioned earlier, the threshold was judged as not having been crossed.[157] In this case, the son and his wife had looked after his mother. The deciding factor seems to have been that the son and his wife had lived rent-free in the deceased's house and that the mother had left him her disposable share in the form of a legacy, which he inherited in addition to the compulsory share he was already entitled to.[158] The court saw the help and assistance that the son had provided as 'counterpart' for the benefits he had received during her lifetime and on her death. Thus, where a child receives certain benefits, including rent-free accommodation in the parents' home and testamentary gifts, as well as lifetime ones, the services may well be regarded as 'normal' and thus as not exceeding the required

[152] See, for instance, the discussion of Canadian enrichment cases examined in Chapter 6, of § 612 BGB in Chapter 8, but also the New Zealand TPA 1949 in Chapter 7.
[153] Chamoulaud-Trapiers *Les fruits et revenus* (1999) 768.
[154] M Tchendjou, D 1995, J, 624ff.
[155] The same is true for Germany. See section II.
[156] CA de Paris, Pôle 3, chambre 1, 11 December 2013, RG no 13-00847.
[157] Cass 1re civ, 23 January 2001, no 98-22937 (n 148), case note R Le Guidec.
[158] The disposable share or portion is that part of the estate that a deceased can freely dispose of. See Pérès, 'Compulsory Portion in France' in *Comparative Succession Law 3* (2020) 86.

threshold. This confirms that French courts tend to focus on the existence of an economic imbalance.

The assistance provided was held not to have exceeded the demands of filial piety also in a later case of 2012, decided by the *Cour d'appel* in Nîmes.[159] In this instance, the problem seems to have been the nature of the services performed by the son, which were not regarded as substantial enough, rather than the mutual benefits he had obtained. Here, a son had undertaken regular visits to his mother over the course of a period of about ten years, which he claimed had enriched her. The son had provided the court with a table in which he had listed the kilometres he had travelled to see his mother, demanding payment of an amount of €134,000 which he had quantified by applying an indemnity for each kilometre. The court concluded that there was no evidence that the numerous and regular visits made by the son exceeded the requirements of filial piety. Where the child's performance is not substantial, as it appears to have been the case here, a claim is unlikely. It may also be more difficult to establish a claim where there is evidence that the parents were independent and autonomous and perfectly capable of looking after themselves.[160] Thus, as we have seen with other forms of redress (e.g. Canadian enrichment law), when evaluating whether the assistance provided by a child exceeds her duties, the benefits obtained by the promisee, the nature and intensity of the services she has performed, but also the parents' physical conditions can play a role.[161]

F. Quantifying the award

In France, it is a matter for the *juges du fond* to establish the indemnity in an *actio de in rem verso*. There are two limits to the quantification beyond which the *juges* is unable to go. The upper limit is represented by the value of the enrichment and the lower by the value of the impoverishment. Within this frame, the sum awarded will be the lesser between the two.[162] This double limit has now been enshrined in

[159] CA Nîmes, Chambre civile 1, section B, 21 June 2012, RG no 11-02235.

[160] Cass 1re civ, 16 December 2015, no 11-20708. In this case there were conflicting documents concerning the state of the parents' health. The documents or witnesses did not confirm that a third person was required to look after them and to live with them (which the claimant did). It was further unclear whether the irregularity in the claimant's professional employment was truly linked to the assistance she had provided to her parents. See also CA d'Orléans, 26 January 2009, RG no 07-03311, where the claim was rejected on the basis of a lack of documentation establishing that the physical or mental state of the claimant's grandfather would have required the presence of a third person with him, or that his other children and grandchildren refused to provide him with the assistance that might have been required had he remained in his home.

[161] The physical conditions of the promisor clearly matter for the purposes of an adjustment of the intestate share based on § 2057a BGB or a claim based on §§ 677ff ABGB, both discussed in Chapter 11.

[162] This principle is now enshrined in the new Article 1303 of the Code civil which establishes that: 'Apart from the situation of management of another's affairs and undue payment, a person who benefits from an unjustified enrichment to the detriment of another person must indemnify the person who is thereby made the poorer to an amount equal to the lesser of the two values of the enrichment and the impoverishment.'

the new Article 1303 of the Code civil. An exception has, however, been introduced by Article 1303-4 of the Code civil, which establishes that in case of bad faith of the enriched, the compensation due is equal to the highest of these two values. As for the date of assessment, the new Article 1303-4 of the Code civil also establishes that '[t]he impoverishment found on the day of the expenditure, and the enrichment as it remains on the day of the demand, are assessed on the day of judgment'. In any event, the amount can be reduced if the impoverishment is a consequence of the fault of the person who has suffered the impoverishment. This is established by Article 1303-2(2) of the Code civil.

In the testamentary context, quantifying the reward is of course not always straightforward.[163] French courts seem to have been guided by the enrichment cases brought by spouses or cohabitants who have worked in the business of their partner. However, this has been criticized. François Boulanger,[164] for instance, regards the analogy that the *Cour de cassation* has drawn between cases in which the spouse or cohabitant works in the business of the partner and those in which a child assists her parents as misguided because of the difficulty to measure the 'loss' that the presence of one's parent in one's home gives rise to. However, putting a price on the assistance or services performed in the domestic context always poses certain challenges and cannot therefore be a reason for not protecting the interest of the person providing such assistance. Also, the two situations are not fundamentally different.

As we saw, mutual benefits in the form of rent-free accommodation or legacies and even lifetime gifts, are being taken into consideration when evaluating the impoverishment and whether the performance exceeds the threshold of filial piety. But they also play a role when quantifying the amount of the recovery, unless they were an instance of a *donation rémunératoire*. Such a gift made in remuneration is not to be accounted for, but in order for a donation to be qualified as such, the services or work provided have to precede the donation.[165] In other words, it must be clear that the donation represented a remuneration for a service already performed.

While legacies matter for the purpose of the quantification, the compulsory share a child is entitled to is not counted against an award and this seems to be the correct approach. As we saw, this is not the case in Germany, where the compulsory share is subtracted from an award based on the *condictio ob rem* (though apparently not if the claim is based on 812 I, 1, 1 BGB). If the compulsory share is counted against the award, the principle that descendants should be treated equally would be frustrated, and we know that equal treatment of descendants is an

[163] The quantification presented, for instance, a problem in Cass 1re civ, 20 January 2004, no 01-03799 because the medical certificate, albeit showing that the parents needed assistance, did not quantify the amount of care needed.

[164] Boulanger (2005).

[165] CA de Versailles, 28 February 2013.

important principle behind the prohibition of contracts to make wills in France.[166] Also, the compulsory share is entirely unrelated to any merit so that even those descendants who do not assist their parents benefit.

Normally, the claimant obtains a monetary compensation and is treated as a creditor of the estate. This is important because it means that she will benefit prior to the successors under the will or on intestacy. However, it seems that a successful claim may not always necessarily lead to a monetary payment. This is what happened in the *Cour de cassation* decision of 3 November 2004.[167] In this case, the litigation arose between two sisters, one of whom, Christiane, had housed and assisted her father. While looking after him she had received lifetime gifts. During that time, the father had also made considerable withdrawals from his bank account, and it was unclear how that money had been spent. In addition, Christiane had been awarded the disposable portion in her father's will. Notwithstanding these benefits, the Court of Appeal of Rennes found that Christiane had been impoverished at the expense of the deceased. Importantly, the court also held that, rather than recovering the value of the enrichment, she should be exempted from having to account for the donations (both direct and indirect) that she had received from the deceased. The sister (Alice) contested the finding of the Court of Appeal, arguing that the benefits obtained by the claimant had to be accounted for, but the appeal was rejected by the *Cour de cassation*. The decision was criticized in legal scholarship for it creates an exemption to the rule that, except for exceptional instances, gifts made during lifetime need to be accounted for by donees who are also compulsory heirs.[168] In deciding to exempt Christiane from accounting for what she had received during her lifetime, rather than allowing her to recover the value of the deceased's enrichment, the *Cour de cassation* had interfered with the rules that regulate the administration of the estate, including those dealing with the calculation of the compulsory shares. The decision was further criticized because the disposable portion that was left to Christiane was transformed into a compensatory liberality, which led to unexpected tax benefits for Christiane.[169] However, the decision seems to be an outlier.

When the claim arises (i.e. whether already during lifetime) appears to be unclear, for French courts have been silent on the point. So far at least, case law in this context seems to only deal with claims that have been brought against the estate.[170]

[166] See Chapter 2, section II.B.3.

[167] Cass 1re civ, 3 November 2004, no 01-15176, Bull civ I, no 248; JCP G 2005 II 10024, note F Boulanger. The decision is commented by Gelot (2005).

[168] For details, see Pérès, 'Compulsory Portion in France' in *Comparative Succession Law 3* (2020) 102ff.

[169] Gelot (2005).

[170] Everaert-Dumont (2003).

G. Reception of the judicial developments

The discussion so far has already revealed that the jurisprudential development whereby children who assist their parents may obtain the value of the enrichment has met with mixed feelings. A number of scholars have deemed the development a step in the right direction.[171] After all, in the past, the *Cour de cassation* had been criticized for not allowing for any sort of protection of children who have assisted their parents.[172] Others have approved the intervention, but have argued for a more cautious approach when applying enrichment law in the testamentary context,[173] suggesting that courts should take into account the state of the parents' health and require a higher threshold where they are not in need.[174] At the same time, some scholars have regarded any intervention of the law in this area sceptically,[175] in part because they are concerned about the risk of commodification of the parent–child relationship,[176] and because in their view a minute and careful accounting of what can be claimed back, and of the benefits obtained by the parents, represents an in-road into privacy.[177]

However, even though the number of cases in which the action has been invoked has risen over the past two decades or so, French courts have granted the claim only in a few instances. In other words, the interventions have been specific and piecemeal, and the requirements interpreted in a restrictive manner, and there is currently no sign that the doctrine will be extended at will. On the contrary, there is rather ground for an argument that French courts have been too narrow in their approach and have not gone far enough, leaving a number of deserving children without protection. For this reason, the French notaries have called for a legislative intervention in this area. During the ninety-fifth *Congres Des Notaires De France*, under the title 'Demain, la famille', which was held in Marseilles in May 1999,[178] it was proposed to recognize a *créance d'assistance* in favour of children who have provided assistance to their parents. The suggestion has met with the support of

[171] Patarin (1995). See also Chamoulaud-Trapiers *Les fruits et revenus* (1999) 773 who regards this as being in line with the principle of equality among children. Equally, Le Guidec (1995).

[172] See section III.D.2.

[173] Sériaux has suggested that the descendant should provide evidence of the fact that his or her actions where not motivated by a gratuitous intent. See Sériaux, 'Enrichissement sans cause' (1995).

[174] Zalewski in *L'entraide familiale* (2012) 241–242.

[175] Hauser (1999); Libchaber (2001).

[176] Another concern expressed by Monteillet-Geffroy *Les conditions de l'enrichissement* (2001) 206 is that the developments have led to a '*fragilisation du droit*' because to ascertain whether or not there is an enrichment is ultimately the decision of the *juge du fond*. Nonetheless, Monteillet-Geffroy also suggests that (205) this approach could be extended to other circumstances and other family members. Similar concerns are raised by Tchendjou (154) 625. Yet in principle Tchendjou approves of the decision as it is based on principles of equity. See also Sériaux 'Des limites' (1995).

[177] Libchaber (2001).

[178] 95e Congrès des notaires de France, 9–12 mai 1999, Demain la famille, 2e comm, 381 reported by R Le Guidec, in JCP 1999, I, 189, 2247. In 2014 the Notaries repeated the proposal in their annual report.

some legal scholars,[179] some of whom have suggested codifying existing case law in which enrichment claims are being granted to the child.[180] So far, however, the legislature has been reluctant to intervene. At the request of the notaries, in August 2014, M Dominique Baert[181] had submitted a query to the French Ministry of Justice asking whether the government intended to consolidate case law in the area and to provide the *créance d'assistance* with a legislative framework, but the answer was negative.[182] The Ministry argued that legislation was unnecessary, given that courts are already providing a satisfactory solution, and that recognition of such a credit could be prejudicial to a peaceful distribution of estates, and lead to disputes. But, as argued before,[183] the floodgates argument should not stand in the way of the protection of the interests of those who are in a vulnerable situation and at risk of exploitation. Rather, it is important to set clear parameters that they must meet. For the Ministry, 'the law already ensures a fair balance between voluntary family assistance, which should be free of charge, and assistance that may give rise to compensation'. However, whether this is true is rather doubtful. The Ministry's response further unhelpfully suggests that problems can be pre-empted if the deceased recognizes the existence of such a claim in her will,[184] or provides for a lump sum in compensation for the child. This advice seems to ignore the fact that families do not necessarily talk openly about estate planning, that many testators do not want to part with assets during their lifetime, and that, even if they agree to make a will, wills can always be revoked. Also, especially in France, testation rates are very low.[185] Moreover, in the case of a remuneration in the context of a will, the claimant would not rank as a creditor but only take after the creditors have been paid. By contrast, the claimant who brings a successful *actio de in rem verso* is to be treated as a creditor of an indemnity that forms part of the *passif successoral* to be subtracted from the *actif successoral* prior to its distribution. Her interest therefore

[179] Monteillet-Geffroy *Les conditions de l'enrichissement* (2001) 122–124. See Chamoulaud-Trapiers *Les fruits et revenus* (1999) 670ff and 685ff who is in favour of generalizing the *créance de salaire différée* outside the agricultural context because in her view, the unjustified enrichment approach showcases certain limitations. One of the risks (687) is indeed that the other party argues, for instance, that the claimant has acted in his or her own interest or at her own risk and peril, e.g. hoping to inherit the future assets or conserving the family patrimony. Here see the parallel with some of the discussion that took place in Germany in section II.

[180] Everaert-Dumont (2003).

[181] Published in *Journal Officiel de la République Française* of 26 August 2014, 7111. See also the query submitted by M Marc Le Fur in 2015 (*Journal Officiel de la République Française* of 28 July 2015, 5716) which was met with the same response. See *Journal Officiel de la République Française* of 7 June 2016, 5139.

[182] The response was published in *Journal Officiel de la République Française* of 23 August 2016, 7531.

[183] See especially the discussion in Chapter 4.

[184] However, the controversial decision of the *Cour de cassation* in Cass 1re civ, 20 January 2004, no 01-03799 shows that even if the will contains a clause recognizing a debt, this can pose problems and lead to different interpretations. See the comment by Gelot (2005) who points out that the clause in the holograph will could be read either as the acknowledgement of the assistance, or as a specific legacy which leads to different practical and fiscal consequences.

[185] Fewer than 10% of the estates are transferred by will. Pérès, 'Intestate Succession in France' in *Comparative Succession Law 2* (2015).

ranks with that of other ordinary unsecured creditors but prevails over that of testate and intestate successors. Thus, an intervention along the lines of the *créance de salaire différé*, which will be discussed in Chapter 10, is in the interest of promisees, especially as they would then be treated as secured creditors.

H. Summary

The fact that French courts are now prepared to grant redress to a child who has cared for parents in old age through the law of enrichment is certainly to be welcomed and may come to the aid of a person who, in exchange for such services, has been promised a testamentary disposition, even if all they can claim is the value of the parents' enrichment. Exactly what triggered the jurisprudential development, whether or not the scholarly criticism had a role to play, is unclear. Interestingly, Mika Oldham sees the decision as an expression of an intention to 'encourage children to make sacrifices to help and support their ageing parents'.[186] In other words, there may well be broader public policy concerns that may have brought about this development. In addition, it is possible that the fact that in the *arrêt Fouret* the claimant was the son, rather than the daughter, played a role.

Irrespective of that, it is suggested here that French courts do not go far enough in extending protection. Compensation is in fact only possible in very limited circumstances. Although this type of action does not depend on the parents' needs and is therefore more widely available than a claim based on the duty of alimony enshrined in Article 205 of the Code civil,[187] because of the way the requirements have been interpreted by the courts, an enrichment claim cannot presently offer a universal solution. In practice, cases in which the claimant has been successful are relatively few. Generally speaking, it seems that while, at first, French courts seemed to be sympathetic towards children who assisted their parents, more recently they appear to have adopted a stricter approach when interpreting the requirements that a child must meet.[188]

Even though there is no need to provide either a promise or reliance, with this type of claim it can be difficult and potentially embarrassing for a child to have to prove that her assistance led to both an enrichment of the parent and corresponding impoverishment on her side, and that what she has done exceeds the filial compassion. The focus seems to rest very much on the financial/economic benefits and losses of the parties. Mutual benefits in the form of gifts, but also free accommodation, may therefore present a bar to a claim. By contrast, intangible benefits on the part of the deceased, but also personal losses and sacrifices on the part of the

[186] Oldham (2001) 159–160.
[187] See section III.D.2.
[188] Brault (1998).

promisee may not receive sufficient appreciation. Also, it seems that a claim is only available on death of the parents.

In addition, unlike in Germany, in France (just as in Austria), the enrichment claim can only be brought when the child has no other action in respect of her impoverishment.[189] Thus, if the parents are in need and the child who looks after them has a claim against the siblings (that is the co-debtors of the duty of alimony), the general enrichment claim is precluded. Similarly, where the claimant is a descendant of a farmer and is entitled to a *créance de salaire différé*, no restitution is possible through an *actio de in rem verso*, except for work that exceeds ten years. It is therefore understandable that French notaries have pushed for the recognition of a *créance d'assistance* modelled on the *créance de salaire différé* which, as we will see in Chapters 10 and 11, has a lower threshold.

IV. Concluding summary

In this chapter, we have seen how and when a claim based on the deceased's enrichment may come to the aid of a promisee in certain civil law jurisdictions. However, in Germany, the *condictio ob rem* is relatively rarely applied, as promisees will normally resort to § 612 BGB in order to obtain redress. In Austria, enrichment claims would seem to be more common than, for instance, claims based on an implied service contract,[190] but the principle of subsidiarity can stand in the way of a claim. In France, the *actio de in rem verso* is invoked in the testamentary context, but the analysis has shown that courts are not necessarily willing to extend its scope. Also, due to the principle of subsidiarity, in France, an enrichment claim is only available as a last resort. Hence, the cases in which enrichment law can currently provide protection to a promisee of a testamentary promise are on the whole limited in the civil law jurisdictions examined.

Irrespective of that, is enrichment law suited to the testamentary context? Does it allow for adequate protection of the promisee's interests? The answer seems to be that it is only partly suitable. This is somewhat due to the fact that, generally speaking, with enrichment claims courts seem to take an economic/financial approach. In other words, enrichment law has a monetary feel so that both intangible forms of benefit and personal sacrifices may escape the scope. It may therefore

[189] Article 1303-3 of the Code civil states that 'The impoverished person has no action on this basis where another action is open to him or is legally barred, as in the case of prescription.' This has led to a number of issues regarding the relationship with the *créance de salaire différé* mentioned earlier and discussed in more detail in Chapter 10. Chapter 11 will show that, as far as Austria is concerned, it remains unclear whether the promisee has a choice between an enrichment claim and, for instance, a claim based on §§ 677ff ABGB.

[190] In Italy, some authors have suggested invoking enrichment law in cases not currently covered by the provisions that regulate work carried out in the context of a family business (Articles 230-bis Codice civile). See Spagnoli (2002).

work more naturally where the promisee has, for instance, made financial contributions or improvements, rather than provided services. However, testamentary promises cases frequently involve a promise made in exchange for services. While domestic/household or care work can lead to enrichment, that may be more likely where the promisor did not have to employ someone or was spared the costs of a retirement home.

Another limitation of enrichment claims is that in most jurisdictions, and certainly under German, Austrian, and French law, the promisee can recover only the promisor's enrichment. A promisee will usually want to obtain what she was promised, especially where the value is much higher than the value of her performance or that of the promisor's enrichment. That said, unlike in some common law jurisdictions, in the civil law context, the promisee will hardly ever see her expectation interest fulfilled, and in some cases an enrichment claim may be all she has at her disposal. While an enrichment claim may only lead to a monetary compensation, she will be treated like a creditor, which puts her in a stronger position than the deceased's successors. Her credit may exceed the value of the estate, in which case the heirs of the deceased may have to pay for it. That is better than the position in the context of some other forms of redress that I will explore in Chapter 11 (i.e. § 2057a BGB and §§ 677ff ABGB).

More problematic from the perspective of the promisee is perhaps the fact that in an enrichment claim mutual benefits in the form of free accommodation and food, or other types of lifetime or testamentary benefits, can affect the chances of a claim besides affecting the calculation of the relief. We also saw that in Germany, though not in France, the compulsory share the claimant is entitled to will be detracted. While mutual benefits are also taken into consideration with some of the other forms of redress examined in this book (e.g. in the case of a proprietary estoppel claim), they are not taken into account where courts imply, for instance, a service contract. Thus, in Germany, the promisee is likely to obtain a higher amount if she bases her claim on § 612 BGB. In addition, in the case of an enrichment claim, the promisor may have defences that are not available in other contexts.

Arguably, framing a claim in terms of unjustified enrichment may also represent certain psychological hurdles. It might be uncomfortable to have to prove that a parent has made a gain at the expense of the child or that the child has suffered an impoverishment, for instance, as a consequence of the fact that they have taken the parent to live with them. It may further feel awkward to have to prove that what the promisee has done exceeds what can be expected of her in a particular situation (e.g. that it exceeds the requirements of filial piety).[191] That said, the requirements are not the same in all jurisdictions. For instance, in Germany a promisee needs to

[191] See also what I said in relation to the need to prove the absence of a juristic reason in Chapter 6.

show that there was a shared purpose and that it was frustrated, which a promisee may well find easier. All in all, it therefore seems that in Germany, and especially in France, enrichment law does not usually represent the approach that is best suited to the testamentary context.

10
Establishing a claim to deferred wages for up to ten years

I. Introduction

The discussion in Chapter 9 has shown that, in France, certain promisees may be able to resort to enrichment law to obtain redress. However, unlike in other jurisdictions, the instances where that is possible are limited to very specific circumstances and, due to the principle of subsidiarity, only where no other claim is available. For instance, in the domestic and care context, an enrichment claim is precluded where the promisee, who has fulfilled her duty to pay alimony to her parents, has a claim for reimbursement of the incurred expenses against her siblings.[1] By contrast, in the agricultural context, an enrichment claim is barred where the promisee is entitled to a 'deferred salary' against the estate, that is a *créance de salaire différé*,[2] which will be the focus of this chapter. However, as we will see, this affects only a limited number of people who are eligible to apply under the legislation.

I should mention from the outset that in order to claim a deferred salary against the estate, there is no need to prove the existence of a promise. Indeed, a promise is entirely irrelevant to a claim and does not affect either the eligibility or the extent of the relief. This is because the purpose of the legislative provisions regulating the *créance de salaire différé* is to give economic recognition to work carried out by certain family members on the deceased's farm, irrespective of any expectations engendered by the deceased. For this reason, the cases we will come across in this chapter do not mention any promises. Nonetheless, a discussion of the *créance de salaire différé* has been included in this book because a promisee who has worked on the farm of her ascendants may want to resort to it.

This chapter analyses who can obtain protection under the provisions regulating the *créance de salaire différé* and what requirements they must meet, with a view to establishing the extent to which promisees may be able to avail themselves of this protection. We will see that, while in many ways this approach fits the testamentary context and accounts for some of its specificities, it is narrow in scope in

[1] See Chapter 9, section III.D.2.
[2] Law 29 July 1939.

Claiming a Promised Inheritance. Alexandra Braun, Oxford University Press. © Alexandra Braun 2022.
DOI: 10.1093/oso/9780198757252.003.0011

terms of the context in which it applies and eligible claimants. The analysis will, in fact, show that an entitlement to a deferred salary can only be asserted by a limited number of people—that is by direct descendants, the descendant's spouse (though only in limited circumstances), and the spouse of a farmer—who have worked on the deceased's farm without being adequately remunerated.[3] Also, for the purposes of the *créance*, work does not include domestic work carried out on the farm, but only farming work. And it does not apply outside the farming context. Thus, many promisees would not be able to avail themselves of the protection it offers. We will further see that, although the requirements imposed by law are generally not that difficult to meet, this approach is usually of limited assistance because it is impossible to obtain a transfer of the promised asset, and those eligible to bring a claim can only claim wages for up to ten years' worth of their work. Any work provided for a period that is longer than that cannot be compensated through the *créance de salaire différé*. Also, a claim for deferred wages can only be brought on death of the farming ascendant, which means that the promisee is likely to have to wait for a considerable period of time and she is not protected against lifetime transfers.

At the same time, the promisee is treated as a secured creditor, which will give her significant protection. What is more, the promisee's motives are entirely irrelevant, and she does not need to prove that her work has enriched the deceased, or that it exceeds a certain threshold, all of which is to her advantage. There is also no risk that the close nature of the relationship with the ascendant, or indeed her gender, will pose any problems (e.g. in terms of proving that there was no donative intent etc).

Before examining the relative provisions and exploring the advantages and disadvantages of this particular approach, it is useful to briefly trace the background and rationale behind the legislation enacted in 1939. While Belgian law has followed the French model by introducing a similar set of provisions,[4] the focus of this chapter is on French law, where there is considerable case law.

[3] Unlike in Germany and in Austria, in France, courts do not seem to have been prepared to imply an employment relationship in order to grant redress where there is a blood relationship between the parties. See Chamoulaud-Trapiers *Les fruits et revenus* (1999) 680, n 2177 citing Cass soc, 10 June 1960, Bull civ V, no 609, 473 and Cass soc, 13 June 1984, Bull civ V, no 246.

[4] See Law 28 December 1967 *relative à l'octroi d'un salaire différé dans l'agriculture et l'horticulture*, art 1 et 4 § 1er, MB, 20 January 1968, 579. For details, see Delnoy & Moreau *Les Libéralités et les succession* (2018) 367–373; Delnoy (1976). In 2003, the Netherlands introduced a provision into their new civil code (Article 4:36 of the BW) that provides children with compensation for the work carried out in the household or the business of their parents. Although this new institution is sometime referred to as *créance à salaire différé*, the provision is more akin to the German § 2057a BGB, and therefore discussed in Chapter 11.

II. Origins and rationale

While the origins of the French *créance de salaire différé* seem to lie in different practices dating back to the *Ancien Droit*, as well as in later case law,[5] the legislative provisions regulating the *créance* were first introduced in 1939. In the beginning, they were part of family law but later were included in the *Code rural et de pêche maritime* (Code for rural matters and maritime fishing) where they are enshrined in Articles L321-13–L321-21-1.

There were two reasons why specific legislation was passed in 1939 to compensate descendants who had worked on a farm. First, the desire to avoid inequality of treatment of descendants,[6] where one (or more) of them had worked gratuitously on their parents' farm, which is then divided among all forced heirs (as they were back then).[7] After all, the work does not just enrich the deceased personally, but rather the patrimony of the entire family, whose close members all take a share. Second, there was a need to prevent descendants of farmers from abandoning the rural areas for larger cities.[8] In other words, there were wider public policy objectives informing this particular legislative intervention,[9] including the sustainability of farming, which is often difficult without the help of the next generation.

For many years, in France, the provisions introduced in 1939 were devoid of practical impact, meaning that they were invoked only in very limited circumstances. The main reason would appear to have been that the reward that the legislature had originally established for descendants was regarded as inadequate. Although the provisions were significantly reformed in 1960,[10] it is only with the changes introduced on 4 July 1980 that the *créance* obtained the success the drafters had always envisaged.[11] This is visible in an increasing number of cases in which descendants claim a deferred salary.[12]

Originally, the 1939 legislation offered protection only to descendants (and their grandchildren) and in some cases the descendant's spouse. Thus, surviving

[5] Not only were there practices in place in the north of France whereby descendants who had worked on a farm were compensated, it would also seem that prior to the 1939 legislation, courts used to grant an enrichment claim to descendants who had worked gratuitously on their parents' farm. For details, see De Bermond de Vaulx (1965); Prévault in *Études dédiées à Alex Weill* (1983) 434.

[6] Monteillet-Geffroy *Les conditions de l'enrichissement* (2001) 105.

[7] French law has moved from a system of forced heirship to a one of compulsory heirship. For details, see Pérès, 'Compulsory Portion in France' in *Comparative Succession Law 3* (2020).

[8] Roussel (2013) para 5.

[9] Similarly, in Belgium, where the legislation was passed almost thirty years later, on 28 December 1967 (n 4), the need was felt to provide for a more equal distribution between descendants who had provided work in farming businesses and those who had not, but also to incentivize the continuation of family businesses, including farms.

[10] Law no 60-808, 5 August 1960, art 10, Journal Officiel 7 August 1960.

[11] Law no 80-502, 4 July 1980, art 38, Journal Officiel 7 July 1980. In Belgium, the 1967 legislation was reformed in 1985 along the lines of the French legislation. Law 12 August 1985 *modifiant la loi du 28 décembre 1967 relative à l'octroi d'un salaire différé dans l'agriculture et l'horticulture*, MB 1 October 1985, 14193.

[12] Savatier (1996) 205, spéc § 1 et 2; Roussel (2010).

spouses of farmers were not covered by the 1939 legislation, nor were other family members, let alone those outside the family circle who may have provided work on the farm. However, fifty years later, in 1999, a comparable action was granted to spouses of the head of a farm, or of a partner in a business (*associé exploitant une société*) the purpose of which is farming,[13] who have participated in the business activity or the cultivation of the farm without remuneration.[14] For this purpose, the 1999 legislation added Article L321-21-1 to the provisions of the *Code rural et de pêche maritime*.

Outside these specific instances, the *créance de salaire différé* cannot be invoked, for as mentioned in Chapter 9,[15] French courts have not been willing to extend the scope of the legislation. Protection must therefore be sought through other means, which in the case of France, will usually be enrichment law, though that is not always possible. Thus, only the work provided by a limited category of people and only in certain contexts is currently remunerated through the provisions on the *créance de salaire différé*.

III. Scope of the legislation

Article L321-13 of the French *Code rural et de pêche maritime* establishes that direct descendants of a farmer (or their descendants), who are over the age of eighteen and who have participated directly and effectively in the cultivation of the farm of their ascendant without taking a share in the profits or losses, or receiving money wages in return for their collaboration, are deemed beneficiaries of an 'employment contract with deferred salary'.

The claim arises only at the moment of the ascendant's death.[16] Thus, descendants have to wait until the death of the farming parent before they can bring the claim, meaning there is no protection during the lifetime of the deceased parent. Compensation will therefore often come late in their lives.

The principal beneficiary of the *créance de salaire différé* is the descendant of an *exploitant agricole*, that is to say a farmer. In the absence of a legislative definition of *exploitant agricole*, French courts have applied the provisions where the activity carried out is agricultural in nature, irrespective of whether or not the farmer is the owner of the farm, or whether farming represents her sole activity. What matters

[13] Law no 99-574, 9 July 1999, art 35, Journal Officiel 10 July 1999 et rect. Journal Officiel 20 October 1999, which introduced Article L321-21-1 of the Code.

[14] In 1989, the French legislature has awarded a similar claim to the spouse (but not the descendant) of the head of an artisanal or commercial enterprise who has participated directly and effectively in the activity of the enterprise for at least ten years, without receiving a salary or participating in benefits and losses of the enterprise. See Law no 89-1008, 31 December 1989, art 14, I, Journal Officiel 2 January 1990.

[15] Chapter 9, section III.A.

[16] The same is true in Belgium. See Article 1, Law 28 December 1967 (n 4).

is that the debtor (the farmer) is an ascendant in direct line of the person bringing the claim.

It can occur that both the son and the grandson of a farmer work on the farm, and, if both fulfil the conditions set out by law, both are entitled to a claim against the farmer's estate. It is also possible that several ascendants cultivate the farm either together[17] or one following the other (e.g. where the father dies, and the farm is then run by the surviving mother). In either case, the descendant has only one claim.[18] In other words, she cannot, for instance, demand the payment both on the father's and then on the mother's death. However, unless she has worked only for one of them, the descendant may demand all or part of her deferred salary on death of the first ascendant. Alternatively, she may prefer to defer settlement to the moment of the death of the surviving ascendant, for the whole or the balance that is due. Thus, while the descendant has only one claim, she gets a choice as to which estate to bring the claim against. In addition, we will see that the legislation also offers protection, albeit a very limited one, to both the descendant's spouse and the surviving spouse of the farmer. This chapter focuses primarily on the protection that the general regime introduced in 1939 provides for descendants with a brief treatment of the protection provided to the descendant's spouse and to the farmer's surviving spouse.

IV. Requirements for a descendant's claim to arise

There are three requirements that a descendant in the direct line must meet for a claim to arise against the estate of the ascendant/s:[19] (i) she must be over the age of eighteen when working on the farm; (ii) she must have directly and effectively participated in the cultivation of the farm or agricultural business; and (iii) she must not have taken a share in the benefits or participated in the losses, nor have received a monetary salary in exchange for her collaboration. The analysis will show that the second and third requirements can pose some difficulties. Nonetheless, the threshold descendants must meet is not particularly high, especially because their

[17] Cass 1re civ, 7 November 1995, Bull civ I, no 399; Defrénois 1996, art 36278, no 40, 416, obs G Champenois; Defrénois 1996, art 36396, no 1, 1145, obs F Roussel; Defrénois 1996, art 36400, 1209, note X Savatier; RTD civ 1998, 961, obs J Patarin; JCP 1998, éd N, 722, note D-G Brelet.

[18] Cass 1re civ, 28 January 1997, 130, obs J-M Gilardeau, C Pitaud and D Rochard; Dr famille 1997, comm 112, obs B Beignier; Defrénois 1997, art 36640, no 131, 1094, obs G Champenois; JCP G 1997, I, 4021, no 4, obs R Le Guidec; JCP G 1997, II, 22913, note F Roussel; RTD civ 1998, 961, no 2, obs J Patarin. See also Cass 1re civ, 23 January 2008, no 06-21301; Bull civ I, no 29; RD rur 2008, comm 30, note F Roussel; Rev Lamy droit civil 2008, no 2925, 53, obs J-R Binet; JCP N 2008, no 30–35, 1262, note F Roussel.

[19] The Belgian legislation protects both descendants and the spouse of the *exploitant* as well as the descendant's spouse. It requires that the claimant is eighteen years old and has assisted the deceased for at least five years, which is not a requirement in France, providing a normal activity that was not remunerated. See Article 1 Law 28 December 1967 (n 4).

motives are irrelevant, and they do not need to prove that they were induced to work on the farm or that their work has enriched the deceased.

A. The descendant must be of full age

As for the first requirement, in order to be able to benefit from the provisions regulating the *créance*, it is necessary that the descendant in the direct line is at least eighteen years old when working on the farm. It follows that any work carried out on the farm before she has reached that age will not be taken into consideration when calculating the debt, even if it was valuable and substantive. This is in contrast with some of the family provision legislation cases that I have examined in Chapter 5, where adult children have been able to obtain a court order on the basis of work they carried out on their parents' farm while they were minors.[20]

Should the descendant, who has reached the age of eighteen and has worked on the farm, predecease the ascendant, her right to claim the outstanding wages passes to her own children.[21] In other words, where the descendant dies before being able to present a claim to the deferred wages, or in all those cases in which the claim was not yet granted or liquidated at the time of the death of the descendant, they are not lost but can be claimed by the children of the descendant entitled to the claim,[22] with the exclusion of all the other heirs, and irrespective of the order of death. For this purpose, it is entirely irrelevant whether or not the children have themselves worked on the farm.[23] This suggests that the descendant's right to the wages arises already during the lifetime of the farmer, even if the claim can only be brought on the ascendant's death—a point I shall return to later.[24]

B. Direct and effective participation

Not only must the descendant have been of full age when providing work on the farm, it is further required that she directly and effectively participated in the cultivation of the farm, though it is not necessary that she has performed up until the death of the ascendant. Put differently, the focus is on the performance that the

[20] See Chapter 5.

[21] Article L321-14 *Code rural et de pêche maritime*. In Belgium, it also passes to the surviving spouse. See Article 4, Law 28 December 1967 (n 4).

[22] Cass 1re civ, 28 May 1968, Bull civ I, no 156; D 1968, 542, note A Breton; JCP G 1968, II, 15652, note M D; RTD civ 1968, 743, obs R Savatier. See also, CA Limoges, 22 December 1965, D 1966, somm 62 and Cass 1re civ, 15 May 2008, Bull civ I, no 133; RD rur 2008, comm 199, note R Le Guidec; JCP N 2009, 1102, note F Roussel; RTD civ 2009, 151, no 2, obs M Grimaldi.

[23] Cass 1re civ, 19 November 2002, no 00-15923: JurisData no 2002-016415; Bull civ I, no 281; JCP N 2003, 1341, obs B Grimonprez; RD rur 2004, 623, obs H Bosse-Platière and R Le Guidec.

[24] See section IX.

descendant provides and there is no need for a promise. But what does it mean to 'participate' directly and effectively in the cultivation of a farm? It appears that French courts have adopted a broad notion of 'participation', to include all types of activities of an agricultural nature. Such a wide interpretation would seem to be justified by the fact that, due to the principle of subsidiarity, a descendant who qualifies for a claim under the 1939 legislation is barred from bringing an enrichment claim.[25] Also, unlike with an enrichment claim, here the descendant can only claim wages for up to ten years' worth of work, which is perhaps why courts can be more liberal when interpreting the requirements. That said, the notion of 'participation' is not so broad so as to include, for instance, domestic work carried out on a farm, which is a serious limitation of the provision, for it is unclear whether an enrichment claim can be brought in such cases, leaving the descendant potentially without any protection.

In order to be 'direct', the participation has to be carried out personally by the descendant and not by her spouse or her own children. In addition, the work of the descendant must also be effective. What is clear is that 'effective' does not mean that the value of the farm must have been improved, or its value increased, as per § 2057a BGB, which, as we will see in Chapter 11, fulfils a similar function to the *créance*. In other words, no relevance seems to be placed on the question of whether the work has enriched the value of the farm, which in many ways is beneficial from the point of view of a beneficiary. In fact, in previous chapters we saw that proving an enrichment (especially of someone in a close relationship) can sometimes be difficult, including from a psychological point of view.[26] Nonetheless, the interpretation of the term 'effective' has posed difficulties and given rise to litigation. On several occasions, the French *Cour de cassation* has established that occasional or seasonal contributions to the farm are insufficient.[27] In other words, the activity has to be carried out 'habitually', though not necessarily daily.[28] At the same time, the descendant's participation does not have to be exclusive of any other activity,[29] on condition that the work on the farm is not merely occasional.

In the past, no compensation was granted where, for instance, the claimant had worked full-time both as a chauffeur and an insurance agent while also helping on the farm.[30] A claim was further excluded where the descendant had helped on the

[25] Le Guidec & Bosse Platière (2010) 5.

[26] See the discussion in Chapters 6 and 9.

[27] See Cass 1re civ, 3 March 1970 no 68-14077, Bull civ I, no 77; D 1970, 301, note A Breton (hereafter Cass 1re civ, 3 March 1970). More recently, see Cass 1re civ, 20 June 2012, no 11-20217; D 2012, 2055, obs B Vassalo and Cass 1re civ, 6 November 2013, no 12-25239, note Roussel (2014).

[28] Cass 1re civ, 10 June 1980, Bull civ I, no 180 in which case the court found that some gardening activity carried out during leisure time was not sufficient to support the claim. See also Cass 1re civ, 22 October 2002, no 00-22458, Bull civ I, no 241, JCP G 2003, I, 180, no 3, obs R Le Guidec dealing with household tasks.

[29] Cass 1re civ, 3 March 1970 (n 27).

[30] Cass 1re civ, 10 June 1980, JCP G 1980, IV, 325.

farm while working full-time in a factory.[31] However, in 2009, the *Cour de cassation* held that, in order for a daughter of the deceased to bring a successful claim, her work on the farm did not have to be carried out full-time.[32] The part-time work on the farm entitled her to compensation. Thus, in this sense, the meaning of 'effective' has changed and the requirement has been relaxed over time.

While it is entirely appropriate that a descendant who works part-time rather than full-time on the farm should be compensated, this has created problems in terms of calculating the award, as the assumption of the drafters of the legislation seems to have been that the descendant always works full-time. This is reflected in the way in which the debt is to be calculated. As will be seen later, the calculation of the debt is established by law without any reference to the quality and, importantly, the duration and intensity of the work. Even so, in a decision of 24 September 2014,[33] the *Cour de cassation* not only confirmed the position taken in the 2009 decision but also approved the Court of Appeal's judgment that had quantified the amount awarded to the descendant at 50% of the legal cap (*plafond legal*).[34] Thus, where the work is part-time rather than full-time, the calculation will be adjusted.

From the perspective of the descendant, being able to bring a claim based on part-time work is of course highly desirable. However, the 2009 decision could potentially make it more difficult for a descendant to prove her case, as she may now have to prove not only that her work was performed effectively, that is more than occasionally, but also the proportion of time actually spent on the farm. Thus, the relaxation of the requirement from full-time to part-time work could potentially lead to potential difficulties in practice.

C. Lack of participation in the profits or losses of the farm or payment of wages

As to the third requirement, the descendant must have carried out the work on the farm without receiving adequate remuneration. This matches, as we saw, the requirement under the New Zealand Law Reform (Testamentary Promises) Act 1949 (hereafter New Zealand TPA 1949), and § 612 BGB.[35] It is also important that the descendant did not take a share in the profits or participate in the losses of the farm.

[31] CA Bordeaux, 1re ch, 14 December 1991, JCP G 1993, IV, no 192, 23. The claim was rejected in CA Agen, 28 October 1998, JCP N 1999, 1054, obs Pitaud; RD ru 1999, 253.

[32] Cass 1re civ, 8 July 2009, no 08-13972; Bull civ I, no 169; Bull Inf C cass 1er févr. 2010, no 146, 56. For an analysis, see Le Guidec & Bosse Platière (2010) 4. The *Cour de cassation* has taken a similar decision in Cass 3e civ, 30 October 2006, no 04-20694. In this case the award was calculated on the basis of half of the annual rate.

[33] Cass 1re civ, 24 September 2014, 13-11082 and 13-16777.

[34] For more details, see section V.

[35] See Chapters 7 and 8. It is further a requirement for the application of § 2057a BGB and §§ 677ff ABGB discussed in Chapter 11.

In other words, the descendant cannot have been a partner in the farming business. This does not mean that the provisions do not find application where some remuneration was paid, so long as it was inferior to the amount foreseen by the legislature.[36] In other words, the descendant can claim the difference. What is more, because the relief as established by law is regarded as a minimum that should be awarded to the descendant, the claim is not barred by additional benefits inherent to a life on a farm, such as food or rent-free lodging, though, as we will see, such benefits are accounted for already by how the wages are calculated.

Importantly, the provisions do not exclude that descendants who fall within the scope of the 1939 legislation inherit from their ascendants or benefit from certain lifetime gifts, which seems right unless such gifts were intended to compensate the descendant for the work carried out on the farm. This was established in a case in 1989 in which the *Cour de cassation* held that the fact that a descendant had received bare ownership of a property by way of a lifetime gift did not bar the court from recognizing a *créance* in his favour.[37] The court felt that, because the bare ownership did not confer on the son the enjoyment of the fruits or income of the donated property, the donation did not have the purpose nor the effect of compensating him and his wife for their work on the farm. In this sense, a claim based on the 1939 legislation is probably more advantageous than, for instance, a claim based on the *actio de in rem verso* discussed in Chapter 9.

However, proving the third requirement is not entirely without its problems. In fact, in July 2013, Senator François Marc submitted a query to the French Ministry of Justice enquiring whether the government envisages to reform the conditions that the claimant must meet in order to bring a successful claim.[38] In doing so, emphasis was placed on the fact that, in practice, some claimants are facing technical difficulties in showing that they were not profiting in any way from the farming activity, for they must establish not only the absence of payment of wages but also of benefits in kind that are comparable to remuneration. However, the governmental response was to leave matters as they are, on the basis that proof can be provided by any means (including the production of bank statements or the production of the various administrative, social, tax, and accounting declarations that farmers must make).[39] Rather unhelpfully, the governmental response also pointed to the fact that problems could be avoided if the ascendant simply made a *donation-partage* (a lifetime gift made in view of the future succession).[40] This suggestion

[36] Cass 1re civ, 16 July 1985, Bull civ I, no 225; Defrénois 1985, 1479, obs Champenois; RD rur 1987, 486, obs R Le Guidec.

[37] Cass 1re civ, 18 October 1989, no 88-10238: JCP N 1990, Prat 1643, no 5, comment by P Catala.

[38] Published in *Journal Officiel de la République Française* of 18 July 2013, 2096.

[39] Published in *Journal Officiel de la République Française* of 20 March 2014, 784.

[40] This is referred to in Article L321-17 of the *Code rural et de pêche maritime*. Article L321-19 establishes that 'In order to facilitate the administration of this proof, the parties may each year make a declaration at the town hall, which must be stamped by the mayor who will issue a receipt'. But again, this depends very much on the ascendant's willingness to collaborate.

seems to overlook that, in practice, people do not usually want to part with their assets during their lifetime, even if they can retain an interest in them.[41] Also, they generally do not want to formalize such arrangements. Even so, on the whole and compared with other forms of redress, the threshold that a descendant must meet here does not seem to be very high. But of course, that is not all that matters, which brings me to the next point.

V. Quantification of the relief

How is the award that a descendant can claim by way of deferred wages quantified? Here we see a marked difference with most, if not all, other forms of redress analysed in this book, for the French legislature establishes exactly how it is to be calculated leaving no discretion to the courts and imposing an artificial limit of ten years. It fixes an annual rate of pay calculated on the assumption that work is carried out full-time.

When the *créance* was reformed in 1980, the French legislature established that the annual rate of pay is equal to, for each year of participation (starting from the age of eighteen), the value of two-thirds of the amount corresponding to 2080 times the hourly rate of the minimum wage growth (SMIC = *taux du salaire minimum interprofessionnel de croissance*),[42] in force either on the day of the division following the date of the death or no later than the date of settlement of the claim, where the settlement takes place during the lifetime of the farmer, that is through a *donation-partage* mentioned earlier.[43]

The reason why the descendant is only to be paid two-thirds of the maximum established by law is to make allowance for the fact that normally, the descendant would have benefited from free accommodation and food, though of course that is not necessarily always the case, for example, where the work is part-time and the child lives elsewhere. As mentioned earlier, if the claimant has worked only part-time for the ascendant, she can only benefit from partial wages, proportionate to the time that was effectively spent on the farm.[44]

Whether the descendant has worked part-time or full-time, the amount she can claim is capped at the value of the estate so that in the event that the deferred debt exceeds the value of the estate, the other successors do not have to pay for the debt from their own pocket.[45] From the perspective of the claimant, this is obviously

[41] See the discussion in Chapter 1.

[42] Thus, per year: (*SMIC horaire* × 2080) x 2/3.

[43] Article L321-13(2) *Code rural et de pêche maritime* as reformed by the law of 1980.

[44] In 2014, the *Cour de cassation* decided to award an amount calculated at 50% of the *plafond legale*. See n 33.

[45] Roussel (2013). The same applies to the surviving spouse who has lived in a patrimonial regime of community of assets.

unsatisfactory, not least because the successors are likely to have benefited from her work.

This calculation applies irrespective of the quality or intensity of the work carried out, so long as it was direct and effective. As we saw, 'effective' does not mean that it has to have enriched the ascendant's farming business. This is to the clear advantage of the descendant who does not have to prove that her work has enriched the estate or that she was impoverished. At the same time, if her work has brought about an enrichment that exceeds the wages that she may obtain, she cannot bring an enrichment claim and has no other way of claiming the difference.

While periods of work inferior to a year can be indemnified,[46] a significant limitation of this particular form of redress is that the maximum a descendant can obtain is ten years' worth of wages.[47] Thus, even though a descendant may have rendered services for more than ten years, she will not be able to obtain payment for a longer period of time. This limit is considered absolute, and courts have no power to make any adjustments, which is problematic in those cases where the descendant has spent all her life on the farm and built her life around it. Exactly why this limit is imposed is unclear. If one of the objectives of the provisions was to obtain equality of treatment of descendants, then it would have been important not to impose a limit on the amount that can be claimed. But perhaps the reason is that otherwise farming may simply not be viable, especially since more than one direct descendant can claim deferred wages against the estate. One must also remember that the provisions were not intended to deal with instances in which a person provides work on the farm in exchange for a promise of the transfer of the farm. In fact, in many ways it seems to be geared towards work carried out by descendants in their youth.

VI. Time limit

The provisions in the *Code rural et de pêche maritime* do not mention a time limit, but it has been suggested that the applicable time limit is the one established by the *droit commun*, which is five years, and runs from the moment of the opening of the succession of the farmer.[48] In any case, the descendant must bring her claim prior to the moment at which the division of the estate has become final,[49] for any later requests cannot be admitted.[50]

[46] Cass 1re civ, 6 April 1994, no 92-11800; Bull civ I, no 148; RTD civ 1994, 917, no 3, obs J Patarin; Defrénois 1995, art 36109, no 92, 826, obs G Champenois; RD rur 1996, 178, obs R Le Guidec.

[47] The same is true in Belgium. However, Article 2 Law 28 December 1967 (n 4) also states that the deferred wage is fixed at half the gross wage of a skilled agricultural worker, taking as a basis the highest wage in force during the actual period of work for which the deferred wage can be claimed. Thus, the basis of the calculation is different in the two jurisdictions.

[48] Le Guidec & Bosse Platière (2010) 12.

[49] Cass 1re civ, 10 October 1995, Bull civ I, no 358.

[50] Cass 1re civ, 14 June 2000, no 98-18303; RD rur 2001, 50.

Problems sometimes arise in practice when both ascendants are farmers, and one of them has predeceased the other. It would seem that in such a case the fact that the action against the first to die is statute barred does not affect the action against the surviving ascendant, so long as the descendant had an action against both, that is so long as she has worked for both of them.[51] This is possible, for instance, where one dies and the other continues the farming business.

Having examined the requirements for a descendant to succeed, as well as the details as to the quantification of the relief, I will briefly outline when the descendant's spouse can bring a claim and what the position of the surviving spouse of the farmer is.

VII. Instances in which the spouse of the descendant can bring a claim

There are two sets of circumstances in which the spouse of a descendant of a farmer may have a claim against the estate of the farmer. Article L321-15 of the *Code rural et de pêche maritime* establishes that if the descendant is married and her spouse also works on the farm, at the same time and in the same manner as the descendant (thus under the same conditions established by Article L321-13 set out earlier), each spouse shall be deemed to be a beneficiary of a contract of employment with deferred salary. Thus, in this case, the spouse, albeit not being a descendant of the farmer, is entitled to bring her own claim against the farmer's estate. However, this is only possible where both have worked on the farm. Where, for instance, a daughter-in-law has worked on the farm of her parents-in-law but her husband has not, she will not be able to present a claim under the 1939 legislation. In Chapter 9 we saw that where such a scenario has arisen, the *Cour de cassation* was prepared to grant an enrichment claim instead.[52]

In 2019, the *Cour the cassation* specified that for the debt to arise it is further necessary that the spouses have participated in the farming at the same time,[53] meaning that a claim is precluded if they contribute at different times. This interpretation was based on the fact that Article L321-15 mentions that the spouse has to 'also participate' (*participe également*) and that the entitlement of the descendant's spouse is derivative in the sense that it is an extension of the descendant's

[51] Cass 1re civ, 17 October 2018, no 17-26725. In this case the son had worked for the father, who had died in 1976, but had only brought the claim when his mother died, over thirty years later. The son had not worked for the mother and his claim was therefore judged to be statute-barred.

[52] Cass 1re civ, 14 March 1995, JCP G 1995, II, 22516, note F Roussel; JCP N 1995, II, 1433, note Moreau; RTD civ 1996, 160, note J Mestre; RTD civ 1996, 215, note J Patarin; D 1996, jurispr 137, note Barabé-Bouchard; Defrénois 1996, 468, note J-L Fillette. For details, see Chapter 9, section III.C.

[53] Cass 1re civ, 29 May 2019, no 18-18376.

entitlement. However, this limitation exposes the descendant's spouse to the risk of exploitation where the couple does not provide work at the same time.

Moreover, in case of divorce or separation attributed to the exclusive fault of the spouse who is not the descendant of the farmer, she will automatically lose her right to bring a claim even though she has performed work on the farm. This is again unsatisfactory and reflects a desire to keep wealth within the blood family. It follows, that on the basis of Article L321-15 a claim for deferred wages can only be brought by the descendant's spouse where both spouses have worked on the farm, at the same time, and there was no decree declaring the divorce or attributing the separation to the responsibility of the spouse of the farmer's descendant.

By contrast, Article L321-16 of the *Code rural et de pêche maritime* deals with the instance in which a married descendant predeceases the ascendant farmer leaving behind a spouse and one or more children who are below the age of eighteen. In such a case, the surviving spouse can claim deferred wages but only if she participated in the cultivation of the farm on the same conditions as set out by Article L321-13, meaning directly and effectively and without remuneration. While the provision does not specify whether the surviving spouse must have started work on the farm prior to the descendant's death, there is nothing in the article to suggest that she does, so that it would seem that she can start work after the descendant's (that is her partner's) death.[54] The amount she can claim concerns, however, only the period between the death of her spouse and the moment when the youngest surviving child reaches the age of eighteen or completes her agricultural studies,[55] and in any case for no longer than ten years. This is yet another limitation that seems difficult to justify. If the point is to compensate the descendant's spouse for her work, then it should not matter how old her children are. However, the provision seems to pursue other policy objectives, such as ensuring the maintenance of the children of the (already deceased) descendant, and keeping wealth within the family.

VIII. Protection of the surviving spouse of the farmer

The protection that the legislation affords to the surviving spouse of the farmer is less strong that that enjoyed by the descendant. Unlike a descendant, a spouse can only bring a claim if she has worked on the farm for at least ten years without having received a salary or being associated with the profits and losses of the farm.[56] What is more, unlike the descendant she benefits from a right to claim an amount equal to three times the minimum annual growth wage in force on the day of death, but

[54] Roussel (2013) para 59.
[55] This was judged by some as being discriminatory. See Patarin (1996).
[56] See Article L321-21-1 *Code rural et de pêche maritime*. For a discussion, see Rochard (1999).

only up to a limit of 25% of the estate assets. In other words, she gets potentially less by way of compensation. Moreover, the potential rights the spouse has in the distribution of the estate and the liquidation of the patrimonial regime are diminished by her credit.[57]

IX. Nature and source of the *créance de salaire différé*

It is somewhat unclear exactly when the statutory claim to deferred wages arises. Article L321-17 merely establishes that the beneficiary of the implied contract exercises her right *after* the ascendant's death. It is from the time of the ascendant's death that the five-year limitation period runs, though the claim must be brought prior to the moment at which the division of the estate has become final. In the past, French courts have explicitly stated that the claim arises only on the ascendant's death, at which point the payment becomes due.[58] Thus, claims of deferred wages by the descendant during the lifetime of the ascendant are precluded.[59] And, because of the subsidiary nature of the *actio de in rem verso*, the descendant cannot obtain immediate (i.e. earlier) payment by arguing, for instance, that the ascendant has been enriched at their expense, unless, of course, the 1939 legislation does not apply.

However, in 2012, the *Cour the cassation* changed its position by reaching the conclusion that, although the claim only becomes due (and thus actionable) on death of the ascendant farmer, it arises already during lifetime.[60] Thus, a distinction was introduced between the moment at which the credit arises and the moment at which it is actionable. This explains why, as noted earlier, the descendant's claim can pass to her descendants, should she predecease the ascendant.[61] The fact that the claim arises already during lifetime would further explain why the ascendant

[57] For more detail, see Roussel (2013) para 3.

[58] Cass 1re civ, 19 February 1985, Bull civ I, no 70, Defrénois 1985, 1164, obs G Champenois, RTD civ, 1986, 162, obs J Patarin; Cass 1re civ, 7 November 1995, Bull civ I, no 399; Defrénois 1996, art 36278, no 40, 416, obs G Champenois; Defrénois 1996, art 36396, no 1, 1145, obs F Roussel; Defrénois 1996, art 36400, 1209, note X Savatier; RTD civ 1998, 961, obs J Patarin; JCP 1N 998, 722, note D-G Brelet; Cass 1re civ, 13 April 1999, JCP N 1999, 1289, note G Rivière; D 2000, jur 527, note H Péroz; Dr et patrimoine 2001, no 92, chron no 2820, 107, note F Roussel; Cass 1e civ, 20 November 2001, JCP 2002, éd G, I, 178, obs R Le Guidec; JCP N 2002, 1187, note B Grimonprez.

[59] Cass 1re civ, 16 July 1997, Bull civ I, no 254; RD rur 1998, 208, no 4, obs F Roussel; Defrénois 1998, art 36765, no 45, 412, obs G Champenois; RTD civ 1998, 961, no 2, obs J Patarin; Cass 1re civ, 30 October 2006, Bull civ I, no 455; RD rur 2007, comm 62, note M-O Gain; JCP N 2007, 1232, note F Roussel.

[60] Cass 1re civ, 18 January 2012, Bull civ I, no 10, D 2012, 851 avis O Falletti and 854, note F Roussel; JCP N 2012, no 8, 1118, note R Le Guidec and H Bosse-Platière; RTD civ 2012, 350, no 1, obs M Grimaldi; AJ Famille 2012, 153, obs P Hilt; Gaz Pal 16-17 mars 2012, 51, note J Casey; RLDC 2012, 4598, obs A Paulin; RDC 2012, 843, obs R Libchaber; D 2012, 2477, no 2, obs J Revel; Defrénois 2012, art 111C5, 1201, obs G Champenois.

[61] Cass 1re civ, 15 May 2008, nos 07-13179 and 07-13330, Bull civ I, no 133. Grimaldi (2009) therefore calls it an 'anomalous succession'.

debtor can decide to extinguish her debt already during her lifetime through a *donation-partage*[62] in the form of a cash payment or a transfer of a piece of property, such as a parcel of land, buildings, life or dead stock, partnership units, agricultural funds, and so on. If the ascendant decides to compensate the descendant during her lifetime, both parties must agree that the transaction represents a payment of the due wages and that it extinguishes the debt. Otherwise, the descendant can obtain the deferred wages while also retaining the lifetime gift. However, if they agree, but the descendant nonetheless brings a claim on the death of the farmer, she needs to prove that any payments or transfers made during lifetime are inferior to the value of the deferred debt.[63]

Since the descendant's entitlement becomes actionable only on the death of the ascendant farmer, the *créance* is often described as having a *nature successoral*. It is disputed whether the right is a credit against the estate 'contre la succession' or a 'droit dans la succession', that is a right to inherit. Since the claimant does not have to accept the inheritance in order to bring a claim (in fact she does not need to be an heir in order to be able to bring a claim), the deferred wages are usually seen as a credit against (*contre*) the succession, that is the estate.[64] This is preferable for it means that the descendant ranks as a creditor and does not take under the farmer's succession (as opposed to an heir or legatee),[65] thereby affording the descendant greater protection.

The wages form part of the *passif successoral* and are thus subtracted from the *activ succcesoral* prior to the distribution of the estate to the heirs. Not only is the descendant a creditor, she is a secured creditor because the legislation explicitly establishes that the credit is (automatically) secured through a *privilège général* (general liens) over movables (Code civil, Article 2331, 4°), a *privilège général* over immovables (Code civil, Article 2375, 2°), and a *hypothèque légale* (legal mortgages) over immovables.[66] This puts the descendant in a strong position not just vis-à-vis successors but also other creditors of the estate. If more than one descendant brings a claim against the ascendant and the estate is insufficient (which may well be the case if more than one child has worked on the farm), the claims will be reduced proportionally. It follows that the *créance* is not treated in the same manner as other debts of the deceased, but still better than if the claimant were to bring an *actio de in rem verso*.

Just as the nature of the descendant's right is debated, so is the nature of the *créance* itself. In particular it is unclear what the source of the debt is. Although the

[62] Roussel (2013) para 89.
[63] Cass 1re civ, 14 April 2010, no 09-12209; RD rur 2010, comm 89, note F Roussel.
[64] In this sense, Terré et al *Droit civil* (2014) 1011.
[65] See Grimaldi (2009).
[66] Article L321-21 *Code rural et de pêche maritime*. The legal mortgage must be registered in the land register, and shall rank from the date of the registration. However, it is not possible to register the mortgage during the life of the farming ascendant. Castella (2010).

specific subsection in the *Code rural et de pêche maritime* dealing with the participation in the farm is entitled '*le contrat de travail à salaire différé*' (the employment contract with deferred salary), and Article L321-13 explicitly speaks of a contract, so that one may be inclined to see a parallel with the German § 612 BGB,[67] it is generally doubted whether it is really possible to talk of a genuine contract in this case. Some authors have, for instance, argued that there cannot be a contract, given that the existence of a contract between the parties would automatically prevent the application of the provisions.[68] Also, Article L321-20 specifies that general rules concerning employment contracts do *not* apply to the *créance*. It has further been excluded that the relationship can be qualified as a partnership (*société*), for the provisions explicitly require that the descendant has *not* participated in the benefits and losses of the farming business.[69] Hence, several scholars have suggested that the source of the farmer's debt (and thus of the descendant's credit) is non-contractual.

Equally discounted is the possibility of linking the *créance* to the law of quasi-contracts.[70] Although some authors take the view that its rationale is similar to that underpinning enrichment law, and that its initial objective was to counter the tendency of courts which facilitated the recourse to the *actio de in rem verso* in similar cases,[71] there is no need to prove an enrichment. In fact, as has been mentioned, the quality and the value of the work do not matter so that the source of the obligation does not seem to be the ascendant's enrichment.

Instead, while some authors have suggested to qualify the *créance* as a charge against the estate, the majority view seems to qualify it as a statutory right to claim a credit against the ascendant's estate.[72]

X. Conclusion

As noted earlier, the 1939 legislation was not intended to address testamentary promises cases. Indeed, no evidence of a promise or reliance is required, and, as the discussion showed, French law regards such promises as entirely without legal effect,[73] due to the prohibition of succession pacts. Nonetheless, the 1939 legislation may come to the aid of a person who has acted upon an informal promise of a

[67] See Chapter 8.
[68] Malaurie *Les Successions* (2010) 481.
[69] Roussel (2013) para 9.
[70] Malaurie *Les Successions* (2010) 481.
[71] Roussel (2013) para 9. This is interesting because, in Germany, the use of the *condictio ob rem* was counterbalanced by resorting to § 612 BGB. See Chapters 8 and 9.
[72] More recently it has been defined as a *dette à terme* that is a debt with an uncertain suspensive term that arises during the lifetime of the ascendant but becomes due only at the moment of the death of the ascendant. See Roussel (2012) spéc no 8, 856 in a note to Cass 1re civ, 18 January 2012, no 10-24892; Grimaldi (2012); Terré et al *Droit civil* (2014) 1010.
[73] See Chapter 2.

bequest and who, unlike in other jurisdictions examined in this book, is left with relatively little protection in France. This is especially so given that an enrichment claim is available only in very limited circumstances and only if there is no other avenue available to the promisee. But does this particular form of redress address the specificities of the testamentary context in a satisfactory way? In many ways it does.

From the perspective of a promisee of a testamentary promise, bringing a claim under the 1939 legislation has indeed certain advantages, in that there is no need for her to prove a promise, let alone in writing, and there is no need to prove reliance. Another advantage is that it does not matter whether the performance started before or after the promise. There is also no risk that the motives informing her behaviour, or the close nature of her relationship with the ascendant, or indeed her gender, pose any problems (e.g. in terms of proving that there was no donative intent etc). What is more, the promisee does not need to show an enrichment or corresponding impoverishment with all the practical and psychological difficulties that that can entail. Her performance does not have to have been valuable, nor does it need to have enriched the ascendant.

What the claimant needs to show is that she has participated directly and effectively in the cultivation of the farm or in the agricultural business, without having received either a salary or a share in the benefits of the farm. While the first two requirements seem to be straightforward, except perhaps where the descendant had a full-time job elsewhere,[74] the third requirement can sometimes cause practical difficulties. According to Article L321-19, proof of the work can be given by any means. Where annual declarations certified by the mayor have been made, a claim will be straightforward, though problems may arise where the ascendant is not willing to make such declarations or where the descendant has received some benefits that could potentially be qualified as remuneration.

What is beneficial from the descendant's point of view is that the credit can be cumulated with what the person receives by way of compulsory heirship and lifetime gifts, and that mutual benefits in the form of lodging and food are not counted against the amount paid, though they are already taken into consideration in the calculation. Moreover, the payment is exempt from income tax,[75] and the amount is secured against other creditors of the estate.

Arguably, the fact that the law establishes how the award is to be calculated provides certainty, which claimants do not have where courts are given discretion (e.g. we saw potential difficulties with an estoppel claim but also claims under the New Zealand legislation).[76] But, of course, certainty also means that there is no flexibility. For instance, irrespective of how substantial or valuable the work has been,

[74] See section IV.B.
[75] On tax, see Roussel (2013) paras 110ff.
[76] See Chapters 4 and 7.

the payment will be the same. The compensation is completely unconnected to the quality and intensity of the work carried out and from the expectation or promised asset. Also, potentially the wages may be inferior to the value of the enrichment of the ascendant, but the descendant is prevented from bringing an enrichment claim. However, one of the biggest limitations is that the descendant (or her spouse or the farmer's surviving spouse) can only ever claim the salary for a period of up to ten years, even if her services were rendered for a longer period of time. Thus, if by acting on a promise a promisee has worked all her life on the farm, the value of what she will be able to claim will normally be below the value of the promised asset or the value of her performance. Another disadvantage is that the descendant cannot bring a lifetime claim and she can only obtain payment for work carried out after she has turned eighteen. Finally, the value of the estate represents the upper limit. Thus, potentially she is in a worse position than someone not caught by the special legislation who can bring an enrichment claim.

Another significant limitation of this approach is its limited scope. It is specific to the agricultural world, and to farm work, and only benefits certain family members. Among these, descendants are protected best. They are certainly better off than the farmer's spouse, who must have performed work for at least ten years in order to benefit from deferred wages, and there is a further cap on what she can claim. Daughters- and sons-in-law who work on the farm have very limited protection, and the legislation does not even apply to farm workers, other types of relatives, friends, and neighbours who work for little or no pay. They will not be able to bring a claim under the current legislation and the French Government appears to have no intention of extending its scope.[77] That said, as mentioned in Chapter 9, in some instances French courts have filled the gap by applying enrichment law, though this happens only in a very specific fashion.[78] Finally, even though the term 'participation' is interpreted in a broad manner, it excludes domestic work on a farm. Again, the *Cour de cassation* has refused to extend the scope of the regime so as to apply it, for instance, to domestic work carried out by the daughter of a farmer,[79] or to work carried out by a female caregiver.[80] Thus, while the *créance* may well come to the aid of promisees, and in many ways fits the testamentary context, it also has its limitations.

Interestingly, the French (and Belgian) legislation bears some resemblance to German cases applying § 612 BGB, which I discussed in Chapter 8,[81] even though in France, the courts do not technically speaking imply a service contract. What

[77] See text at n 39.
[78] See Chapter 9, section III.
[79] Cass 1re civ, 19 March 1975, Bull Civ I, no 177; Cass 1er civ, 22 October 2002 (n 28).
[80] Cass 1re civ, 7 October 1981, RD rural 1982, 113.
[81] See Chapter 8.

they have in common is that in both cases the claimant obtains wages, but in this case the wages are limited to ten years and the descendant does not receive payment for leave. Both approaches involve a certain level of fiction, except that in the case of the *créance à salaire différé*, the claim only ever arises on death, so that there is no need to imply an agreement that payment of the wages is deferred until then.

11
Establishing a claim on the basis of § 2057a BGB and §§ 677ff ABGB

I. Introduction

In this final chapter I will examine two further modes of redress that can come to the aid of a promisee. One is drawn from German law (§ 2057a BGB), and the other from Austrian law (§§ 677ff ABGB). Even though neither of these legislative solutions was developed to specifically address cases of unfulfilled informal testamentary promises, and thus no mention is made of promises, a promisee may nonetheless rely on them to obtain redress. While their scope of application is relatively narrow, and the protection offered on the whole limited, both legislative interventions are interesting. They represent attempts to acknowledge the importance of work and services provided by certain family members, and thus contributions to the estate, including in the form of domestic and care services that would otherwise remain unremunerated. In that sense they are similar to the *créance de salaire différé*, examined in Chapter 10, though the *créance* applies only in the agricultural context.

On the basis of § 2057a BGB, during the partitioning of the estate, an intestate descendant can claim an adjustment of her share for work, services, and contributions provided to the deceased. By contrast, §§ 677ff ABGB allow certain family members who have cared for the deceased during the last years prior to her death to claim a statutory care legacy. The analysis will show that just like the *créance de salaire différé*, §§ 677ff ABGB impose an artificial limit on the amount that can be claimed, in this case for care services provided for up to three years. By contrast, under § 2057a BGB courts have considerable discretion in establishing the amount of the adjustment of the descendant's intestate share. However, the scope of the provision is so narrow that it is hardly invoked in practice. Just like the *créance de salaire différé*, both provisions offer protection only after the promisor's death. However, unlike for the *créance de salaire différé*, for both forms of redress the fact that the promisee's performance enriches the estate plays a role. In the case of § 2057a BGB, another objective is to ensure that distribution among intestate heirs is as equal as possible.

Even though their scope and requirements, as well as the way in which the award is calculated, are different, I will examine them together in this chapter because they are functionally comparable. Also, the Austrian provisions of §§ 677ff ABGB

Claiming a Promised Inheritance. Alexandra Braun, Oxford University Press. © Alexandra Braun 2022.
DOI: 10.1093/oso/9780198757252.003.0012

were somewhat inspired by the German § 2057a BGB and, as we will see, they offer an approach that is along the lines of some of the reform proposals that were discussed in German legal scholarship, but that were never implemented in Germany.

II. Compensating the promisee on the basis of § 2057a BGB

A. Scope and rationale of the provision

In Chapter 8 we saw that, in Germany, claims by promisees of an unfulfilled testamentary promise are usually dealt with through the application of § 612 BGB. This provision allows for an employment contract to be implied so that the promisee can demand payment of wages for the services provided to the deceased. However, where such a claim is unavailable,[1] for instance, because the promisee has not performed services but rather made financial contributions or improvements to the deceased's property, and no claim exists based on any other ground (e.g. the promisor's unjustified enrichment discussed in Chapter 9), German law offers certain promisees the possibility of obtaining some form of redress through § 2057a BGB. This option is, however, only available to descendants and only if their parent dies intestate. § 2057a(1) and (2) BGB establish that:

> (1) A descendant who, as a result of work over a long period in the household, occupation or business of the deceased, of substantial financial contributions or in another way has to a particular degree contributed to the preservation or increase of the property of the deceased, may, in the partitioning, demand adjustment between the descendants who inherit as heirs on intestacy together with him; section 2052 applies with the necessary modifications. This also applies to a descendant who cared for the deceased for a long period.
> (2) An adjustment may not be demanded if adequate payment was made or agreed for the work, or to the extent that the descendant, on account of his work, has a claim on another legal basis. It does not conflict with the duty to adjust advancements if the work was done under sections 1619 and 1620.

§ 2057a BGB, apparently inspired by a similar provision enshrined in Swiss law,[2] is not meant to compensate promisees whose expectations of a future inheritance have been frustrated. Rather, it falls within the set of provisions that regulate the community of heirs in the context of intestate succession, and that deal with the

[1] An adjustment based on § 2057a BGB has subsidiary character. See Bosch (1972) 173.

[2] See former Article 633 of the Swiss Civil Code which has been replaced by Articles 334, 334bis, and 603(2) ZGB. For a discussion, see Imhof *Die neuen Bestimmungen zum Lidlohn* (1975). The Swiss provisions offer a stronger protection than § 2057a BGB, including because the children (and grandchildren) are being treated as creditors.

adjustment, or the so-called collation, among co-heirs.[3] The provisions preceding § 2057a BGB concern payments or advancements which the deceased has made to intestate heirs during her lifetime, and which the latter will have to account for. By contrast, § 2057a BGB deals with payments, work, care services, or financial contributions rendered by descendants (not also other intestate heirs), which have preserved or increased the deceased's property, and which they can demand to be considered when their intestate share is established.

When § 2057a BGB was first introduced back in 1969,[4] it was intended primarily to ensure that marital children would not be treated like extra-marital ones. The drafters of the provision had acted on the assumption that certain types of work or services performed in the household or family business would typically be provided by marital children rather than non-marital ones, for it was considered more likely that marital children would be living in the household of their deceased father.[5] With time, this provision has, however, become a means of ensuring that any descendants (whether marital or not), who have provided work or services for the deceased, are adequately 'compensated' for their efforts.[6] In other words, § 2057a BGB ensures equality of treatment among intestate descendants where one of them has provided work or services for the parents, and their contribution has preserved, and increased, the parents' property, and the others have not. Although initially the objective seems to have been to reward the contribution that descendants were providing, especially in the context of small family businesses or the rural/agricultural context,[7] of late § 2057a BGB has been increasingly viewed as a means to ensure that elderly people are cared for at home, rather than in care homes.[8] Thus, the rationale underpinning this particular legislative provision has changed over time.

Interestingly, although this legislative provision was never intended to deal with instances of unfulfilled promises, it would appear that it was designed to at least counter the fact that, quite often, the provision of services among family members has no basis in contract law and that there are gaps in their protection due to either evidential difficulties (e.g. difficulties of proving an agreement) or the fact that contractual claims are easily statute barred.[9] In this sense, § 2057a BGB was an

[3] See Lohmann, '§ 2057a Ausgleichungspflicht bei besonderen Leistungen eines Abkömmlings' in *Beck'scher Online-Kommentar BGB* (2021) Rn 1; Ann, 'BGB § 2057a Ausgleichungspflicht' in *Münchener Kommentar zum BGB* (2020) Rn 1; Damrau (1969) 580.

[4] Article 1 Nr 90 of the *Nichtehelichen Gesetz* of 19 August 1969, BGBl I S 1243 entered into force on 1 July 1970. For an explanation of the history of its origins, see BT-Drucksache V/4179, Nr 82. For a discussion of the background, see Zimmermann, 'Intestate Succession in Germany' in *Comparative Succession Law 2* (2015) 181, 207–208; Rapp in *Erbrecht und Vermögensnachfolge* (2012) 295ff.

[5] Lutter *Erbrecht des nichtehelichen Kindes* (1972) 102; Ann, 'BGB § 2057a Ausgleichungspflicht' in *Münchener Kommentar zum BGB* (2020) Rn 1; Ludyga (2009) 290.

[6] It is not really a 'compensation' in the technical sense of the word, but rather an adjustment. See Doering-Striening (2012) 534.

[7] Röthel *Ist unser Erbrecht noch zeitgemäß?* (2010) 59. See BT-Drucksache V/4179, 6 zu Nr 83a.

[8] Teschner (2017) 62, argues that this emerges from the reform of the provision that has entered into effect in 2010. See further OLG Schleswig 22 November 2016 – 3 U 25/16, BeckRS 2016, 115280 = NJW 2017, 1891 = ZEV 2017, 400 2016, [43].

[9] Paetel *Die erbrechtliche Ausgleichung von Pflegeleistungen* (2009) 19.

acknowledgement not of the vulnerability of promisees but rather of descendants who provide services and work in the family context that remain unremunerated, whether or not they are provided on the basis of a promise.

It should, however, be stressed that § 2057a BGB does not provide the descendant with an independent claim against other co-heirs. Rather, the descendant can argue that adjustments should be made in her favour when the estate is divided,[10] though only where she does not have any other claim at her disposal. In addition, an adjustment is possible only if: (i) the deceased has died intestate or has made a will under which the descendant receives her statutory share (i.e. the share she would be entitled to in case of intestacy);[11] and (ii) the person demanding the adjustment is a descendant of the deceased,[12] and inherits together with other descendants. Also, it should be noted that the deceased can expressly exclude or change the operation of § 2057a BGB in her testamentary disposition, for the provision is based on the testator's presumed intention that she would like to treat her descendants equally,[13] something which she may not in fact want. Thus, all in all, the scope of, and the protection provided by § 2057a BGB is limited, which is one of the reasons why it has met with considerable criticism of the legal community. The limited scope may also explain why, overall, there are few reported cases in which § 2057a BGB has been invoked. This was even more so the case when § 2057a BGB only protected those carers who had given up their employment, and who had provided the care themselves.[14] Fortunately, as we will see, these requirements were dropped in 2009 and there are some recent cases dealing specifically with instances of the provision of care. These cases are interesting not least because, arguably, German courts have taken a somewhat liberal approach when interpreting the requirements and quantifying the adjustment,[15] which seems to suggest that they are aware of the limitations of the provision and the need to provide greater recognition of the value of care. The scope of the provision aside, the protection § 2057a BGB provides is on the whole inadequate, also because it cannot be invoked during the promisor's lifetime and because the descendant will not be treated as a creditor of the deceased.

[10] § 2042 BGB in the context of a *Feststellungsklage* (declaratory judgment).

[11] See § 2052 BGB.

[12] Those who represent the descendant (that is to say primarily the grandchildren of the deceased) can also demand an adjustment.

[13] Werner, '§ 2057 a BGB' in *Staudinger, Kommentar zum BGB* (1996) Rn 4; Paetel *Die erbrechtliche Ausgleichung von Pflegeleistungen* (2009) 18.

[14] The extent to which the provision will come into play in the context of work carried out in the deceased's business has been doubted by Röthel *Erbrecht* (2020) 345. Röthel suggests that where the deceased owned a business, intestacy will be rare. Röthel *Ist unser Erbrecht noch zeitgemäß?* (2010) 59 further points out that where the collaboration of a descendant is significant, some form of remuneration is usually agreed upon, but acknowledges that § 2057a BGB is likely to have greater importance in the context of care cases.

[15] See OLG Schleswig 22 November 2016 (n 8).

B. The requirements of § 2057a BGB

For the reasons set out earlier, § 2057a BGB does not require proof of a promise nor of an agreement with the deceased, and compensation does not depend on reliance or an inducement. Nonetheless, it can be invoked by a promisee and, all other avenues failing, can sometimes prove useful. In the pages that follow, I will examine the requirements for a descendant to be able to demand an adjustment. We will see that, given the dearth of case law, some questions remain unanswered. The analysis will further show that, while the descendant's motives do not matter, which is to be welcomed, one of the difficulties they might face is the need to show that what they have done exceeds what is 'normal' in their position, that is in the context of a parent–child relationship. A 'special performance' is therefore usually required, but, as with other forms of redress, what counts as such is not always easy to establish or predict.

1. Work, care services, or substantial financial contributions

While the first sentence of § 2057a(1) BGB outlined earlier specifically mentions work carried out in the household, the occupation or business (meaning an agricultural or commercial business) of the deceased, as well as financial or other types of contributions,[16] the second sentence speaks specifically of the provision of care for the deceased. Little can be gleaned from the legislation, as no definitions are provided, but 'work' seems to include both mental and physical activities. What counts as 'care' is somewhat contentious, however. Doubts have, for instance, been raised in relation to services that are not technically speaking 'care' services, but that are provided in the household and that benefit the person in need of care, such as the provision of food. In establishing what qualifies as care for the purposes of § 2057a BGB, German courts have often been guided by whether or not local health care services have deemed the deceased as requiring care.[17] In other words, services provided by the descendants were regarded as amounting to care services when the deceased had formally qualified as in need of care for the purposes of the Social Code (SGB XI).[18] Thus, it is not necessarily the type of activity but the fact that the person is in need that can qualify certain services as care services for the purpose of § 2057a BGB.

[16] Lohmann, '§ 2057a Ausgleichungspflicht bei besonderen Leistungen eines Abkömmlings' in *Beck'scher Online-Kommentar BGB* (2021) Rn 7 mentions also a loan without interest.

[17] For instance, the OLG Schleswig 15 June 2012 – 3 U 28/11, NJW-RR 2013, 205 = ZEV 2013, 86ff was guided by the fact that the deceased was qualified by the local medical services as 'Plegestufe I' (care level I). In this case, the son had cared for the deceased first in her flat and then in his own house. See also OLG Frankfurt 19 March 2013 – 11 U 134/11, BeckRS 2013, 22801.

[18] § 14 SGB XI defines the concept of 'need of care' in the following manner: 'In need of care are those persons who require medical treatment for their independence or abilities and who need help from others. They must be persons who cannot independently compensate or cope with physical, cognitive or psychological impairments or health-related stresses or requirements. The need for long-term care must be long-term, presumably for at least six months, and at least the severity specified in § 15.'

In a decision of 2016, the Higher Regional Court (*Oberlandesgericht*, hereafter OLG) of Schleswig established that, given that the purpose of § 2057a BGB is to avoid the placement of the person in a care home, or the provision of care through professional services, what counted as care was not just the fact that, in that particular case the son had prepared meals and assisted with the mobility of the deceased mother. The mere presence of the son also amounted to care service within the meaning of § 2057a BGB insofar as he provided general companionship and ensured the welfare of the deceased in the event of a sudden need of assistance.[19] By considering these intangible benefits, the court arguably strengthened the protection of descendants who provide such care,[20] which is important and similar to what we have seen to be the case under the New Zealand Law Reform (Testamentary Promises) Act 1949 (hereafter the New Zealand TPA 1949).[21]

Work and care aside, adjustments may also be demanded in case of substantial financial contributions that the descendant has made to her parents. What is meant by 'substantial' will depend on the circumstances of the deceased, but the purpose behind such contributions seems to be irrelevant.[22] Aside from financial contributions, an adjustment may further be demanded where the descendant has contributed in another way to the preservation or increase of the deceased's property, such as, for instance, through the provision of a guarantee on a loan, or the granting of a usufruct. Thus, § 2057a BGB captures a wide range of contributions and performances rendered by the promisee for the benefit of the deceased, arguably even wider than the New Zealand TPA 1949.

2. Work or care must be provided for a long period of time

A descendant intending to rely on § 2057a BGB on the basis of work or care services, rather than financial or other contributions, needs to have provided these for a long period of time. What this means is not clearly defined in the legislation. It is likely that when the intensity of the work or care provided is considerable, and the daily efforts substantial, a short period of time is sufficient. Conversely, where the work or care services are less intensive, a longer period of time may be required,[23] though where one is to draw the line is difficult to know. Case law concerning care services would suggest that such services do not have to be provided continuously,[24] but that occasional assistance is

[19] OLG Schleswig 22 November 2016 (n 8) [50]. For a discussion of the case, see Kollmeyer (2017) 1849.

[20] In the decision of the LG Magdeburg 20 October 2010 – 9 O 1070/01, BeckRS 2011, 20919, juris Rn 74 it was held to be sufficient that the son had ensured that his mother (who was incontinent) would wear clean clothes, that the flat would be heated, and that there would be food in the house.

[21] See Chapter 7.

[22] Ann, 'BGB § 2057a Ausgleichungspflicht' in *Münchener Kommentar zum BGB* (2020) Rn 22.

[23] In relation to care, see Teschner (2017) 65.

[24] See OLG Frankfurt 19 March 2013 (n 17), where one of the daughters had cared for the deceased on weekends from 2006 until the death of the promisor in 2008, and the other daughter during

insufficient.[25] We saw that the same is the case with the *créance de salaire différé*.[26] Thus, difficulties may arise where a descendant has, for instance, provided care only during holidays, even though since 2010, it is no longer necessary that she must have given up her employment to care for the deceased.

3. Contribution to the preservation or increase of the value of the property of the deceased ...

The descendant's work, care services, financial, or other contributions must have contributed to the preservation or increase of the property of the deceased. In other words, the property of the deceased must have been preserved, or there must have been an enrichment or increase of its value.[27] Here we can see a clear difference with the *créance de salaire différé*, which requires the work to be effective but it need not have enriched the deceased.[28] From the perspective of the promisee, having to prove an enrichment can be difficult both on a practical and psychological level.

While the mere fact that the descendant has provided considerable work or care services does not lead to a presumption of an enrichment of the assets of the deceased, it is often seen as proof of such an enrichment or increase of the value of the deceased's property. For instance, in the case of care, the estate has been found to have been preserved, or increased in value where the deceased did not have to spend resources on professional care or for accommodation in a care home.[29] That of course sets the threshold rather high and does not capture a number of cases where the descendant provides invaluable services to the parent.

4. ... to a particular degree

Not only must the contribution lead to a preservation or increase of the value of the deceased's property, § 2057a BGB speaks of a 'particular degree'. Exactly what that means is somewhat unclear, for the provision is silent on this point. Courts have stated that the contribution must be significant. It must be a 'special performance' (*Sonderleistung*) or a performance that amounts to something *extra*,[30] which is language similar to that employed by the New Zealand courts when speaking of domestic services.[31] As we saw with regards to New Zealand, but also in connection

weekdays. Both were compensated. But see also the decision of the LG Magdeburg 20 October 2010 (n 20), which has taken a different view.

[25] Paetel *Die erbrechtliche Ausgleichung von Pflegeleistungen* (2009) 68–69.
[26] See Chapter 10.
[27] This was doubted in OLG Düsseldorf 22 August 1997 – 7 U 251/96, OLGR Düsseldorf 1998, 81.
[28] See Chapter 10, section IV.B.
[29] OLG Schleswig 15 June 2012 (n 17).
[30] On the question, see also the obiter statements in the BGH decision of 8 March 2006 – IV ZR 263/04, (2006) NJW-RR 877.
[31] See Chapter 7, section II.A.

with other forms of redress,[32] defining what is normal and what is special is open to interpretation.

According to the OLG Celle (1996), a descendant is entitled to an adjustment where the services (care services in this particular case) exceed 'what can normally be expected from a descendant'.[33] Equally the District Court (*Landgericht*) Magdeburg (2010) stressed that what is provided in the context of the *normal* parent–child relationship cannot be compensated.[34] However, without any further guidance, such statements are not particularly helpful. Again, we see here societal expectations playing a role. Thus, as is the case with other forms of redress explored in this book, the crux of the problem lies in establishing what is to be regarded as *normal* and what counts as *extra*, and therefore what can be expected of the descendant. Much would seem to depend, as always, on the context and thus on the particular family or relationship in question, and on the type of performance provided.

It is clear that the descendant's performance has to exceed what is required of her on the basis of the duty of maintenance that German law imposes on lineal relatives (§ 1601ff BGB),[35] or, as we saw before,[36] the duty that children belonging to the household have to contribute to the household and business of their parents (§ 1619 BGB). The District Court of Magdeburg (2010) spoke in fact of a performance that exceeds such obligations imposed on descendants (*überobligatorische Leistungen*).[37] This, as we will see later,[38] is different under the Austrian statutory care legacy. Importantly, in the case of § 2057a BGB, the work or care service must also go beyond any performances that other descendants may have provided to the deceased.[39] In other words, where all descendants have provided work or services, only those performances exceeding the performances of the others, both in duration and intensity, can be adjusted.

Regarding care services in particular, the conditions would seem to be met where the deceased would have had to employ someone had the descendant not provided assistance,[40] though this is not a necessary requirement for a descendant to succeed. As mentioned earlier, prior to 2010,[41] in order to be able to demand an

[32] See the discussions in Chapters, 6, 8, and 9.

[33] OLG Celle 20 May 1996 – 7 W 58/95, OLGR Celle 1996, 214ff. The concept of 'special performances' is referred to also in OLG Oldenburg 1 December 1998 – 5 U 126/98, FamRZ 1999, 1466, 1467. The court rejected the son's argument that he had worked for the deceased and provided financial contributions, arguing, amongst other things, that his claim was not sufficiently substantiated.

[34] LG Magdeburg 20 October 2010 (n 20) [74].

[35] §§ 1601ff BGB provides that lineal relatives are under an obligation to maintain each other.

[36] See the analysis in Chapters 6 and 9.

[37] LG Magdeburg 20 October 2010 (n 20) [74].

[38] See section III.B.

[39] In this sense, OLG Oldenburg 1 December 1998 (n 33). Lohmann, '§ 2057a Ausgleichungspflicht bei besonderen Leistungen eines Abkömmlings' in *Beck'scher Online-Kommentar BGB* (2021) Rn 4.

[40] OLG Naumburg 24 March 1999 – 5 U 249/98, BeckRS 1999, 31024642.

[41] *Gesetz zur Änderung des Erb—und Verjährungsrechts* of 23 September 2009 (BGBl I S 3142) that has entered into force on 1 January 2010.

adjustment it was necessary for the descendant to have given up her professional income. The reasoning behind this requirement was precisely the need to draw a line between services that needed to be remunerated and those that could be regarded as *normal* or expected in the familial context. However, this requirement has since been abolished, so that no financial sacrifice in the form of a loss of job is required on the part of the descendant, which means that the focus now lies on the descendant's care services, rather than on her professional sacrifice. Requiring the descendant to give up her job sets a very high bar and fails to protect those who, on top of their full-time job, provide work and services. Furthermore, it seems that it is no longer necessary that the services are provided personally, it being sufficient that the descendant has paid for the care provided by third parties.

Thus, it seems that the 2009 reform has somewhat broadened the scope of the protection of the provision, which is to be welcomed. Even so, it is still very narrow and there are several challenges a promisee who wants to rely on § 2057a BGB would need to overcome.

5. Lack of adequate compensation

§ 2057a(2) BGB establishes that no adjustment can be demanded where the work or care services rendered have been adequately compensated during the lifetime of the parent or where adequate remuneration has been agreed upon, for example, in the form of an express or implied employment contract.[42] This does not, however, exclude an adjustment where the descendant has, for instance, received only partial payment.[43] It is important in this regard to mention that it is up to the other intestate descendants (the co-heirs) to prove that the descendant who demands an adjustment of her share has received adequate compensation for her work or care services. Thus, the onus of proof shifts, which is of benefit to the promisee and is a clear difference to other forms of redress (e.g. the *créance de salaire différé*).

However, § 2057a BGB cannot be invoked where the promisee has a claim for compensation against the estate on another legal basis,[44] for example, on the basis of a contract of employment, § 612 BGB (and thus an implied contract of services),[45] or the *condictio ob rem*.[46] In other words, § 2057a BGB provides a subsidiary

[42] Here we see an analogy with the requirements of the New Zealand TPA 1949 (Chapter 7), of § 612 BGB (Chapter 8), the *créance de salaire différé* (Chapter 10), and the Austrian care legacy discussed later in this chapter.

[43] That was the case in the decision of the LG Konstanz 18 December 2009 – 5 O 249/08 E, ZErb 2010, 93 where the daughter had cared for her mother for a period of about seven years and, in order to do so, had given up her job. She was paid a monthly salary of €733 which the court regarded as inadequate, awarding her an additional €30,000.

[44] § 2057a(2) BGB.

[45] Chapter 8.

[46] Chapter 9, section II.

claim that can be brought solely where no other claim is available, or where such claims are statute barred.[47]

This leaves little scope for invoking the provision and may explain why there is relatively little case law. Nonetheless, § 2057a BGB can be useful where the requirements for the application of § 612 BGB, or those of a claim based on the *condictio ob rem*, cannot be met.

C. Quantifying the adjustment

The way in which the amount of the adjustment is determined under § 2057a BGB is not clearly outlined by the legislature. § 2057a BGB merely establishes that the gratuitous work or care performed by a descendant is to be compensated by way of adjustments in the partitioning between the other descendants (but not the spouse) who inherit together on intestacy.[48] The descendant who has provided work or care services can demand to receive more than the other descendants who are co-heirs, so long as the deceased has not directed otherwise in her will. This is in fact a possibility and weakens the protection that § 2057a BGB is able to provide. Exactly how much more a descendant can seek is not specified, as decisions are made on the basis of considerations of equity. Thus, courts have a discretion in making the adjustment. § 2057a(3) BGB explicitly states that the amount of the adjustment is to be assessed in such a way as is equitable with regard to the duration and scope of the work, and the value of the estate. These two pointers aside, nothing more is said.

The question is therefore what represents the starting point of the court's evaluation and what is the upper limit. It would seem that an award of the entire estate is excluded, not least because the claim has to be evaluated against the value of the estate.[49] In a decision of 9 December 1992,[50] the *Bundesgerichtshof* (hereafter BGH) acknowledged that the majority of legal scholars reject the idea that the adjustment under § 2057a BGB can amount to the entire estate but had left the possibility open. By contrast, the OLG Schleswig (2012) categorically denied the possibility that the adjustment could lead to an award of the whole estate.[51] At the

[47] Bosch (1972) 173. The decision of the OLG Schleswig 15 June 2012 (n 17) had dealt with a case in which an enrichment claim was rejected but § 2057a BGB was successfully invoked.

[48] The person who acquires the inheritance (*Erbteilserwerber* § 2376 BGB) is also affected, as is the heir of a co-heir who has a duty to pay for the adjustment. See Ann, 'BGB § 2057a Ausgleichungspflicht' in *Münchener Kommentar zum BGB* (2020) Rn 14 who suggests that the deceased can impose a duty to make an adjustment on the spouse.

[49] OLG Schleswig 15 June 2012, NJW-RR 2013, 205, 206 (n 17).

[50] See BGH 9 December 1992 – IV ZR 82/92, BGH NJW 1993, 1197, 1198. In this particular case, the amount of the adjustment paid to the person who had worked in the agricultural business of the deceased had amounted to more than half of the estate.

[51] OLG Schleswig 15 June 2012 (n 17). The same position was taken a few years earlier by the LG Magdeburg 20 October 2010 (n 20).

same time, the OLG Schleswig also established that the value of the enrichment (or of the preservation of the property of the deceased) does not represent the upper limit, but that it is only the starting point.[52] This suggests that an adjustment based on § 2057a BGB is potentially preferable to a claim based on the *condictio ob rem*, except for the fact that in the latter case the claimant counts as a creditor, whereas here she does not. Thus, while on the basis of § 2057a BGB a promisee could not receive the entire estate, she could potentially obtain more than the economic value of her work for the deceased.

Apparently, the German legislature intentionally omitted a requirement that individual performances and their value should be determined with precision, opting instead in favour of a discretion of the courts, which are to take a holistic approach,[53] including, as we will see, intangible benefits. In a decision of 9 December 1992,[54] the BGH confirmed that it is not necessary to list and count all individual items, including mutual benefits, and this has been followed also in later decisions. Thus, German courts are not engaged in a mere mathematical exercise or in a 'netting off', as we observed under the New Zealand TPA 1949 (Chapter 7). Dealing specifically with care services, the OLG Schleswig, in the aforementioned decision, confirmed that a holistic approach should be taken.[55] It further suggested that an approach in three stages should be adopted. First, attention should be paid to the duration and the extent of the descendant's performance, in particular the duration of her daily efforts, and the extent to which the estate has been preserved. Next, the court should consider the immaterial (intangible) value of the descendant's performance (in this case, care services) for the deceased as well as any disadvantages experienced by the caring descendant,[56] but also potential benefits she has obtained in the form of free accommodation and gifts. This, as we saw, is different in the case of a claim based on § 612 BGB, where such benefits do not affect the amount of wages the promisee can claim. Finally, just as with the New Zealand TPA 1949, though not with § 612 BGB or an enrichment claim, according to the OLG Schleswig, courts must consider the economic situation of the other intestate heirs and of those entitled to a compulsory share in the estate, as well as the value of the whole estate.

[52] Ibid.

[53] Bericht des Rechtsausschusses, BT-Drucksache 5/4179 Nr 83a. Lohmann, '§ 2057a Ausgleichungspflicht bei besonderen Leistungen eines Abkömmlings' in *Beck'scher Online-Kommentar BGB* (2021) Rn 10. While the unsuccessful reform proposal of 2009 required compensation to be quantified on the basis of specific principles (in particular on the basis of § 36 Abs 3 SGB XI), this proposal was rejected. See Bill of 30 May 2008 (BT-Drucksache 16/8954).

[54] BGH 9 December 1992, BGH NJW 1993, 1197, 1198 (n 50)

[55] OLG Schleswig 15 June 2012 (n 17).

[56] Ibid, [89]. In this particular case, there was evidence that, on several occasions, the deceased had said how important it had been to her that she could stay at home rather than being cared for in a care home. Some authors have criticized the decision precisely for giving value to something that cannot be measured in numbers, see Trappe (2017) 207. Supportive of the approach taken by the OLG, are Ruby & Schindler (2017) 382–383.

Whether courts will follow this approach in the future remains to be seen. In any case, it would appear that they have considerable leeway in quantifying the amount of the adjustment, which has met with criticism. It has, for instance, been argued that the lack of clear criteria entails the risk that the adjustments are arbitrary and uncertain. Some authors have also argued that this has led to increased litigation,[57] though it is unclear whether this is really borne out by case law.

D. Nature of the right to an adjustment

An adjustment made on the basis of the German § 2057a BGB is not seen as a debt against the estate (in the sense of § 1967 BGB), and the descendant applying for an adjustment is not a creditor of the deceased. The interests of the deceased's creditors therefore prevail. From the perspective of the promisee, this is not a desirable situation and is another reason why § 2057a BGB cannot offer a satisfactory solution to cases of unfulfilled testamentary promises.

The adjustment does not normally have consequences for testate heirs because the provision only comes into play when there is no will, unless the testator has made a will leaving the statutory shares in which case the beneficiaries under the will are treated as if there was no will. However, the interests of the other intestate descendants (though not that of the surviving spouse) are affected because the amount that is adjusted on the basis of § 2057a BGB is subtracted from the net value of the estate before the intestate shares are determined.[58] Consequently, the compulsory shares are also affected, their value being half of what the heir would be entitled to in case of intestacy.[59]

As has been noted, it is disputed whether the adjustment under § 2057a BGB can amount to the entire estate at the expense of other compulsory heirs. Certainly, the OLG Schleswig has suggested that courts should take into account the economic situation of compulsory heirs.[60]

E. Attempts at reforming the provision

Over the years, § 2057a BGB has met with considerable criticism. The point about judicial discretion aside, there seems to be a consensus that the provision does not go far enough, and that the German legislature missed the opportunity to

[57] In this sense Kollmeyer (2017) 1851 and Ludyga (2009) 291. Increased litigation was also predicted by Damrau (1969) 580.

[58] § 2057a(4) BGB. See Paetel *Die erbrechtliche Ausgleichung von Pflegeleistungen* (2009) 10ff.

[59] Zimmermann, 'Compulsory Portion in Germany' in *Comparative Succession Law 3* (2020) 268, 284. Ludyga (2009) 293–294.

[60] OLG Schleswig 15 June 2012 (n 17).

significantly improve it in the context of the 2009 reform. Indeed, one major point of criticism is that § 2057a BGB continues to benefit only descendants, even though the 2009 reform proposal had suggested that the scope of its application should be extended so as to capture all statutory heirs.[61] Some authors felt that even that was not going far enough, as it would have continued to neglect, for instance, the position of those who do not qualify as statutory heirs under German law, such as neighbours, cohabitants, and, especially, daughters-in-law who frequently end up looking after the parents of their husbands.[62] Consequently, a number of German legal scholars suggested a variety of changes to § 2057a BGB. These included recommendations to introduce a statutory legacy (*gesetzliches Vermächtnis*),[63] which is the solution that, as we will see, the Austrian legislature has favoured in the recent succession law reform.[64]

However, ultimately none of the suggestions were adopted and, in the end, § 2057a BGB was only marginally modified. As a consequence, cohabitants, siblings but also daughters-in-law, who seek some form of compensation (whether or not they are promisees) must continue to bring a claim arguing that the deceased was either unjustly enriched at their expense or that a service contract with the deceased can be implied from the circumstances on the basis of § 612 BGB. Some of these alternative claims may well be in their interest, for instance, because an adjustment based on § 2057a BGB is likely to be lower than the wages payable on the basis of § 612 BGB.[65] And as noted earlier, in the case of an adjustment based on § 2057a BGB, the descendant is not a creditor. Nonetheless, it is regrettable that the provision has such a narrow scope.

F. Conclusion

There is no doubt that § 2057a BGB does not represent a satisfactory solution for those who, acting on a promise of an inheritance, have suffered detriment because

[61] The Bill of 30 May 2008 (BT-Drucksache 16/8954) was planning to introduce a new § 2057b, but the proposal was not included in the later Bill presented on 24 January 2009. As to who counts as an intestate heir under German law, see Zimmermann, 'Intestate Succession in Germany' in *Comparative Succession Law 2* (2015).

[62] Röthel *Ist unser Erbrecht noch zeitgemäß?* (2010) A 60 has pleaded for a stronger compensation of care provided by cohabitants and daughters-in-law. Others have gone further and have suggested extending the protection also to people outside the family, such as neighbours and friends. Otte (2008) 261; Muscheler (2008) 105–112, 109 and Keim (2008) 2072–2077. See also Windel (2008) 305–308. This position was also shared by the German *Bundesrat*, which favoured a widening of the circle of people who could benefit so as to include third parties. See RegE 2008, BT-Drucksache 16/8954, 31.

[63] In this sense Otte (2008) 261 but also Kanzleiter in *Hereditare 9* (2019). However, Ludyga (2009) sees the statutory legacy as an infringement of the deceased's testamentary freedom. Muscheler (2008) 105 is also critical of it arguing that this can probably not be brought in line with the deceased's presumed intention.

[64] See section III.

[65] See Chapter 8, section V.

the promise remained unfulfilled. Although there is no need to prove a promise or some form of tacit agreement, or indeed reliance, a promisee who wants to invoke the protection provided by the provision needs to show that, as a result of care services or work in the deceased's household or business over a long period of time, or because of substantial financial or other contributions, she has to a particular degree contributed to the preservation or increase of the value of the property of the deceased. In doing so, she must prove that her performance exceeded any duties she may have had towards the promisor, as well as any performances rendered by other descendants, and that it went beyond what is normally to be expected given the particular context, that is her relationship with the deceased parent. As we saw earlier, a 'special performance' is required, but what that means is frequently difficult to establish. Here societal expectations again play a critical role.

Of advantage to the promisee is the fact that the descendant does not have to give exact proof of the individual performances and their value, and that the other descendants have the burden to prove that she has received adequate remuneration for her work or services. Also, under § 2057a BGB, German courts have discretion in determining the adjustment. They are prepared to take into account intangible benefits that have accrued to the deceased. They further consider any disadvantages experienced by the caring descendant, which shows that the focus is not only on the financial enrichment or financial impoverishment, as is, for instance, often the case in enrichment claims. That said, for the purposes of an adjustment, German courts also consider the situation of other intestate successors as well as of those entitled to a compulsory share.

However, § 2057a BGB does not provide the descendant with an independent claim against the other co-heirs but merely with a right to an adjustment. This right applies only to descendants, only vis-à-vis other descendants, and only in the context of intestacy. By contrast, an enrichment claim, or one based on § 612 BGB, can be brought during the promisor's lifetime and against all other co-heirs. What is more, § 2057a BGB operates only when the descendant cannot bring any other type of claim, whether contractual or based on enrichment law. Another problem is that the deceased can exclude or modify the application of the provision,[66] which is, for instance, much more difficult to do in the case of the Austrian care legacy discussed later. Finally, the descendant is not treated as a creditor and may therefore not obtain an adjustment if the funds are insufficient.[67] Nonetheless, other avenues failing, § 2057a BGB can be a useful provision for descendants of a deceased promisor. Indeed, the fact that there is now a greater number of cases brought by

[66] Lohmann, '§ 2057a Ausgleichungspflicht bei besonderen Leistungen eines Abkömmlings' in *Beck'scher Online-Kommentar BGB* (2021) Rn 1. The heirs too can all agree to make other arrangements.

[67] In other words, there is no obligation on the estate in the sense of §1967 BGB (*Nachlassverbindlichkeit*).

carers suggests that it has some utility. In some cases, it may be their only way to obtain compensation for their services or work.

It is interesting to note that the Dutch Civil Code of 2003, contains a similar provision in Article 4:36(1) BW. Just like § 2057a BGB, Article 4:36(1) BW is part of the law of intestacy and is framed in similar terms to § 2057 a BGB. It establishes that:

> a child (stepchild, foster child, child-in-law or grandchild) of the deceased who, having attained the age of majority, performed work in the deceased's household, professional practice or business, without having received appropriate remuneration for such work, may claim a lump sum constituting fair compensation.

Just like § 2057a BGB, Article 4:36(1) BW applies to assistance provided with the running of a farm, and in the household. It only aids children and grandchildren and not spouses or other relatives, let alone anyone else. It further seems that, just like in Germany, the work in question has to have been *long-term* work in the deceased's professional practice, business, or household. Although there is no reference to an enrichment, another criterion derived from the discussion in Parliament is that the descendant's work must be of 'economic value'. However, unlike the German solution, the Dutch provision grants a claim to compensation and not simply a right to demand an adjustment in the context of the partitioning of the estate. The Dutch provision speaks of fair compensation. Thus, here too courts have considerable discretion. Wilbert Kolkman has argued that this requirement introduces a particular level of uncertainty, which seems to have been a point of criticism of the provision.[68] That said, it would seem that, in practice, courts have been cautious in applying Article 4:36 BW. Just as is the case with § 2057a BGB, there is limited case law, which may well be largely due to the limited scope of these provisions. In section III we will see that Austria has also felt the need to provide compensation, in particular for care services by family members, but that it has chosen a different solution.

III. Compensating the promisee on the basis of §§ 677ff ABGB

A. Background and rationale

Unlike the German BGB, the Austrian ABGB does not explicitly rule out the validity of a contract to make a will. Nonetheless, contracts to make a will are regarded

[68] Kolkman, 'Compulsory Portion and Family Provision in the Netherlands' in *Comparative Succession Law 3* (2020) 335.

as invalid.[69] Just as in Germany, informal testamentary promises are made in exchange for work on farms, work or services provided in the household, or care services. Where such promises remain unfulfilled, in Austria, just as in Germany, the promisee can try to establish the existence of an implied employment contract with the promisor,[70] or she can argue that the latter has been unjustly enriched at her expense.[71] In addition, in Austria, a promisee who has cared for the deceased promisor during the last years prior to her death may have the possibility of obtaining redress by claiming a statutory care legacy (*Pflegevermächtnis*) against the promisor's estate. This possibility was introduced in the course of the succession law reform of 2015.[72] The new § 677 ABGB establishes that:

> a person who is close to the deceased and who has cared for the latter for at least six months in the last three years prior to his death for a not insignificant degree, shall be entitled to a statutory legacy, unless a donation has been made or remuneration agreed.

The purpose behind the introduction of this legislative provision was, in the words of the drafters, a desire to remedy:

> the fact that not infrequently sacrificial and extensive services performed by relatives fall by the wayside. Often care services are rendered to the deceased out of an obligation to provide assistance or due to moral reasons that are valuable both from an emotional, but also a monetary perspective, but no compensation has been provided.[73]

Thus, the provision is a response to the awareness that care services provided by family members often remain unremunerated. Another objective behind the introduction of this statutory care legacy seems to have been the fact that neighbouring Germany provides some form of protection for carers through § 2057a BGB.[74] Yet, the Austrian legislature did not follow the German model, which, as we saw, grants descendants a right of adjustment in case of intestacy. Instead, Austria introduced a statutory care legacy that operates irrespective of whether or not there is intestate or testate succession, and that benefits a wider range of people who can demand

[69] See OGH 3 Ob 531/79. See also Fischer-Czermak and Pierer, '§ 552' in *Großkommentar zum ABGB* (2021) Rn 11ff.

[70] This claim is based on § 1152 ABGB. See the analysis in Chapter 8.

[71] See § 1435 ABGB. See Chapter 9, section II.

[72] For a detailed analysis of the statutory care legacy, see Christandl, '§§ 677–678', in *Großkommentar zum ABGB* (2021) 196–235. See also Christandl & Nemeth (2020).

[73] See ErläutRV zu § 677 ABGB.

[74] This is highlighted by Wendehorst, 'Compulsory Portion and other Aspects of Family Protection in Austria' in *Comparative Succession Law 3* (2020) 255. In Austrian literature the topic was discussed especially after the German reform of 2009. For example, see Wendehorst (2010); Wendehorst *Reform II* (2010) 34ff.

payment of compensation for up to three years of their care services. This solution is precisely what some legal scholars had suggested Germany should introduce when it reformed § 2057a BGB in 2009. However, in the end the German reform was modest. At the same time, it should be mentioned that the German provision is much more broadly conceived and does not apply only to cases of care.

While it would seem that the protection of the interests of family members who have cared for the deceased was a major selling point of the entire Austrian succession law reform,[75] and that it met with considerable favour among the public,[76] the end result is perhaps less path-breaking than one might have hoped for, for reasons I will discuss later. Nonetheless, and even though §§ 677ff ABGB do not specifically deal with testamentary promises, the statutory care legacy can be a means through which a promisee can try to obtain at least some form of redress, though only if she has cared for the promisor during the last three years prior to her death, and only if she falls within the circle of people covered by the provision.

In the pages that follow, I explore briefly who can benefit and the requirements that they must meet to be successful, before evaluating the statutory care legacy from the perspective of promisees. We will see that, on the whole, the requirements are not difficult to meet. Also, and importantly, demanding compensation is not usually costly unless the carer has to file a case in court. In fact, compensation can be demanded in the course of the probate procedure (*Verlassenschaftsverfahren*) that opens automatically when a person dies. This means that a claim in court is necessary only if the *Gerichtskommissär* in charge of the probate procedure cannot reach a consensual agreement between the heirs and the carer. Still, we will also see that the statutory care legacy is not without its problems, for the carer will only be compensated for the care provided during the last three years prior to the death of the person she has cared for, and she will not be regarded as a creditor of the deceased. The deceased's debtors are paid first. In fact, her claim only arises on the death of the person she has cared for. Finally, as we will see, only a limited number of people can claim a care legacy.

B. Scope and requirements

The Austrian care legacy can benefit people who were close to the deceased and, more precisely, intestate heirs of the deceased (i.e. the spouse and registered partner, children and grandchildren, parents, siblings, grandparents and great grandparents, uncles and aunts, and cousins), but also the spouse, registered partners, or cohabiting partners of the deceased's intestate heirs, as well as the cohabiting partner of the deceased herself, and the children of the cohabiting partner. Hence, unlike

[75] Fischer-Czermak in *Das neue Erbrecht* (2015) 38.
[76] Eccher *Erbrechtsreform* (2017) 87.

under the German § 2057a BGB discussed earlier, a much wider range of carers can benefit, including stepchildren or daughters-in-law, though not, for instance, neighbours or friends.

For a care legacy to arise, the care must have been provided within the last three years preceding the deceased's death, for at least six months, and it must have been more than insignificant. According to the explanatory notes, the 'more than insignificant' test is usually met if the care was provided on average for more than twenty hours per month.[77] Exactly how this will work in practice is currently debated. Although the requirement of twenty hours for at least six months is arguably low, one must remember that the promisee is only entitled to a legacy for the care provided during the last three years. In other words, any care provided prior to that moment will not be compensated through §§ 677ff ABGB. The provision does not therefore provide adequate protection to those who provided care for longer than three years, which is a significant limitation. They will have to bring an enrichment claim, unless it is possible to imply an employment contract, but of course such claims are linked to higher costs.[78]

At the same time, the notion of 'care' is broad. For instance, the Austrian legislature does not require that the claimant provide nursing services. Care can consist of other forms of support, provided that the deceased needed care within the meaning of the relevant social security laws.[79] Whether the care must have been provided by the relevant family member in person, or whether it is sufficient that the relevant family member provided the financial means, is unclear and subject to debate.[80] It is to be hoped though that personal care will not be made a necessary requirement, just as is the case under § 2057a BGB and the New Zealand TPA 1949. It should be sufficient that the person has, for instance, paid for the care.[81]

§ 677 ABGB explicitly states that no care legacy is granted where the carer received adequate remuneration or similar benefits. As we saw, the same requirement must be met for a claim to be brought on the basis of the New Zealand TPA 1949, § 612 BGB, § 2057a BGB and the *créance de salaire différé*. Where remuneration has been the object of a contractual promise but was never paid, the carer needs to file a contractual claim against the estate.[82] However, according to the drafters of the Austrian succession law reform, the fact that the carer was under a statutory duty to support the deceased, for example, under the provisions requiring mutual support between spouses or partners or parents and children, does *not* stand in the way of a claim to a statutory legacy.[83] Additionally, unlike with § 2057a BGB, the

[77] ErläutRV § 688 BlgNR 25, GP 17.
[78] See Chapters 8 and 9.
[79] Deixler-Hübner in *Erbrecht NEU* (2015); ErläutRV 688 BlgNR 25, GP 17.
[80] Kiener (2015); Stefula (2016).
[81] For a different view, see Christandl, '§§ 677–678', in *Großkommentar zum ABGB* (2021) Rn 64.
[82] The preparatory works speak of a service contract. ErläutRV 688 BlgNR 25, GP 17.
[83] ErläutRV 688 BlgNR 25, GP 17. The situation is different in Germany, where the courts speak of an *überobligatorische Leistung*.

performance does not have to exceed the carer's obligation. Neither does the promisee have to prove that her performance exceeded what could normally be expected of her, as is necessary under § 2057a BGB, or that there is a nexus, as is necessary if an employment contract is to be implied. Equally, the carer's motives are entirely irrelevant, which is important given that motives are often mixed. Indeed, a statutory legacy may be awarded also when the carer and the deceased have explicitly agreed that the care would be provided for free. What matters is that the care was provided on average for more than twenty hours per month and not why it was provided. This is important and removes some of the obstacles that promisees are often required to overcome.

Unlike with § 2057a BGB, the deceased can exclude the care legacy only in exceptional cases that allow her to disinherit the relevant person.[84] Whether a testator should at all be able to exclude the care legacy is of course debatable; after all, the care legacy is not a gift but rather compensation for something that the carer has earned. Interestingly, while the care legacy can only be excluded in exceptional cases, if the deceased so establishes in her will, benefits under the will or under intestacy can reduce the care legacy. As Gregor Christandl has pointed out, this has serious implications.[85] It means that by a will and without specific reasons, a testator can remove all benefits linked to the legacy, for the legacy becomes part of the intestate share of the carer.

Importantly, the carer is entitled to the statutory care legacy in addition to any compulsory share she may be entitled to. This must be right, for compulsory heirship is not based on merits and there is a risk of unfairness, especially as the care services may have enriched the estate that is then distributed to all heirs. Finally, a competing claim based on unjustified enrichment is not regarded as a relevant benefit that would automatically exclude or diminish the care legacy.[86] That said, as we will see, the question of whether or not the carer is entitled to both claims, and to choose one over the other, is subject to debate in Austrian literature.

C. Quantifying the care legacy

According to § 678(1) ABGB, the size of the legacy depends on the type, duration, and extent of the care provided, though what is meant by that will have to be clarified by the courts and may well be an aspect that will lead to future litigation. However, the explanatory notes specify that the legacy will be quantified primarily, though not only, on the basis of the benefit obtained by the deceased, in particular

[84] Fischer-Czermak in *Das neue Erbrecht* (2015) 41.

[85] Christandl, '§§ 677–678', in *Großkommentar zum ABGB* (2021) 215, Rn 48.

[86] Wendehorst, 'Compulsory Portion and other Aspects of Family Protection in Austria' in *Comparative Succession Law 3* (2020) 257.

any savings on the part of the estate,[87] for example, in the form of payments for services provided by another person, though not the costs of professional care. This suggests that the deceased's enrichment represents the basis or starting point, but that a promisee can potentially obtain more than the value of the enrichment, as is the case with § 2057a BGB. However, the Austrian provisions do not mention fairness and the Austrian courts do not therefore have the same level of discretion that German courts have.

It is further noticeable that the value of the estate does not play a role in the context of the quantification, which is different from the position in Germany.[88] In other words, unlike in the case of § 2057a BGB, the value of the estate does not represent the upper limit when quantifying the statutory care legacy. From the viewpoint of the promisee this is beneficial because where the legacy exceeds the value of the estate, the heir/s may have to pay for it, for instance, in a case where they have accepted the inheritance without limiting their liability.[89]

D. Relationship with other claims

What is the relationship between the statutory care legacy and other possible claims that a promisee may have under Austrian law? The drafters of the Austrian succession law reform explicitly refer to enrichment claims, stating that 'the carer may at best also be entitled to enrichment claims according to 1435. She has the freedom of choice between the two claims and can also reject the legacy based on 677.'[90] This is, as we saw, different under German law where the promisee can ask for compensation under § 2057a BGB only where no other claim is available to her.

The reference by the Austrian drafters to enrichment claims, and especially the mention of a choice on the part of the carer, has generated considerable debate in Austrian legal literature. While many authors seem to take the view that a carer has and should have a choice between an enrichment claim and one based on §§ 677ff ABGB, some deny this choice on the basis that the enrichment claim is subsidiary to the latter claim and that the care legacy must therefore come first.[91] Having such a choice is, however, important for the promisee, especially where the estate has insufficient assets. This is because an enrichment claim takes priority over the interests of legacies,[92] and the promisee ranks as a creditor of the deceased, which she does not do if she brings a claim based on §§ 677ff ABGB.

[87] ErläutRV 688 BlgNR 25, GP 17.

[88] For Wendehorst, 'Compulsory Portion and other Aspects of Family Protection in Austria' in *Comparative Succession Law 3* (2020) 257 it is 'both remarkable and problematic that the explanatory notes declare the size of the estate to be of no relevance'.

[89] See Deixler-Hübner in *Erbrecht NEU* (2015) 41; Fischer-Czermak in *Das neue Erbrecht* (2015) 40.

[90] ErläutRV 688 BlgNR 25, GP 17.

[91] Eccher *Erbrechtsreform* (2017) 88 but also Christandl & Nemeth (2016).

[92] Wendehorst, 'Compulsory Portion and other Aspects of Family Protection in Austria' in *Comparative Succession Law 3* (2020) 256.

By contrast, no mention is made by the drafters of the possibility for a claimant to imply an employment contract, but that may be because, unlike in Germany, in Austria there appears to be limited case law at least in recent years.[93] Even so, where such a contract is implied, the promisee is again treated as a creditor.

E. Conclusion

Austrian legal scholars have overall been rather critical of the newly introduced care legacy. Besides the fact that the legislation has left open a number of questions, according to Christiane Wendehorst, many scholars fear that the new care legacy will create considerable problems in practice.[94] Yet, at least so far, it does not seem that the provision has led to major problems and litigation is very limited. Wendehorst herself has expressed the concern that a significant number of individuals will bring a claim against the estate, especially because the threshold is arguably low, both in terms of the definition of 'care' adopted and the requirement of an average of (only) twenty hours per month.[95] However, there does not seem to be a risk that estates are exhausted because the carer can only ever be compensated for up to three years' worth of service.

The Austrian statutory care legacy also has important benefits. The burden of proof is not overly onerous, and the promisee does not have to show that she has acted on the basis of an expectation to be compensated. In other words, her motives do not play a role. Neither does she need to prove that her performance exceeded what can *normally* be expected of her, nor that it exceeded her own obligations towards the deceased. Also, the promisee does not have to show that the deceased's estate has been enriched, which as we saw in Chapter 9 can be difficult both from a practical and psychological standpoint. The legacy is payable in addition to the compulsory share and can only be excluded by the deceased in limited circumstances, though we saw that the deceased can decide that the care legacy has to be accounted for against the intestate share, which is less than satisfactory. Finally, the value of the estate is not the upper limit, so that the heir/s may have to make up for the difference, and potentially the carer can obtain more than the value of the enrichment.

That said, one disadvantage of the statutory care legacy is that the promisee will not be able to obtain the promised asset, though that is, of course, also the case with claims based on the enrichment of the deceased or an implied service contract. More importantly, the legacy can only be demanded for the care that is provided

[93] See Chapter 8.
[94] Wendehorst, 'Compulsory Portion and other Aspects of Family Protection in Austria' in *Comparative Succession Law 3* (2020) 259.
[95] Ibid.

during the three years prior to the promisor's death. While care rendered during the last few years may arguably often be more demanding, it is highly unsatisfactory that the carer cannot bring a claim for the entirety of her services. Thus, the statutory care legacy does not solve the really hard cases where family members sacrifice their lives for significantly longer than three years. As this book shows, such cases are not uncommon in practice.

However, an enrichment claim can be brought for all the services exceeding the three years, though restitution is due only for those services which exceed the family duty. Also, an enrichment claim requires the carer to go to court, which involves costs. By contrast, the costs of demanding a statutory care legacy are relatively low because, as we saw, a claim in court is necessary only if the *Gerichtskommissär* in charge of the probate procedure cannot find a consensual agreement between the heir/s and the carer. This is a significant advantage. On the other hand, in the case of an enrichment claim, or one based on an implied employment contract, the promisee would rank as a creditor of the deceased. Instead, with the care legacy she benefits only after the debts have been paid, which is a significant limitation. In this sense, other avenues may be preferable. But whether or not the promisee has a choice between claims is, as we have seen, unclear, at least with regards to an enrichment claim.

All in all, the protection offered under the Austrian care legacy seems to be preferable to that provided, for instance, by § 2057a BGB, though it is not as effective as it could be and does, in my view, currently not go far enough. What is more, unlike § 2057a BGB, it only covers care services and does not extend to other types of services or work.

Concluding summary of Part III

Part III has shown that, besides a proprietary estoppel claim or a claim based on Canadian unjust enrichment law, there are various other ways in which a promisee may obtain a monetary award based either on the value of her performance or the value of her enrichment. However, we also saw that in some cases the promisee gets less because the law imposes some artificial limits to the amount that can be claimed. This is the case with the *créance de salaire différé*, where the award cannot exceed ten years' worth of wages, and the Austrian statutory care legacy, where the carer can only be compensated for up to three years of care services, even if they have worked or performed services for much longer.

Of the various approaches examined in this part, several are the product of legislative developments, and three of them stem from the area of succession law. Of them only one, the New Zealand TPA 1949, is able to capture a broad range of testamentary promises. In fact, neither the French provisions on the *créance de salaire différé* nor the German § 2057a BGB, nor the Austrian §§ 677ff ABGB, offer comprehensive regulation comparable to that provided by the New Zealand TPA 1949. Unlike the New Zealand TPA 1949, they apply in very specific contexts and/or benefit specific family members and are aimed at addressing cases of unremunerated services irrespective of any promise. By contrast, the New Zealand TPA 1949 deals directly with informal testamentary promises.

The German § 2057a BGB and the Austrian statutory care legacy enshrined in §§ 677ff ABGB, which I examined last, were primarily a response to the fact that often work and care services provided in the family context are not adequately remunerated. In addition, the German provision aims to ensure equality of treatment of the deceased's intestate successors in the sense that those who have not provided a performance for the deceased should not get more than those who have. Equality of treatment of descendants was also a concern behind the French and Belgian *créance de salaire différé*. § 2057a BGB seems to also have been a response to the fact that services performed by descendants are usually not performed on a contractual basis.[1] Though the German legislature did not talk specifically of promises, it appears to have been aware of the informal nature of arrangements in the family/domestic context. This is confirmed also by the extensive interpretation of § 612 BGB by both the German BGH and the BAG analysed in Chapter 8, which was constructed in a way

[1] Paetel *Die erbrechtliche Ausgleichung von Pflegeleistungen* (2009) 19.

to protect those who, in the expectation of an inheritance, provide certain services. This construction was a response partly to the void created by § 2302 BGB which, as we saw, prohibits contracts to make a future will, and partly to the limits of the protection provided by German enrichment law in these cases. In fact, as Chapter 9 has shown, bringing an enrichment claim is not always easy, not just in German law but also under French law. The French developments in the area of enrichment law appear to be a response to the significant gaps in the protection of children who assist their parents in old age. Similarly, the New Zealand legislation was a response to the harshness of contract law and the fact that many promisees were left without protection. Thus, it seems that both legislatures and courts have been sensitive to gaps in the protection provided by the law if not specifically to promisees, then to those who provide work or care in the family context, be it in the home, a business, or on a farm, without being adequately remunerated. In addition, it seems that some of the legislative or jurisprudential developments signify an increased awareness of the fact that the economic value of domestic and care work is often unrecognized. And in some cases, there are also broader policy reasons at work, for example, in the case of the *créance de salaire différé*, which was aimed at ensuring that farming remains viable and the younger generation would not leave the countryside for the big cities.

From the promisee's perspective, some of these forms of redress can work well, for example, because they do not require proof of a promise or of reliance, but the price to pay is usually that they will not receive the promised asset. Nonetheless, they can assist a promisee by offering at least some relief. Even so, certain solutions work better than others. For instance, some of the approaches analysed are very narrow in scope (e.g. the *créance de salaire différé*, § 2057a BGB and §§ 677ff ABGB) and will only protect certain promisees. That said, other approaches (e.g. § 612 BGB and the New Zealand TPA 1949) are able to cater for a broader range of promisees. While both have certain weaknesses, on the whole they are attuned to the specificities of the context in which testamentary promises are made. By contrast, the analysis has shown that enrichment law is perhaps less suited to this context, not least because of the defences available to the promisor and the difficulty, at least in France, of having to prove enrichment and corresponding impoverishment, but also the focus on financial aspects. At the same time, the promisee would count as a creditor, which is highly desirable from the promisee's perspective. In fact, in some of the approaches analysed, promisees are creditors (e.g. in the case of a claim based on enrichment law, § 612 BGB and the *créance de salaire différé*) while in others they are not (e.g. in the case of a claim based on the New Zealand TPA 1949, § 2057a BGB and §§ 677ff ABGB). Where they are treated as a creditor their position is stronger than that of testate and intestate successors, compulsory heirs, or, in the case of common law jurisdictions, applicants under the family provision legislation (and in the case of New Zealand, also claimants under the TPA 1949). Where they are not treated as a creditor, they run a greater risk that not enough funds are in the estate. And thus, their protection will be weaker, which is another aspect to consider when seeking redress.

Concluding reflections

I. Summary

The aim of this book has been to bring into sharper focus the perspective of promisees of testamentary promises often neglected by legal scholarship. The book has considered the personal stories of promisees as they emerge from reported cases—stories which provide the reader with an insight into the dynamics of the relationships between promisees and promisors, the motivations underpinning informal promises of an inheritance, and why these promises might remain unfulfilled.

This book has shown that testamentary promises (broadly understood) represent a social phenomenon that is of practical importance and societal benefit. They are made in all sorts of contexts and can often be critical in procuring and negotiating assistance especially in the care and farming context—contexts in which such assistance is likely to continue to be in demand. Thus, they are usually part of an intergenerational exchange that can yield benefits (of both financial and non-financial nature) for both the promisor and the promisee.

The analysis has further revealed that promises of an inheritance are a social practice that can be found across legal traditions, irrespective of whether or not the specific jurisdiction allows testators to enter into a pact or contract to make a future will or whether or not it limits testamentary freedom through forced or compulsory heirship provisions. Some civil law legislatures may have hoped that they can do away with the challenges posed by promises of an inheritance by simply forbidding formally binding ones.[1] However, as we have seen, such prohibitions have not stopped people from expressing, and acting on, informal promises of a future inheritance. At the same time, the analysis has also revealed that even while common law jurisdictions allow parties to enter into a legally binding contract to make a future will, this does not necessarily mean that promisees enjoy greater protection. We saw that contract law does not always offer effective protection.[2] More importantly, contracts are not easily entered into in the domestic context, because people tend not to formalize arrangements with family members and friends even when they involve economic exchanges, and because of the flexibility that is required for the arrangement to work over time. There is often a considerable time lag between the moment of the promise and the promisors' death. As a consequence, a

[1] Chapter 2.
[2] Chapter 3.

promisee can rarely rely on the protection provided by contract law. Hence, both in common and civil law traditions courts are confronted with situations where an informal promise of an inheritance has been made and acted upon but has remained unfulfilled. This does not, however, mean that promisees are left without protection.

While the law generally tends to privilege the perspective of testators, donors, and promisors, and despite the absence in most legal systems of a specific legal regime aimed at dealing with informal testamentary promises, the analysis has shown that promisees can usually resort to a variety of private law doctrines that are the product of judicial developments and, in some cases, legislative interventions. In fact, the picture portrayed in this book is not just one of vulnerable promisees and their frustrated testamentary expectations, but also one of courts, and sometimes legislatures, being prepared to protect the interests of promisees in a variety of different ways.

New Zealand aside, such legislative interventions have been most common in civil law jurisdictions. They have usually first been made in the agricultural context,[3] or that of small family businesses, before being directed towards domestic and care services, but have often been piecemeal and narrow in scope. They have frequently been an expression of a desire to protect those who provide unremunerated work or services in the family or domestic context (including family farms or agricultural businesses), irrespective of a testamentary promise. This means that they do not usually lead to the award of the promised asset.[4] In the absence of specific legislation, courts have protected promisees by adapting, developing, and sometimes stretching existing private law doctrines belonging to the law of unjust or unjustified enrichment, property, employment, and, to a lesser extent, family and succession law. We saw that, for instance, in relation to the development of the common law doctrine of proprietary estoppel, the broad application of the family provision legislation in Australia, and enrichment law in common law Canada. In the civil law context, Germany is a good example. German courts have applied enrichment law to situations in which testamentary promises have remained unfulfilled and have also interpreted § 612 BGB dealing with service contracts so as to adapt it to cases where the work was provided on the basis of a promise of a future inheritance.

What justifications underpin these legislative and judicial interventions? The answer is not straightforward because the rationale is not always openly revealed;

[3] For instance, we saw that in France, already in 1939, the legislature recognized the need to compensate children performing unremunerated work on the parents' farm, irrespective of any promise, and that in the 1960s, Belgium followed with a similar provision (Chapter 10). And, in 1969, Germany introduced § 2057a BGB, which allows for an adjustment of the intestate share both in case of work and care services rendered for the deceased (Chapter 11).

[4] We can see that, for instance, with the 2009 reform of the German § 2057a BGB, but also the introduction in 2003 of the Dutch Article 4:36(1) BW 2003 and of the Austrian statutory care legacy in 2015 (Chapter 11).

there is often more than one rationale, and it may change over time.[5] However, on the whole, there are several broad justifications, which are not necessarily mutually exclusive: (i) preventing unconscionable behaviour on the part of the promisor/risk of exploitation; (ii) protecting reliance; (iii) remunerating unremunerated work; (iv) preventing the promisor's enrichment; and (v) treating the promisor's successors equally. These justifications aside, there are also other broader policy reasons for intervening both in the farming and in the care context.

The developments traced in this book seem to suggest an increased appreciation of services and work carried out in the domestic context, including by family members. Even so, not all types of performances seem to be valued in the same manner. Generally, domestic work including care work, often carried out by women, is still frequently underrated and those providing such work are often less likely to obtain the promised asset,[6] among other reasons because the law regularly struggles to give value to intangible benefits. Indeed, this book has shown that different promisees enjoy different levels of protection even when they are equally meritorious. Some have fewer forms of redress at their disposal or have to overcome societal expectations based on the nature of their relationship with the promisor, the type of performance rendered when acting on the promise, or their gender. Hence, depending on the context and jurisdiction involved, some promisees are better off than others.

Although the comparison shows that the approaches offered map only partly onto different legal traditions, overall, the likelihood of a promisee receiving the promised asset seems higher in the common law tradition, partly because of the role of equity and the fact that several doctrines grant courts considerable discretion in determining the relief. While this often makes the outcome unpredictable, we saw that from the promisee's perspective, judicial discretion is not necessarily a bad thing given how context-specific the cases are. In the civil law jurisdictions analysed in this book, prohibitions of contracts or pacts to make a future will usually stand in the way of promisees obtaining the promised asset, so that they can normally only claim the value of their performance, that of the promisor's enrichment, or less. While forced/compulsory heirship provisions may temper the risk that at least certain promisees go empty handed, such provisions can potentially prevent promisors from fulfilling their promise.

It follows that across both common and civil law traditions, the legal framework within which testamentary promises operate is complex—certainly much more complex than the legal framework for lifetime promises. At times, the framework is also incoherent and inconsistent.[7] This may well discourage some promisees

[5] See Chapters 5 and 7. See also the rationale underpinning the German § 2057a BGB (discussed in Chapter 11).

[6] Chapter 2.

[7] For instance, we saw in Chapter 3 that with some of the solutions examined in this book, a promisee might be better off when the promise is broken than when it is kept. And the analysis in Chapter 7 has

who have a genuine claim from going to court and leave others who seek justice without adequate protection. At the same time, the fact that the state of the law is not always consistent and coherent, and the legal framework patchy not just across legal traditions, but also within individual jurisdictions, is perhaps not altogether surprising, given that the factual situations are very heterogeneous and complex, ranging from cases in which there is a clear and express promise or arrangements, to ones where the promise is vague and generic, or where the promise needs to be implied from conduct performed over a long period of time. In some cases, the promise precedes the performance by the promisee, while in others, it is difficult to know which came first. And, often, more than one promise is made over time. Moreover, the parties' behaviour can be motivated by a range of different reasons, including the prospect of a financial reward, altruistic concerns, as well as love and affection. Also, any decision about the distribution of the estate has implications for the administration of the estate, and consequently for creditors and successors of the promisor and her estate. In a sense therefore, the state of the law may reflect, to some extent, the ambiguities and complexities of social practices. It is therefore perhaps all too easy to 'blame' legislatures and courts for the way in which the law has developed. After all, the factual scenarios they are confronted with in this context do not always easily fit into existing doctrinal categories, so that courts may be required to straddle definitional boundaries and to push doctrines beyond their original scope. In other words, there is no easy solution to the problems that testamentary promises can give rise to.

II. Leaving it to the parties

One way of dealing with testamentary promises cases would be to leave it to the parties and to decide that, unless they enter a legally binding contract to make a will, the promisee is not provided any legal protection. However, this book has shown that not all jurisdictions allow for contracts to make a will. Even if they did, and one were to abolish the prohibitions of pacts and contracts to make a future will, the contractual approach is not an answer to the problems that promisees of informal testamentary promises face. This is not to say that if the parties want to, they should not be given the opportunity to formalize their testamentary arrangements. There can no doubt be advantages to that. My point is rather that this will only be possible if both parties are prepared to enter into a legally binding contract. In other words, it does not overcome the difficulties created when promisors refuse to formalize the agreement. In those cases, a promisor could still take advantage of the promisee. Legal systems could, of course, provide incentives for parties to

shown that the positions of promisees under the New Zealand Law Reform (Testamentary Promises) Act 1949 vis-à-vis others with an interest in the estate is neither consistent nor clear.

set up legally binding agreements concerning a future inheritance. However, even then, there would still be a power imbalance, for the promisee is unlikely to be able to dictate the conditions for the agreement. As Thompson put it, albeit in the context of nuptial agreements, 'inequalities caused by the relationship of power between parties entering such agreements are likely to be reproduced and reinforced, particularly on gender lines'.[8]

Also, the book has shown that while a contract to make a will would potentially allow parties to determine the details of their agreement,[9] it also has its challenges. Death is an unknown factor and the time span between the promise and the promisors' death is often long. The parties would, therefore, need to insert detailed conditions to deal with various unforeseen circumstances and rules about the termination of the contract. However, the reality of the cases analysed in this book show that much of what happens between the parties over a long time cannot be easily cast in contractual terms. Also, we know that both care and work on the farm often start off with small contributions that increase over time. At what point, then, should the contract be concluded? Thus, a contractual arrangement may not necessarily be in the interest of either of the parties.

Another possibility could be to push parties to enter into binding lifetime agreements.[10] However, most promisors are reluctant to give up control and to depart with assets during their lifetime, and some are simply unable to do so.[11] They therefore want to defer the transfer for as long as possible. Incentives would need to be put in place that make such mechanisms attractive.[12] There are of course ways in which promisors can be left with a certain amount of control over their asset (e.g. through a usufruct or a trust). However, all these structures assume again that both parties are willing to formalize their arrangement, which is precisely what they do not usually want.[13] Thus, ways need to be found to cater for the fact that in the domestic context, promises of an inheritance are usually made informally and these informal promises are being relied upon. In fact, this book has argued that lack of formality of testamentary arrangements involving a future inheritance should not stand in the way of protecting promisees who have acted on a testamentary promise, lest we are happy for them to bear the risk that on the promisor's death they may discover that the promise was not kept even though they have performed all this time. Also, if we insist on formal contracts to make a will, only the interests

[8] Thompson (2018) 623.

[9] Nield (2007) 304.

[10] For instance, through a 'contratto di mantenimento' in Italy or a *Verpfründungsvertrag* in Switzerland. Chinese law has introduced so-called 'legacy support agreements' through Article 31 of the Law of Succession of the People's Republic of China. For an analysis, see Foster (1999). For lifetime agreements, see more generally Hall (2001–2002); Hall (2003).

[11] See the analysis in Chapter 1.

[12] For instance, in Germany, tax incentives seem to have led to an increase in lifetime transfer of family farms.

[13] See the analysis in Chapter 1.

of promisees who manage to get, or insist on, not only a clear agreement as to the obligations of both parties, as well as the subject matter of the promise, but also something in writing, will be safeguarded. In other words, insisting on formalities risks rewarding promisees who are lucky, courageous, or strategic. It would also mean that promisors (and their successors) could avoid liability by insisting on the lack of formality of their agreement. How, then, can we protect promisees of informal testamentary promises?

Ideally, any form of redress would avoid court proceedings, for they can work as a deterrent, not least because of the costs and length of the proceedings. Here the Austrian statutory care legacy (discussed in Chapter 11) is particularly interesting because in the normal case it avoids the court room, but that is because Austria has a probate procedure in place that is lacking in many civil law jurisdictions.[14] Even if court proceedings cannot be avoided, where possible, ways should be sought to make them cost-effective, speedy, and possibly private.[15]

III. Putting in place a legal framework

Putting in place a legal framework is, however, no easy feat. In fact, one important conclusion to be drawn from the analysis carried out in this book is that no universal approach that fits all factual scenarios, let alone across legal traditions, is possible or perhaps even desirable. Even so, there are important factors that ought to be paid attention to when considering how to tackle testamentary promises cases and how best to protect the promisee's interests. These observations are offered tentatively—drawing on the lessons I have learnt in the course of writing this book—and keeping in mind that any specific legal response will need to be tailored to the relevant legal context.

A. Establishing a claim

It is important to ensure that statements are not taken out of context, and that assertions of promises that never took place are not enforced. At the same time, we have seen that testamentary promises are often vague and generic, not just because of the context in which they are made, but also because of the uncertainty of death. Thus, a certain flexibility will be required for the arrangement to work over time. Any requirement for the promisee to have to prove a promise would need to make allowance for that. In other words, if proof of a promise is required,

[14] See Chapter 11.

[15] As Chapter 5 dealing with family provision orders has shown, in some jurisdictions, the applications are not heard in open court so that privacy is protected.

a very broad understanding of 'promise' would need to be put in place. Here the New Zealand Law Reform (Testamentary Promises) Act 1949 (hereafter the New Zealand TPA 1949) discussed in Chapter 7 could provide a useful model. How flexible the requirements are is likely to depend on the type of relief that promisees can potentially obtain, for example, on whether or not they can claim the promised asset or merely compensation for the value of their performance, or the promisor's enrichment.

Arguably, one potential issue with informal promises is the lack of evidence as to the promisor's capacity to make a promise, as well as the risk of undue influence. Wills require either formalities or witnesses that act as safeguards, but, of course, these are often absent in these instances. However, most of the cases discussed in this book show that promises are not usually made very late in the promisor's life. Also, arguably the doctrine of undue influence will protect promisors against undue influence from the promisee.

In most of the cases examined in this book it has not been difficult to identify a performance on the part of the promisee. Yet, we also saw the importance of focusing not only on the financial benefits for the promisor, or financial losses (or impoverishment) on the part of the promisee, but also the value of intangible benefits for the promisor, and the personal sacrifices many promisees make both in the care and agricultural context. In fact, too great an emphasis on financial aspects privileges certain performances (e.g. work on a farm, or the improvement of the promisor's property) over others (e.g. domestic and care services).

Given that a line must be drawn somewhere in terms of how substantial the performance has to be, as clear as possible guidelines should be given as to what threshold the promisee needs to meet and thus what can be regarded as 'substantial' (and thus also whether work and services have to be provided personally or can be paid for). The fact that work or services are provided part-time or on weekends should not work against the promisee. A holistic approach should be taken instead. Also, the availability of a claim should not depend upon whether the promisee moved in with the promisor (and thus lived rent free) or the promisor moved in with her, though mutual benefits of this kind could be considered at the time of quantifying the relief. In the context of care, but also farming, it is simply often inevitable that promisor and promisee live under one roof, and not infrequently the one provided by the promisor.

Where a nexus is required between the promise and the performance, it ought to be borne in mind that in most cases there is not necessarily a chronological sequence between them. Sometimes the performance starts at a lower level before a promise is being made. Thus, to require that the promisor starts performing only after the promisee may work unfairly against certain promisees. More importantly, provision should be made for the fact that, as noted earlier, the parties' motives for agreeing an exchange between a promise of a future inheritance and a performance are often mixed. To require that a promisee must prove that she has acted only or primarily because of the promise, and thus the prospect of a future inheritance, or that she has not acted out of love or affection (as with an enrichment claim), can create both practical and psychological challenges.[16] One possibility is to establish that the promisee's motives do not matter, as is the case with the New Zealand TPA 1949.[17] Alternatively, one could impose an objective standard or place the burden of disproving reliance, or absence of a donative intent, on the promisor or her successors.

B. Granting relief

In terms of how much a promisee should gain, some flexibility will be needed if justice is to be obtained in each individual case. Fairness often comes with a certain degree of flexibility, but that of course may also mean that the cases vary greatly and that the rules become more complex. From the perspective of the promisee, obtaining the promised asset is usually preferable not just because of its economic value but also the emotional attachment that promisees often have (e.g. to the family home, family business, or farm). One needs to also remember that in these cases, promisees often hope that the inheritance will secure their future existence, even if they act also partly out of love and affection for the promisor. Not infrequently, the prospect of an inheritance is appealing because its value is frequently greater than the wealth the promisee will be able to accumulate through their work. In addition, as Shelly Kreiczer-Levy has argued, 'the dynastic aspect explains the importance of inheriting property, rather than receiving compensation for the care'.[18] A further issue with not awarding the promised asset is that compensation of the value of the performance, or the value of the promisor's enrichment, does not always do justice where the promisee has worked for the promisor for many years and made substantial sacrifices. Indeed, frequently promisees make greater sacrifices and 'put up' with more than, for instance, an employee would. They may not have worked on the farm, or in the business, or cared for the promisor, had they known that they would only obtain the value of their performance or that of the benefit of the promisor's enrichment. The fact that the promisee's expectations were engendered by the promisor's promise, even if the promise was made informally, also favours an award of the promised asset. Finally, the promisor, too, may have intended the promised inheritance to not only compensate the promisee for her performance, but also to provide for her future. It is, in fact, important to

[16] Chapter 2.
[17] Chapter 7.
[18] Kreiczer-Levy (2019) 522. See also Conway in *Emotional Dynamics of Law and Legal Discourse* (2016).

remember that the promise may remain unfulfilled for a variety of reasons that are not necessarily attributable to the promisor.[19]

At the same time, if the expectation interest is always fulfilled there is also the risk that promisees obtain the asset irrespective of the length and intensity of their performance. It could, of course, be argued that this is a risk the promisor should bear. Since she is usually dead when the claim is brought, it arguably no longer matters to her, but, of course, it matters to her successors and creditors. One way of dealing with this problem could be to require a certain proportionality between the nature of the promise and the length and nature of the performance. In other words, the clearer the promise, the more substantial the performance (both in terms of intensity and duration), the stronger the argument that the promised asset should be awarded. Here the developments of the doctrine of proprietary estoppel discussed in Chapter 4 are interesting. The question, then, is whether the starting point should be the expectation interest or the value of the performance. Given that the actions of the promisee are fostered by the promisor's behaviour, the expectation interest should arguably be the starting point.

The fact that in some jurisdictions the promisee may be entitled to a forced or compulsory share in the promisor's estate should, in my view, not matter for the purpose of the existence of a claim, nor the quantification of the award.[20] The rationale for such an entitlement is entirely unconnected to the meritoriousness of the claim. Mutual benefits (e.g. in the form of free accommodation), legacies, but also lifetime gifts that the promisor makes to the promisee, could be deducted if they were intended to partially fulfil the promise.

C. Balancing the interests of the promisee with other interests

For a promisee what matters is not only what she needs to prove, and whether or not she can claim the promised asset or merely compensation, but also what her position is vis-à-vis others with an interest in the estate. We saw that in some cases promisees have a proprietary claim, so that they will be in a very strong position, including with regards to third-party transferees. Many forms of redress analysed in this book put the promisee in the position of a creditor, but there are also several where that is not the case, meaning that her protection is less effective. However, it seems that promisees should be treated as creditors for otherwise there is a risk that they go empty handed. In other words, their interests should take priority over those of successors (whether intestate or testate), including forced/compulsory

[19] See Chapter 1.

[20] For instance, the *créance de salaire différé* may be claimed in addition to the compulsory share (Chapter 10). See the difference between the German and the French enrichment law (Chapter 9) and § 612 BGB (Chapter 8).

heirs, whose entitlement is not based on merits or needs and who would usually benefit from the promisee's performance. More problematic is the question how to solve a potential conflict with regards to applicants under the family provision legislation, especially if they are in need, which we saw is not always a requirement. Arguably, the interests of the applicants should be balanced against that of promisees. Where there is more than one promisee, they could both take a share in the promisor's estate, irrespective of whether the promise was expressed in the form of a contract or not. We have seen that the issue has arisen in some common law jurisdictions and that, in the absence of clear guidance, courts have often struggled.[21]

IV. Concluding thoughts

This enquiry has revealed that testamentary promises lead to tensions between a person's testamentary freedom (including the free revocability of the will) and commitments she may have made in view of her death, especially when these commitments have been acted upon by a promisee. But they also reveal a tension between family solidarity and friendship on the one hand, and expectations of a remuneration on the other. This book has therefore challenged the assumption that a clear line can be drawn between bargains and gifts, and gratuitous and non-gratuitous transactions, and shows that these distinctions are overly simplistic. Indeed, more likely than not, testamentary promises are non-donative in nature and represent a kind of *gratuité intéressée*.[22] For that very reason they do not fit comfortably within the broader category of 'gift promises' or 'gratuitous promises'—something which warrants further investigation.

The book has further shown that testamentary promises not only involve different motivations and considerations from lifetime promises but also affect different interests. This is not always sufficiently acknowledged in legal scholarship. In other words, the testamentary context, and testamentary promises as such, deserve separate attention. The analysis has also demonstrated that, as Melanie Leslie has argued,[23] wills cannot be properly viewed as purely unilateral acts. There is often a testamentary arrangement lurking in the background and the will may well be intended to remunerate those who have provided services or work or financial support. Thus, this book is an invitation to further study gifts (whether lifetime or testamentary) including 'remunerative' ones, as well as to explore various types of promises that are usually lumped together under the heading of 'gift promises' or 'gratuitous promises'.

[21] See the analysis in Chapters 3 and 7.

[22] Guével in *Mélanges en l'honneur du professor G Goubeaux* (2009); Braun in *L'abnégation en droit civil* (2017).

[23] Leslie (1999).

The analysis in this book has also put into question the model of the rational actor. Contrary to prevailing assumptions, even though testamentary promises are made in the domestic context, and usually among family members and friends, and the promisor promises to leave a future gift in the form of an inheritance, promisors often act rationally or even strategically. In other words, the fact that they are made in the domestic/family context does not mean that promisors automatically act without careful consideration. At the same time, the book has argued that promisors are perhaps more generous because they usually have nothing to lose. We have also seen that promisees are vulnerable, among other reasons, because of the emotional ties they usually have with the promisor. The reality is thus much more complex than a rational actor model allows for.

The book has argued that the moral quality of the law is impoverished if the law protects primarily the promisor and her testamentary freedom. Yet, succession law debates are often focused primarily on the private autonomy of testators in opposition to the protection of family members, whether based on their status or need. Much less attention is usually paid to the role of unremunerated services or work they may have provided.[24] However, this book has argued that the promisor's testamentary freedom should not foreclose protection of the promisee if the latter has acted on the promise. In other words, a promisor should not be free to dispose of her assets if she has made a promise and a performance has been rendered in exchange. The reason for that is that the promisor has voluntarily assumed an obligation towards the promisee by making a promise (broadly understood) and accepting the promisee's performance.

The book also invites a broader discussion of the basis of forced/compulsory heirship provisions, which can stand in the way of promisors who want to keep their promise, as well of prohibitions of pacts or contracts of a future inheritance which prevent parties from formalizing their agreement if they want to do so. In fact, as it stands, in many jurisdictions a testator cannot bind herself as to the content of her future will, nor can she relinquish her power to change or revoke her will, for reasons that are not necessarily always convincing. Thus, this book has raised wider questions about when a person's freedom of disposition can and should be limited and whether testators should be allowed to bind themselves if they wish to do so.[25]

The book has further shown that the role that gender and notions of intergenerational equality and relationality play in the testamentary context deserve greater attention than they currently receive. What would testamentary freedom look like if it were analysed through the lens of relational theories? The book has demonstrated that when it comes to inheritance, not just the economic value of the promised asset or inheritance matter but, for instance, also the emotional attachment of

[24] See Foster (1998–1999), who is in favour of a behaviour-based model.
[25] See also Dutta (2020).

both the promisor and the promisee to the promised asset. This attachment, then, explains, at least in part, why promisors do not want to give up control over what they own by making a lifetime transfer or entering a legally binding agreement and why promisees may rely on informal testamentary promises.

The analysis has also alerted us to the fact that a certain number of wealth transfers on death happen in hidden ways and not necessarily through succession law. In fact, succession law may not always be the best way to protect the promisee's interests. Here, the comparative enquiry is particularly useful for it forces us to move away from, and look beyond, formal categories and doctrinal structures, and brings into sharper focus the context-sensitive factors that should be paid attention to. Importantly, the analysis has shown that comparative lawyers should pay attention to both formal and informal social practices. After all, social practices do not always correspond to the legal framework in place.[26] Indeed, what would a comparative account of succession law, written from the perspective of various informal social practices, look like?

[26] See Chapter 2. Hyland *Gifts* (2009) 114, has also argued that social practice refuses to conform to the categories the law seeks to impose.

Bibliography

Anderson, R, and Hepworth, M, 'Retirement from Farming: Some Economic and Social Considerations' (1980) 13 Farm Management Review 1 (cit Anderson & Hepworth (1980))

Ann, C, 'BGB § 2057a Ausgleichungspflicht bei besonderer Leistung eines Abkömmlings' in *Münchener Kommentar zum BGB* (8th edn, CH Beck 2020) (cit Ann, 'BGB § 2057a Ausgleichungspflicht' in *Münchener Kommentar zum BGB* (2020))

Atherton, R, 'New Zealand's Testator's Family Maintenance Act of 1900—The Stouts, the Women's Movement and Political Compromise' (1990) 7 Otago Law Review 202 (cit Atherton (1990))

Atiyah, PS, *Promises, Morals, and the Law* (Clarendon Press 1981) (cit Atiyah *Promises* (1981))

Atkinson, TE, *Handbook of the Law of Wills* (West Publishing Co 1937) (cit Atkinson *Handbook of the Law of Wills* (1937))

Barlow, RFD, Wallington, RA, Meadway, SL, and MacDougald, JAD, *Williams on Wills*, vol 1 (20th edn, LexisNexis 2014) (cit Barlow et al *Williams on Wills I* (2014))

Baron, JB, 'Gifts, Bargains, and Form' (1988–1989) 64 Indiana Law Journal 155 (cit Baron (1988–1989))

Battes, R, 'Erfüllungsansprüche trotz beiderseits bewußtem Formmangel—Zugleich ein Beitrag zur Abgrenzung zwischen vertraglicher und außergeschäftlicher Haftung' [1969] JuristenZeitung 683 (cit Battes (1969))

Battes, R, 'Der erbrechtliche Verpflichtungsvertrag im System des Deutschen Zivilrechts—Ziele, Dogmatik und praktische Auswirkungen des § 2302 BGB' (1978) 178 Archiv für die civilistische Praxis 337 (cit Battes (1978))

Baudry-Lacantinerie, G, and Barde, L, *Traité théorique et pratique de droit civil*, vol 1 (3rd edn, L. Larose (Paris) 1906) (cit Baudry-Lacantinerie & Barde *Traité théorique et pratique I* (1906))

Beale, H (ed) *Chitty on Contracts, vol 1, General Principles* (33rd edn, Sweet & Maxwell 2020) (cit Beale *Chitty on Contracts* (2020))

Beardsley, RL, 'Evidence—The Dead Man's Statute: State Legislatures and Courts Conflict' (2001) 25 American Journal of Trial Advocacy 217 (cit Beardsley (2001))

Bentham, J, *Theory of Legislation* (6th edn, London 1890) (cit Bentham *Theory of Legislation* (1890))

Bernheim, BD, Shleifer, A, and Summers, LH, 'The Strategic Bequest Motive' (1985) 93 Journal of Political Economy 1045 (cit Bernheim et al (1985))

Beuthien, V, 'Das fehlerhafte Arbeitsverhältnis als bürgerlich-rechtliches Abwicklungsproblem' [1969] Recht der Arbeit 161 (cit Beuthien (1969))

Biehler, H, *Equity and the Law of Trusts in Ireland* (6th edn, Thomson Reuters 2016) (cit Biehler *Law of Trusts in Ireland* (2016))

Bosch, FW, 'Erbrechtliche Probleme des "Nichtehelichengesetzes"' [1972] Zeitschrift für das gesamte Familienrecht 169 (cit Bosch (1972))

Boulanger, F, 'Enrichissement sans cause et conditions de l'indemnisation d'un enfant pour l'aide et l'assistance apportées à ses parents' (2005) La Semaine Juridique—Édition Notariale et Immobilière 1209 (cit Boulanger (2005)).

Bourdieu, P, *The Logic of Practice* (Stanford University Press 1990) (cit Bourdieu *Logic of Practice* (1990))

Brault, J-C, 'L'intention libérale dans les relations familiales' [1998] La Semaine Juridique—Édition Notariale et Immobilière 14265 (cit Brault (1998))

Braun, A, 'Formal and Informal Testamentary Promises: A Historical and Comparative Perspective' (2012) 76 Rabels Zeitschrift für Ausländisches und Internationales Privatrecht 994 (cit Braun 'Formal and informal testamentary promises' (2012))

Braun, A, 'Towards a Greater Autonomy for Testators and Heirs: Some Reflections on Recent Reforms in France, Belgium and Italy' [2012] Zeitschrift für Europäisches Privatrecht 461 (cit Braun 'Towards a Greater Autonomy' (2012))

Braun, A, and Röthel, A (eds), *Passing Wealth on Death. Will-Substitutes in Comparative Perspective* (Hart Publishing 2016) (cit Braun & Röthel *Passing Wealth on Death* (2016))

Braun, A, 'Will-Substitutes in England and Wales' in Braun, A, and Röthel, A (eds), *Passing Wealth on Death. Will-Substitutes in Comparative Perspective* (Hart Publishing 2016) 51 (cit Braun in *Passing Wealth on Death* (2016))

Braun, A, 'Testamentary Promises Between Selflessness and Self-interest' in Hulin, A-S, and Leckey, R (eds), *L'abnégation en droit civil* (Editions Yvon Blais 2017) 21 (cit Braun in *L'abnégation en droit civil* (2017))

Brian, H, 'The Family Agreement—a Collision Between Love and the Law' [2002] Australian Law Reform Commission Reform Journal 23 (cit Brian (2002))

Bright, S, and McFarlane, B, 'Proprietary Estoppel and Proprietary Rights' [2005] Cambridge Law Journal 449 (cit Bright & McFarlane (2005))

Burckhardt, J, *Der Ausgleich für Mitarbeit eines Ehegatten im Beruf oder Geschäft des anderen (§ 1356 II BGB)* (Gieseking 1971) (cit Burckhardt *Ausgleich für Mitarbeit eines Ehegatten* (1971))

Burns, F, '*Giumelli v Giumelli* Revisited: Equitable Estoppel, the Constructive Trust and Discretionary Remedialism' (2001) 22 Adelaide Law Review 123 (cit Burns (2001))

Burns, P, 'Testamentary Promises: Development of the Law' [1965] New Zealand Law Journal 200 (cit Burns (1965))

Bydlinski, F, 'Lohn—und Kondiktionsansprüche aus zweckverfehlenden Arbeitsleistungen' in Wilburg, W, *Festschrift zum 60. Geburtstag von Walter Wilburg* (Leykam Verlag 1965) 45 (cit Bydlinski in *Festschrift zum 60. Geburtstag von Walter Wilburg* (1965))

Caccavale, C, 'Contratto e Successioni' in Roppo, V (ed), *Trattato del Contratto, Vol VI, Interferenze* (Giuffrè 2006) 481 (cit Caccavale in *Trattato del Contratto VI* (2006))

Caemmerer, E, von, 'Bereicherung und unerlaubte Handlung' in Dölle, H, Rheinstein, M, and Zweigert, K, *Festschrift für Ernst Rabel*, vol 1 (Mohr Siebeck 1954) 333 (cit Caemmerer in *Festschrift für Ernst Rabel I* (1954))

Campbell, ID, 'Promises to Make Testamentary Provisions' (1947) 23 New Zealand Law Journal 221 (cit Campbell (1947))

Canaris, C-W, 'Atypische Faktische Arbeitsverhältnisse' [1967] Betriebs-Berater 165 (cit Canaris (1967))

Canaris, C-W, *Die Vertrauenshaftung im deutschen Privatrecht* (CH Beck 1971) (cit Canaris *Vertrauenshaftung* (1971))

Carroll, E, '"The Assurances Are Only Half the Story ... " Proprietary Estoppel and Testamentary Capacity in James v James' [2018] Conveyancer and Property Lawyer 192 (cit Carroll (2018))

Castella, C, 'Retour sur le contrat de salaire différé du descendant au vu de la jurisprudence récente: observations sur la pérennité d'une singularité du monde agricole' (May 2010) Revue de droit rural, étude 10 383 (cit Castella (2010))

Chalmers, R, 'The Future of Unjust Enrichment in Common Law Canada' [2017] Restitution Law Review 3 (cit Chalmers (2017))

Chamoulaud-Trapiers, A, *Les fruits et revenus en droit patrimonial de la famille* (Pulim 1999) (cit Chamoulaud-Trapiers *Les fruits et revenus* (1999))

Christandl, G, and Nemeth, K, 'Das neue Erbrecht—ausgewählte Einzelfragen' [2016] Österreichische Notariats-Zeitung 5 (cit Christandl & Nemeth (2016))

Christandl, G, 'Will-Substitutes in Italy' in Braun, A, and Röthel, A (eds), *Passing Wealth on Death. Will-Substitutes in Comparative Perspective* (Hart Publishing 2016) 131 (cit Christandl in *Passing Wealth on Death* (2016))

Christandl, G, and Nemeth, K, 'Austrian Succession Law Rewritten: A Comparative Analysis' [2020] European Review of Private Law 149 (cit Christandl & Nemeth (2020))

Christandl, G, '§§ 677–678' in Fenyves, A, Kerschner, F, and Vonkilch, A (eds), *Großkommentar zum ABGB—Klang* (3rd edn, Verlag Österreich 2021) 196 (cit Christandl, '§§ 677–678' in *Großkommentar zum ABGB* (2021))

Coester, M, '§ 1619 BGB' in von Staudinger, J (eds), *Kommentar zum Bürgerlichen Gesetzbuch mit Einführungsgesetz und Nebengesetzen* (De Gruyter Neubearbeitung 2007) (cit Coester, '§ 1619 BGB' in *Staudinger, Kommentar zum BGB* (2007))

Conway, H, 'Where There's a Will ... : Law and Emotion in Sibling Inheritance Disputes' in Conway, H, and Stannard, J (eds), *The Emotional Dynamics of Law and Legal Discourse* (Hart Publishing 2016) 35 (cit Conway in *Emotional Dynamics of Law and Legal Discourse* (2016))

Conway, H, and Stannard, J, 'The Emotional Dynamics of Property Law' in Bandes, SA, Lyneé Madeira, J, Temple, KD, and Kidd White, E (eds), *Research Handbook on Law and Emotions* (Elgar 2021) 229 (cit Conway and Stannard in *Research Handbook on Law and Emotions* (2021))

Conway, SF, McDonagh, J, Farrell, M, and Kinsella, A, 'Cease Agricultural Activity Forever? Understanding the Importance of Symbolic Capital' (2016) 44 Journal of Rural Studies 164 (cit Conway et al (2016))

Coote, B 'Testamentary Promises Jurisdiction in New Zealand' in Northey, JF (ed), *A G Davis Essays in Law* (Butterworths, 1965) 1 (cit Coote in *Essays in Law* (1965))

Core, P, 'The Contractualisation of Care in an Ageing World' in Beverley, C, and Herring, J (eds), *Ageing, Gender and Family Law* (Routledge 2018) 34 (cit Core in *Ageing, Gender and Family Law* (2018))

Croucher, RF, 'Contracts to Leave Property by Will and Family Provision after *Barns v* Barns (2003) 196 ALR 65—Orthodoxy or Aberration?' (2005) 27 Sydney Law Review 263 (cit Croucher (2005))

Croucher, RF, 'Conflicting Narratives in Succession Law—A Review of Recent Cases' (2007) 14 Australian Property Law Journal 179 (cit Croucher (2007))

D'Angelo, A, *Le promesse unilaterali. Artt. 1987–1991* (Giuffrè 1996) (cit D'Angelo *Le promesse unilaterali* (1996))

Dal Pont, GE, *Equity and Trusts in Australia* (6th edn, Thomson Reuters 2015) (cit Dal Pont *Equity and Trusts* (2015))

Dal Pont, GE, and Mackie, KF, *Law of Succession* (2nd edn, LexisNexis Butterworths 2017) (cit Dal Pont & Mackie *Succession* (2017))

Damrau, J, 'Erbersatzanspruch und Erbausgleich. Zur Neuregelung des Erbrechts im "Nichtehelichengesetz"' [1969] Zeitschrift für das gesamte Familienrecht 579 (cit Damrau (1969))

Danneman, G, *The German Law of Unjustified Enrichment* (OUP 2009) (cit Danneman *Unjustified Enrichment* (2009))

Davey, M, 'Testamentary Promises' (1988) 8 Legal Studies 92 (cit Davey (1988))

Davis, AG, 'The Law Reform (Testamentary Promises) Act, 1949 (NZ)' (1950) 13 The Modern Law Review 353 (cit Davis (1950))

Dawson, JP, *Gifts and Promises* (Yale University Press 1980) (cit Dawson *Gifts and Promises* (1980))

De Bermond de Vaulx, J-M, 'Le contrat de travail à salaire différé (Origine et régime depuis la loi d'orientation agricole du 5 août 1960)' [1965] La Semaine Juridique—Édition Générale 1893 (cit De Bermond de Vaulx (1965))

De Giorgi, MV, *I patti sulle successioni future* (Jovene 1976) (cit De Giorgi *I patti sulle successioni future* (1976))

De Groot, JK, and Nickel, BW, *Family Provision in Australia* (5th edn, LexisNexis Buttterworths 2017) (cit De Groot & Nickel *Family Provision in Australia* (2017))

Deixler-Hübner, A, 'Familienrechtliche Aspekte des Erbrechts' in Deixler-Hübner, A, and Schauer, M (eds), *Erbrecht NEU* (LexisNexis ARD ORAC 2015) 43 (cit Deixler-Hübner in *Erbrecht NEU* (2015))

Deixler-Hübner, A, '§10 Das Pflegevermächtnis' in Gruber, M, Kalss, S, Müller, K, and Schauer, M (eds), *Erbrecht und Vermögensnachfolge* (2nd edn, Verlag Österreich 2018) 358 (cit Deixler-Hübner in *Erbrecht und Vermögensnachfolge* (2018))

Delnoy, P, 'Le salaire différé dans l'agriculture et l'horticulture' [1976] Annales de la Faculté de droit, d'économie et de sciences sociales de Liège 55 (cit Delnoy (1976))

Delnoy, P, and Moreau, P, *Les Libéralités et les succession* (6th edn, Larcier 2018) (cit Delnoy & Moreau *Les Libéralités et les succession* (2018))

Descheemaeker, E, 'The New French Law of Unjustified Enrichment' [2017] Restitution Law Review 77 (cit Descheemaeker (2017))

Dienstbühl, C, 'Der Pflegevergütungsanspruch nach § 612 BGB in der erbrechtlichen Auseinandersetzung' [2009] Zeitschrift für die gesamte erbrechtliche Praxis 178 (cit Dienstbühl (2009))

Dixon, M, 'Estoppel: A Panacea for All Wills' [1999] Conveyancer and Property Lawyer 46 (cit Dixon (1999))

Dixon, M, 'Proprietary Estoppel and Formalities in Land Law and the Land Registration Act 2002' in Cooke, E (ed), *Modern Studies in Property Law*, vol 2 (Hart Publishing 2003) 168 (cit Dixon in *Modern Studies II* (2003))

Dixon, M, 'Estoppel and Testamentary Freedom' [2008] Conveyancer and Property Lawyer 65 (cit Dixon (2008))

Dixon, M, 'Proprietary Estoppel: The Law of Farms and Families (Editorial)' [2019] Conveyancer and Property Lawyer 89 (cit Dixon (2019))

Doering-Striening, G, 'Häusliche Pflege von Eltern—was bringt sie "fürsorgenden" Kindern ein?' [2012] Familienrecht und Familienverfahrensrecht 531 (cit Doering-Striening (2012))

Du Plessis, J, *The South African Law of Unjustified Enrichment* (Juta 2012) (cit Du Plessis *Unjustified Enrichment* (2012))

Dutta, A, 'Die Zulässigkeit erbrechtlicher Selbstbindungen' [2020] Zeitschrift für die gesamte Privatrechtswissenschaft 20 (cit Dutta (2020))

Eccher, B, *Die österreichische Erbrechtsreform* (Verlag Österreich 2017) (cit Eccher *Erbrechtsreform* (2017))
Eisenberg, MA, 'Donative Promises' (1979) 47 University of Chicago Law Review 1 (cit Eisenberg (1979))
Eisenberg, MA, 'The World of Contract and the World of Gift' (1997) 85 California Law Review 821 (cit Eisenberg (1997))
Enderlein, W, 'Die Dienstpflicht des Hauskindes als Folge seiner Unterhaltsgemeinschaft mit den Eltern' [2000] Archiv für die civilistische Praxis 565 (cit Enderlein (2000))
Errington, A, and Lobley, M, 'Handing Over the Reins. A Comparative Study of International Farm Transfers' (2002) Paper presented to the Agricultural Economics Society Annual Conference (cit Errington & Lobley (2002))
Esser, J, *Schuldrecht*, vol 2 (Verlag CF Müller Karlsruhe 1969) (cit Esser *Schuldrecht II* (1969))
Everaert-Dumont, D, 'L'assistance aux parents âgés: quand le dévouement devient source d'indemnisation ou de rémunération' [2003] Petites affiches 8 (cit Everaert-Dumont (2003))
Farber, DA, and Matheson, JH, 'Beyond Promissory Estoppel: Contract Law and the "Invisible Handshake"' (1985) 52 University of Chicago Law Review 903 (cit Farber & Matheson (1985))
Farnsworth, EA, 'Reasons for Regret' in Gorla, G (ed), *Scintillae Iuris. Studi in Memoria di Gino Gorla, III* (Giuffrè 1994) 1877 (cit Farnsworth in *Scintillae Iuris* (1994))
Farnsworth, EA, 'Promises to Make Gifts' (1995) 43 American Journal of Comparative Law 359 (cit Farnsworth (1995))
Farnsworth, EA, *Changing your Mind: The Law of Regretted Decisions* (Yale University Press 1998) (cit Farnsworth *Changing your Mind* (1998))
Fehr, E, and Gächter, S, 'Fairness and Retaliation: The Economics of Reciprocity' (2000) 14 Journal of Economic Perspectives 159 (cit Fehr & Gächter (2000))
Fehr, E, and Fischbacher, U, 'The Nature of Human Altruism' (2003) 425 Nature 785 (cit Fehr & Fischbacher (2003))
Fehr, E, and Schmidt, KM, 'The Economics of Fairness, Reciprocity and Altruism. — Experimental Evidence and New Theories' in Kolm, SG, and Ythier, JM (eds), *Handbook of the Economics of Giving, Altruism and Reciprocity*, vol 1 (North Holland 2006) 615 (cit Fehr & Schmidt in *Handbook of the Economics of Giving I* 2006))
Fellows, ML, 'His to Give; His to Receive; Hers to Trust: A Response to Carol M Rose' (1992) 44 Florida Law Review 329 (cit Fellows (1992))
Fenn, H, 'Die juristische Qualifikation der Mitarbeit bei Angehörigen und ihre Bedeutung für die Vergütung' [1968] Zeitschrift für das gesamte Familienrecht 291 (cit Fenn (1968))
Fenn, H, *Die Mitarbeit in den Diensten Familienangehöriger* (Bad Homburg v.d.H. 1970) (cit Fenn *Mitarbeit* (1970))
Fillette, J-L, 'Enrichissement sans cause' [1996] Defrénois 468 (cit Fillette (1996))
Fineman, MA, and Grear, A (eds), *Vulnerability: Reflections on a New Ethical Foundation for Law and Politics* (Ashgate 2013) (cit Fineman & Grear *Vulnerability* (2013))
Fischer-Czermak, C, 'Ehegattenerbrecht, Rechte des Lebensgefährten und Abgeltung von Pflegeleistungen' in Rabl, C, and Zöchling-Jud, B (eds), *Das neue Erbrecht. Erbrechts-Änderunggesetz* 2015 (Manz 2015) 38 (cit Fischer-Czermak in *Das neue Erbrecht* (2015))
Fischer-Czermak, C, and Pierer, J, '§ 552' in Fenyves, A, Kerschner, F, and Vonkilch, A (eds), *Großkommentar zum ABGB—Klang §§ 552–646* (3rd edn, Verlag Österreich 2021) 29 (cit Fischer-Czermak and Pierer, '§ 552' in *Großkommentar zum ABGB* (2021))
Flynn, L, and Lawson, A, 'Gender, Sexuality and the Doctrine of Detrimental Reliance' [1995] Feminist Legal Studies 105 (cit Flynn & Lawson (1995))

Forbes-Chilibeck, E, 'Have You Heard the One about the Farmer's Daughter? Gender-bias in the Intergenerational Transfer of Farm Land on the Canadian Prairies' (2005) 24 Canadian Woman Studies/Les Cahiers De La Femme 26 (cit Forbes-Chilibeck (2005))

Foster, FH, 'Towards a Behaviour-Based Model of Inheritance?: The Chinese Experiment' (1998–1999) 32 UC Davis Law Review 77 (cit Foster (1998–1999))

Foster, FH, 'Linking Support and Inheritance: A New Model from China' (1999) Wisconsin Law Review 1199 (cit Foster (1999).

Freedman, CD, 'Unjust Enrichment Claims against the Estate Based on the Provision of Services to the Deceased' (2010) 29 Estates, Trusts & Pensions Journal 163 (cit Freedman (2010))

Friedman, GHL, 'Part Performance of Contracts and *Quantum Meruit Claims* for Services Rendered' (1980) 6 Estates and Trusts Reports 105 (cit Friedman (1980))

Friedman, LM, *Dead Hands. A Social History of Wills, Trusts, and Inheritance Law* (Stanford University Press 2009) (cit Friedman (2009))

Fuller, LL, 'Consideration and Form' (1941) 41 Columbia Law Review 799 (cit Fuller (1941))

Gallanis, TP, and Gittler, J, 'Family Caregiving and the Law of Succession: A Proposal' (2011–2012) 45 University of Michigan Journal of Law Reform 761 (cit Gallanis & Gittler (2011–2012))

Gardner, S, 'The Remedial Discretion in Proprietary Estoppel' (1999) 115 Law Quarterly Review 438 (cit Gardner (1999))

Gardner, S, 'The Remedial Discretion in Proprietary Estoppel—Again' (2006) 122 Law Quarterly Review 492 (cit Gardner (2006))

Gasson, R, and Errington, A, *The Farm Family Business* (Wallingford: CAB International 1993) (cit Gasson & Errington *Farm Family Business* (1993))

Gazzoni, FM, 'Patti successori: conferma di una erosione' [2001] Rivista del notariato 232 (cit Gazzoni (2001))

Gelot, B, 'Enrichissement sans cause' (2005) Defrénois 224 (cit Gelot (2005))

Gerckens, FJ, 'Zum Mißbrauch der Testierfreiheit im Landwirtschaftsrecht' [1955] Zeitschrift für das gesamte Familienrecht 163 (cit Gerckens (1955))

Ghezzi, G, 'Legato per remunerazione di servizi resi' [1961] Rivista Trimestrale di Diritto e Procedura Civile 803 (cit Ghezzi (1961))

Ghezzi, G, 'Ordinamento della famiglia, impresa familiare e prestazione di lavoro' [1976] Rivista Trimestrale di Diritto e Procedura Civile 1358 (cit Ghezzi (1976))

Glennon, L, 'Displacing the Conjugal Family in Legal Policy—A Progressive Move?' (2005) 17 Child and Family Law Quarterly 141 (cit Glennon (2005))

Glister, J, 'Lifetime Wealth Transfer and the Equitable Presumptions of Resulting Trust and Gift' (2018) 103 Iowa Law Review 1971 (cit Glister (2018))

Godbout, JT, *The World of the Gift* (McGill-Queen's Press 1998) (cit Godbout *World of the Gift* (1998))

Goetz, CJ, and Scott, RE, 'Enforcing Promises: An Examination of the Basis of Contract' (1980) 89 Yale Law Journal 1261 (cit Goetz & Scott (1980))

Goodnow, JJ, and Lawrence, JA, 'Inheritance Norms for Distributions of Money, Land, and Things in Families' (2010) 1 Family Science 73 (cit Goodnow and Lawrence (2010))

Gordley, J (ed), *The Enforceability of Promises in European Contract Law* (CUP 2001) (cit Gordley *Enforceability of Promises* (2001))

Gordley, J, *Foundations of Private Law. Property, Tort, Contract, Unjust Enrichment* (OUP 2006) (cit Gordley *Foundations of Private Law* (2006))

Gordon-Bouvier, E, 'Crossing the Boundaries of the Home: A Chronotopical Analysis of the Legal Status of Women's Domestic Work' [2019] International Journal of Law in Context 1 (cit Gordon-Bouvier (2019))

Gordon-Bouvier, E, *Relational Vulnerability. Theory, Law and the Private Family* (Palgrave Macmillan 2020) (cit Gordon-Bouvier *Relational Vulnerability* (2020))

Gorla, G, *Il contratto* (Giuffrè 1954) (cit Gorla *Il contratto* (1954))

Granger, C, 'Doctrine of Part Performance—English and Canadian Attitudes' (1969) 3 Ottawa Law Review 664 (cit Granger (1969))

Grimaldi, M, 'La créance de salaire différé ne se transmet qu'aux enfants' [2009] Revue trimestrielle de droit civil 151 (cit Grimaldi (2009))

Grimaldi, M, 'Revirement de jurisprudence: la créance de salaire différé est une créance à terme qui, exigible au décès de l'exploitant, naît de son vivant, et qui constitue donc une dette de sa communauté universelle' [2012] Revue trimestrielle de droit civil 350 (cit Grimaldi (2012))

Grimaldi, M, *Droit Civil Successions* (7th edn, LexisNexis, 2017) (cit Grimaldi *Droit Civil Successions* (2017))

Grziwotz, H, 'Bereicherungsanspruch wegen Zweckverfehlung in Erwartung eines späteren Eigentumserwerbs' [2013] Mitteilungen des Bayerischen Notarvereins 471 (cit Grziwotz (2013))

Guével, D, 'La gratuité intéressée: oxymore d'avenir' in Cachard, O, and Henry, X, *Mélanges en l'honneur du professor G Goubeaux* (Dalloz 2009) 229 (cit Guével in *Mélanges en l'honneur du professor G Goubeaux* (2009))

Gulliver, AG, and Tilson, CJ 'Classification of Gratuitious Transfers' (1941) 51 Yale Law Journal 1 (cit Gulliver & Tilson (1941))

Günther, G, *Das Rechtsverhältnis zwischen Bauer und mitarbeitendem Sohn* (Carl Heymanns Verlag KG 1966) (cit Günther *Das Rechtsverhältnis* (1966))

Haas, U, and Holla, M, 'Ausgleich für die enttäuschte Erberwartung' [2002] Zeitschrift für Erbrecht und Vermögensnachfolge 169 (cit Haas & Holla (2002))

Hall, MI, 'The Care Agreement: Transfer of Property in Exchange for the Promise of Care and Support' (2001–2002) 21 Estates, Trusts & Pensions Journal 209 (cit Hall (2001–2002))

Hall, MI, 'Care for Life: Private Care Agreements between Older Adults and Friends or Family Members' [2003] Elder Law Review 9; (2003) 2 Elder Law Review 24 (cit Hall (2003))

Hartog, H, *Someday All This Will Be Yours. A History of Inheritance and Old Age* (Harvard University Press 2012) (cit Hartog *Someday* (2012))

Hauser, J, 'L'établissement et l'entretien des enfants majeurs: une famille à titre onéreux?' [1999] Defrénois 1217 (cit Hauser (1999))

Hayton, D, 'By-Passing Testamentary Formalities' (1987) 46 Cambridge Law Journal 215 (cit Hayton (1987))

Herring, J, *Law and the Relational Self* (CUP 2020) (cit Herring *Relational Self* (2020))

Herring, J, 'Relational Autonomy and Family Law' in Wallbank, J, Choudhry, S, and Herring, J (eds), *Rights, Gender and Family Law* (Routledge 2010) 257 (cit Herring in *Rights, Gender and Family Law* (2010))

Hoerder, D, Van Nederveen Meerkerk, E, and Neunsinger, S (eds), *Towards a Global History of Domestic and Caregiving Workers* (Brill 2015) (cit Hoerder et al *Towards a Global History* (2015))

Hofri-Winogradow, A, and Kaplan, RL, 'Property Transfers to Caregivers: A Comparative Analysis' (1997) 103 Iowa Law Review 1997 (cit Hofri-Winogradow & Kaplan (1997))

Honey, R, and Evans, M, 'Great Expectations: Inheritance, Equity and the Family Farm' (2007) 9 The Agricultural Industry 47 (cit Honey & Evans (2007)).

Hopkins, N, 'Estoppel and Restitution: Drawing a Divide' in Cooke, E (ed), *Modern Studies in Property Law: Volume II* (Hart Publishing, 2001) 145 (cit Hopkins in *Modern Studies II* (2001))

Humbert, H, 'Die formlose Bestimmung des Hoferben' [1956] NJW 1857 (cit Humbert (1956))

Hutchison, D, 'Succession Agreements in South African and Scots Law' in Reid, KGC, and de Waal, MJ (eds), *Exploring the Law of Succession: Studies National, Historical and Comparative* (Edinburgh University Press 2007) 226 (cit Hutchison in *Exploring the Law of Succession* (2007))

Hyland, R, *Gifts: A Study in Comparative Law* (OUP 2009) (cit Hyland *Gifts* (2009))

Imhof, BM, *Die neuen Bestimmungen zum Lidlohn* (Dissertation, Freiburg 1975) (cit Imhof *Die neuen Bestimmungen zum Lidlohn* (1975))

Izuhara, M, 'Negotiating Family Support? The "Generational Contract" between Long-term Care and Inheritance' (2004) 33 Journal of Social Policy 649 (cit Izuhara (2004)).

Jansen, N, 'Farewell to Unjustified Enrichment?' (2016) 20 Edinburgh Law Review 123 (cit Jansen (2016))

Jarman, T, and Sweet, C, *A Treatise on Wills* (6th edn, Sweet & Maxwell 1910) (cit *Jarman on Wills* (1910))

Jöchl, L, 'Das Pflegevermächtnis' [2016] Zeitschrift für Verbraucherrecht 44 (cit Jöchl (2016))

Kanzleiter, R, 'Leer ausgegangen? In der Verfügung von Todes wegen nicht bedacht trotz aufopfernder Leistung für den Erblasser zu dessen Lebzeiten?' in Muscheler, K (ed), *Hereditare—Jahrbuch für Erbrecht und Schenkungsrecht*, vol 9 (Mohr Siebeck 2019) 23 (cit Kanzleiter in *Hereditare 9* (2019))

Kaser, M, *Das Römische Privatrecht*, vol 1 (2nd edn, CH Beck 1971) (cit Kaser *Das Römische Privatrecht I* (1971))

Kaser, M, *Das Römische Privatrecht*, vol 2 (CH Beck 1975) (cit Kaser *Das Römische Privatrecht II* (1975))

Kasirer, N, 'Honour Bound' (2001) 47 McGill Law Journal 237 (cit Kasirer (2001))

Keating, A, *Keating on Probate* (5th edn, Thomson Reuters 2015) (cit Keating *Probate* (2015))

Keim, C, 'Testamentsgestaltung bei "missratenen" Kindern. Neue Möglichkeiten durch die geplanten Änderungen im Pflichtteilsrecht?' [2008] NJW 2072 (cit Keim (2008))

Kerridge, R, *Parry and Kerridge, The Law of Succession* (13th edn, Sweet & Maxwell 2016) (cit Kerridge *Parry and Kerridge* (2016))

Kerridge, R, 'Family Provision in England and Wales' *Comparative Succession Law 3* (2020) 384 (cit Kerridge, 'Family Provision in England and Wales' in *Comparative Succession Law 3* (2020))

Kiener, M, 'Abgeltung von Pflegeleistungen naher Angehöriger—Das Pflegevermächtnis' [2015] Österreichische Zeitschrift für Pflegerecht 188 (cit Kiener (2015))

Kohn, NA, 'For Love and Affection: Elder Care and the Law's Denial of Intra-Family Contracts' (2019) 54 Harvard Civil Rights-Civil Liberties Law Review 211 (cit Kohn (2019))

Kolkman, W, 'Compulsory Portion and Family Provision in the Netherlands' in *Comparative Succession Law 3* (2020) 319 (cit Kolkman, 'Compulsory Portion and Family Provision in the Netherlands' in *Comparative Succession Law 3* (2020))

Kollmeyer, D, 'Ausgleich von Pflegeleistungen unter Abkömmlingen' [2017] NJW 1849 (cit Kollmeyer (2017))
Korven, KS, 'Returning to its Rural Beginnings: Unjust Enrichment and the Constructive Trust from the Perspective of a Farm Child' (1993) 57 Saskatchewan Law Review 429 (cit Korven (1993))
Kössinger, W, '§ 1' in Niede, H, and Kössinger, W, *Handbuch der Testamentsgestaltung* (5th edn, CH Beck 2015) (cit Kössinger, '§ 1' in *Handbuch der Testamentsgestaltung* (2015))
Krebber, S, 'Die Sicherung erbrechtlicher Erwerbsaussichten im Lichte erbrechtlicher Prinzipien' (2004) 204 Archiv für die civilistische Praxis 149 (cit Krebber (2004))
Kreiczer-Levy, S, 'Parents and Adult Children: The Elusive Boundaries of the Legal Family' (2019) 44 Law & Social Inquiry 519 (cit Kreiczer-Levy (2019))
Kreitner, R, *Calculating Promises: The Emergence of Modern American Contract Doctrine* (Stanford University Press 2007) (cit Kreitner *Calculating Promises* (2007))
Kroeschell, K, 'Rechtsprobleme der bäuerlichen Hofübergabe' in Universität (Göttingen). *Rechts—und Staatswissenschaftliche Fakultät Göttinger Festschrift für das Oberlandesgericht Celle* (Schwartz Verlag 1961) 99 (cit Kroeschell in *Göttinger Festschrift* (1961))
Kropholler, J, 'Die Rechtsnatur der Familienarbeit und die Ersatzpflicht bei Verletzung oder Tötung des mitarbeitenden Familienangehörigen' [1969] Zeitschrift für das gesamte Familienrecht 240 (cit Kropholler (1969))
Kroppenberg, I, 'Anmerkungen' [2014] JuristenZeitung 50 (cit Kroppenberg (2014))
Kull, A, 'Reconsidering Gratuitous Promises' (1992) 21 Journal of Legal Studies 39 (cit Kull (1992))
Kupisch, B, 'Leistungskondiktion bei Zweckverfehlung—Teil 2' [1985] Juristenzeitung 163 (cit Kupisch (1985))
Küpper, W, '§ 1967 BGB—Erbenhaftung, Nachlassverbindlichkeiten' in *Münchener Kommentar zum BGB* (8th edn, CH Beck 2020) (cit Küpper, '§1967 BGB—Erbenhaftung, Nachlassverbindlichkeiten' in *Münchener Kommentar zum BGB* (2020))
Langbein, JH, 'Substantial Compliance with the Wills Act' (1975) 88 Harvard Law Review 489 (cit Langbein (1975))
Langbein, JH, 'The Nonprobate Revolution and the Future of the Law of Succession' (1983–1984) 97 Harvard Law Review 1108 (cit Langbein (1983–1084))
Larenz, K, and Canaris, C-W, *Lehrbuch des Schuldrechts, Band II/2 Besonderer Teil* (13th revised edn, CH Beck 1994) 151 (cit Larenz & Canaris *Schuldrecht II* (1994))
Le Guidec, R, 'Successions et libéralités' [1995] La Semaine Juridique—Édition Générale 3876 (cit Le Guidec (1995))
Le Guidec, R, and Bosse Platière, H, 'Droit patrimonial de la famille' [December 2010] Revue de droit rural, chronique 2 (cit Le Guidec & Bosse Platière (2010))
Learmonth, A, Ford, C, Fletcher, T, Clark, M, and Shuman, M, *Theobald on Wills* (19th edn, Sweet & Maxwell 2021) (cit Learmonth et al *Theobald on Wills* (2021))
Lee, WA, 'Contracts to Make Wills' (1971) 87 Law Quarterly Review 358 (cit Lee (1971))
Lee, WA, 'Wills Contract to Leave Property by Will—Jurisdiction to Make TFM Order Interfering with Benefit' (1972) 46 Australian Law Journal 191 (cit Lee (1972))
Leleu, YH, 'Les pactes successoraux en droit comparé' in Chambre des Notaires de l'Arrondissement Tongeren. *Congrès des Notaires Les relations contractuelles internationales. Le rôle du notaire* (Antwerpen-Apeldoorn 1995) 545 (cit Leleu in *Les relations contractuelles internationales* (1995))
Leonard, B, Kinsella, A, O'Donoghue, C, Farrell, M, and Mahon, M, 'Policy Drivers of Farm Succession and Inheritance' (2017) 61 Land Use Policy 147 (cit Leonard et al (2017))

Lescaillon, A, 'Les rapports entre codébiteurs d'aliments' [1990] La Revue des huissiers de justice 949 (cit Lescaillon (1990))

Leslie, MB, 'Enforcing Family Promises: Reliance, Reciprocity and Relational Contract' (1999) 77 North Carolina Law Review 551 (cit Leslie (1999))

Lettmaier, S, *Broken Engagements. The Action for Breach of Promise of Marriage and the Feminine Ideal, 1800–1940* (OUP 2010) 10 (cit Lettmaier *Broken Engagements* (2010))

Libchaber, R, 'Enrichissement sans cause: Note sous Cour de cassation, première Chambre civile, 23 janvier 2001' [2001] Répertoire du Notariat Defrénois 719 (cit Libchaber (2001))

Lieb, M, *Die Ehegattenmitarbeit im Spannungsfeld zwischen Rechtsgeschäft, Bereicherungsausgleich und gesetzlichem Güterstand* (Mohr Siebeck 1970) (cit Lieb *Ehegattenmitarbeit* (1970))

Litman, MM, 'The Emergence of Unjust Enrichment as a Cause of Action and the Remedy of Constructive Trust' (1988) 26 Alberta Law Review 407 (cit Litman (1988))

Lobley, M, 'Succession in the Family Farm Business' (2010) 13 Journal of Farm Management 839 (cit Lobley (2010))

Locke, J, *Second Treatise of Government* (Raleigh, N.C.: Alex Catalogue 2001) (cit Locke *Second Treatise of Government* (2001))

Logar, T, 'Exploitation as Wrongful Use: Beyond Taking Advantage of Vulnerabilities' (2010) 25 Acta Anal 329 (cit Logar (2010))

Lohmann, I, '§ 2057a Ausgleichungspflicht bei besonderen Leistungen eines Abkömmlings' in Hau, W, and Poseck, R (eds), *Beck'scher Online-Kommentar BGB* (57th edn, CH Beck 2021) (cit Lohmann, '§ 2057a Ausgleichungspflicht bei besonderen Leistungen eines Abkömmlings' in *Beck'scher Online-Kommentar BGB* (2021))

Lord Neuberger of Abbotsbury, 'The Stuffing of Minerva's Owl? Taxonomy and Taxidermy in Equity' (2009) 68 Cambridge Law Journal 537 (cit Lord Neuberger (2009))

Lorenz, W, '§ 812' in *J von Staudingers Kommentar zum Bürgerlichen Gesetzbuch mit Einführungsgesetz und Nebengesetzen* (13th edn, De Gruyter 1996) 143 (cit Lorenz, '§ 812' in *Staudinger, Kommentar zum BGB* (1996))

Lüdtke-Handjery, E, and von Jeinsen, U (eds), *Höfeordnung* (11th edn, CH Beck, 2015) (cit Lüdtke-Handjery & Jeinsen, *Höfeordnung* (2015)

Ludyga, H, 'Die Berücksichtigung von Pflegeleistungen gemäß § 2057a BGB nach der Erbrechtsreform' [2009] Zeitschrift für die Steuer—und Erbrechtspraxis 289 (cit Ludyga (2009))

Lurger, B, '§ 1435 ABGB' in Kletečka, A, and Schauer, M (eds), *ABGB-ON* (Manz 2016) (cit Lurger, '§ 1435 ABGB' in *ABGB-ON* (2016))

Lutter, M, *Das Erbrecht des nichtehelichen Kindes* (Alfred Metzner Verlag 1972) (cit Lutter *Erbrecht des nichtehelichen Kindes* (1972))

MacQueen, H, and Hogg, M, 'Donations in Scots Law' [2012] Juridical Review 1 (cit MacQueen & Hogg (2012))

MacQueen, H, 'Cohabitants in the Scottish Law of Unjustified Enrichment' [2019] Acta Juridica 419 (cit MacQueen (2019))

Malaurie, P, *Les Successions. Les Libéralités* (4th edn, Defrénois 2010) (cit Malaurie *Les Successions* (2010))

Malaurie, P, Aynès, L, Stoffel-Munck, P, *Droit des obligations* (11th edn, LGDJ 2020) (cit Malaurie et al *Droit des obligations* (2020))

Malaurie, P, *La Famille* (7th edn, Defrénois 2020) (cit Malaurie *La Famille* (2020))

Malek, HM, *Phipson on Evidence* (18th edn, Sweet & Maxwell 2013) (cit Malek *Phipson on Evidence* (2013))

Margrave-Jones, CV, *Mellows: The Law of Succession* (5th edn, Butterworths 1993) (cit Margrave-Jones *Mellows Succession* (1993))

Martyn, JGR, Evans-Gordon, J, Learmonth, A, Ford, C, and Fletcher, T, *Theobald on Wills* (18th edn, Sweet & Maxwell 2016) (cit Martyn et al *Theobald on Wills* (2016))

Masson, A, and Pestieau, P, 'Bequest Motives and Models of Inheritance: A Survey of Literature' in Erreygers, G, and Vandevelde, T (eds), *Is Inheritance Legitimate? Ethical and Economic Aspects of Wealth Transfers* (Berlin: Springer 1997) 54 (cit Masson & Pestieau in *Is Inheritance Legitimate?* (1997))

Mauger-Vielpeau, L, 'Les sujets et l'objet de la dette alimentaire' [2010] Petites affiches 21 (cit Mauger-Vielpeau (2010))

Mauss, M, *The Gift: Forms and Functions of Exchange in Archaic Societies* (I Cunnison transl, WW Norton 1967) (cit Mauss *The Gift* (1967))

McBride, NJ, *The Humanity of Private Law: Part I: Explanation* (OUP 2019) (cit McBride *Humanity of Private Law I* (2019))

McFarlane, B, 'Proprietary Estoppel: The Importance of Looking Back' in Davies, PS, and Pila, J (eds), *The Jurisprudence of Lord Hoffmann* (Hart Publishing 2015) 331 (cit McFarlane in *Jurisprudence of Lord Hoffmann* (2015))

McFarlane, B, and Sales, P, 'Promises, Detriment, and Liability: Lessons from Proprietary Estoppel' (2015) 131 Law Quarterly Review 610 (cit McFarlane & Sales (2015))

McFarlane, B, 'Proprietary Estoppel: Undermining the Law of Succession?' in B Häcker, B and Mitchell, C (eds), *Current Issues in Succession Law* (Hart Publishing 2016) 77 (cit McFarlane in *Current Issues* (2016))

McFarlane, B, *The Law of Proprietary Estoppel* (2nd edn, OUP 2020) 487 (cit McFarlane *Proprietary Estoppel* (2020))

McFarlane, B, Hopkins, N, and Nield, S, *Land Law. Text, Cases and Materials* (5th edn, OUP 2021) (cit McFarlane et al *Land Law* (2021))

McGregor-Lowndes, M, and Hannah, F, 'Reforming Australian inheritance Law: Tyrannical Testators vs Greying Heirs?' (2009) 17 Australian Property Law Journal 62 (cit McGregor-Lowndes & Hannah (2009))

McGee, J (ed), *Snell's Equity* (33rd edn, Sweet & Maxwell 2015) (cit McGee *Snell's Equity* (2015))

McInnes, M, *The Canadian Law of Unjust Enrichment and Restitution* (LexisNexis 2014) (cit McInnes *Canadian Law of Unjust Enrichment* (2014))

McInnes, M, 'Improvements to Land, Equity, Proprietary Estoppel, and Unjust Enrichment' (2016) 2 Canadian Journal of Comparative and Contemporary Law 421 (cit McInnes (2016))

McLachlin, B, 'Restitution in Canada' in Cornish, WR, Nolan, RC, O'Sullivan, J, and Virgo, GJ (eds), *Restitution Past, Present and Future. Essays in Honour of Gareth Jones* (Hart Publishing 1998) 275 (cit McLachlin in *Restitution Past, Present and Future* (1998))

Medicus, D, *Bürgerliches Recht* (23rd revised edn, Vahlen 2011) (cit Medicus *Bürgerliches Recht* (2011))

Mee, J, 'The Limits of Proprietary Estoppel: *Thorner v Major*' (2009) 21 Child and Family Law Quarterly 367 (cit Mee (2009))

Mee, J, 'The Role of Expectation in the Determination of Proprietary Estoppel Remedies' in Dixon, M (ed), *Modern Studies in Property Law*, vol 5 (Hart Publishing 2009) 389 (cit Mee in *Modern Studies V* (2009))

Mee, J, 'Proprietary Estoppel and Inheritance: "Enough is Enough"?' [2013] Conveyancer and Property Lawyer 280 (cit Mee (2013))

Mee, J, 'Thorner v Major (2009): Proprietary Estoppel and Inheritance' in Sloan, B (ed), *Landmark Cases in Succession Law* (Hart Publishing 2019) 191 (cit Mee in *Landmark Cases* (2019))

Miller, G, 'Provision for Adult Children under the Inheritance (Provision for Family and Dependants) Act 1975' [1995] Conveyancer and Property Lawyer 22 (cit Miller (1995))

Miller, G, *The Machinery of Succession* (2nd edn, Dartmouth Publishing Co Ltd 1996) 219 (cit Miller *The Machinery* (1996))

Mischkowski, D, Stone, R, and Stremitzer, A, 'Promises, Expectations, and Social Cooperation' (2019) 62 Journal of Law and Economics 687 (cit Mischkowski et al (2019))

Miserre, R, *Die 'culpa in testando': Möglichkeiten und Grenzen einer Vertrauenshaftung im Erbrecht* (Gieseking Verlag 2002) (cit Miserre *Die 'culpa in testando'* (2002))

Monteillet-Geffroy, M, *Les conditions de l'enrichissement sans cause dans les relations de famille* (Lille: ANRT 2001) (cit Monteillet-Geffroy *Les conditions de l'enrichissement* (2001))

Montoux, D, 'Pension Alimentaire. —Conditions d'exercice. —Caractères particuliers', Fasc. 10 [1 March 2005] JurisClasseur Notarial Formulaire > V° Pension alimentaire (cit Montoux (2005))

Mowbray, J, Tucker, L, Le Poidevin, N, Brightwell, J, and Simpson, E, *Lewin on Trusts* (18th edn, Sweet & Maxwell 2007) (cit Mowbray et al *Lewin on Trusts* (2007))

Müller-Glöge, R, '§ 612 BGB Vergütung' in *Münchener Kommentar zum BGB* (8th edn, CH Beck 2020) (cit Müller-Glöge, '§ 612 BGB Vergütung' in *Münchener Kommentar zum BGB* (2020))

Muscheler, K, 'Die geplanten Änderungen im Erbrecht, Verjährungsrecht und Nachlassverfahrensrecht' [2008] Zeitschrift für Erbrecht und Vermögensnachfolge 105 (cit Muscheler (2008))

Muscheler, K, *Erbrecht,* vol 1 (Mohr Siebeck 2010) (cit Muscheler *Erbrecht I* (2010))

Nield, S, '"If You Look after Me, I Will Leave You My Estate": The Enforcement of Testamentary Promises in England and New Zealand' (2000) 20 Legal Studies 85 (cit Nield (2000))

Nield, S, 'Testamentary Promises, A Test Bed for Legal Frameworks of Unpaid Caregiving' (2007) 58 Northern Ireland Legal Quarterly 287 (cit Nield (2007))

Nikisch, A, *Arbeitsrecht*, vol 1 (3rd revised edn, Mohr Siebeck 1961) (cit Nikisch *Arbeitsrecht I* (1961))

Nozick, RS, 'The Statute of Frauds: Can a Lost Will be a Sufficient 'Memorandum'? What Constitutes Acts of Part Performance?' (1978) 2 Estates and Trusts Reports 165 (cit Nozick (1978))

Oldham, M, 'Financial Obligations within the Family—Aspects of Intergenerational Maintenance and Succession in England and France' (2001) 60 Cambridge Law Journal 128 (cit Oldham (2001))

Oosterhoff, AH, Freedman, CD, McInnes, M, and Parachin, A, *Oosterhoff on Wills* (8th edn, Thomson Reuters 2016) (cit Oosterhoff et al *Oosterhoff on Wills* (2016))

Otte, G, 'Bessere Honorierung von Pflegeleistungen—Plädoyer für eine Vermächtnislösung' [2008] Zeitschrift für Erbrecht und Vermögensnachfolge 260 (cit Otte (2008))

Oughton, R, *Tyler's Family Provision* (3rd edn, LexisNexis 1997) (cit Oughton *Tyler's Family Provision* (1997))

Paciocco, D, 'The Remedial Constructive Trust: A Principled Basis for Priorities over Creditors' (1989) 68 Canadian Bar Review 315 (cit Paciocco (1989))

Paetel, A, *Die erbrechtliche Ausgleichung von Pflegeleistungen und anderen Sonderleistungen, eine Auseinandersetzung mit § 2057a BGB und dem geplanten § 2057b BGB* (Verlag Dr Kovač 2009) (cit Paetel *Die erbrechtliche Ausgleichung von Pflegeleistungen* (2009))

Patarin, J, 'Composition du passif successoral: l'indemnisation, *de in rem verso*, de l'héritier dont l'aide et l'assistance apportées à ses parents excèdent les exigences de la piété filiale' [1995] Revue trimestrielle de droit civil 407 (cit Patarin (1995))

Patarin, J, 'L'action d'enrichissement sans cause exercée contre la succession d'un exploitant agricole par l'épouse d'un descendant à défaut de droit au contrat de travail à salaire différé' [1996] Revue trimestrielle de droit civil 215 (cit Patarin (1996))

Patterson, WM, *Law of Family Protection and Testamentary Promises* (5th edn, LexisNexis New Zealand 2021) (cit Patterson *Law of Family Protection* (2021))

Pearson, ST, *The Testamentary Promises Act. To Be or Not to Be?* (Dissertation October 2011) (cit Pearson *Testamentary Promises Act* (2011))

Peart, N, '*Re Welch*: The Boundaries of the Testamentary Promises Act' [1991] New Zealand Law Journal 77 (cit Peart (1991))

Peart, N, and Borkowski, A, 'Provision for Adult Children on Death—The Lesson from New Zealand' (2000) 12 Child & Family Law Quarterly 333 (cit Peart & Borkowski (2000))

Peart, N, 'Where There is a Will, There is a Way—A New Wills Act for New Zealand' (2007) 15 Waikato Law Review 26 (cit Peart (2007))

Peart, N, 'New Zealand's Succession Law: Subverting Reasonable Expectations' (2008) 37(4) Common Law World Review 356 (cit Peart (2008))

Peart, N, 'Testamentary Formalities in Australia and New Zealand' in *Comparative Succession Law* 1 (2011) 329 (cit Peart, 'Testamentary Formalities in Australia and New Zealand' in *Comparative Succession Law 1* (2011))

Peart, N, 'Re Welch (1990): Enforcing Testamentary Promises' in Sloan, B (ed), *Landmark Cases in Succession Law* (Hart Publishing 2019) 211 (cit Peart in *Landmark Cases* (2019))

Peart, N, and Vines, P, 'Family Provision in New Zealand and Australia' in *Comparative Succession Law* 3 (2020) 450 (cit Peart & Vines, 'Family Provision in New Zealand and Australia' in *Comparative Succession Law 3* (2020))

Pérès, C, 'Intestate Succession in France' in *Comparative Succession Law 2* (2015) 33 (cit Pérès, 'Intestate Succession in France' in *Comparative Succession Law 2* (2015))

Pérès, C, 'Compulsory Portion in France' in *Comparative Succession Law 3* (2020) 78 (cit Pérès, 'Compulsory Portion in France' in *Comparative Succession Law 3* (2020))

Philipps, L, 'Helping Out in the Family Firm: The Legal Treatment of Unpaid Market Labor' (2008) 23 Wisconsin Journal of Law, Gender & Society 65 (cit Philipps (2008))

Pierron, J, 'Quelques aspects du recours entre codébiteurs d'aliments' [1949] La Semaine Juridique—Édition Générale 784 (cit Pierron (1949))

Popovici, A, and Smith, LD, 'Family Provision in Canada' in *Comparative Succession Law 3* (2020) 507 (cit Popovici & Smith, 'Family Provision in Canada' in *Comparative Succession Law 3* (2020))

Posner, EA, 'Norms, Formalities, and the Statute of Frauds: A Comment' (1996) 144 University of Pennsylvania Law Review 1971 (cit Posner (1996))

Posner, EA, 'Altruism, Status, and Trust in the Law of Gifts and Gratuitous Promises' [1997] Wisconsin Law Review 567 (cit Posner (1997))

Posner, RA, 'Gratuitous Promises in Economics and Law' (1977) 6 Journal of Legal Studies 411 (cit Posner (1977))

Potter, C, and Lobley, M, 'Aging and Succession on Family Farms' (1992) 32 Sociologia Ruralis 317 (cit Potter & Lobley (1992))

Preis, U, '§ 612 BGB' in Müller-Gölge, R, Preis, U, and Schmidt, I (eds) *Erfurter Kommentar zum Arbeitsrecht* (20th edn, CH Beck 2020) (cit Preis, '§ 612 BGB' in *Erfurter Kommentar zum Arbeitsrecht* (2020))

Prévault, J, 'Vers un élargissement du concept de salaire différé' in *Études dédiées à Alex Weill* (Dalloz-Litec 1983) 433 (cit Prévault in *Études dédiées à Alex Weill* (1983))

Richardi, R, and Fischinger, P, '§ 612 BGB' in *J von Staudingers Kommentar zum Bürgerlichen Gesetzbuch mit Einführungsgesetz und Nebengesetzen* (De Gruyter Neubearbeitung 2011) (cit Richardi & Fischinger, '§ 612 BGB' in *Staudinger, Kommentar zum BGB* (2011))

Raoul-Cormeil, G, Veaux-Fournerie, P, and Veaux, D, 'Successions. —Pacte sur succession future', Fasc 20 [11 May 2011] JurisClasseur Civil Code Art 721 à 724-1 (cit Raoul-Cormeil et al (2011))

Rapp, M, 'Die Ausgleichung von Pflegeleistungen—Geschichte einer verunglückten Gesetzgebung' in Damrau, J, and Muscheler, K (eds), *Erbrecht und Vermögensnachfolge: Festschrift für Manfred Bengel und Wolfgang Reimann* (CH Beck 2012) 295 (cit Rapp in *Erbrecht und Vermögensnachfolge* (2012))

Reid, KGC, de Waal, MJ, and Zimmermann, R (eds), *Comparative Succession Law, Volume 1: Testamentary Formalities* (OUP 2011) (cit *Comparative Succession Law 1* (2011))

Reid, KGC, de Waal, MJ, and Zimmermann, R, 'Testamentary Formalities in Historical and Comparative Perspective' in *Comparative Succession Law 1* (2011) 432 (cit Reid, de Waal & Zimmermann, 'Testamentary Formalities in Historical and Comparative Perspective' in *Comparative Succession Law 1* (2011))

Reid, KGC, de Waal, MJ, and Zimmermann, R (eds), *Comparative Succession Law, Volume 2: Intestate Succession* (OUP 2015) (cit *Comparative Succession Law 2* (2015))

Reid, KGC, de Waal, MJ, and Zimmermann, R, 'Intestate Succession in Historical and Comparative Perspective' in *Comparative Succession Law* 2 (2015) 444 (cit Reid, de Waal & Zimmermann, 'Intestate Succession in Historical and Comparative Perspective' in *Comparative Succession Law 2* (2015))

Reid, KGC, de Waal, MJ, and Zimmermann, R (eds), *Comparative Succession Law, Volume 3: Mandatory Family Protection* (OUP 2020) (cit *Comparative Succession Law 3* (2020))

Reid, KGC, 'Mandatory Family Protection in the Common Law Tradition' in *Comparative Succession Law 3* (2020) 707 (cit Reid, 'Mandatory Family Protection in the Common Law Tradition' in *Comparative Succession Law 3* (2020))

Reid, KGC, de Waal, MJ, and Zimmermann, R, 'Mandatory Family Protection in Historical and Comparative Perspective' in *Comparative Succession Law 3* (2020) 737 (cit Reid, de Waal & Zimmermann, 'Mandatory Family Protection in Historical and Comparative Perspective' in *Comparative Succession Law 3* (2020))

Resta, G, 'Gratuità e solidarietà: fondamenti emotivi e "irrazionali"' [2014] Rivista critica del diritto privato 39 (cit Resta (2014))

Richardson, N, 'Testamentary Promises in New Zealand' [March 2003] International Family Law 42 (cit Richardson (2003))

Ripert, G, *La règle morale dans les obligations civiles* (LGDJ Paris 1949) (cit Ripert (1949))

Rivier, M-C, 'Inégalités dans l'entretien des parents par les enfants majeurs' in Dekeuwer-Défossez, F, and Choain, C (eds), *Les Enjeux De la transmission entre générations. Du don pesant au du vindicatif* (Septentrion 2005) 141 (cit Rivier in *Les Enjeux De la transmission entre générations* (2005))

Rochard, D, 'Loi d'orientation Agricole—La créance de salaire différé du conjoint survivant' [1999] Juris-Classeur Périodique 1509 (cit Rochard (1999))

Rödl, C, *Ehegattenmitarbeit im deutschen und französischen Recht. Eine rechtsvergleichende Untersuchung zum Entgeltanspruch für die Mitarbeit im Beruf des Ehegatten ohne ausdrücklichen Vertrag* (Gieseking 1998) (cit Rödl *Ehegattenmitarbeit* (1988))

Roemer, 'Zur formlosen Hoferbenbestimmung in der Rechtssprechung des BGH' [1957] Deutsche Notar-Zeitschrift 283 (cit Roemer (1957))

Romani, A-M, 'Enrichissement sans cause' (2018) Répertoire de droit civil (cit Romani (2018))
Rose, CM, 'Giving, Trading, Thieving, and Trusting: How and Why Gifts become Exchanges, and (More Importantly) Vice Versa' (1992) 44 Florida Law Review 295 (cit Rose (1992))
Roth, M, 'Private Pflege' in Becker, U, and Roth, M (eds), *Recht der Älteren* (De Gruyter 2013) 455 (cit Roth in *Recht der Älteren* (2013))
Röthel, A, *Ist unser Erbrecht noch zeitgemäß? Gutachten A zum 68. Deutschen Juristentag* (CH Beck 2010) (cit Röthel *Ist unser Erbrecht noch zeitgemäß?* (2010))
Röthel, A (ed), *Verträge in der Unternehmerfamilie: Privatautonomie in Nähebeziehungen* (CH Beck 2014) (cit Röthel *Verträge in der Unternehmerfamilie* (2014))
Röthel, A, *Erbrecht* (18th edn, CH Beck 2020) (cit Röthel *Erbrecht* (2020))
Roussel, F, 'Des difficiles rapports entre salaire différé et actio de in rem verso' (1996) 11 La Semaine Juridique—Édition Notariale et Immobilière 417 (cit Roussel (1996))
Roussel, F, 'La vivacité du contrat de travail à salaire différé' [2010] Revue de droit rural, repère 2 (cit Roussel (2010))
Roussel, F, 'Naissance de la créance de salaire différé' [2012] Recueil Dalloz 854 (cit Roussel (2012))
Roussel, F, 'Le salaire différé, dette personnelle de l'exploitant' [2014] Recueil Dalloz 259 (cit Roussel (2014))
Roussel, F, 'Successions agricoles. —Salaire différé', Fasc. 40 [October 2013] JurisClasseur Civil Code Art. 831 à 834 (cit Roussel (2013))
Ruby, G, and Schindler, A, 'ZEV-Report Zivilrecht' [2017] Zeitschrift für Erbrecht und Vermögensnachfolge 382 (cit Ruby & Schindler (2017))
Sanders, A, *Statischer Vertrag und dynamische Vertragsbeziehung: Wirksamkeits—und Ausübungskontrolle von Gesellschafts—und Eheverträgen* (Gieseking 2008) (cit Sanders *Statischer Vertrag* (2008))
Savatier, X, 'Enrichissement sans cause' [1994] Defrénois 1511 (cit Savatier (1994))
Savatier, X, 'Réflexions sur le salaire différé à la lumière de la jurisprudence récente de la Cour de cassation' *Rapport de la Cour de cassation 1996* (Doc. fr., Paris 1997) (cit Savatier (1996))
Schauer, M, 'Familie und Erbrecht' in Deixler-Hübner, A (ed), *Handbuch Familienrecht* (Linde Verlag 2015) 689 (cit Schauer in *Handbuch Familienrecht* (2015))
Schmidt, JP, *Itinera hereditatis: Strukturen der Nachlassabwicklung in historisch-vergleichender Perspective* (Mohr Siebeck 2021) (cit Schmidt, *Itinera hereditatis* (2021).
Schulz, F, *Classical Roman Law* (Oxford 1951) (cit Schulz *Classical Roman Law* (1951))
Schwab, M, '§ 812 BGB' in *Münchener Kommentar zum BGB* (8th edn, CH Beck 2020) Rn 461 (cit Schwab, '§ 812 BGB' in *Münchener Kommentar zum BGB* (2020))
Sériaux, A, 'Des limites de la piété filiale' [1995] La Semaine Juridique—Édition Génerale 22425 (cit Sériaux, 'Des limites' (1995))
Sériaux, A, 'Enrichissement sans cause et devoir de secours envers les parents: Note sous Cour de cassation, première Chambre civile, 12 juillet 1994, Fouret contre Madame Courtois' [1995] La Semaine Juridique—Édition Notariale et Immobilière 1658 (cit Sériaux, 'Enrichissement sans cause' (1995))
Shavell, S, 'An Economic Analysis of Altruism and Deferred Gifts' [1991] Journal of Legal Studies 401 (cit Shavell (1991))
Sheppard, AW, 'Contracts to Make Wills and the Family Protection Act 1955: Is the Promisee a Creditor or a Beneficiary' (1985) 15 Victoria University Wellington Law Review 157 (cit Sheppard (1985))

Silbaugh, KB, 'Commodification and Women's Household Labor' in Albertson Fineman, M, and Dougherty, T (eds), *Feminism Confronts Homo Economicus: Gender, Law and Society* (Cornell University Press 2005) 338 (cit Silbaugh in *Feminism Confronts Homo Economicus* (2005))

Sloan, B, 'Estoppel and the Importance of Straight Talking' [2009] Conveyancer and Property Lawyer 154 (cit Sloan (2009))

Sloan, B, 'Proprietary Estoppel: Recent Developments in England and Wales' (2010) 22 Singapore Academy of Law Journal 110, 131–135 (cit Sloan (2010)).

Sloan, B, 'Due Rewards or Undue influence?' Property Transfers Benefitting Informal Carers' [2011] Restitution Law Review 37 (cit Sloan 'Due Rewards' (2011))

Sloan, B, 'Testamentary Freedom and Caring Adult Offspring in England & Wales and Ireland' in Boele-Woelki, K, Miles, J, and Scherpe, JM (eds), *The Future of Family Property in Europe* (Intersentia 2011) 251 (cit Sloan in *Future of Family Property in Europe* (2011))

Sloan, B, 'Unjust Enrichment Claims by Informal Carers' [2011] Elder Law Journal 298 (cit Sloan 'Unjust Enrichment Claims' (2011))

Sloan, B, *Informal Carers and Private Law* (Hart Publishing 2012) (cit Sloan *Informal Carers* (2012))

Sloan, B, 'Reversing Testamentary Dispositions in Favour of Informal Carers' in Häcker, B, and Mitchell, C (eds), *Current Issues in Succession Law* (Hart Publishing 2016) 189 (cit Sloan in *Current Issues* (2016))

Sloan, B, *Borkowski's Law of Succession* (4th edn, OUP 2020) (cit Sloan *Borkowski's Law of Succession* (2020))

Smith, L, 'The State of the Law of Unjust Enrichment in Common Law Canada' (2015) 57 Canadian Business Law Journal 39 (cit Smith (2015))

Söllner, A, 'Der Bereicherungsanspruch wegen Nichteintritts des mit einer Leistung bezweckten Erfolges' (1963) 16 Archiv für die civilistische Praxis 20 (cit Söllner (1963))

Spagnoli, C, 'Note in tema di impresa familiare, lavoro gratuito ed azione di arricchimento senza causa' [2002] Diritto di Famiglia e delle Persone 672 (cit Spagnoli (2002))

Sparks, BM, 'Historical Development of the Law of Contracts to Devise or Bequeath' (1953–1954) 42 Kentucky Law Journal 573 (cit Sparks (1953–1954))

Sparks, BM, 'Problems in the Formation of Contracts to Devise or Bequeath' (1954–1955) 40 Cornell Law Quarterly 60 (cit Sparks (1954–1955))

Sparks, BM, 'Contract to Devise or Bequeath as an Estate Planning Device' (1955) 20 Missouri Law Review 1 (cit Sparks (1955))

Sparks, BM, *Contracts to Make Wills* (New York University Press 1956) (cit Sparks *Contracts to Make Wills* (1956))

Spierin, B, *Succession Act 1965 and Related Legislation: A Commentary* (5th edn, Bloomsbury Professional 2017) (cit Spierin *Succession Act* (2017))

Stefula, M, 'Die Abgeltung von Pflegeleistungen—Das Pflegevermächtnis nach dem ErbRÄG 2015' [2016] Zeitschrift für Familien—und Erbrecht 118 (cit Stefula (2016))

Stoljar, SJ, 'A Rationale of Gifts and Favours' (1956) 19 Modern Law Review 237 (cit Stoljar (1956))

Stoljar, SJ, 'Enforcing Benevolent Promises' (1989–1990) 12 Sydney Law Review 17 (cit Stoljar (1989–1990))

Süss, R, *Erbrecht in Europa* (4th edn, Zerb Verlag 2020) (cit Süss *Erbrecht in Europa* (2020))

Tattersall, L, 'A Portable Palm Tree: Proprietary Estoppel in *Davies v Davies* (CA)' (2016) 30 Trust Law International 237 (cit Tattersall (2016))

Terré, F, Lequette, Y, and Gaudemet, S, *Droit civil. Les successions. Les libéralités* (4th edn, Dalloz 2014) (cit Terré et al *Droit civil. Les successions* (2014))

Terré, F, and Fenouillet, D, *Droit civil. La famille* (9th edn, Dalloz 2018) (cit Terré & Fenouillet *Droit civil. La famille* (2018))

Terré, F, Simler, P, Lequette, Y, and Chénedé, J, *Droit civil. Les obligations* (12th edn, Dalloz 2019) (cit Terré et al *Droit civil. Les obligations* (2019))

Teschner, A, '§ 2057a BGB—Pflegeleistungen im Lichte der Rechtsprechung (Teil 1)' [2017] Zeitschrift für die Steuer—und Erbrechtspraxis 61 (cit Teschner (2017))

Thomale, C, *Leistung als Freiheit. Erfüllungsautonomie im Bereicherungsrecht* (Mohr Siebeck 2012) (cit Thomale *Leistung als Freiheit* (2012))

Thomale, C, 'BGH: Vererblichkeit des Bereicherungsausgleichs wegen Zweckverfehlung' [2013] Lindenmaier-Möhring—Kommentierte BGH-Rechtsprechung (LMK) 347486 (cit Thomale (2013))

Thompson, MP, 'Estoppel: A Return to Principle' [2001] Conveyancer and Property Lawyer 78 (cit Thompson (2001))

Thompson, MP, 'Estoppel: Reliance, Remedy and Priority' [2003] Conveyancer and Property Lawyer 157 (cit Thompson (2003))

Thompson, S, 'Feminist Relational Contract Theory: A Model for Family Property Arrangements' (2018) 45 Journal of Law and Society 617 (cit Thompson (2018))

Titmuss, R, *The Gift Relationship: From Human Blood to Social Policy* (Phanteon Books 1971) (cit Titmuss *The Gift of Relationship* (1971))

Toti, B, 'La nullità del testamento esecutivo del patto successorio' [1985] Rivista del Notariato 9 (cit Toti (1985))

Trappe, S, and Renners, S, 'Die Vergütung von Pflegeleistungen als Gegenstand arbeitsrechtlicher Auseinandersetzungen?' [2012] Zeitschrift für Erbrecht und Vermögensnachfolge 301 (cit Trappe & Renners (2012))

Trappe, S, 'Ausgleich von Pflegeleistungen im Erbfall' [2017] Zeitschrift für die gesamte erbrechtliche Praxis 206 (cit Trappe (2017))

Tucker, H, 'Colorado Dead Man's Statute: Time for Repeal or Reform' (2000) 29 Colorado Lawyer 45 (cit Tucker (2000))

Uchiyama, T, Lobley, M, Errington, A and Yanagimura, S, 'Dimensions of Intergenerational Farm Business Transfers in Canada, England, the USA and Japan' (2008) 10 Japanese Journal of Rural Economy 33 (cit Uchiyama et al (2008))

Vismara, G, *Storia dei patti successori*, vol 1 (Milano 1942) (cit Vismara *Storia dei patti successori I* (1942))

Vogelsang, H, '§ 67 Grundlagen und Bemessung der vertraglichen Arbeitsvergütung' in Ahrendt, M, Koch, U, Linck, R, Treber, J, and Vogelsang, H, *Schaub Arbeitsrechts-Handbuch* (18th edn, CH Beck 2019) (cit Vogelsang, '§ 67' in *Schaub Arbeitsrechts-Handbuch* (2019))

Von Jhering, R *Law in Daily Life—A Collection of Legal Questions Connected with the Ordinary Events of Everyday Life* (Clarendon Press 1904) (cit Jhering *Collection of Legal Questions* (1904))

Voyce, M, 'The Impact of the Testator's Family Maintenance Legislation as Law and Ideology on the Family Farm' (1993) 7 Australian Journal of Family Law 191 (cit Voyce (1993))

Voyce, M, '"Domestic Promises" and the Division of Farming Property in Australia' (2014) 14 Macquarie Law Journal 149 (cit Voyce '"Domestic Promises"' (2014))

Voyce, M, 'Family Provision, The Family Farm and Rural Patriarchy: Three Actors in Search of a Play?' (2014) 19 Deakin Law Review 347 (cit Voyce 'Family Provision' (2014))

Voyce, M, 'Testamentary Promises, Family Provision and the Family Farm' (2014) 8 Elder Law Review 1 (cit Voyce 'Testamentary Promises' (2014))

Walker, R, 'Which Side "Ought to Win"? Discretion and Certainty in Property Law' [2008] Singapore Journal of Legal Studies 229 (cit Walker (2008))
Wallbank, J, and Herring, J (eds), *Vulnerabilities, Care and Family Law* (Routledge 2014) (cit Wallbank & Herring *Vulnerabilities* (2014))
Wallis, E, 'Outdated Form of Evidentiary Law: A Survey of Dead Man's Statutes and a Proposal for Change' (2005) 53 Cleveland State Law Review 75 (cit Wallis (2005))
Waters, DWM, 'The Constructive Trust in Evolution: Substantive and Remedial' (1990–1991) 10 Estate & Trust Journal 334 (cit Waters (1990–1991))
Waters, DWM, Smith, L, Gillen, M, *Waters' Law of Trusts in Canada* (5th edn Carswell Thomson Reuters 2021) (cit Waters et al *Waters' Law of Trusts in Canada* (2021))
Weber, M, 'Bereicherungsansprüche wegen enttäuschter Erwartung?' [1989] JuristenZeitung 25 (cit Weber (1989))
Weimar, P, 'Inheritance Contracts and Public Policy' (1994) 4 Journal of South African Law 787 (cit Weimar (1994))
Weimar, P, 'Erbvertrag und gute Sitten' in García y García, A, and Weimar, P (eds), *Miscellanea Domenico Maffei*, vol 4 (Keip Verlag Goldback 1995) 231 (cit Weimar in *Miscellanea Domenico Maffei IV* (1995))
Weiner, AB, *Inalienable Possessions: The Paradox of Keeping While-Giving* (Berkeley: University of California Press 1992) (cit Weiner *Inalienable Possessions* (1992))
Wells, RP, *Testamentary Promises: A New Approach* (PhD Thesis, King's College London 2007) (cit Wells *New Approach* (2007))
Wells, RP, 'Testamentary Promises and Unjust enrichment' [2007] Restitution Law Review 37 (cit Wells 'Testamentary Promises' (2007))
Wendehorst, C, 'Die Reform des österreichischen Erbrechts' in *Verhandlungen des 17. Österreichischen Juristentages*, vol 2 (Manz 2010) 20 (cit Wendehorst *Reform II* (2010))
Wendehorst, C, 'Nach der deutschen Erbrechtsreform: Anregungen für Österreich?' [2010] Zeitschrift für Familien—und Erbrecht 138 (cit Wendehorst (2010))
Wendehorst, C, '§ 812' in Bamberger, HG, Roth, H, Hau, W, and Poseck, R (eds), *Beck'scher Online-Kommentar BGB* (44th edn, CH Beck 2017) (cit Wendehorst, '§ 812' in *Beck'scher Online-Kommentar BGB* (2017))
Wendehorst, C, 'Compulsory Portion and other Aspects of Family Protection in Austria' in *Comparative Succession Law 3* (2020) 233 (cit Wendehorst, 'Compulsory Portion and other Aspects of Family Protection in Austria' in *Comparative Succession Law 3* (2020))
Werner, O, '§ 2057 a BGB' in *J v Staudinger, Kommentar zum Bürgerlichen Gesetzbuch mit Einführungsgesetz und Nebengesetzen* (13th edn, De Gruyter 1996) (cit Werner, '§ 2057 a BGB' in *Staudinger, Kommentar zum BGB* (1996))
Wessman, MB, 'Retraining the Gatekeeper: Further Reflections on the Doctrine of Consideration' (1995–1996) 29 Loyola of Los Angeles Law Review 713 (cit Wessman (1995–1996))
Wieacker, F, 'Stillschweigende Hoferbenbestimmung' (1956) Deutsche Notar-Zeitschrift 115 (cit Wieacker (1956))
Wieacker, F, 'Hoferbenbestimmung durch schlüssiges oder sozialtypisches Verhalten?' (1957) Zeitschrift für das gesamte Familienrecht 287 (cit Wieacker (1957))
Windel, PA, 'Wie ist die häusliche Pflege aus dem Nachlass zu honorieren?' [2008] Zeitschrift für Erbrecht und Vermögensnachfolge 305 (cit Windel (2008))
Wöhrmann, O and Graß, C (eds), *Das Landwirtschaftserbrecht* (11th edn, Luchterhand, 2019) (cit Wöhrmann & Graß *Das Landwirtschaftserbrecht* (2019))
Wong, S, 'Would You "Care" to Share Your Home?' (2007) 58 Northern Ireland Legal Quarterly 268 (cit Wong (2007))

Yorio, E, and Thel, S, 'The Promissory Basis of Section 90' (1991) 101 Yale Law Journal 111 (Yorio & Thel (1991))

Zalewski, V, 'L'aide à un membre de sa famille: indemnisation ou rémunération' in Le Borgne-Uguen, F, and Rebourg, M (eds), *L'entraide familiale: régulations juridiques et sociales* (PUR 2012) 235 (cit Zalewski in *L'entraide familiale* (2012))

Zankl, W *Das gesetzliche Vorausvermächtnis des Ehegatten: Österreichisches Recht und Rechtsvergleichung* (Manz Verlag 1996) (cit Zankl *Gesetzliche Vorausvermächtnis des Ehegatten* (1996))

Zelizer, VA, 'The Purchase of Intimacy' (2000) 25 Law & Social Inquiry 817 (cit Zelizer (2000))

Zimmermann, R, *The Law of Obligations. Roman Foundations of the Civilian Tradition* (Clarendon Press 1996) (cit Zimmermann *Law of Obligations* (1996))

Zimmermann, R, 'Intestate Succession in Germany' in *Comparative Succession Law* 2 (2015) 181 (cit Zimmermann, 'Intestate Succession in Germany' in *Comparative Succession Law 2* (2015))

Zimmermann, R, 'Compulsory Portion in Germany' in *Comparative Succession Law 3* (2020) 268 (cit Zimmermann, 'Compulsory Portion in Germany' in *Comparative Succession Law* 3 (2020)

Zoll, F, 'Testamentary Formalities in Poland' in *Comparative Succession Law* 1 (2011) 270 (cit Zoll, 'Testamentary Formalities in Poland' in *Comparative Succession Law 1* (2011))

Zoppini, A, *Le successioni in diritto comparato* (UTET 2002) (cit Zoppini *Le successioni* (2002))

Zweigert, K, and Kötz, H, *An Introduction to Comparative Law* (T Weir tr, 3rd edn, OUP 1998) (cit Zweigert & Kötz *Introduction to Comparative Law* (1998))

Index

For the benefit of digital users, indexed terms that span two pages (e.g., 52–53) may, on occasion, appear on only one of those pages.